P9-DZN-435

PRENTICE HALL FINANCE SERIES

Personal Finance
Keown, *Personal Finance: Turning Money into Wealth*
Trivoli, *Personal Portfolio Management: Fundamentals & Strategies*
Winger/Frasca, *Personal Finance: An Integrated Planning Approach*

Investments
Alexander/Sharpe/Bailey, *Fundamentals of Investments*
Fabozzi, *Investment Management*
Fischer/Jordan, *Security Analysis and Portfolio Management*
Haugen, *Modern Investment Theory*
Haugen, *The New Finance*
Haugen, *The Beast on Wall Street*
Haugen, *The Inefficient Stock Market*
Sharpe/Alexander/Bailey, *Investments*
Taggart, *Quantitative Analysis for Investment Management*
Winger/Frasca, *Investments*

Portfolio Analysis
Alexander/Sharpe/Bailey, *Fundamentals of Investments*
Fischer/Jordan, *Security Analysis and Portfolio Management*
Haugen, *Modern Investment Theory*
Sharpe/Alexander/Bailey, *Investments*

Options/Futures/Derivatives
Hull, *Introduction to Futures and Options Markets*
Hull, *Options, Futures, and Other Derivatives*

Risk Management/Financial Engineering
Hull, *Financial Engineering and Risk Management*
Mason/Merton/Perold/Tufano, *Cases in Financial Engineering*

Fixed Income Securities
Van Horne, *Financial Market, Rates and Flows*
Handa, *FinCoach: Fixed Income* (software)

Bond Markets
Fabozzi, *Bond Markets, Analysis and Strategies*
Van Horne, *Financial Market Rates and Flows*

Capital Markets
Fabozzi/Modigliani, *Capital Markets: Institutions and Instruments*
Van Horne, *Financial Market Rates and Flows*

Corporate Finance, Survey of Finance, & Financial Economics
Bodie/Merton, *Finance*
Emery/Finnerty/Stowe, *Principles of Financial Management*
Emery/Finnerty, *Corporate Financial Management*
Gallagher/Andrew, *Financial Management: Principles and Practices*
Haugen, *The New Finance: The Case Against Efficient Markets*

Keown/Martin/Petty/Scott, *Basic Financial Management*

Keown/Martin/Petty/Scott, *Foundations of Finance: The Logic and Practice of Financial Management*

Shapiro/Balbirer, *Modern Corporate Finance: A Multidisciplinary Approach to Value Creation*

Van Horne, *Financial Management and Policy*

Van Horne/Wachowicz, *Fundamentals of Financial Management*

International Finance

Baker, *International Finance: Management, Markets, and Institutions*

Grabbe, *International Financial Markets*

Rivera-Batiz/Rivera-Batiz, *International Finance and Open Economy Macroeconomics*

Capital Budgeting

Aggarwal, *Capital Budgeting Under Uncertainty*

Bierman/Smidt, *The Capital Budgeting Decision*

Mergers/Acquisitions/Takeovers

Hill/Sartoris, *Short Term Financial Management*

Weston/Siu/Johnson, *Takeovers, Restructuring, and Corporate Governance*

Short-Term Finance

Hill/Sartoris, *Short Term Financial Management*

Taxes

Scholes/Wolfson, *Taxes and Business Strategy: A Global Planning Approach*

Insurance

Black/Skipper, *Life and Health Insurance*

Dorfman, *Introduction to Risk Management and Insurance*

Rejda, *Social Insurance and Economic Security*

Financial Markets and Institutions

Arshadi/Karels, *Modern Financial Intermediaries and Markets*

Dietrich, *Financial Services and Financial Institutions*

Fabozzi/Modigliani/Ferri/Jones, *Foundations of Financial Markets and Institutions*

Kaufman, *The U.S. Financial Systems*

Van Horne, *Financial Market Rates and Flows*

Commercial Banking

Arshadi/Karels, *Modern Financial Intermediaries and Markets*

Dietrich, *Financial Services and Financial Institutions*

Sinkey, *Commercial Bank Financial Management*

Entrepreneurial Finance

Adelman/Marks, *Entrepreneurial Finance*

Vaughn, *Financial Planning for the Entrepreneur*

Cases in Finance

May/May/Andrew, *Effective Writing: A Handbook for Finance People*

Financial Statement Analysis

Fraser/Ormiston, *Understanding Financial Statements*

Finance Center

For downloadable supplements and much more . . . visit us at www.prenhall.com/financecenter

THIRD EDITION

Takeovers, Restructuring, and Corporate Governance

J. Fred Weston

The Anderson School
University of California, Los Angeles

Juan A. Siu

The Anderson School
University of California, Los Angeles

Brian A. Johnson

The Anderson School
University of California, Los Angeles

Upper Saddle River, NJ 07458

Library of Congress Cataloging-in-Publication Data

Weston, J. Fred (John Fred)
  Takeovers, restructuring, and corporate governance / J. Fred Weston, Juan A. Siu,
Brian A. Johnson.–3rd ed.
    p. cm.
  Includes bibliographical references and index.
  ISBN 0–13–026505–5
    1. Consolidation and merger of corporations–United States–Finance.   2. Consolidation
and merger of corporations–United States–Management.   I. Siu, Juan A.   II. Johnson,
Brian A.   III. Title

HG4028.M4 W47 2001
338.8'3'0973–dc21   00–034694

Senior Editor: Maureen Riopelle
Managing Editor (Editorial): Gladys Soto
Editor-in-Chief: PJ Boardman
Editorial Assistant: Cheryl Clayton
Assistant Editor: Holly Jo Brown
Media Project Manager: Bill Minick
Executive Marketing Manager: Lori Braumberger
Production/Manufacturing Manager: Gail Steier de Acevedo
Production Coordinator: Maureen Wilson
Manufacturing Buyer: Natacha St. Hill Moore
Senior Prepress/Manufacturing Manager: Vincent Scelta
Cover Design: Bruce Kenselaar
Composition: Carlisle Communications, Ltd.

10 9 8 7 6 5 4 3
ISBN 0-13-026505-5

To my wife Bernadine, with love, Fred
To my family, with my greatest gratitude, Juan
To my parents, Craig and Carol, love, Brian

Brief Contents

Contents

Cases in Text

Preface

M&As IN THE NEW ECONOMY

Takeovers, restructuring, and corporate governance activities continue to accelerate. New industries like e-commerce and biotechnology have been exploding; old industries are being transformed. The New Economy has been characterized by interactions between the "new economy" firms and the "old economy" firms. The announcement of the merger between America Online and Time Warner in January 2000 quickly followed by Time Warner's proposal to acquire the music business of the EMI Group was appropriate symbolism for the new millennium. It combined new economy and old economy firms in an international setting. But other equally significant industry transformations have been taking place. Telecommunications and media firms are converging. Computers and the Internet industries are characterized by explosive growth in multiple segments with some firms achieving competitive advantage while competitive thrusts continue to challenge.

Powerful change forces have been driving the increased M&A activity. Foremost is technological change, impacting every industry. Changes in transportation and communications have produced the internationalization of markets. The globalization of competition and its increased intensity have produced deregulation in airlines, financial services, telecommunications, and even the traditional electrical and other public utilities industries. But the massive change forces have also impacted the pharmaceutical, chemical, auto, tire, and petroleum industries as well as those described above. Business firms will need to continue to adjust to the strong change forces. The ways of doing business will continue to change. The forms of competition will continue to multiply and its intensity will continue to increase. Relations with suppliers, workers, consumers, and other stakeholders will continue to evolve. These forces are not likely to diminish in the years ahead. The M&A subject, therefore, will continue to grow in importance.

Dramatic events in mergers, takeovers, restructuring, and corporate control fill the newspaper headlines almost daily. Mergers, takeovers, restructuring, and corporate control issues have become central public and corporate policy issues. To some, M&As, restructuring, and corporate control activities represent a new industrial force that will lead the United States and other economies that practice these arts to new heights of creativity and productivity. To others, these same activities are regarded as a blight on our economy—a symptom of the larger malaise evidenced by greed and gambling that is rotting the core of American society. M&As are increasingly used in China to attempt to improve the performance of the state-owned enterprises. Regardless of which view is held, M&As, restructuring, and corporate control represent major forces in the modern financial and economic environments. These are areas with potential for both good and harm.

Merger and acquisition activity has continued to stimulate a veritable deluge of published materials. Compact summaries of these materials or synthesis articles cannot cover the material adequately. In this book we seek to provide a more complete treatment of the leading topics related to mergers, takeovers, restructuring, and corporate control. In the future, shifts in the levels of these activities may occur with fluctuations in the economy and with changing regulatory environments. However, takeovers, restructuring, and leveraged buyouts will continue to be major forces in the economy. Additionally, some key topics such as valuation, cost of capital, and strategic financial planning—essential to the subject of financial economics—enter into the analysis of takeovers and restructuring. Therefore, important analytical concepts must be mastered.

POINT OF VIEW

We try to be objective in our analysis of M&A activity. We see some positive benefits from increased emphasis on financial strategy and restructuring. Undoubtedly, there have been excesses such as typically occur in exploding markets. We have to separate the good from the bad. We come not to praise, criticize, or condemn but to increase understanding. Our central aim is to provide a conceptual framework that will help the reader put into perspective events that are headlined almost daily in the financial and general press and increase his or her understanding of them.

The main audience we have in mind is the academic user. Increasingly, M&A courses deal with all or part of the subject matter of this book. For that reason, we have included end-of-chapter questions to stimulate discussion and to emphasize the key subject matter. We have also kept in mind two other audiences—businesspeople and the general public, including legislators and other policy makers. We have tried to keep the level of treatment accessible by avoiding excessive jargon. We have tried to develop the technical materials from the ground up so that both the academic reader and the general reader will be able to master the material and, we hope, experience intellectual growth in the process.

What we think will be of value to academics and businesspeople is the ability to answer natural and practical questions that arise. For the bidding firm, how much will my early investment in the target increase in value if I use cash as a method of payment? What if I use stock? For the target, what is a reasonable premium for me to expect from a bidder? How much will my firm increase in value if I engage in a sell-off or divestiture? What will be the effect on a firm's share price on average if it engages in stock repurchase? What will be the impact on my firm's share price if it makes a stock or debt issue? What will the share price effect be if a proxy contest is started? What will be the effect of paying greenmail? What value changes take place with going private, particularly through a leveraged buyout? If my firm establishes two classes of stock, which one will have the greater value—the one that pays more income, or the one that has more voting power?

There is a rich body of conceptual and empirical material that can provide a basis for answering such questions. This book attempts to bring that material together in a systematic way. At the same time it tries to lay bare the theory or principles and the logical analysis that give meaning to the empirical findings. These and related materials will provide the general reader with a basis for understanding and judgment about the flow of proposals to alter public policy toward M&As and corporate restructuring that are introduced into every session of Congress.

CHANGES IN THE THIRD EDITION

We have updated the text with new empirical data and literature citations. In some cases we have summarized groups of articles into their main findings. In other cases, where individual articles develop their own distinct new findings, we discuss them individually. We have striven to tighten the conceptual framework that provides perspective on groups of articles in individual subject areas.

We have streamlined the valuation material, orienting it more fully to M&A decisions and case studies, by introducing many more cases in the text and as end-of-chapter exercises. We plan to continue to do more along these lines in the *Study Guide to Takeovers, Restructuring, and Corporate Governance* and in future editions.

In this third edition, at least 50 percent of the material is new or rewritten. We have class-tested the manuscript with gratifying results. Students have requested permission to make copies for friends who are doing corporate internships before taking their M&A course. Students and practitioners have told us that reading the materials has improved the breadth and maturity of their understanding of the M&A field.

This book applies materials from business finance and financial economics, business economics, strategy, accounting, and law. It demonstrates the application of a wide range of concepts from diverse fields. A framework for performing M&A analysis is provided. Many applications are developed through case studies and examples. The book helps develop the intellectual maturity for sound judgments on M&A analysis and decisions.

SUPPLEMENTARY MATERIALS

An important companion piece to this text is the related *Study Guide to Takeovers, Restructuring, and Corporate Governance*. Our *Study Guide* contains outlines that provide an overview of the subject matter of each chapter and illustrative problems and solutions that seek to help the student understand how to apply the main ideas contained in the book itself. The main goal of the *Study Guide* is to help students develop a conceptual framework for analyzing the subject matter of the M&A field.

A comprehensive *Instructor's Manual* contains six parts: suggestions for teaching the M&A course; solutions to end-of-chapter questions and cases; true–false questions for each chapter; illustrative examinations; and sample material of our PowerPoint Presentation Graphics.

We have also developed a softcover compilation of *Cases on Takeovers, Restructuring, and Corporate Governance*. This provides coverage of a wide range of cases, especially the most recent blockbusters.

APPRECIATION

We are grateful to the following people for their helpful comments on the first edition: Nickolaos Travlos, Boston College; Michael J. Sullivan, Florida State University; Kenneth W. Wiles, University of Texas at Austin; George J. Papaioannou, Hofstra University; Douglas V. Austin, University of Toledo; Maclyn L. Clouse, University of Denver; Matthew Spiegel and Michael Salinger, Columbia University; Nikhil P. Varaiya, Southern Methodist University; Robert F. Bruner, University of Virginia; and Ralph A. Walkling, Ohio State University.

For help on the second edition, we thank Michael F. Toyne, La Salle University; Kent Hickman, Gonzaga University; and Yun W. Park, Saint Mary's University.

For contributions to the third edition, we thank Mark Mitchell, Harvard University; J. Harold Mulherin, Penn State University; Ted Azami, Cal State at Long Beach; Theodore Peridis, York University; Mark Shrader, Gonzaga University; David Ikenberry, Rice University; and R.M. Karanjia, University of Notre Dame.

We extend our appreciation also to the many scholars whose writings have enriched the literature on M&As and corporate control. They are listed in the Author Index, and those with multiple citations deserve our special gratitude. We were also helped by scholars whose writings and discussions have stimulated our thinking: Armen Alchian, Edward Altman, Antonio Bernardo, Michael Brennan, Bhagwan Chowdhry, Bradford Cornell, Harry DeAngelo, Jack Farrell, Julian Franks, David Hirshleifer, Patricia Hughes, John Matsusaka, Jeff Pontiff, Richard Roll, Eduardo Schwartz, James Seward, Walt Torous, and Ivo Welch. Particular thanks to Kwang S. Chung, our coauthor on the first edition, and to Matthias Kahl for his corrections and many penetrating comments.

We received assistance from associates in our M&A Research Program at The Anderson School at UCLA. They include Vickie Ho, Miriam Jin, Elizabeth Kwon, Nicole Madani, Shirley Ng, and Stacie Papp.

This book memorializes Marilyn McElroy, who was our associate for 28 years.

We appreciate the complete cooperation of the people at Prentice Hall, particularly Maureen Riopelle, Senior Finance Editor, and her associates, Cheryl Clayton, Holly Brown, and Gladys Soto.

This subject is so dynamic and the flow of articles and other materials is so voluminous that there will be a need for future updating. We invite reactions, comments, and suggestions from our readers.

J. Fred Weston
Juan A. Siu
Brian A. Johnson

J. Fred Weston
The Anderson School at UCLA
258 Tavistock Ave.
Los Angeles, CA 90049-3229
Tel. (310) 472-5110
Fax. (310) 472-9471
Email jweston@anderson.ucla.edu

The Takeover Process

THE PACE OF MERGER ACTIVITY

After reaching $2.7 trillion in 1998, world M&A activity increased by another 25.9% to $3.4 trillion in 1999, as shown in Table 1.1. The first quarter of 2000 appears to be running ahead of 1999. So M&A activity continues to grow. U.S. M&A activity is strong and characterized by blockbusters such as AOL and Time Warner in which AOL offered stock valued at $165 billion on the announcement date of 1/10/2000. But as shown in Table 1.1, M&A activity abroad now exceeds the U.S. and is growing even faster.

It is useful to put these numbers in historical perspective as shown in Table 1.2. Merger activity in the 1980s was considered shockingly high. The peak year during the 1980s was 1988, when merger activity (in 1992 dollars) was $287 billion. The 1998 level (in constant dollars) was 366% of the peak year of the 1980s. The 1999 constant dollar level of $1,239.7 billion was 118% of the 1998 level.

Furthermore, individual transactions are becoming larger. The largest mergers announced from April 1998 through October 1999 are listed in Table 1.3. The MCI WorldCom bid for Sprint heads the list at $115 billion. All of these top 10 deals exceed $50 billion. Table 1.3 also illustrates the internationalization of merger activity. The Vodafone Group, a British company, acquired AirTouch Communications, an American company, illustrating a cross-border transaction. The increased merger

Table 1.1   Worldwide M&A Activity, 1998-1999 ($ Trillions)

	1998	1999	% Increase
World	$2.70	$3.40	25.9%
U.S.	$1.19	$1.43	20.2%
Rest of World*	$1.51	$1.97	30.5%

*Non-U.S. targets and acquirers.
Source: Estimates of Wachtell, Lipton, Rosen & Katz and authors.

Table 1.2 Merger Announcements: The Mergerstat Series

(1)	(2)	(3)	(4)	(5)	(6)	(7)	
			Number of Transactions Valued at				
Year	Total Dollar Value Paid ($ Billion)	Number Total	$100 Million or More	$1,000 Million or More	GDP Deflator (1992 = 100)	1992 Constant Dollar Consideration	Percent Change
1979	43.5	2,128	83	3	55.3	78.7	17%
1980	44.3	1,889	94	4	60.4	73.3	−7%
1981	82.6	2,395	113	12	66.1	125.0	70%
1982	53.8	2,346	116	6	70.2	76.6	−39%
1983	73.1	2,533	138	11	73.2	99.9	30%
1984	122.2	2,543	200	18	75.9	161.0	61%
1985	179.6	3,001	270	36	78.6	228.5	42%
1986	173.1	3,336	346	27	80.6	214.8	−6%
1987	163.7	2,032	301	36	83.1	197.0	−8%
1988	246.9	2,258	369	45	86.1	286.8	46%
1989	221.1	2,366	328	35	89.7	246.5	−14%
1990	108.2	2,074	181	21	93.6	115.6	−53%
1991	71.2	1,877	150	13	97.3	73.2	−37%
1992	96.7	2,574	200	18	100.0	96.7	32%
1993	176.4	2,663	242	27	102.6	171.9	78%
1994	226.7	2,997	383	51	105.1	215.7	25%
1995	356.0	3,510	462	74	107.8	330.2	53%
1996	494.9	5,848	640	94	110.2	449.1	36%
1997	656.0	7,804	871	120	112.3	584.1	30%
1998	1,192.0	7,809	906	158	113.4	1,051.1	80%
1999	1,426.9	9,278	1,097	195	115.1	1,239.7	18%
Annual Average							
1970–1980	22.8	3,126	39	1	42.8	50.9	3%
1981–1989	146.2	2,534	242	25	78.2	181.8	20%
1990–1992	92.0	2,175	177	17	97.0	95.2	−19%
1993–1999	647.0	5,701	657	103	109.5	577.4	46%

Source: Houlihan Lokey Howard & Zukin, *Mergerstat Review,* Los Angeles, CA, annual volumes.

activity in Europe is illustrated by the Total Fina acquisition of Elf Aquitaine, both French companies. The industries represented in Table 1.3 are telecommunications (six companies), oil (two), and financial services (two).

The daily newspapers continue to be filled with case studies of mergers and acquisitions (M&As), tender offers (both friendly and hostile), spin-offs and divestitures, corporate restructuring, changes in ownership structures, and struggles for

Table 1.3   Top 10 Mergers

Rank	Acquirer	Acquired	Announcement Date	Amount ($billion)	Industry
1	MCI WorldCom	Sprint	Oct. 1999	$ 115.0	Telecommunications
2	Exxon	Mobil	Dec. 1998	78.9	Oil
3	Travelers Group	Citicorp	Apr. 1998	72.6	Financial services
4	SBC Commun.	Ameritech	May 1998	62.6	Telecommunications
5	NationsBank	BankAmerica	Apr. 1998	61.6	Financial services
6	Vodafone Group	AirTouch Commun.	Jan. 1999	60.3	Telecommunications
7	AT&T	MediaOne Group	Apr. 1999	56.0	Telecommunications
8	AT&T	Tele-Communications	June 1998	53.6	Telecommunications
9	Total Fina	Elf Acquitaine	July 1999	53.5	Oil
10	Bell Atlantic	GTE	July 1998	53.4	Telecommunications

corporate control. The Securities and Exchange Commission (SEC) is active in pursuing insider trading cases. In recent years, leverage ratios for some companies have increased and newer forms of financing have proliferated, including an increase in the use of bonds with ratings below the first four grades (below Baa3 by Moody's or BBB by Standard & Poor's, referred to as high yield or "junk" bonds). Thus, the traditional subject matter of M&As has been expanded to include takeovers and related issues of corporate restructuring, corporate control, and changes in the ownership structure of firms. For brevity, we refer to these and related activities as M&As.

CHANGE FORCES

Merger activities throughout history have been related to the economic and cultural characteristics of their time and place. The increasing pace of merger activity throughout the world in recent years is related to the powerful change forces listed in Table 1.4.

Overriding all are technological changes, which include computers, computer services, software, servers, and the many advances in information systems, including the Internet. Improvements in communication and transportation have created a global economy. Nations have adopted international agreements such as the General Agreement on Tariffs and Trade (GATT) that have resulted in freer trade. The growing forces of competition have produced deregulation in major industries such as financial services, airlines, and medical services.

The next set of factors relates to efficiency of operations. Economies of scale spread the large fixed cost of investing in machinery or computer systems over a larger number of units. Economies of scope refer to cost reductions from operations in related activities. In the information industry, these would represent economies of activities in personal computer (PC) hardware, PC software, server hardware,

Table 1.4   The Seven Change Forces

1. Technological change
2. Globalization and freer trade
3. Deregulation
4. Economies of scale, economies of scope, complementarity, and the need to catch up technologically
5. Changes in industry organization
6. Individual entrepreneurship
7. Rising stock prices, low interest rates, strong economic growth

server software, the Internet, and other related activities. Another efficiency gain is achieved by combining complementary activities—for example, combining a company strong in research with one strong in marketing. Mergers to catch up technologically are illustrated by the series of acquisitions by AT&T.

The fifth major force stimulating M&A and restructuring activities comprises changes in industry organization. An example is the shift in the computer industry from vertically integrated firms to a horizontal chain of independent activities. Dell Computers, for example, has been very successful concentrating on PC sales with only limited activities in the many other segments of the value chain of the information industry.

The sixth major force is represented by individual entrepreneurship, which has responded to opportunities and, in turn, created further dynamism in industrial activities. Examples are Bill Gates at Microsoft, Andrew Grove at Intel, Jack Welch at General Electric, John Chambers at Cisco Systems, and Bernie Ebbers at MCI WorldCom, among the many.

Finally, the economic and financial environments have been favorable for deal making. Strong economic growth, rising stock prices, and relatively low interest rates have favored internal growth as well as a range of M&A activities.

ISSUES RAISED BY M&A ACTIVITY

Mergers and industrial restructuring activities have raised important issues both for business decisions and for public policy formulation. No firm is regarded safe from the possibility of takeover. Mergers and acquisitions may be critical to the healthy expansion of business firms as they evolve through successive stages of growth and development. Both internal and external growth may be complementary in the long-range evolution of firms. Successful entry into new product markets and into new geographic markets may require M&As at some stage in the firm's development. Successful competition in international markets may depend on capabilities obtained in a timely and efficient fashion through M&As.

Some have argued that mergers increase value and efficiency and move resources to their optimal uses, thereby increasing shareholder value. Others are skeptical. They argue that acquired companies are already efficient and that their subsequent performance after acquisition is not improved. Yet others aver that the gains to shareholders merely represent a redistribution away from labor and other stakeholders. Another view is that the M&A activity represents the machinations of speculators who reflect the frenzy of a "casino society." This speculative activity is said to increase debt unduly and to erode equity, resulting in an economy highly vulnerable to economic instability.

Even individual businesspeople have expressed skepticism of the power of mergers. Warren Buffett observed:

Many managements apparently were overexposed in impressionable childhood years to the story in which the imprisoned handsome prince is released from a toad's body by a kiss from a beautiful princess. Consequently, they are certain their managerial kiss will do wonders for the profitability of Company T[arget]. . . . Investors can always buy toads at the going price for toads. If investors instead bankroll princesses who wish to pay double for the right to kiss the toad, those kisses had better pack some real dynamite. We've observed many kisses but very few miracles. Nevertheless, many managerial princesses remain serenely confident about the future potency of their kisses—even after their corporate backyards are knee-deep in unresponsive toads . . .

We have tried occasionally to buy toads at bargain prices with results that have been chronicled in past reports. Clearly our kisses fell flat. We have done well with a couple of princes—but they were princes when purchased. At least our kisses didn't turn them into toads. And, finally, we have occasionally been quite successful in purchasing fractional interests in easily identifiable princes at toadlike prices.

In this volume, we seek to sort out these opposing views. We offer guidelines for such practical matters as M&A planning by firms and the valuation of combining firms. Further, the theory and empirical evidence have implications for social and economic policies toward mergers. Thus, this work provides a framework for the evaluation of alternative business and social policies involving M&As.

In this chapter, we provide a framework for understanding the many aspects of mergers and takeovers. We cover the topics of merger and tender offer terminology, types of mergers from an economic standpoint, mergers in a legal framework, and the nature of tender offers.

MERGER AND TENDER OFFER TERMINOLOGY

The words **merger** and **tender offer** are frequently used, but the distinctions are not precise. In general, "mergers" refers to negotiated deals that meet certain technical and legal requirements. "Tender offer" usually means that one firm or person is making an offer directly to the shareholders to sell (tender) their shares at specified prices. In one sense, the word merger refers to negotiations between friendly parties who arrive at a mutually agreeable decision to combine their companies. However, in practice, one firm in a merger may be stronger and may dominate the transaction. Similarly, tender offers can be friendly or hostile. In either mergers or tender offers, the negotiations may start out friendly and become hostile. Conversely, negotiations may start out hostile and become friendly. In addition, there may be wide variations in attitudes in either direction as negotiations proceed. However, mergers are mostly "friendly." Some tender offers are "hostile" in the sense that an offer is made to the shareholders without the approval of the board of directors.

As a practical matter, it is useful to have some language to describe the M&A activities. Definitions are arbitrary but useful. In general, mergers reflect various forms of combining companies through some mutuality of negotiations. In tender offers the bidder directly contacts shareholders, inviting them to sell (tender) their shares at an offer price. The directors of the company may or may not have endorsed the tender offer proposal. These distinctions are reflected in a practical way in business practice. That segment of investment banking firms engaged in providing advice on these activities is usually referred to as the Mergers and Acquisitions (M&A) Department. In this sense, mergers and tender offers are two forms of **takeovers.** It is appropriate, therefore, to refer to these activities interchangeably as takeovers or M&As or M&A activity.

With the foregoing as background, we describe some characteristics of mergers and then follow with a section in which some technical aspects of tender offers are discussed. Then we discuss the concept of restructuring, which involves changes in organizations or policies to alter the firm's approach to achieving its long-term objectives. Describing the activities related to the words and concepts conveys a practical understanding of their meaning. With experience, a judgmental feel for or understanding of how these terms are used is developed. They provide some useful handles for organizing data and studying some important phenomena. However, the terms should be used thoughtfully and not in a mechanical way.

TYPES OF MERGERS FROM AN ECONOMIC STANDPOINT

Economists have grouped mergers based on whether they take place at the same level of economic activity—exploration, production or manufacturing, wholesale distribution, or retail distribution to the ultimate consumer. The element of relatedness is also important in defining economic categories of mergers.

Horizontal Mergers

A horizontal merger involves two firms that operate and compete in the same kind of business activity. Thus, the acquisition in 1999 of Mobil by Exxon represented a horizontal combination or merger. Forming a larger firm may have the benefit of economies of scale. The argument that horizontal mergers occur to realize economies of scale is, however, not sufficient to be a theory of horizontal mergers. Although these mergers would generally benefit from large-scale operation, not all small firms merge horizontally to achieve economies of scale. Further, why do firms decide to merge at a particular time? Why do they choose a merger rather than internal growth? Because a merger theory should have implications with respect to these aspects, it must be more than a theory of large firm size or a theory of horizontally integrated operations.

Horizontal mergers are regulated by the government for possible negative effects on competition. They decrease the number of firms in an industry, possibly making it easier for the industry members to collude for monopoly profits. Some believe that horizontal mergers potentially create monopoly power on the part of the combined firm, enabling it to engage in anticompetitive practices. It remains an empirical question whether horizontal mergers take place to increase the market power of the combined firm or to seek to augment the firm's capabilities to become a more effective competitor.

Vertical Mergers

Vertical mergers occur between firms in different stages of production operation. In the oil industry, for example, distinctions are made between exploration and production, refining, and marketing to the ultimate consumer. In the pharmaceutical industry one could distinguish between research and the development of new drugs, the production of drugs, and the marketing of drug products through retail drugstores.

There are many reasons why firms might want to be vertically integrated. There are technological economies such as the avoidance of reheating and transportation costs in the case of an integrated iron and steel producer. Transactions within a firm may eliminate the costs of searching for prices, contracting, payment collecting, and advertising and may also reduce the costs of communicating and of coordinating production. Planning for inventory and production may be improved due to more efficient information flow within a single firm. When assets of a firm are specialized to another firm, the latter may act opportunistically. Expropriation can be accomplished by demanding the supply of a good or service produced from the specialized assets at a price below its average cost. To avoid the costs of haggling that arise from expropriation attempts, the assets are owned by a single vertically integrated firm. Divergent interests of parties to a transaction can be reconciled by common ownership.

The efficiency and affirmative rationale of vertical integration rests primarily on the costliness of market exchange and contracting. The argument, for instance, that uncertainty over input supply is avoided by backward integration reduces to the fact that long-term contracts are difficult to write, execute, and police.

Conglomerate Mergers

Conglomerate mergers involve firms engaged in unrelated types of business activity. Thus, the merger between Mobil Oil and Montgomery Ward was generally regarded as a conglomerate merger. Among conglomerate mergers, three types have been distinguished. Product extension mergers broaden the product lines of firms. These are mergers between firms in related business activities and may also be called concentric mergers. A geographic market extension merger involves two firms whose operations have been conducted in nonoverlapping geographic areas. Finally, the other conglomerate mergers that are often referred to as pure conglomerate mergers involve unrelated business activities. These would not qualify as either product extension or market extension mergers.

Investment Companies

By contrasting four categories of companies, the economic functions of conglomerate mergers may be illuminated. The four categories are: (1) investment companies such as mutual funds, (2) financial conglomerates which operate as internal capital markets, (3) managerial conglomerates in which staff groups in general management functions such as research, legal, and human resources provide services to diversified segments of operations, (4) concentric companies in which diversified activities are related to core activities. A fundamental economic function of investment companies is to reduce risk by diversification. Combinations of securities whose returns are not perfectly correlated reduce portfolio variance for a target rate of return. Because investment companies combine resources from many sources, their power to achieve a reduction in variance through portfolio effects is greater than that of individual investors. In addition, the managements of investment companies provide professional selection from among investment alternatives.

Conglomerate firms differ fundamentally from investment companies in that they control the entities to which they make major financial commitments. Two important characteristics define a conglomerate firm. First, a conglomerate firm controls a range of activities in various industries that require different skills in the specific managerial functions of research, applied engineering, production, marketing, and so on. Second, the diversification is achieved mainly by external acquisitions and mergers, not by internal development.

Within this broader category, two types of conglomerate firms can be distinguished. Financial conglomerates provide a flow of funds to each segment of their operations, exercise control, and are the ultimate financial risk takers. In theory, financial conglomerates undertake strategic planning but do not participate in operating decisions. Managerial conglomerates not only assume financial responsibility and control but also play a role in operating decisions and provide staff expertise and staff services to the operating entities.

Financial Conglomerates

The characteristics of financial conglomerates may be further clarified by comparisons with investment companies. The financial conglomerate serves at least five distinct economic functions. First, like investment companies, it improves risk/return ratios through diversification. Second, it avoids "gambler's ruin" (an adverse run of losses that might cause bankruptcy). If the losses can be covered by avoiding gambler's ruin, the financial conglomerate maintains the viability of an economic activity with long-run value. Without this form of risk reduction or bankruptcy avoidance, the assets of the operating entity might be shifted to less productive uses because of a run of losses at some point in its development.

Third, a potential contribution by financial conglomerates derives from their establishing programs of financial planning and control. Often, these systems improve the quality of general and functional managerial performance, thereby resulting in more efficient operations and better resource allocation for the economy.

Fourth, if management does not perform effectively but the productivity of assets in the market is favorable, then the management is changed. This reflects an effective competitive process because assets are placed under more efficient management to ensure more effective use of resources. This contributes to improved resource allocation.

Fifth, in the financial planning and control process, a distinction is made between performance based on underlying potentials in the product market area and results related to managerial performance. Thus, adverse performance does not necessarily indicate inadequate management performance. If management is competent but product market potentials are inadequate, executives of the financial conglomerate will seek to shift resources by diverting internal cash flows from the unfavorable areas to areas more attractive from a growth and profitability standpoint. From the standpoint of the economy as a whole, resource allocation is improved.

Managerial Conglomerates

Managerial conglomerates carry the attributes of financial conglomerates still further. By providing managerial counsel and interactions on decisions, managerial conglomerates increase the potential for improving performance. One school of management theory holds that the generic management functions of planning, organizing, directing, and controlling are readily transferable to all types of business firms. Those managers who have the experience and capability to perform general management functions can perform them in any environment.

This theory argues for management transferability across a wide variety of industries and types of organizations, including government, nonprofit institutions, and military and religious organizations. To the extent that this proposition is valid, it provides a basis for the most general theory of mergers. When any two firms of unequal management competence are combined, the performance of the combined firm will benefit from the impact of the superior management firm, and the total performance of the combined firm will be greater than the sum of the individual parts. This interaction defines **synergy** in its most general form. In the managerial conglomerate, these economic benefits are achieved through corporate headquarters that provide the individual operating entities with expertise and counsel on the generic management functions.

Concentric Companies

The difference between the managerial conglomerate and the concentric company is based on the distinction between the general and specific management functions. If the activities of the segments brought together are so related that there is carryover of specific management functions (manufacturing, finance, marketing, personnel, and so on) or complementarity in relative strengths among these specific management functions, the merger should be termed concentric rather than conglomerate. This transferability of specific management functions across individual segments has long been exemplified by the operations of large, multiproduct, multiplant firms in the American economy. The characteristic organizational structure of these firms has included senior vice presidents who perform as staff specialists to corresponding functional executives in operating departments.

Definitions are inherently arbitrary. Is there any reason to distinguish between managerial conglomerates and concentric companies? The two types have in common a basic economic characteristic. Each transfers general management functions over a variety of activities, using the principle of spreading a fixed factor over a larger number of activities to achieve economies of scale and to lower the cost function for the output range. Concentric companies achieve these economic gains in specific management functions as well as in general management functions. A priori, the potential economies for the concentric companies might be expected to be larger. But the magnitude of economies gained in general rather than specific management functions may vary by industry and by industry mix. Further, in the multiproduct, multiplant firms that have achieved economies of carryover of both specific and general management functions, the interactions may be so great that it is impossible to differentiate between the two.

Similarly, a managerial conglomerate that originally provided expertise on general management functions may increasingly act on specific management functions as its executives become more familiar with the operations of the individual entities. Financial conglomerates also may increasingly provide staff service for both general and specific management functions.

Additional illustrations will clarify these concepts and their economic implications. If one company has competence in research, manufacturing, or marketing that can be applied to the product problems of another company that lacks that particular competence, a merger will provide the opportunity to lower cost functions. For example, firms seeking to diversify from advanced technology industries may be strong on research but weaker on production and marketing capabilities than firms in industries with less advanced technology.

To this point we have described the different kinds of mergers and explained some of the reasons why they appear to take place. In the following section we look at mergers within a legal framework.

MERGERS IN A LEGAL FRAMEWORK

From a legal standpoint, the **statutory merger** is the basic form of transaction. The transaction is governed by the statutory provisions of the state or states in which the parties to the merger are chartered. The main elements of a statutory merger are the percentage vote required for approval of the transaction, who is entitled to vote, how the votes are counted, and the rights of the voters who object to the transaction or its terms.

The Delaware statute is typical of the merger provisions found in most states. After the boards of directors have approved the transaction, it is submitted for ratification to the shareholders of the respective corporations. Prior to the 1960s, most states required approval by two-thirds of the shareholders who possessed the right to vote. In 1962 the model Business Corporation Act provided for a majority vote. In 1967 the state of Delaware adopted the majority vote provision. Other states that provide for a majority vote include California, Michigan, and New Jersey. The state of New York, in contrast, still requires a two-thirds majority for approval of a takeover proposal. In a merger, the traditional legal doctrine was that the minority must agree to the terms approved by the majority. The minority still has the right to sue on a number of issues such as the fairness of the pricing of ownership interests.

After approval by the majority of those with voting rights, the act of "merger" takes place upon the filing of appropriate documents with the states in which the participant companies are chartered. One corporation survives; the others go out of existence. The surviving company assumes the assets and liabilities of the merging firms. When the Nabisco Corporation merged with Standard Brands, Standard Brands was dissolved and Nabisco survived. Nabisco itself was subsequently acquired by the RJ Reynolds tobacco company to form RJR Nabisco. In some combinations, a new entity is created. For example, when Burroughs and Sperry combined in May 1986, the new company adopted the name Unisys, a name completely unrelated to the former names of the merging companies.

The law also makes provision for a **short-form merger.** The legal procedures are streamlined and shareholder approval is not required. In such a transaction, the ownership of the corporation is concentrated in the hands of a small group, usually referred to as insiders. The threshold ownership requirement is usually 90%.

Sometimes the identity of one of the companies in the merger transaction is preserved. For example, when General Motors bought Electronic Data Systems (EDS) from Ross Perot, EDS became a subsidiary of General Motors. In 1995 General Motors announced that it was going to spin off or divest its EDS subsidiary.

Furthermore, when one firm controls a number of other firms held in the form of subsidiaries, the parent firm is referred to as a holding company. Each of the subsidiaries remains a separate legal entity. In a holding company system, the parent has a controlling interest in each of the subsidiaries.

The percentage of ownership required for a controlling interest varies. If a target has widely dispersed ownership, holdings of 10% to 20% probably give the parent effective control. Ownership of more than 50% conveys certain control. If a parent owns 80% or more of the shares of its subsidiary, the financial results of the subsidiary can be consolidated for income tax purposes.

The preceding discussion conveys much of the terminology of the legal rules governing merger transactions. Many of the same principles apply to tender offers.

THE NATURE OF TENDER OFFERS

In a tender offer, the bidder typically seeks the approval of the company management and board of directors of the target company, but makes an offer directly to shareholders of the target firm. The bidder's obtaining 50% or more of the shares of the target firm is equivalent to having received shareholder approval. In this case, the shareholders have voted with their pocketbooks.

In a merger, the traditional legal doctrine held that the minority must agree to the terms negotiated. In a tender offer, the offer is extended to the individual shareholders so that management and the board of directors can be bypassed. The law is still not clear on whether merger doctrine applies. In some cases, after the bidder has obtained control, the terms may be "crammed down" on the minority. Sometimes the acquirer may decide not to complete the buyout. In this case, there is a "freeze-in" problem in that the minority is subject to the decisions of the majority holders. The minority always has the right to bring legal action if it feels that it has been treated inequitably.

There are different kinds of tender offers with different kinds of provisions. The financial press from time to time reports detailed tender offers, summarizing the provisions of the documents sent directly to shareholders. These, in effect, are public notices of the proposals mailed to the shareholders. The tender offer may be conditional or unconditional. For example, the offer may be contingent on obtaining 50% of the shares of the target. The tender offer may be restricted or unrestricted. A restricted tender offer prespecifies the number or percentage of shares the bidder will take. An "any-or-all" tender offer is both unconditional and unrestricted.

If the tender offer is restricted, oversubscription may result in prorating by the bidder. For example, assume that the bidder tenders for 60% of a target company's 1,000 shares of stock and that 80% of the total shares are offered. The bidder may decide to accept all 800 or to accept only 600 shares, which is 75% of the amount tendered by the shareholders. Then, for example, if shareholder A offered 100 shares, the bidder would buy only 75.

The law requires a 20-day waiting period during which the target company shareholders may make their decision to offer their shares for sale. The bidder would then have to wait until after the 20-day waiting period to calculate the proration percentage. If the bidder decides to extend the offer, the proration period is also automatically extended.

Another complication arises when other bidders compete with the first bidder—a contested offer. The law requires that when a new tender offer is made, the stockholders of the target company must have 10 business days to consider that new offer. The effect is to extend the initial offer period. For example, suppose 18 days has elapsed since the first offer. If a second bid is made, the shareholders have an additional 10 days, which is equivalent to 28 days on the first bid and 10 days on the second bid. If the second bid occurred 5 days after the first bid was made, the original 20-day waiting period is not extended because 5 + 10 is less than the original 20-day waiting period.

Another variation is the use of a two-tier tender offer. The first tier, typically for cash, is to obtain 50% or more of the target's stock to obtain control. In the second tier, a smaller value may be offered because control has already been established. The second tier is often paid in securities such as debt rather than cash or equity of the bidder.

A variation of the two-tier offer is the "three-piece suitor." The three steps are (1) an initial toehold; (2) a tender offer to obtain control; and (3) after control and a majority of shareholders have tendered, a freeze-out purchase of the minority shareholders.

The preceding by no means describes all of the different types of tender offers or merger patterns, nor does it cover the multitude of legal issues that may become involved. We simply convey the general patterns. The details would require legal and accounting expertise of a very high order.

RISK ARBITRAGE IN M&A ACTIVITY

Arbitrage is defined as purchasing in one market for immediate sale in another at a higher price. Thus, arbitragers take advantage of temporary price discrepancies between markets. By their actions, the differences are eliminated, driving prices up by their purchases in one market and driving prices down by their sales in the other.

Arbitragers may take offsetting positions in one security in two markets or in equivalent securities in one or two markets, to make profits without assuming any risk under the theory of pure arbitrage.

In the area of mergers and acquisitions, risk arbitrage is the practice of purchasing (speculating in) the stock of takeover targets for short-term (though not immediate) resale at a higher price. On average, target shareholders earn excess returns in the range of 20% or more in successful takeovers. By taking a position in the stock of target firms, risk arbitragers are, in effect, betting on the outcome of contests for corporate control. Thus, the term *risk arbitrage* is used differently from the true or original concept of arbitrage.

Illustrative Example

An example will illustrate the arbitrage operation. When a tender is announced, the price will rise toward the offer price. For example, bidder B selling at $100 may offer $60 for target T now selling at $40 (a 50% premium). After the offer is announced, the arbitrage firm (A) may short B and go long in T. The position of the hedge depends on price levels after the announcement. Suppose B goes to $90 and T to $55. If the arbitrage firm (A) shorts B and goes long on T, the outcome depends on a number of alternatives. If the tender succeeds at $60, the value of B may not change or may fall further, but the value of T will rise to $60, resulting in a profit of at least $5 per share of T for A. If the tender fails, T may fall in price but not much if other bids are made for T; the price of B may fall because it has "wasted" its search and bidding costs to acquire T. Thus, A may gain whether or not the bid succeeds. If the competition of other bidders causes B to raise its offer further, A will gain even more, because T will rise more and B will fall. (Remember that A is short on B and long on T.)

During the stock market crash of October 1987, it was reported that the arbitrage departments of most investment banking firms suffered large losses. The prices of both B and T decreased. It was likely that T fell more than B, because B was likely to reduce or withdraw its offer and acquisition activity dried up in the initial general uncertainty following the market crash. If the arbitrage department (A) was not hedged, but simply long on T, its losses would be even larger.

The increased incidence of hostile takeover activity via cash tender offers in the late 1970s created more opportunities for risk arbitrage and led to dramatic growth of the industry. These participants include both freestanding arbitrage funds and partnerships as well as the arbitrage departments now found in most brokerage houses, investment banks, and many other financial institutions. Ivan Boesky's famous (now infamous) arbitrage fund was started in 1975 with an initial investment of $700,000, which grew to over $1 billion by November 1986, for a compound annual growth rate of 93.6%.

The Nature of the Arbitrage Business

Traditionally, arbitragers have responded to announced takeover bids. They evaluate the offer and assess its probability of success relative to the value of the target. They must consider the likelihood and consequences of a bidding war between alternative potential acquirers, various takeover defenses, a white knight, and so on. However, the arbitragers do not have the luxury of time to perform their analyses; they must act early enough to capture the gains inherent in the transaction. Numerous empirical studies document that target firm stock prices begin to rise even before the first public announcement of a takeover bid.

Information is the principal raw material in the arbitrage business. The vast majority of this information comes from careful analysis of publicly available documents, such as financial statements and filings with the SEC and/or regulatory agencies. Arbitragers buy expert advice from lawyers and industry specialists. They may hire investment bankers to assist in their assessment of the offer. In some cases, the investment bankers involved in the transaction may double-check their own assessment of valuation against that of the arbitragers. They attempt to get all available information from the investment bankers representing the target and bidding firms and from the participants themselves. This phase of information gathering may cross over the boundary into the gray area of insider trading if the pursuit is too vigorous.

With the increased pace in recent years, arbitragers have in some cases attempted to anticipate takeover bids to establish their stock positions in advance of any public announcement, thus increasing their potential return. To do so, they try to identify undervalued firms that would make attractive targets and to track down rumors of impending bids; they may monitor price increases that might signal someone is accumulating stock in a particular company to ferret out potential bidders before the 5% disclosure trigger at which the purchaser has to announce his or her intentions. The risk of taking a position based upon this type of activity is clearly greater. Also, if one firm in an industry is acquired, other firms in the industry may be expected to become targets.

Arbitrage Funds

The basic philosophy of an arbitrage fund is to eliminate market risk taking an arbitrage position in connection with multiple merger and takeover transactions. It does prior intensive research in order to mitigate deal risk and does not invest in rumors. The firm takes a position when there has been a public announcement that two firms are likely to sign a definitive merger agreement. At this point it is likely that there has been some rise in the market price of the target and some decline in the market price of the bidder. As long as the terms of the merger agreement make it likely that the market price of one merger partner is out of line with the other, an arbitrage position can profitably be taken. The main risk is whether the deal is completed and on a timely basis. Investing in 10 to 20 transactions at a given time, plus the prior research, reduces the unfavorable impact if a particular deal is not completed. The goal of such funds is to generate 10% to 15% annual returns in all market environments. The operations of these newer funds are quite different from the aggressive positions in individual transactions taken by some of the well-known arbitrage firms in the 1980s.

SUMMARY

This chapter has summarized some basic terminology and concepts, providing a foundation for developing further knowledge and understanding of M&As. Merger activity is driven by economic and cultural trends. Recent change forces driving mergers include globalization, technology, deregulation, a strong economic environment (high stock prices, low interest rates), and changes in industry organization. In tender offers, the bidder directly contacts shareholders, inviting them to sell (tender) their shares at an offer price. Mergers usually involve some mutuality of negotiations. In practice, the acquiring company may make a successful tender offer for the target followed by a formal merger of the two companies.

From an economic standpoint, different types of mergers or tender offers are grouped on the basis of the stage of economic activity and the degree of relatedness of the firms. Horizontal mergers involve firms operating in the same kind of business activity. Vertical mergers take place between firms in different stages of production operations. Pure conglomerate mergers involve firms engaged in unrelated types of business activity. Financial conglomerates develop financial planning and control systems for groups of segments that may be otherwise unrelated from a business standpoint. Financial conglomerates operate as an internal capital market in assigning funds to segments; future allocations of funds will depend on the performance of the segments. Managerial conglomerates provide managerial counsel and interactions with their segments. Concentric companies carry the idea further in having staff expertise in specific managerial functions such as production, marketing, and finance.

Statutory mergers meet the formal legal requirements of the state or states in which the parties to the merger are chartered. After the approval of the tender offer followed by a merger agreement or the approval of a merger directly, the act of merger takes place upon the filing of appropriate documents with the state or states. Tender offers may have various types of conditions or restrictions.

Risk arbitrage in connection with M&As is the practice of making short-term gains from the relationship between the takeover bid price and the relative prices of the bidder's and target's stock. The announcement of a merger or tender offer causes the stock price of the target to rise because the bidder pays a premium. Arbitragers generally will take a long position in the target stock and a short position in the bidder stock, especially if they are out of line. For example, if the bidder offers to trade 1.5 shares for 1 share of the target and, net of commissions, the bidder stock sells for $10 and the target stock sells for $14.25, the arbitrager can lock in a $0.75 gain by shorting 1.5 shares of the bidder and going long on one share of the target stock. If anything, the spread is likely to move in favor of the arbitrager. The big risk is that the deal may not be completed. Arbitragers also attempt to establish their stock positions before the runup of the target's stock price by trying to anticipate takeover announcements through careful research.

QUESTIONS

1.1 What is the difference between a merger and a tender offer?

1.2 What are some of the potential synergy advantages of horizontal mergers?

1.3 How do the economic advantages of vertical mergers differ from those of horizontal mergers?

1.4 Are there valid distinctions between pure conglomerates, managerial conglomerates, and a concentric company? If so, what are they?

1.5 An arbitrage firm (A) notes that a bidder (B) whose stock is selling at $30 makes an offer for a target (T) selling at $40 to exchange 1.5 shares of B for 1 share of T. Shares of T rise to $44; B stays at $30. A sells 1.5 B short for $45 and goes long on T at $44. One month later the deal is completed with B at $30 and T at $45. What is A's dollar and percentage annualized gain, assuming a required 50% margin and 8% cost of funds on both transactions?

Merger Process Information in Proxy Statements

A rich source of information about the merger process is contained in the proxy statements to shareholders issued in connection with reviews by the U.S. Securities and Exchange Commission (SEC). These proxy statements include the designation of a future shareholders' meeting at which approval of the transaction is solicited. Also, the statements give the details of the merger agreement, company backgrounds, reasons for the merger, and opinions of legal and financial advisors. These proxy statements are available in hard copy from the companies involved. They are also available on the Internet at the SEC Web page (www.sec.gov) within the EDGAR database.

To illustrate the vast amount of information available in the proxy statements to mergers, we examine the proxy for World-Com's acquisition of MCI. Many proxy statements begin with a list of questions and answers addressing potential concerns of investors. This provides a quick reference that avoids some of the "legalese" of the rest of the document. In the WorldCom/MCI proxy, the questions addressed concerns including: the benefits of the merger, the other bids for MCI by British Telecommunications (BT) and GTE, how to vote on the merger, the terms of the deal, the tax consequences, dividends, regulatory approval, and other topics. These questions occupied about the

first 3 pages of the WorldCom proxy statement (out of 135 pages before appendices).

Following the investors' questions section is generally a summary of the topics covered in the rest of the material. In the case of the WorldCom proxy statement, the summary provides a 10 page overview of the following 120 pages. It gives descriptions of the businesses, information about the shareholders' meetings, terms of the deal, and most of the other topics covered in the comprehensive proxy statement.

The proxy statement is very detailed. A proxy statement probably will address more issues and concerns than any individual investor will have. This is necessary to hopefully prevent liability if the firms are sued for not disclosing some piece of information. The WorldCom/MCI proxy contains a description of the risks associated with the transaction. It cautions investors about the risks concerning "forward-looking statements." It also lists 13 risk factors particular to the merger. These include: uncertainties in integrating the acquired companies and achieving cost savings, risks associated with regulation and obtaining government approvals of the merger, dilution of voting interest for WorldCom shareholders, risks of international business, etc.

Most merger proxy statements give a very detailed outline of the merger agreement. MCI agreed to accept $51 in World-Com stock. However, the firms included a table detailing how that consideration would increase if the value of WorldCom stock exceeded a certain point, or fall if the stock fell below a designated value. As long as WorldCom remained within a window between $29 and $41, MCI would receive $51 of WorldCom stock.

The "Background of the Merger" section is an account of the negotiations between the two merging firms. In the case of WorldCom/MCI, this section begins as far back as 1994, when BT took a 20% stake in MCI. It details the merger agreement between BT and MCI (announced 8/21/97), and the subsequent announcements of the WorldCom (10/1/97) and GTE (10/15/97) offers. The background includes details about board meetings and decisions, and meetings between the senior management of the merging firms. WorldCom had extensive negotiations with MCI, as well as with BT to arrive at a deal to buy BT's shares of MCI.

The "Reasons for the Merger" detail management's views of the gains created by the merger. This section often includes estimates of synergies and a description of the overall strategic motivations for the merger. WorldCom and MCI looked to combine two leaders in long distance telecommunications as well as to capitalize on the booming Internet industry. The combined company would provide extensive telecommunications services. Synergies were projected to be $2.5 billion in 1999 and $5.6 billion in 2002.

The "Opinion of Financial Advisor" sections give insight into some of the findings of the investment banks involved in the deal. Salomon Smith Barney, WorldCom's advisor, used analyses including historical stock price performance, historical exchange ratio analysis, synergy analysis, and business division analysis. MCI used at least two advisors, Lazard Freres and Lehman Brothers, who did similar analyses of the deal.

Merger proxy statements also address the issues of taxability and accounting treatment. The tax section usually tries to cover any possible scenario that would require payment of taxes. Accounting treatment details the effects of purchase or pooling on the resulting financial statements of the combined firm. The WorldCom/MCI deal was non-taxable to most shareholders. It was accounted for under the purchase method of accounting.

The accounting method will be reflected in the "Pro Forma Financial Information" section, which attempts to capture what the financials of the future combined firm will look like. However, as the WorldCom/MCI proxy states the financials "are presented for comparative purposes only and are not intended to be indicative of actual results . . . nor do they purport to indicate results which may be attained in the future."

The foregoing is only a small portion of the information contained within a merger proxy statement. To illustrate, a partial list of the Table of Contents from the World-Com/MCI proxy gives an indication of how much information is readily available.

MCI WorldCom Proxy Table of Contents

continued

QUESTIONS

One of the valuable benefits of going through a proxy statement is that it gives you a good feel and understanding of the takeover process. With that objective in mind, the following questions require selection of one of the large mergers from 1999. Go to the EDGAR database on the SEC Web page (www.sec.gov) and look for "S-4" or "DEF14A" forms dated a few months after the merger announcement date for the company you select.

Choose one of the following mergers:

Approximate Announcement Date	Buyer	Seller
10/5/99	MCI WorldCom	Sprint
1/15/99	Vodafone Group	AirTouch Communications
5/6/99	AT&T	MediaOne Group
5/17/99	Qwest Communications	US West
9/6/99	Viacom	CBS

A1.1   Was this a pooling or a purchase?

A1.2   Was it taxable or non-taxable?

A1.3   What was the method of payment (stock, cash, debt)?

A1.4   Describe the major products of each company. Classify the transaction as related (10), unrelated (1), or somewhere in between (with a number). Give reasons.

A1.5   The Federal Trade Commission classifies mergers and tender offers as horizontal, vertical, or conglomerate. Explain what each of these terms means, and classify this one.

A1.6   Summarize the reasons given for the transaction. If there is an estimate of synergies, summarize the dollar amounts with the specific sources of savings.

A1.7   What does the proxy say about what happens if the merger agreement is terminated?

A1.8   What does the proxy say about the rights of dissenting shareholders?

A1.9   What does the proxy say about the exercise of executive stock options as a result of the merger?

A1.10 Summarize the methods of valuation employed by the financial advisor to each of the companies. If comparable companies or transactions are cited, list them and explain the ratios used. Describe and explain the Discounted Cash Flow (DCF) method or methods used by the financial advisors as the basis for the fairness opinion.

The AOL and Time Warner Merger

This Appendix provides a summary of the AOL merger with Time Warner (TWX) as a symbol of important new directions in M&A activities. The AOL-TWX combination is an illustration of the broader industry implications of combining "new economy" companies with "old economy" companies. Many regard the merger as a precursor to more pervasive impacts of the Internet companies on more traditional industries.

A merger between America Online (AOL) and Time Warner was announced 1/10/2000. A new company named AOL Time Warner Inc. was the planned outcome of the merger. AOL shareholders would receive 1 new share for each AOL and TWX shareholders would receive 1.5 new shares for 1 TWX share.

The merger captured the imagination of the public. AOL agreed to pay stock worth about $165 billion for Time Warner, a 70% premium. At the announcement, it was estimated that the market value of the combined companies would be $350 billion. As important as the large value of the deal was the combination of "new economy" and "old economy" companies. AOL's stock price had boomed in the 1990s as a hot Internet stock. Investors saw its potential for significant future earnings growth based on its implementation of technology. Meanwhile, Time Warner was a leader of old-line media, owning publishing, television, cable, movie, and other entertainment properties. Although AOL only brought 18% of the rev-

enues and 30% of the operating cash flows to the table, AOL shareholders would own 55% of the combined firm.

New technologies had been crucial in transforming the industries of both AOL and Time Warner. The Internet industry had undergone a rapid transformation in the 1990s. In the early part of the decade, it was seen as a kind of virtual library. The Internet would be the means to exchange tremendous amounts of academic information easily. The introduction of Netscape Navigator in 1994 made the Internet more accessible to the masses. During the late 1990's, e-commerce became a central function of the Internet, with shopping online becoming "the next big thing." Many analysts believe the AOL Time Warner merger is the sign that multimedia entertainment will be the next major step for the Internet and a precursor to combining more old and new economy industries.

For all the promise of the Internet as a source of multimedia entertainment, there are many challenges to be overcome. While some believe that internet sources will eventually replace print media, many find it cumbersome to read from a computer screen for long periods of time. Television on demand (where consumers pay to watch programming of their own choosing) has long been a dream for media companies, but so far it has never been effectively implemented. The movie and music industries have experienced challenges from the Internet in the form of piracy. In particular, some consumers are finding it easier to download their favorite songs from the Internet than to purchase CDs. However, virtually all these multimedia activities are eased by faster Internet connections, sparking the conversion to broadband.

The reasons for the AOL Time Warner merger reflect the challenges that both companies face in the changing business environment. AOL was a content distributor. As an Internet service provider (ISP), monthly fees are the source of 70% of its revenues. AOL faces competition from Microsoft and from free/low-cost Internet access providers. In order to continue its profit growth, AOL could no longer rely on subscription revenue. Instead, AOL had to pursue increased advertising and e-commerce. It needed unique content and services to distinguish itself from its competitors.

Furthermore, AOL was constricted in a world shifting toward high-speed Internet connections. AOL currently relies on dial-up modems using regular telephone lines. The speed restrictions are a bottleneck for multimedia content delivery. Since AOL doesn't own any high speed lines, it would have been forced to hash out deals with companies that do (e.g., AT&T). Once it became clear the broadband cable internet access could become the future of the ISP industry, AOL became the most vocal supporter of government intervention to force cable firms to open their cables to outside ISPs. This would allow firms like AOL to offer its services to the cable customers of other firms without having to own the "pipes" that carry the information to the home. Uncertainty concerning the future of open access was a motivation for AOL to acquire its own cable system.

TWX was a content producer and a broadband content distributor. Its revenues

were growing at 10% to 15% per year. Any opportunity for higher growth would require developing a successful Internet business. So far, it had no clear Internet strategy, and had been frustrated by its inability to exploit its cable and media assets more effectively in the Internet. Its interactive TV, Full Service Network, failed. Its Pathfinder website was a fiasco. Its broadband distribution business over cable lines through its partial ownership of the Internet provider Road Runner had not grown as rapidly as was hoped. Thus, the merger answered AOL's concerns on how it would implement its broadband strategy without owning content or having access to high-speed lines. It allows TWX to leverage its entertainment assets more effectively online with the benefit of AOL Internet resources and expertise.

The merger will link AOL's broad customer relationships to TWX's content and service distribution. The premier Internet distribution company in the world will be paired with the leading owner of copyrights in the world. AOL brings its worldwide Internet services, AOL and CompuServe, with a combined 22.2 million subscribers base or 54% of the total ISP business; also portal sites such as Netscape Netcenter and AOL.COM; web browsers like Netscape Navigator and Communicator; and several leading Internet brands such as ICQ and A.I.M. instant messaging, Digital City, AOL MovieFone and MapQuest.com.

TWX brings the second largest U.S. cable television system with 13 million subscribers in Time Warner Cable and 350,000 subscribers in its partially-owned broadband Internet provider, Road Runner; print media businesses which include Time Inc. with 33 magazines such as *Entertainment Weekly, Fortune, Life, People, Sports Illustrated,* and *Time,* with estimated 120 to 130 million readers and a 21% share of the 1998 consumer magazine advertising dollars; the eighth-largest book publishing business which includes Book-of-the-Month Club, Time Life, Little Brown and Warner Books; television broadcasting with 10 cable channels that include CNN with a global reach of more than 1 billion, HBO with 30 million subscribers, TNT and TBS with 75 million homes, and the WB Network; movie and television production such as Warner Bros. and New Line Cinema with 8% of the domestic film market; and music with Warner Music Group which accounted for 16% of all records sold. The new company will embrace nearly all types of media including cable, magazine, movies, music, and online, offering new opportunities for cross-promotion and expanded e-commerce.

It was estimated that the combination would save $1.0 billion in 2001. Potential cost savings would arise from administrative savings and from substantially lower advertising and promotion costs. The new management team states that layoffs are unlikely and the intention is to expand the company. In the future, broadband strategies could represent substantial savings; for example, it could dramatically cut manufacturing and shipping costs associated with audio and video delivery.

Perhaps due to skepticism about the estimates of synergies, or the overall strategic vision of the merger, the market had a negative initial reaction to the announcement of the merger. Although TWX stock took off, due to the large premium, AOL stock suffered, as illustrated by Figure 1B.1. On February 19, 2000, AOL stock reached its low point of 54 and began to recover. By late March, AOL was trading at over 80% of its pre-merger levels. Some people attributed the loss of value to the fact that investors did not yet "get" the merger. In some mergers, the complexity of the deal makes it hard to immediately recognize future revenue sources, cost savings, and other synergies that may arise. The AOL Time Warner deal was further complicated by the fact that AOL was covered by internet financial analysts, and Time Warner was covered by media financial analysts. There were no analysts who were fully conversant with both businesses.

The above provides a summary of the economic and business aspects of the transaction. Strong views have been expressed on other issues. One concern is media independence. Another is editorial integrity. These issues were raised directly by Jim Lehrer in his 1/12/00 interview with Steve Case, head of AOL, and Gerald Levin, head of TWX. Levin assured Jim Lehrer that Henry Luce had left a legacy that Time was to be operated not only in the interest of shareholders, but also in the interest of the public. Case emphasized that AOL would support the public service objective. He argued that individual segments of the combined firm in the future would be even more independent of other segments to demonstrate their integrity.

Some critics fear that a small number of firms increasingly control viewer choices. Others argue the opposite. In earlier decades, viewers were limited to the offerings of four major networks; today every viewer has a multiplicity of choices. At least dozens of choices are possible through cable television, although the majority of cable channels are owned by the few large media firms that control the networks. Thus, critics argue that while the number of choices have increased, there are fewer viewpoints represented in deciding what those choices will be. The AOL Time Warner merger is an indicator that the Internet may fall under the same media influences that control television and other media outlets. Indeed, the merger gave rise to speculation about other firms that could follow the same "new" and "old" media combination strategy. Prominently mentioned were Yahoo! and Disney as potential partners.

Figure 1B.1 Stock Price AOL and TWX

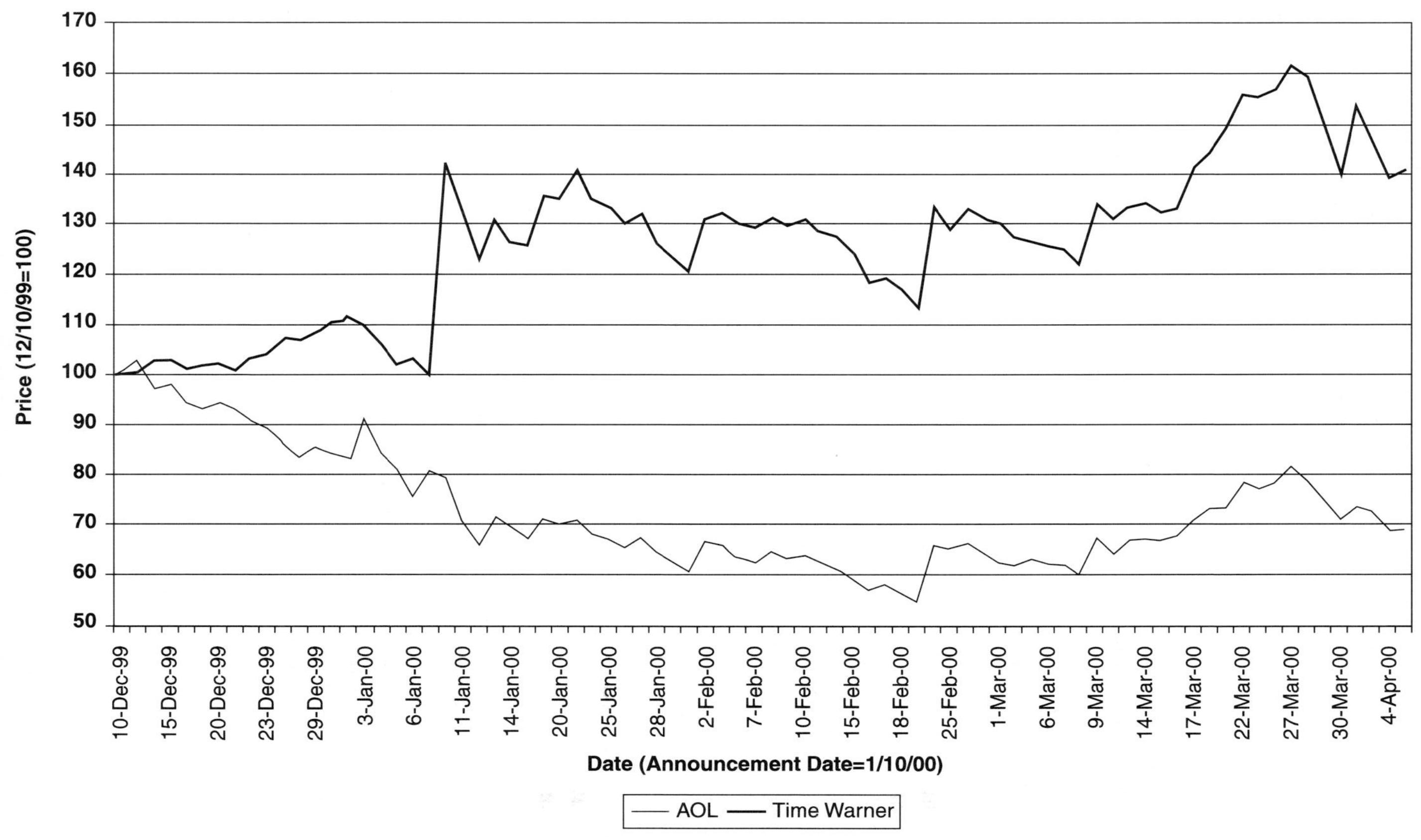

The convergence between TV, the PC, and the Internet will continue to evolve. No one knows for sure what the nature of the ultimate development will be. Many firms and interest groups will shape the future of the media industry. Other media firms are going to have to decide if they will follow Time Warner and seek a strong internet partner, or if they will continue independently. Cable providers like AT&T and the new AOL Time Warner will have to resolve the debate with Internet service providers to determine who will bring broadband internet access into people's homes. Entertainment firms will have to coordinate with technology firms if they are to achieve interactive television. Such dynamic interactions will be shaped by mergers, joint ventures, strategic alliances, and other forms of interfirm relationships.

QUESTIONS

B1.1 Are there likely to be major problems of combining different cultures in this combination of "bricks and clicks"?

B1.2 Discuss the issue of the integration of diverse compensation structures between Time Warner and AOL.

The Legal and Regulatory Framework

This chapter discusses the laws and rules or regulations promulgated to cover securities trading and takeover activity. We discuss securities trading generally as well as takeover activity, the central focus of this book, because the two are so interlinked that they really cannot be separated. Indeed, the laws that were enacted to regulate takeover activity were made a part of the original securities acts enacted in the early 1930s. We also examine the leading cases related to the laws we cover, because they give more explicit content to the nature of the law and its intent.

THE MAIN SECURITIES LAWS

Because wide price fluctuations are likely to be associated with merger and acquisition activity, public policy has been concerned that investors be treated fairly. Legislation and regulations have sought to carry over to the takeover activity of recent decades the philosophy of the securities acts of the 1930s. The aim is prompt and full disclosure of relevant information in the effort to achieve a fair "playing field" for all participants. Some of the earlier legislation remains fully applicable, but it has been augmented with changes in statutes and regulations.

Because the takeover laws are so closely interlinked with securities laws generally, we begin with a summary of the major securities laws. This provides a framework to which we can relate the laws, rules, and regulations governing takeover activity.

Federal Securities Laws

The federal securities laws consist mainly of seven statutes:

> Securities Act of 1933 (SA)
>
> Securities Exchange Act of 1934 (SEA)
>
> Public Utility Holding Company Act of 1935 (PUHCA)
>
> Trust Indenture Act of 1939 (TIA)
>
> Investment Company Act of 1940 (ICA)
>
> Investment Advisers Act of 1940 (IAA)
>
> Securities Investor Protection Act of 1970 (SIPA)

We first summarize what each of the laws covers to provide an overview of the pattern of legislation. We then develop some of the more important provisions in greater detail. Six of the seven major acts were enacted beginning in 1933. There is a reason for the timing. The stock market crash of 1929 was followed by continued depressed markets for several years. Because so many investors lost money, both houses of Congress conducted lengthy hearings to find the causes and the culprits. The hearings were marked by sensationalism and wide publicity. The securities acts of 1933 and 1934 were the direct outgrowth of the congressional hearings.

The Securities Act of 1933 regulates the sale of securities to the public. It provides for the registration of public offerings of securities to establish a record of representations. All participants involved in preparing the registration statements are subject to legal liability for any misstatement of facts or omissions of vital information.

The Securities Exchange Act of 1934 established the Securities and Exchange Commission (SEC) to administer the securities laws and to regulate practices in the purchase and sale of securities.

The purpose of the Public Utility Holding Company Act of 1935 was to correct abuses in the financing and operation of electric and gas public utility holding company systems and to bring about simplification of the corporate structures and physical integration of the operating properties. The SEC's responsibilities under the act of 1935 were substantially completed by the 1950s.

The Trust Indenture Act of 1939 applies to public issues of debt securities with a value of $5 million or more. Debt issues represent a form of promissory note associated with a long document setting out the terms of a complex contract and referred to as the **indenture.** The 1939 act sets forth the responsibilities of the indenture trustee (often a commercial bank) and specifies requirements to be included in the indenture (bond contract) for the protection of the bond purchasers. In September 1987 the SEC recommended to Congress a number of amendments to establish new conflict of interest standards for indenture trustees and to recognize new developments in financing techniques.

The Investment Company Act of 1940 regulates publicly owned companies engaged in the business of investing and trading in securities. Investment companies are subject to rules formulated and enforced by the SEC. The act of 1940 was amended in 1970 to place additional controls on management compensation and sales charges.

The Investment Advisers Act of 1940, as amended in 1960, provides for registration and regulation of investment advisers, as the name suggests.

The Securities Investor Protection Act of 1970 established the Securities Investor Protection Corporation (SIPCO). This corporation is empowered to supervise the liquidation of bankrupt securities firms and to arrange for payments to their customers.

The Securities Act Amendments of 1975 were passed after four years of research and investigation into the changing nature of securities markets. The study recommended the abolition of fixed minimum brokerage commissions. It called for increased automation of trading by utilizing data processing technology to link markets. The SEC was mandated to work with the securities industry to develop an effective national market system to achieve the goal of nationwide competition in securities trading with centralized reporting of price quotations and transactions. It proposed a central order routing system to find the best available price.

In 1978 the SEC began to streamline the securities registration process. Large, well-known corporations were permitted to abbreviate registration statements and to disclose information by reference to other documents that had already been made public. Before these changes, the registration process often required at least several weeks. After the 1978 changes, a registration statement could be approved in as short a time as two days.

In March 1982, Rule 415 provided for shelf registration. Large corporations can register the full amount of debt or equity they plan to sell over a two-year period. After the initial registration has been completed, the firm can sell up to the specified amount of debt or equity without further delay. The firm can choose the time when the funds are needed or when market conditions appear favorable. Shelf registration has been actively used in the sale of bonds, with as much as 60% of debt sales utilizing shelf registration. Less than 10% of the total issuance of equities have employed shelf registration.

In 1995 the Private Securities Litigation Reform Act (PSLRA) was enacted by Congress. This law placed restrictions on the filing of securities fraud class action suits. It sought to discourage the filing of frivolous claims. In late 1998 the Securities Litigation Uniform Standards Act (SLUSA) was signed into law. It had been found that some class action plaintiffs had been circumventing PSLRA by filing suits in state courts. SLUSA establishes a uniform national standard to be applied to securities class actions and makes clear that such suits will be the exclusive jurisdiction of the federal courts. SLUSA forces all class action plaintiffs alleging securities fraud to provide greater detail on the basis for their claims. It enables defendant companies to delay the expenses of discovery of evidence until the complaint has withstood a motion to dismiss. The 1998 act seeks to protect companies against unfounded securities fraud class actions. This reduces the pressure on defendant companies to enter into a settlement to avoid the litigation expenses that otherwise would be incurred.

THE OPERATION OF THE SECURITIES ACTS

The Securities Act of 1933 has primary responsibility for recording information. Section 5 prevents the public offering and sale of securities without a registration statement. Section 8 provides for registration and permits the statement to automatically become effective 20 days after it is filed with the SEC. However, the SEC has the power to request more information or to issue a stop order, which delays the operation of the 20-day waiting period.

It is the Securities Exchange Act of 1934 (SEA) that provides the basis for the amendments that were applicable to takeover activities. Section 12(j) empowers the SEC to revoke or suspend the registration of a security if the issuer has violated any provisions of the 1934 act. The SEC imposes periodic disclosure requirements under Section 13. The basic reports are (1) Form 10-K, the annual report; (2) Form 10-Q, the quarterly report; and (3) Form 8-K, the current report for any month in which specified events occur.

Section 14 governs proxy solicitation. Prior to every meeting of its security holders, they must be furnished with a proxy statement containing specified information. The SEC provides procedural requirements for proxy contests. Under SEA Rule 14a-8, any security holder may require management to include his or her proposal for action in the proxy statement. If management opposes the proposal, it must include in the proxy material a statement by the security holder not more than 200 words in length in support of his or her proposal.

TENDER OFFER REGULATION—THE WILLIAMS ACT

Prior to the late 1960s, most intercorporate combinations were represented by mergers. This typically involved "friendly" negotiations by two or more firms. When they mutually agreed, combination of some form might occur. During the conglomerate merger movement of the 1960s, corporate takeovers began to occur. Some were friendly and not much different from mergers. Others were hostile and shook up the business community.

In October 1965 Senator Harrison Williams introduced legislation seeking to protect the target companies. These initial efforts failed, but his second effort, initiated in 1967, succeeded. The Williams Act, in the form of various amendments to the Securities Exchange Act of 1934, became law on July 29, 1968. Its stated purpose was to protect target shareholders from swift and secret takeovers in three ways: (1) by generating more information during the takeover process that target shareholders and management could use to evaluate outstanding offers; (2) by requiring a minimum period during which a tender offer must be held open, thus delaying the execution of the tender offer; and (3) by explicitly authorizing targets to sue bidding firms.

Section 13

Section 13(d) of the Williams Act of 1968 required that any person who had acquired 10% or more of the stock of a public corporation must file a Schedule 13D with the SEC within 10 days of crossing the 10% threshold. The act was amended in 1970 to increase the SEC powers and to reduce the trigger point for the reporting obligation under Section 13(d) from 10% to 5%. Basically, Section 13(d) provides management and the shareholders with an early warning system.

The filing requirement does not apply to those persons who purchased less than 2% of the stock within the previous 12 months. Due to this exemption, a substantial amount of stock can be accumulated over years without having to file Schedule 13D. Institutional investors (registered brokers and dealers, banks, insurance companies, and so forth) can choose to file Schedule 13G instead of Schedule 13D if the equity securities were acquired in the ordinary course of business. Schedule 13G is an abbreviated version of Schedule 13D.

The insider trading scandals of the late 1980s produced calls for a reduction below 5% and a shortening of the 10-day minimum period for filing. However, shortening the period would not stop the practice of "parking" violations that was uncovered in the Boesky investigation. Under parking arrangements, traders attempt to hide the extent of their ownership to avoid the 5% disclosure trigger by "parking" purchased securities with an accomplice broker until a later date. A related practice is to purchase options on the stock of the target; this is equivalent to ownership because the options can be exercised whenever the holder wishes to take actual ownership.

Section 14

Sections 13(d) and 13(g) of the Williams Act apply to any large stock acquisitions, whether public or private (an offering to less than 25 people). Section 14(d) applies only to public tender offers but applies whether the acquisition is small or large, so its coverage is broader. The 5% trigger rule also applies under Section 14(d). Thus, any group making solicitations or recommendations to a target group of shareholders that would result in owning more than 5% of a class of securities registered under Section 12 of the Securities Act must first file a Schedule 14D with the SEC. An acquiring firm must disclose in a Tender Offer Statement (Schedule 14D-1) its intentions and business plans for the target as well as any relationships or agreements between the two firms. The schedule must be filed with the SEC "as soon as practicable on the date of the commencement of the tender offer"; copies must be hand-delivered to the target firm and to any competitive bidders; the relevant stock exchanges (or the National Association of Securities Dealers for over-the-counter stocks) must be notified by telephone (followed by a mailing of the schedule).

Note, however, that the language of Section 14(d) refers to *any* group making recommendations to target shareholders. This includes target management, which is prohibited from advising target shareholders as to how to respond to a tender offer until it too has filed with the SEC. Until target management has filed a Schedule 14D-9, a Tender Offer Solicitation/Recommendation Statement, they may only advise shareholders to defer tendering their shares while management considers the offer. Companies who consider themselves vulnerable often take the precaution of preparing a fill-in-the-blanks schedule left with an agent in Washington, to be filed immediately in the event of a takeover attempt, allowing target management to respond swiftly in making public recommendations to shareholders. Thus, Section 14(d) (1) provides both the early warning system and information that will help target shareholders determine whether or not to tender their shares. SEA Sections 14(d) (4)–(7) regulate the terms of a tender offer, including the length of time the offer must be left open (20 trading days), the right of shareholders to withdraw shares that they may have tendered previously, the manner in which tendered shares must be purchased in oversubscribed offers, and the effect of the bidder changing the terms of the offer. The delay period, of course, also gives shareholders time to evaluate the offer, but, more important, it enables management to seek out competing bids.

Also, SEA Section 14(e) prohibits misrepresentation, nondisclosure, or any fraudulent, deceptive, or manipulative acts or practices in connection with a tender offer.

INSIDER TRADING OVERVIEW

The SEC has three broad categories under which insider trading, fraud, or illegal profits can be attacked. Rule 10b-5 is a general prohibition against fraud or deceit in security transactions. Rule 14e-3 prohibits trading in nonpublic information in connection with tender offers. The Insider Trading Sanctions Act of 1984 applies to insider trading more generally. It states that those who trade on information not available to the general public can be made to give back their illegal profits and pay a penalty of three times as much as their illegal activities produced. To date, the term insider trading has not been clearly delineated by the SEC. The ambiguity of the three sources of power that may be used by the SEC in the regulation of insider trading gives the SEC considerable discretion in its choice of practices and cases to prosecute. Also, the SEC is empowered to offer bounties to informants whose information leads to the recovery of illegal gains and payment of a civil penalty.

It should be noted also that the traditional regulation of insider trading was provided for under SEA Sections 16(a) and 16(b). Section 16(a) applies to officers, directors, and any persons who own 10% or more of any class of securities of a company. Section 16(a) provides that these corporate insiders must report to the SEC all transactions involving their purchase or sale of the corporation's stock on a monthly basis. Section 16(a) is based on the premise that a corporate insider has an unfair advantage by virtue of his or her knowledge of information that is generated within the corporation. This information is available on a privileged basis because he or she is an officer, a director, or a major security holder who is presumed to have privileged communications with top officers in the company. Section 16(b) provides that the corporation or any of its security holders may bring suit against the offending corporate insider to return the profits to the corporation because of insider trading completed within a six-month period.

The Racketeer Influenced and Corrupt Organizations Act of 1970 (RICO)

The Racketeer Influenced and Corrupt Organizations Act of 1970 (RICO) was originally aimed at unions. It provides for triple damages, as do the antitrust laws. It has also been applied to securities trading in famous cases such as the legal action against Michael Milken. Its requirements are simple: (1) conspiracy and (2) repeated transactions. If more than one person is involved, it is a conspiracy. If, in addition, repeated acts occur, the two requirements for the applicability of RICO have been met. Its provisions are truly draconian.

The act is now aimed at companies that engage in acts that defraud consumers, investors, or public bodies such as cities or states and authorizes triple damages for winning plaintiffs. Furthermore, in a criminal suit brought by any representative of the Department of Justice, RICO permits the court to order that all of the assets of the accused be seized while the case is still being tried. This gives the prosecutor tremendous power. From a practical standpoint, it means that a mere accusation brought under RICO can bring the business of any accused to a halt. If its assets are seized, particularly if it is engaged in securities transactions, it no longer has the means of conducting business. Hence, whether the accused is guilty or not, there is tremendous pressure to settle, because the alternative is to have its business disrupted. And even if after months and months of trial the accused is found innocent, it is small solace, because the disruption may have resulted in irreparable damage to its business.

Table 2.1   Summary of Securities Laws and Regulations

Rule 10b-5:	Prohibits fraud, misstatements, or omission of material facts in connection with the purchase or sale of any security.
Section 13(d):	Provides early warning to target firms of acquisitions of their stock by potential acquirers: 5% threshold, 10-day filing period. Applies to all large stock acquisitions.
Section 14(d) (1):	Requirements of Section 13(d) extended to *all public tender offers.* Provides for full disclosure to SEC by any group making recommendations to target shareholders.
Section 14(d) (4)–(7):	Regulates terms of tender offers: length of time offer must be held open (20 days), right of shareholders to withdraw tendered shares, and so on.
Section 14(e):	Prohibits fraud and misrepresentation in context of tender offers. Rule 14e-3 prohibits trading on nonpublic information in tender offers.
Section 16(a):	Provides for reporting by corporate insiders on their transactions in their corporations' stocks.
Section 16(b):	Allows the corporation or its security holders to sue for return of profits on transactions by corporate insiders completed within a six-month period.
Insider Trading Sanctions Act of 1984:	Provides for triple damages in insider trading cases.
Racketeer Influenced and Corrupt Organizations Act of 1970 (RICO):	Provides for seizure of assets upon accusation and triple damages upon conviction for companies that defraud consumers, investors, and so on.

We have thus brought together in one place the whole array of laws, rules, and regulations that apply to securities trading including the takeover process. For convenience of reference, we summarize them briefly in Table 2.1.

COURT CASES AND SEC RULES

To this point we have described the main statutory provisions that specify the various elements of fraud and insider trading in connection with trading in securities and takeover activities. The full meaning of these statutes is brought out by the subsequent court interpretations and SEC rules implementing the powers granted the SEC by the various statutes.

Liability Under Rule 10b-5 of the 1934 Act

As we have indicated, Rule 10b-5, issued by the Securities and Exchange Commission under the powers granted to it by the 1934 act, is a broad, powerful, and general securities antifraud provision. In general, for Rule 10b-5 to apply, a security must be involved. Technical issues have arisen as to what constitutes a security. If securities are involved, all transactions are covered, whether on one of the securities exchanges or over the counter. A number of elements for a cause of action have been set forth in connection with Rule 10b-5, as follows.

1. There must be fraud, misrepresentation, a material omission, or deception in connection with the purchase or sale of securities.
2. The misrepresentation or omission must be of a fact as opposed to an opinion. However, inaccurate predictions of earnings may be held to be misrepresentations, and failure to disclose prospective developments may be challenged.
3. The misrepresentation or omission must be material to an investor's decision in the sense that there was a substantial likelihood that a reasonable investor would consider the fact of significance in his or her decision.
4. There must be a showing that the plaintiff actually believed the misrepresentation and relied upon it and that it was a substantial factor in his or her decision to enter the transaction.
5. The plaintiff must be an actual purchaser or an actual seller to have standing.
6. Defendant's deception or fraud must have a sufficiently close nexus to the transaction so that a court could find that the defendant's fraud was "in connection with" the purchase or sale by plaintiff.
7. Plaintiff must prove that the defendant had scienter. "Scienter" literally means knowingly or willfully. It means that the defendant had a degree of knowledge that makes the individual legally responsible for the consequences of his or her act and that he or she had an actual intent to deceive or defraud. Negligence is not sufficient.

These elements represent requirements for a successful suit under Rule 10b-5. Some of the elements were developed in a series of court decisions. The main thrust of Rule 10b-5 concerns fraud or deceit. The Supreme Court set forth the scienter requirement in two cases: *Ernst and Ernst v. Hochfelder,* 425 US 185 (1976); and *Aaron v. SEC,* 446 US 680 (1980).

In addition to its use in fraud or deceit cases, a number of interesting cases have brought out the meaning and applicability of Rule 10b-5 in connection with insider trading. For the present, we refer to insider trading merely as purchases or sales by persons who have access to information that is not available to those with whom they deal or to traders generally. However, there are many court decisions about what constitutes insider trading and a continual stream of proposals in Congress to clarify the meaning of the term.

An early case was *Cady, Roberts & Co.,* 40 SEC 907 (1961). In this case, a partner in a brokerage firm received a message from a director of the Curtiss-Wright Corporation that the board of directors had voted to cut the dividend. The broker immediately placed orders to sell the Curtiss-Wright stock for some of his customers. The sales were made before news of the dividend cut was generally disseminated. The broker who made the transactions was held to have violated Rule 10b-5.

The Texas Gulf Sulphur Corp. case of 1965 was classic [*SEC v. Texas Gulf Sulphur Company,* 401 F.2d 833 (2d Cir. (1968)]. A vast mineral deposit consisting of millions of tons of copper, zinc, and silver was discovered in November 1963.

However, far from publicizing the discovery, the company took great pains to conceal it for over five months, to the extent of issuing a false press release in April 1964 labeling proliferating rumors as "unreliable . . . premature and possibly misleading." Meanwhile, certain directors, officers, and employees of Texas Gulf Sulphur who knew of the find bought up quantities of the firm's stock (and options on many more shares) before any public announcement. The false press release was followed only four days later by another that finally revealed publicly the extent of the find. In the company's defense, it was alleged that secrecy was necessary to keep down the price of neighboring tracts of land that they had to acquire in order to fully exploit the discovery. However, the SEC brought and won a civil suit based on Rule 10b-5.

The next case is *Investors Management Co.,* 44 SEC 633 (1971). An aircraft manufacturer disclosed to a broker-dealer, acting as the lead underwriter for a proposed debenture issue, that its earnings for the current year would be much lower than it had previously publicly announced. This information was conveyed to the members of the sales department of the broker-dealer and passed on in turn to major institutional clients. The institutions sold large amounts of the stock before the earnings revisions were made public. Again the SEC won the suit.

In the next two cases we cover, the SEC lost. The first case involved one of the leading investment banking corporations, Morgan Stanley. The Kennecott Copper Corporation was analyzing whether or not to buy Olinkraft, a paper manufacturer. Morgan Stanley began negotiations with Olinkraft on behalf of Kennecott. Later, Kennecott decided it did not wish to purchase Olinkraft. The knowledge that Morgan Stanley had gained in its negotiations led it to believe that one of its other clients, Johns-Manville, would find Olinkraft attractive. In anticipation of this possibility, Morgan Stanley bought large amounts of the common stock of Olinkraft. When Johns-Manville subsequently made a bid for Olinkraft, Morgan Stanley realized large profits. A suit was brought against Morgan Stanley. However, the court held that Morgan Stanley had not engaged in any improper behavior under Rule 10b-5.

In the next case, Raymond Dirks was a New York investment analyst who was informed by a former officer of Equity Funding of America that the company had been fraudulently overstating its income and net assets by large amounts. Dirks conducted his own investigation, which corroborated the information he had received. He told the SEC and a reporter at the *Wall Street Journal* to follow up on the situation and advised his clients to sell their Equity Funding shares. The SEC brought an action against Dirks on grounds that if a tippee has material information knowingly obtained from a corporate insider, he or she must either disclose it or refrain from trading. However, the U.S. Supreme Court found that Dirks had not engaged in improper behavior [*Dirks v. SEC,* 463 US 646 (1983)]. In Texas Gulf Sulphur, the law made it clear that trading by insiders in shares of their own company using insider knowledge is definitely illegal. But the court held that it was not illegal for Raymond Dirks to cause trades to be made on the basis of what he learned about Equity Funding because the officer who conveyed the information was not breaching any duty and Dirks did not pay for the information.

So the first principle is that it is illegal for insiders to trade on the basis of inside information. A second principle that has developed is that it is illegal for an outsider to trade on the basis of information that has been "misappropriated." The misappropriation doctrine began to develop in the famous Chiarella case [*United States v. Chiarella* 445 US 222 (1980)]. *United States v. Chiarella* was a criminal case. Vincent Chiarella was the "markup man" in the New York composing room of Pandick Press, one of the leading U.S. financial printing firms. In working on documents, he observed five announcements of corporate takeover bids in which the targets' identities had presumably been concealed by blank spaces and false names. But Chiarella made some judgments about the names of the targets, bought their stock, and realized some profits. Chiarella was sued under Rule 10b-5 on the theory that, like the officers and directors of Texas Gulf Sulphur, he had defrauded the uninformed shareholders whose stock he had bought. Chiarella was convicted in the lower courts, and his case was appealed to the Supreme Court. In arguing its case before the Supreme Court, the government sought to strengthen its case. It argued that even if Chiarella did not defraud the persons with whom he traded, he had defrauded his employer, Pandick Press, and its clients, the acquiring firms in the documents he had read. He had misappropriated information that had belonged to Pandick Press and its clients. As a result he had caused the price of the targets' stock to rise, thereby injuring his employer's clients and his employer's reputation for reliability. The Supreme Court expressed sympathy with the misappropriation theory but reversed Chiarella's conviction because the theory had not been used in the lower court.

However, in the next case that arose, the SEC used its misappropriation theory from the beginning and won in a criminal case. A stockbroker named Newman was informed by friends at Morgan Stanley and Kuhn Loeb about prospective acquisitions. He bought the targets' shares and split the profits with his friends who had supplied the information. He was convicted under the misappropriation theory on grounds that he had defrauded the investment banking houses by injuring their reputation as safe repositories of confidential information from their clients. He had also defrauded their clients because the stock purchases based on confidential information had pushed up the prices of the targets.

The misappropriation theory also won in a case very similar to Chiarella. Materia was a proofreader at the Bowne Printing firm. Materia figured out the identity of four takeover targets and invested in them. This time the SEC applied the misappropriation theory from the start and won [*SEC v. Materia,* 745 F.2d 197 (2d Cir. (1984)].

The SEC also employed the misappropriation theory in its criminal case against a *Wall Street Journal* reporter, R. Foster Winans, the author of the newspaper's influential "Heard on the Street" column. Along with friends, Winans traded on the basis of what they knew would appear in the paper the following day. Although his conviction was upheld by the Supreme Court, the 4–4 vote could not be mistaken for a resounding affirmation of the misappropriation doctrine, and there are those who suspect that without the mail and wire fraud involved in the Winans case, the outcome might have been different. Rulings in later cases strengthened the misappropriation doctrine.

OTHER DISCLOSURE REQUIREMENTS

Regulations and legislation have been applied to all phases of trading activity generally. We next describe some additional aspects of disclosure including interpretation and implementation of the regulations.

Disclosure Requirements of Stock Exchanges

In addition to the disclosure and notification requirements of federal and state securities regulation, the various national and regional stock exchanges have their own internal disclosure requirements for listed companies. In general, these amount to notifying the exchanges promptly (that is, by telephone) of any material developments that may significantly affect the trading volume and/or price of the listed firm's stock.

The exchanges are naturally reluctant to halt trading in a stock, particularly because institutional investors may continue to trade in the "third market" during a halt. However, it sometimes does so to allow the public time to digest important information that would otherwise result in an order imbalance. A listed company may also request a trading halt. Target companies have sometimes requested halts as a defensive strategy to buy time to find another bidder (a white knight) or to force the initial bid higher. As a result, the NYSE has implemented a policy to limit the length of such voluntary halts. Once a halt is requested, a company has 30 minutes to disclose its news, after which the exchange, not the company, decides when to reopen trading.

Disclosure of Merger Talks

On April 4, 1988, the Supreme Court ruled by a 6–0 vote (three justices not participating) that investors may claim damages from a company that falsely denied it was involved in negotiations that resulted in a subsequent merger. Such denials would represent misleading information about a pending merger, which would provide investors who sold stock during the period with a basis for winning damages from the company officers.

The case involved the acquisition by Combustion Engineering of Basic Inc. Executives of Combustion Engineering began talks with Basic officers in 1976. The talks continued through 1977 and into early 1978, when Basic stock was selling for less than $20 per share. The stock began to rise in price, and in response to rumors of a merger Basic issued three public statements denying that its officers knew of any reason for the rise in the price of its stock. It issued a denial as late as November 6, 1978.

On December 19, 1978, Basic's board voted to approve the sale of the company to Combustion at $46 per share. Some shareholders filed suit against Basic's board, claiming that they were misled into selling their stock at the low premerger price. A district court judge in Cleveland rejected their suit, but a federal appeals court reinstated the suit in 1986 on grounds that the statements made were both significant and misleading. The Supreme Court returned the case to the district court judge for trial. The Supreme Court decision written by Justice Blackmun stated that federal securities laws require that investors be informed about "material developments." What is "material" depends on the facts of the case, but corporate boards may not deny merger talks that reach the point of board resolutions, instructions to investment bankers, and actual negotiations between principals (Savage, 1988).

In a footnote, Justice Blackmun appeared to suggest that refusing to comment might shield a board. Apparently silence is not misleading under Rule 10b-5 of the Securities Exchange Act. This has been interpreted as saying that either the board must put a sufficiently tight lid on any information about mergers that no rumors get started or, if there are leaks, the board must issue accurate statements of information. The decision appeared to be consistent with the spirit of federal laws and regulations governing securities transactions. Mergers simply represent an area of particular importance because of the large price fluctuations frequently associated with such activity.

REGULATION OF TAKEOVER ACTIVITY BY THE STATES

Before the Williams Act of 1968, there was virtually no state regulation of takeover activity. Even by 1974 only seven states had enacted statutes in this area. This is surprising because states are the primary regulators of corporate activity. The chartering of corporations takes place in individual states. State law has defined a corporation as a legal person subject to state laws. Corporate charters obtained from states define the powers of the firm and the rights and obligations of its shareholders, boards of directors, and managers. However, states are not permitted to pass laws that impose restrictions on interstate commerce or that conflict with federal laws regulating interstate commerce.

Early state laws regulating hostile takeovers were declared illegal by the courts. For example, in 1982 the U.S. Supreme Court declared illegal an antitakeover law passed by the state of Illinois. The courts held that the Illinois law favored management over the interests of shareholders and bidders. The Illinois law was also found to impose impediments on interstate commerce and was therefore unconstitutional.

Recent Developments

To the surprise of most observers, the Supreme Court in April 1987 upheld the Indiana Act. The Indiana Act provides that when an acquiring entity or bidder obtains shares that would cause its voting power to reach specified threshold levels, the bidder does not automatically obtain the voting rights associated with those shares. The transfer of voting rights must receive the approval of a majority of shareholders, not including the shares held by the bidder or insider directors and officers of the target company. A bidder can request a special shareholders meeting that must be held within 50 days of the request, with the expenses of the meeting to be borne by the bidder.

Critics of the Indiana Act regard it as a delaying tactic that enables the target to delay the process by at least 50 days. The special requirements in connection with voting make the outcome of the tender offer much more uncertain. The Indiana Act was tested in a case brought by Dynamics Corporation of America chartered in Connecticut. It announced a tender offer to increase its holdings of CTS Corporation (incorporated in Indiana) from 9.6% to 27.5%. CTS invoked the Indiana Act. Dynamics would not be able to vote either the additional shares or the initial 9.6%. Dynamics filed suit arguing that the Indiana Act was preempted by the Williams Act and violated the interstate commerce clause. Dynamics won in the U.S. district court and in the appeals court, but the decision was reversed in the U.S. Supreme Court.

Other states passed acts more moderate than the Indiana Act. The New York–New Jersey pattern provides for a five-year moratorium preventing hostile bidders from doing a second-step transaction such as merging a newly acquired company with another (Veasey, 1988).

A Delaware law was enacted in early 1988. It followed the New York–New Jersey model. The Delaware moratorium on second-step transactions is only for three years, and it does not apply if the hostile bidder obtains the approval of the board of the target company and a two-thirds vote of the other stockholders for the transaction to proceed. The board of a Delaware corporation may also vote to "opt out" of the statute within 90 days of its effective date (Veasey, 1988).

The Delaware statute was regarded as having great significance because more than half of the Fortune 500 companies are incorporated in Delaware. Also, Delaware's statutes and regulations of corporations are widely regarded as a national model. But in this instance it is argued that Delaware acted because the Delaware state legislators "apparently feared an exodus of companies in search of protection elsewhere" (Bandow, 1988, p. 2).

Issues with Regard to State Takeover Laws

One reason put forth for state takeover laws is that they permit shareholders a more considered response to two-tier and partial tender offers. The other argument is that the Williams Act provides that tender offers remain open for only 20 days. It is argued that a longer time period may be needed when the target is large to permit other bidders to develop information to decide whether or not to compete for the target.

However, in practice it has been found that 70% of the tender offers during the years 1981 to 1984 were for all outstanding shares. The other 30% of the offers were split between two-tier and partial offers. The proportion of two-tier offers declined over the period of the study (Office of the Chief Economist, SEC, April 1985).

Furthermore, many companies have adopted fair price amendments that require the bidder to pay a fair price for all shares acquired. Under the laws of Delaware, Massachusetts, and certain other states, dissenting shareholders may request court appraisal of the value of their shares. To do so, however, they must file a written demand for appraisal before the shareholders meeting to vote on the merger. Tendering shareholders must not vote for the merger if they wish to preserve the right to an appraisal.

Critics also point out that state antitakeover laws have hurt shareholders. Studies by the Office of the Chief Economist of the SEC found that when in 1986 New Jersey placed restrictions on takeovers, the prices for 87 affected companies fell by 11.5% (Bandow, 1988). Similarly, an SEC study found that stock prices for 74 companies chartered in Ohio declined an average of 3.2%, a $1.5 billion loss, after that state passed restrictive legislation. Another study estimated that the New York antitakeover rules reduced equity values by 1%, costing shareholders $1.2 billion (Bandow, 1988).

For these reasons, critics argue that the state laws protect parochial state interests rather than shareholders. They argue that the states act to protect employment and increase control over companies in local areas. Furthermore, they argue that state laws are not needed. If more shareholder protection were needed, all that would be required would be to amend the Williams Act, by extending the waiting period from 20 to 30 days, for example. It is argued further that securities transactions clearly represent interstate commerce. Thus, it is difficult to argue that the state laws are not unconstitutional. By limiting securities transactions, they impede interstate commerce.

The goal is to achieve a balance. Certainly it is desirable to protect the interests of shareholders. However, it must be recognized that two-tier offers and partial offers are used to prevent free-riding. In the absence of two-tier pricing and post-takeover dilution, shareholders know that their shares will not decline in value if the takeover succeeds. So individual small shareholders will wait until after the takeover in hopes that the changes made by the acquirer will increase the value of the stock. Most individual shareholders may behave this way. Then this "free-rider" behavior will prevent takeovers from being accomplished.

Similarly, if states make takeovers more difficult, the advantage is that time can be extended so that competing bids may be made. The data show that competing bids lead to higher prices for target shareholders. On the other hand, if the impediments to takeover are increased too greatly, bidders will be discouraged from even making the effort. In this case target shareholders will lose all benefits. The argument then concludes that state takeover laws are unnecessary. Applicable federal laws should seek to strike a balance between protecting shareholders and stimulating reasonable competing bidding activity, but not to the point where all bidding activity is discouraged.

It has also been argued that federal laws should prevent "abusive takeovers" where "speculative financing" may be involved. But the critical concepts are ambiguous. What is regarded as abusive or speculative varies with the viewpoints of different decision makers. There may, however, be legitimate concerns that rising debt ratios, whether or not associated with takeovers or restructuring, may amplify financial problems when a future economic downturn takes place.

ANTITRUST POLICIES

Antitrust actions have increased along with the rise in merger activity. This can readily be documented from the annual reports of the Department of Justice (DOJ) and the Federal Trade Commission (FTC), available from their Web sites. The DOJ and the FTC have overlapping jurisdictions but manage to reach compromises on allocations of antitrust cases.

In 1998, the DOJ challenged 51 mergers. The DOJ blocked Lockheed Martin from acquiring Northrop Grumman. This would have been an $11.6 billion acquisition. The DOJ permitted WorldCom's $44 billion acquisition of MCI only on condition that MCI agree to sell its Internet business for $1.75 billion. The DOJ filed suit to block the attempt by Primestar to acquire the direct broadcast satellite assets of News Corporation and MCI. As a consequence, the companies abandoned the transaction.

During 1998 the DOJ obtained $267 million in fines for antitrust violations. This was a record high, exceeding the previous 1997 record of $205 million. Most of these fines grew out of criminal cases involving international cartels. A number of U.S. and foreign companies paid fines for participating in an international cartel to fix the price and allocate market shares worldwide for graphite electrodes used in electric arc furnaces to melt scrap steel. An agreement to fix the wholesale price of vitamins resulted in fines levied against Swiss, German, Japanese, and U.S. drug companies. Archer Daniels Midland along with Swiss, German, and Japanese companies were fined for fixing the prices of lysine and citric acid.

The FTC reported that it had also achieved a record year in antitrust enforcement in 1998. It stopped or required modifications in merger agreements in 32 large transactions. The FTC successfully blocked two mergers involving pharmaceutical wholesalers: the acquisition by McKesson Corp. of AmeriSource Health Corp. and the acquisition by Cardinal Health of Bergen Brunswig Corp. The FTC negotiated a settlement in which S.C. Johnson agreed to divest a portion of the assets it would gain in its $1.125 billion acquisition of DowBrands, including Dow's "Spray 'n Wash," "Spray 'n Starch," and "Glass Plus" brands. In Tenet Healthcare, the FTC obtained an injunction against a proposed merger between the only two commercial acute care hospitals in Butler County, Missouri. The FTC also issued a complaint against Summit Technology and VISX, Inc. the only two firms authorized to sell the equipment and technology used for laser eye surgery. The FTC charged that they had formed a joint venture to pool their patents rather than compete against one another.

The above examples demonstrate that in considering possible merger transactions, antitrust considerations are an important part of the planning process. For these reasons we review the relevant antitrust statutes and the policies promulgated by the DOJ and the FTC.

THE BASIC ANTITRUST STATUTES

The two basic antitrust laws are the Sherman Act of 1890 and the Clayton Act of 1914.

Sherman Act of 1890

This law was passed in response to the heightened merger activity around the turn of the century. It contains two sections. Section 1 prohibits mergers that would tend to create a monopoly or undue market control. This was the basis on which the DOJ stopped the merger between Staples and Office Depot. Section 2 is directed against firms that had already become dominant in their markets in the view of the government. This was the basis for actions against IBM and AT&T in the 1950s. Both firms were required to sign consent decrees in 1956 restricting AT&T from specified markets and requiring that IBM sell as well as lease computer equipment. Under Section 2, IBM and AT&T were sued again in the 1970s. The suit against IBM, which had gone on for 10 years, was dropped in 1983. The suit against AT&T resulted in divestiture of the operating companies, effective 1984.

The Microsoft case illustrates the policies of the Department of Justice under Section 2 of the Sherman Act. Parallel to DOJ's suits against IBM during the 1970s, the DOJ turned its attention to Microsoft during the decade of the 1990s. We begin with a summary timeline.

Timeline of the Microsoft Case

1990		Federal Trade Commission (FTC) opens an antitrust investigation of Microsoft. The FTC investigates whether Microsoft's pricing policies illegally thwarted competition and whether Microsoft had written its operating system source code to hinder competing applications.
1993	February	The FTC deadlocks on bringing charges against Microsoft in a 2–2 vote.
	July	The FTC again is unable to reach a decision.
	August	The FTC drops its inquiry on Microsoft. The Department of Justice (DOJ) announces that it will take over the case.
1994	July	In a settlement with the DOJ, Microsoft agrees to alter several business practices, including its licensing agreements with computer makers.
1995	February	U.S. District Judge Sporkin rejects the Microsoft–DOJ settlement on the grounds that it does not do enough to curtail Microsoft's anticompetitive actions.
	April	DOJ sues to block Microsoft's acquisition of Intuit, maker of Quicken personal finance software.
	May	Microsoft drops its planned acquisition of Intuit.
	June	Microsoft announces that the DOJ is investigating Microsoft Network, its online service.
		Federal appeals court upholds the 1994 settlement and removes Judge Sporkin from the case.
	August	U.S. District Judge Jackson approves the 1994 settlement.
		Microsoft launches Windows 95.
1996	July	Caldera Inc. sues Microsoft, alleging that Microsoft excludes competitors from selling rival DOS operating systems.
	September	Microsoft announces that the DOJ is investigating the bundling of Internet Explorer, its Internet browser, and Windows 95.
1997	August	The DOJ approves Microsoft's acquisition of WebTV Networks Inc.
		Microsoft invests $150 million in rival Apple Computer Inc., drawing DOJ scrutiny.
		DOJ announces that it is investigating Microsoft's video-streaming business, which allows users to get high-quality video and sound from the Internet.

	October	The European Commission opens a probe on Microsoft.
		The DOJ sues Microsoft for violating the 1994 agreement. It charges that Microsoft violates the agreement by requiring computer makers to include Internet Explorer if they want to license Windows 95.
	November	Texas sues Microsoft for impeding its investigation.
	December	Judge Jackson issues a preliminary injunction that prohibits Microsoft from requiring computer makers to install Internet Explorer. Jackson appoints Harvard Law professor Lawrence Lessig as a special master to advise him on a final ruling.
		Microsoft appeals the ruling.
		Microsoft later agrees to comply with the order. It provides computer makers with two new options; however, both options weaken computer performance.
		The DOJ charges that the new options do not meet the requirements of the preliminary injunction; it requests that Microsoft be held in contempt of court.
1998	January	The contempt charges are settled by Microsoft and the DOJ.
	February	Lessig is removed from his post by an appeals court while the court considers Microsoft's appeal.
		A Texas judge rules in Microsoft's favor, saying it did not hinder the state's investigation.
	March	Bill Gates and other industry executives testify before a Senate panel investigating Microsoft's practices.
	April	Federal appeals court hears arguments on Microsoft's appeal of the 1997 injunction.
	May	U.S. and 20 states sue Microsoft.
		Microsoft requests to delay hearing; judge sets September trial date.
	June	A federal appeals court rules that Microsoft did not violate a previous agreement with the government when it combined Windows 95 and Internet Explorer.
	July	Microsoft countersues all 20 states.
	August	Probe begins to determine whether Microsoft illegally pressured Intel and Apple.

September	Microsoft and the DOJ ask for a three-week delay due to pretrial preparations.
	Jackson announces that he may have Lessig write a "friend of the court" brief summarizing his views of the case.
	Microsoft serves subpoenas to authors David Yoffie and Michael Cusumano seeking notes and tapes of their interviews with Netscape employees.
October	Internet Explorer overtakes Netscape Navigator in market share.
	Court rejects Microsoft's attempt to obtain the notes and tapes of the two authors.
	Trial is delayed until October 19.
October 19	Trial begins in Washington, D.C.

Preliminary Findings on the Microsoft Case

On November 5, 1999, U.S. District Judge Thomas Penfield Jackson issued a 207-page "Findings of Facts." His materials were generally summarized in the press into four points. (1) Microsoft (MSFT) has a monopoly in the market for personal operating systems with more than a 90% market share. (2) At a meeting on June 25, 1995, MSFT met with Netscape to make an illegal offer to divide the market for Internet browser software. (3) MSFT bundled its Internet browser to its monopoly product, the Windows operating system, in an attempt to stifle competition. (4) MFST illegally used its market power to pressure personal computer makers like Compaq and Internet service providers like America Online into exclusionary agreements not to distribute or promote Netscape's browser.

Shortly thereafter, Judge Jackson appointed Richard Posner, chief judge of the U.S. Court of Appeals in Chicago, as a mediator. His mission was to achieve some compromises in the positions of the Department of Justice and Microsoft. On April 2, 2000, Judge Posner indicated that it was not possible to reach a resolution of the opposing positions. On April 3, 2000, Judge Jackson issued his findings of law that Microsoft was guilty of the first three items in the preceding paragraph, but had not engaged in exclusionary behavior in connection with the Internet browser business.

Some argue that the true economic facts are the opposite of what Judge Jackson set forth. One study found that software prices rose 35% when WordPerfect was the dominant word processor but fell 75% after MSFT took the lead. It is argued that Judge Jackson defined the market too narrowly. It did not include Apple's market share of 10%. Sun Microsystems' sales were up 30% in 1998. Hand-held computer system sales rose 61% in 1998. Linux has 10 million users and has captured 17% of the server market. Sun's Java programming language is becoming increasingly formidable in Internet use. Linux has a 31% market share of the operating systems in Web-based servers. The AOL–Netscape merger suggests that browsers in e-commerce offer the greatest growth opportunity. Internet commercial traffic will be driven by portals where AOL-Netscape is the leader, with MSFT in tenth place.

Prospective developments in the Internet include application service providers creating packages that run on Web servers. Some argue that MSFT will have zero leverage in a world where applications are written so that any browser can run them and any operating system can access them.

With regards to tying arrangement and exclusionary contracts, a rebuttal has also been offered. Two tests of tying are technology that disables other products and contractual agreements that foreclose other products. MSFT uses neither. It uses bundling, which is nonexclusive. MSFT does not prevent original equipment manufacturers (OEMs) from adding Netscape or any other browsers. Netscape and AOL together have 58% of the browser market.

Its competitors have argued that MSFT has been highly aggressive. In rebuttal, it is argued that PC users have benefited and innovations have exploded in many directions. Software application programmers complain that their task would be made easier if MSFT would fully disclose the code to its operating system. To force MSFT to do so would violate the fundamental principles of intellectual property rights.

The arguments and counterarguments are highly controversial. They are only summarized here to provide a basis for the reader to make further investigations and to formulate independent conclusions.

Clayton Act of 1914

The Clayton Act created the Federal Trade Commission for the purpose of regulating the behavior of business firms. Among its sections, two are of particular interest. Section 5 gives the FTC power to prevent firms from engaging in harmful business practices. Section 7 involves mergers. As enacted in 1914, Section 7 made it illegal for a company to acquire the stock of another company if competition could be adversely affected. Companies made asset acquisitions to avoid the prohibition against acquiring stock. The 1950 amendment gave the FTC the power to block asset purchases as well as stock purchases. The amendment also added an incipiency doctrine. The FTC can block mergers if it perceives a tendency toward increased concentration—that the share of industry sales of the largest firms appeared to be increasing.

Hart-Scott-Rodino Act of 1976

The Hart-Scott-Rodino Act of 1976 (HSR) consists of three major parts. Its objective was to strengthen the powers of the DOJ and FTC by requiring approval before a merger could take place. Before HSR, antitrust actions were usually taken after completion of a transaction. By the time a court decision was made, the merged firms had been operating for several years so it was difficult to "unscramble the omelet."

Under Title I, the DOJ has the power to issue civil investigative demands in an antitrust investigation. The idea here is that if the DOJ suspects a firm of antitrust violations it can require firms to provide internal records that can be searched for evidence. We have seen cases in which firms were required to provide literally boxcar loads of internal files for review by the DOJ under Title I.

Title II is a premerger notification provision. If the acquiring firm has sales or assets of $100 million or more and the target firm has sales or assets of $10 million or more, or vice versa, information must be submitted for review. Before the takeover can be completed, a 30-day waiting period for mergers, 15 days for tender offers, is required to enable the agencies to render an opinion on legality. Either agency may request a 20-day extension of the waiting period for mergers or a 10-day extension for tender offers.

Title III is the Parens Patriae Act—each state is the parent or protector of consumers and competitors. It expands the powers of state attorneys general to initiate triple damage suits on behalf of persons (in their states) injured by violations of the antitrust laws. The state itself does not need to be injured by the violation. This gives the individual states the incentive to increase the budgets of their state attorneys general. A successful suit with triple damages can augment the revenues of the states. In the Microsoft case, the attorneys general of 22 states joined in the suit filed by the DOJ.

The prenotification required by Title II is an important part of the merger process. For example, in 1998, out of 7,809 merger announcements, filings were required for 4,728 transactions. This implies that 61% of total transactions involved targets with total assets in excess of $10 million; the other 39% were relatively small deals. About 70% of the filings were reviewed and permitted to proceed before the end of the statutory 30-day waiting period. About 14% (662) of the transactions were assigned to either the DOJ or the FTC for further substantive review. Of the 662, the DOJ or FTC issued "second requests" for 142 of the submissions. A second request is traumatic for applicants because onerous investigations may result. Furthermore, about half of the second request cases (67) in 1998 resulted in about 50 formal actions taken against the merger and about 17 abandonments.

The legal literature and our own experience suggest actions by the parties to a merger that may improve the odds of approval by the review authorities. Companies should follow a proactive strategy during the 30-day review period. The HSR process should be viewed as an educational endeavor to provide the necessary information to the government staff attorneys. The staff attorneys should be contacted with an offer to voluntarily provide additional information. A briefing package should fully develop the business reasons for the merger. Under the guidance of attorneys, high level business executives should be made available for informal presentations or staff interviews.

In response to a second request, the companies should start with a rolling production of material. Two copies of the organization charts for both companies should be provided, with the second copy annotated with names of core groups of employees identified as sources of information. Relevant documents identified in discussions with staff should be promptly offered.

The overriding approach should be for the lawyers and executives to convey a factual, logical story, emphasizing the industry dynamics that make the transaction imperative for the preservation of the client as a viable entity for providing high quality products to its customers at fair prices. The presentation should demonstrate how the industry dynamics require the transaction to enable the firm to fulfill its responsibilities to consumers, employees, the communities in which it has its plants and offices, and its owners and creditors.

THE ANTITRUST GUIDELINES

In the merger guidelines of 1982, and successively in 1987, 1992, and 1996, the spirit of the regulatory authorities was altered. In the merger guidelines of 1968, concentration tests were applied somewhat mechanically. With the recognition of the internationalization of competition and other economic realities, the courts and the antitrust agencies began to be less rigid in their approach to antitrust. In addition to the concentration measures, the economics of the industry were taken into account. For example, in its July 8, 1995 issue, the *Economist* had a lead article entitled, "How Dangerous Is Microsoft?" (pp. 13–14). In an article on antitrust in the same issue, the *Economist* commented that Microsoft held 80% of its market but advised that the trustbusters should analyze the economics of the industry.

The guidelines sought to assure business firms that the older antitrust rules that emphasize various measures of concentration would be replaced by consideration of the realities of the marketplace. Nevertheless, the guidelines start with measures of concentration. For many years, the antitrust authorities, following the academic literature, looked at the share of sales or value added by the top four firms. If this share exceeded 20% (in some cases even lower), it might trigger an antitrust investigation.

Beginning in the 1982 guidelines the quantitative test shifted to the Herfindahl-Hirschman Index (HHI), which is a concentration measure based on the market shares of all firms in the industry. It is simply the sum of the squares of market shares of each firm in the industry. For example, if there were 10 firms in the industry and each held a 10% market share, the HHI would be 1,000. If one firm held a 90% market share, and the nine others held a 1% market share, the HHI would be 8,109 ($90^2 + 9 \times 1$). Notice how having a dominant firm greatly increases the HHI. The HHI is applied as indicated by Table 2.2.

A merger in an industry with a resulting HHI of less than 1,000 is unlikely to be investigated or challenged by the antitrust authorities. An HHI between 1,000 and 1,800 is considered to represent moderate concentration. Investigation and challenge depend on the amount by which the HHI increased over its premerger level. An increase of 100 or more may invite an investigation. An industry with a postmerger HHI above 1,800 is considered a concentrated market. Even a moderate increase over the premerger HHI is likely to result in an investigation by the antitrust authorities.

Table 2.2   Critical Concentration Levels

Postmerger HHI	Antitrust Challenge to a Merger?
Less than 1,000	No challenge—industry is unconcentrated.
Between 1,000 and 1,800	If HHI increased by 100, investigate.
More than 1,800	If HHI increased by 50, challenge.

But, beginning in 1982, the guidelines had already recognized the role of market characteristics. Particularly important is the ability of existing and potential competitors to expand the supply of a product if one firm tries to restrict output. On the demand side, it is recognized that there are usually close substitutes for any product, so a high market share of the sales of one product does not give the ability to elevate price. Quality differences, the introduction of new products, and technological change result in product proliferation and close substitutes. The result is usually fluctuating market shares. For these reasons, concentration measures alone are not a reliable guide to measure the competitiveness of an industry.

Other Market Characteristics

Most important is whether entry is easy or difficult. If output can be increased by expansion of noncooperating firms already in the market or if new firms can construct new facilities or convert existing ones, an effort by some firms to increase price would not be profitable. The expansion of supply would drive prices down. Conditions of entry or other supply expansion potentials determine whether firms can successfully collude regardless of market structure numbers.

Next considered is the ease and profitability of collusion, because there is less likelihood that firms will attempt to coordinate price increases if collusion is difficult or impossible. Here the factors to consider are product differences (heterogeneity), frequent quality changes, frequent new products, technological changes, contracts that involve complicated terms in addition to price, cost differences among suppliers, and so on. Also, DOJ challenges are more likely when firms in an industry have colluded in the past or use practices such as exchanging price or output information.

Nonhorizontal Mergers

The guidelines also include consideration of nonhorizontal mergers. Nonhorizontal mergers include vertical and conglomerate mergers. The guidelines express the view that while nonhorizontal mergers are less likely than horizontal mergers to create competitive problems, "they are not invariably innocuous." The principal theories under which nonhorizontal mergers are likely to be challenged are then set forth. Concern is expressed over the elimination of potential entrants by nonhorizontal mergers. The degree of concern is greatly influenced by whether conditions of entry generally are easy or difficult. If entry is easy, effects on potential entrants are likely to be small. If entry is difficult, the merger will be examined more closely.

The guidelines set forth three circumstances under which vertical mergers may facilitate collusion and therefore be objectionable: (1) If upstream firms obtain a high level of vertical integration into an associated retail market, this may facilitate collusion in the upstream market by monitoring retail prices. (2) The elimination by vertical merger of a disruptive buyer in a downstream market may facilitate collusion in the upstream market. (3) Nonhorizontal mergers by monopoly public utilities may be used to evade rate regulation.

Private Antitrust Suits

The attitudes of business competitors have always had a strong influence on antitrust policy. Writers have pointed out that even when government was responsible for most antitrust actions, the investigations usually followed complaints that had been lodged by competitors against the behavior of other firms that were making life difficult for them in the marketplace (Ellert, 1975, 1976).

But it is also argued that the private lawsuit has always been a temptation to lawyers. The cost of litigation is so high that the threat of a private lawsuit can sometimes be used as blackmail to pressure the prospective defendant to make a cash settlement (Grundman, 1987). Some basic statistics on private antitrust cases were developed under the auspices of the Georgetown Law School (Pitofsky, 1987; White, 1988). Most private antitrust cases are Sherman Act cases in which plaintiffs challenge cartel behavior. The average private triple damage case takes about 1.5 years to complete compared with nine months for the average civil case, including relatively minor court cases. The median award in private antitrust cases is $154,000, about the same as the median award in civil litigation.

State Antitrust Activity

Another development said to be stimulated by the changed policies of the federal antitrust agencies has been an increase in state activity. The arguments here are also complex and require careful analysis. In the first place the increased power of the states was granted in the Hart-Scott-Rodino (HSR) Act of 1976 described earlier in this chapter. This was four years before antitrust policies by the federal agencies began to change in 1980. In addition, the federal government gave $10 million to the states to increase their antitrust enforcement efforts under HSR. The Department of Justice reported that during the grant period the number of state actions increased from 206 in 1977 to over 400 in 1979 (Ewing, 1987). Again, all of this increase in activity was before the change in policies by the federal antitrust agencies after 1980.

The activity of the states has been increasing. The state attorneys general have formed the National Association of Attorneys General (NAAG), which has published both merger and vertical restraint guidelines. In addition, it is developing a legislative program to change by statute the content of the federal antitrust laws.

Although the state attorneys general have been cooperating, there is potential chaos in having 50 different antitrust laws to which business operations may be subject. While cooperation between the state attorneys general may mitigate this problem, some risk remains. Whenever jobs are threatened in any locality either by the functioning of active free markets or by merger activity, there is a risk that parochial views will prevail over what is best for the national economy (Ewing, 1987).

REGULATORY BODIES

Several industries in the United States remain subject to regulation. Generally, regulated industries are still subject to antitrust review, requiring cooperation between the regulatory bodies involved. Our summary coverage will be limited to railroads, commercial banking, and telecommunications.

Railroads

The Interstate Commerce Commission, established in 1887, had long regulated the railroad industry. Under the ICC Termination Act of 1995, it was replaced by the Surface Transportation Board (STB). The STB has final authority on antitrust matters, but must file notices with the Justice Department, which may file objections at STB hearings. Among the tests the STB is required to consider are (1) the effect on adequacy of transportation, (2) the effect on competition among rail carriers, and (3) the interests of rail carrier employees affected by the proposed transaction.

The Department of Justice strongly opposed the Union Pacific–Southern Pacific merger, but, after gaining the approval of the STB, the deal was completed in 1996. In October 1996, CSX offered $92.50 in cash for 40% of Conrail and stock for the remaining 60%. The Norfolk Southern Railroad shortly made an all cash offer of $100 per share. A bidding war ensued coupled with legal skirmishes. The STB urged the participants to negotiate an agreement in which two balanced east-west lines would be created. In the resulting compromise, CSX acquired what was the old New York Central Railroad and Norfolk Southern acquired the old Pennsylvania Railroad system. The two examples demonstrate the strong role of the STB.

Commercial Banks

Banking is another industry subject to regulation. The Board of Governors of the Federal Reserve System (FED) has broad powers over economic matters as well as antitrust. With regard to bank mergers, three agencies may be involved. The Comptroller of the Currency has jurisdiction when national banks are involved. The FED makes decisions for state banks that are members of the Federal Reserve System. The Federal Deposit Insurance Corporation (FDIC) reviews mergers for state chartered banks that are not members of the FED, but are insured by the FDIC. In conducting its reviews, each agency takes into account a review provided by the Department of Justice.

Bank mergers have long been subject to Section 7 of the Clayton Act of 1914. Modifications were enacted by the Bank Merger Act of 1966. Past bank mergers were legalized. Any merger approved by one of the three regulatory agencies had to be challenged within 30 days by the Attorney General. The Act of 1966 provided that anticompetitive effects could be outweighed by a finding that the transaction served the "convenience and needs" of the community to be served. The convenience and needs defense is not applicable to the acquisition by banks of non-banking businesses. The review by one of the three agencies substitutes for filing under Hart-Scott-Rodino of 1976.

Telecommunications

The Federal Communications Commission (FCC) has primary responsibility for the radio and television industries. Mergers in these areas are subject to approval by the FCC, which defers to the Department of Justice and the FTC on antitrust aspects. The Federal Communications Act of 1996 provided for partial deregulation of the telephone and related industries, with rather complicated provisions affecting the role of the former operating companies of the Bell System with their relatively strong monopoly positions in their regional markets.

INTERNATIONAL ANTITRUST

Most of the developed countries of the world have some form of merger control. Cross border transactions will be subject to the multiple jurisdictions of the home countries of bidders and targets. At the end of February 2000, the International Competition Policy Advisory Committee released its two-year study. It recommended that the more than 80 nations conducting antitrust enforcement make more explicit what their antitrust policies are. They proposed faster approval of transactions that do not present obvious problems. They recommended that the U.S. "second-request" process, in which the U.S. antitrust agencies ask for more information about a merger, should be streamlined. The report noted that about one-half of the mergers reviewed by the U.S. Federal Trade Commission or Justice Department have an international component.

While variations in statutes and administrative bodies and procedures are observed, a central theme is market share percentages. The advisory committee report recommended that the merger-size threshold be raised to reduce the number of reviews. It also recommended that more definite timelines for the review process be established. But antitrust authorities may even take action when a purely foreign transaction is perceived to have an impact in domestic markets.

United Kingdom

The Monopolies and Mergers Act of 1965 created the Monopolies and Mergers Commission (MMC) (Gray and McDermott, 1989). A new era in merger control was established by the Fair Trading Act of 1973 in the United Kingdom (UK). The Act created an Office of Fair Trading (OFT) headed by a Director General (DG). The DG of the OFT is required to review all mergers in which the combined firm would have a 25% market share or where the assets of the target exceed 30 million British pounds. After review by the OFT, its DG advises the Secretary of State for Trade and Industry whether a referral should be made to the MMC. The Secretary of State has discretion whether or not to make the referral. If a referral is made to the MMC, the current bid lapses, but may be renewed if the MMC approves. The MMC review may take as long as six months. Its report is made to the OFT and the Secretary of State. If the MMC recommends approval, the Secretary of State cannot override. However, if the MMC recommends prohibition, the Secretary of State is not required to accept its findings, but such instances are rare. As a practical matter a referral to the MMC, which lapses the current bid and involves a long time lag, is likely to kill the transaction.

Japan

Immediately after the conclusion of World War II, the United States attempted to reduce the role of Japanese business groups (keiretsu). Also, a proposed merger requires a filing with a Japanese FTC. The government has 30 days to review the antitrust implications and can extend the review period another 60 days. But in a stock for stock transaction, approval by the government is not required. The reasoning is that advanced review is not needed in a stock transaction which is more easily reversed. But the government can still make an antitrust challenge within 90 days after the transaction.

As in the United States, the review focuses on market share. A combined market share below 25% is not likely to be challenged. A market share above the critical level is likely to be reviewed. The government is probably more flexible in reaching a compromise with the merging companies than are the U.S. antitrust agencies.

Europe

The European Union Merger Regulation grants the European Commission (EC) exclusive authority to review the antitrust implications of transactions which affect the economy of the European Community. Transactions have a community impact if total sales of the combined firm are greater than $4.5 billion annually and the EU sales of each party are greater than $250 million. However, if two-thirds of the revenues of each firm are achieved in a single EU country, the EC will defer to that country's antitrust authorities.

Premerger notification is required. The Minister of Competition of the EU requires a three-week waiting period, but can extend it. The Commission is required to decide upon further investigation within the waiting period and must render an approval decision within five months. The critical issue is whether the combination will create or strengthen a dominant position.

A dramatic example of the international reach of the EU competition policy is provided by the Boeing–McDonnell Douglas merger, announced in December 1996. U.S. defense procurement outlays between 1988 and 1996 had declined by more than 50%. A series of consolidating mergers had taken place among U.S. defense contractors. The EU competition commissioner was concerned that Boeing's position in the commercial aviation market would be further strengthened. But the main concern was Boeing's aggressive program of signing exclusive purchase contracts with major U.S. airlines that would have made it more difficult for Airbus to increase its share of the U.S. commercial aviation market. On May 21, 1997, the EU issued its objections, requiring concessions to avoid its stopping the transaction. The EU had the authority to impose substantial fines, including the seizure of Boeing planes in Europe. Boeing made the requisite concessions to obtain approval from the EU Competition Commissioner. This case illustrates the potentially far reach of international antitrust to a merger between two U.S. firms.

On February 9, 2000, it was announced that UK's Vodafone AirTouch filed materials with the European Commission related to its $181 billion acquisition of Germany's Mannesmann. The filing of Vodafone was said to be related to concessions with regard to Orange, the number 3 mobile phone operator in Britain, which had been acquired by Mannesmann in 1999.

REGULATION BY PUBLICITY

Three in-depth studies [DeAngelo, DeAngelo, and Gilson (DDG), 1994, 1996; DeAngelo and DeAngelo (DD), 1998] document some propositions developed by Michael Jensen on the politics of finance (Jensen, 1979, 1991, 1993).

Seizure of the First Executive Corporation and First Capital Life

In their 1994 study, DDG described the experience of the First Executive Corporation (FE) and its main subsidiary, the Executive Life Insurance Company (ELIC). In 1974 Fred Carr took over as chief executive officer of FE. Under his direction, ELIC's total assets grew from 355th in rank to 15th in 1988. Measured by insurance in force, FE grew from $700 million in 1974 to $60 billion in 1989.

This spectacular growth came from two major sources. One was innovative products such as single-premium deferred annuities. Another important innovation was interest-sensitive whole life products that put competitive pressure on traditional insurers locked into long-term and low-risk assets with low returns. On the management side, FE and ELIC followed some innovative cost reduction methods. The other major competitive advantage developed was to invest in higher yielding junk bonds, which grew to 65% of the assets of ELIC. Until January 1990, ELIC enjoyed an AAA rating from Standard & Poor's with comparable ratings from Moody's and Best.

Carr was a tough competitor. His letters to stockholders criticized his competitors for their stodginess and refusal to mark assets to market values. The aggressive behavior by Carr was especially inflammatory because it was accompanied by a substantial increase in market share.

In 1989, when Milken and the Drexel Company became the target of regulatory and legal actions, the junk bond market in its entirety was unfavorably impacted. In 1989 the Congressional enactment of the Financial Institutions Reform Recovery and Enforcement Act (FIRREA) essentially forced the S&Ls to dispose of their junk bonds and caused the junk bond market to collapse. Although Carr had been calling for "mark-to-market" accounting in his letters to shareholders for many years, the timing of the enactment of the legislation made what otherwise might have been a minor adjustment a major collapse.

The competitors to ELIC publicized these adverse developments and encouraged the policyholders of FE and ELIC to cash in their policies, resulting in the equivalent of a bank run. The financial press ran numerous feature articles dramatizing the difficulties of FE. This adverse publicity gave John Garamendi, the insurance commissioner of California, a basis for placing ELIC in conservatorship on April 11, 1991. This seizure caused further policy surrender requests. Ultimately, in March 1992, California regulators sold $6.13 billion (par value) of ELIC's junk bonds for $3.25 billion; this was at least $2 billion below their then current value.

Ironically, the more traditional insurers experienced declines in their real estate portfolios that were 2.5 times the decline in junk bonds. Furthermore, while junk bonds, real estate, and mortgages bottomed out toward the end of 1990, the value of junk bonds increased in value by almost 60% by July 1992, while real estate and mortgages had recovered by less then 20%. Without regulatory intervention, FE and ELIC would have been fully solvent within a year and a half after the junk bond market bottomed out. Insurance companies and S&Ls with heavy investments in real estate and mortgages experienced continued difficulties.

The story of First Capital Life is similar (DDG, 1996). The seizure of First Capital Life and its parent First Capital Holdings was related to the investment of 40% of its portfolio in junk bonds. DDG state that their evidence suggests that regulatory seizure reflected the targeting of insurers that had invested in junk bonds. However, these companies did not experience differentially poorer financial positions compared with other insurers.

The Hostile Takeover of the Pacific Lumber Company

In 1986 the Pacific Lumber Company (PL), the largest private owner of old redwood trees, was acquired in a leveraged hostile takeover by the MAXXAM Group headed by Charles Hurwitz, regarded as a corporate raider. The event resulted in a dramatic barrage of negative media coverage, linking junk bonds and takeover greed to the destruction of the redwoods.

In their careful analysis of the facts, DD (1996) reach a more balanced conclusion. They point out that basic timber economics explains the behavior of MAXXAM and the predecessor owners of PL. Timber economics predict that old growth forests will be harvested first because they will yield virtually no further growth in harvestable timber volume. Timber economic principles predict that under any private ownership, old growth forests will be harvested, a process that had been taking place for at least 100 years before the 1986 takeover of PL. Their study presents evidence that shows that 91% of PL's old growth redwoods had already been logged by the time of the takeover and that both the old and new managements had similar timetables for the remaining acreage. Junk bonds and takeovers would have little effect on these timetables. DD outline the correct policies for saving the redwoods. One is to raise funds to purchase the old growth acreage for public holding. The other is to raise funds to purchase previously logged land to grow new redwood forests. These eminently sensible prescriptions were lost in the hysteria over the change of ownership of the Pacific Lumber Company.

Regulation by the Politics of Finance

The clinical studies of ELIC, First Capital Life, and PL illustrate how the use of junk bonds resulted in regulation by the politics of finance. The ultimate explanation for the bad reputation of junk bonds is that potentially they could finance the takeover of any firm that was not performing up to its potential. Thus, junk bonds became a vigilant monitoring instrument to pressure managements to achieve a high level of efficiency in the companies under their stewardship. The junk bond takeover threat was unsettling to the managers of the leading companies in the United States. Widespread animosity toward the use of junk bonds developed. Junk bonds filled an important financing gap for new and risky growth companies. Their use in takeovers led to value enhancement for shareholders. But these three case studies illustrate how junk bond use became a lightning rod for widespread hysteria, animosity, and pressures on government regulators to limit and penalize their use.

SUMMARY

Regulation of securities trading is closely related to regulation of merger and acquisition activity, because takeovers are carried out by means of the securities markets. Special characteristics of securities that make them vulnerable to being used fraudulently mandate regulation to increase public confidence in securities markets. The earliest securities legislation in the 1930s grew out of the collapse of confidence following the stock market crash of 1929. The Securities Act of 1933 called for registration of public offerings of securities. The Securities Exchange Act of 1934 established the Securities and Exchange Commission to regulate securities market practices; it also specified disclosure requirements for public companies (Section 13) and set out the procedural requirements for proxy contests. A number of other securities laws in the late 1930s and 1940s applied to public utilities, bond indenture trustees, and investment companies.

The Securities Act of 1933 and Securities Exchange Act of 1934 provided the framework for subsequent regulation. Most of the more recent legislation has been in the form of amendments to these two acts. The Williams Act of 1968 amended the 1934 act to regulate tender offers. Two main requirements were a filing with the SEC upon obtaining 5% ownership and a 20-day waiting period after making a tender offer. The disclosure requirements aim to give the target shareholders information that will enable them to receive more of the gains associated with the rise in the share price of the takeover target. The 20-day waiting period gives the target more time to evaluate the offer and/or tailor a defense or seek multiple bids. Empirical studies on the impact of tender offer regulation on shareholder returns almost universally document significantly higher returns for target shareholders and lower (or negative) returns for bidder shareholders. To the extent that successful tender offers continue to take place, the legislation has achieved its goal of benefiting target shareholders. The risk, however, is that reductions in the returns to bidding firms reduce their incentives to engage in the kind of information-producing activities that lead to beneficial takeovers; thus, the lot of target shareholders in those tender offers that *might* have taken place is not improved.

Historically, insider trading has little to do with M&A activity; it refers to the trading in their own companies' stock by corporate officers, directors, and other insiders. It is largely controlled by Section 16 of the Securities Exchange Act, which requires insiders to report such transactions to the SEC on a regular basis. However, the volatility of stock price changes in connection with M&As creates opportunities for gains by individuals who may not fit the traditional definition of insiders. Rule 10b-5 is a general prohibition of fraud and deceit in the purchase or sale of securities. Rule 14e-3 applies to insider trading, particularly in connection with tender offers. The Insider Trading Sanctions Act of 1984 provides for triple damage penalties in insider trading cases, as does the Racketeer Influenced and Corrupt Organizations Act of 1970 (RICO), which also allows immediate seizure of assets and which is invoked in some of the more notorious cases of insider trading. The SEC rules are somewhat ambiguous, but it is illegal to trade on inside information, whether obtained as a result of one's fiduciary relationship to a firm or through misappropriation.

In addition to federal regulation of M&A activity, a number of states have enacted legislation to protect corporations headquartered within their boundaries. States are the primary regulators of corporate activities. However, there are problems in state regulation of takeovers. Securities markets represent interstate commerce, and state regulations that interfere with interstate commerce are, by definition, unconstitutional. Others argue that state regulations are not necessary, that federal regulations and corporate antitakeover amendments provide sufficient protection. There is even evidence that shareholders are damaged by restrictive state legislation that limits takeovers.

Antitrust policies in the United States continue to be suspicious of large firms and merger activity. Yet the increasing dynamism of the economy has intensified the forces of market competition. Some fundamental economic factors have changed.

1. International competition has clearly increased, and many of our important industries are now international in scope. Concentration ratios must take into account international markets and will be much lower than when measured on the assumption of purely domestic markets.

2. The pace of technological change has increased, and the pace of industrial change has increased substantially. This requires more frequent adjustments by business firms, including many aspects of restructuring that include acquisitions and divestitures.

3. Deregulation in a number of major industries requires industrial realignment and readjustments. These require greater flexibility in government policy.

4. New institutions, particularly among financial intermediaries, represent new mechanisms for facilitating the restructuring processes that are likely to continue.

Many see merger activity as a natural expression of strong change forces. Mergers during the 1980s and 1990s were associated with extraordinary growth in employment and in gross domestic product. Through mergers and restructuring, firms all over the world have become more efficient. In light of the increased dynamism of their environments and the greater intensity of competitive forces, firms should not be restricted by antitrust policies from making required adjustments to economic turbulence. (See publications by Weston, 1953, 1973, 1978, 1980a, 1980b, 1982)

QUESTIONS

2.1 What is the rationale for tender offer regulation?

2.2 Discuss the pros and cons of trading halts as a measure to deal with significant information about a listed firm.

2.3 Discuss the pros and cons of *state* regulation of mergers and tender offers.

2.4 List and briefly explain the product characteristics and/or management decision variables that make collusion within an industry more difficult.

2.5 What other factors are considered along with the Herfindahl-Hirschman Index in the government's decision to initiate an antitrust case?

Case 2.1 Broader Board Responsibilities

An area of great practical importance to directors involved in the sale of their company is the obligation to prove that they received the best possible price for their shareholders. One reason this problem arises is that a target may receive a very attractive proposal from a bidder. The board of the target and some of its key shareholders may believe the offer is a very attractive one. To prove to other shareholders that the offer is the best that could be achieved, the board of the target might test the market (shop around) for other possible bidders. Or they might hire an investment banker or some other financial intermediary to test the market or even to conduct an auction.

But one risk is that if the market feels that the target is being shopped, it may suspect some weakness and potential problems at the target. If no other offers are forthcoming or if other offers come in at much lower prices, the first bidder may lower his offer because his position has been clearly strengthened. Another possibility is that the initial bidder may drop out as soon as the target checks other alternatives rather than continue to incur the additional expenses required to investigate and evaluate the deal with the target.

The basic problem is that if bidding is costly, then the decision of the potential bidder to make an investigation is influenced by the probability that the investigation is influenced by the probability that the investigated investments will be profitable. There are advantages to the target to encourage bids by reducing the investment risk of potential acquirers. Four types of techniques have been used to provide this kind of encouragement (Gilson and Black, 1995, pp. 1020–1023). One is a *no-shop* agreement by the target. This prohibits the target from seeking other bids or providing nonpublic information to third parties. A related agreement commits the target management to use its best efforts to secure shareholder approval of the offer by the bidder. These protections to the acquirer are subject to a **fiduciary out** when the target receives a legal opinion that the fiduciary duty of the target board requires it to consider competitive bids.

Another protection is the payment of a **breakup or termination fee** to the initial bidder. For example, the termination fee Paramount Communications agreed to pay to Viacom, the favored acquirer, was $100 million. The termination fee reflects investigation expenses and the executive time involved in formulating an offer as well as opportunity costs of alternative investment options not pursued.

Another protection to a bidder is a *stock lockup* such as an option to buy the target's stock at the first bidder's initial offer when a rival bidder wins. This technique was used in the bidding contest between U.S. Steel (later USX) and Mobil Oil for the acquisition of Marathon Oil. In this case, Mobil had made an initial hostile bid. Marathon granted USX the right to purchase 10 million newly issued Marathon shares for $90 per share, which was the competing offer by USX. If Mobil or some other firm ultimately acquired Marathon for $95 per share, for example, the gain to USX would have been $5 times 10 million shares, or $50 million.

Still another method of encouraging the initial bidder is to grant a *crown jewels lockup*. USX was also granted an option to purchase for $2.8 billion Marathon's 48% interest in the oil and mineral rights to the Yates Field in western Texas, one of the richest domestic oil wells ever discovered.

QUESTION

1. What are the four techniques used to encourage bidders?

57

Case 2.2   Van Gorkom

The creation of techniques to favor an early bidder plus the economic environment of competitive bids raise practical and legal issues. How does the board of directors of the target demonstrate that it obtained the best price? A series of court cases illustrate the nature of the issues involved. The lead case in this area is *Smith v. Van Gorkom,* 488 A.2d 858 (Del. (1985)). The plaintiff Smith represented a class action brought by the shareholders of the Trans Union Corporation (Trans Union). Van Gorkom had been an officer of Trans Union for 24 years during most of which he was either chief executive officer (CEO) or chairman of the board. Trans Union was a diversified company, but most of its profits came from its railcar leasing business. The company had difficulty generating sufficient taxable income to offset increasingly large investment tax credits (ITCs). Beginning in the late 1960s, Trans Union followed a program of acquiring many companies to increase available taxable income. A 1980 report considered still further alternatives to deal with the ITC problem. Van Gorkom was approaching 65 years of age and mandatory retirement.

One of the alternatives was a leveraged buyout. The chief financial officer (CFO) of Trans Union ran some numbers at $50 a share and $60 a share to check whether the prospective cash flows could service the debt in a leveraged buyout (LBO). The numbers indicated that $50 would be easy but that $60 would be difficult. Van Gorkom took a midway $55 price and met with Jay Pritzker, a well-known takeover investor and social acquaintance. Van Gorkom explained to Pritzker that the $55 share price represented a substantial premium and would still enable the buyer to pay off most of the loan in the first five years. Van Gorkom stated that to be sure the $55 was the best price obtainable, Trans Union should be free to accept any better offer. Pritzker stated that his organization would serve as a "stalking horse" for an "auction contest" only if Trans Union would permit Pritzker to buy 1.75 million shares at (the current) market price, which Pritzker could then sell to any higher bidder. After many discussions and negotiations, Salomon Brothers over a three-month period ending January 21, 1981 tried to elicit other bids. GE Credit was interested but was unwilling to make an offer unless Trans Union first rescinded its merger agreement with Pritzker. Kohlberg Kravis Roberts (KKR) had also made an offer but had withdrawn it.

Ultimately the Pritzker offer was submitted to the vote of shareholders. Of the outstanding shares, 69.6% voted in favor of the merger; 7.55% voted against; 22.85% were not voted. The class action suit was then brought. The defendants argued that the $55 represented a 60% premium and established the most reliable evidence possible, a marketplace test that the price was more than fair. Nevertheless, the court concluded that the directors of Trans Union had breached their fiduciary duty to their stockholders on two counts: (1) their failure to inform themselves of all information relevant to the decision to recommend the Pritzker merger and (2) their failure to disclose all material information that a reasonable stockholder would consider important in evaluating the Pritzker offer. Interestingly enough, the court's measure of damages was the amount by which the fair value of the transaction exceeded $55 per share, and the case was ultimately settled for about $23.5 million.

Within a few months after the Trans Union decision, the Delaware legislature amended the Delaware general corporate law to provide directors with more protection in connection with a transaction such as the Trans Union. The new law made three points: (1) Once it was recognized that a company was "in play," meaning it was going to be sold, the directors had the responsibility to get the best price for shareholders. (2) The directors should be equally fair to all bidders. (3) The decision should not be tainted by the self-interest of management or directors.

It was in the same year, 1985, that the Delaware Supreme Court was confronted with the issues of *Unocal v. Mesa.* In the Uno-cal case the directors paid a large special dividend to all shareholders except Mesa. The court distinguished Unocal as a case in which the directors were seeking to preserve the company. To do this, the court held that the directors had the right to take defensive actions in the face of a hostile takeover attempt. In particular, the court held that Mesa had made a two-tier offer with a second-tier price less than the first tier, so it was coercive.

QUESTION

1. On what basis did the courts conclude that the directors of Trans Union had breached their fiduciary duty to their stockholders?

Case 2.3   Revlon Inc. v. Pantry Pride

The defendant in the Revlon case, 506 A.2d 173 (Del. (1986)), was technically MacAndrews & Forbes Holdings, which was the controlling stockholder of Pantry Pride. Ronald O. Perelman, chairman and CEO of Pantry Pride, met with the head of Revlon in June 1985 to suggest a friendly acquisition of Revlon. Perelman indicated that Pantry Pride (PP) would offer $45 per share. Revlon's investment banker (in August 1985) advised that $45 was too low and that Perelman would use junk bond financing followed by a bust-up of Revlon, which would bring as much as $70 a share. As defensive actions, Revlon was advised to repurchase at least one-sixth of its shares and to adopt a poison pill.

In October, Revlon received a proposal from Forstmann Little and the investment group Adler & Shaykin. The directors agreed to an LBO plan. Each shareholder would receive $56 cash per share, and management would receive a substantial stock position in the new company by the exercise of their Revlon golden parachutes. Some initial bids and counterbids by Pantry Pride and Forstmann Little took place. At this point the court observed that the duty of the board had changed from the preservation of Revlon as a corporate entity to getting the best price for the shareholders. This made the case different from Unocal. The Revlon board had granted Forstmann Little (1) a lockup option to purchase certain Revlon assets, (2) a no-shop provision to deal exclusively with Forstmann, and (3) a termination fee of $25 million. The Delaware Supreme Court concluded that it agreed with the Court of Chancery that the Revlon defensive measures were inconsistent with the directors' duties to shareholders.

QUESTION

1. What was the reasoning of the court in *Revlon Inc. v. Pantry Pride?*

Case 2.4 Maxwell Communications v. Macmillan

Macmillan was a large publishing company. In May 1987 Robert Maxwell had made a hostile bid for another publishing company, Harcourt Brace Jovanovich, Inc., which was defeated by a leveraged recap. Fearing that Maxwell would make a hostile bid, the management of Macmillan decided to restructure the company so as to increase its share of stock ownership to block a Maxwell takeover.

On October 21, 1987, the Bass Group of Texas announced that it had acquired 7.5% of Macmillan's stock. At a special board meeting, management painted an uncomplimentary picture of the Bass Group. Offers and counteroffers took place. On July 20, 1988, Maxwell intervened in the Bass–Macmillan bidding contest with an all-cash offer of $80 per share. Macmillan did not respond but instead started negotiations for Kohlberg Kravis Roberts (KKR) to do an LBO of Macmillan. In the subsequent offers and counteroffers, Macmillan gave preferential treatment to KKR in a number of ways. KKR asked for a "no-shop rule" and a lockup option to purchase eight Macmillan subsidiaries for $950 million. Maxwell countered by stating that he would always top whatever bid was made by KKR. Maxwell sued, requesting an injunction against the lockup option. A lower court denied the injunction.

The Supreme Court of Delaware concluded that the Macmillan board had not been neutral. To conduct a fair auction to get the best price for shareholders, fairness to all bidders must be achieved. The higher court reversed the lower court's decision thus allowing Maxwell's motion for a preliminary injunction. This blocked the sale of the eight Macmillan subsidiaries to KKR. Maxwell succeeded in acquiring Macmillan in 1988 for $2,335 million.

QUESTION

1. What was the reasoning in the Macmillan decision?

Case 2.5 Paramount v. Time

In *Paramount Communications, Inc. v. Time, Inc.,* Fed.Sec.L. Rep. (CCH) ¶94.514 (Del.Ch. (1989)) and 571 A.2d 1140 (Del. (1990)), the Revlon and Macmillan case issues were visited again. The Supreme Court of Delaware reached a different decision. The court held that Time did not expressly resolve to sell the company. The exchange of stock between Time and Warner did not contemplate a change in corporate control. Although the Paramount offer had a higher dollar value, the Time board argued that it was following a program of long-term share value maximization for its shareholders. The court therefore upheld the right of the Time board to not accept the Paramount offer.

QUESTION

1. On what basis did the court uphold the right of Time's board of directors not to accept the Paramount offer?

Case 2.6   Paramount v. QVC Network

This case is cited as 637 A.2d 34 (Del. (1993)). Paramount had a strategic vision in trying to acquire Time. It would have given Paramount entry into the cable television industry. Failing to acquire Time, Paramount negotiated an acquisition of Viacom. The form of the transaction sought to avoid any implication of a change in control of Paramount. Paramount tried to avoid the Revlon trigger and sought to take advantage of that avoidance by providing Viacom with important lockups. Viacom was controlled by Sumner Redstone, who essentially owned about 90% of the company. Viacom's equity coinvestors in the Paramount–Viacom transaction included NYNEX and Blockbuster Entertainment Corporation.

After some preliminary negotiations, on September 12, 1993, the Paramount board approved a merger agreement. It was understood that Martin Davis, the head of Paramount, would be the CEO of the combined company and Redstone would be its controlling stockholder. The merger agreement included a no-shop provision. It provided a termination fee to Viacom of $100 million. It granted Viacom an option to purchase about 20% of Paramount's outstanding common stock at $69.14 per share if any of the triggering events related to the termination fee occurred.

Despite the attempts to discourage a competing bid, Barry Diller, the chairman and CEO of QVC Network, along with several equity coinvestors including Bell South and Comcast, proposed a merger paying $30 in cash and about 0.9 share of QVC common to total $80 per share. This started counterbids by Viacom and further bids by QVC. In their final offers, the Paramount management disparaged some aspects of the QVC bid but failed to mention that it was $1 billion higher than the best Viacom offer. The Supreme Court of Delaware held that the directors of Paramount had breached their fiduciary duty in not getting the best possible price. Rather than seizing opportunities to get the highest price, the Paramount directors walled themselves off from material information and refused to negotiate with QVC or to seek other alternatives. The bidding war continued, but ultimately Viacom became the successful buyer of Paramount.

QUESTION

1. What was the reasoning of the court in the *Paramount v. QVC* decision? How did that affect Viacom?

Case 2.7   Sandoz-Gerber

We have seen legal subtleties weave their way through a number of major merger transactions. The decisions of the court seem inconsistent to some. To others, each of the court decisions had a valid factual basis for distinguishing between distinct and different circumstances. To wrap up this story, when Gerber Products was acquired by Sandoz, a major Swiss drug firm, in May 1994, there were no stock option lockups

(Steinmetz, 1994). It was generally recognized that the Paramount decision had an impact. It was pointed out that the purchase of Syntex by Roche Holdings for $5.4 billion had no option agreements whatsoever. In the Sandoz–Gerber deal, there was a $70 million breakup fee. Takeover lawyers have commented that as long as the compensation of stock options and breakup fees were under 2.5% of the deal's value, the courts probably would not find preferential treatment. The $70 million Sandoz breakup fee represented 1.9% of the $3.7 billion deal value.

QUESTION

1. How did the previous court decisions affect the size of the breakup fee in the acquisition of Gerber Products by Sandoz?

◻ REFERENCES

Bandow, D., "Curbing Raiders Is Bad for Business," *New York Times,* February 7, 1988, p. 2.

DeAngelo, Harry, and Linda DeAngelo, "Ancient Redwoods and the Politics of Finance: The Hostile Takeover of the Pacific Lumber Company," *Journal of Financial Economics,* 47, 1998, pp. 3–53.

———, and Stuart C. Gilson, "The Collapse of First Executive Corporation Junk Bonds, Adverse Publicity, and the 'Run on the Bank' Phenomenon," *Journal of Financial Economics,* 36, 1994, pp. 287–336.

———, "Perceptions and the Politics of Finance: Junk Bonds and the Regulatory Seizure of First Capital Life," *Journal of Financial Economics,* 41, 1996, pp. 475–511.

Economist, "How Dangerous Is Microsoft?" July 8, 1995, pp. 13–14.

———, "Thoroughly Modern Monopoly," July 8, 1995, p. 76.

Ellert, J. C., "Antitrust Enforcement and the Behavior of Stock Prices," Ph.D. dissertation, Graduate School of Business, University of Chicago, June 1975, pp. 66–67.

———, "Mergers, Antitrust Law Enforcement and Stockholder Returns," *Journal of Finance,* 31, 1976, pp. 715–732.

Ewing, Ky P., Jr., "Current Trends in State Antitrust Enforcement: Overview of State Antitrust Law." *Antitrust Law Journal,* 56, April 1987, pp. 103–110.

Gilson, Ronald J., and Bernard S. Black, *The Law and Finance of Corporate Acquisitions,* 2nd ed., Westbury, NY: The Foundation Press, Inc., 1995.

Grass, A., "Insider Trading Report Addresses Reform of Section 16," *Business Lawyer Update,* July/August 1987, p. 3.

Gray, S. J., and M. C. McDermott, *Mega-Merger Mayhem,* London: Paul Chapman Publishing Ltd., 1989.

Grundman, V. Rock, Jr., "Antitrust: Public vs. Private Law," *Restructuring and Antitrust,* The Conference Board Research Bulletin No. 212, 1987, pp. 5–13.

Jensen, Michael C., "Toward a Theory of the Press," in Karl Brunner, ed., *Economics and Social Institutions,* Boston, MA: Martinus Nijhoff Publishing, 1979, pp. 267–287.

———, "Corporate Control and the Politics of Finance," *Journal of Applied Corporate Finance,* 4, 1991, pp. 13–33.

———, "The Modern Industrial Revolution, Exit, and the Failure of Internal Control Systems," *Journal of Finance,* 48, 1993, pp. 831–880.

Office of the Chief Economist, Securities and Exchange Commission, "The Economics of Any-or-All, Partial, and Two-Tier Tender Offers," April 1985.

Pitofsky, Robert, "Antitrust: Public vs. Private Law," *Restructuring and Antitrust,* The

Conference Board Research Bulletin No. 212, 1987, pp. 5–13.

Savage, D. G., "Justices Say Firm Can't Lie About Merger Talks," *Los Angeles Times,* March 8, 1988, pp. 1, 17.

Steinmetz, Greg, "Stock-Option Lockups Are Absent From Takeover Deals," *Wall Street Journal,* May 24, 1994, pp. C1, C21.

U.S. Department of Justice, "1985 Vertical Restraints Guidelines," *The Journal of Reprints for Antitrust Law and Economics,* 16, 1986, pp. 3–57.

———, "1984 Department of Justice Merger Guidelines," *The Journal of Reprints for Antitrust Law and Economics,* 16, 1986, pp. 61–115.

———, "1982 Department of Justice Merger Guidelines," *The Journal of Reprints for Antitrust Law and Economics,* 16, 1986, pp. 119–165.

———, "1982 Federal Trade Commission Horizontal Merger Guidelines," *The Journal of Reprints for Antitrust Law and Economics,* 16, 1986, pp. 169–185.

———, "1980 Antitrust Guide Concerning Research Joint Ventures," *The Journal of Reprints for Antitrust Law and Economics,* 16, 1986, pp. 189–303.

———, "1977 Antitrust Guide for International Operations," *The Journal of Reprints for Antitrust Law and Economics,* 16, 1986, pp. 307–375.

———, "1977 Guidelines for Sentencing Recommendations in Felony Cases Under the Sherman Act," *The Journal of Reprints for Antitrust Law and Economics,* 16, 1986, pp. 379–397.

———, "1968 Department of Justice Merger Guidelines," May 30, 1968, p. 12.

Veasey, N., "A Statute Was Needed to Stop Abuses," *New York Times,* February 7, 1988, p. 2.

Weston, J. Fred, *The Role of Mergers in the Growth of Large Firms,* Berkeley: University of California Press, 1953.

———, *Concentration and Efficiency: The Other Side of the Monopoly Issue,* Special Issues in the Public Interest No. 4, New York: Hudson Institute, 1978.

———, "Section 7 Enforcement: Implementation of Outmoded Theories," *Antitrust Law Journal,* 49, August 1980a, pp. 1411–1450.

———, "International Competition, Industrial Structure and Economic Policy," Chapter 10 in I. Leveson and J. W. Wheeler, eds., *Western Economies in Transition.* Hudson Institute, Boulder, CO: Westview Press,. 1980b.

———, "Trends in Anti-Trust Policy." *Chase Financial Quarterly,* 1, Spring 1982, pp. 66–87.

———, and Stanley I. Ornstein. *The Impact of the Large Firm on the U.S. Economy,* Lexington, MA: Heath Lexington Books, January 1973.

White, Lawrence J., ed., *Private Antitrust Litigation,* in Richard Schmaler, ed., *Regulation of Economics Series,* Cambridge, MA: MIT Press, 1988.

Legal Due Diligence Preliminary Information Request*

GENERAL OBSERVATIONS

The checklist that follows is a relatively extensive and generic due diligence information request form. It is probably longer than most and longer than generally necessary (except for larger transactions involving a target company that owns real estate and may be involved in an environmentally sensitive business). A form such as this is almost certain to intimidate the typical target company. The acquiring company's management and counsel must thoughtfully customize any due diligence information request form, taking into account such factors as what is truly material to the buyer as well as the target company's level of tolerance.

It should be emphasized further that despite its considerable length and the wide range of subjects covered, this due diligence outline is limited to legal aspects. Of course, many types of business activities and operations are inextricably tied to the legal issues treated. In addition, the wide range of topics treated in the other chapters of this volume need to be evaluated in the merger planning and implementation analysis. Mr. Weiner has emphasized in his lectures to the Merger Week programs at the Anderson School, UCLA: "The goal is to achieve the greatest increase in value from the merger transaction while minimizing all types of risks."

TABLE OF CONTENTS

---

*This legal due diligence checklist was provided by Jeffrey M. Weiner of Kimball & Weiner LLP, Los Angeles, California, who have kindly granted permission to use their copyrighted material (and in turn acknowledge their debt to lawyers who have preceded them in due diligence checklist drafting, particularly a committee of the American Bar Association's Business Law Section).

LEGAL DUE DILIGENCE PRELIMINARY INFORMATION REQUEST LIST

1. CORPORATE AND ORGANIZATIONAL

1.1 Certified copy of articles/certificate of incorporation of [company name] (the "Company"), as currently in effect.

1.2 Certified copy of bylaws of the Company, as currently in effect.

1.3 Copy of minute books of the Company.

1.4 Copy of stock books and stock transfer ledgers of the Company.

1.5 List of states and foreign countries in which the Company is qualified to do business, including names and addresses of registered agents and list of states and foreign countries in which the trade names of the Company are registered.

1.6 Long-form good standing certificate, including payment of taxes for state of incorporation and every state and foreign country in which the Company is qualified to do business.

1.7 List of states and foreign countries in which tax returns are filed because of the ownership of property or conduct of business by the Company.

1.8 List of states and foreign countries, if any, in which the Company is not qualified to do business and does not file tax returns but in which it maintains an office, any inventory or equipment, employees, or an agent who is a resident of any state in which he or she solicits orders.

1.9 Current organizational chart for the Company and subsidiaries, operating divisions, and hierarchy of officers.

1.10 All names under which the Company or any predecessor has done business in the past five years.

2. SUBSIDIARIES

2.1 List of subsidiaries of the Company.

2.2 Certified copies of articles/certificates of incorporation and bylaws of each subsidiary, and access to minute books and stock transfer ledgers of each subsidiary.

2.3 Information requested in item 1, shown separately for each subsidiary.

3. SECURITIES

3.1 Statement of outstanding and treasury shares of common stock, preferred stock (including a complete description of the rights attaching to preferred shares), and any other securities of the Company and each subsidiary.

3.2 Stockholders list, giving name and address of each stockholder of the Company and its subsidiaries and of any voting trustees, his or her affiliation with the Company, the type of security held, the date of issue by the Company, the consideration received by the Company, and the number of shares of such security owned by each such stockholder or trust.

3.3 List of holders of any options or rights to purchase any securities of the Company (including warrants), giving name, number of options held, option prices, date(s) of grant, expiration dates, position in the Company or subsidiary, and number of shares owned (excluding those subject to option).

3.4 Copies of all stock option agreements, stock option plans, and warrants.

3.5 Copies of all stockholder agreements and all other agreements with respect to securities of the Company or its subsidiaries.

3.6 All reports to stockholders of the Company prepared within the past five years.

3.7 Indication of whether there are any stockholders or stock certificates whose whereabouts are unknown, or any stockholders from whom it will be difficult to obtain approval of the transaction or stock certificates, as appropriate.

3.8 Description of all contractual restrictions on transfer of the Company's capital stock or assets.

3.9 Copies of registration rights or preemptive rights agreements.

4. BUSINESS DESCRIPTIONS

4.1 All market studies, feasibility studies, analyses, and similar reports concerning the Company prepared within the past five years.

4.2 All marketing and other descriptive brochures regarding the Company prepared within the past five years.

4.3 All press releases issued by the Company during the past five years, and any press clippings that refer to the Company, if available.

4.4 Recent analyses of the Company or its industries prepared by investment bankers, engineers, management consultants, accountants, or others, including marketing studies, credit reports, and other types of reports, financial or otherwise.

5. FINANCING DOCUMENTS

5.1   List and brief description of all long-term and short-term debt and other financial obligations (including capitalized leases, guarantees, indemnity undertakings, and other contingent obligations) to which the Company and each subsidiary is a party, and copies of all related material documentation.

5.2   List of all mortgages, liens, pledges, security interests, or other encumbrances to which any property (real or personal) of the Company and each subsidiary is subject, and copies of all related material documentation.

5.3   All correspondence with lenders and other debt security holders for the past five years (including all consents, notices, or waivers of default from lenders with respect to borrowings by the Company).

5.4   Any presentations given to creditors in connection with obtaining credit or prepared for potential lenders in connection with any proposed financings.

6. FINANCIAL STATEMENTS

6.1   Audited financial statements, both consolidated and consolidating, for the Company and its subsidiaries for the past five fiscal years.

6.2   All unaudited interim financial statements of the Company prepared since the date of the most recent audited financial statements.

6.3   Separate consolidating statement for significant subsidiaries or divisions.

6.4   Brief description of contingent liabilities involving the Company.

6.5   Name of accountants and length of relationship with accountants; indicate whether the accountants own any interest in or hold any position with the Company or its subsidiaries.

6.6   Management financial reports to the directors, or any board committee, of the Company prepared during the past five years.

6.7   Correspondence with the Company's accountants prepared or received during the past five years, including all management letters from accountants.

6.8   Brief description of depreciation policy.

6.9   Brief description of nature of prepaid or deferred income or expenses.

6.10 Copy of any sales projections and estimates, and copy of current budget and any budget projections, including a discussion of any assumptions used.

6.11 Brief description of any change in accounting policies or procedures during the past five years.

6.12 Brief description of outstanding commitments for capital expenditures in excess of $ _____ .

6.13 Any documents relating to material write-downs or write-offs of notes, accounts receivable, or other assets other than in the ordinary course of business.

7. TAX MATTERS

7.1 Copies of all federal, state, local, and foreign income and franchise tax returns filed by the Company and its subsidiaries for the past five years concerning the business, assets, or income of the Company.

7.2 All correspondence with the Internal Revenue Service or state or local tax authorities concerning adjustments or questioning compliance.

7.3 List of returns and the years thereof that have been audited by federal, state, or local tax authorities, and copies of related determination letters.

7.4 List of state and local taxes to which the Company or any subsidiary is subject with respect to the business, assets, or income of the Company, showing assessment date, date return is to be filed, and date tax is due.

7.5 Description and copies of all agreements, consents, elections, and waivers filed or made with the IRS or other taxing authorities.

7.6 List and description of all pending or threatened disputes with regard to tax matters involving the Company or any of its subsidiaries.

7.7 Copies of S corporation elections, IRS notices of acceptance, and any other information pertinent to the Company's S corporation status, where applicable.

7.8 Copies of any tax indemnification, tax sharing, or tax allocation agreements involving the Company and other members of an affiliate group, including any joint venture agreements that have the effect of tax allocation agreements, and a statement setting forth how such agreements were carried out for the past five fiscal years.

7.9 Copies of all legal or accounting tax opinions received by the Company during the past five fiscal years relating to the Company's tax reporting.

8. OFFICERS AND DIRECTORS, EMPLOYEES, BENEFIT PLANS, AND LABOR DISPUTES

8.1 Name, address, and telephone numbers (home and business) of each director and officer of the Company and each subsidiary (and, if applicable, principal occupation), and aggregate compensation at present and for the previous fiscal year.

8.2 Copies of all liability insurance policies for directors and officers of the Company and each subsidiary.

8.3 Number of persons employed by the Company and by each subsidiary in terms of function (executive, sales, clerical, research, labor, or other appropriate classification).

8.4 Name and address of each person who has a power of attorney to act on behalf of the Company or any subsidiary. Furnish copies.

8.5 List of all labor union contracts and collective bargaining arrangements to which the Company or any subsidiary is a party, the number of employees covered by each agreement, and the anticipated expiration dates. Furnish copies.

8.6 Brief description of "labor unrest" situations, all pending or threatened labor strikes, or other trouble experienced by the Company and its subsidiaries during the past five fiscal years.

8.7 List and brief description of the current status of all unfair labor practices complaints lodged during the past three fiscal years against the Company and its subsidiaries.

8.8   Brief description of any pending or threatened request for arbitration, grievance proceedings, labor disputes, strikes, or disturbances affecting the Company or any subsidiary, and history of recent union negotiations.

8.9   All performance bonus plans adopted by the board of directors of the Company during the past five years.

8.10   a. Brief description and copies of all employee benefit plans, group life insurance plans, major medical plans, medical reimbursement plans, supplemental unemployment benefit plans or welfare plans (for hourly employees) or salary continuation plans, or other perquisites, and a brief description of policy regarding bonuses, salary review, severance pay, moving expenses, tuition reimbursement, loans, advances, vacations, holiday, sick leaves, and other benefits.

       b. For each pension or profit-sharing plan, including multiemployer plans, if any, furnish copies of plan documents, including amendments (and a description of any changes in these plans proposed, agreed upon, or under consideration); actuarial reports, if applicable; trust instruments and trust balance sheets, if any; summary plan descriptions; the latest application for determination to the IRS; any IRS determination letter; and the latest Annual Report on Form 5500, 5500-C, or 5500-K. For each pension plan that is a "multiemployer plan," furnish a statement of the employer's "withdrawal liability" under ERISA §4211.

8.11   Details on any terminated pension plans and unfunded pension liabilities.

8.12   a. List of all employees of the Company who received compensation exceeding $50,000 in the last fiscal year, giving name, date of birth, date hired, position, and compensation for the last fiscal year, and, to the extent available, similar information for all other employees and for retired employees who are receiving or will be entitled to receive any payment not described previously in item 8.9.

       b. Description of all written or oral employment or consulting agreements (other than union contracts) to which the Company or any subsidiary is a party or bound, and copies of any written agreements (except for employment contracts that can be terminated at will by the Company or a subsidiary without cost or liability).

       c. Brief description of all confidentiality, noncompetition, or similar agreements between the Company or any subsidiary and any of their present or former officers, employees, directors, consultants, or agents. If any are in writing, furnish copies.

       d. Brief description of all consulting and management agreements, arrangements, or understandings to which the Company or any subsidiary is a party. If any are in writing, furnish copies.

       e. Description of all deferred compensation programs affecting officers, directors, or employees of the Company. State the amount accrued and/or paid during the most recent fiscal year under such programs and amounts of accruals thereunder through a recent date.

8.13   A description of the manner in which the Company fulfills its workers' compensation and unemployment compensation insurance obligations in each state (i.e., insured or self-insured, etc.).

8.14   Documents representing or relating to workers' compensation or disability policies, and any material claims with respect thereto.

8.15   Copy of employee handbook or any similar document.

9. PROPERTIES, LEASES, AND INSURANCE

9.1   a. List of real estate owned, leased, or used by the Company, stating whether owned or leased (whether as lessor or lessee), and brief description of property, structures, zoning, estoppel letters, reversions or remainders, lease provisions (including assignment and renewal), use, and location. Furnish copies of mortgages, deeds, surveys, maps, rights of way, easements, leases, and other contracts.

     b. Copies of title insurance policies or lawyers' abstract reports covering real estate.

     c. Copies of zoning variances and local permits.

9.2   a. List of fixed assets, machinery, and equipment (whether owned, leased, or used by the Company), giving for each material asset or group of assets cost, depreciation reserve, method of depreciation, insured value, estimated remaining useful life, condition suitability for use, and (if available) appraised value.

     b. List of automobiles, trucks, and other registered equipment owned, leased, or used by the Company, giving a brief description of equipment and lease provisions (if any), year made, state of registration, registration number, cost, estimated remaining useful life, and insured value.

     c. List of premises at which any assets of the Company are currently located or located from time to time, including (without limitation) terminals, plants, storage facilities, sales offices, and warehouses, and any related written agreements.

     d. Brief description of portfolio investments of the Company (except in subsidiaries), including cost basis and current value.

     e. All currently effective purchase contracts, leases, or other arrangements concerning material items of equipment used by the Company.

     f. All appraisals of any material property of the Company.

9.3   Copies of all material leases of or security agreements for personal property of the Company, including conditional sales contracts, equipment leases, financing agreements, and factoring agreements.

9.4   List of all insurance policies relating to the business assets or properties of the Company (including directors' and officers' liability insurance), giving insurance company, policy number, term of coverage, property or risk covered, appraised value of covered property (where appropriate), extent of coverage, annual premium, and amount of premiums that are prepaid or are unpaid from prior years. Furnish copies of all policies.

9.5   A description of all insurance claims over $ _____ in amount currently pending.

9.6   Schedule of Company's loss experience per insurance year.

10. INTELLECTUAL PROPERTY (PATENTS, TRADEMARKS, COPYRIGHTS, TRADE SECRETS)

10.1   Schedule of patent registrations and applications, identifying each patent by title, registration (application) number, date of registration (application), and country.

10.2   Schedule of trademark and service mark registrations and applications, identifying each mark, including date of registration (application), registration (application) number, status, and country or state where registered. Where registration has not been sought, identify the mark and its date of first use anywhere in the United States.

10.3   Schedule of copyright registrations and applications, identifying each copyright by title, registration number, and date of registration.

10.4   Manual or other written document detailing the procedures for maintaining the secrecy of trade secrets.

10.5   Licensing agreements, merchandising agreements (naming Company as licensee or licensor), or assignments relating to patents, technology, trade secrets, trademarks (service marks), and copyrights.

10.6   Communications to or from third parties relating to the validity or infringement of any of Company's intellectual property.

10.7   Studies or reports relating to the validity or value of Company's intellectual property and the licensing or merchandising thereof.

10.8   Agreements pursuant to which any intellectual property has been sold or transferred by or to the Company and evidence of recording thereof.

11. CONTRACTS AND ARRANGEMENTS

11.1   All standard sales and purchase orders and other forms of agreements used by the Company.

11.2   All warranty agreements, including all forms of product warranties, of the Company currently in force for completed and executory material contracts.

11.3   List and description of all significant oral contracts and commitments.

11.4   All currently effective guarantees given by the Company concerning the payment or performance of obligations of third parties.

11.5   All sales agency and distribution agreements.

11.6   A list of all contracts and commitments under which a default has occurred or is claimed to have occurred, setting forth the following:

   a. Nature of default

   b. Name of party in default

   c. Monetary amount claimed

   d. Current status of contract or claim

11.7   A list of all contracts subject to renegotiation (indicating those contracts currently being renegotiated).

11.8   All agreements to which the Company or any subsidiary is (or was within the past five years) a party and in which any officer, director, employee, or shareholder of any such companies has (or had) an interest (whether directly or indirectly).

11.9   Copies of all agreements not to be performed within three months or involving over $ _____ whether or not entered into in the ordinary course of business, except (a) agreements for the sale of merchandise or standard sales order forms entered into in the ordinary course of business and (b) agreements referred to elsewhere herein.

11.10 Copies of all contracts with advertising or public relations agencies.

11.11 A list of all significant suppliers (representing in excess of 5% of annual purchases) of the Company, with an indication of the amount paid to each such supplier during the Company's most recent fiscal year and the estimated number of alternative suppliers.

11.12 All executory contracts, as amended to date, with each of the above referenced suppliers, and all related purchase orders.

11.13 Brief description of contractual or customary credit terms available from suppliers and manufacturers, and copies of all agreements with suppliers and manufacturers.

11.14 List and brief description of all agreements and arrangements with distributors, dealers, sales agents, or representatives. Furnish copies of all such written agreements.

11.15 List and brief description of all agreements and arrangements whereby the Company or any subsidiary acts as a distributor. Furnish copies of all such written agreements.

11.16 List and brief description of all agreements relating to the supply of [principal raw material] and other raw materials and supplies. Furnish copies of all such written agreements.

11.17 Copies of all forms of product warranties or guarantees, if any, given by the Company or any of its subsidiaries.

11.18 Copies of all agreements and other documentation relating to the acquisition of any business constituting a part of the Company, or sale or proposed sale of any business owned by it in the past five years.

11.19 Copies of joint venture or partnership agreements to which the Company or any subsidiary is a party.

11.20 Copies of all franchise or distribution agreements between the Company or any of its subsidiaries and any third party concerning the manufacture, sale, or distribution of the Company's or its subsidiaries' products or services. If any such agreements are oral, summarize the terms thereof.

11.21 Copies of all agreements, not previously listed, with suppliers, independent agents, salespersons, or others involving the payment of commissions or other consideration or discounts with respect to the manufacture, sale, or distribution of the Company's or its subsidiaries' products or services. If any such agreements are oral, summarize the terms.

11.22 Brief description of any contracts restricting the ability of the Company or any subsidiary to compete in any line of business with any person or entity, or committing the Company or any subsidiary to continue in any line of business.

11.23 Advise if there are any facts or circumstances that may give rise to the cancellation or termination of, or claim for damages or loss under, any of the agreements, arrangements, or understandings referred to herein.

11.24 List and description of all leases, licenses, and other agreements involving the payment of more than $ _____ in the aggregate, currently in the process of negotiation.

11.25 Copies of agreements granting to the Company any right of first refusal to acquire any business or assets or pursuant to which the Company has granted any such rights.

11.26 List of material terms of all contracts and arrangements for (a) trucking and other delivery and (b) warehouse space.

11.27 Copies of all material research and development agreements.

11.28 All technology license agreements to which the Company is a party as licensor or licensee.

11.29 Documents relating to the Company's internal determinations as to whether it can, or should, fulfill a particular contract.

12. LITIGATION

12.1 List and brief description of each threatened or pending claim, lawsuit, arbitration, or investigation involving a claim for relief of $ _____ or more against the Company, any subsidiary, or any of their respective officers or directors.

12.2 List and brief description of any pending or threatened (a) claim or litigation involving alleged violations of laws or regulations for the health or safety of employees or others, (b) governmental or administrative proceeding, (c) equal employment opportunity claim or litigation, (d) antitrust claim or litigation, (e) claim or litigation seeking injunctive relief, or (f) other material claim or litigation to which, in either case, the Company or any subsidiary is a party.

12.3 A copy of all complaints, answers, and other material pleadings concerning any litigation not fully covered by insurance.

12.4 All letters from counsel to the Company to accountants relating to litigation or contingent liabilities involving the Company.

12.5 All correspondence relating to actual or alleged infringement by the Company of intellectual property rights of others.

12.6 List and brief description of all outstanding judgments, decrees, or orders to which the Company or any subsidiary is subject.

12.7 Copy of most recent response to auditors' request for information about litigation and/or contingent liabilities of the Company.

12.8 All material governmental permits, licenses, etc., of the Company.

12.9 Documents pertaining to any litigation involving an officer or director of the Company concerning bankruptcy, crimes, securities law, or business practice (past five years).

12.10 Description of any investigations of the Company, pending or threatened, by any federal, state, local, or foreign authorities.

12.11 All correspondence with, reports of or to, filings with, or other material information about any other regulatory bodies that regulate a material portion of the Company's business.

13. ENVIRONMENTAL AND RELATED MATTERS

13.1 All internal Company reports concerning environmental matters relating to current or former Company properties.

13.2 Copies of any applications, statements, or reports filed or given by the Company or any of its subsidiaries with or to the Federal Environmental Protection Agency, any state department of environmental regulations, or any similar state or local regulatory body, authority, or agency.

13.3 All notices, complaints, suits, or similar documents sent to, received by, or served upon the Company or any of its subsidiaries by the Federal Environmental Protection Agency, any state department of environmental regulation, or any similar state or local regulatory body, authority, or agency.

13.4 All Company or outside reports concerning compliance with waste disposal regulations (hazardous or otherwise).

13.5 Copies of all permits, shipping authorizations, manifests, and waste stream authorizations.

13.6 Description of any processes of facilities currently or previously operated by the Company or any subsidiary (or by others on property currently owned by the Company or any subsidiary) that generate or are suspected of generating any hazardous material.

13.7 All pollution control capital expenditure reports (including budget requests) for the past five years.

13.8 All annual reports, manifests, or other documents relating to hazardous waste or pesticide management over the past five years.

13.9 All documents relating to equipment using PCBs, spills of PCBs, or worker exposure to PCBs, and all documents relating to the existence or removal of asbestos.

13.10 Any public records reflecting existing or recent environmental problems.

14. RECEIVABLES

14.1 Brief description of customary sales credit terms.

14.2 Brief description of aging of accounts receivable, giving collections since aging date and brief statement of reasons for receivables in excess of $ _____ past due.

14.3 Names of customers owing in excess of $ _____ .

14.4 Description of basis for establishing bad debt reserve.

15. INVENTORIES

15.1 List of products and services currently sold by the Company and its subsidiaries, together with applicable prices and discounts.

15.2 Brief description of inventory pricing procedure.

15.3 List of major sources of supply for material, dollar purchases from each in the last fiscal year, and brief description of available alternative supply sources for material items.

16. ACQUISITION DOCUMENTS AND SALES OF SECURITIES

16.1 All other agreements pursuant to which the Company has acquired securities or has issued (or may be obligated to issue) securities.

16.2   All private placement memoranda, prospectuses, or other documentation relating to the offering or acquisition of securities by the Company.

16.3   All reports to, documents filed with, and correspondence with the Securities and Exchange Commission for the past five years.

16.4   All reports to, documents filed with, and correspondence with any state securities commission.

16.5   All agreements and other documentation concerning any sale of material assets (including any agreements in principle) to which the Company is a party.

16.6   Copies of all agreements and plans entered into by the Company or any of its subsidiaries relating to the acquisition of, or merger with, a business or an interest in any business, whether by acquisition of shares, acquisition of assets, or otherwise.

17. TRANSACTIONS WITH OFFICERS, ETC.

17.1   List and statement of amounts and other essential terms of any indebtedness or other obligations of or to the Company or its subsidiaries to or from any officer, director, stockholder, or employee.

17.2   List and description of assets or properties used by the Company in which any officer, director, stockholder, or employee has any interest.

17.3   List of all material transactions between the Company and its officers, directors, stockholders, or employees not disclosed under items 17.1 or 17.2.

18. CUSTOMERS

List of major customers, showing percentage of sales to each customer accounting for more than 5% of sales for any product line or service within the past fiscal year.

19. FILINGS AND REPORTS

To the extent not covered elsewhere, copies of all filings and reports in the last three years made with or submitted to any governmental agencies.

20. LICENSES

20.1   List of all federal, state, local, and foreign governmental permits, licenses, and approvals (excluding those listed elsewhere herein) either held or required to be held by the Company or its subsidiaries for the conduct of their businesses.

20.2   All correspondence, reports, and notices relating to laws and regulations administered by any federal, state, local, or foreign governmental agency for the past five years.

21. CONSENTS

21.1   List and brief description of any of the Company contracts, leases, security agreements, licenses, authorizations, etc., that may require the consent of any third party (including any governmental agency or instrumentality) to the proposed transactions.

21.2 Indicate any other notification required to be given to or consents required from any third party (including any governmental agency or instrumentality) in connection with the proposed transactions.

22. MISCELLANEOUS

22.1 List of all bank accounts and safe deposit boxes, naming authorized signatories.

22.2 List of memberships in trade associations.

22.3 List of all requirements and obligations imposed on the Company by the proposed or effective rules and regulations of any governmental agency.

QUESTIONS

A2.1 Is due diligence restricted to legal matters?

A2.2 What is the fundamental nature of legal due diligence?

A2.3 What are important procedural aspects of due diligence?

A2.4 What are three legal documents that are critical in the due diligence process?

A2.5 What are the issues involved in formulating a letter of intent?

A2.6 Is the scope of due diligence limited to information provided by the parties to the transaction?

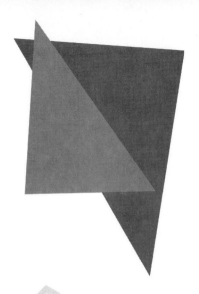

Accounting for M&As

The analysis of M&As and restructuring must begin with the accounting numbers. This is a necessary first step if only to get behind the numbers to see what is really going on. The rules follow the recommendations of professional accounting organizations. Securities and Exchange Commission (SEC) approval is required in connection with financial statements issued to investors.

The Financial Accounting Standards Board (FASB) of the Financial Accounting Foundation is a cooperative private research organization financed by individuals and corporations. The FASB issues statements on accounting policy that have become recognized as accounting standards. They are policies that the SEC itself has usually adopted.

CHANGES IN ACCOUNTING FOR BUSINESS COMBINATIONS

In May 1999 the FASB voted unanimously to eliminate pooling of interests as a method of accounting for business combinations. The change will be effective for business combinations taking place after the FASB issues a final standard and procedures, expected to take place in late 2000. It released a formal proposal for comment in August 1999. We first analyze the difference between alternative methods of accounting for mergers to provide a basis for discussing the reasons for the policy changes.

HISTORICAL BACKGROUND

On August 2, 1970, the 18-member Accounting Principles Board (APB) of the American Institute of Certified Public Accountants issued Opinion 16, which deals with guidelines for corporate mergers, and Opinion 17, which deals with goodwill arising from mergers. The recommendations, which became effective October 31, 1970,

Much appreciation to Professors Jack Farrell, Patricia Hughes, and Bruce Miller of the accounting department at The Anderson School, University of California, Los Angeles, for considerable assistance on this chapter.

modify and elaborate on previous pronouncements on the pooling of interests and purchase methods of accounting for business combinations. These 1970 rules still prevail, although discussion memoranda and related statements have been issued periodically.

On August 19, 1976, the FASB issued a lengthy "Discussion Memorandum on Accounting for Business Combinations and Purchased Intangibles." It consisted of 178 pages of text plus Appendixes A through J consisting of an additional 154 pages. Later FASB publications dealt with rules for preparing consolidated statements, for example, "Statement of Financial Accounting Standards No. 94, Consolidation of All Majority-Owned Subsidiaries, an amendment of ARB No. 51, with related amendments to APB Opinion 18 and ARB No. 43, Chapter 12." On August 26, 1994, in the Financial Accounting Series, FASB published "Preliminary Views, Consolidation Policy," No. 140-B. Comprehensive item-by-item comparisons of the Generally Accepted Accounting Principles (GAAP) in Canada, Mexico, and the United States were published in the Financial Accounting Series in December 1994 as No. 144-B, entitled "Financial Reporting in North America. Highlights of a Joint Study." The GAAP for business combinations as well as consolidation and equity accounting followed the earlier rules adopted in 1970.

In a business combination, one company will usually be the "acquiring firm," with the other company being described as the acquired or "target" firm. Although there are many ways to structure a business combination, one board of directors and one CEO usually end up with control over the combined operations. When the operations of two companies are placed under common control through any form of business combination, financial reporting rules require that financial statements (at the date of combining) present numbers from the combining of two accounting systems.

Accounting Principles Board Opinion 16, "Accounting for Business Combinations," prescribes two accounting methods for recording the acquisition of a "target" company by an "acquiring" company:

1. The pooling of interests method of accounting, which requires that the original "historical cost" basis of the assets and liabilities of the target company be carried forward.
2. The purchase method of accounting, which requires that a new "historical cost" basis be established for the assets and liabilities of the target company.

A second major difference between the two methods has to do with the reporting of earnings:

1. In the pooling of interests method of accounting, earnings of the combined entities are combined for any reporting periods. If in a subsequent financial report data for a prior year are included, it would reflect the accounting for a pooling of interests combination.
2. In the purchase method of accounting, earnings of the acquired company are reported by the acquirer only from the date of acquisition forward.

In its status report of April 22, 1997, the FASB described its project to reconsider the 1970 APB Opinions 16 and 17. It stated that more than 50 issues related to business combinations and tangible assets had been considered by its

Emerging Issues Task Force (EITF). A *Wall Street Journal* article at about the same time (April 15, 1997) commented that business firms were seeking to have the rules changed to make it easier to use pooling accounting but that the FASB was considering proposals to restrict more narrowly the use of pooling. One objection to pooling is that it ignores the new market values that have been established by the merger or acquisition transaction itself. Another criticism is that in a pooling the financial statements do not record what the buyer paid. Some companies have sought to use pooling to avoid recording goodwill. Since 1992, in deals valued at over $500 million, 130 have been recorded as poolings versus 159 purchase acquisitions (55%). Smaller acquisitions are mostly purchases. The analysis in this chapter seeks to provide background for evaluating the proposals to restrict the use of pooling versus those seeking the expansion of the use of pooling.

OVERVIEW OF POOLING VERSUS PURCHASE

Pooling of Interests

Twelve criteria are prescribed to determine whether the conditions for the pooling of interests treatment are satisfied. If all of them are met, the combination is, in theory, a merger between companies of comparable size, and the **pooling of interests** method must be employed. In practice, comparable size is not a compelling requirement. Accounting practice with SEC approval permits some flexibility. The tests are as follows.

1. None of the combining companies has been a subsidiary or division of another corporation within two years.
2. The combining companies have no significant equity investments (greater than 10%) in one another.
3. The combination is effected in a single transaction or is completed in accordance with a specific plan within one year after the plan is initiated.
4. Payment is effected by one corporation offering and issuing only common stock in exchange for substantially all (meaning 90% or more) of the voting common stock interest of another company.
5. None of the combining companies changes the equity interest of its voting common stock for two years before the plan to combine is initiated or between the dates the combination is initiated and consummated.
6. None of the combining companies reacquires shares of its voting stock except for purposes other than business combinations.
7. The ratio of the interest of an individual common stockholder to those of other common stockholders in the combination is unchanged before and after the combination.
8. Voting rights in the combined company are exercisable by the stockholders.
9. The combined corporation does not agree to issue additional shares of stock or other consideration on any contingency at a later date to former stockholders of the combining companies.
10. The combined corporation does not agree to retire or reacquire any of the common stock issued to effect the combination.

11. The combined corporation does not enter into other financial arrangements—such as a guaranty of loans secured by stock issued in the combination, which in effect negates the exchange of equity securities—for the benefit of former stockholders of a combining company.

12. The combined corporation does not intend to dispose of a significant part of the assets of the combining companies—other than disposals in the normal course of business or to eliminate duplicate facilities or excess capacity—within two years after the combination.

Previous to the issuance of APB Opinion 16, a stimulus to pooling was the opportunity to dispose of assets acquired at depreciated book values, selling them at their current values and recording subsequent profits on sales of assets. Opinion 16 attempted to deal with this practice by the requirement that sales of major portions of assets not be contemplated for at least two years after the merger has taken place. For example, suppose firm A buys firm B, exchanging stock worth $100 million for assets worth $100 million but carried at $25 million. After the merger, A could, before the change in rules, sell the acquired assets and report the difference between book value and the purchase price, or $75 million, as earned income. Thus, pooling could be used to manipulate accounting measures of net income.

Purchase Accounting

In purchase accounting, one company is identified as the buyer and records the company being acquired at the price it actually paid. All identifiable assets acquired and liabilities assumed in a business combination should be assigned a portion of the cost of the acquired company, normally equal to their fair values at the date of acquisition. In taxable transactions, the new stepped-up basis is depreciable for tax accounting. The excess of the cost of the acquired company over the sum of the amounts assigned to identifiable assets acquired less liabilities assumed should be recorded as goodwill. This goodwill account was required under the old rules to be written off, for financial reporting, over some reasonable period but no longer than 40 years. Under the new FASB proposals, the new write-off period would be shortened to 20 years.

Under a 1993 tax law change, if an acquisition is made by the purchase of the assets of the acquired company, any resulting goodwill can be amortized over 15 years for tax accounting. The intention of the 1993 tax law change was to come closer to the tax deductibility of goodwill write-offs provided by foreign countries such as Japan, Switzerland, and Germany. In some countries, goodwill can be written off directly to shareholders' equity for financial reporting (bypassing the income statement); under some circumstances the total of goodwill can be written off in the year of the acquisition, which maximizes the tax shelter benefits on cash flows.

As we demonstrate in the next section, when purchase accounting is employed, reported net income is usually lower than under pooling of interests accounting. This is because of an increased depreciation charge or amortization of goodwill. However, cash flows will be higher under purchase accounting if any of the depreciation or amortization is tax-deductible.

ACCOUNTING FOR POOLING VERSUS PURCHASE

In a series of statements issued on April 29, May 18, and September 30, 1999, the Financial Accounting Standards Board (FASB) described proposals to eliminate pooling of interests accounting for business combinations. It indicated that the review process would be completed and the new rules would become effective by the end of 2000. To provide a basis for evaluating the FASB proposal to ban pooling of interests accounting, we first explain the nature of pooling vs. purchase accounting.

We now illustrate the different accounting treatments under pooling versus purchase. Our treatment focuses on the central financial and economic implications of the alternative treatments and does not include some of the fine points of the accounting treatments found in advanced accounting texts or the technicalities covered in case books on the legal aspects of pooling versus purchase.

We use a case example starting with the financial statements of the acquiring firm (A) and the target firm (T) as shown in Table 3.1. We choose to use the same set of data to illustrate both pooling and purchase to highlight the contrasts. The spirit of the pre-2000 accounting regulations for pooling is that the acquiring firm and target firm would be approximately the same size. Thus, the combined firm would reflect a continuity of the influence of both companies. In a purchase, the target firm would be much smaller and would be absorbed into the operations of the acquiring firm.

The historical choice of purchase versus pooling had some judgmental factors involved. For example, AT&T succeeded in having its acquisition of NCR treated as a pooling of interests. At the time of its unsolicited bid for NCR on December 2, 1990, AT&T was six times larger, with a 1989 revenue of $36 billion versus $6 billion for NCR. Observing the differences in revenues and stock market values, the *Wall Street Journal* commented that AT&T "could swallow NCR with barely a gulp" (December 3, 1990, p. A3). Nevertheless, AT&T succeeded in obtaining SEC approval to have the acquisition treated as a pooling.

Chevron's market value was $11 billion when it bought Gulf in 1984 for $13.3 billion. Yet Chevron treated the acquisition as a purchase. It is convenient to use the same set of input data to illustrate the two methods. But after 2000 the pooling method may no longer be permitted.

The illustrative data in our example in Table 3.1 show A to be roughly double the size of T. Firm A has net income of $40,000; T, $20,000. Each firm has 20,000 shares outstanding, so A has earnings per share of $2 versus $1 for T. We postulate that the price-to-earnings ratio for A is 15 and for T it is 20. Hence, the indicated market price per share of A is $30, and for T, $20. The book value per share of A is $240,000 divided by 20,000, which is $12, versus $6 for the target. The market-to-book ratio for the acquiring firm is $30/$12 = 2.5 times; for the target it is $20/$6 = 3.3 times.

Illustration of Pooling Accounting

For illustrative purposes, let us assume further that A buys T by exchanging one share of its stock for one share of the target stock. This represents a 50% premium to T in market value, reflecting its higher growth prospects implied by its higher valuation multiple. In Table 3.2, we present balance sheets to illustrate pooling of

Table 3.1 Initial Financial Data for Merging Firms

Initial Balance Sheets	Acquiring Firm		Target Firm	
Current assets		$210,000		$110,000
Land		50,000		20,000
Plant and equipment	200,000		100,000	
Less: accumulated depr.	60,000		30,000	
Net plant and equipment		140,000		70,000
Goodwill				
Total assets		$400,000		$200,000
Interest-bearing debt	40,000		20,000	
Other current liabilities	60,000		30,000	
Long-term debt	60,000		30,000	
Total liabilities		160,000		80,000
Common stock (Par $4)	80,000		(Par $2) 40,000	
Paid-in capital	100,000		50,000	
Retained earnings	60,000		30,000	
Shareholders' equity		$240,000		$120,000
Total claims on assets		$400,000		$200,000
Initial Income Statements				
Sales		$800,000		$400,000
Operating costs less depr. and amort.		703,333		351,667
EBITDA*		96,667		48,333
Depreciation (D)**		20,000		10,000
Amortization of goodwill (A)				
Net operating income (NOI) = EBIT		76,667		38,333
Interest cost @ 10%		10,000		5,000
Earnings before taxes		66,667		33,333
Taxes @ 40%		26,667		13,333
Net income		$40,000		$20,000

Earnings before interest, taxes, depreciation, and amortization.
**Ten-year life, so 10% of the gross plant and equipment account.*

interests accounting for this combination. Under a pooling of interests, the accounting treatment is simply to combine the balance sheets of the two companies. The target firm shows common stock with a total par value of $40,000 (20,000 shares with a par value of $2 per share). Thus, the acquiring firm issues 20,000 additional shares with a par of $4 per share or a book total of $80,000 in acquiring T. When added to the original $80,000 par value of the acquiring firm, the consolidated book total under pooling will be $160,000. To obtain this amount, a credit of $40,000 to the common stock account is required to add to the sum of the existing

Table 3.2   Balance Sheets to Illustrate Pooling of Interests Accounting for a Combination*

	Acquiring Firm		Target Firm	*Adjustment Pooling* Debit	*Adjustment Pooling* Credit	Consolidated Pooling
Current assets		$210,000	$110,000			$320,000
Net fixed assets		190,000	90,000			280,000
Total assets		$400,000	$200,000			$600,000
Current liabilities		$100,000	$50,000			$150,000
Long-term debt		60,000	30,000			90,000
Common stock	80,000	40,000			$40,000[(1)]	160,000
Paid-in capital	100,000	50,000		$40,000[(1)]		110,000
Retained earnings	60,000	30,000				90,000
Shareholders' equity (SHE)	240,000	120,000				360,000
Total claims on assets		$400,000	$200,000	$40,000	$40,000	$600,000

*Accounting texts and practice use an investment account among other intermediate steps. The final result is as shown here.

[(1)]Issued 20,000 shares at $4 par to buy the target firm to give a total of 40,000 shares at par of $4, totaling $160,000. Summing the common stock accounts of A and T gives $120,000, so an additional credit of $40,000 is required. The offsetting debit is to the paid-in capital account (i.e., paid-in capital serves as the "plug").

$80,000 for A and the existing $40,000 for T. The offsetting debit of $40,000 is to the combined paid-in capital. So the consolidated total paid-in capital is reduced from $150,000 to $110,000.

Retained earnings are simply added to obtain $90,000 for the combined companies. This illustrates one of the advantages of pooling. If the target company shows a large amount in retained earnings, and if the acquiring firm wished to strengthen the retained earnings account, it could do so by using the pooling method. This is one of the reasons given for AT&T's strong preference for the use of pooling in its acquisition of NCR (Lys and Vincent, 1995).

In summary, we see from Table 3.2 that pooling simply amounts to adding the individual asset and liability amounts. There is no change in the historical cost basis of either company. Additional shares of common stock issued by the acquiring firm may cause the consolidated common stock account to be different than the simple sum for the A and T accounts, so a credit or debit may be required. The offsetting credit or debit will be to the paid-in capital account. Usually retained earnings will be the sum of the two or more companies involved in the merger or acquisition. It is possible that if a debit were required to the paid-in capital account that exhausted the total, any remaining debit would be made to the retained earnings account.

Illustration of Purchase Accounting

The nature of purchase accounting is shown in Table 3.3. We illustrate a taxable transaction in which one or more of the 12 criteria for the use of pooling of interests accounting were not met. As before, A buys T for 20,000 shares of A with a

Table 3.3 Consolidated Balance Sheet, Purchase Accounting All "Excess" to Depreciable Assets

	Acquiring Firm	Target Firm	Adjustment Purchase Debit	Adjustment Purchase Credit	Consolidated Purchase (All "Excess" to Depreciable Assets)
Current assets	$210,000	$110,000			$ 320,000
Land	50,000	20,000			70,000
Plant and equipment	200,000	100,000	480,000 (2)	30,000 (2)	750,000
Less: accumulated depr.	60,000	30,000	30,000 (2)		60,000
Net plant and equipment	140,000	70,000			690,000
Goodwill					
Total assets	$400,000	$200,000			$1,080,000
Interest-bearing debt	40,000	20,000	40,000 (1)		60,000
Other current liabilities	60,000	30,000	50,000 (1)		90,000
Long-term debt	60,000	30,000	30,000 (1)		90,000
Total liabilities	160,000	80,000			240,000
Common stock	80,000	40,000		80,000 (3)	160,000
Paid-in capital	100,000	50,000		520,000 (4)	620,000
Retained earnings	60,000	30,000			60,000
Shareholders' equity (SHE)	240,000	120,000			840,000
Total claims on assets	$400,000	$200,000	$630,000	$630,000	$1,080,000

(1) Paid $30 each for 20,000 shares = $600,000. Eliminate SHE of target of $120,000. The $600,000 less $120,000 equals $480,000 to asset write-ups or to goodwill or some combination of the two.

(2) The difference between the market value of $600,000 paid and the elimination of the net worth accounts of the target is $480,000. The gross plant and equipment account is debited $480,000, and the accumulated depreciation account for the target is eliminated by a debit of $30,000 with an offsetting credit of $30,000. In the consolidated column, gross plant and equipment is $200,000 plus $100,000 plus $450,000, totaling $750,000. The accumulated depreciation is only that of the acquiring firm in the amount of $60,000. Net plant and equipment is therefore $690,000.

(3) The common stock account of the acquiring firm (A) was 20,000 shares with a par value of $4, totaling $80,000. Firm A issued 20,000 new shares at a par of $4 to buy T. The consolidated common stock account, therefore, would be $160,000, shown in the column for the consolidated company.

(4) The total debits were $600,000. A credit of $80,000 was made to the common stock account. So it is necessary to make an additional credit of $520,000 to the paid-in capital account.

market value of $30 per share, a total value of $600,000. This cost of the acquired company is assigned to the assets acquired and liabilities assumed. If the cost of the acquired company exceeds the amounts assigned to identifiable assets less liabilities assumed, this difference is recorded as goodwill. In practice, it is likely that some of the excess of the amount paid over the net worth of the acquired firm would be assigned to identifiable assets. To illustrate the different consequences of pooling versus purchase accounting, we analyze the two extreme cases, in which (1) all of the excess is assigned to identifiable and depreciable assets, and (2) none is so assigned, so the excess is entirely goodwill. We first discuss the case in which all of the excess is assigned to depreciable assets, as shown in Table 3.3.

The adjustments in purchase consolidation accounting designated by the superscript (1) in Table 3.3 represent the elimination of the net worth accounts of the target by debits totaling $120,000. The difference between the market value of $600,000 paid and the elimination of the net worth accounts of the target is $480,000. In note (2) in Table 3.3, the gross plant and equipment account is debited $480,000 and the accumulated depreciation account for the target is eliminated by a debit of $30,000. In the consolidated column, gross plant and equipment is A's $200,000 plus T's $100,000 plus the net step-up of $450,000, totaling $750,000. The accumulated depreciation is only that of the acquiring firm in the amount of $60,000. The consolidated net plant and equipment is therefore $690,000, as shown.

The common stock account of A was 20,000 shares with a par value of $4, totaling $80,000. Table 3.3 shows a credit of $80,000 to the common stock account. This represents the 20,000 new shares of A issued to buy T. Because these 20,000 shares have a par value of $4 each, the credit [(3) in Table 3.3] to the book common stock account is $80,000. For the combined company, there are now 40,000 shares of stock outstanding—the 20,000 original shares of A and the additional 20,000 shares it issued to buy T. With a par value of $4, the book total of common stock is therefore $160,000 for the combined company. The difference between the $600,000 and the $80,000 credit to the common stock is $520,000, representing the additional credit [(4) in Table 3.3] that must be made to the paid-in capital account for the combined company.

Recall that in Table 3.2, for pooling accounting the total assets were simply the sum of the total assets of the combining companies, $600,000. In Table 3.3, under purchase accounting, the total consolidated assets for the combined companies is $1,080,000. This new total represents the total under pooling accounting of $600,000 plus the $480,000 representing the excess of the total value paid less the book value of net worth purchased.

In Table 3.4, we show the balance sheet effects of assigning all of the excess to goodwill rather than to depreciable assets as was done in Table 3.3. The excess of $480,000 is assigned to a goodwill account rather than to depreciable assets. The accumulated depreciation account of the target firm is eliminated. The combined net value of plant and equipment is $210,000.

Table 3.4 Consolidated Balance Sheet, Purchase Accounting All "Excess" to Goodwill

	Acquiring Firm	Target Firm	Adjustment Purchase Debit	Adjustment Purchase Credit	Consolidated Purchase (All "Excess" to Goodwill)
Current assets	$210,000	$110,000			$ 320,000
Land	50,000	20,000			70,000
Plant and equipment	200,000	100,000		30,000 [2]	270,000
Less: accumulated depr.	60,000	30,000	30,000 [2]		60,000
Net plant and equipment	140,000	70,000			210,000
Goodwill			480,000 [1]		480,000
Total assets	$400,000	$200,000			$1,080,000
Interest-bearing debt	40,000	20,000			60,000
Other current liabilities	60,000	30,000			90,000
Long-term debt	60,000	30,000			90,000
Total liabilities	160,000	80,000			240,000
Common stock	80,000	40,000	40,000 [1]	80,000 [3]	160,000
Paid-in capital	100,000	50,000	50,000 [1]	520,000 [4]	620,000
Retained earnings	60,000	30,000	30,000 [1]		60,000
Shareholders' equity (SHE)	240,000	120,000			840,000
Total claims on assets	$400,000	$200,000	$630,000	$630,000	$1,080,000

[1] Paid $30 for 20,000 shares = $600,000. Eliminate SHE of target of $120,000. The $600,000 less $120,000 equals $480,000 to goodwill.

[2] The accumulated depreciation account of the target firm is eliminated by a debit with an offsetting credit of $30,000.

[3] The common stock account of the acquiring firm (A) was 20,000 shares with a par value of $4, totaling $80,000. Firm A issued 20,000 new shares at a par of $4 to buy T. The consolidated common stock account, therefore, would be $160,000, shown in the column for the consolidated company.

[4] Total of $600,000 debits less credit of $80,000 requires a credit of $520,000 to paid-in capital.

86

Effects of Pooling Versus Purchase on Income Measurement

We now consider the effects of pooling versus purchase on the consolidated income statements. The first two columns of Table 3.5 repeat the information for A and T from the statement of facts presented in Table 3.1. The consolidated income statement *under pooling* shown in column 3 would be the summation, item by item, of each account in the income statement except for the per share figures. Earnings per share for the combined company would be the initial combined net income of $60,000 divided by the 40,000 shares now outstanding, which gives $1.50 for earnings per share.

Shareholders of T, who are now shareholders of the combined firm, now have a claim on earnings per share that is increased by 50% over the dollar per share earnings before the acquisition. This is because T shareholders had a 100% claim to $20,000 earnings prior to the combination. With 20,000 shares outstanding, this was earnings per share (EPS) of $1. After the combination, the former T shareholders have a 50% claim to $60,000. For the 20,000 shares of the combined company they now own, this represents $1.50 per share. In this example, T shareholders have earnings accretion of $0.50 per share while the A shareholders have earnings dilution of $0.50 per share. This results from the facts of this particular example. More generally, the earnings accretion per share need not be exactly equal to the earnings dilution per share of the company with the lower price-to-earnings ratio (P/E). Many different patterns are observed in practice.

Columns 4, 5, and 6 analyze the income statement effects of purchase accounting under alternative assumptions. In column 4, all of the excess of the purchase price over the book net worth acquired is assigned to depreciable assets. In Table 3.3, the balance sheet under purchase accounting showed the net $450,000 excess added to the gross plant and equipment accounts, resulting in a total gross plant and equipment of $750,000. Because the 10-year life assumption is continued from Table 3.1, the tax-deductible depreciation will be 10% of the $750,000 or $75,000 as shown. We then calculate net income and cash flows in total and on a per share basis.

In column 5, all of the excess is assigned to goodwill and qualifies for the 15-year write-off permitted by the tax law change of 1993. Hence, the depreciation charge continues at $30,000. In addition, the $480,000 goodwill is amortized over 15 years, representing $32,000 as shown. We calculate EPS and cash flow per share.

If all of the excess were assigned to goodwill and it did not qualify for tax deductibility, we would have column 6. The depreciation expenses are 10% of $20,000 plus one-seventh of the gross value and net value of the plant and equipment acquired from the target firm. EBIT would become $115,000, and earnings before taxes $100,000. After deduction of $40,000 for taxes and $24,000 for amortization of goodwill, the reported net income would be $36,000 or $0.90 per share. Cash flows would be $90,000 (net income of $36,000 plus depreciation of $30,000 and amortization of $24,000) or $2.25 per share. The cash flows per share would be the same as in column 3 under pooling, because both lack the tax shelter benefit of the amortization of goodwill.

These results illustrate the generalization we presented at the beginning of the analysis. In every case, net income is lower under purchase accounting than under

Table 3.5 Income Statements for Pooling vs. Purchase

| | Acquiring Firm (1) | Target Firm (2) | Consolidated, Pooling Accounting (3) | CONSOLIDATED PURCHASE ACCOUNTING* | | |
				All "Excess" to Depreciable Assets (4)	All "Excess" to Goodwill Depreciable Over 15 Years (5)	Nondeductible (6)
Sales	$800,000	$400,000	$1,200,000	$1,200,000	$1,200,000	$1,200,000
Operating cost	703,333	351,667	1,055,000	1,055,000	1,055,000	1,055,000
EBITDA	96,667	48,333	145,000	145,000	145,000	145,000
Depreciation	20,000	10,000	30,000	75,000	30,000	30,000
Amortization (deductible)					32,000	
EBIT	76,667	38,333	115,000	70,000	83,000	115,000
Interest cost @ 10%	10,000	5,000	15,000	15,000	15,000	15,000
Earnings before taxes	66,667	33,333	100,000	55,000	68,000	100,000
Taxes @ 40%	26,667	13,333	40,000	22,000	27,200	40,000
Amortization (not deduct.)						24,000
Net income	$40,000	$20,000	$60,000	$33,000	$40,800	$36,000
Earnings per share	$2.00	$1.00	$1.50	$0.83	$1.02	$0.90
Cash flows**	$60,000	$30,000	$90,000	$108,000	$102,800	$90,000
Cash flows per share	$3.00	$1.50	$2.25	$2.70	$2.57	$2.25

*This assumes that the purchase was completed on the first day of the fiscal year. In column 4, the depreciation charge is the new gross plant and equipment total of $750,000 times 10%. In column 5, the amortization of goodwill on the tax return is shown as a tax deduction amortized over 15 years. In column 6, the depreciation charge of $30,000 is composed of the $20,000 in the $200,000 gross assets of A and one-seventh (the remaining life of the assets of T is 7 years) of $70,000, which is the postacquisition gross and net value of the target's depreciable assets now owned by the combined company; 20 years is the period for the nondeductible amortization.

**Cash flows are defined as net income plus depreciation and amortization. The cash flows in purchase accounting exceed the cash flows in pooling by the tax shield of 0.4($45,000) = $18,000 for column 4 and 0.4($32,000) = $12,800 for column 5.

88

pooling accounting. This is because of the deductions made for amortization of goodwill or increased depreciation expenses. However, when amortization or increased depreciation are deductible for tax purposes, they shelter cash flows. In columns 4 and 5, where purchase accounting provides for increased tax shelter, cash flows are larger than under pooling accounting. In column 6, where the goodwill amortization is not tax deductible, cash flows are the same as under pooling accounting.

Intermediate cases in which part of the excess is assigned to depreciable assets and part to goodwill would follow the patterns developed in Table 3.5. Because the results would fall between the cases we have analyzed, they can be pursued as problem exercises.

EFFECTS ON LEVERAGE

In pooling, because assets and claims on assets are simply added, total assets and total claims on assets are the sum of the individual component firms. Leverage measured by debt-to-equity ratios at book values would remain unchanged. For the example in Table 3.2, the ratio of debt to equity for the component firms and for the combined firm is 2/3, or 67%.

In purchase accounting when stock is used, the result is shown in Table 3.3. The debt-to-equity ratio for the component firms is again 2/3, or 67%. In the consolidated firm, the debt-to-equity ratio is 240/840, which is 29%. Thus, in a purchase when stock is used as the medium of payment, the leverage ratio declines. The intuition behind this is that the net worth of the combined firm is increased by the actual market value of the purchase price of the target firm less the debt of the book net worth accounts of the target firm. As shown in Table 3.3, the difference between the purchase price of $600,000 and the credit of $80,000 to the common stock account is $520,000, which is added to the paid-in capital account, increasing the net worth in the combined firm. This causes the debt-to-equity ratio to decline.

The Time Warner acquisition of the Turner Broadcasting System provides an example. On page 113 of the September 6, 1996 proxy statement issued by Time Warner in connection with the Turner acquisition, a pro forma consolidated balance sheet is presented. It shows that as a result of the transaction, goodwill was increased by $6.4 billion. The Turner shareholders' equity of $500 million was eliminated. Paid-in capital in the combined accounts was increased by $6.4 billion. As a result of the transaction, the shareholders' equity of Time Warner increased from $3.8 billion to $9.9 billion because of the large credit to the paid-in capital account to offset the debit of $6.4 billion to the goodwill account in the "New Time Warner" pro forma balance sheet of June 30, 1996.

If the method of payment in a purchase is cash, leverage is increased rather than decreased. This is shown in the simple example in Table 3.6. The acquiring firm has $25 excess cash. The debt-to-equity ratio of the acquirer was the debt (net of excess cash) of $25 divided by the $50 equity, or 50%. It acquires for $25 a target firm with a net worth of $10. In the adjustments, the shareholders' equity of the target ($10) is eliminated. The cash used to make the transaction is credited. A debit of $15 is made either to depreciable assets or to a goodwill account. The new total assets are $110. The new debt-to-equity ratio is 60/50, which is 120%, a rise from 50%.

Table 3.6   Effect on Leverage of a Cash Purchase

	Acquirer	Target	Adjustments Debit	Adjustments Credit	Combined Firm
Excess cash	$ 25			$25	$ 0
Other assets	75	$20			95
Goodwill			$15		15
Total assets	$100	$20			$110
Total debt	50	10			60
Shareholders' equity	50	10	10		50
Total claims	$100	$20	$25	$25	$110

THE FASB PROPOSAL TO ELIMINATE POOLING

In the FASB's August 31, 1999 Financial Accounting Series No. 200-B, six reasons were given for eliminating pooling:

1. The pooling method provides investors with less information—and less-relevant information—than that provided by the purchase method.
2. The pooling method ignores the values exchanged in a business combination, whereas the purchase method reflects them.
3. Under the pooling method, financial statement readers cannot tell how much was invested in the transaction, nor can they track the subsequent performance of the investment.
4. Having two methods of accounting makes it difficult for investors to compare companies when they have used different methods to account for their business combinations.
5. Because future cash flows are the same whether the pooling or purchase method is used, the boost in earnings under the pooling method reflects artificial accounting differences rather than real economic differences.
6. Business combinations are acquisitions and should be accounted for as such, based on the value of what is given up in exchange, regardless of whether it is cash, other assets, debt, or equity shares.

The FASB is essentially arguing that the pooling method provides less relevant information than purchase accounting. By having two different methods of accounting, comparability between financial statements of companies is diminished. Yet it is widely recognized that acquiring firms prefer the pooling method. The considerable evidence is systematically presented by Walter (1999).

Empirical Studies of Pooling Versus Purchase

Despite the evidence of a preference for the use of the pooling method, empirical research has established that the stock prices of acquiring firms are not penalized when the purchase method of accounting is used. In fact, previous studies, including our own, find that stock price reactions to the use of purchase accounting are more positive than for pooling accounting. However, generally, the reaction in favor of purchase accounting is not statistically significant.

One possible advantage of pooling is that the transactions are generally non-taxable, because stock is exchanged for stock. But the research studies of nontaxable transactions included both pooling and purchase samples. Stock price reactions were not statistically different for pooling vs purchase transactions.

The preference for the use of pooling stems from the concern about the negative impact of purchase accounting on reported net earnings per share. FASB's proposed reduction in the goodwill write-off period from 40 years to 20 years implies a greater negative impact on reported earnings per share (EPS). It appears that the FASB will permit companies to report two separate EPS numbers, one of which would exclude the goodwill amortization charge. Some companies have reported cash EPS numbers in their financial releases. This facilitates the use of the relevant cash flow numbers. But it will also be necessary that regulators and rating agencies use cash earnings in setting standards. For example, debt indentures base dividend rules on GAAP earnings.

The most important consideration should be whether a proposed merger makes sense from an economic standpoint and creates value. The purpose of combining companies is to achieve improvements that the individual companies could not have achieved independently. If the merger was soundly conceived and effectively implemented, then the combined cash flows should be greater than the simple sum of the constituent firms. Conversely, a combination that did not make sense from an economic standpoint or that was not implemented effectively could result in combined cash flows less than the sum of the cash flows of the individual companies. In this longer term perspective, even if an acquisition results in initial dilution in earnings per share for the stockholders of one of the companies, the merger still may make business and economic sense. The initial dilution can be regarded as an investment that will have a payoff in future years in the form of magnified cash flows for the combined company. Thus, we do not expect the elimination of pooling to have a significantly negative impact on mergers soundly conceived and effectively implemented.

SUMMARY

The use of the purchase method in financial accounting results in lower reported net income. When the excess of the price paid over the target net worth is assigned to depreciable assets or to deductible amortization of goodwill, cash flows will be higher by the tax shelter effects of the increased depreciation or amortization of goodwill.

When all of the excess paid in purchase accounting is assigned to goodwill whose amortization is not tax deductible, the cash flows are the same under both pooling and purchase accounting. The elimination of pooling accounting should not have a significantly negative impact on mergers that increase value.

QUESTIONS

3.1 Why is reported net income lower under purchase accounting than under pooling of interests accounting?

3.2 Are actual cash flows different in financial accounting for pooling versus purchase if the 40-year write-off period for non-tax-deductible amortization of goodwill is used?

3.3 Why are cash flows higher under purchase accounting when the amortization of goodwill is deductible for tax purposes under the conditions of the 1993 law changes?

3.4 Summarize the studies on the effects of pooling versus purchase on stock prices.

3.5 Rework Table 3.3 when the terms of the merger are 0.9 share of the acquirer (A) for one share of target (T).

3.6 Discuss some likely consequences of the elimination of pooling of interests as a method of accounting for mergers if the FASB proposal becomes effective.

Case 3.1   AT&T's Acquisition of NCR

In 1991, after about six months of offers by AT&T and resistance by NCR, NCR agreed to be acquired for $7.5 billion in a stock-for-stock transaction. During the negotiations, the market value of AT&T stock declined by between $3.9 billion and $6.5 billion. The purchase price at $111 per share was regarded as a substantial overpayment. On November 7, 1990, the day before a *Wall Street Journal* article reported a rumor of AT&T's interest in acquiring NCR, NCR closed at $48 per share. When AT&T made its initial bid of $90 on December 3, 1990, NCR called the offer "grossly inadequate," but stated that it would "carefully consider a financially sound proposal."

AT&T paid a documented $50 million and possibly as much as $500 million to satisfy the requirements of pooling accounting. By using the pooling method, earnings per share were about 17% higher than un-der purchase accounting, but cash flows were unchanged. For further details, see the *Wall Street Journal,* December 3, 1990, "AT&T Makes Unsolicited $6.03 Billion Bid For NCR After Merger Discussion Stall" (also see Lys and Vincent, 1995).

QUESTIONS

1. Why did AT&T persist in its efforts to acquire NCR for about six months and continue to raise its bid price when "the market" reaction predicted that it was an unsound acquisition with negative synergies?

2. Why would AT&T go to extra expenses of over $50 million to use pooling accounting rather than purchase accounting even though the method of accounting had no effect on cash flows?

Case 3.2 Wells Fargo Acquisition of First Interstate Bancorporation

On October 17, 1995, Wells Fargo Bank (WF) made an unsolicited bid for the First Interstate Bancorporation (FIB), both operating mainly in California. First Interstate Bancorporation rejected the bid as inadequate. It solicited a second bidder (white knight), the First Bank System (FBS) of Minneapolis, Minnesota, with branches in that area. The wealth effects of the WF initial bid are shown in Part A.

Part A. Wells Fargo Initial Bid	WF	FIB	FBS
1. October 3, 1995—Preannouncement (1) prices	$207	$105	$51
2. Number of shares (millions)	47	76	127
3. Total market value (billions) (1 × 2)	$9.7	$8.0	$6.5
4a. October 17, 1995—Initial WF offer	0.625 FIB		
4b. Dollar value to FIB (1 × 4a)		$129.375/sh	
5. Postannouncement price	$229	$140	
5a. Price change per share (5 − 1)	$22	$35	
5b. Shareholder wealth effect (billions) (2 × 5a)	$1.03	$2.66	
5c. New total market value (billions) (2 × 5)	$10.76	$10.64	

The results of the white knight bid by FBS on November 6, 1995, are shown in Part B.

Part B. FBS Bid	WF	FIB	FBS
6. November 6, 1995—FBS merger agreement			2.6/FIB
6a. Postannouncement (2) price	$211	$127	$51
6b. Implied dollar value of FIB		FBS offer: 2.6($51) = $132.60/sh	
6c. WF counteroffer		WF offer: 0.625($211) = $131.88/sh	

Further bids by WF are shown in Part C.

Part C. WF Further Bids	WF	FIB	FBS
7a. November 6, 1995—WF raises offer to 0.65		0.65($211) = $137.15/sh	
7b. November 13, 1995—WF raises offer to 0.667		0.667($211) = $140.74/sh	

On January 19, 1996, the SEC ruled that FBS could not use pooling accounting because its share repurchase program violated one of the conditions for the use of pooling. The price effects are shown in Part D.

Part D. SEC Rules that FBS Cannot Use Pooling	WF	FIB	FBS
8. January 19, 1996—SEC ruling			
9. From January 17, 1996 to January 23, 1996— Stock price movements	$215 to $229	$136.75 to $149.25	$48.25 to $50.50

The wealth effects of WF's winning bid on January 24, 1996, are shown in Part E.

Part E. WF Winning Bid	WF	FIB	FBS
10. January 24, 1996—WF and FIB agree to merge			$51.75
10a. Value of FIB		0.667($229) = $152.74/sh	
11. January 24, 1996—Prices less initial prices	$229 − $207 = $22/sh	$149.25 − $105 = $44.25/sh	$51.75 − $51 = $0.75/sh
12. Deflate by 6% rise in NASDAQ Bank stock index (October 3, 1995 to January 24, 1996)	$229/1.06 = $216/sh	$149.25/1.06 = $140.80/sh	$51.75/1.06 = $48.82/sh
12a. Price change based on deflated prices	$216 − $207 = $9/sh	$140.80 − $105 = $35.80/sh	$48.82 − $51 = −$2.18/sh
13a. Wealth effect, nominal (millions)	47($22) = $1,034	76($44.25) = $3,363	127($0.75) = $95.25
13b. Wealth effect, deflated (millions)	47($9) = $423	76($35.80) = $2,720.8	127(−$2.18) = −$276.86

Wells Fargo estimated that they could save at least a billion dollars a year by combining overlapping offices. This was not possible for FBS because it was located in a different geographic area. One attraction of FIB was that its average interest cost on deposits in the first half of 1995 was 2.49% annualized, the lowest of 42 big regional banks. Wells Fargo's cost of funds was 3.14%, and that of FBS, 3.71%. For FBS, the inexpensive deposits of FIB were especially attractive because FBS was "an aggressive lender hungry for funds" (Tom Petruno, "Suitors Covet First Interstate's Low-Cost Deposits," *Los Angeles Times,* November 10, 1995, pp. D1, D12).

The offers by both WF and FBS were exchanges of stock. In the attempt to make its stock exchange offer more attractive, FBS had embarked on an open market share repurchase program of 73 million shares. But FBS was planning to treat the acquisition as a pooling of interests transaction for financial accounting purposes. It was announced on January 20, 1996, that the SEC ruled that to qualify for pooling accounting FBS could not buy back its own stock for two years (Saul Hansell, "S.E.C. Deals a Blow to First Bank's Bid for First Interstate," the *New York Times,* January 20, 1996, pp. 17, 31).

On January 25, 1996, it was announced that WF and FIB had agreed to merge under the terms described in the chronology above. Wells Fargo planned to use purchase accounting that involved a write-off of goodwill, reducing reported net income by $400 million per year. First Interstate Bancorporation had contracted to pay FBS a $200 million fee if their agreement was not consummated. In the early stages of counterbidding, WF sued to have this agreement declared illegal. After its merger agreement with FIB, WF paid the $200 million to FBS in two installments.

For additional background, see the *Wall Street Journal,* the *New York Times,* and the *Los Angeles Times* from October 3, 1995, to March 5, 1996 and the following journal articles:

Davis, Michael L, "The Purchase vs. Pooling Controversy: How the Stock Market Responds to Goodwill," *Journal of Applied Corporate Finance,* 9, Spring 1996, pp. 50–59.

Houston, Joel F., and Michael D. Ryngaert, "The Value Added by Bank Acquisitions: Lessons from Wells Fargo's Acquisition of First Interstate," *Journal of Applied Corporate Finance,* 9, 1996, pp. 74–82.

QUESTIONS

1. Why were greater savings available to WF as compared with FBS?
2. Compare the two methods of accounting that FBS and WF planned to use.
3. What were the wealth effects of the transaction, and what are their implications?

◻REFERENCES

Financial Accounting Standards Board, Financial Accounting Series, No. 172-A, April 22, 1997, Status Report No. 287, p. 3.

Financial Accounting Standards Board, Financial Accounting Series, No. 200-B, August 1999.

Lys, Thomas, and Linda Vincent, "An Analysis of Value Destruction in AT&T's Acquisition of NCR," *Journal of Financial Economics,* 39, 1995, pp. 353–378.

Walter, John R., "Pooling or Purchase: A Merger Mystery," Federal Reserve Bank of Richmond *Economic Quarterly,* 85/1, 1999, pp. 27–46.

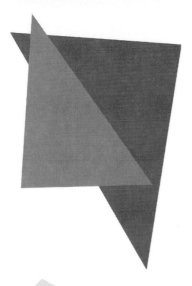

Tax Planning Options

Aconsiderable literature has been produced on the relationship between taxes and takeovers. This chapter provides a synthesis and assesses the results of the studies to date. The following topics are covered: taxable versus nontaxable or tax-deferred acquisitions, the Tax Reform Act of 1986, and the question of whether tax gains cause acquisitions, which includes considerations of early empirical tests of tax effects, later empirical studies of tax effects, and taxes and LBOs.

TAXABLE VERSUS NONTAXABLE OR TAX-DEFERRED ACQUISITIONS

The basic tax rule is simple. If the merger or tender offer involves exchanging the stock of one company for the stock of the other, it is a nontaxable transaction. If cash or debt is used, it is a taxable transaction. In practice, many complications exist.

The Internal Revenue Code makes a technical distinction between three types of "acquisitive tax-free reorganizations," which are defined in Section 368 of the code. They are referred to as type A, B, and C reorganizations. A type A reorganization is a statutory merger or consolidation. In a merger, target firm shareholders exchange their target stock for shares in the acquiring firm; in a consolidation, both target and acquiring firm shareholders turn in their shares and receive stock in the newly created company.

Type B reorganizations are similarly stock-for-stock exchanges. Following a type B reorganization, the target may be liquidated into the acquiring firm or maintained as an independent operating entity.

Type C reorganizations are stock-for-asset transactions with the requirement that at least 80% of the fair market value of the target's property be acquired. Typically, the target firm "sells" its assets to the acquiring firm in exchange for voting stock in the acquiring firm; the target then dissolves, distributing the acquiring firm's stock to its shareholders in return for its own (now-canceled) stock.

In practice, a three-party acquisition technique is employed. The parent creates a shell subsidiary. The shell issues stock, all of which is bought by the parent with cash or its own stock. The target as the third party is bought with the cash or stock of the parent held by the subsidiary. The advantage of creating the subsidiary as an intermediary is that the parent acquires control of the target through the subsidiary without incurring responsibilities for the known and possibly unknown liabilities of the target. The transaction still qualifies as an A reorganization. The target firm may remain in existence if the stock of the parent is used in the acquisition. Because the parent-acquirer shareholders are not directly involved, they are denied voting and appraisal rights in the transaction. In a reverse three-party merger, the subsidiary is merged into the target. The parent stock held by the subsidiary is distributed to the target's shareholders in exchange for their target stock. This is equivalent to a B reorganization.

The "tax-free" reorganization actually represents only tax deferral for the target firm shareholders. If the target shareholder subsequently sells the acquiring firm's stock received in the transaction, a capital gains tax becomes payable. The basis for the capital gains tax is the original basis of the target stock held by the target shareholder. If the former target shareholder dies without selling the acquiring firm's stock, the estate tax laws establish the tax basis as the value at time of death.

In Table 4.1, the main implications of nontaxable versus taxable acquisitions are summarized. In a nontaxable (tax-deferred) reorganization, the acquiring firm can generally use the net operating loss (NOL) carryover and unused tax credits of the acquired firm. However, even though the value of the shares paid may be greater than the net book values of the assets acquired, no write-up or step-up of the depreciable values of the assets acquired can be made. For the shareholders of the target firm, taxes are deferred until the common shares received in the transaction are sold. Thus, the shareholders can defer the taxes.

In taxable acquisitions, the acquiring firm may assign the excess of purchase price over the book value of equity acquired to depreciable assets, as described under purchase accounting. The acquiring firm, however, is unable to carry over the NOLs and tax credits. The shareholders of the target firm in a taxable acquisition must recognize the gain over their tax basis in the shares. If, in addition, the target firm has used accelerated depreciation, a portion of any gain that is attributable to excess depreciation deductions will be recaptured to be taxed as ordinary income rather than capital gains, the amount of recapture depending on the nature of the property involved. (Ginsburg, 1983)

Table 4.1 Nontaxable vs. Taxable M&As

	Acquiring Firm	**Target Firm**
A. Nontaxable reorganizations	NOL carryover Tax-credit carryover Carryover asset basis	Deferred gains for shareholders
B. Taxable acquisitions	Stepped-up asset basis Loss of NOLs and tax credits	Immediate gain recognition by target shareholders Depreciation recapture of income

THE TAX REFORM ACT OF 1986

The Tax Reform Act of 1986 (TRA 1986) made many fundamental amendments to the prevailing 1954 code. Corporate income tax rates have been only slightly modified since TRA 1986. TRA 1986 also had a number of impacts on merger and acquisition transactions. (1) It severely restricted the use of net operating loss carryovers. (2) The preferential rate on corporate capital gains was repealed. (3) A minimum tax was imposed on corporate profits. (4) The General Utilities doctrine was repealed. (5) Greenmail payments could not be deducted.

Net Operating Loss (NOL) Carryovers

The Tax Reform Act of 1986 provides that if there is a greater than 50% ownership change in a loss corporation within a three-year period, an annual limit on the use of NOLs will be imposed. The amount of an NOL that may be used to offset earnings is limited to the value of the loss corporation at the date of ownership change multiplied by the long-term tax-exempt bond rate. For example, assume a loss corporation is worth $10 million immediately before an ownership change, the tax-exempt bond rate is 7% , and the corporation has a $5 million loss carryforward. Then $700,000 ($10 million $\times$ 7%) of the NOL can be used annually to offset the acquiring firm's taxable income.

In addition, a loss corporation may not utilize NOL carryovers unless it continues substantially the same business for two years after the change in ownership. If this requirement is not met, all of the losses are generally disallowed (Curtis, 1987).

Minimum Tax on Corporate Profits

Before the Tax Reform Act of 1986, a corporation paid a minimum tax on specific tax preferences in addition to its regular tax. The old add-on minimum tax is replaced by an alternative minimum tax with a flat rate of 20%. Thus, corporations pay taxes to at least 20% of their income above the exemption amount. This has a negative impact on leveraged buyouts and acquisitions of mature companies for which effective tax rates are below 20%.

General Utilities Doctrine

Under the General Utilities case decided in the 1930s and incorporated in later code sections, corporations did not recognize gains when they sold assets in connection with a "complete liquidation" in the sense of legal technicalities. This required adoption of a plan of liquidation and sale with distribution of assets within a 12-month period. Distribution of assets in kind in liquidation was also not subject to tax. The provisions were repealed by the TRA of 1986. Most of the exemptions from the new rules are for relatively small and closely held corporations or provide for limited transitional periods (Wood, 1987).

Greenmail

The Tax Reform Act of 1986 also limited the extent to which amounts paid as greenmail to corporate raiders could be deducted for tax purposes. This change and the others listed previously move in the direction of being less favorable to merger and acquisition activity.

STOCK VERSUS ASSET PURCHASES

Tax considerations are part of the general topic, structuring the deal. One issue is the effects on buyers and sellers of a stock versus asset purchase in a taxable transaction. We use a specific example to illustrate the factors involved.[1] The selling company in this example is a regular C corporation, not an LLC or S corporation. The other data assumed are listed below:

Purchase price, stock	$ 100 million
Purchase price, assets	$ 100 million
Liabilities of seller	$ 25 million
Basis in assets (seller)	$ 60 million
Basis in shares (of seller)	$ 50 million
Corporate tax rate (federal and state)	40%
Individual tax rate (federal and state)	25%
Applicable discount factor	10%

Based on the above data the net proceeds to the shareholders of the selling firm are compared in Table 4.2.

Table 4.2

	(1) Acquisition of Stock	(2) Acquisition of Assets
Assumed purchase price	$ 100	$ 100
Assumed liabilities	—	25
Total purchase price	$ 100	$ 125
Basis in assets		(60)
Gain		65
Corporate tax rate		40%
Tax on sale of assets		26
Net to shareholders (SH)	$ 100	74
Basis in shares	(50)	(50)
Capital gain	50	24
Tax rate on individual	25%	25%
Tax on individual on sale	12.50	6
Net proceeds to seller SH	**$ 87.50**	**$ 68**

---

[1] Our presentation is based on the booklet "Tax Considerations—Mergers & Acquisitions," by Deloitte & Touche LLP, March 24, 1999.

The explanation for the acquisition of stock alternative is straightforward. The assumed purchase price is $100. The tax basis for the shareholders of the seller is $50. Their capital gain is $50. With an assumed federal plus state capital gains tax of 25%, the tax to the shareholders would be $12.50. The net proceeds to the seller shareholders would be $87.50.

If the transaction is an acquisition of assets, the seller corporation must be included in the analysis. If the buyer pays $100 for the assets, its assumption of the liabilities of the corporation is added to the purchase price. We postulate that the seller corporation has a tax basis of $60 in the assets sold. Its gain is therefore $65. With a combined state and federal corporate income tax rate of 40%, the tax on the sale of the assets would be $26. The amount available to the target shareholders would be $74. Their tax basis was postulated to be $50, so the capital gain would be $24. With the same individual tax rate of 25% (as above), the net proceeds to the seller shareholders would be $68.

The buyer may prefer the acquisition of assets to avoid unknown liabilities of the seller for which the buyer would otherwise be liable. In this asset acquisition with purchase accounting, the buyer is able to step up the tax basis of the assets acquired. The excess of the purchase price of $125 over the seller's original basis in assets can be allocated first to tangible assets and the remainder to goodwill. The purchaser will have a step-up for both book and tax purposes. In the present example it is assumed that all of the differential is assigned to goodwill, depreciable for tax purposes over 15 years.

The tax benefits of the step-up may influence the purchase price in a competitive corporate control market. The present value of the tax benefit may be added to the purchase price. The calculation of the present value of the tax benefit is as follows.

Purchase price	$ 100
Assumed liabilities	25
Total purchase price	$ 125
Basis in assets	(60)
Goodwill	65
Life of tax benefit	15
Annual tax benefit	4.333
Expected future tax rate	40%
Actual cash savings	1.733
Discount rate	10%
PV of tax benefit	**$ 13.18**

The goodwill of $65 is spread over 15 years, resulting in an annual tax benefit of $4.333. Using an expected future tax rate of 40%, the annual tax benefits would be $1.733. With a 10% discount factor, the present value of an annuity of $1 for 15 years would be 7.6061 to be multiplied times $1.733. The result is a present value of tax benefits of $13.18. If competition forces the buyer to pay this additional amount, the purchase price of assets becomes $113. The total purchase price becomes $138. The net proceeds to the selling shareholders would rise from $68 to $74.

Even if the tax benefits to the buyer of the asset step-up in the purchase of assets are passed on to the selling shareholders, they still receive less than they would have from the sale of stock. For relatively small firms the major shareholders are likely to be the founding executives. Tax and legal advisors usually counsel the closely held small corporations to be formed as limited liability corporations (LLC) or S corporations. For both LLCs and S corporations, income from the entity flows directly to the shareholders. This avoids the double taxation that otherwise occurs when the business is sold as an asset acquisition.

DO TAX GAINS CAUSE ACQUISITIONS?

Gilson, Scholes, and Wolfson (GSW) (1988) make the most comprehensive analysis of the possibility that acquisitions are fostered by the tax system. Another way of posing the issue is whether acquisitions represent the best method of achieving tax gains. GSW present a lengthy discussion of a number of possibilities. We greatly compress their highly sophisticated analysis for our discussion.

GSW focus on three main types of tax gains from acquisitions under the pre-1986 tax code: increased leverage, net operating loss carry-forwards (NOLs), and the basis increase on acquired assets. Leverage can be easily disposed of because there is no clear reason why a company cannot leverage itself without an acquisition, for example, by issuing debt and repurchasing stock.

Net operating losses could be utilized under perfect markets by issuing equity and buying taxable debt. The NOLs could be used to offset the taxable interest income. GSW indicate that various types of transaction costs may prevent this simple utilization of NOLs but also inhibit acquisitions. Some NOLs expire unused, which is evidence that the transaction costs of utilizing NOLs either by acquisitions or other transactions are substantial. Again, under perfect markets (no information costs and no transactions costs), a firm could sell assets and buy them to achieve the basis step-up, or sale-and-leaseback transactions could be used. However, if acquisitions are motivated primarily by efficiency considerations, the basis step-up simply adds to the gains from acquisition. Thus, if the acquisition improves efficiency, any subsidy involved in the tax gains adds to the value increases.

Empirical studies of tax effects confirm the predictions of the GSW analysis. Tax factors are of significant magnitude in less than 10% of merger transactions. Individual case studies yield similar results. Even when tax effects are significant, they are not the main motivation for merger transactions. (Hayn, 1989).

A possible qualification of the role of taxes is in *going private* transactions, such as leveraged buyouts (LBOs) and management buyouts (MBOs). The initial financial structures of LBOs and MBOs can be as high as 90% debt. Although the tax savings from such high debt ratios can be substantial, systematic studies show that debt is paid down as rapidly as possible. The main objective is to achieve value increases so that the companies can be taken public again within three to five years. The proceeds from such public offerings are usually applied to pay down debt even further. All of this is evidence that tax savings from high leverage is not the dominant influence.

Furthermore, there are more dimensions to the analysis. Jensen, Kaplan, and Stiglin (1989) considered a broader range of effects of LBOs on tax revenues of the U.S. Treasury. They listed five sources of incremental tax revenues. First, capital gains taxes are paid on the realized capital gains of shareholders. Second, the LBO may sell off assets, realizing taxable capital gains. Third, the interest income from the LBO debt payments is subject to tax. Fourth, the LBO increases operating income, which gives rise to incremental taxes. Fifth, by using capital more efficiently, additional taxable revenues are generated in the economy. The negative effects are the increased tax deductions from the additional debt and the lower personal tax revenues because LBOs pay little or no dividends.

Jensen, Kaplan, and Stiglin (1989) drew on the data in Kaplan (1989), which covered 48 of the 76 LBOs greater than $50 million in size announced during the years 1979 to 1985. They developed the tax revenue implications of the average LBO based on Kaplan's study. They concluded that, on average, LBOs generated tax increases that were almost twice the size of the tax losses they created. They estimated that the average LBO involved a purchase of $500 million, which generated $227 million in present value (using a 10% discount factor) of tax revenue increases versus $117 million in present value of tax losses to the treasury.

They made similar estimates for the R. J. Reynolds–Nabisco leveraged buyout. They estimated that in present value terms the increased revenue to the treasury was $3.76 billion. They observed that these payments were more than eight times the $370 million in federal taxes paid by RJR Nabisco in 1987 (Jensen, Kaplan, and Stiglin, 1989, p. 733). A *Fortune* magazine article (Newport, 1988) obtained similar results from their analysis of the tax effects of LBOs.

SUMMARY

Tax considerations affect the planning and structuring of corporate combinations. Even in M&As undertaken for other motives, transactions are structured to maximize tax benefits while complying with internal revenue code regulations. In some individual instances, the tax benefits may have been substantial and may have had a major impact. Unfavorable tax rulings by the IRS have also led to the abandonment of some proposed M&As. But tax effects are not the dominant influence in merger and acquisition decisions.

In LBOs, taxes could have a significant influence because of the higher leverage employed. However, such leverage increases could also have been accomplished without LBOs. Furthermore, LBOs reduce leverage from cash flows and from subsequent public offerings of equity. As will be shown in Chapter 13 on LBOs, leverage is used as a device to increase the ownership position and to motivate key managers.

In addition, when broader aspects of the tax effects of LBOs are taken into account, the tax benefits appear to go to the U.S. Treasury. Studies of LBOs also demonstrate that there are always important elements of a "business turnaround" in forming the LBO. Empirical studies of LBOs demonstrate substantial improvements in operating performance. The lasting gains from LBOs result from improving performance rather than from tax benefits alone.

QUESTIONS

4.1 How can personal taxation affect mergers?

4.2 Discuss the advantages and disadvantages of stock-for-stock versus cash-for-stock transactions from the viewpoint of acquired and acquiring firm shareholders.

4.3 How do a firm's growth prospects affect its potential for being involved in a tax-motivated merger?

4.4 A selling company is a regular C corporation. Given the following data, calculate the net proceeds to the shareholders of the selling firm if the buyer makes a stock acquisition versus an acquisition of assets.

Purchase price, stock	250
Purchase price, assets	250
Liabilities of seller	100
Basis in assets (seller)	150
Basis in shares (shareholders of seller)	125
Marginal corporate tax rate (federal and state)	35%
Individual capital gains tax rate (federal and state)	24%

REFERENCES

Curtis, M. R., "Tempered Benefits on NOLs and Capital Gains," *Mergers & Acquisitions,* 21, January/February 1987, pp. 48–49.

Gilson, R. J., M. S. Scholes, and M. A. Wolfson, "Taxation and the Dynamics of Corporate Control: The Uncertain Case for Tax-Motivated Acquisitions," Chapter 18 in J. C. Coffee, Jr., L. Lowenstein, and S. Rose-Ackerman, eds., *Knights, Raiders, and Targets,* New York: Oxford University Press, 1988, pp. 271–299.

Ginsburg, M. D., "Taxing Corporate Acquisitions," *Tax Law Review,* 38, 1983, pp. 177–319.

Hayn, C., "Tax Attributes as Determinants of Shareholder Gains in Corporate Acquisitions," *Journal of Financial Economics,* 23, 1989, pp. 121–153.

Jensen, M., S. Kaplan, and L. Stiglin, "The Effects of LBO's on Tax Revenues," *Tax Notes,* February 6, 1989, pp. 727–733.

Kaplan, S., "Management Buyouts: Evidence on Taxes as a Source of Value," *Journal of Finance,* 44, July 1989, pp. 611–632.

Newport, J. P., Jr., "Why the IRS Might Love Those LBOs," *Fortune,* December 5, 1988, pp. 145–152.

Wood, R. W., "General Utilities Repeal: Injecting New Levies Into M&A," *Mergers & Acquisitions,* 21, January/February 1987, pp. 44–47.

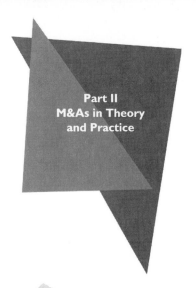

C h a p t e r 5

Strategic Processes

The nature of strategy will first be illustrated by two examples, Cisco Systems, Inc. and Intel. Cisco is one of the exciting success stories in the exploding high technology area of the New Economy. One dollar invested in Cisco in February 1990 would have grown in value nine years later, in March 1999, to $384.77, a compound annual rate of increase of 93.75%—almost a doubling in stock value every year! Cisco began by selling basic Internet routers to corporate customers. A router is a specialized computer that regulates traffic on the Internet and picks the most efficient route for each packet. When information is sent through the Internet, it is broken into smaller pieces, called packets. Each packet travels independently through an Internet path; when packets arrive at their destination, they are reassembled. Cisco evolved from a single-product company in routers to become a complete data networking solutions provider.

What is most relevant for our subject is that between September 21, 1993 and October 26, 1999, Cisco engaged in over 50 acquisitions. Most of the acquisitions were of relatively small size, in the range of $40 million to $400 million. Their underlying strategy was to acquire the technology and people to enable Cisco to perform an increasing role in the data networking industry. Cisco does not become attached to only one type of technology. It concentrates on meeting customer needs, with an emphasis on customer service. Its acquisition strategy is defined by four main criteria: shared vision, beating competitors to the market, innovation, and chemistry.

Chemistry or culture as explained by Michael Volpi, Cisco's vice president of business development, is of key importance. He points out that technology in their industry lasts only 18 months, so continued innovation is a necessity. Judgments are required, so debate and disagreements occur on the road to reaching decisions. The personalities involved have to be able to achieve bonding in the crucible of aggressive policy formulation. Cisco usually finances its acquisitions with its stock, and executives must be with the company for four years before they can exercise their options. Voluntary attrition at Cisco, including personnel from acquired companies, is less than 5%. The acquisition strategy at Cisco is a dynamic process.

This chapter benefited from the presentations on Structure and Strategy by William G. Ouchi to the Anderson School—UCLA biennial Merger Week Programs.

Another example of strategy is provided by Intel. This is described in detail by its former chief executive, Andrew S. Grove (1996). In 1984, Intel found that Japanese companies were producing higher quality memory chips for computers at lower costs and prices. Yet the role of memories in Intel strategy involved two strongly held beliefs. One was that Intel always developed and refined their technologies on memory products first where they were easier to test. After new technology had been debugged on memories, it was then applied to microprocessors and other products. Memory stores information inside a computer; the central processing unit (CPU) processes instructions, performs calculations, and manages the flow of information through a computer—it's the brains.

The second belief was that the sales force needed a full product line to successfully compete for customers. Nevertheless, in the face of much resistance, Intel's basic strategy was shifted from memory to microprocessors. This made some equipment and plant available for expansion of microprocessor production. But plants more specialized to the production of memory units were shut down. Some executives and memory developers were able to make the transition to microprocessors; others moved to different companies. The years 1984 through 1986 represented a period of depressed profitability and transition for Intel. More people and more space were assigned to building a new generation of microprocessors based on the Intel 386 chip. The changed strategy guided Intel to impressive growth and profitability.

Examples like the above and many others document the critical role of strategy. A central proposition is illustrated. Acquisition and restructuring policies and decisions must be formulated within the framework of a company's overall strategic plans and processes. So this chapter begins with the formulation of strategy. We then discuss the relationship between strategy and organizational structure.

STRATEGY

Various approaches to strategy are presented in the literature. All agree on a general view. Strategy defines the central plans, policies, and culture of an organization in terms of a long-term horizon. The orientation of strategic decisions involves the future of the firm. Although the horizon is the long view, strategy, to be implemented properly, must also take account of mid-term and short-run decisions and actions.

Strategy is formulated in many different ways. The strategic planning process can be performed on the basis of a set of formal procedures and/or informally in the minds of managers. Strategy is not static. Individual strategies, plans, policies, or procedures are formulated, but they are not the whole story. Strategic planning is a behavior and a way of thinking, requiring diverse inputs from all segments of the organization. Everyone must be involved in the strategic planning processes.

Ultimate Responsibility

Because strategic planning is concerned with the future of the organization, it follows that ultimate responsibility resides in the top executive (or executive group). Although many others perform important roles and have responsibilities for strategic planning processes, the chief executive (or group) must take ultimate responsi-

Table 5.1   Essential Elements in Strategic Planning Processes

1. Assessment of changes in the organizational environment.
2. Evaluation of company capabilities and limitations.
3. Assessment of expectations of stakeholders.
4. Analysis of company, competitors, industry, domestic economy, and international economies.
5. Formulation of the missions, goals, and policies for the master strategy.
6. Development of sensitivity to critical external environmental changes.
7. Formulation of internal organizational performance measurements.
8. Formulation of long-range strategy programs.
9. Formulation of mid-range programs and short-run plans.
10. Organization, funding, and other methods to implement all of the preceding elements.
11. Information flow and feedback system for continued repetition of all essential elements and for adjustments and changes at each stage.
12. Review and evaluation of all processes.

bility for its success or failure. The chief executive officer (CEO) or executive group is responsible for the strategic planning process for the firm as a whole; the top manager of a division must be responsible for strategic planning for that division and for conforming it to the strategic planning for the organization as a whole.

Basic Steps in Strategic Planning

Although different approaches to strategic planning may be found, they all include the steps set forth in Table 5.1, which lists the critical activities involved in strategic planning processes. These procedures are described at length in the vast literature on strategy. Whether these represent formal or informal procedures, they are elements to be covered in strategic planning. In each of these activities, both staff and line personnel have important responsibilities in the strategic decision-making processes.

DIVERSITY IN STRATEGIC PLANNING PROCESSES

Some general elements required for any strategic planning activity have been identified. In other aspects of strategic planning, wide diversity is encountered. A number of different activities and aspects are involved in strategic planning.

Monitoring the Organizational Environment

A key to all approaches to strategic planning is continuous monitoring of the external environment. The environmental monitoring should encompass both domestic and international dimensions and include analysis of economic, technological, political, social, and legal factors. Different organizations give different emphasis and weight to each of the categories.

Stakeholders

Strategic planning processes must take into account the diverse stakeholders of the organization. These are the individuals and groups that have an interest in the organization and its actions. They include customers, stockholders, creditors, employees, governments, communities, media, political groups, educational institutions, the financial community, and international entities.

Writers disagree on the appropriate stake of each of the groups listed. One view is that the firm need only maximize profit or shareholder stock values to maximize the long-run interests of every group. Another is that by properly balancing the interests of major stakeholders the long-range interests of all will be maximized.

Organizational Cultures

How the organization carries out the strategic thinking and planning processes also varies with its culture. Illustrative organizational cultures include:

1. Strong top leadership versus team approach.
2. Management by formal paperwork versus management by wandering around.
3. Individual decisions versus group consensus decisions.
4. Rapid evaluation based on performance versus long-term relationship based on loyalty.
5. Rapid feedback for change versus formal bureaucratic rules and procedures.
6. Narrow career paths versus movement through many areas.
7. Risk taking encouraged versus "one mistake and you're out."
8. Big-stakes (bet-your-company) decisions versus low-risk activities.
9. Narrow responsibility assignments versus "everyone in this company is a salesman (or cost controller, or product quality improver, and so on)."
10. Learn from the customer versus "we know what is best for the customer."

The above list conveys the wide differences in corporate cultures and how the strategic thinking and planning processes may be affected. Failure to mesh divergent cultures may be a major obstacle to the full realization of the potentials of a merger (*Economist*, 1997).

Alternative Strategy Methodologies

We draw a distinction between different strategy methodologies and different analytical frameworks employed in developing strategy. First, some alternative approaches to methodologies used in strategy formulation are considered in Table 5.2.

The first 12 in the list are described somewhat more fully in the following pages. The remainder are well known or self-explanatory and do not require elaboration.

WOTS UP Analysis

Identifying strengths and weaknesses and opportunities and threats would appear to be easily accomplished. However, much subjectivity is involved. Different managers may have different judgments. Even though opportunities may exist, the differences in cost may require a careful balancing of considerations. On balance, this approach may provide a useful starting point for developing a strategic planning process and for stimulating strategic thinking in an organization.

Table 5.2   Alternative Strategy Methodologies

1. SWOT or WOTS UP: Inventory and analysis of organizational strengths, weaknesses, environmental opportunities, and threats.
2. Gap analysis: Assessment of goals versus forecasts or projections.
3. Top-down and/or bottom up: Company forecasts versus aggregation of segments.
4. Computer models: Opportunity for detail and complexity.
5. Competitive analysis: Assess customers, suppliers, new entrants, products, and product substitutability.
6. Synergy: Look for complementarities.
7. Logical incrementalism: Well-supported moves from current bases.
8. Muddling through: Incremental changes selected from a small number of policy alternatives.
9. Comparative histories: Learn from the experiences of others.
10. Delphi technique: Iterated opinion reactions.
11. Discussion group technique: Stimulating ideas by unstructured discussions aimed at consensus decisions.
12. Adaptive processes: Periodic reassessment of environmental opportunities and organizational capability adjustments required.
13. Environmental scanning: Continuous analysis of all relevant environments.
14. Intuition: Insights of brilliant managers.
15. Entrepreneurship: Creative leadership.
16. Discontinuities: Crafting strategy from recognition of trend shifts.
17. Brainstorming: Free-form repeated exchange of ideas.
18. Game theory: Logical assessments of competitor actions and reactions.
19. Game playing: Assign roles and simulate alternative scenarios.

Gap Analysis

In the assessment of goals versus forecasts or projections, goals may be formulated first. These may be expressed in quantitative terms, such as sales of $2 billion by 20XX or net income of $100 million by 20XX or a return on shareholder equity of 15%. But a reasonable assessment of the future based on the firm's existing capabilities may indicate that these goals cannot be achieved by the target dates. The divergence may stimulate an assessment of whether the goals should be revised or how the organization could augment its capabilities in order to close the gap between goals and projections.

Top-Down Versus Bottom-Up Forecasts

In the history of strategic planning, a variety of approaches can be observed. In some companies overall projections are made with requirements assigned to individual segments so that the overall company results can be achieved. At the other extreme, the projections of individual segments could be added up, with the result representing the outlook for the company as a whole. Good practice avoids both extremes.

There is evidence that successful companies begin with planning premises formulated at the overall corporate level. These planning premises begin with the outlook for the economy and the industry, translated into what appears plausible for the particular firm. The planning premises are supplied to the individual segments, who use them as a basis for their own individual forecasts. The individual segment forecasts are aggregated to provide an outlook for the company as a whole. Meetings and discussions between the corporate level and the individual segments take place. A communication process is developed, and iterations of meetings continue until a consensus is reached. The desired goal is a company plan that is understood and reasonable from the standpoint of the various segments and results in an overall company outlook that is satisfactory from the standpoint of top management.

Computer Models

Computer models provide the opportunity for considerable detail and complexity. However, the models must reflect a theory or logic to guide their content. Otherwise, there is a great risk that the methodology will be overwhelmed by the resulting complexity.

Competitive Analysis

A number of approaches to competitive analysis may be found (see, for example, Porter, 1979). Our approach is conveyed by Figure 5.1. A firm's competitive position is determined by 11 important factors involved in demand and supply conditions. On the demand side, what is critical is the degree of feasible product substitutability. On the supply side, the nature and structure of costs are critical. Of particular importance is the ability to switch among suppliers of inputs. This may be critically affected by switching costs—the costs involved in shifting from one supplier to another. Supply competition from existing firms including their potentials for capacity expansion are also major influences on the competitive position of the firm. Complementary firms are important. Is there a threat that your business could be carried out in another way?

Synergy

Synergy represents the $2 + 2 = 5$ effect. The concept of synergy was highly regarded at an earlier period but then subsequently came into disrepute. What is critical is how the extra gains are to be achieved. One example of synergy is found in the history of the pharmaceutical industry; after World War II the major firms shifted from producing bulk chemicals for others to process to an emphasis on basic research and packaging products that were ready for final sale. They also needed a sales organization. After a number of years, synergistic mergers took place between companies strong in research or marketing and companies that had complementary strengths and weaknesses. Synergy can be a valid concept if it has a basis in reality.

Logical Incrementalism

After extensive field interviews, Quinn (1977, 1980) concluded that major changes in strategy are carried out most effectively when they can be broken down into numerous small changes, made on an incremental basis. In addition, he emphasized that a number of steps are required to involve the organization as broadly as possible. The process he emphasized also called for the exercise of effective leadership qualities.

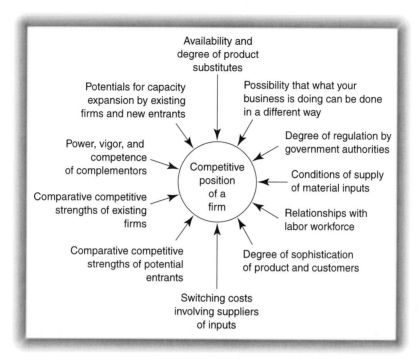

Figure 5.1   Competitive Analysis

Muddling Through

Another form of the incremental approach is one Lindblom (1959, 1965) called "muddling through." He also used the term *disjointed incrementalism* to describe the process. The basic idea is that instead of attempting to evaluate a wide range of alternatives, decision makers should focus on those policy alternatives that differ incrementally from existing policies. An iterative process is then employed to formulate and implement decisions.

Comparative Histories

The methodology of comparative histories is widely used by many firms in monitoring the behavior of their rivals. It was used in a fundamental research mode by Chandler (1962) in an analysis of the interrelationships among the economic environments of firms, their strategies, and their organizational structures. Chandler compared the histories of organizational changes among 50 large companies during a century beginning with the period after the Civil War in the United States. From his studies he developed theories about the relationship between a firm's strategy and its organizational structure at various stages of development. Individual firms continuously monitor the policies, actions, and reactions of rivals.

Delphi Technique

A questionnaire developed to obtain information on problems or issues is distributed by mail to informed individuals. The responses are summarized into a feedback report, which is returned to the same people with a second questionnaire designed to probe more deeply into the ideas generated by the first questionnaire. Several iterations can be performed.

Discussion Group Technique

The group leader begins with a statement of the problem. An unstructured group discussion ensues for the purpose of generating ideas. Information and judgments are generated. The goal is to reach a consensus decision or to make a decision based on a majority voting procedure.

Adaptive Processes

In some sense all approaches to strategy employ adaptive processes. The approach was first formalized by Ansoff (1965). The nature of the problem is structured on a tentative basis. Analysis is facilitated by a series of checklists or the analysis of matrix relationships. Successive iterations take place until a basis for formulating policies and reaching decisions is achieved. The method emphasizes developing a strong information feedback system to achieve flexibility in the organization's capability to adjust to its environmental changes. This approach is especially important in merger analysis.

The remainder of the approaches in Table 5.2 do not require further elaboration. The list conveys the profusion of methodologies encountered in strategic planning. The particular approaches to strategy adopted by individual firms and consultants involves selection from alternative strategy methodologies as listed in Table 5.2 combined with different groups of alternative analytical frameworks of the kind discussed next.

Alternative Analytical Frameworks

Many different alternative analytical frameworks are employed in the formulation of strategy. Their nature is indicated by the list in Table 5.3.

Most of the items in Table 5.3 are self-explanatory. We will describe the many applications of matrix patterns of strengths and weaknesses or alternative approaches to markets.

A simple approach is the product–market matrix shown in Figure 5.2. It is based on the relatedness concept that is widely used in formulating strategy. The thrust of Figure 5.2 is that in developing new product markets the lowest risk is to stay "close to home." The highest risk is to venture forth into unrelated products and unrelated markets. This analysis clearly depends on how risk is defined. It may be very risky to stay where you are, if, for example, the prospects for growth of existing products and markets are unfavorable and the industry has excess capacity. This represents a strong motive for mergers to gain entry to markets with more favorable growth opportunities.

Table 5.3   Alternative Analytical Frameworks

1. Product life cycles: Introduction, growth, maturity, decline stages with changing opportunities and threats.
2. Learning curve: Costs decline with cumulative volume experience resulting in competitive advantages for the firm that moves most quickly.
3. Competitive analysis: Industry structure, rivals' reactions, supplier–customer relations, product positioning.
4. Cost leadership: Low-cost advantages.
5. Product differentiation: Develop product configurations that achieve customer preference.
6. Value chain analysis: Control cost outlays to add product characteristics valued by customers.
7. Niche opportunities: Specialize to needs or interests of customer groups.
8. Product breadth: Carryover of organizational capabilities.
9. Correlations with profitability: Statistical studies of factors associated with high profitability measures.
10. Market share: High market share associated with competitive superiority.
11. Product quality: Customer allegiance and price differentials for higher quality.
12. Technological leadership: Keep at frontiers of knowledge.
13. Relatedness matrix: Unfamiliar markets and products involve greatest risk.
14. Focus matrix: Narrow versus broad product families.
15. Growth–share matrix: Aim for high market share in high growth markets.
16. Attractiveness matrix: Aim to be strong in attractive industries.
17. Global matrix: Aim for competitive strength in attractive countries.
18. Resource-based view (RBV):   Capabilities are inimitable.

Product / Market	Present	Related	Unrelated
Present	Low risk		High risk
Related			
Unrelated	High risk		Highest risk

Figure 5.2   Product–Market Matrix

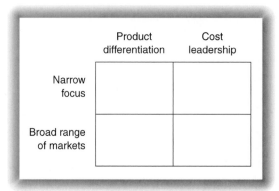

Figure 5.3   Competitive Position Matrix

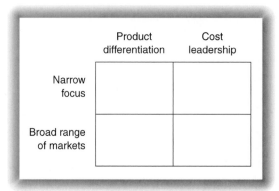

Figure 5.4   Growth–Share Matrix

Figure 5.3 portrays one formulation of a competitive position matrix. It suggests a choice of emphasis between product differentiation and cost leadership. In addition, the focus may be on a narrow market segment or niche or product representation to provide presence in a broad range of markets.

The matrix shown in Figure 5.4, the growth–share matrix, has been associated particularly with the Boston Consulting Group. Products for which the firm has a high market share in an industry with favorable growth rates are potential "stars" with high profitability. As an industry matures, its growth slows, so that if a firm continues to have high market share the attractive profits are available for investment in markets with more favorable growth rates, and the products become "cash cows." Products and markets with low growth where the firm has a small market share are "dogs," and the firm should discontinue such products, according to the simple product portfolio approach.

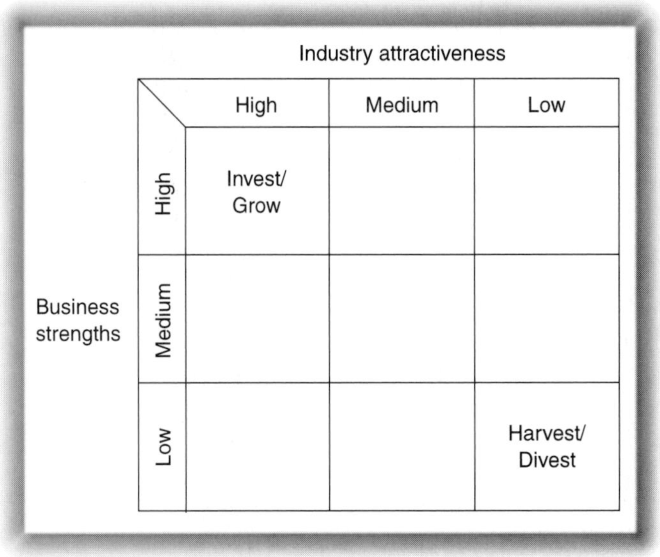

Figure 5.5 Strength–Market Attractiveness Matrix

A variant of the growth–share matrix is the strength–market attractiveness matrix shown in Figure 5.5. The greatest opportunities for investment and growth are where the outlook for an industry is attractive and the firm has high capabilities for performance in that industry. Where the industry outlook is unfavorable and the firm has weakness in such markets, the firm should divest or close down such businesses.

Figure 5.6 moves the analysis to an international basis. In the international setting the most attractive countries in terms of growth or political stability in which the firm has competitive strengths offer the most favorable growth opportunities. The opposite, of course, occurs in countries of low attractiveness where the firm's competitive strengths are low.

In our view the preceding examples of the matrix approach to strategy represent in spirit the checklist approach to formulating alternatives. They are useful devices for suggesting factors to take into account in formulating strategies.

The different analytical frameworks set forth in Table 5.3 are not mutually exclusive. In strategic planning a wide range of analytical approaches may usefully be employed. Their use is facilitated by a checklist and an adaptive approach to strategic planning. Practicing consultants as well as individual firms have employed a combination of methodologies and analytical approaches with considerable success.

APPROACHES TO FORMULATING STRATEGY

Many different schools of thought in the strategy field can be observed. Each represents some combination of the methodologies and/or analytical frameworks in the preceding lists. Three approaches are discussed more fully to illustrate how alternative

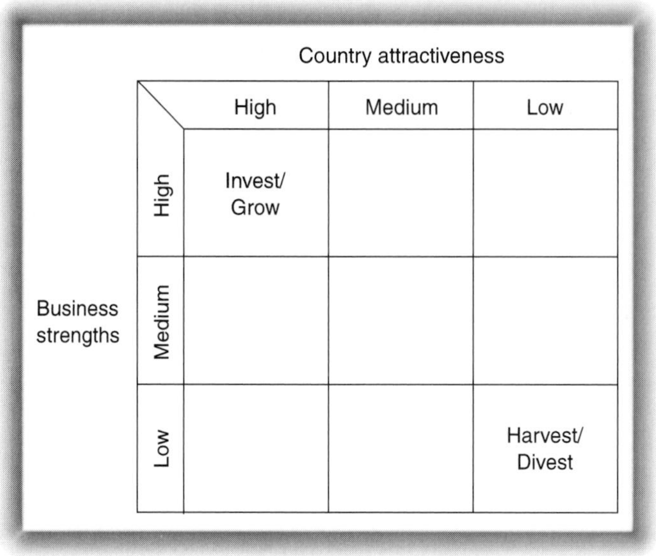

Country attractiveness			
	High	Medium	Low
High	Invest/ Grow		
Medium			
Low			Harvest/ Divest

Business strengths

Figure 5.6 Strength–Country Attractiveness Matrix

methodologies and analytical frameworks are used in practice. They are (1) the Boston Consulting Group approach, (2) the Porter approach, and (3) adaptive processes.

The Boston Consulting Group

The Boston Consulting Group (BCG) historically emphasized three concepts: the experience curve, the product life cycle, and portfolio balance (Boston Consulting Group, 1985; Henderson, 1984; Thomas, 1986).

The experience curve represents a volume–cost relationship. It is argued that as the cumulative historical volume of output increases, unit costs will fall at a geometric rate. This is said to result from specialization, standardization, learning, and scale effects. The firm with the largest cumulative output will have lower costs, suggesting a strategy of early entry and price policies to develop volume.

The product life cycle concept holds that every product or line of business proceeds through four phases: development, growth, maturity, and decline. During the first two stages, sales growth is rapid and entry is easy. As individual firms gain experience and as growth slows in the last two stages, entry becomes difficult because of the cost advantages of incumbents. In the decline phase of the product line (as other product substitutes emerge), sales and prices decline; firms that have not achieved a favorable position on the experience curve become unprofitable and either merge or exit from the industry.

Related to the product life cycle is the concept of portfolio balance. In the early stages of the product life cycle, rapid growth may require substantial investments. Such business segments are likely to require more investment funds than are generated by current profitability levels. As the requirements for growth diminish, profits may generate more funds than are necessary for current investment requirements. Portfolio balance seeks to combine attractive investment segments (stars) with cash-generating segments (cash cows), eliminating segments with unattractive prospects (dogs). Overall, total corporate cash inflows will roughly balance total corporate investments.

In recent years, the Boston Consulting Group has distinguished itself with newer approaches to strategy. Its executives have published innovative materials on the impact of the Internet and other technological innovations on the economics of information, "blowing apart the foundations of traditional business strategy" (Evans and Wurster, 1997, 2000). Implications for reconstructing value chain analysis are also developed. Other BCG publications have emphasized performance measurement by the use of "cash flow return on investment" (CFROI) and its implications for valuation.

The Porter Approach

Over the years, Michael Porter developed concepts that have become standard in strategy analysis. Michael Porter's (1980, 1985, 1987) approach has three parts: (1) Select an attractive industry, (2) develop a competitive advantage through cost leadership and/or product differentiation, and (3) develop attractive value chains.

First, Porter (1987, p. 46) defines an attractive industry or strategic group as one in which

> entry barriers are high, suppliers and buyers have only modest bargaining power, substitute products or services are few, and the rivalry among competitors is stable. An unattractive industry like steel will have structural flaws, including a plethora of substitute materials, powerful and price-sensitive buyers, and excessive rivalry caused by high fixed costs and a large group of competitors, many of whom are state supported.

The difficulty of generalizing about industries is demonstrated by Porter's example. During the 1970s and 1980s, minimills flourished, and by 1988 some major steel firms had returned to profitability. In addition, there appears to be an inconsistency in that high fixed costs are considered to be an entry barrier in Porter's theory (Weston, 1978, 1982).

Second, Porter formulates a matrix for developing generic strategies. Competitive advantage may be based on cost leadership or on product differentiation. Cost advantage is achieved by consideration of a wide range of checklist factors including BCG's learning curve theory. The focus of cost advantage or of product differentiation can be on narrow market segments, or niches (for autos, the luxury car market—Cadillac, Continental, BMW, Mercedes, and so on), or on broader market groups (compact and standard cars) or across the board (GM).

Porter's third key concept is "the value chain." A matrix relates the support activities of infrastructure, human resource management, technology development, and procurement to the primary activities of inbound logistics, operations, outbound logistics, marketing, sales, and service. The aim is to minimize outlays in adding characteristics valued by customers.

Adaptive Processes

Other writers have been more eclectic than the preceding two approaches. These writers view strategy more as an adaptive process or way of thinking (see, for example, Ansoff, 1965; Bogue and Buffa, 1986; Quinn, Mintzberg, and James, 1988; Steiner, 1979; Steiner, Miner, and Gray, 1986). Some writers also emphasize the uniqueness of each firm. "In essence, the concept is that a firm's competitive position is defined by a bundle of unique resources and relationships and that the task of general management is to adjust and renew these resources and relationships as time, competition, and change erode their value" (Rumelt, 1984, p. 557). Mergers perform a role in these renewal efforts.

More generally the adaptive processes orientation involves matching resources to investment opportunities under environmental uncertainty compounded with uncertain competitors' actions and reactions. The methodology for dealing with these kinds of "ill-structured problems" requires an iterative solution process. Most managers in an organization have responsibilities for the inputs and studies required for the repeated "going around the loop" in the strategic planning processes outlined in Table 5.1.

In performing the iterated checklist procedures, difficult questions are encountered. For example, is the firm maximizing its potential in relation to its feasible environment? Is there a gap between the firm's goals and prospects based on its present capabilities? Should the firm attempt to alter its environment or capabilities or both? Should the firm change its missions? What will be the cost of each alternative? What are the risks and unknowns? What are the rewards of success and penalties of failure?

The methodology involves not closed-form mathematical solutions but **processes.** It involves ways of thinking that assess competitors' actions and reactions in relation to the changing environments. The process approach is especially applicable to merger analysis because it is difficult to find out all that is needed when combining with another entity.

EVALUATION OF THE ALTERNATIVE APPROACHES

Although some approaches emphasize generalizations, all make heavy use of checklists that have evolved into expert systems. Writers who have emphasized strategy implementation have recently shifted from a list of precepts to an emphasis on flexibility.

Checklists and Iterations

The adaptive processes methodologies emphasize the use of checklists to stimulate insights, and the BCG and Porter approaches to strategy formulation also rely heavily on similar techniques. For example, in his book *Competitive Strategy* (1980), Michael Porter utilized 134 checklists and checklist-like diagrams—one about every three pages. In his later *Competitive Advantage* (Porter, 1985), the number had expanded to 187 checklists and checklist-like diagrams—about one every 2.5 pages. Stryker (1986) (adaptive approach) had 174 checklists in 269 pages—one checklist per 1.5 pages. Thus, the process of strategic planning includes the art of making checklists, going around the loop iteratively, with the expectation that the thinking stimulated will lead to useful insights and sound strategies, policies, and decisions.

The BCG and Porter approaches emphasize prescriptions. However, in their actual implementation they employ checklists not limited to the generalizations each emphasizes. In practice, all approaches to strategy become relatively eclectic.

With the greater use of computers in strategic planning, the different approaches appear to have more and more elements in common. Expert systems and other decision support systems have been developed. These represent a disciplined approach to strategic planning in which rules are used to guide implementation of the iterated checklist approach, making use of ideas from a wide range of philosophical perspectives (Chung and Davidson, 1987).

Some Recent Developments

Publications by writers who have popularized strategy implementation exhibit a recent change in emphasis. In *In Search of Excellence,* Peters and Waterman (1982) asserted that the precepts for success could be reduced to a short checklist: (1) bias for action; (2) close to the customer; (3) autonomy and entrepreneurship; (4) productivity improvement; (5) hands-on, value-driven; (6) stick to core businesses; (7) simple form, lean staff; and (8) loose–tight properties.

Peters and Waterman (1982) admonished their readers to learn how the best-run American companies use eight basic principles to stay "on top of the heap!" Although *In Search of Excellence* was a commercial success, it also received criticisms (Carroll, 1983; Johnson, Natarajan, and Rappaport, 1985; Ramanujam and Venkatraman, 1988). Of particular interest to business economists was the analysis in the cover story of the November 5, 1984 issue of *Business Week* entitled, "Who's Excellent Now? Some of the Best-Seller's Picks Haven't Been Doing So Well Lately." *Business Week* (p. 74) studied the 43 "excellent" companies and concluded that many had encountered difficulties. The article observed:

> Of the 14 excellent companies that had stumbled, 12 were inept in adapting to a fundamental change in their markets. Their experiences show that strict adherence to the eight commandments—which do not emphasize reacting to broad economic and business trends—may actually hurt a company.

Peters and Waterman appear to acknowledge the deficiencies in their earlier prescriptive approach by shifting their emphasis in later publications. In *The Renewal Factor,* Waterman (1987) emphasizes flexibility; he quotes with approval the executive who stated that he wanted his managers to be "Fred Astaires—intellectually quick, nimble, and ready to act" (p. 6). Similarly, Peters, Waterman's coauthor of *In Search of Excellence,* in his 1987 publication, begins, "There are no excellent companies. The old saw 'If it ain't broke, don't fix it' needs revision. I propose: 'If it ain't broke, you just haven't looked hard enough.' Fix it anyway" (Peters, 1987, p. 1). Similarly, two executives associated with the Boston Consulting Group proposed that to manage for increased competitiveness companies need to "make decisions like a fighter pilot" (Hout and Blaxill, 1987, p. 3).

But flexibility and rapid adjustments are more the stuff of tactics, not strategy! We believe that these developments in the literature on implementing strategy continue to suffer from the criticism conveyed by the *Business Week* article previously quoted. They make inadequate use of perspectives offered by economic analysis. Economics is forward looking, projecting market and supply conditions and patterns. Economic analysis can help identify prospective changes in such areas as demand, product differentiation, market growth segments, and behavior of rivals. Analysis of supply conditions can help identify areas of potential cost changes and thus targets for cost control. Economic analysis can delineate critical monitoring variables to indicate when changes in economic directions are likely to occur. Given this information, trade-off analysis (the bread and butter of economic marginal analysis) can identify and analyze alternative paths of action and their consequences. In short, economics aids in dealing with uncertainty and in anticipating change rather than reacting to events after they have occurred.

Economics seeks an understanding of environmental developments to identify the trends and discontinuities important to strategy formulation and implementation, as well as providing a framework within which flexibility and adjustments can be achieved efficiently. From the preceding analysis of alternative approaches to strategy, we can now develop guidelines for formulating a merger strategy.

FORMULATING A MERGER STRATEGY

The literature on long-range strategic planning indicates that one of the most important elements in planning is continual reassessment of the firm's environment. To determine what is happening in the environment, the firm should analyze its industry, competitors, and social and political factors.

Industry analysis allows the firm to recognize the key factors required for competitive success in the industry and the opportunities and threats present in the industry. From competitor analysis, the firm determines the capabilities and limitations of existing and potential competitors and their probable future moves. Through these analyses and with additional consideration of societal factors, the firm's strengths and weaknesses relative to present and future competitors can be ascertained.

The purpose of the environmental reassessment is to provide the firm with a choice among strategic alternatives. For this choice, the firm then considers whether its current goals and policies are appropriate to exploit industry opportunities and to deal with industry threats. At the same time, it is necessary for the firm to examine whether the goals and policies match the managerial, technological, and financial resources available to the firm, and whether the timing of the goals and policies appropriately reflects the ability of the organization to change.

The firm then works out feasible strategic alternatives given the results of the analyses. The current strategy (represented by its goals and policies) may or may not be included in the set of feasible alternatives. A strategic choice is made from this set such that the chosen strategy best relates the firm's situation to external opportunities and threats. Mergers represent one set of alternatives.

A brilliant exposition of how a company must be alert to important changes is set forth by Andrew S. Grove, President and CEO of Intel Corporation. Grove (1996) describes how a firm must adjust to six forces: existing competitors, potential competitors, complementors, customers, suppliers, and industry transformations. He presents illuminating case studies of the approach to strategy that we have called eclectic adaptive processes.

Business Goals

General goals may be formulated with respect to size, growth, stability, flexibility, and technological breadth. Size objectives are established in order to use effectively the fixed factors the firm owns or buys. Size objectives have also been expressed in terms of critical mass. Critical mass refers to the size a firm must achieve to attain cost levels that enable the firm to operate profitably at market prices.

Growth objectives may be expressed in terms of sales, total assets, earnings per share, or the market price of the firm's stock. These are related to two valuation objectives. One is to attain a favorable price/earnings multiple for the firm's shares. A second is to increase the ratio of the market value of a firm's common stock to its book value.

Two major forms of instability can be distinguished. The first is exemplified by the defense market, which is subject to large, erratic fluctuations in its total size and abrupt shifts in individual programs. Another form of instability is the cyclical instability that characterizes producers of both industrial and consumer durable goods.

The goal of flexibility refers to the firm's ability to operate in a wide variety of product markets. Such flexibility may require a breadth of research, manufacturing, or marketing capabilities. Of increased interest in recent years is technological breadth. With the increased pace of technological change in the U.S. economy, a firm may consider it important to possess capabilities in the rapidly advancing technologies.

Goals may be stated in general or specific terms, but both are subject to quantification. For example, growth objectives may be expressed in relationship to the growth of the economy or the firm's industry. Specific objectives may be expressed in terms of percentage of sales in specified types of markets. The quantification of goals facilitates comparisons of goals with the potential for achieving them.

Efforts to achieve multiple goals suggest a broader range of variables in the decision processes of the firm. Decisions require judgments of the nature of future environments, the policies of other firms with respect to the dimensions described, and new needs of customers, technologies, and capabilities. In short, to the requirements of operating efficiency and optimal output adjustments has been added the increased importance of the planning processes.

Aligning the Firm to Its Changing Environment

When it is necessary to take action to close a prospective gap between the firm's objectives and its potential based on its present capabilities, difficult choices must be made. For example, should the firm attempt to change its environment or capabilities? What will be the costs of such changes? What are the risks and unknowns? What are the rewards of success? What are the penalties of failure? Because the stakes are large, an iterative process is employed. A tentative decision is made. The process is repeated, perhaps from a different management function orientation, and at some point, the total-enterprise point of view is brought to bear on the problem. At some point, decisions are made and must involve entrepreneurial judgments. Mergers may help or hurt.

The emphasis is on the effective alignment of the firm with its environments and constituencies. Different approaches may be emphasized. One approach seeks to choose products related to the needs or wants of the customer that will provide large markets. A second approach focuses on technological bottlenecks or barriers, the solution of which may create new markets. A third strategy chooses to be at the frontiers of technological capabilities on the theory that some attractive product fall-out will result from such competence. A fourth approach emphasizes economic criteria including attractive growth prospects and appropriate stability.

If it is necessary for the firm to alter its product–market mix or range of capabilities to reduce or close the strategic gap, a diversification strategy may be formulated. Thus, the key connection between planning and diversification or mergers lies in the evaluation of current managerial and technological capabilities relative to capabilities required to reach objectives.

Thus far in the chapter, we have focused on strategy as the vision that guides the firm. We also reviewed alternative philosophies of strategy. We next turn to the relationships between strategy and structure and their implications for merger decisions.

STRATEGY AND STRUCTURE

A substantial literature discusses the relationship between strategy and structure. Some authors hold that structure determines strategy—the firm can access only those strategies that it is organized to undertake. Our view is that there is a feedback relationship between structure and strategy. The focus of our analysis here is on organizational architecture. We describe alternative organizational structures with emphasis on their implications for acquisition strategies. First we describe the advantages and disadvantages of different types of organizational structures.

The unitary form, or U-form (Figure 5.7) is highly centralized under the president. It is broken into functional departments, and no department can stand alone. The president must stay close to the departments to know what needs to be improved, because there is no easy way to measure each as a profit center. A long-term vision is often left solely to the president. Although this form allows rapid decision making, it is usually only successful in small organizations. It is difficult for the U-form to handle multiple products. Acquired firms have to fit into the limited span

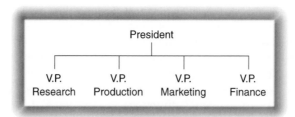

Figure 5.7 The Unitary Form of Organization

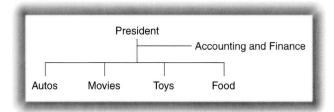

Figure 5.8   The Holding Company Form of Organization

of control of the top executive group. Acquisitions are likely to be horizontal or very closely related activities. The new units are likely to be consolidated fully into the unitary organization.

The holding company, or H-form, is arranged, as shown in Figure 5.8, around various unrelated operating businesses. The leadership of the firm is able to evaluate each unit individually and can allocate resources according to projected returns. The firm has superior knowledge of the situation of each unit, allowing it to act as an "inside investor."

The holding company arrangement makes it possible for firms to acquire relatively unrelated activities. Each of the dissimilar operations is permitted to function almost as an independent company. The risk is that the H-form may be less than fully effective because of the requirement to guide activities that are widely diverse.

The multidivisional organization, or M-form, lies between the centralization of the U-form and the decentralization of the H-form. Each division is autonomous enough to be judged as a profit center, but all divisions share some endowments such as production or marketing. Hewlett Packard, before it restructured in 1999, was arranged along product lines such as computers and measurement products. While these divisions were largely separate, they shared electrical engineering technology, as well as some facets of production (see Ouchi, 1984, for insights and extensions).

The multidivisional firm can handle related product and geographic market extensions. Its structure is represented in Figure 5.9. The acquisition of a firm with a related product line might result in designating it as a separate division. Since the products are related, the same functional staff groups may be able to serve the new division effectively. At some point, groups of divisions may have elements in common and require their own thrust with support staff groups having the required specialized knowledge. This appeared to be what developed at Hewlett Packard when it restructured in 1999, separating the computer-related activities from the non-computer-related products. The latter group of activities were placed in a new company called Agilent. The new company had its own stock, a portion of which was sold to the public and was well received.

The matrix form of organization, as shown in Figure 5.10, consists of functional departments such as finance, manufacturing, and development. The employees of these functional departments are assigned to subunits that are organized around products, geography, or some other criterion. In such an organization,

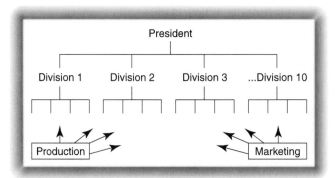

Figure 5.9   The Multidivisional Form of Organization

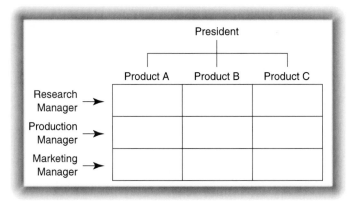

Figure 5.10   The Matrix Form of Organization

employees report to a functional manager as well as a product manager. The matrix form is most effective in firms characterized by many new products or projects. Intel, as of 1992, was structured around five major product groups.

The matrix form represents another way to handle the acquisition of related products or to engage in geographic market expansion. However, as new product groups are added, a heavier burden is placed on the communication system. The possibility of disputes and conflicts arising from multiple lines of authority is likely to be increased.

VIRTUAL INTEGRATION

A new method of organization has been developed by firms such as Dell, which are pursuing "virtual integration." Under such a system, the links of the value chain are brought together by an informal arrangement among suppliers and customers. Dell establishes close ties with suppliers, enabling many of the benefits of vertical integration. Shipments of the components that Dell needs can be easily arranged through the Internet or a networked computer system. This same type of arrangement allows Dell to fully serve customers in ordering, services, or any other needs.

A qualification to such an arrangement being considered a "form of organization" is that it involves multiple firms, which likely have a variety of organizational forms. However, it is important to realize that virtual integration represents a blurring of company boundaries. As communication strengthens the ties between different firms in a value chain, it is easier to envision grouping them as an "organization." Indeed, a firm's networks help create "inimitable" value in the resource-based view of the firm (Gulati, Nohria, and Zaheer, 2000; Lippman and Rumelt, 1982).

SUMMARY

In the process approach to strategy, each firm has a set of capabilities and opportunities. The firm must seek to exploit these effectively in relation to its changing environments. It must recognize that the dynamics of competition and economic change will require continuous reassessment of its position and realignment to its new challenges and opportunities. In this view the firm is required to make strategic decisions in the face of much uncertainty and considerable risk, especially with respect to mergers.

In this process view of strategy, divestitures represent a form of strategic adjustment process. Numerous case studies demonstrate that many divestitures were planned in advance in order to retain the desired parts of an acquisition. Or divestitures can represent a method of making acquisitions and paying them off in part or sometimes entirely by the segments sold off. At a minimum this may help make the diversification effort a low-cost one. Hence, it is erroneous to conclude that divestitures represent management mistakes.

Internal and external investment programs may be successful or unsuccessful. Firms may try either or both approaches in their efforts to increase shareholder value. The generalization of writers on strategic planning contain valuable insights for helping firms carry out strategies with a higher degree of efficiency than they otherwise would have been able to attain. The critical need is a rapid information feedback system in the firm to improve its capabilities for adapting to change, correcting errors, and seizing new opportunities. It is in this framework that merger and takeover decisions are made.

A substantial literature develops the relationship between strategy and the structure of firms. Organizational form can be critical to implementing strategy. Our view is that there is a feedback relationship between strategy and structure. The unitary form is highly centralized under the president. The holding company form is very decentralized and usually includes unrelated businesses. The multidivisional form has different units that share some common functions. The matrix form is organized around various products or projects. Virtual integration is a developing method of blurring the lines between organizations.

QUESTIONS

5.1 What is strategy?

5.2 What is an attractive industry according to Porter?

5.3 What does Porter mean by "competitive advantage" through cost leadership? Through product differentiation?

5.4 What are entry barriers, and what is their significance?

5.5 What is the adaptive approach to strategy? (Include a discussion of the role of checklists and iterative processes.)

5.6 Discuss different types of business goals.

5.7 What is meant by aligning a firm to its environment(s)?

5.8 Why does a firm seek to continue to exist after its main products are either obsolete or out of favor for health or other reasons?

5.9 What factors resulted in the conglomerate merger movement of the 1960s?

5.10 Explain the unitary (U) form of organization, the holding company (H) form, and the multidivisional (M) form of organization. Describe the strengths and limitations of each form.

5.11 Explain what is meant by virtual integration taking place between firms resulting from modern communications systems such as the Internet.

Case 5.1   Merck Acquisition of Medco

On July 28, 1993, Merck & Co., then the world's largest drug manufacturer, announced that it planned to acquire, for $6.6 billion, Medco Containment Services Inc., the largest prescription benefits management company (PBM) and marketer of mail order medicines in the United States. This merger reflected fundamental changes taking place in the pharmaceutical industry.

GROWTH IN MANAGED CARE

Perhaps the most significant change involves the growth of managed care in the health care industry. Managed care plans typically provide members with medical insurance and basic health care services, using volume and long-term contracts to negotiate discounts from health care providers. In addi-

tion, managed care programs provide full coverage for prescription drugs more frequently than do traditional medical insurance plans. Industry experts estimate that by the turn of the century 90% of Americans will have drug costs included in some kind of managed health care plan and 60% of all outpatient pharmaceuticals will be purchased by managed care programs.

The responsibility for managing the provision of prescription drugs is often contracted out by the managed care organizations to PBMs. The activities of PBMs typically include managing insurance claims, negotiating volume discounts with drug manufacturers, and encouraging the use of less expensive generic substitutes. The management of prescription benefits is enhanced through the use of formularies and drug utilization reviews. Formularies are lists of drugs compiled by committees of pharmacists and physicians on behalf of a managed care organization. Member physicians of the managed care organization are then strongly encouraged to prescribe from this list whenever possible. Drug utilization reviews consist of analyzing physician prescribing patterns and patient usage. They can identify when a patient may be getting the wrong amount or kind of medicine and when a member physician is not prescribing from a formulary. Essentially, this amounts to an additional opportunity for managed care or PBM administrators to monitor costs and consolidate decision-making authority.

The key aspect of the shift to managed care is that the responsibility for payment is linked more tightly to decision making about the provision of health care services than it is in traditional indemnity insurance plans. The implications for drug manufacturers are far-reaching. With prescription decision-making authority shifting away from doctors to managed care and PBM administrators, drug manufacturers' marketing strategies will similarly shift their focus from several hundred thousand doctors to a few thousand formulary and plan managers. This, in turn, will result in a dramatic reduction in the sales forces of pharmaceutical manufacturers.

Several other significant changes in industry structure are expected to occur. Many industry experts predict that managed care providers will rely on a single drug company to deliver all of its pharmaceutical products and services rather than negotiating with several drug companies. This will favor those firms with manufacturing, distribution, and prescription management capabilities. In addition, many experts believe that only a handful of pharmaceutical companies will exist on the international scene in a few years. They point to intense competition, lower profits, and a decrease in the number of new drugs in the "research pipeline" as contributing factors.

BENEFITS OF THE ACQUISITION

Merck & Co. and Medco Containment Services Inc. believe that a merger between the two firms will create a competitive advantage that will allow for their survival. Merck executives identify Medco's extensive database as the key factor motivating the merger. Medco maintains a computer profile of each of its 33 million customers, amounting to 26% of all people covered by a pharmaceutical benefit plan. Medco clients include one hundred Fortune 500 companies, federal and state benefit plans, and 58 Blue Cross/Blue Shield groups and insurance companies.

Numerous opportunities exist for Merck to utilize the information contained in Medco's database. First, the database will allow Merck to identify prescriptions that may be switched from a competitor's drug to a Merck drug. Merck pharmacists will then suggest the switch to a patient's doctor. This prospect of increasing sales is enormous. Second, the database will allow Merck to identify patients who fail to refill prescriptions. The failure to refill needed prescriptions amounts to hundreds of millions of dollars in lost sales each year. Finally, Merck will be able to use Medco's computerized patient record system as a real-life laboratory with the goal of proving that some Merck drugs are worth the premium price charged. This will take place by identifying who takes what pill and combining that information with the patient's medical records. This may allow Merck to establish the supremacy of its products.

Additional benefits of the merger include $1 billion annual savings in redundant marketing operations and a reduction in Merck's sales force as a result of more precise marketing strategies brought about by Medco's database and the industry emphasis on marketing to plan managers instead of doctors. Merck & Co.'s acquisition of Medco Containment Services Inc. is essentially an attempt to increase market share in an industry with decreasing prices by capitalizing on the most valuable asset in the pharmaceutical industry—information. It is also intended to increase its competitive position in the growing managed care arena by aligning itself with a PBM.

Merck & Co.'s strategy was quickly emulated when British drug maker SmithKline Beecham announced plans to acquire Diversified Pharmaceutical Services Inc., one of the four largest drug wholesalers in the United States, from United Healthcare for $2.3 billion, and Roche Holdings Ltd. reported that it planned to acquire Syntex Corporation. Also, in the summer of 1994, Eli Lilly and Company announced its intention to acquire PCS Health Systems from McKesson Corp. for

$4 billion. These mergers were not only a reaction to the changing industry structure but caused the change to accelerate.

QUESTIONS

1. What was the major force driving this acquisition?
2. What is the role of prescription benefits management (PBM) companies?
3. What role was envisaged for the use of Medco's database?
4. What competitive reactions took place in response to Merck's acquisition of Medco?

Case 5.2   Acquisition of Lotus Development Corp. by IBM

Lotus Development Corp., the second largest PC software firm, was taken over via a hostile bid by IBM Corp. in 1995 for $3.52 billion.

THE TAKEOVER PROCESS

Previous Relations Between IBM and Lotus

According to executives familiar with the situation, Jim Manzi, the CEO of Lotus Development Corp., offered to sell the company's desktop software applications to IBM but did not want to sell the entire company. In August 1994, Manzi suggested to James Cannavino, IBM's top strategist at the time, a joint venture in desktop applications or the sale of that part to IBM. IBM declined the offer. In January 1995, Manzi repeated the offer to the new IBM senior vice president in charge of the software group, John M. Thompson. Thompson offered to acquire the entire company, to which Manzi responded that Lotus was not for sale. Manzi ruled out anything but a minority stake

for IBM of Lotus's communications business. The two met for the last time in March, when Manzi again objected to the acquisition.

Announcement of the Bid

On June 5, 1995, IBM announced its first ever hostile bid in the form of a $60 cash per share tender offer. That day, Lotus's stock price soared $29 from $32.375, closing at $61.375 on the NASDAQ (a 90% premium), while IBM stock dropped $2.625 from $93.875, closing at $91.25 on the NYSE (a 2.8% decline).

The bid was the culmination of months of strategy. In April 1995, IBM analyzed the fit of Lotus products with IBM software and decided to pursue Lotus. IBM realized that Lotus Development Corp. wanted to remain independent if they were to be acquired. With this in mind, Louis V. Gerstner, Jr., the chairman of IBM, approved the hostile deal on May 12. On May 22 IBM incorporated White Acquisition Corp., a subsidiary specifically created to execute the acquisition of Lotus. On June 5, 1995, IBM sent a message promising Lotus employees that they would not be assimilated into IBM after the merger. IBM agreed to this stipulation because they did not want to lose key Lotus employees such as the software developer of Lotus Notes, Raymond Ozzie.

Shortly after 8 A.M. on the morning of the bid, IBM's Delaware law firm filed a lawsuit challenging Lotus's poison pill. The activated Lotus pill with a trigger set at 15% would have dramatically increased the number of Lotus shares and the cost of the acquisition to a potential acquirer. At 8:25 A.M., Gerstner informed Manzi of the bid. Manzi agreed to consider the offer, knowing that he was not promised a position should Lotus be acquired. At 8:30 A.M., IBM informed the exchanges on which IBM and Lotus traded, the NYSE and NASDAQ, respectively. Gerstner also called the CEO of Hewlett Packard and chairman of AT&T, two partners of Lotus who were also potential white knights, to inform them of IBM's intent.

At a 1:30 P.M. press conference, Gerstner spoke of the three different ages of computing. The first age of computing, the mainframe, was dominated by IBM, whereas the second age of personal computers remained very competitive. The race is currently on for dominance of the third age, networked computing. Networked computing allows users of different software and hardware platforms to work together in a collaborative manner. A network offers the user-friendliness and the applications of a desktop along with the security, dependability, and capacity of a large-scale system. IBM's acquisition of Lotus is an attempt to gain a significant share of the networked computing market.

In addition to the press conference on June 5, IBM took the first steps toward consent solicitation to put pressure on the Lotus board. Lotus bylaws permitted shareholders to vote at any time on whether to retain the board. With

the threat of being ousted, the Lotus board would be forced to pay careful attention to the wishes of the shareholders. Shareholders were likely to want the premium, given the recent poor performance of the company stock. Institutions held the bulk of Lotus's stock. Directors and officers held only 3.3% of Lotus's stock, but 2.54% of that number, or 1.2 million shares, was held by Manzi, the largest individual holder of Lotus stock.

The announcement of the bid appeared to be anticipated given the 11% rise in the Lotus stock price on Friday, June 2, which triggered an SEC insider trader investigation. Rumors that IBM might acquire Lotus had existed for several months prior to the bid.

Acceptance of the Offer

On Sunday, June 11, Lotus accepted a sweetened $64 a share, or $3.52 billion, offer from IBM. The final price represented four times Lotus's 1994 revenues. IBM anticipated writing off approximately $1.8 billion in goodwill after a one-time charge. Also under the terms of the deal, Manzi would remain the CEO of Lotus and become a senior vice president of IBM. He would be allowed to run Lotus with a high degree of independence in addition to receiving a $78 million windfall from his Lotus stock.

In Manzi's own words, he was staying on, not in a "transitional role," but rather to help make Lotus Notes the industry standard for network software, to protect Lotus employees, and to protect the Lotus organization (Glenn Rifkin, "How Shock Turned to Deal for Lotus Chief," *The New York Times,* June 13, 1995, p. D6). Though analysts were surprised that Manzi would remain in charge of Lotus, they predicted that he would not stay with the company for long. Analysts spoke of the clash of egos they felt would occur between Gerstner and Manzi.

Manzi said that the previously announced restructuring of Lotus into four business units would still take place in spite of the merger. Some Lotus employees may have favored the merger because of the stability involved in joining IBM's team, the capital IBM could invest in the company, and the soaring value of their Lotus stock options. Prior to the merger Lotus's future looked grim. Lotus was vulnerable due to its recent poor performance, lack of a white knight, and corporate bylaws that allowed a direct appeal to Lotus shareholders. Lotus shares traded at 66% below their 1994 high, and efforts to find a white knight may have been impeded by the fact that Lotus was a competitor of the powerful Microsoft, with which very few companies were able or willing to compete.

On July 5, 1995, the acquisition was finally completed.

STRATEGIC ANALYSIS OF THE ACQUISITION

Previous History of Lotus

Lotus was founded by a college dropout named Mitch Kapor in 1982. Eight months later the company successfully introduced Lotus 1-2-3, the first spreadsheet program to translate numbers into graphics. In 1983 a McKinsey and Company consultant by the name of Jim Manzi was assigned to help manage Lotus's rapid growth. Later that year Manzi joined the Lotus board as vice president of marketing and sales. In 1986 Kapor left the firm and made Manzi his successor.

In the early 1980s the Lotus 1-2-3 spreadsheet package was the most popular PC business application. But because Lotus was slow to develop a version of 1-2-3 for Windows, many users switched to Microsoft Excel or Borland's Quattro Pro for Windows.

The growing popularity of Windows created other problems for Lotus as well. Late in developing software suites, the company tried to rectify this through acquisitions. In 1990 Lotus acquired Samna Corp. and its Ami Pro word processing line for $65 million,

and in March 1991 Lotus purchased cc:Mail. Also, in June 1994 Lotus acquired SoftSwitch Inc. for $70 million in stock, or 1.3 million shares. Unfortunately, these acquisitions did little to help improve Lotus's weakened state.

The reduction in its desktop applications and continued reputation for being weak on marketing and updating programs contributed to Lotus's subsequent decline. Lotus's desktop software accounted for two-thirds of its revenues, so it was particularly troublesome when in 1994 these revenues declined 20% to $620 million. In the first quarter of 1995 Lotus lost another $17.5 million due in part to a 50% price cut on Notes announced in January 1995. The price cut was intended to increase the market share of Notes before the release of MS Exchange.

The company's troubles prompted Manzi to announce a restructuring on April 19, 1995. Cost cuts and reorganization meant layoffs and low employee morale. In two weeks, Lotus eliminated 32 high level positions, with lower level layoffs expected in the near future. This restructuring was directed by Richard S. Braddock, a powerful outside director and former president of Citicorp.

Motivations Behind the Merger

The main motivation behind the acquisition was IBM's desire to own Lotus's network software program called Notes. Released in December 1989, Notes had propelled Lotus to a 65% market share in groupware, a market that was anticipated to grow from $500 million to $5 billion by the end of the decade. In 1994 sales of Notes nearly doubled to $350 million, with the majority coming from existing customers. By January 1995 one million people used Notes in 4,500 companies, and third-party companies had created over 700 commercial applications that work with Notes. Moreover, the Notes customer base had increased because although it was originally available only on OS/2 servers it could now run on Windows NT and other operating systems.

Primarily used by large corporations and large networks, groupware enables groups of workers to communicate with one another and to share or have access to the same data. It is often used as the central framework for managing entire corporate systems and can be customized for use as a platform on which to build additional applications.

QUESTIONS

1. What were IBM's strategic strengths and weaknesses in the computer industry?
2. What role was the acquisition of Lotus expected to perform?
3. What has been IBM's performance since this acquisition?

◈ REFERENCES

Ansoff, H. Igor, *Corporate Strategy*, New York: McGraw-Hill, 1965.

Bogue, Marcus C., III, and Elwood S. Buffa, *Corporate Strategic Analysis*, New York: The Free Press, 1986.

Boston Consulting Group, *The Strategy Development Process*, Boston: The Boston Consulting Group, 1985.

Carroll, D. T., "A Disappointing Search for Excellence," *Harvard Business Review*, 61, November–December 1983, pp. 78–88.

Chandler, Alfred D., Jr., *Strategy and Structure: Chapters in the History of the American Industrial Enterprise*, Cambridge, MA: The M.I.T. Press, 1962.

Chung, Mary, and Alistair Davidson, "Business Experts," *PCAI*, 1, Summer 1987, pp. 16–21.

Economist, "Why Too Many Mergers Miss the Mark," January 4, 1997, pp. 57–58.

Evans, Philip, and Thomas Wurster, "Strategy and the New Economics of Information," *Harvard Business Review*, September–October 1997.

Evans, Philip, and Thomas Wurster, *Blown to Bits*, Boston: Harvard Business School Press, 2000.

Grove, Andrew S., *Only the Paranoid Survive: How to Exploit the Crisis Points That Challenge Every Company and Career*, New York: Currency Doubleday, 1996.

Gulati, R., N. Nohria, and A. Zaheer, "Strategic Networks," *Strategic Management Journal*, March 2000, pp. 203–215.

Henderson, Bruce D., *The Logic of Business Strategy*, Cambridge, MA: Ballinger, 1984.

Hout, Thomas M., and Mark F. Blaxill, "Make Decisions Like a Fighter Pilot," *New York Times*, November 15, 1987, Sec. 3, p. 3.

Johnson, W. Bruce, Ashok Natarajan, and Alfred Rappaport, "Shareholder Returns and Corporate Excellence," *Journal of Business Strategy*, 6, Fall 1985, pp. 52–62.

Lindblom, Charles E., "The Science of 'Muddling Through'," *Public Administration Review*, 19, Spring 1959, pp. 79–88.

———, *The Intelligence of Democracy: Decision Making Through Mutual Adjustment*, New York: The Free Press, 1965.

Lippman, S., and R. Rumelt, "Uncertain Imitability: An Analysis of Interfirm Differences in Efficiency Under Competition," *The Bell Journal of Economics*, 13, 1982, pp. 418–438.

Ouchi, William. *The M-Form Society: How American Teamwork Can Recapture the Competitive Edge*. Reading, Mass.: Addison-Wesley, 1984.

Peters, Thomas J., *Thriving on Chaos*. New York: Alfred A. Knopf, Publishers, 1987.

———, and Robert H. Waterman, Jr., *In Search of Excellence*, New York: Harper & Row, 1982.

Porter, Michael E., "How Competitive Forces Shape Strategy," *Harvard Business Review*, 57, March–April 1979, pp. 137–145.

———, *Competitive Strategy*, New York: The Free Press, 1980.

———, *Competitive Advantage,* New York: The Free Press, 1985.

———, "From Competitive Advantage to Corporate Strategy," *Harvard Business Review,* May–June 1987, pp. 43–59.

Quinn, James Brian, "Strategic Goals: Process and Politics," *Sloan Management Review,* Fall 1977, pp. 21–37.

———, *Strategies for Change: Logical Incrementalism,* Homewood, IL: Irwin, 1980.

———, Henry Mintzberg, and Robert M. James, *The Strategy Process,* Englewood Cliffs, NJ: Prentice Hall, 1988.

Ramanujam, Vasudevan, and N. Venkatraman, "Excellence, Planning, and Performance," *Interfaces,* 18, May–June 1988, pp. 23–31.

Rumelt, Richard P., "Towards a Strategic Theory of the Firm" Chapter 26 in R. B. Lamb, ed., *Competitive Strategic Management,* Englewood Cliffs, NJ: Prentice Hall, 1984.

Steiner, George A., *Strategic Planning,* New York: The Free Press, 1979.

———, John B. Miner, and Edmund R. Gray, *Management Policy and Strategy,* 3rd ed., New York: Macmillan, 1986.

Stryker, Steven C., *Plan to Succeed: A Guide to Strategic Planning,* Princeton, NJ: Petrocelli Books, 1986.

Thomas, Lacy Glenn, III, ed., *The Economics of Strategic Planning,* Lexington, MA: Lexington Books, 1986.

Waterman, Robert H., Jr., *The Renewal Factor,* New York: Bantam Books, 1987.

Weston, J. Fred, *Concentration and Efficiency: The Other Side of the Monopoly Issue,* Special Issues in the Public Interest No. 4, New York: Hudson Institute, 1978.

———, "Section 7 Enforcement: Implementation of Outmoded Theories," *Antitrust Law Journal,* 49, 1982, pp. 1411–1450.

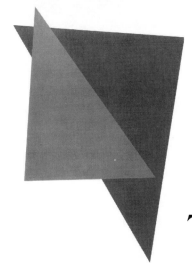

Theories of Mergers and Tender Offers

Almost daily the *Wall Street Journal, Business Week,* and other financial publications report major merger and takeover events. Some are alarmed by all this activity. Others see resources being redeployed to their highest value uses. This chapter seeks to explain the reasons for merger and takeover activity.

SIZE AND RETURNS TO SCALE

Since mergers increase the size of firms it is useful to summarize the relationship between size and production efficiency. These basic concepts are relevant in analyzing a number of theories of mergers discussed subsequently in this chapter.

The basic physical relationship between volume and surface area produces economies of scale. Well-known applications are in pipelines, chemicals, and pharmaceuticals in which cylindrical or spherical containers are used. Consider the use of a spherical container. The cost of a sphere is related to the materials required for its surface area, which is equal to $4\pi r^2$, where π is the constant 3.1416 and r is the radius of the sphere. The volume and output of the sphere is $(4\pi r^3)/3$. Simple numerical examples demonstrate that doubling the radius raises output by a factor of 8 while the costs related to surface area increase by a factor of four.

There is another natural economy of scale in holding inventories and replacement parts. If demand is subject to random influences, the statistical law of large numbers will hold. The larger the scale of operations, the lower the required investment in inventories in relation to the average quantity sold.

Important economies of scale have been widely observed in operations such as auto body stamping plants. For larger production volumes, costly dies can be made more durable and greater degrees of automation utilized.

Learning experience curves were observed in airplane production to reduce costs. The Boston Consulting Group emphasized that cumulative volume was associated with lower costs. These learning curve benefits are applicable particularly in production of commodity chemicals. Thus, a firm much farther along on the learning curve can confer benefits to another firm in the same product line, but at an earlier stage of production experience. The learning curve is a relationship between average costs and the cumulative units produced. In the early stages of producing a new product, practice and experience will cause costs to decline. But after a considerable time period during which the cumulative volume has become large, these learning curve benefits would be expected to become smaller and smaller. A study by Marvin Lieberman (1984) estimated economies of scale and learning effects for the chemical processing industry. Between the 1950s and 1970s, he found that for each doubling in plant size, average production costs fell by about 11%. For each doubling of cumulative volume, average production costs fell by 27%.

Another important source of returns to scale is specialization. This was observed by Adam Smith in his famous example of producing pins. Firms of larger size may be able to organize production into specialist groups which become more efficient. For example, in a firm with 10 employees, each might be responsible for performing several types of jobs. In a firm with 1,000 employees, groups of employees might specialize in only one type of task. At some size of operations the cost of coordinating the specialist groups may increase to the point where returns to scale may become decreasing. This is why incremental or marginal costs may at first be declining and then begin to rise.

We have described some examples of returns to scale. These concepts are reflected in the economists' depiction of long run average costs first declining and then rising at some point. Mathematically, when average costs are declining, incremental or marginal costs are less than average costs and pulling down average costs. When average costs are rising, marginal costs lie above average costs and are rising. So with increasing (decreasing) returns to scale, average costs are greater (smaller) than marginal costs. The relationships can also be expressed by production functions. A simple production function with constant returns to scale would be $Q=C^{2/3}*L^{1/3}$, where Q is output quantity, C is the capital input, and L is the labor input. For C=8 and L=27, the quantity of output would be 12. If we double each of the inputs, output would become 24. This illustrates that under constant returns to scale doubling inputs doubles output.

We next illustrate increasing returns to scale. We change the exponent of the capital factor of production to 3/4 so that the production function becomes $Q=C^{3/4}*L^{1/3}$. Note that in this example, the sum of the exponents is greater than one. For constant returns to scale in the previous paragraph, the sum was one. Using the same input quantities for capital and labor, total output is 14.27. When we double the two input quantities to 16 and 54, total output becomes 30.24, more than double. If the sum of the exponents were less than one, doubling the inputs would result in less than doubling the outputs.

Returns to scale should be distinguished from spreading fixed costs over a larger number of units, which represents better capacity utilization. For example, in industries such as steel and autos, consolidating mergers have taken place to reduce industry capacity. One possibility is that some plants may be closed, so the remaining plants may produce more units getting the benefits of spreading fixed costs over a larger volume. A restructuring write-off may be associated with the plants closed, but levels of reported cash flows or net income in the future can be improved. The industry sales to capacity relationship is also adjusted favorably. With less excess capacity ruinous price cutting may be mitigated.

We have also observed fragmented industries, such as waste management and water filtration, in which firms have been rolled up into larger units. An important factor has been the availability of expertise in the top management functions that could be applied to the smaller units acquired. Gains in purchasing and in marketing were also possibilities. This illustrates indivisibilities. The creation of an able management team requires an investment. It is advantageous to spread this investment over a larger number of activities.

Another important influence is the role of the Internet. Dell Computers, for example, has achieved great economies by assembling a network of parts and component suppliers through Internet communications. Major manufacturers have arranged to have suppliers submit bids communicated and assembled by use of the Internet. Purchasing transaction costs are reduced for the buyers as well as the sellers. But revenues for suppliers may be reduced even more. Similarly, strategic networks and alliances in which the boundaries of firms overlap may be important sources of economies (Gulati, Nohria, Zaheer, 2000).

We have distinguished between returns to scale and spreading fixed costs over a larger number of units. Another distinction is between economies of scale and economies of scope. Economies of scope enable a firm to produce related additional products at lower cost because of experience with existing products. One example is the pharmaceutical industry, where adding products to a therapeutic product class, such as antibiotics, benefits from production experience and better utilization of the marketing organization. Similarly, in the automobile industry adding the production of pick-up trucks and various types of vans benefited from the experience in producing automobiles.

A firm that has achieved lower costs because of economies of scale and/or the ability to spread fixed costs over a larger number of units and/or the advantages of learning experience may be said to have organization capital. In this sense, organizational capital is information assets that accumulate over time to enhance productivity. Organization capital includes information used in assigning employees to appropriate tasks, in forming teams of employees, and the information each employee acquires about other employees in the organization (Prescott and Visscher, 1980).

Organization capital is distinguished from organization reputation. **Organization reputation** is the implicit contractual relationships between the firm and its stakeholders, which include customers, employees, creditors, and stockholders. A distinction is made between explicit contractual claims and implicit contractual claims. Explicit contractual claims are illustrated by wage contracts and product warranties. Implicit claims are the tacit assurances of consistent product quality to customers and job security to employees. Clearly, organization reputation has value. In this sense, it is a part of the firm's organization capital.

Three types of human capital resources are available to the firm as inputs for production. The first of these human capital resources may be termed generic managerial capabilities to represent the combination of organization learning in the generic managerial functions and the relevant organization capital. The second is called industry-specific managerial capabilities. The third type includes all others and can be called nonmanagerial human capital (Rosen, 1972).

Given that the three types of human resources are specialized to the firm to some extent, we need to examine the implications and degrees of their specificity. The jobs of nonmanagerial production workers are specified according to the details of the production facility. Once a team of workers is organized with each worker assigned to a different job based on specific information on their characteristics, the team is specialized to the facility. Therefore, it is specialized to the firm's production establishment or can at best be transferred to a similar establishment. A merger between firms, even firms in related industries, will therefore not include the transfer of nonmanagerial human capital between the firms. Its transfer between firms is feasible only in horizontal mergers.

Industry-specific managerial capabilities can be transferred to other firms in related industries without impairing the team effect, as they are not identified with a particular establishment. The requirement that managers be transferred as a team is satisfied by a merger initiated to carry over industry-specific managerial capabilities. The team-effect portion of organization capital will be preserved through a merger, but the other type of organization capital (that is, employee-embodied firm-specific information) has to be reacquired for the new setting of the acquired or combined firm. Mergers between firms are therefore more efficient at transferring these capabilities than the movements through the labor market of individual managers. Mergers thus cause the supply of managerial capabilities in the market to be more elastic.

Generic managerial capabilities can, of course, be carried over even through a merger with a firm in an unrelated industry. Again, to the extent that team effects are important, a merger that can preserve these effects is more efficient than inter-firm movements of managers as individuals. However, there are reasons to believe that invoking a merger to acquire or to carry over generic managerial resources will not be as compelling as in the case of industry-specific resources. First, the team size to produce generic managerial service is in general smaller than that for managerial resources related to production and marketing. Thus, the organization of a managerial team for control, coordination, and planning requires less time than the organization of a team for other managerial capabilities. Second, information on top-level managers who perform the control and coordination functions may be more public than on lower level managers for production and marketing functions. Third, managers for generic functions can come from even remotely related industries, whereas managers in specific function areas should have experience in closely related industries.

MODELS OF THE TAKEOVER PROCESS

Many factors can potentially influence the structure of formal models of the merger and takeover processes. These are listed in Table 6.1.

An infinite number of models could be constructed by selecting alternative combinations of the variables or assumptions in Table 6.1. We illustrate the kinds of models that can be constructed, but we cover only a small sample of the models published and described in working papers. We have selected those aspects of models that can most readily be communicated to nonspecialists in the literature of bargaining, games, and auctions. Other aspects are so technical that their study is most appropriate in courses and writings for specialized study of such subjects.

Table 6.1   Variables in Models of the Merger and Takeover Processes

1. Choice of model: (a) Microeconomics—competition or market power; (b) bargaining; (c) game theory; (d) auctions.
2. Form of auction: English, Dutch, or other.
3. Form of game.
4. Bargaining: (a) Does it take place? (b) If so, what forms or types?
5. Form of equilibrium: Pooling, separating, sequential?
6. Incentives of shareholders, managers, and bidders.
7. Friendly (merger) or unfriendly (tender).
8. Form of tender: (a) Unconditional bid for any and all shares; (b) conditional bid on acquiring a specified number, percentage, or control.
9. Form of two-part bids: (a) Front- and back-end bids revealed in bid; (b) only front end revealed; (c) competition from multiple bidders.
10. Degree to which bids provide information or signal to shareholders, managers, and bidders.
11. Atomistic versus finite shareholders.
12. If finite shareholders, how did they acquire their position?
13. Kinds and amounts of transactions costs in multiple or successive bids.
14. Investigation costs of first bidder and subsequent bidders.
15. Legislative, regulatory, and other rules of the game as they affect transactions, investigation, and other aspects of bargaining, games, or auctions.
16. Degree of synergy between target and bidder and potential bidders.
17. Reservation values of target and explanations of how they were established.
18. Degree to which target could restructure without another firm.
19. Amount, kinds, and values of information provided by target to some or all bidders.
20. Private information of target about its value; private information of bidder on the profitability of takeover.
21. Effects of taxes on the forms of transactions included in the models.
22. Effects of costs of investigation on actions of bidders.
23. Disadvantages or advantages to target and bidders of eliminating some bidders, and circumstances under which elimination can be accomplished, if ever.
24. Influence of method of financing—cash, securities. If securities, what forms of debt and equity, and combinations, are used?
25. Degree to which prices paid incorporate earn-outs and bonuses.

FREE-RIDER PROBLEM, INITIAL SHAREHOLDING, AND THE EQUILIBRIUM BID

In a diffusely held corporation, it may not pay a small shareholder to make expenditures on monitoring the performance of its management. The reason for this is that shareholders could simply free-ride on the monitoring efforts of other shareholders and share in the resulting improvements of the firm's performance.

Grossman and Hart (1980) argue that this free-rider problem also reduces the incentives of outsiders without any shareholdings to be engaged in a costly takeover of the diffusely held firm in order to improve its performance. The small ("atomistic") shareholders will not accept any offer price below the new revised price that should obtain as a result of the improvement. They reason that their individual decision to accept or reject the tender offer does not affect the success of the offer and that if the offer succeeds they will fully share in the improvement brought about by the takeover.

One solution to the free-rider problem is to allow the bidder to dilute the value of the remaining, nontendered shares of the target firm after takeover. The dilution could be allowed explicitly by limiting the rights of minority shareholders through a corporate charter amendment (Grossman and Hart, 1980). Or the bidder might be able to achieve dilution by supplying overpriced inputs to the target or buying underpriced products or other assets from the target. The anticipated dilution induces shareholders to tender their shares at a price below that reflecting the post-takeover improvements. The bidder will be able to profit from the takeover if dilution is possible.

Another method used to avoid the free-rider problem, and one theoretically equivalent to dilution, is to announce a two-tier offer. In such an offer the bidder will buy target shares up to a certain percentage of the firm at a first-tier price and, after the takeover, buy the remaining shares at a lower, second-tier price. The second-tier price will be lower than the value of the target shares under the anticipated improvements, so the takeover will be profitable for the bidder. However, the average price paid may represent a division (equitable) of the improvement in value that conceivably might have been contained in a single price offer were it not for the free-rider problem.

In a study critical of the atomistic stockholder models that emphasize the free-rider problem, Bagnoli and Lipman (1988) argue that when there are finitely many stockholders the bidder can overcome the free-rider problem. They show that for a finite number of stockholders, some stockholders must be pivotal in the sense that they do recognize that they may affect the outcome of the bid. In their model, making some stockholders pivotal is crucial, because it forces them to choose whether or not the bid succeeds. Hence, they cannot free-ride, so exclusionary devices such as dilution and two-tier offers are not necessary for successful takeovers.

A third way of avoiding the free-rider problem, which does not require dilution, is for a large shareholder (or an outsider after "secretly" accumulating a large fraction of the equity) to make a tender offer. This is the subject of the analysis by Shleifer and Vishny (1986), Hirshleifer and Titman (1990), and Chowdhry and Jegadeesh (1994). They will gain from the rise in the price of the shares they already own.

A FRAMEWORK

In addition to the broad models discussed in the previous sections, many individual theories or explanations for mergers and takeovers have been formulated. They can be summarized into three major categories as shown by Table 6.2 (Berkovitch and Narayanan (BN), 1993). The first column of Table 6.2 lists the three major motives for mergers and takeovers on the basis of whether value changes are positive, zero, or negative. The value changes refer to movements in the prices of the securities of companies as a result of mergers, takeovers, divestitures, spin-offs, share repurchases, or other significant developments affecting the outlook for a firm. The gains can be measured as percentage returns or in absolute dollar amounts. How these "event returns" are measured is described in Appendix B to this chapter.

Table 6.2   Pattern of Gains Related to Takeover Theories

Motive	(1) Total Gains	(2) Gains to Target	(3) Gains to Acquirer
I. Efficiency or synergy	+	+	+
II. Hubris (winner's curse, overpay)	0	+	−
III. Agency problems or mistakes	−	+	−

Source: Berkovitch and Narayanan, 1993

Total gains can be positive because of efficiency improvements, synergy, or increased market power. The hubris theory (Roll, 1986) postulates that total gains are zero and that acquiring firms overpay. Total gains may be negative as a result of agency problems or mistakes. When agency factors motivate an acquisition or merger, managers take the action in their own self-interest even to the detriment of the company.

By definition, then, total gains are positive for synergy, zero for hubris, and negative for agency problems. Column 2 of Table 6.2 lists gains to targets. All empirical studies show positive gains for groups of targets. For each of the three categories of theories, the entry would be a plus. We next consider the gains to the acquirer. With synergy or efficiency, the total gains from the merger are positive. If the value increases are shared to any degree, the gains to both the target and the bidder would be positive. Of course, when the total gains are positive, it is possible that the premium paid by the bidder could be greater than the total gains, resulting in negative gains to the bidder. But overpaying puts us in the second category of hubris, in which gains to targets are positive but the gains to bidders are negative. In the third category of agency problems or mistakes, total gains are negative. Because gains to targets are positive, the returns to the acquirer or bidding firm would necessarily be negative.

Table 6.2 provides a beginning framework for analyzing the reasons for mergers and takeovers. It centers attention on the very important issue of whether the total gains are positive, negative, or negligible. But some redistribution elements are not encompassed by it. A full overview of theories of M&As is presented in Table 6.3.

SOURCES OF VALUE INCREASES FROM M&AS

We shall discuss each of the four major sections of Table 6.3. We begin with the sources of total value increases.

Efficiency Increases

Efficiency improvements can result from combining firms of unequal managerial capabilities. A relatively efficient bidder may acquire a relatively inefficient target. Value can be increased by improving the efficiency of the target. Or the bidder may seek a merger with a target firm because the management of the target firm can improve the efficiency of the bidder. The target firm may have relatively better growth

Table 6.3   Theories of M&As

I. Total value increased
    1. Efficiency increases
    2. Operating synergy
    3. Diversification
    4. Financial synergy
    5. Strategic realignments
    6. The q-ratio
    7. Information
    8. Signaling
II. Hubris: Acquirer overpays for target.
III. Agency: Managers make value-decreasing mergers to increase size of firm.
IV. Redistribution
    1. Taxes—redistribution from government
    2. Market power—redistribution from consumers
    3. Redistribution from bondholders
    4. Labor—wage renegotiation
    5. Pension reversions

opportunities than the bidder or vice versa. Sometimes the combination will achieve a more efficient critical mass. The investments in expensive specialized machinery may be large. Combining firms may achieve better utilization of large fixed investments. Plants that have old or inefficient-sized equipment may be shut down after the merger.

Operating Synergy

The theory based on operating synergy assumes that economies of scale do exist in the industry and that prior to the merger the firms are operating at levels of activity that fall short of achieving the potential for economies of scale. Economies of scale arise because of indivisibilities, such as people, equipment, and overhead, that result in lower costs if spread over a large number of units of output. Thus, in manufacturing operations, heavy investments in plant and equipment typically produce such economies. For example, costly machinery such as the large presses used to produce automobile bodies requires optimal utilization. The research and development departments of chemical and pharmaceutical companies often must have a large staff of highly competent scientists who could develop and oversee a larger number of product areas. In marketing, having one organization cover the entire United States may yield economies of scale because of the increase in the ratio of calling-on-customer time to traveling time, which in turn is due to the higher density of customers who can be called on by the same number of salespeople.

One potential problem in merging firms with existing organizations is the question of how to combine and coordinate the good parts of the organizations and eliminate what is not required. The merger announcement may say that firm A is strong in research and development but weak in marketing, while firm B is strong in marketing but weak in research and development, and the two firms combined will complement each other. Analytically, this implies underutilization of some existing factors and inadequate investment in other factors of production. (Because the economies are jointly achieved, the assignment of the contributions of each firm to the merger is difficult both in theory and in practice.)

Managerial economies in production, research, marketing, or finance are sometimes referred to as economies in the specific management functions. It has also been suggested that economies may be achieved in generic management activity such as the planning and control functions of the firm. It is argued that firms of even moderate size need at least a minimum number of corporate officers. The corporate staff with capabilities for planning and control is therefore assumed to be underutilized to some degree. Acquisitions of firms just approaching the size where they need to add corporate staff would provide for fuller utilization of the corporate staff of the acquiring firm and avoid the necessity of adding such staff for the other firm.

Another area in which operating economies may be achieved is in vertical integration. Combining firms at different stages of an industry may achieve more efficient coordination of the different levels. The argument here is that costs of communication and various forms of bargaining can be avoided by vertical integration (Arrow, 1975; Klein, Crawford, and Alchian, 1978; Williamson, 1975).

Diversification Motives

Diversification may be sought by managers and other employees for preservation of organizational and reputational capital and for financial and tax advantages.

First, in contrast to the position of shareholders, who can diversify across firms in the capital market, executives and other employees of the firm have only a limited opportunity to diversify their labor income sources. In general, employees need to make firm-specific investments. Most of their knowledge acquired while working for the firm may be valuable to the firm but not to others. Typically employees are more productive in their current job than in other firms because of their specialized knowledge. They are compensated for these firm-specific investments. Thus, they value stability in their job and greater opportunity to acquire specialized knowledge and to get higher pay. This latter opportunity normally comes with promotion in the firm. Diversification of the firm can provide managers and other employees with job security and opportunities for promotion and, other things being equal, results in lower labor costs.

This diversification argument also applies to an owner-manager whose wealth is concentrated in his or her firm. The owner-manager may not want to sell ownership shares in the firm for reasons of corporate control. An undiversified owner will require a higher risk premium in investments and make smaller investments than otherwise optimal (Fama and Jensen, 1985). Thus, diversification at the firm level (that is, diversification of the firm itself) is valuable for such an owner-manager or, in general, for shareholders who hold a controlling interest and are undiversified.

Second, in the modern theory of the firm, information on employees is accumulated within the firm over time. This information is firm-specific to the extent that its transfer to outside firms or the market involves costs. The information is used for efficient matching of employees and jobs or of employees themselves for a particular job. This implies that managerial and other teams are formed in the firm. When a firm is liquidated, these teams are destroyed and the value of the organization is lost. If the firm is diversified, the teams can be transferred from unprofitable business activities to growing and profitable activities. Diversification may ensure smooth and efficient transition of the firm's activities and the continuity of the teams and the organization.

Third, firms have reputational capital that customers, suppliers, and employees utilize in establishing their relationships with the firm. Reputation is acquired over time through firm-specific (and thus nonsalvageable) investments, ethical behavior in advertising, research and development, fixed assets, personnel training, organizational development, and so on. Diversification can help preserve the firm's reputational capital, which will cease to exist if the firm is liquidated.

Fourth, as in the discussion of financial synergy and tax effects below, diversification can increase corporate debt capacity and decrease the present value of future tax liability. These effects are a result of the decrease in cash flow variability due to the merger.

Diversification can be achieved through internal growth as well as mergers. However, mergers may be preferred to the internal growth avenue to diversification under certain circumstances. The firm may simply lack internal growth opportunities owing to a lack of requisite resources or to potential excess capacity in the industry. Timing may be important, and mergers can provide diversification more quickly.

Empirical studies find that the average diversified firm has been worth less than a portfolio of comparable single-segment firms (Berger and Ofek, 1995; Lang and Stulz, 1994). A number of explanations have been offered to explain the discount. One is that external capital markets allocate resources more efficiently than internal capital markets. Price signals are generated by competitive capital markets to guide the flow of resources. Without such price information managers make inferior decisions in internal allocations. A second reason could be that there are political influences that result in subsidizing underperforming divisions within a firm.

A third explanation for the diversification discount is that managers of multiple activities are not as well informed about each activity as the managers of a single-product firm. Fourth, securities analysts are said to be less likely to follow multisegment firms because of inadequate information on the individual segments. Fifth, without external market measures of performance, managers of segments cannot be adequately evaluated. Stock options cannot be granted on the basis of segment contributions. Hence, the incentives and motivations of managers of segments are not as high as those of managers of single-segment firms.

A sixth hypothesis uses the basic valuation relationship that asset prices are a function of expected future cash flows discounted at a required or expected return (Lamont and Polk, 1999). A diversified firm with a high expected rate of return (relative to single-segment firms) has a low value (a discount). The empirical studies by Lamont and Polk find that excess values do forecast future returns. "Firms with discounts have higher subsequent returns than firms with premia. The diversification discount puzzle is, at least in part, an expected return phenomenon as well as an expected cash flow phenomenon" (p. 4).

Financial Synergy

One source of financial synergy is the lower costs of internal financing in comparison with external financing. Firms with large internal cash flows and small investment opportunities have excess cash flows. Firms with low internal funds generation and large growth opportunities have a need for additional financing. Combining the two may result in advantages from the lower costs of internal funds availability.

Previous empirical findings appear to support this internal funds effect. Nielsen and Melicher (1973) found that the rate of premium paid to the acquired firm as an approximation to the merger gain was greater when the cash flow rate of the acquiring firm was greater than that of the acquired firm. This implied that there was redeployment of capital from the acquiring to the acquired firm's industry. The investment literature also indicates that internal cash flows affect the rate of investment of firms (Nickell, 1978).

Another proposition is that the debt capacity of the combined firm can be greater than the sum of the two firms' capacities before their merger, and this provides tax savings on investment income. Still another possible dimension is economies of scale in flotation and transaction costs of securities (Levy and Sarnat, 1970). Changes in the economic and financial environments may permit higher levels of debt than those employed historically. Debt ratios increased during the 1980s in an economy of sustained growth and large tax advantages to debt. Tax law changes after 1986 and the recession of 1989 to 1990 resulted in more equity financing and a reduction in book leverage ratios in the early 1990s. (McCauley, Ruud, Iacono, Chapter 5, 1999).

Strategic Realignments

The increased merger activity of 1992 to 1996 was said to be motivated by strategic considerations. Here the emphasis is on acquiring new management skills to augment the capabilities of the firm in relation to new growth areas or to meet new competitive threats. New capabilities and new markets could be developed internally. However, the speed of adjustment can be improved through merger activity.

The q-Ratio

The q-ratio is defined as the ratio of the market value of the firm's securities to the replacement costs of its assets. One frequently discussed reason that firms stepped up acquisition programs in the late 1970s was that entry into new product market areas could be accomplished on a bargain basis. Inflation had a double-barreled impact. For various reasons, including inflation, stock prices were depressed during the 1970s and did not recover until the latter part of 1982 as the level of inflation dropped and business prospects improved. The second impact of inflation was to cause current replacement costs of assets to be substantially higher than their recorded historical book values. These twin effects resulted in a decline of the q-ratio, because the market value of the firm's securities fell and the replacement costs of its assets increased.

In the late 1970s and early 1980s the q-ratio had been running between 0.5 and 0.6. If a company wished to add to capacity in producing a particular product, it could acquire the additional capacity more cheaply by buying a company that produced the product rather than building brick-and-mortar from scratch. If firm A sought to add capacity, this implied that its marginal q-ratio was greater than 1. But if other firms in its industry had average q-ratios of less than 1, it was efficient for firm A to add capacity by purchasing other firms. For example, if the q-ratio was 0.6 and if in a merger the premium paid over market value was even as high as 50%, the resulting purchase price was 0.6 times 1.5, which equals 0.9. Thus, the average purchase price would still be 10% below the current replacement costs of the assets acquired. This potential advantage would provide a broad basis for the operation of the undervaluation theory in years when the q-ratio was low.

When a firm's q-ratio is high this implies superior management. A high q-ratio firm may be bought by a low q-ratio firm seeking to augment its managerial capabilities.

Information

The shares of the target firm in a tender often experience upward revaluation even if the offer turns out to be unsuccessful (Bradley, 1980; Dodd and Ruback, 1977). A hypothesis based on this empirical observation posits that new information is generated as a result of the tender offer and the revaluation is permanent. Two forms of this information hypothesis can be distinguished. One is that the tender offer disseminates information that the target shares are undervalued and the offer prompts the market to revalue those shares. No particular action by the target firm or any others is necessary to cause the revaluation. This has been called the "sitting-on-a-goldmine" explanation (Bradley, Desai, and Kim, 1983). The other is that the offer inspires target firm management to implement a more efficient business strategy on its own. This is the "kick-in-the-pants" explanation. No outside input other than the offer itself is required for the upward revaluation.

An opposing view holds that the increase in share value of the target firm involved in an unsuccessful offer is due to the expectation that the target firm will subsequently be acquired by another firm. The latter would have some specialized resources to apply to the target resources. Bradley, Desai, and Kim (1983, 1988) examined the data to determine whether the information hypothesis or the latter (synergy) explanation is acceptable. They found that the share prices of the target firms that did not subsequently receive acquisition offers within five years of the initial unsuccessful offer fell back to their preoffer level. The share prices of those targets that received a subsequent bid increased further. They interpret this result as indicating that the information hypothesis is not valid. A permanent revaluation of the target shares occurs when the target resources are combined with the resources of an acquiring firm, or at least when the control of the target resources is transferred to the acquiring firm.

But Roll (1987, pp. 74–91) suggested that the data were equally consistent with an information explanation. He observed that the appearance of a rival bid increased the probability that there existed positive nonpublic information about the target firm. It also decreased the probability that the initial bidder had exclusive possession of the information.

Signaling

A distinction may be drawn between information and signaling. When a firm receives a tender offer, this conveys information to the market that a bidder sees value in the firm greater than its prevailing market price. The information conveyed to the market by the bid did not represent the motive of the bidder, which was to make an advantageous purchase. On the other hand, in a share repurchase when management holds a significant proportion of the stock and does not tender stock at the premium in the repurchase price, it is signaling that the company's shares are undervalued. In the original theory of signaling by Spence (1973, 1974), higher quality labor in terms of intelligence or aptitudes would receive greater returns from education and training than lower quality labor. Hence, the level of education of a laborer was a signal not only of more training but also of higher innate abilities. Lower quality labor would have negative returns on investment in education and training. Thus, it was advantageous for some to signal but disadvantageous for others. As a result, the signal would convey meaningful and correct information. In a share repurchase, firms with undervalued stock are signaling. It would not be advantageous for the control group of companies with overvalued stock to pay a premium in a share repurchase, because it would not recoup the premium paid.

WINNER'S CURSE AND HUBRIS

The winner's curse concept has a long history in the literature on auctions. When there are many bidders or competitors for an object of highly uncertain value, a wide range of bids is likely to result. For example, suppose that many oil companies are bidding on the drilling rights to a particular parcel of land. Given the difficulty of estimating the actual amount of oil in the land, the estimates of the oil companies will vary greatly. The highest bidder will bid and typically pay in excess of the expected value of the oil on the property. The winning bidder is, therefore, "cursed" in the sense that its bid exceeds the value of the tract, so the firm loses money. Capen, Clapp, and Campbell (1971), based on their analysis of sealed-bid competitive lease sales, presented a diagram that depicted the ratio of high estimate to true value as a function of the degree of uncertainty and the number of bidders. For example, with 10 bidders for leases on a large-uncertainty oil project (Arctic), the ratio of high estimate (bid) to true value was about 3.5 times.

Roll (1986) analyzed the effect in takeover activity. Postulating strong market efficiency in all markets, the prevailing market price of the target already reflected the full value of the firm. The higher valuation of the bidders (over the target's true economic value), he states, resulted from **hubris**—their excessive self-confidence (pride, arrogance). Hubris is one of the factors that caused the winner's curse phenomenon to occur.

Even if there were synergies, competition between bidders was likely to result in paying too much. Even when there was a single bidder, the potential competition of other bidders could cause the winning bidder to pay too much. Roll (1986) hypothesized that even without competition, managers committed errors of overoptimism in evaluating merger opportunities due to hubris.

AGENCY PROBLEMS

Jensen and Meckling (1976) formulated the implications of agency problems. An agency problem arises when managers own only a fraction of the ownership shares of the firm. This partial ownership may cause managers to work less vigorously than otherwise and/or to consume more perquisites (luxurious offices, company cars, memberships in clubs) because the majority owners bear most of the cost. Furthermore, the argument goes, in large corporations with widely dispersed ownership there is not sufficient incentive for individual owners to expend the substantial resources required to monitor the behavior of managers.

Agency problems arise basically because contracts between managers (decision or control agents) and owners (risk bearers) cannot be written and enforced at no cost. Resulting (agency) costs include (1) costs of structuring a set of contracts, (2) costs of monitoring and controlling the behavior of agents by principals, (3) costs of bonding to guarantee that agents will make optimal decisions or principals will be compensated for the consequences of suboptimal decisions, and (4) the residual loss, that is, the welfare loss experienced by principals, arising from the divergence between agents' decisions and decisions to maximize principals' welfare. This residual loss can arise because the costs of full enforcement of contracts exceed the benefits.

Takeovers as a Solution to Agency Problems

The agency problems may be efficiently controlled by some organizational and market mechanisms. Fama and Jensen (1983) hypothesize that when a firm is characterized by separation of ownership and control, decision systems of the firm separate decision management (initiation and implementation) from decision control (ratification and monitoring) in order to limit the power of individual decision agents to expropriate shareholders' interests. Control functions are delegated to a board of directors by the shareholders, who retain approval rights on important matters, including board membership, mergers, and new stock issues.

Compensation arrangements and the market for managers may also mitigate the agency problem (Fama, 1980). Compensation can be tied to performance through such devices as bonuses and executive stock options. Managers carry their own reputation, and the labor market sets their wage levels based on performance reputation.

The stock market gives rise to an external monitoring device because stock prices summarize the implications of decisions made by managers. Low stock prices exert pressure on managers to change their behavior and to stay in line with the interests of shareholders (Fama and Jensen, 1983).

When these mechanisms are not sufficient to control agency problems, the market for takeovers provides an external control device of last resort (Manne, 1965). A takeover through a tender offer or a proxy fight enables outside managers to gain control of the decision processes of the target while circumventing existing managers and the board of directors. Manne emphasized mergers as a threat of takeover if a firm's management lagged in performance either because of inefficiency or because of agency problems.

Managerialism

In contrast to the view that mergers occur to control agency problems, some observers consider mergers as a manifestation of agency problems rather than as a solution. The managerialism explanation for conglomerate mergers was set forth most fully by Mueller (1969). Mueller hypothesized that managers are motivated to increase the size of their firms. He assumes that the compensation to managers is a function of the size (sales) of the firm, and he argues that managers therefore adopt a lower investment hurdle rate. In a study critical of earlier evidence, Lewellen and Huntsman (1970) present findings that managers' compensation is significantly correlated with the firm's profit rate, not its level of sales. Thus, the basic premise of the Mueller theory may not be valid.

The managerialism theory argues that the agency problem is not solved and that merger activity is a manifestation of the agency problems of inefficient, external investments by managers. An alternative view of the firm takes the opposite position on the role of mergers.

The modern theory of the firm suggests that firms exist because the market is not frictionless. Economies of scale arise out of indivisibilities. Managements are organized as teams based on firm-specific information on individual characteristics. Firm reputation is valuable because information is costly. Transaction costs lead to integration of operations. The existence of these imperfections (indivisibilities, information costs, and transaction costs) make it inefficient to have individual productive inputs move individually and separately across firms. Takeovers and mergers may be one means of efficiently redeploying corporate resources across firms while minimizing transaction costs and preserving organizational values. Product and labor market efficiency would not automatically result in changing market conditions and would require reallocation of resources across economic activities. Mergers and takeovers may represent one of the reallocation processes necessary to maintain or restore efficiency.

The Free Cash Flow Hypothesis (FCFH)

The problem of agency costs discussed in the preceding section also gives rise to the free cash flow hypothesis. Michael Jensen (1986, 1988) considered the agency costs associated with conflicts between managers and shareholders over the payout of free cash flow to be a major cause of takeover activity. According to Jensen, shareholders and managers (who are their agents) have serious conflicts of interest over the choice of corporate strategy. Agency costs resulting from these conflicts of interest can never be resolved perfectly. When these costs are large, takeovers may help reduce them, according to Jensen.

Jensen's free cash flow hypothesis (FCFH) is that the payout of free cash flow can serve an important role in dealing with the conflict between managers and shareholders. Jensen defines free cash flow as cash flow in excess of the amounts required to fund all projects that have positive net present values when discounted at the applicable cost of capital. He states that such free cash flow must be paid out to shareholders if the firm is to be efficient and to maximize share price. The payout of free cash flow (FCF) reduces the amount of resources under the control of managers and thereby reduces their power. In addition, they are then more likely to be subject to monitoring by the capital markets when they seek to finance additional investments with new capital.

In addition to paying out the current amount of excess cash, Jensen considers it important that managers bond their promise to pay out future cash flows. An effective way to do this is by debt creation without retention of the proceeds of the issue. Jensen argues that by issuing debt in exchange for stock, for example, managers bond their promise to pay out future cash flows more effectively than any announced dividend policy could achieve. Jensen emphasizes that the control function of debt is most important in organizations that generate large cash flows but whose outlook involves low growth or an actual reduction in size.

Jensen recognizes that increased leverage involves costs. It increases the risk of bankruptcy costs. There are agency costs of debt as well. One is for the firm to take on highly risky projects that benefit shareholders at the expense of bondholders. He defines an optimal debt-to-equity ratio where the marginal costs of debt are equal to the marginal benefits of debt.

For evidence Jensen begins with a review of a wide range of financial transactions. He cites an earlier study by Smith (1986a, 1986b) of 20 studies of stock price changes at announcements of transactions that involved a change of capital structure or dividend behavior. In a preliminary to a review of the evidence, he restates the prediction of the FCFH. For firms with positive FCF, stock prices will increase with unexpected increases in payouts to shareholders and decrease with unexpected decreases in payouts. The hypothesis predicts further that increasing tightness of debt service constraints, requiring the payout of future FCF will also increase stock prices.

Jensen argues that in virtually all of the 32 cases he summarizes, the direction of the effect on share price agreed with the predictions of the free cash flow hypothesis. Jensen states that his predictions do not apply to firms that have more profitable projects than cash flow to fund them. Nor does the theory apply to growth firms, only to firms that should be exiting some of their activities. Similarly, Jensen argues that in leveraged buyouts the high debt ratios taken on caused the increase in share price. But successful LBOs usually involved a turnaround—an improvement in company performance (Kaplan, 1989). Also, in LBOs the executive group was provided with a large ownership stake in the company, which would have substantial value if the LBO succeeded. It is likely that the incentives provided by the strong ownership stake and other characteristics of LBO situations accounted for the rise in value in addition to the bonding effects of the high debt ratios.

REDISTRIBUTION

The Berkovitch and Narayanan (BN) framework reflected in Table 6.2 does not include forms of redistribution such as taxes and market power or breach of trust (redistribution) with respect to bondholders and labor.

Tax Gains

Tax savings may be another motive for mergers, representing a form of redistribution from the government or public at large. Mergers may be used to substitute capital gains for ordinary income. In chapter 4, we discussed the role of the carryover of net operating losses and the value of tax credits that would otherwise be unused. We also discussed the use of a stepped-up tax basis for assets after a merger.

The empirical evidence establishes that tax benefits from a merger may be substantial. However, the evidence also establishes that tax advantages are not likely to be the major reason. Successful mergers are based on sound business and economic principles. Taxes are likely to be a reinforcing influence rather than the major force in a sound merger.

Market Power

An objection that is often raised to permitting a firm to increase its market share by merger is that the result will be "undue concentration" in the industry. The argument in brief is that if four or fewer firms account for a substantial percentage of an industry's sales, these firms will recognize the impact of their actions and policies on one another. This recognized interdependence will lead to a consideration of actions and reactions to changes in policy that will tend toward "tacit collusion." As a result, the prices and profits of the firms will contain monopoly elements. Thus, if economies from mergers cannot be established, it is assumed that the resulting increases in concentration may lead to monopoly returns. If economies can be demonstrated, then a comparison of increased efficiencies versus the effects of increased concentration must be made.

While some economists hold that high concentration, however measured, leads to some degree of monopoly, other economists hold that increased concentration is generally the *result* of active and intense competition. They argue further that the intense competition continues among large firms in concentrated industries because the dimensions of decision making with respect to prices, outputs, types of product, quality of product, service, and so on are so numerous and of so many gradations that neither tacit nor overt collusion could possibly be achieved.

When the antitrust authorities determine a merger to be anticompetitive in some sense, they can block the merger, as discussed in chapter 2. They can also block the merger by delays. Or they can approve it only if certain conditions are met, such as selling off part of the assets acquired.

Redistribution from Bondholders

Most of the studies find no evidence that shareholders gain in mergers and tender offers at the expense of bondholders (Asquith and Kim, 1982; Dennis and McConnell, 1986; Kim and McConnell, 1977). Even in debt-for-common stock exchanges, most of the evidence indicates that there is no negative impact on bondholders even though leverage has been increased. However, in leveraged buyouts in which debt is increased by very high orders of magnitude, there is evidence of negative impacts on bondholders (McDaniel, 1986; Warga and Welch, 1993). There is also dramatic evidence of negative effects on bondholders in individual cases and in patterns of downgrading

Table 6.4   Labor Cost Savings in the TWA Takeover (M = Million)

(1)	(2)	(3) Annual	(4) Total	(5)	(6)
		Annual	Total Annual	Rate	Annual
	Number of	Wage	Annual	Rate	Annual
Category	Employees	Rates	Wage Bill	Reductions	Savings
Pilots	3,000 @	$90,000 =	$270M	33%	$ 90M
Machinists	9,000 @	38,000 =	342M	15%	50M
Flight attendants	6,000 @	35,000 =	210M	28.5%	60M
				Total savings	$200M

(the *Wall Street Journal,* October 25, 1988). But the losses to bondholders, on average, represent only a small fraction of the gains to shareholders.

Redistribution from Labor

Redistribution from labor to shareholders has also received attention (Shleifer and Summers, 1988). The problem was formalized by Williamson (1988). The issues can be delineated by a case example based on the TWA–Icahn study outlined by Shleifer and Summers and covered in some detail in the press. The stylized facts can be summarized as shown in Table 6.4.

The original annual salary levels of the TWA pilots, machinists, and flight attendants are shown in column 3. When these are multiplied by the number of employees shown in column 2, we obtain the total annual wage bill shown in column 4. Column 5 is a stylized estimate of the salary cuts achieved by Icahn after he obtained control of TWA. They represent the percentage rate reductions in the annual compensation rates shown in column 3. Applying the rate reductions to the total annual wage bill yields the annual savings shown in column 6. The total annual savings appear to be roughly $200 million per year. The gains from the savings are shown in Table 6.5.

Before the takeover, TWA had 33 million shares of common stock outstanding, whose market price was $8 per share, giving a total market value of $264 million. The final block of shares obtained in the takeover were priced at $24. The gains to the participants can therefore be calculated. For the roughly 6.5 million shares Icahn purchased at an average price of $12, his gain would be the difference between $24 and $12, or $12 per share. For the 6.5 million shares Icahn purchased at $18, his gain would be $6 per share. The total gains to Icahn would therefore be $117 million. Similarly, the gains to the original shareholders are shown in column 3 of Table 6.5. The gains per share represent the difference between the $8 price and the Icahn purchase price. The gains to the original shareholders total $411 million. When these gains are added to the original value of the company, we obtain a total value for TWA after the takeover of $792 million.

Whether "breach of trust" or redistribution occurs depends on a number of variables, as shown in Table 6.6. The labor costs that were subsequently reduced

Table 6.5　Gain from Savings (M = Million)

(1) Original Icahn Purchases	(2) Gains to Icahn	(3) Gains to Shareholders	
6.5M @ $12	$12 × 6.5M = $ 78M	$ 4 × 6.5M = $ 26M	
6.5M @ $18	$ 6 × 6.5M = 39M	10 × 6.5M = 65M	
20.0M @ $24	0M	16 × 20M = 320M	
	$117M	$411M	
		117M	
		Gains	$528M
		Original value	264M
		Total value	$792M

Table 6.6　Alternative Sources of Increases in Value

Labor Costs	Product Market	Product Quality
Union power	Regulated	Down
Firm-specific productivity	Monopoly	Same
Management inefficiency	Competitive	Up

could have reflected union power, the firm-specific productivity of the employees, or a form of management inefficiency. Another set of variables that influences the interpretation of the case is whether the product markets in which airline services were being sold were competitive, monopolized, or operated under government regulation. A third set of variables to consider is whether, as a consequence of the takeover, the quality of the product services sold went down, went up, or remained the same.

In their analysis of the case, Shleifer and Summers (1988) gave emphasis to the interpretation that the high labor costs may have reflected the firm-specific productivity developed by the employees. With deregulation, new airline entrants hired employees at much lower rates than unionized airlines such as TWA were paying. But if the unionized employees at TWA were more efficient because of their firm-specific skills, the real cost of labor would not necessarily be any higher for TWA than for its nonunionized rivals. Under this scenario, Shleifer and Summers observed that a breach of trust is involved. This says that as a consequence of the takeover, investments made by employees to develop firm-specific skills are not paid their full value when previous labor contracts are broken by the new control group. If breach of trust is involved, then employees would take this into account when writing contracts in the future. It would affect their supply price. The consequence would be that labor costs in the airline industry would rise and prices to airline passengers and other users would be increased in the long run.

Another possible scenario is that the higher union wages at TWA reflect the previous period of regulation. One theory holds that in a regulated industry, employees, whether unionized or not, are able to extract wage increases. It is argued that either management will be soft on wage demands or the pressure of regulatory bodies will cause management to accept higher wages, which, in turn, the regulator permits to be passed on in higher prices. With subsequent deregulation, the competition of new entrants with lower costs will result in lower prices for products and services. The lower prices of competitors pressure firms with high-wage unionized employees to force wage reductions if they are to stay in business. To meet the lower prices of competitors, the monopoly rents that were formerly paid to unionized labor must be reduced. Under this scenario, lower employee compensation rates would not represent a breach of trust, but a restoration of more competitive conditions. It could be argued that the rise in share prices then simply enables shareholders to earn competitive returns on their investments. Consumers benefit from the lower competitive prices. The degree of the benefit to consumers and the extent to which the returns to shareholders are competitive depend on whether full competitive conditions are achieved in the airline industry. There appear to be some elements of regulation and supply restriction in space allocations at airport terminals. This would prevent the full realization of the competitive assumptions of the present scenario.

Still a third scenario, in addition to the "breach of trust" and the "end of regulation" theories, is the management inefficiency explanation. In this scenario the problem is that one of the manifestations of managerial inefficiency is the failure to bargain effectively with labor. The new competition with deregulation stimulates takeovers to provide new and efficient management. If the new management efficiencies include bargaining employee compensation down to competitive levels, shareholders should earn competitive rates of return and prices to consumers should be reduced to competitive levels. The price reductions might be expressed to some degree in the form of improved product quality.

Thus, whether the value increases associated with mergers and takeovers represent redistribution, particularly from labor, depends on which scenario is correct. If union power is reflected in monopoly rents to employees, then the employee cost reductions do not represent a breach of trust. They represent a movement from monopoly elements to competitive elements in the industry. If management inefficiency is involved, the introduction of efficient managers moves the industry from inefficiency to efficiency gains. Thus, whether breach of contract or other forms of expropriation are involved depends on the facts of individual industry circumstances.

Pension Fund Reversions

Pontiff, Shleifer, and Weisbach (PSW) (1990) studied another aspect of breach of trust. Their sample of 413 successful tender offers executed from March 1981 through May 1988 was taken from Jarrell (1988). This sample was matched to a list of pension plan reversions over $1 million from the Pension Benefit Guarantee Corporation (PBGC). In the two years following hostile takeovers, 15.1% of acquirers executed pension asset reversions compared with 8.4% in friendly takeovers.

Reversions occurred mostly in unit-benefit plans in which pension benefits are based on final wages (a pension bond). Reversions are less likely in flat-benefit plans based on number of years worked (no pension bond). Viewing the pension plan agreement as an implicit contract, terminations or returning excess funding to the firm benefits shareholders, and workers lose. Event return analysis finds positive returns to shareholders at the announcement of a pension plan termination. Pontiff, Shleifer, and Weisbach (1990) suggest that the stock market is surprised by this transfer of cash to the shareholders and expects that the funds will be used in positive net present value (NPV) projects. Similarly, share prices rise on reversion announcements, indicating that the market expects the funds to be used more in the shareholders' interest. Reversions, on average, account for about 11% of the takeover premium in cases in which they actually occurred. Pontiff, Shleifer, and Weisbach conclude that reversions are not a major source of takeover gains.

SUMMARY

Many theories have been advanced to explain why mergers and other forms of restructuring take place. Efficiency theories imply social gains from M&A activity in addition to the gains for participants. The **differential efficiency** theory says that more efficient firms will acquire less efficient firms and realize gains by improving their efficiency; this implies excess managerial capabilities in the acquiring firm. Differential efficiency would be most likely to be a factor in mergers between firms in related industries where the need for improvement could be more easily identified. The related **inefficient management** theory suggests that target management is so inept that virtually any management could do better, which could be an explanation for mergers between firms in unrelated industries.

The **operating synergy** theory postulates that there are economies of scale or of scope and that mergers help achieve levels of activities at which these economies can be obtained. It includes the concept of complementarity of capabilities. For example, one firm might be strong in R&D but weak in marketing, while another has a strong marketing department without the R&D capability. Merging the two firms would result in operating synergy. The **financial synergy** theory hypothesizes complementarities between merging firms, not in management capabilities but in matching the availability of investment opportunities to internal cash flows. A firm in a declining industry will produce large cash flows because there are few attractive investment opportunities. A growth industry has more investment opportunities than cash with which to finance them. The merged firm will have a lower cost of capital due to the lower cost of internal funds as well as possible risk reduction, savings in flotation costs, and improvements in capital allocation.

Diversification as a motive for mergers differs from shareholder portfolio diversification. Shareholders can efficiently spread their investments and risk among industries, so there is no need for firms to diversify for the sake of their shareholders.

Managers and other employees, however, are at greater risk if the single industry in which their firm operates should decline; their firm-specific human capital is not transferable. Therefore, firms may diversify to encourage firm-specific human capital investments that make their employees more valuable and productive and to increase the probability that the organization and reputation capital of the firm will be preserved by transfer to another line of business owned by the firm in the event its initial industry declines. The average diversified firm has been valued at a discount compared to a portfolio of comparable single-segment firms. Alternative explanations are found in the literature.

The theory of **strategic alignment to changing environments** says that mergers take place in response to environmental changes. External acquisitions of needed capabilities allow firms to adapt more quickly and with less risk than developing capabilities internally.

The **undervaluation** theory states that mergers occur when the market value of target firm stock for some reason does not reflect its true or potential value or its value in the hands of an alternative management. The q-ratio is also related to the undervaluation theory. Firms can acquire assets for expansion more cheaply by buying the stock of existing firms than by buying or building the assets when the target's stock price is below the replacement cost of its assets. Some bidders may seek targets with high q's to obtain the capabilities that create value.

The **information** theory attempts to explain why target shares seem to be permanently revalued upward in a tender offer whether or not it is successful. The information hypothesis says that the tender offer conveys information to the market that the target shares are undervalued. Alternatively, the tender offer sends information to target management that inspires them to implement a more efficient strategy on their own. Another school holds that the revaluation is not really permanent but only reflects the likelihood that another acquirer will materialize for a synergistic combination.

Positive valuation errors in bidding for companies represent the winner's curse. Roll (1986) analyzes the effect in takeover activity. Postulating strong market efficiency in all markets, the prevailing market price of the target already reflects the full value of the firm. The higher valuation of the bidders (over the target's true economic value), he states, results from hubris—their excessive self-confidence (pride, arrogance). Hubris is one of the factors that causes the winner's curse phenomenon to occur in takeover bids.

Agency problems may result from a conflict of interest between managers and shareholders or between shareholders and debt holders. A number of organization and market mechanisms serve to discipline self-serving managers, and takeovers are viewed as the discipline of last resort. **Managerialism,** on the other hand, views takeovers as a manifestation of the agency problem rather than its solution. It suggests that self-serving managers make ill-conceived combinations solely to increase firm size and their own compensation. The hubris theory is another variant on the agency cost theory; it implies acquiring firm managers commit errors of over-optimism (winner's curse) in bidding for targets.

Jensen's **free cash flow** hypothesis says that takeovers take place because of the conflicts between managers and shareholders over the payout of free cash flows. The hypothesis posits that free cash flows (that is, cash flows in excess of investment needs) should be paid out to shareholders, reducing the power of management and subjecting managers to the scrutiny of the public capital markets more frequently. Debt-for-stock exchange offers are viewed as a means of bonding the managers' promise to pay out future cash flows to shareholders.

Another theory of the value increases to shareholders in takeovers is that the gains come at the expense of other stakeholders in the firm. Expropriated stakeholders under the **redistribution** hypothesis may include bondholders, the government (in the case of tax reductions), and employees.

Tax effects can be important in mergers, although they do not play a major role in explaining M&A activity overall. Carryover of net operating losses and tax credits, stepped-up asset basis, and the substitution of capital gains for ordinary income are among the tax motivations for mergers. Looming inheritance taxes may also motivate the sale of privately held firms with aging owners.

The **market power** theory holds that merger gains are the result of increased concentration leading to collusion and monopoly effects. Empirical evidence on whether industry concentration causes reduced competition is not conclusive. There is much evidence that concentration is the result of vigorous and continuing competition, which causes the composition of the leading firms to change over time.

QUESTIONS

6.1 Briefly explain how the various efficiency theories of mergers differ and how they are alike.

6.2 Explain the differences between managerial synergy, operating synergy, and financial synergy, and their relationships to different types of mergers.

6.3 How are agency problems and managerialism related? What is the hypothesized effect of each on merger activity?

6.4 Discuss the hubris hypothesis in terms of efficiency theories of mergers.

6.5 What is the rationale for the use of such measures as the four-firm concentration ratio and the Herfindahl index?

6.6 How do tax considerations affect mergers and their structuring?

6.7 What is the "breach of trust" theory of merger gains?

6.8 Using option pricing theory, why is leverage likely to increase after two firms with uncorrelated cash flow streams combine?

Case 6.1   Boeing's Acquisition of McDonnell Douglas

On December 16, 1996, Boeing agreed to acquire McDonnell Douglas by paying 0.65 share of Boeing for each share of McDonnell Douglas. The deal was valued at $13.3 billion. It was stated that the combined employment of 200,000 was not expected to be reduced, although a redeployment of workers would take place. In 1995 Boeing had commercial aircraft sales of about $14 billion and $5.6 billion from defense and space contracts. McDonnell Douglas had commercial aircraft revenues of about $4 billion with about $10 billion in military aircraft and other defense revenues. St. Louis would be the headquarters for the defense operations; Seattle would be the headquarters for the commercial.

It was stated that this acquisition would enable Boeing to develop a better balance in its mix between commercial and defense business. The executives judged that they would be stronger competitors in the world commercial aviation business. Seventy percent of Boeing's commercial business was outside the United States; fifty percent for McDonnell Douglas. Savings of at least a billion dollars a year would be achieved by combining the defense operations. Employment in research and development (R&D) was expected to increase rather than decrease.

On the day of the announcement of the acquisition (December 16, 1996), the common stock of Boeing rose by about $6 per share and the price of McDonnell Douglas stock rose by about $10 a share. The number of common shares of Boeing outstanding was about 344 million. For McDonnell Douglas the number of shares was 223.6 million.

QUESTIONS

1. By how much did the market value of the two companies increase on the announcement date?
2. Why did "the market" evaluate this combination as value-increasing?
3. What subsequently happened, and why?

REFERENCES

Arrow, K. J., "Vertical Integration and Communication," *Bell Journal of Economics,* 6, Spring 1975, pp. 173–183.

Asquith, P., and E. H. Kim, "The Impact of Merger Bids on the Participating Firms' Security Holders," *Journal of Finance,* 37, 1982, pp. 1209–1228.

Bagnoli, Mark, and Barton Lipman, "Successful Takeovers without Exclusion," *Review of Financial Studies,* 1, 1988, pp. 89–110.

Berger, Philip G., and Eli Ofek, "Diversification's Effect on Firm Value," *Journal of Financial Economics,* 6, 1995, pp. 39–66.

Berkovitch, Elazar, and M. P. Narayanan, "Motives for Takeovers: An Empirical Investigation," *Journal of Financial and Quantitative Analysis,* 28, September 1993, pp. 347–362.

Bradley, M., "Interfirm Tender Offers and the Market for Corporate Control," *Journal of Business,* 53, October 1980, pp. 345–376.

———, A. Desai, and E. H. Kim, "The Rationale Behind Interfirm Tender Offers: Information or Synergy?" *Journal of Financial Economics,* 11, April 1983, pp. 183–206.

———, "Synergistic Gains from Corporate Acquisitions and Their Division Between the Stockholders of Target and Acquiring Firms," *Journal of Financial Economics,* 21, 1988, pp. 3–40.

Capen, E. C., R. V. Clapp, and W. M. Campbell, "Competitive Bidding in High-Risk Situations," *Journal of Petroleum Technology,* 23, June 1971, pp. 641–653.

Chowdhry, Bhagwan, and Narasimhan Jegadeesh, "Pre-Tender Offer Share Acquisition Strategy in Takeovers," *Journal of Financial and Quantitative Analysis,* 29, 1994, pp. 117–129.

Dennis, Debra K., and John J. McConnell, "Corporate Mergers and Security Returns," *Journal of Financial Economics,* 16, 1986, pp. 143–187.

Dodd, P., and R. Ruback, "Tender Offers and Stockholder Returns: An Empirical Analysis," *Journal of Financial Economics,* 5, December 1977, pp. 351–374.

Fama, E. F., "Agency Problems and the Theory of the Firm," *Journal of Political Economy,* 88, April 1980, pp. 288–307.

————, and M. C. Jensen, "Separation of Ownership and Control," *Journal of Law and Economics,* 26, 1983, pp. 301–325.

————, "Organizational Forms and Investment Decisions," *Journal of Financial Economics,* 14, 1985, pp. 101–119.

Grossman, S. J., and Q. D. Hart, "Takeover Bids, the Free-Rider Problem and the Theory of the Corporation," *Bell Journal of Economics,* 11, Spring 1980, pp. 42–64.

Gulati, R., N. Nohria, and A. Zaheer, "Strategic Networks," *Strategic Management Journal,* 21, March 2000, pp. 199–201.

Hirshleifer, David, and Sheridan Titman, "Share Tendering Strategies and the Success of Hostile Takeover Bids," *Journal of Political Economy,* 98, 1990, pp. 295–324.

Jarrell, G. A., Testimony in the Case of *RP Acquisition Corp. v. Staley Continental and Michael Harkins.* Testimony in the United States District Court for the District of Delaware (Civil Action No. 88-190), 1988.

Jensen, M. C., "Agency Costs of Free Cash Flow, Corporate Finance and Takeovers," *American Economic Review,* 76, May 1986, pp. 323–329.

————, "The Takeover Controversy: Analysis and Evidence," Chapter 20 in J. C. Coffee, Jr., L. Lowenstein, and S. Rose-Ackerman, eds., *Knights, Raiders, and Targets,* New York: Oxford University Press, 1988.

————, and W. Meckling, "Theory of the Firm: Managerial Behavior, Agency Costs and Ownership Structure," *Journal of Financial Economics,* 3, October 1976, pp. 305–360.

Kaplan, Steven, "The Effects of Management Buyouts on Operating Performance and Value," *Journal of Financial Economics,* 24, 1989, pp. 217–254.

Kim, E. H., and J. McConnell, "Corporate Merger and the Coinsurance of Corporate Debt," *Journal of Finance,* 32, 1977, pp. 349–365.

Klein, B., R. Crawford, and A. Alchian, "Vertical Integration, Appropriable Rents, and the Competitive Contracting Process," *Journal of Law and Economics,* 21, October 1978, pp. 297–326.

Lamont, Owen A., and Christopher Polk, "The Diversification Discount: Cash Flows vs. Returns," NBER working paper no. 7396, October 1999.

Lang, Larry, and Rene Stulz, "Tobin's Q, Corporate Diversification, and Firm Performance," *Journal of Political Economy,* 102, 1994, pp. 1248–1280.

Levy, H., and M. Sarnat, "Diversification, Portfolio Analysis and the Uneasy Case for Conglomerate Mergers," *Journal of Finance,* September 1970, pp. 795–802.

Lewellen, W. G., and B. Huntsman, "Managerial Pay and Corporate Performance," *American Economic Review,* 60, September 1970, pp. 710–720.

Lieberman, M. B., "The Learning Curve and Pricing in the Chemical Processing Industries," *Rand Journal of Economics,* 15, 1984, pp. 213–228.

McCauley, R. N., J. S. Ruud, F. Iacono, *Dodging Bullets,* Cambridge, MA, MIT Press: 1999.

McDaniel, Morey W., "Bondholders and Corporate Governance," *The Business Lawyer,* 41, February 1986, pp. 413–460.

Manne, H. G., "Mergers and the Market for Corporate Control," *Journal of Political Economy,* 73, April 1965, pp. 110–120.

Mueller, D. C., "A Theory of Conglomerate Mergers," *Quarterly Journal of Economics,* 83, 1969, pp. 643–659.

Nickell, S. J., *The Investment Decisions of Firms,* Oxford, England: Cambridge University Press, 1978.

Nielsen, J. F., and R. W. Melicher, "A Financial Analysis of Acquisition and Merger Premiums," *Journal of Financial and Quantitative Analysis,* 8, March 1973, pp. 139–162.

Pontiff, Jeffrey, Andrei Shleifer, and Michael S. Weisbach, "Reversions of Excess Pension Assets after Takeovers," *RAND Journal of Economics,* 21, Winter 1990, pp. 600–613.

Prescott, E. C., and M. Visscher, "Organization Capital," *Journal of Political Economy,* 88, June 1980, pp. 446–461.

Roll, Richard, "The Hubris Hypothesis of Corporate Takeovers," *Journal of Business,* 59, April 1986, pp. 197–216.

———, "Empirical Evidence on Takeover Activity and Shareholder Wealth," Chapter 5 in Thomas E. Copeland, ed., *Modern Finance & Industrial Economics,* New York: Basil Blackwell, 1987, pp. 74–91.

Rosen, Sherwin, "Learning by Experience as Joint Production," *Quarterly Journal of Economics,* August 1972, pp. 366–382.

Shleifer, A., and L. H. Summers, "Breach of Trust in Hostile Takeovers," Chapter 2 in A. J. Auerbach, ed., *Corporate Takeovers: Causes and Consequences,* Chicago: University of Chicago Press, 1988.

Shleifer, Andrei, and Robert W. Vishny, "Large Shareholders and Corporate Control," *Journal of Political Economy,* 94, June 1986, pp. 461–488.

Smith, Clifford W., Jr., "Investment Banking and the Capital Acquisition Process,"

Journal of Financial Economics, 15, January/February 1986a, pp. 3–29.

———, "Raising Capital: Theory and Evidence," *Midland Corporate Finance Journal,* Spring 1986b, pp. 6–22.

Spence, A. Michael, "Job Market Signalling," *Quarterly Journal of Economics,* 87, August 1973, pp. 355–379.

———, "Competitive and Optimal Responses to Signals: Analysis of Efficiency and Distribution," *Journal of Economic Theory,* 7, March 1974, pp. 296–332.

Warga, Arthur, and Ivo Welch, "Bondholder Losses in Leveraged Buyouts," *Review of Financial Studies,* 6, 1993, pp. 959–982.

Williamson, O. E., *Markets and Hierarchies: Analysis and Antitrust Implications,* New York: Free Press, 1975.

———, "Comment," Chapter 2 in A. J. Auerbach, ed., *Corporate Takeovers: Causes and Consequences,* Chicago: University of Chicago Press, 1988, pp. 61–67.

Appendix A

A Chemical Industry Case Study

The chemical industry provides an excellent case study illustrating the concepts of Chapter 5 on strategy and Chapter 6 on theories of M&A. This appendix illustrates how patterns of restructuring and M&As have evolved in the chemical industry.

CHANGE FORCES

The major change forces that have propelled the increased pace of economic adjustment processes are technological change, the globalization of markets, and favorable financial and economic environments. The new technologies include advances in computers and related products that have transformed industrial processes, product proliferation, and new ways of doing business, illustrated by the Internet and "the Wal-Mart way." Improvements and cost reductions in communication and transportation have created a global economy. Industry boundaries have become blurred, with new competitive impacts coming from diverse and changing sources. These growing forces of competition have been reflected in deregulation in major industries such as financial services, medical services, and airlines and other forms of transportation. Strong economic growth, relatively favorable interest rate and financing environments, and rising equity and asset prices have facilitated the adjustment processes described.

CHARACTERISTICS OF THE CHEMICAL INDUSTRIES

Although the adjustment processes have followed the same general patterns exhibited by other segments of the economy, distinctive characteristics have influenced how the change forces have operated in the chemical industry. A rich literature is available on the characteristics of the chemical industries (see References to this appendix).

"Mergers and acquisitions" (M&As) as a shorthand for adjustment and adaptive processes in firms are related to the economic characteristics of their industries. The U.S. chemical industry produces almost 2% of U.S. gross domestic product, making it the largest contributor to GDP among U.S. manufacturing industries (Arora, Landau, and Rosenberg, 1998, p. 6). The chemical industry is a high tech, R&D-oriented industry that receives about 12% of patents granted annually. It produces over 70,000 different products. Few industries exhibit the diversity and complexity of the chemical industry.

Certain characteristics are significant for an understanding of M&A processes within the chemical industries: The industry has many distinctive segments, a number of which overlap with the oil and other energy industries as well as with pharmaceuticals and life sciences products. Two major types of firms have been identified: *All-around* companies operate in many areas. *Focused* firms operate in downstream specialized segments.

Research and development performs a key role in the long-term viability of chemical firms. Because new R&D discoveries often do not fit into the firm's core businesses, the organization may require time to adjust effectively to the new products and may delay achieving significant economies of scope. A series of R&D efforts that result in "dry holes" will have a negative impact on sales and profitability, making the firm vulnerable to takeover.

In the chemical industry, innovations are imitated relatively rapidly by large competitors. The commoditization of products may occur relatively soon after innovations. This results in the familiar economic pattern of cobweb responses. Favorable profit margins induce large additions to capacity in existing and new entry firms, resulting in downward pressures on prices and returns. This problem has been aggravated in those segments of the chemical industry in which the process development of new products is performed by specialized engineering firms (SEFs) capable of installing turnkey chemical production plants. This speeds the diffusion of process information, making it more difficult for innovators to long sustain a competitive advantage. These market processes take place in a global setting and can affect even niche segments of the industry.

Chemical companies interact with other industries. As petrochemicals became a high percentage of chemical company production, oil refining and the chemical industry converged. Large oil companies were able to expand into the chemical industry more easily than the chemical companies could expand into oil refining. (Siu and Weston, 1996). The switch from coal to oil allowed the development of many organic chemicals, which revolutionized the industry with new products. In recent years, some firms shifted from oil to life sciences products. Synergies between the chemical business and life sciences activities have not been well established.

Chemicals is a "keystone" industry. Many products are related to chemicals. As an R&D-intensive industry, the chemical industry has been a source of new technologies that have diffused over many other industries. Chemicals are building blocks at every level of production in major economic segments of agriculture, construction, manufacturing, and the service industries (Arora, Landau, and Rosenberg, 1998). Chemical industry technological innovations have been important in individual industries, specifically textiles, petroleum refining, agriculture, rubber, automobiles, metals, health services, and construction.

The international competitiveness of other U.S. industries depends upon a strong U.S. chemical industry that can supply critical products at high quality and competitive prices. For a number of chemical products, competition in foreign markets requires operations in foreign countries. Acquisitions are often a least cost method of establishing operations abroad and/or a method of acquiring new capabilities and new product lines.

One of the adverse economic trends affecting the chemical industry stems from the changing structure of the economy. The increase in the service industries relative to manufacturing, construction, basic industries, and other major users of chemicals has caused a decline in the growth of chemical shipments in response to changes in GDP growth (U.S. Department of Commerce/ITC, 1999). In the 1960s, a 1% change in GDP growth was associated with a 2.9% change in growth of chemical shipments. By 1998, the 2.9% ratio had declined to 0.9%. Chemical shipments are not keeping up with the growth in the economy.

Thus, secular trends represent a retardation factor for chemical industry growth. This is a massive influence difficult to overcome. This negative secular influence is aggravated further by the relative rapidity of commoditization of new products.

Entry into the chemical industries has been relatively easy. As noted, oil and gas companies have made substantial expansion into important segments of the chemical industry. The boundaries between pharmaceutical and chemical firms are blurred. Many important pharmaceutical firms started life as chemical companies. Important entrants into individual segments of the chemical industry have been established chemical, oil, and pharmaceutical firms. Thus, although some individual chemical firms may have a large market share in individual product segments of the chemical industry, their price and production policies are severely constrained by active and potential entrants. An important economic implication is that the relevant market for measuring the economic position of individual companies is the global chemical industry, not individual product segments in individual national markets. Especially important are foreign firms, many of which can make rapid entry by acquiring domestic firms whose capabilities provide an immediate market position with the potential for powerful expansion by combining strengths.

In many cases new entrants into a segment have purchased activities divested by an established chemical firm. This is an empirical pattern for which the explanations are complex. Differences in bundles of capabilities and environments cause some activities to shrivel and fade in one firm and yet expand and thrive in another. Thus, substantial evidence supports the conclusion that entry into chemical industries is relatively easy, and movement between segments is continuously taking place.

M&AS IN THE CHEMICAL INDUSTRY

Mergers and acquisitions have historically performed a significant role in the evolution of the chemical industry. In Germany in 1926, the largest producers of organic chemicals consolidated into IG Farben. Apparently this was the response of large dye makers to increasing competition from American companies (Da Rin, 1998). After World War II, the Allied powers restructured German industry. IG Farben was broken into its major constituent firms: Bayer, BASF, and Hoechst.

Also in 1926, the British government induced a merger to form Imperial Chemical Industries (ICI). Brunner, Mond was combined with another strong firm, Nobel, and joined with much weaker firms, United Alkali and the British Dye Corporation. This powerful aggregation had immediate access to the public equity markets. But ICI suffered declines in market share over the years. A possible explanation is underperforming management with a lack of effective corporate governance due to its widely diffused ownership (Da Rin, 1998). In 1993 ICI spun off Zeneca, its pharmaceutical division. In May 1997 ICI bought four companies whose sales were 20% of ICI but whose operating profits were 68% of ICI. The four companies were National Starch, Quest, Unichema, and Crosfields. ICI's planned sale of $1 billion of chemical assets to DuPont and NL Industries in early 1999 was blocked by the U.S. Federal Trade Commission.

At the end of World War I, DuPont had substantial liquid assets from the wartime profits of its explosives division. This strong financial position and effective management led to both innovation and diversification. This history is set forth in a detailed study covering the history of DuPont from 1902 to 1980 (Hounshell and Smith, 1988).

During the 1980s, DuPont was involved in over 50 acquisitions and joint ventures, investing more than $10 billion. A major part of this investment was the purchase of Conoco and Consolidation Coal. In 1998 DuPont began spinning off Conoco. In 1999 it spent $7.7 billion to buy the 80% of Pioneer Hi-bred International it did not already own. *Fortune* Magazine (April 26, 1999, p. 154) called this "trading oil for corn," saying that DuPont "hopes to use the corn grown with Pioneer seeds as the feedstocks for its bio-engineered chemicals." A DuPont release of July 7, 1999, announced plans to consolidate its coatings manufacturing facilities and to reorganize "other business activities" over a period of nine months following the $1.8 billion acquisition of Herberts, a European coatings supplier.

These brief capsule histories of three major firms in the chemical industry illustrate the full panoply of acquisitions, alliances, restructuring, divestitures, and spin-offs. In the *Fortune* list of the global 500 (August 3, 1998), DuPont was ranked number 1 in chemicals, with sales of $41.3 billion. The offspring of IG Farben were ranked in the next three positions, each of which had sales of about $32 billion. Dow was fifth, with sales of $20 billion. ICI held the sixth position, with sales of $18 billion. It is interesting to note that ranks 7 through 12 were each from different countries, with sales of $15.4 billion for Rhone-Poulenc (France), $14.1 billion for Mitsubishi Chemical (Japan), $13.9 for Montedison (Italy), $13.6 for Norsk Hydro (Norway), $12.3 billion for Akzo Nobel (Netherlands), and $11.6 billion for Henkel (Germany).

The size, complexity, dynamism, and turbulence of the chemical industry would be expected to produce a high level of merger activity. Our studies demonstrate that in any given year in the United States, five industries account for about 50% or more of total M&A activity by dollar value

(*Mergerstat,* annual volumes). Yet, between 1981 and 1998, the category chemical, paints, and coatings was in the top five in only one year, placing number 5 in 1986. Over the total period 1981 to 1998, chemicals, paints, and coatings ranked 17th, accounting for some $83 billion of M&A activity in relation to a U.S. total for the 18 years of $4.7 trillion. The top three industries were banking and finance with $641 billion, communications with $385 billion, and oil and gas with $345 billion.

A partial resolution of the paradox between the size and complexity of the chemical industry and its relatively low ranking in M&A activity is provided by classification ambiguities. For example, a Chemical Manufacturer's Association listing of 31 mergers and acquisitions of over $500 million in 1998 includes pharmaceutical and other life sciences firms as well as oil and gas industry combinations. The two major producers of M&A statistical compilations, Mergerstat and the Securities Data Corporation, have separate categories for the latter two groups. Using the broader definition of chemical and related industries as a category establishes this area as one of the top ranking ones in M&A activity. Change forces have impacted industries generally but have had greater effect in industries such as chemicals that are characterized by a high rate of innovations in both processes and products as well as relatively easy entry conditions.

A number of important roles have been played by M&As in the chemical industry. They have been (1) to strengthen an existing product line by adding capabilities or extending geographic markets; (2) to add new product lines; (3) to make foreign acquisitions to obtain new capabilities or a needed presence in local markets; (4) to obtain key scientists for the development of particular R&D programs; (5) to reduce costs by eliminating duplicate activities and shrinking capacity to improve sales-to-capacity relationships; (6) to divest activities that were not performing well; (7) to harvest successful operations in advance of competitor programs to expand capacity and output; (8) to round out product lines; (9) to strengthen distribution systems; (10) to move the firm into new growth areas; (11) to expand to the critical mass required for effective utilization of large investment outlays; (12) to create broader technology platforms; and (13) to achieve vertical integration.

In summary, M&As may enable firms to revisit and refresh their strategic visions. M&As may also reduce the time required to catch up to other firms that have developed new technologies, new processes, and new products. M&As enable a firm to make changes more rapidly. The cost of new projects is known at the time of purchase. By obtaining a going organization, the delays in the learning process are reduced or avoided.

However, M&As and internal new product programs are not mutually exclusive. One can reinforce the other. A disadvantage of internal programs is that the firm may lack the requisite experience, it may not have an effective operating organization in place, and the time required for achieving a profitable market position is uncertain.

Acquisitions have different kinds of disadvantages. Despite due diligence, it is impossible for the buyer to know as much about what is being acquired as the seller. Implementing two organizations is not easy. Considerable executive talent and time commitments are required. Implementation problems are magnified if the organizational cultures are different. This is often a serious challenge in cross-border transactions.

Joint ventures have been used widely in the chemical industries. Since the areas of expertise are so diverse, it is difficult for a firm to embrace all of them. Often the size of the investment and the risks involved may be reduced by combining the different areas of expertise and capabilities of different companies. Joint ventures, strategic alliances, and the joint use of facilities can minimize investment outlays and magnify capabilities. For every merger, there are many more joint venture types of activities. By forming alliances and joint ventures, outlays and risks are reduced, learning may be achieved, and returns can be attractive.

We emphasize that M&As represent a shorthand for a wide range of adjustments and adaptations to changing technologies, changing markets, and changing competitive thrusts. The many forms of restructuring include spin-offs and split-ups to realign organization systems. The goal is to group activities so that the benefits of relatedness, focus, and the development of distinctive and superior expertise in each area of activity can be achieved. Organization restructuring is also used to group related activities and to better measure their performance. Compensation systems can thereby be more effectively related to performance.

Restructuring and M&As include changes in financial policies and effectiveness. One aspect is to review cost structures to improve the utilization of investments in receivables, inventories, and plant and equipment. The other side of this coin is effective utilization of financing sources. Dow Chemical is legendary for its innovative use of dividend policy, equity financing, and aggressive debt leverage to facilitate its growth.

The chemical industry has also made considerable use of highly leveraged restructuring such as leveraged buyouts (LBOs) and management buyouts (MBOs) (Lane, 1993). The key logic of LBOs (covered in chapter 16) can be summarized. A company is identified that has stable earnings or earnings growth potential from an improvement in strategy, operations, or management (a turnaround potential). High leverage is initially employed to finance investment requirements needed for the turnaround and to buy out previous owners. Management is given an opportunity to buy equity shares representing a significant fraction of the shrunken ownership base. The stable or augmented future cash flows are used to pay down debt and to increase the portion of cash flows available to equity holders. The aim is to increase equity prices so that within at least three years the company could be taken public again, realizing large gains to the organizers of the buyout and management.

In the early 1980s there were opportunities to buy segments or companies at low price-to-cash flow multiples, with opportunities to improve efficiency and financial performance. Early successes led to the expansion of large buyout funds, which in turn led to competition for the dwindling opportunities and payment of higher price-to-cash flow multiples. LBO activity revived in the 1990s with greater sophistication and more direct participation by financial investors. Cain Chemical and Vista Chemical were financial groups active in the chemical industry.

A scaled-down version of LBOs has been the use of share repurchases. The most prevalent form is open market repurchases of a firm's own shares. The announcement of share repurchases is taken as a signal of future improvements in cash flows. Such announcements on average have stimulated significant immediate share price increases as well as superior market performance in the ensuing three years. The subsequent improvement in cash flows makes share repurchase announcements credible signals on average.

However, some manipulative financial engineering may also be involved. The reduction in the number of shares outstanding will increase reported earnings per share even if total net income does not increase. For given net income levels, the ratio

of net income to shareholders' equity is artificially increased when the market-to-book ratio exceeds 1, since the reduction of book equity is magnified. For example, if book equity is $10 per share and the market price is $30 per share, the reduction in shareholders' equity from a share repurchase will be $30 per share, according to usual accounting practice, shrinking book equity per share by a factor of 3. For the share repurchase practice to remain a credible signal of improved future cash flows, this mechanical aspect must be supported by substance—superior operating performance and good cash flows. One positive aspect is that returning funds to shareholders may create confidence that management is responsibly giving shareholders the opportunity to invest the funds in alternatives that may provide higher returns. Another positive impact is that share repurchases may be regarded as a signal of broader management efforts to improve the efficiency and profitability of the firm.

We find evidence that M&As and restructuring in their broadest meaning have been important in the chemical industries. In one study we analyzed the chemical companies followed by Value Line in three groups: basic chemicals, diversified chemicals, and specialty chemicals. We found that every firm in their listings had engaged in one or more of the forms of restructuring—M&As in the broad sense described above. The results are summarized in Table 6A.1.

It is clear that each of these firms from this Value Line sample has engaged in some form of acquisition, divestiture, joint venture, share repurchase, etc. These many forms of M&A and restructuring in the chemical industry parallel similar activities in other industries. The nature of the adjustment processes can be made more spe-

Table 6A.1   M&A Adjustments in the Value Line Chemical Industries

Company	Restructuring Activity
Basic Chemical Companies	
Dow Chemical	Acquired Mycogen
DuPont	Divestiture of Conoco
Union Carbide	Repurchased shares
Diversified Companies	
Air Products	Repurchased shares
Eastman Chemical	Made deal to acquire Lawter International
W. R. Grace	Purchased Sealed Air
Imperial Chemical (ICI)	Sold commodity chemical divisions
Minnesota Mining and Manufacturing	Repurchased shares
Norsk Hydro	Made tender offer for Saga Petroleum
Novo-Nordisk	Various joint ventures
PPG Industries	Made or announced 15 acquisitions since 1997
Pall Corp.	Repurchased shares
Rhone-Poulenc	Planned merger with Hoechst
Specialty Companies	
Airgas	Acquired Oxygen Sales & Service
Crompton & Knowles	Agreed to merger with Witco Corp.
Engelhard	Repurchased shares
Great Lakes Chemical	Purchased NSC Technologies
Hercules	Purchased BetzDearborn
International Flavors and Fragrance	Divesting aroma chemicals
Morton International	Purchased by Rohm & Haas
Nalco Chemical	Purchased by Suez Lyonnaise
Praxair	Acquired division of GP Industries
RPM	Repurchased shares
Rohm & Haas	Purchased Morton International
Sherwin-Williams	Purchased Marson Chilena
Sigma-Aldrich	Purchased Genosys
Valspar	Acquired Dexter

cific. Table 6A.2 briefly describes the reasons for M&A activities listed in Table 6A.1, augmented by a Chemical Manufacturers Association (CMA) list of 31 M&A deals of over $500 million that took place in 1998.

The diverse reasons for the merger activities described in Table 6A.2 are summarized in Table 6A.3. They reflect general change forces as well as the particular characteristics of the chemical industry. The central influences are improving technology, broadening capabilities, adjusting to industry structure change, responding to the pressures of commoditization of products.

Table 6A.2   Chemical Industry—Reasons for Merging or Divesting

Companies	Reasons	Type*
Dow Chemical/Mycogen	Leverage Mycogen's biotech capabilities throughout Dow and merge agricultural and medicine operations.	A, C, F, H
DuPont/Conoco (spin-off)	To avoid the volatility of the oil and gas industry.	F, J
Eastman/Lawter	To pursue growth opportunities in specialty chemicals, which are characterized by higher earnings and lower cyclicality.	A, C, F, I
W.R. Grace/Sealed Air	Combines specialty chemical business for synergies, expanded global reach, ability to compete in changing marketplace.	F, I
Imperial Chemical (divestitures)	Strategic shift toward speciality products and paints.	B, I
Norsk Hydro/Saga Petroleum	Greater activity, lower cost, and increased expertise in the oil and gas industry.	F
PPG Industries (15 acquisitions)	To sustain growth with profitable acquisitions in higher margin businesses.	A, B, C, I
Rhone-Poulenc/Hoechst	Focus on life sciences and divest all remaining chemical businesses.	A, B, I, J
Airgas/Oxygen Sales and Service	Invest in core distribution segment.	D, F
Crompton & Knowles/Witco	Consolidated industry size increases strategic options and lowers cost of capital.	C, F
Hercules/Betz Dearborn	Combined company will be able to meet paper manufacturers' growing demand for integrated services.	K
Rohm & Haas/Morton	Expanded product lines, greater technical depth, and broader geographic reach.	C, K
Suez Lyonnaise/Nalco	Will be better able to provide customers with range of services they desire; will take advantage of cross-selling opportunities.	F, K
Praxair/GP Industries	Strategic acquisition that is part of company focus on healthcare as a key growth area.	B, C, I
Sherwin-Williams/Marson Chilena	Acquisition is part of the companies' continued interest in Chile and South America.	D
Sigma-Aldrich/Genosys	Acquisition is part of Sigma's strategy to move into the molecular biology field.	A, B, I
Lyondell/Arco Chemical	Gains preeminent global market position in propylene oxide. Goal is to reduce cyclicality of earnings by broadening the product mix. Provides a platform for future domestic and international growth.	D, F
Equistar II (combination)	Diversify product line, improve distribution network.	F, K

*See Table 6A.3.

Table 6A.3   Reasons for Mergers

A. Technologically dynamic industries to seize opportunities in industries with developing technologies
B. To develop a new strategic vision
C. To apply a broad range of capabilities and managerial skills in new areas
D. International competition—to establish presence in foreign markets and strengthen position in domestic market
E. Deregulation—relaxation of government barriers
F. Industry excess capacity and need to cut costs
G. Industry roll-ups—consolidation of fragmented industries
H. Change in strategic scientific segment of the industry
I. Shift from overcapacity area to area with more favorable sale-to-capacity ratios
J. Exit a product area that has become commoditized to area of specialty
K. Combined company can better meet customers' demands for a wide range of services; strengthens distribution systems.

These examples illustrate the multiple roles that M&As have performed in the adjustment processes in the chemical industry (Filipello, 1999).

EFFECTS ON CONCENTRATION

Concern has been expressed that the rising tide of M&A activity might have undesirable impacts on industry structures. Specifically, the issue has been raised of whether increases in industry concentration will have adverse effects on competition. Considerable evidence has demonstrated that the degree of concentration does not predict the nature or intensity of competition in an industry (see Weston, 1978). Nevertheless, some still believe in this numbers game, so it will be addressed.

In our description of the nature of the chemical industry, it was established that the relevant market for analysis would be the world industry. We begin with the U.S. market because of the availability of reliable data. We then make estimates for the world market.

Concentration will be measured by the HHI, an index named after the economists who developed it, Herfindahl and Hirschman. This is the measure adopted in the antitrust guidelines first issued by the Federal Trade Commission and Department of Justice in 1982 and retained in subsequent modifications. The HHI is measured by the sum of the squares of the market shares of all firms in an industry. For example, if there were 20 firms in an industry, each with a market share of 5%, the HHI would be 20×25, or 500. If only 10 firms, each with a market share of 10%, the HHI would be 10×100 which equals 1,000. With 50 firms with a market share of 2% each, the HHI would be 50×4, which equals 200. This illustrates that more concentration results in a higher index, and less concentration, in a lower index. Of course, assigning equal market shares is artificial, but it simplifies the arithmetic.

The guidelines have specified critical levels for the HHI. Below 1,000, concentration is considered sufficiently low that no further investigation is required to determine the possible effects of a merger or joint venture on competition. If a premerger HHI was between 1,000 and 1,800 and the index has been increased by 100 or more, the merger will be investigated. If the industry HHI was more than 1,800 and has been increased by at least 50, the merger will be challenged. Thus, if the industry consisted of one firm with 40% and six firms each with 10% of industry revenues and one of the six was acquired by the largest firm, the new HHI would be 50 squared plus 500, resulting in an industry measure of 3,000. It would clearly violate the antitrust guidelines, because the HHI exceeded 1,800 to begin with and was increased by 800 points.

Using data of annual chemical sales in the United States by firm presented in *Chemical & Engineering News (C&EN)*, we calculated HHIs for the U.S. chemical industry. The HHI in 1980 was 178, declining to 148 in 1990 and to 102 in 1998. Obviously, the HHI for the U.S. chemical industry is far below the critical 1,000 specified in the guidelines. Furthermore, the trend has been strongly downward. How can the HHI decline when M&A activity is increasing? The

answer lies in the intensity of competition. Manifestations include divestitures, spinoffs, carve-outs, and downsizing, among others. Also, in the chemical industry, many new firms have come into being as a result of divestitures.

We attempted to estimate the HHI for the world chemical industry. Compilations of chemical industry firms in the *Fortune* global list and other sources do not break out chemical sales as C&EN does for chemical sales in the United States. *Fortune* and other compilers overstate chemical sales, as the total company sales include products other than chemicals. These compilations may also not include in their chemical industry groupings petroleum and pharmaceutical companies with substantial sales in chemicals. Our best judgment of the HHI for the world chemical market is that it is significantly below the critical 1,000 level and that it is probably declining for the same reasons that the HHI for the U.S. market has been declining over time—new entries and competitive forces that have reduced firm size inequalities.

We conclude that concentration in the chemical industries has been relatively low and decreasing over time. Mergers and acquisitions and related activities in chemicals reflect the forces of change and the dynamics of competitive actions and reactions. The pace of new product introductions has increased. Product life cycles have been shortened. The numbers of competitors have increased. Competitors from one industry segment are invading other industry segments. Industry boundaries continue to blur. Concentration has declined and competition has intensified in the evolution of the chemical industries.

SUMMARY

The high rate of M&A activity is being propelled by powerful change forces supported by favorable economic and financing environments. Rapid advances in technologies have led to the globalization of markets and increased intensity of competition. These forces have been magnified in the chemical industry, the most R&D-intensive in the economy.

The innovation activities in the chemical industry are reflected in its high ranking in the annual number of patents granted. Research and development efforts represent activities of high risk that should be associated with high returns—a basic principle of financial economics. But the achievement of such results has faced formidable challenges in the chemical industry. A secular problem has been that structural changes in the economy have produced relatively higher growth in the service industries (where chemicals are less important) than in the other major users of chemicals. This problem is compounded by the rapidity with which innovations by one chemical firm are diffused to competitors. Innovative products become commodities in relatively short periods of time. Thus, the impacts of the major change forces are even stronger in the chemical industry.

As a consequence, the chemical industry throughout its long history has been characterized by adjustments and restructuring. The many forms of restructuring—mergers, joint ventures, cross-border transactions, divestitures, spin-offs, share repurchase programs—are actively employed by chemical companies. They represent competitive responses to turbulent environments and vigorous competitive moves and countermoves.

QUESTIONS

A6.1   Explain why the chemical industry's share of gross domestic product has been declining.

A6.2   What has been the impact of the specialized engineering firms (SEFs) in the industry?

REFERENCES

Arora, Ashish, Ralph Landau, and Nathan Rosenberg, eds., *Chemicals and Long-Term Economic Growth*, New York: John Wiley & Sons, 1998.

Chemical and Engineering News publications.

Chemical Manufacturers Association publications.

Da Rin, Marco in Arora, Ashish, R. Landau, and N. Rosenberg, eds., *Chemicals and Long-Term Economic Growth*, New York: John Wiley & Sons, 1998, p. 320.

Donaldson, Lufkin, and Jenrette, *Specialty Chemicals*, June 21, 1999.

Filipello, A. Nicholas, "The Evolution of Restructuring: Seizing Change to Create Value," *Business Economics,* January 1999, pp. 25–28.

"The Fortune Global 500," *Fortune,* Aug. 3, 1998, p. F-17.

Houlihan Lokey Howard and Zukin, *Mergerstat Review,* annual volumes.

Hounshell, D. A., and J. K. Smith, *Science and Strategy: DuPont R&D 1902–1980,* Cambridge, U.K.: Cambridge University Press, 1988.

Lane, Sarah J., "Corporate Restructuring in the Chemicals Industry," in Margaret M. Blair, ed., *The Deal Decade,* Washington, D.C.: The Brookings Institution, 1993, pp. 239–287.

Siu, Juan A., and J. Fred Weston, "Restructuring in the U.S. Oil Industry," *Journal of Energy Finance & Development,* Vol. 1, No. 2, 1996, pp. 113–131.

Standard & Poor's, *Industry Surveys.*

Taylor, Alex, III, "Why DuPont Is Trading Oil for Corn," *Fortune,* Apr. 26, 1999, pp. 154–160.

U.S. Department of Commerce/International Trade Administration, *U.S. Industry & Trade Outlook '99,* Chapter 11, New York: McGraw-Hill, 1999.

Value Line Investment Survey, *Ratings & Reports,* April through July 1999.

Weston, J. Fred, *Concentration and Efficiency: The Other Side of the Monopoly Issue,* Special Issues in the Public Interest No. 4, New York: Hudson Institute, 1978.

Measurement of Abnormal Returns

STEPS IN CALCULATION OF RESIDUALS

The first step in measuring the effect of an "event" (announcement of a tender offer, share repurchase, and so on) on stock value is to define an event period. Usually this is centered on the announcement date, which is designated day 0 in event time. The purpose of the event period is to capture all the effects on stock price of the event. Longer periods will make sure that all the effects are captured, but the estimate is subject to more noise in the data. Many studies choose a period like days -40 to $+40$, that is, from 40 days before the announcement to 40 days after the announcement. Note, day 0 is the date the announcement is made for a particular firm and will denote different calendar dates for different firms.

The next step is to calculate a predicted (or normal) return, $\hat{R}_{jt}$, for each day in the event period for each firm. The predicted return represents the return that would be expected if no event took place. There are basically three methods of calculating this predicted return. These are the mean adjusted return method, the market model method, and the market adjusted return method. For most cases the three methods yield similar results. Next the residual, r_{jt}, is calculated for each day for each firm. The residual is the actual return for that day for the firm minus the predicted return, $r_{jt} = R_{jt} - \hat{R}_{jt}$. The residual represents the abnormal return, that

is, the part of the return that is not predicted and is therefore an estimate of the change in firm value on that day, which is caused by the event. For each day in event time the residuals are averaged across firms to produce the average residual for that day, AR_t, where

$$AR_t = \frac{\sum_j r_{jt}}{N}$$

and N is the number of firms in the sample. The reason for averaging across firms is that stock returns are "noisy," but the noise tends to cancel out when averaged across a large number of firms. Therefore, the more firms in the sample, the better the ability to distinguish the effect of an event. The final step is to cumulate the average residual for each day over the entire event period to produce the cumulative average residual or return, CAR, where

$$CAR = \sum_{t=-40}^{40} AR_t$$

The cumulative average residual represents the average total effect of the event across all firms over a specified time interval.

The Mean Adjusted Return Method

In the mean adjusted return method a "clean" period is chosen and the average daily return for the firm is estimated for this period. The clean period may be before the event period, after the event period, or both, but never includes the event period. The clean period includes days on which no information related to the event is released, for example days -240 to -41. The predicted return for a firm for each day in the event period, using the mean adjusted return method, is just the mean daily return for the clean period for the firm. That is:

$$\hat{R}_{jt} = \overline{R}_j = \frac{\sum\limits_{t=-240}^{-41} R_{jt}}{200}$$

This predicted return is then used to calculate the residuals, average residuals, and cumulative average residual as explained above.

The Market Model Method

To use the market model a clean period is chosen and the market model is estimated by running a regression for the days in this period. The market model is:

$$R_{jt} = \alpha_j + \beta_j R_{mt} + \epsilon_{jt}$$

where R_{mt} is the return on a market index (for example, the S&P 500) for day t, β_j measures the sensitivity of firm j to the market—this is a measure of risk, α_j measures the mean return over the period not explained by the market, and ϵ_{jt} is a statistical error term $\Sigma\epsilon_{jt} = 0$. The regression produces estimates of α_j and β_j; call these $\hat{\alpha}_j$ and $\hat{\beta}_j$. The predicted return for a firm for a day in the event period is the return given by the market model on that day using these estimates. That is:

$$\hat{R}_{jt} = \hat{\alpha}_j + \hat{\beta}_j R_{mt}$$

where now R_{mt} is the return on the market index for the actual day in the event period. Because the market model takes explicit account of both the risk associated with the market and mean returns, it is the most widely used method.

The Market Adjusted Return Method

The market adjusted return method is the simplest of the methods. The predicted return for a firm for a day in the event period is just the return on the market index for that day. That is:

$$\hat{R}_{jt} = R_{mt}$$

The market adjusted return method can be thought of as an approximation to the market model where $\hat{\alpha}_j = 0$ and $\hat{\beta}_j = 1$ for all firms. Because $\hat{\alpha}_j$ is usually small and the average $\hat{\beta}_j$ over all firms is 1, this approximation usually produces acceptable results.

Illustrations

The first step for any event study is to determine the date of the announcement. The actual date of the first release of the information to the public is not easily obtainable. The best one can do is to check a source such as the *Wall Street Journal Index (WSJI)* for the earliest date and use an event window sufficient to cover the period. In our example, the events of interest are three major mergers in the oil industry: Chevron–Gulf (March 5, 1984), Mobil–Superior Oil (March 9, 1984), and Imperial Oil–Texaco Canada (January 19, 1989). We chose 40 days prior and 40 days after the earliest announcement date found in the *WSJI*. We refer to $[-40, 40]$ as our event window.

To quantify the effects of the event on the stock returns, we need to calculate the residuals during the event window interval. The residuals are just the difference between the actual stock return and a benchmark of what would have been the expected return if the event had not happened. Three methods are used to calculate the expected return. One is the **mean adjusted return method.** We use the mean return of the stock in a clean period prior to the event window as the expected return. In our example, we took 200 trading

Table 6B.1 Parameters for Measuring Abnormal Returns

			Targets			*Acquirers*		
			Gulf Corp.	Superior Oil	Texaco Canada	Chevron	Mobil	Imperial Oil
M1: Mean adjusted return model	$R1 = r_{jt}$ $= R_{jt} - \bar{R}_j$	$\bar{R}_j$	0.0022	0.0012	0.0015	0.0004	0.0010	−0.0007
M2: Market model method	$R2 = r_{jt}$ $= R_{jt} - \hat{\alpha}_j - \hat{\beta}_j R_{mt}$	$\hat{\alpha}_j$ $\hat{\beta}_j$	0.0015 0.9702	0.0005 1.0807	0.0012 0.6233	−0.0005 1.2096	0.0001 1.3665	−0.0010 0.5136
M3: Market adjusted return method	$R3 = r_{jt}$ $= R_{jt} - R_{mt}$							

days prior to our event window to calculate a mean expected return for each firm. For illustration, let us consider the case of Chevron. The mean return from date −240 to −41 was found to be 0.00037 (see Table 6B.1). Chevron's return on date −40 was 0.0036. Then $R1$, the mean adjusted residual on date −40 will be Chevron's return on date −40 minus the estimated mean return, or 0.0036 − 0.00037 = 0.00323 ≈ 0.003 (see first row $R1$ under Chevron columns in Table 6B.2).

Two is the **market model method.** We use an expected return that takes into account the riskiness of the firm with respect to the market. The procedure involves a regression of the firm return series against a market index. The calculations must involve a period not included in the event window. We again used the 200 trading days returns prior to the event window and regressed them against a market index represented by the value-weighted CRSP index, which represents an aggregate of stocks including dividends traded in the major exchanges such as NYSE and AMEX. The regression of Chevron's returns against the returns of the CRSP index for the period −240 to −41 yielded an intercept $\hat{\alpha}$, of −0.0005 and a slope, $\hat{\beta}$, of 1.2096 (see Table 6B.1). On date −40, Chevron's return was 0.0036 and the CRSP market index

return was 0.00431. $R2$, the market model adjusted residual, for date −40 will be 0.0036 − (−0.0005) − 1.2096(0.00431) = −0.0011 ≈ 0.001 (see first row $R2$ under Chevron column in Table 6B.2).

Three is the **market adjusted return method.** The expected return for any stock is postulated to be just the market return for that particular day. Going back to our Chevron example, $R3$, the market adjusted residual, for date −40 will be 0.0036 − 0.00431 = −0.00071 ≈ −0.001 (see first row $R3$ under Chevron column in Table 6B.2).

Table 6B.2 shows the residuals for the three acquiring firms in our sample using the above three methods. Table 6B.3 is a similar table corresponding to the target companies. The residuals are averaged across firms to obtain an average residual (AR) for each day in the event period. Three average residuals are presented corresponding to each of the above three methods. For example, $AR1$ for the acquiring companies is the average of the mean adjusted residuals: $R1$ Chevron, $R1$ Mobil, and $R1$ Imperial Oil. For date −40, $AR1$ = 1/3[0.003 + (−0.014) + 0.031] = 0.007 (see first row $AR1$ under Average Residuals columns in Table 6B.2). $AR2$ is for the market model. $AR3$ represents the average residuals using the market adjusted method.

Table 6B.2 Event Study for Acquiring Companies

| | RESIDUALS | | | | | | | | | AVERAGE RESIDUALS | | | CAR | | |
| | Chevron Corp. | | | Mobil Corp. | | | Imperial Oil Ltd. | | | | | | | | |
Event Date	R1	R2	R3	R1	R2	R3	R1	R2	R3	AR1	AR2	AR3	CAR1	CAR2	CAR3
-40	0.003	-0.001	-0.001	-0.014	0.013	-0.013	0.031	0.032	0.032	0.007	0.006	0.006	0.007	0.006	0.006
-39	0.000	0.003	0.002	-0.005	0.000	-0.001	0.027	0.026	0.023	0.007	0.010	0.008	0.014	0.016	0.014
-38	0.007	0.012	0.011	-0.005	-0.004	-0.004	0.007	0.004	0.000	0.003	0.004	0.002	0.017	0.020	0.017
-37	0.000	0.001	0.001	0.008	0.004	0.006	0.032	0.035	0.036	0.013	0.014	0.014	0.030	0.033	0.031
-36	0.007	0.008	0.007	0.003	0.006	0.006	0.004	0.002	-0.001	0.005	0.005	0.004	0.035	0.039	0.035
-35	0.007	0.012	0.010	0.025	0.029	0.028	-0.005	-0.009	-0.014	0.009	0.011	0.008	0.043	0.049	0.043
-34	-0.011	-0.010	-0.011	0.003	0.012	0.010	-0.005	-0.010	-0.015	-0.004	-0.003	-0.005	0.039	0.046	0.038
-33	-0.007	-0.010	-0.010	-0.013	0.000	-0.004	0.001	0.002	0.001	-0.007	-0.003	-0.004	0.032	0.043	0.034
-32	-0.018	-0.016	-0.016	0.024	0.020	0.022	0.001	0.002	0.002	0.002	0.002	0.002	0.034	0.046	0.036
-31	0.025	0.029	0.028	-0.005	0.004	0.002	-0.003	-0.003	-0.009	0.007	0.010	0.007	0.041	0.055	0.043
-30	0.017	0.025	0.023	-0.001	0.006	0.004	0.007	0.000	-0.002	0.008	0.011	0.009	0.049	0.067	0.052
-29	0.000	0.011	0.009	-0.001	0.003	0.002	0.001	0.000	-0.001	0.000	0.005	0.003	0.049	0.071	0.055
-28	-0.014	-0.018	-0.017	0.011	0.024	0.021	0.001	0.003	0.004	-0.001	0.003	0.003	0.048	0.074	0.057
-27	0.010	0.018	0.016	0.009	0.008	0.008	-0.005	-0.006	-0.008	0.004	0.007	0.006	0.053	0.081	0.063
-26	-0.004	0.002	0.001	-0.013	-0.007	-0.008	-0.006	-0.004	-0.005	-0.008	-0.003	-0.004	0.045	0.078	0.059
-25	-0.004	0.000	-0.001	0.007	0.004	0.005	-0.009	-0.008	-0.008	-0.002	-0.001	-0.001	0.043	0.077	0.057
-24	0.017	0.028	0.026	-0.005	0.014	0.009	-0.002	-0.001	0.000	0.003	0.014	0.012	0.046	0.090	0.069
-23	0.013	0.013	0.012	-0.022	0.001	-0.004	-0.002	-0.001	0.000	-0.004	0.004	0.003	0.043	0.095	0.072
-22	-0.007	-0.001	-0.003	-0.005	-0.007	-0.006	0.010	0.007	0.003	-0.001	-0.001	-0.002	0.042	0.095	0.070
-21	0.020	0.017	0.018	-0.018	0.005	0.000	0.017	0.013	0.009	0.006	0.012	0.009	0.049	0.107	0.078
-20	-0.017	-0.001	-0.004	-0.005	0.002	0.000	0.016	0.018	0.018	0.002	0.006	0.005	0.046	0.113	0.083
-19	-0.025	-0.005	-0.008	-0.001	-0.007	-0.005	0.004	0.004	0.003	-0.007	-0.003	-0.003	0.039	0.110	0.080
-18	-0.008	-0.009	-0.009	0.003	0.017	0.014	0.001	0.001	0.001	-0.001	0.003	0.002	0.038	0.114	0.082
-17	-0.022	-0.001	-0.005	0.003	-0.009	-0.005	0.010	0.008	0.005	-0.003	-0.001	-0.002	0.035	0.113	0.080
-16	-0.008	-0.002	-0.003	-0.005	-0.003	-0.003	0.007	0.008	0.009	-0.002	0.001	0.001	0.033	0.114	0.081
-15	0.003	-0.002	-0.002	-0.001	0.002	0.001	0.004	0.003	0.002	0.002	0.001	0.001	0.035	0.115	0.082
-14	0.003	0.016	0.013	0.029	0.033	0.032	0.007	0.004	-0.001	0.013	0.017	0.015	0.048	0.133	0.096
-13	0.007	-0.004	-0.002	-0.022	-0.012	-0.014	0.001	0.002	0.002	-0.005	-0.004	-0.005	0.043	0.128	0.092
-12	0.003	0.005	0.005	0.012	0.016	0.015	0.004	0.008	0.011	0.006	0.010	0.010	0.049	0.138	0.102
-11	0.011	0.013	0.012	0.007	0.011	0.010	0.010	0.003	-0.004	0.009	0.013	0.006	0.059	0.147	0.108
-10	0.032	0.036	0.035	-0.001	-0.027	-0.020	0.030	0.029	0.027	0.020	0.013	0.014	0.079	0.160	0.122
-9	0.007	0.016	0.014	0.036	0.021	0.025	0.024	0.022	0.020	0.022	0.020	0.020	0.101	0.179	0.142
-8	0.000	0.003	0.002	0.007	0.026	0.021	0.029	0.028	0.026	0.012	0.019	0.017	0.113	0.198	0.158
-7	0.010	0.013	0.012	-0.001	-0.004	-0.003	-0.013	-0.012	-0.012	-0.001	-0.001	-0.001	0.112	0.198	0.157
-6	0.003	-0.020	-0.016	0.011	0.003	0.005	-0.002	-0.004	-0.007	0.004	-0.007	-0.006	0.116	0.190	0.151
-5	0.037	0.024	0.026	-0.005	-0.014	-0.011	0.009	0.007	0.004	0.014	0.006	-0.006	0.130	0.196	0.158
-4	-0.014	0.003	0.000	-0.025	-0.014	-0.016	0.001	0.000	-0.002	-0.013	-0.003	-0.006	0.117	0.193	0.152
-3	-0.014	-0.016	0.016	-0.021	0.007	0.011	0.001	0.000	-0.002	-0.011	0.008	0.009	0.106	0.185	0.142
-2	-0.027	-0.035	-0.034	-0.005	0.010	0.007	-0.002	-0.001	-0.001	-0.012	-0.008	-0.009	0.094	0.177	0.133

174

−1	−0.007	−0.015	−0.014	0.007	0.004	0.005	0.001	−0.004	−0.009	0.000	−0.005	−0.006	0.094	0.172	0.127
0	0.000	0.009	0.007	−0.005	0.002	0.000	−0.002	−0.003	−0.005	−0.003	0.006	0.001	0.092	0.175	0.128
1	−0.046	−0.033	−0.036	−0.018	−0.031	−0.027	−0.021	−0.021	−0.022	−0.028	−0.028	−0.028	0.064	0.146	0.100
2	−0.008	0.006	0.003	−0.005	−0.010	−0.008	−0.028	−0.024	−0.023	−0.013	−0.009	−0.009	0.050	0.137	0.090
3	0.011	0.008	0.008	0.007	0.002	−0.004	−0.020	−0.025	−0.030	−0.005	−0.007	−0.009	0.045	0.130	0.081
4	0.007	0.013	0.012	0.012	0.002	0.004	0.004	0.003	0.000	0.006	0.006	0.005	0.051	0.136	0.087
5	0.000	−0.012	−0.010	−0.013	−0.002	0.002	0.007	0.003	−0.002	0.006	−0.004	−0.003	0.057	0.132	0.083
6	−0.004	−0.008	−0.008	0.007	0.001	−0.004	0.001	−0.002	−0.006	−0.006	−0.004	−0.006	0.052	0.128	0.077
7	−0.011	−0.010	−0.011	0.028	0.030	0.003	0.001	−0.001	−0.003	−0.001	−0.003	−0.004	0.051	0.125	0.074
8	0.014	0.010	0.010	−0.021	−0.007	0.030	−0.005	−0.009	−0.013	0.012	0.010	0.009	0.063	0.135	0.074
9	0.000	−0.012	−0.011	−0.005	−0.004	−0.010	0.004	0.004	0.003	−0.006	−0.005	−0.006	0.057	0.130	0.083
10	−0.018	−0.007	−0.009	0.007	0.004	−0.004	0.001	0.000	0.003	−0.007	−0.002	−0.003	0.051	0.128	0.077
11	0.014	0.009	0.009	0.005	0.005	0.005	0.001	0.002	−0.001	0.003	0.002	0.001	0.054	0.130	0.073
12	0.000	0.002	0.001	0.007	0.010	0.018	−0.002	−0.004	0.001	0.003	0.003	0.003	0.057	0.132	0.074
13	−0.019	−0.006	−0.008	−0.013	−0.004	0.005	0.005	−0.001	−0.010	−0.008	−0.011	−0.012	0.049	0.121	0.077
14	0.003	0.005	0.004	−0.001	0.004	0.009	0.009	−0.004	−0.001	0.001	0.003	0.003	0.050	0.124	0.065
15	0.018	0.019	0.019	0.003	0.005	−0.006	−0.002	0.004	−0.002	0.006	0.008	0.009	0.056	0.132	0.068
16	0.014	0.011	0.012	−0.001	0.020	0.003	0.001	0.001	0.009	0.000	0.004	0.005	0.056	0.136	0.076
17	0.025	0.009	0.011	−0.009	−0.009	0.005	0.007	0.007	−0.001	0.008	0.005	0.005	0.064	0.141	0.081
18	0.014	0.015	0.015	−0.001	0.000	0.015	0.013	0.007	0.007	0.008	0.009	0.009	0.071	0.150	0.086
19	0.027	0.029	0.029	−0.001	−0.003	−0.009	−0.005	0.009	0.005	0.013	0.019	0.016	0.084	0.170	0.094
20	0.000	0.008	0.006	−0.001	0.011	0.000	−0.002	−0.006	−0.008	−0.005	−0.002	−0.003	0.079	0.167	0.110
21	0.003	0.007	0.006	0.003	0.006	−0.002	−0.011	−0.005	−0.008	0.000	0.001	−0.001	0.079	0.168	0.107
22	−0.014	−0.012	−0.013	0.024	0.001	0.010	−0.011	−0.010	−0.010	−0.009	−0.008	−0.008	0.071	0.160	0.106
23	−0.014	0.005	0.001	0.011	−0.011	0.011	0.001	−0.004	0.002	−0.007	0.004	0.004	0.063	0.164	0.098
24	0.003	0.004	0.003	0.007	−0.005	0.013	0.013	−0.001	−0.007	0.009	0.003	0.004	0.073	0.167	0.102
25	0.010	0.011	0.011	−0.005	0.016	0.003	0.013	0.005	0.009	0.010	0.009	0.011	0.079	0.177	0.106
26	0.010	0.008	0.008	−0.013	0.009	−0.009	0.003	0.010	0.010	0.006	0.006	0.006	0.088	0.183	0.117
27	0.000	0.007	0.005	0.015	−0.004	−0.007	−0.002	−0.004	0.008	−0.003	−0.002	−0.003	0.085	0.180	0.124
28	0.036	0.020	0.023	−0.001	−0.001	0.016	0.025	−0.003	−0.006	0.006	0.004	0.004	0.091	0.184	0.120
29	0.006	0.007	0.007	0.003	0.003	0.006	0.013	0.021	−0.003	0.015	0.015	0.013	0.107	0.199	0.125
30	0.016	0.011	0.011	−0.005	−0.018	−0.002	0.004	0.011	0.016	0.009	0.010	0.009	0.116	0.209	0.138
31	0.009	0.004	0.005	−0.001	0.001	0.001	0.004	−0.001	0.008	0.005	0.000	0.000	0.121	0.207	0.146
32	−0.016	−0.009	−0.010	0.003	−0.009	−0.014	0.004	0.005	−0.007	−0.003	−0.002	−0.001	0.118	0.201	0.145
33	−0.013	−0.013	−0.013	0.003	0.001	0.001	0.013	0.012	0.004	−0.002	−0.006	−0.002	0.116	0.202	0.143
34	−0.023	−0.014	−0.016	−0.005	−0.009	0.001	0.015	0.016	0.011	−0.003	0.001	−0.003	0.113	0.204	0.138
35	0.019	0.013	0.014	−0.016	−0.012	−0.008	0.002	0.002	0.002	0.004	0.002	0.004	0.117	0.206	0.138
36	0.000	−0.004	−0.003	−0.013	−0.010	−0.010	0.017	0.021	0.010	0.008	0.002	0.008	0.125	0.207	0.140
37	0.013	0.001	0.003	−0.009	−0.009	−0.008	0.012	0.012	0.008	0.006	0.001	0.006	0.131	0.210	0.142
38	0.000	0.001	0.001	−0.001	−0.002	−0.010	0.013	0.016	−0.007	0.001	0.003	0.002	0.133	0.215	0.145
39	0.009	0.009	0.009	−0.005	0.005	0.002	−0.002	0.003	0.004	0.003	0.006	0.002	0.135	0.209	0.148
40	−0.010	−0.021	−0.019	−0.001	0.002	−0.002	0.012	0.003	0.012	−0.006	−0.007	−0.003	0.129	0.209	0.144

Source: University of Chicago Center for Research on Security Prices (CRSP) tapes.

Table 6B.3 Event Study for Target Companies

Event Date	RESIDUALS Gulf Corp.			Superior Oil Co.			Texaco Canada Inc.			AVERAGE RESIDUALS			CAR		
	R1	R2	R3	R1	R2	R3	R1	R2	R3	AR1	AR2	AR3	CAR1	CAR2	CAR3
-40	0.054	0.051	0.052	-0.008	-0.007	-0.006	0.019	0.020	0.022	0.022	0.021	0.022	0.022	0.021	0.022
-39	0.006	0.009	0.010	0.015	0.020	0.020	0.022	0.021	0.021	0.014	0.016	0.017	0.036	0.038	0.039
-38	0.035	0.039	0.041	0.002	0.003	0.003	0.010	0.006	0.005	0.016	0.016	0.017	0.052	0.054	0.056
-37	-0.025	-0.024	-0.022	0.012	0.009	0.010	0.006	0.009	0.012	-0.001	-0.002	0.000	0.049	0.052	0.056
-36	0.019	0.020	0.021	-0.014	-0.012	-0.011	-0.009	-0.011	-0.011	-0.001	-0.001	0.000	0.048	0.051	0.055
-35	0.011	0.015	0.016	0.044	0.048	0.048	0.018	0.013	0.011	0.024	0.025	0.025	0.072	0.076	0.081
-34	-0.012	-0.012	-0.010	-0.004	0.002	0.002	0.017	0.012	0.010	0.000	0.001	0.001	0.072	0.077	0.081
-33	-0.007	-0.010	-0.008	-0.017	-0.006	-0.007	0.002	0.003	0.005	-0.007	-0.004	-0.003	0.065	0.073	0.078
-32	-0.007	-0.005	-0.004	-0.001	-0.004	-0.004	-0.013	-0.011	-0.009	-0.007	-0.007	-0.006	0.058	0.066	0.072
-31	-0.028	-0.025	-0.023	0.024	0.031	0.031	0.006	0.001	-0.001	0.001	0.002	0.002	0.059	0.068	0.075
-30	-0.002	0.004	0.006	-0.035	-0.030	-0.030	-0.002	-0.006	-0.008	-0.013	-0.011	-0.011	0.046	0.057	0.064
-29	0.011	0.020	0.022	0.046	0.049	0.050	0.032	0.031	0.032	0.030	0.034	0.035	0.075	0.091	0.099
-28	0.053	0.050	0.052	-0.025	-0.016	-0.016	-0.002	0.001	0.004	0.009	0.012	0.013	0.084	0.103	0.112
-27	0.010	0.016	0.018	0.039	0.038	0.039	-0.002	-0.002	-0.001	0.016	0.018	0.019	0.100	0.120	0.130
-26	-0.010	-0.005	-0.003	-0.016	-0.011	-0.011	-0.002	0.000	0.002	-0.009	-0.005	-0.004	0.091	0.115	0.126
-25	0.050	0.053	0.054	-0.004	-0.007	-0.006	-0.005	-0.004	-0.002	0.013	0.014	0.015	0.104	0.129	0.142
-24	0.007	0.016	0.018	-0.010	0.004	0.004	-0.009	-0.007	-0.004	-0.004	0.005	0.006	0.100	0.134	0.147
-23	-0.009	-0.010	-0.008	-0.020	-0.001	-0.002	-0.002	0.001	0.003	-0.010	-0.004	-0.003	0.090	0.130	0.145
-22	0.036	0.041	0.042	0.011	0.010	0.011	0.006	0.002	0.001	0.018	0.018	0.018	0.108	0.148	0.163
-21	0.048	0.046	0.047	-0.023	-0.004	-0.005	0.016	0.012	0.011	0.014	0.018	0.018	0.122	0.166	0.180
-20	-0.033	-0.020	-0.018	-0.011	-0.005	-0.005	-0.002	0.001	0.003	-0.015	-0.008	-0.007	0.107	0.158	0.174
-19	0.007	0.023	0.025	0.005	0.000	0.001	-0.002	-0.001	0.000	0.003	0.007	0.009	0.110	0.165	0.183
-18	-0.020	-0.021	-0.020	-0.014	-0.003	-0.003	0.006	0.006	0.008	-0.009	-0.006	-0.005	0.101	0.159	0.178
-17	-0.009	0.008	0.010	-0.001	-0.011	-0.010	0.005	0.003	0.003	-0.002	0.000	0.001	0.099	0.159	0.179
-16	0.037	0.042	0.044	0.040	0.042	0.043	0.005	0.007	0.010	0.028	0.031	0.032	0.127	0.190	0.211
-15	0.002	-0.002	-0.001	-0.007	-0.005	-0.005	0.012	0.012	0.012	0.002	0.001	0.002	0.129	0.191	0.213
-14	-0.057	-0.047	-0.045	0.005	0.008	0.009	0.016	0.012	0.010	-0.012	-0.009	-0.009	0.117	0.182	0.204
-13	0.065	0.057	0.058	-0.023	-0.015	-0.015	-0.008	-0.007	-0.005	0.011	0.012	0.013	0.128	0.194	0.217
-12	-0.035	-0.033	-0.031	-0.004	-0.001	-0.001	-0.002	-0.004	0.008	-0.014	-0.010	-0.008	0.115	0.183	0.209
-11	-0.031	-0.029	-0.028	-0.026	-0.024	-0.023	-0.002	-0.009	-0.013	-0.020	-0.021	-0.021	0.095	0.163	0.187
-10	-0.002	0.001	0.002	0.018	-0.003	0.000	0.022	0.021	0.021	0.013	0.006	0.008	0.108	0.169	0.195
-9	-0.028	-0.020	-0.019	0.024	0.012	0.013	-0.002	-0.003	-0.003	-0.002	-0.004	-0.003	0.106	0.165	0.192
-8	0.107	0.110	0.111	-0.009	0.006	0.005	0.005	0.004	0.005	0.034	0.040	0.041	0.140	0.205	0.233
-7	0.094	0.097	0.098	0.008	0.006	0.007	-0.008	-0.007	-0.005	0.031	0.032	0.033	0.172	0.237	0.266
-6	-0.024	-0.042	-0.041	0.030	0.023	0.024	-0.008	-0.004	-0.005	0.002	-0.008	-0.007	0.173	0.229	0.259
-5	0.092	0.081	0.082	-0.019	-0.026	-0.025	-0.011	-0.014	-0.014	0.020	0.014	0.014	0.193	0.243	0.273
-4	0.007	0.021	0.022	0.002	0.010	0.010	0.039	0.038	0.039	0.016	0.023	0.024	0.209	0.266	0.297
-3	-0.004	-0.006	-0.004	-0.016	-0.005	-0.006	-0.009	-0.010	-0.009	-0.010	-0.007	-0.006	0.199	0.259	0.291

-2	0.005	-0.001	0.000	-0.035	-0.023	-0.023	0.006	0.008	0.009	-0.008	-0.005	-0.005	0.191	0.254	0.286
-1	-0.002	-0.008	-0.007	-0.043	-0.046	-0.045	0.002	0.003	-0.005	-0.014	-0.019	-0.019	0.177	0.235	0.267
0	0.016	0.024	0.025	0.049	0.054	0.055	0.002	0.001	0.002	0.022	0.026	0.027	0.199	0.261	0.294
1	-0.023	-0.013	-0.012	0.008	-0.002	-0.001	0.029	0.029	0.030	0.005	0.005	0.006	0.204	0.265	0.300
2	-0.067	-0.056	-0.054	-0.042	-0.046	-0.045	0.002	0.006	0.009	-0.036	-0.032	-0.030	0.168	0.233	0.270
3	0.033	0.030	0.031	-0.001	0.000	0.000	0.002	0.004	-0.006	0.011	0.009	0.008	0.179	0.242	0.279
4	-0.030	-0.025	-0.024	-0.001	-0.015	-0.014	-0.002	-0.003	-0.003	0.014	0.015	0.014	0.165	0.227	0.265
5	0.015	0.006	0.007	0.049	0.038	0.039	0.002	-0.003	-0.004	0.022	0.014	0.014	0.187	0.241	0.279
6	-0.034	-0.038	-0.036	0.011	0.022	0.021	0.000	-0.003	-0.004	-0.008	-0.006	-0.006	0.179	0.235	0.272
7	0.019	0.020	0.022	0.018	0.012	0.013	0.000	-0.002	-0.002	0.012	0.010	0.011	0.192	0.245	0.284
8	0.011	0.007	0.009	0.017	0.019	0.019	-0.002	-0.006	-0.008	0.009	0.007	0.007	0.201	0.252	0.290
9	0.083	0.073	0.074	-0.013	-0.002	-0.002	-0.009	-0.009	-0.007	0.020	0.021	0.022	0.221	0.273	0.312
10	0.006	0.005	0.017	-0.004	-0.003	-0.003	-0.002	-0.001	0.000	0.000	0.004	0.005	0.221	0.276	0.317
11	0.010	0.030	0.007	0.002	0.003	0.004	0.002	-0.002	-0.001	0.003	0.002	0.003	0.224	0.278	0.320
12	0.028	0.008	0.032	-0.010	-0.013	-0.012	0.002	0.003	0.005	0.007	0.007	0.008	0.231	0.285	0.328
13	-0.002	-0.002	0.010	0.008	-0.006	-0.004	-0.002	-0.008	-0.010	0.001	-0.002	-0.002	0.233	0.283	0.326
14	0.001	0.002	0.004	0.011	0.010	0.010	-0.002	0.000	0.002	0.006	0.003	0.004	0.234	0.286	0.330
15	0.001	-0.001	0.000	0.004	0.013	0.013	0.006	0.010	0.014	-0.002	0.008	0.010	0.240	0.295	0.341
16	0.001	0.001	0.000	0.001	0.006	0.006	-0.005	0.003	0.009	0.001	0.003	0.005	0.238	0.297	0.346
17	0.011	-0.001	-0.001	-0.007	-0.003	-0.003	-0.002	-0.002	-0.001	0.001	-0.002	-0.001	0.239	0.295	0.344
18	0.001	-0.002	-0.004	-0.001	0.000	0.001	-0.002	-0.001	0.001	-0.001	0.001	0.002	0.238	0.296	0.346
19	-0.007	0.003	-0.004	-0.001	0.016	0.015	0.004	-0.001	-0.001	-0.001	0.003	0.003	0.237	0.299	0.349
20	0.004	-0.005	-0.004	-0.001	0.000	0.000	-0.003	-0.004	-0.004	0.000	0.002	0.003	0.237	0.301	0.352
21	0.001	0.011	0.013	0.005	0.006	0.006	0.000	-0.003	-0.002	0.002	0.003	0.003	0.239	0.304	0.355
22	-0.001	0.005	0.006	-0.001	-0.003	-0.002	-0.005	-0.004	-0.004	-0.003	-0.002	-0.001	0.237	0.302	0.355
23	-0.005	0.001	0.002	-0.001	0.005	0.005	0.002	0.011	0.018	-0.001	0.009	0.012	0.235	0.310	0.366
24	-0.002	0.010	0.012	-0.001	-0.014	-0.016	0.002	-0.003	-0.003	-0.002	-0.007	-0.006	0.233	0.304	0.360
25	-0.002	-0.002	0.000	-0.004	-0.003	-0.003	0.005	0.014	0.020	0.000	0.003	0.006	0.233	0.307	0.366
26	0.003	-0.001	0.000	-0.001	-0.006	-0.005	0.002	0.002	0.003	0.001	-0.001	0.000	0.234	0.306	0.366
27	-0.004	0.001	0.002	-0.004	0.009	0.008	-0.016	-0.018	-0.018	-0.008	-0.008	-0.007	0.226	0.298	0.359
28	0.003	0.002	0.004	-0.004	0.002	0.002	-0.002	0.001	0.003	-0.001	-0.002	-0.001	0.255	0.295	0.358
29	0.003	-0.010	-0.009	-0.004	-0.001	0.000	-0.002	-0.007	-0.009	0.000	-0.001	-0.001	0.225	0.294	0.357
30	-0.001	0.004	0.005	-0.001	0.006	0.006	0.002	0.000	0.000	0.000	0.001	0.001	0.225	0.295	0.358
31	0.001	-0.005	-0.003	-0.001	-0.006	-0.006	0.024	0.018	0.016	0.008	0.003	0.003	0.233	0.297	0.361
32	-0.010	-0.003	-0.002	0.008	0.006	0.005	-0.034	-0.033	-0.031	-0.012	-0.011	-0.009	0.221	0.287	0.351
33	0.001	-0.004	-0.003	0.002	-0.007	-0.008	-0.005	-0.006	-0.005	-0.001	-0.004	-0.003	0.220	0.283	0.348
34	0.004	0.001	0.003	-0.001	0.001	0.000	0.004	-0.005	-0.003	-0.001	0.002	0.003	0.220	0.285	0.352
35	0.003	0.011	0.013	-0.004	-0.004	-0.004	0.004	0.006	0.008	-0.001	0.000	0.001	0.220	0.285	0.353
36	-0.001	-0.002	-0.001	0.002	-0.008	-0.007	-0.007	-0.011	-0.012	-0.002	-0.007	-0.007	0.218	0.277	0.346
37	0.002	-0.003	-0.002	0.002	-0.002	-0.001	0.000	0.001	0.002	0.002	-0.002	-0.001	0.220	0.275	0.345
38	-0.005	-0.006	-0.005	0.002	0.005	0.005	-0.003	-0.006	-0.006	-0.002	-0.002	-0.001	0.218	0.273	0.344
39	0.002	-0.004	-0.003	0.004	0.007	0.007	0.000	-0.002	-0.004	0.000	0.002	0.002	0.218	0.276	0.346
40	-0.005	-0.014	-0.013	-0.004	-0.005	-0.005	-0.016	-0.004	0.005	-0.009	-0.008	-0.004	0.209	0.268	0.342

Source: CRSP tape.

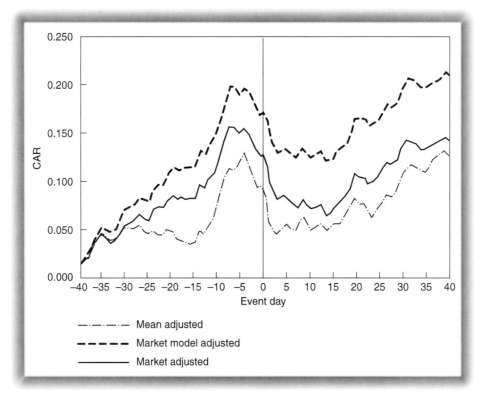

Figure 6B.1   CAR for Acquiring Companies

Finally, the average residuals are cumulated over the entire event period to obtain the cumulative average residual (CAR). For the acquiring firms in Table 6B.2, the cumulative average residual based on the mean adjusted residual is defined as *CAR*1. On day −40, *CAR*1 is equal to 0.007, the *AR*1 on day −40. On day −39, *CAR*1 is equal to the sum of the *AR*1 values on days −40 and −39, or 0.007 + 0.007 = 0.014. On day −38, the corresponding *CAR*1 would be 0.007 + 0.007 + 0.003 = 0.0017, and so on (see the *CAR*1 columns in Table 6B.2). *CAR*2 and *CAR*3 are calculated in the same way.

The residuals, average residuals, and CARs for the target companies shown in Table 6B.3 are calculated by following the same procedures. The CARs in Table 6B.2 for the acquiring firms are graphed in Figure 6B.1. We see a picture of a sharp rise in the CAR values from −40 to −5. A small decline is followed by a strong recovery. For this illustrative sample of three firms, the three methods give somewhat different results, but patterns are quite parallel. Figure 6B.2 graphs the data from Table 6B.3 for target firms. The patterns are again similar, but the CAR values are much larger for the target companies.

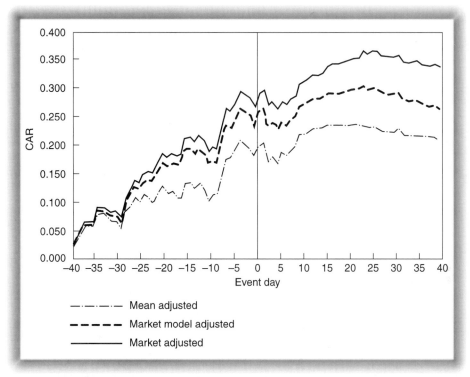

Figure 6B.2   CAR for Target Companies

Absolute Gains and Losses

Residual returns are also known as *abnormal returns* because they represent the return that was unexpected or different from the return that would have been expected if the event had not occurred. The absolute dollar gain or loss at time t (ΔW_t) due to the abnormal return during the event period is defined by

$$\Delta W_t = CAR_t \times MKTVAL_0$$

where $MKTVAL_0$ is the market value of the firm at a date previous to the event window interval and CAR_t is the cumulative residuals to date t for the firm. The percent return times the market value of the firm is the total dollar gain or loss.

Table 6B.4 presents the market adjusted residual returns ($R3$) that were previously displayed in Tables 6B.2 and 6B.3. In Table 6B.4, the $CAR3$ values are the cumulative abnormal returns obtained by cumulating the daily abnormal returns $R3$ for each individual firm.

Table 6B.5 illustrates the absolute dollar gain or loss at days + 1 and + 40 for the six firms of interest. The reference $MKTVAL_0$ is obtained one day prior to the event window interval or at day − 41. Thus, the absolute gain for Chevron on day + 1 was $11,888 million times the CAR from days − 40 to + 1 of 0.083, or a gain of $987 million.

Table 6B.4 Market Adjusted CAR for Individual Companies

	TARGETS						ACQUIRERS					
	Gulf Corp.		Superior Oil		Texaco Canada		Chevron		Mobil		Imperial Oil	
Event Date	R3	CAR3	R3	CAR3	R3	CAR3	R3	CAR3	R3	CAR3	R3	CAR3
−40	0.052	0.052	−0.006	−0.006	0.022	0.022	−0.001	−0.001	−0.013	−0.013	0.032	0.032
−39	0.010	0.063	0.020	0.013	0.021	0.043	0.002	0.001	−0.001	−0.013	0.023	0.055
−38	0.041	0.104	0.003	0.017	0.005	0.048	0.011	0.012	−0.004	−0.018	0.000	0.055
−37	−0.022	0.081	0.010	0.026	0.012	0.060	0.001	0.013	0.006	−0.012	0.036	0.091
−36	0.021	0.102	−0.011	0.015	−0.011	0.049	0.007	0.020	0.006	−0.007	−0.001	0.091
−35	0.016	0.119	0.048	0.063	0.011	0.060	0.010	0.031	0.028	0.022	−0.014	0.077
−34	−0.010	0.108	0.002	0.066	0.010	0.070	−0.011	0.020	0.010	0.032	−0.015	0.061
−33	−0.008	0.100	−0.007	0.059	0.005	0.075	−0.010	0.010	−0.004	0.028	0.001	0.063
−32	−0.004	0.096	−0.004	0.055	−0.009	0.066	−0.016	−0.006	0.022	0.050	0.002	0.064
−31	−0.023	0.073	0.031	0.086	−0.001	0.064	0.028	0.022	0.002	0.051	−0.009	0.056
−30	0.006	0.079	−0.030	0.057	−0.008	0.056	0.023	0.045	0.004	0.055	−0.002	0.054
−29	0.022	0.101	0.050	0.106	0.032	0.088	0.009	0.054	0.002	0.057	0.004	0.053
−28	0.052	0.153	−0.016	0.091	0.004	0.092	−0.017	0.037	0.021	0.078	0.004	0.057
−27	0.018	0.171	0.039	0.130	−0.001	0.091	0.016	0.053	0.008	0.087	−0.008	0.049
−26	−0.003	0.168	−0.011	0.119	0.002	0.092	0.001	0.054	−0.008	0.078	−0.005	0.045
−25	0.054	0.222	−0.006	0.113	−0.002	0.090	−0.001	0.052	0.005	0.084	−0.008	0.037
−24	0.018	0.240	0.004	0.117	−0.004	0.086	0.026	0.078	0.009	0.093	0.000	0.036
−23	−0.008	0.231	−0.002	0.114	0.003	0.089	0.012	0.091	−0.004	0.088	0.003	0.039
−22	0.042	0.273	0.011	0.125	0.001	0.090	−0.003	0.088	−0.006	0.082	0.009	0.048
−21	0.047	0.321	−0.005	0.120	0.011	0.101	0.018	0.106	0.000	0.082	0.018	0.066
−20	−0.018	0.303	−0.005	0.115	0.003	0.103	−0.004	0.102	0.000	0.082	0.003	0.070
−19	0.025	0.328	0.001	0.116	0.000	0.104	−0.008	0.093	−0.005	0.077	0.001	0.070
−18	−0.020	0.309	−0.003	0.113	0.008	0.111	−0.009	0.085	0.014	0.091	0.001	0.070
−17	0.010	0.319	−0.010	0.104	0.003	0.114	−0.005	0.079	−0.005	0.085	0.005	0.075
−16	0.044	0.362	0.043	0.146	0.010	0.124	−0.003	0.077	−0.003	0.082	0.009	0.084
−15	−0.001	0.361	−0.005	0.142	0.012	0.136	−0.002	0.075	0.001	0.084	0.002	0.086
−14	−0.045	0.316	0.009	0.150	0.010	0.147	0.013	0.088	0.032	0.116	−0.001	0.085
−13	0.058	0.374	−0.015	0.136	−0.005	0.142	−0.002	0.086	−0.014	0.102	0.002	0.087
−12	−0.031	0.342	−0.001	0.135	0.008	0.149	0.005	0.091	0.015	0.117	0.011	0.097
−11	−0.028	0.314	−0.023	0.111	−0.013	0.136	0.012	0.103	0.010	0.127	−0.004	0.093
−10	0.002	0.317	0.000	0.111	0.021	0.157	0.035	0.138	−0.020	0.108	0.027	0.120
−9	−0.019	0.298	0.013	0.124	−0.003	0.154	0.014	0.152	0.025	0.133	0.020	0.140
−8	0.111	0.410	0.005	0.129	−0.005	0.159	0.002	0.154	0.021	0.154	0.026	0.166
−7	0.098	0.508	0.007	0.136	−0.005	0.154	0.012	0.166	−0.003	0.152	−0.012	0.155
−6	−0.041	0.466	0.024	0.160	−0.005	0.150	−0.016	0.150	0.005	0.157	−0.007	0.147
−5	0.082	0.548	−0.025	0.135	−0.014	0.136	0.026	0.175	−0.011	0.146	0.004	0.151
−4	0.022	0.571	0.010	0.146	0.039	0.174	0.000	0.175	−0.016	0.130	−0.002	0.150
−3	−0.004	0.566	−0.006	0.140	−0.009	0.165	−0.016	0.159	−0.011	0.119	−0.002	0.148

Lag	(1)	(2)	(3)	(4)	(5)	(6)	(7)	(8)	(9)	(10)	(11)	(12)
−2	0.147	−0.001	0.125	0.007	0.126	−0.034	0.175	0.009	0.117	−0.023	0.567	0.000
−1	0.138	−0.009	0.131	0.005	0.112	−0.014	0.170	−0.005	0.072	−0.045	0.560	−0.007
0	0.134	−0.005	0.131	0.000	0.119	0.007	0.171	0.002	0.126	0.055	0.585	0.025
1	0.112	−0.022	0.104	−0.027	0.083	−0.036	0.202	0.030	0.080	−0.001	0.573	−0.012
2	0.089	−0.023	0.096	−0.008	0.087	0.003	0.211	0.009	0.081	−0.045	0.519	−0.054
3	0.058	−0.030	0.091	−0.004	0.094	0.008	0.205	−0.006	0.066	0.000	0.551	0.031
4	0.059	0.000	0.095	0.004	0.106	0.012	0.202	−0.003	0.105	−0.014	0.527	−0.024
5	0.057	−0.002	0.097	0.002	0.096	−0.010	0.197	−0.004	0.127	0.039	0.534	0.007
6	0.050	−0.006	0.094	−0.004	0.088	−0.008	0.193	−0.004	0.140	0.021	0.498	−0.036
7	0.047	−0.003	0.097	0.003	0.077	−0.011	0.191	−0.002	0.159	0.013	0.519	0.022
8	0.033	−0.013	0.127	0.030	0.087	0.010	0.184	−0.008	0.157	0.019	0.528	0.009
9	0.036	0.003	0.117	−0.010	0.077	−0.011	0.176	−0.007	0.155	−0.002	0.602	0.074
10	0.039	0.003	0.113	−0.004	0.067	−0.009	0.175	0.000	0.158	−0.003	0.620	0.017
11	0.037	−0.001	0.109	−0.004	0.077	0.009	0.179	−0.001	0.146	0.004	0.626	0.007
12	0.039	0.001	0.115	0.005	0.078	0.001	0.169	0.005	0.142	−0.012	0.658	0.032
13	0.028	−0.010	0.097	0.018	0.070	−0.008	0.171	−0.010	0.152	−0.004	0.668	0.010
14	0.027	−0.001	0.102	0.005	0.074	0.004	0.185	0.012	0.165	0.010	0.668	0.001
15	0.025	−0.002	0.111	0.009	0.093	0.019	0.193	0.014	0.171	0.013	0.672	0.004
16	0.034	0.009	0.105	−0.006	0.104	0.012	0.193	0.009	0.168	0.006	0.673	0.000
17	0.033	−0.001	0.108	0.003	0.116	0.011	0.193	−0.001	0.169	−0.003	0.672	−0.001
18	0.040	0.007	0.113	0.005	0.130	0.015	0.192	0.001	0.184	0.001	0.676	0.004
19	0.044	0.005	0.128	0.015	0.159	0.029	0.188	−0.001	0.184	0.015	0.672	−0.004
20	0.036	−0.008	0.119	−0.009	0.165	0.006	0.184	−0.004	0.190	0.000	0.685	0.013
21	0.028	−0.008	0.120	0.000	0.171	−0.013	0.183	−0.004	0.188	0.006	0.691	0.006
22	0.018	−0.010	0.117	−0.002	0.159	0.001	0.200	−0.002	0.193	−0.002	0.693	0.002
23	0.020	0.002	0.127	0.010	0.160	0.003	0.197	0.005	0.179	0.005	0.705	0.012
24	0.017	−0.003	0.138	0.011	0.163	0.011	0.217	−0.014	0.176	−0.014	0.705	0.000
25	0.027	0.010	0.150	0.013	0.174	0.008	0.220	−0.003	0.172	−0.003	0.705	0.000
26	0.035	0.008	0.154	0.003	0.182	0.005	0.202	−0.005	0.164	−0.005	0.708	0.002
27	0.029	−0.006	0.145	−0.009	0.187	0.023	0.205	−0.018	0.166	−0.008	0.711	0.004
28	0.026	−0.003	0.138	−0.007	0.210	0.007	0.197	0.003	0.166	0.002	0.702	−0.009
29	0.042	0.016	0.154	0.016	0.217	0.011	0.197	−0.009	0.172	0.000	0.708	0.005
30	0.050	0.008	0.160	0.006	0.228	0.005	0.212	0.000	0.167	0.006	0.704	−0.003
31	0.043	−0.007	0.159	−0.002	0.233	−0.010	0.181	0.016	0.172	−0.006	0.703	−0.002
32	0.047	0.004	0.159	0.001	0.222	−0.003	0.177	−0.006	0.165	0.006	0.700	−0.003
33	0.058	0.011	0.145	−0.014	0.209	−0.016	0.174	0.006	0.166	−0.007	0.730	0.003
34	0.073	0.015	0.146	0.001	0.193	0.014	−0.181	−0.007	0.162	0.001	0.716	0.013
35	0.076	0.002	0.137	−0.009	0.207	−0.003	0.170	0.001	0.155	−0.004	0.715	−0.001
36	0.092	0.017	0.129	−0.008	0.204	0.003	0.172	−0.004	0.154	−0.007	0.713	−0.002
37	0.104	0.012	0.121	−0.008	0.207	0.001	0.166	−0.007	0.160	−0.001	0.708	−0.005
38	0.116	0.013	0.111	−0.010	0.207	0.009	0.162	−0.001	0.167	0.005	0.705	−0.003
39	0.114	−0.002	0.113	0.002	0.216	−0.019	0.167	0.005	0.162	0.007	0.709	0.004
40	0.125	0.012	0.111	−0.002	0.197			0.005		−0.005	0.696	−0.013

Table 6B.5 Absolute Event Gains (Losses) ($ Million)

	Targets			Acquirers		
	Gulf Corp.	Superior Oil	Texaco Canada	Chevron	Mobil	Imperial Oil
Market value at − 41*	$7,296	$4,867	$3,729	$11,888	$12,052	$6,034
On day + 1						
CAR (market adjusted)**	0.573	0.126	0.202	0.083	0.140	0.112
Dollar gain (loss)	$4,183	$612	$752	$989	$1,254	$673
On day + 40						
CAR (market adjusted)**	0.696	0.162	0.167	0.197	0.111	0.125
Dollar gain (loss)	$5,078	$789	$621	$2,339	$1,341	$757

*Data from CRSP 1995 tape.

**Here the CARs represent the cumulative abnormal returns obtained by cumulating the daily abnormal returns in each of the individual company R3 columns in Tables 6B.2 and 6B.3, which are repeated as the first of the two columns under each company name in Table 6B.4.

Interpretation of Measurements

Residual analysis basically tests whether the return to the common stock of individual firms or groups of firms is greater or less than that predicted by general market relationships between return and risk. Most merger studies in recent years have made use of residual analysis. These studies have sought to test whether merger events provide positive or negative abnormal returns to the participants. The studies of abnormal returns provide a basis for examining the issue of whether or not value is enhanced by mergers.

The studies cover different time periods and different sample sizes. The studies are sometimes limited to conglomerate mergers. Other studies include horizontal and vertical mergers as well. Many studies deal with tender offers only. Some studies use monthly data, some use daily data, and some focus on individual mergers. At least one study analyzes firms engaged in programs of merger and tender offer activity over a period of years (Schipper and Thompson, 1983).

On average, the event studies predict the longer term performance of merging companies. Healy, Palepu, and Ruback (1992) find a strong positive relationship between the abnormal stock returns related to the announcement of mergers and the subsequent postmerger changes in operating cash flows. Their findings support the view that the event returns, on average, represent accurate predictions of the subsequent performance of merging companies.

STATISTICAL SIGNIFICANCE OF EVENT RETURNS

One Day, One Firm

Once the measures of abnormal returns have been estimated, we must interpret these results. Can we infer with a certain level of confidence that the residuals are significantly different from zero? If we assume that the returns for each firm are independently and identically normally distributed, then

$$\frac{r_{jt}}{\hat{S}(r_j)}$$

has a *t*-distribution. [r_{jt} is the residual for firm j on day t; $\hat{S}(r_{jt})$ is the estimated standard deviation of the residuals for firm j using data from the estimation period,

$$\left[\frac{1}{199}\sum_{t=-240}^{-41}(r_{jt}-\bar{r}_j)^2\right]^{1/2}$$

and the degrees of freedom are 199.] For more than 30 degrees of freedom, the *t*-statistic has, approximately, a standard normal distribution. This statistic tests the null hypothesis that the one-day residual for a single firm is equal to zero. Intuitively, we are comparing the value of the residual to its estimated sample standard deviation. Only if this ratio is greater than a specified critical value can we reject the null hypothesis with some degree of confidence. For instance, if this ratio is greater than 1.96, we can say that the one-day residual is significantly different from zero at the 5% level. If the ratio is greater than 2.58, we can reject the null hypothesis at a confidence level of 1%. Table 6B.6 presents the statistical significance (the *t*-stat) of the individual firm's residual on the announcement day (r_{j0}). The positive abnormal returns for Superior Oil are the only ones significant at the 1% level. For the other firms, we cannot reject the null hypothesis of a zero residual.

One Day, Average Over Firms

The corresponding test statistic for the hypothesis that the one-day residual, averaged over three firms,

$$AR_t=\frac{1}{3}\sum_{j=1}^{3}r_{jt}$$

is zero is as follows:

$$\frac{AR_t}{\hat{S}(AR)}=\frac{AR_t}{\left[\dfrac{1}{199}\displaystyle\sum_{t=-240}^{-41}(AR_t-\overline{AR})^2\right]^{1/2}}$$

where the sample standard deviation is

$$\hat{S}(AR)=\left[\frac{1}{199}\sum_{t=-240}^{-41}(AR_t-\overline{AR})^2\right]^{1/2}$$

and

$$\overline{AR}=\frac{1}{200}\sum_{t=-240}^{-41}AR_t$$

In Table 6B.6, the positive average residuals for the target companies are statistically significant. For the acquirers, the small average residuals are not distinguishable from zero.

Over 81 Days, Average Over Firms

The corresponding statistic for the cumulative average residual (CAR) for the three firms and cumulating over 81 days $[-40, +40]$, is

$$\frac{CAR}{\hat{S}(CAR)}=\frac{\displaystyle\sum_{t=-40}^{+40}AR_t}{\displaystyle\sum_{t=-40}^{+40}\hat{S}(AR)}=\frac{\displaystyle\sum_{t=-40}^{+40}AR_t}{\sqrt{81}\hat{S}(AR)}$$

Note that the estimated standard deviation for each day in the event interval is the same because we are using the same estimation period for a sample drawn from independent and identically distributed excess returns. Table 6B.7 presents the CAR for each individual firm and the average CAR for target and acquiring firms. Gulf Corp. is the only company that presents a significant abnormal return during the event interval. Both target and acquiring firms' average CARs are significant, except for the acquirers' average CAR using the mean adjusted return method.

The procedure we used to estimate the test statistics is the simplest to illustrate the calculations of statistical significance. Several adjustment factors must be recognized. For the mean adjusted return model and the market model, the estimation of $\hat{S}$ should be adjusted because the residuals involve prediction errors.

Table 6B.6 One-Day Residuals (Announcement Day) Statistical Significance

			Targets				Acquirers			
		Gulf Corp.	Superior Oil	Texaco Canada	Average	Chevron	Mobil	Imperial Oil	Average
M1: Mean adjusted Return model	$R1 = r_{jt}$ $= R_{jt} - \bar{R}_j$	r_{jo}	0.0158	0.0489	0.0023	0.0223	-0.0004	-0.0051	-0.0020	-0.0025
		s_j	0.0160	0.0236	0.0160	0.0104	0.0172	0.0171	0.0103	0.0083
		t-stat	0.9890	2.0764	0.1430	2.1496	-0.0215	-0.2998	-0.1947	-0.3021
M2: Market model method	$R2 = r_{jt}$ $= R_{jt} - \hat{\alpha}_j - \hat{\beta}_j R_{mt}$	r_{jo}	0.0236	0.0544	0.0014	0.0265	0.0094	0.0018	-0.0028	0.0028
		s_j	0.0144	0.0223	0.0152	0.0103	0.0150	0.0142	0.0094	0.0074
		t-stat	1.6385	2.4381	0.0906	2.5615	0.6264	0.1248	-0.2911	0.3805
M3: Market adjusted return method	$R3 = r_{jt}$ $= R_{jt} - R_{mt}$	r_{jo}	0.0253	0.0546	0.0019	0.0273	0.0074	0.0003	-0.0047	0.0010
		s_j	0.0144	0.0223	0.0155	0.0104	0.0151	0.0145	0.0102	0.0074
		t-stat	1.7589	2.4450	0.1209	2.6126	0.4883	0.0194	-0.4577	0.1326

Table 6B.7 Cumulative Average Residuals [-40, +40] Statistical Significance

			Targets				Acquirers			
		Gulf Corp.	Superior Oil	Texaco Canada	Average	Chevron	Mobil	Imperial Oil	Average
M1: Mean adjusted return model	$R1 = r_{jt}$ $= R_{jt} - \bar{R}_j$	CAR	0.4677	0.0079	0.1518	0.2091	0.1176	-0.0249	0.2932	0.1287
		s_j	0.1436	0.2121	0.1436	0.0935	0.1552	0.1543	0.0926	0.0746
		t-stat	3.2579	0.0370	1.0568	2.2371	0.7579	-0.1613	3.1673	1.7241
M2: Market model method	$R2 = r_{jt}$ $= R_{jt} - \hat{\alpha}_j - \hat{\beta}_j R_{mt}$	CAR	0.5715	0.1235	0.1084	0.2678	0.2470	0.1214	0.2575	0.2086
		s_j	0.1296	0.2008	0.1366	0.0930	0.1348	0.1280	0.0850	0.0663
		t-stat	4.4081	0.6151	0.7934	2.8807	1.8319	0.9481	3.0277	3.1465
M3: Market-adjusted return method	$R3 = r_{jt}$ $= R_{jt} - R_{mt}$	CAR	0.6960	0.1620	0.1667	0.3416	0.1967	0.1113	0.1254	0.1445
		s_j	0.1297	0.2009	0.1392	0.0939	0.1355	0.1301	0.0918	0.0670
		t-stat	5.3678	0.8066	1.1972	3.6372	1.4523	0.8555	1.3660	2.1575

These errors derive from the estimation of the mean return for the mean adjusted model and from the estimation of the regression coefficients for the market model. In addition, we did not take into account the possible changes in the variance outside the estimation period, nor did we consider time dependence or nonnormality in the returns. Finally, there is the possibility of cross-correlation in abnormal returns resulting, for example, from a government regulation that simultaneously impacts a number of different securities. For a more complete exposition of the issues involved in event studies, see Brown and Warner (1980, 1985) and Boehmer et al. (1991).

REFERENCES

Boehmer, E., J. Musumeci, and A. Poulsen, "Event-Study Methodology Under Conditions of Event-Induced Variance," *Journal of Financial Economics,* 30, 1991, pp. 253–272.

Brown, S., and J. Warner, "Measuring Security Price Performance," *Journal of Financial Economics,* 8, 1980, pp. 205–258.

————, "Using Daily Stock Returns: The Case of Event Studies." *Journal of Financial Economics,* 14, 1985, pp. 3–31.

Healy, Paul M., Krishna G. Palepu, and Richard S. Ruback, "Does Corporate Performance Improve After Mergers?" *Journal of Financial Economics,* 31, 1992, pp. 135–175.

Schipper, K., and R. Thompson, "Evidence on the Capitalized Value of Merger Activity for Acquiring Firms," *Journal of Financial Economics,* 11, 1983, pp. 85–119.

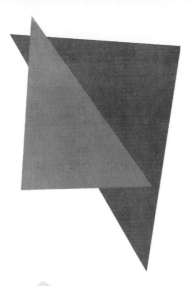

The Timing of Merger Activity

In chapter 6 we presented a number of alternative theories or explanations of why M&As take place. The present chapter starts the process of testing alternative explanations of M&A activity by examining the empirical evidence. We begin by reviewing the major merger movements that have taken place in the United States since the 1890s.

EARLY MERGER MOVEMENTS

Several major merger movements have occurred in the United States (Golbe and White, 1988), and each was more or less dominated by a particular type of merger. All of the merger movements occurred when the economy experienced sustained high rates of growth and coincided with particular developments in business environments. Mergers represent resource allocation and reallocation processes in the economy, with firms responding to new investment and profit opportunities arising out of changes in economic conditions and technological innovations impacting industries. Mergers rather than internal growth may sometimes expedite the adjustment process and in some cases be more efficient in terms of resource utilization.

The 1895 to 1904 Horizontal Mergers

The combination movement at the turn of the century consisted mainly of horizontal mergers, which resulted in high concentration in many industries, including heavy manufacturing industries. The period was one of rapid economic expansion. The 1904 decision of the Supreme Court in the Northern Securities case [193 U.S. 197 (March 1904)] may have contributed to ending this merger wave. In the decision, the Court established that mergers could be successfully attacked by Section I of the Sherman Act, which prohibited "every combination in the form of trust or otherwise" in restraint of trade. It should be noted, however, that the merger activity began its downturn in 1901, as some combinations failed to realize their expectations, and declined further by 1903, when the economy went into recession.

This merger movement at the turn of the century accompanied major changes in economic infrastructure and production technologies (Markham, 1955, p. 156;

Salter and Weinhold, 1980, p. 7). It followed the completion of the transcontinental railroad system, the advent of electricity, and a major increase in the use of coal. The completed rail system resulted in the development of a national economic market, and thus the merger activity represented to a certain extent the transformation of regional firms into national firms.

In addition to the goal of achieving economies of scale, two other motivational factors have been ascribed to this first major merger movement. Stigler (1950) characterized the merger movement as "merging for monopoly." Of 92 large mergers studied by Moody (1904), 78 controlled 50% or more of the market. However, in reviewing the early literature on mergers, Markham (1955) concluded that "out of every five mergers ostensibly monopolistic in character only one resulted in considerable monopoly control" (pp. 161–162) and that "it is certain that many mergers formed during the early merger movement did not have monopoly power as their principal objective and, accordingly, must be explained on other grounds" (p. 162). In reviewing the early literature, authors such as Markham (1955) and Salter and Weinhold (1979) concluded that professional promoters and underwriters or "producers" of mergers added to the magnitude of the merger wave.

Several studies attempted to measure the success of the early mergers in terms of profitability and to determine the reasons for their success or failure. Livermore (1935) attributed success to "astute business leadership" and, in particular, to rapid technological and managerial improvement, development of new products or entry into a new subdivision of the industry, promotion of quality brand names, and commercial exploitation of research. The causes for failure as given by Dewing (1953) included lack of efforts to realize economies of scale by modernizing inherited plant and equipment, increase in overhead costs and lack of flexibility due to large size, and inadequate supply of talent to manage a large group of plants.

The 1922 to 1929 Vertical Mergers

As in the first merger movement, the second wave of mergers also began with an upturn in business activity, in 1922. It ended with the onset of a severe economic slowdown in 1929. Many combinations in this period occurred outside the previously consolidated heavy manufacturing industries. The public utilities and banking industries were among the most active. About 60% of the mergers occurred in the still fragmented food processing, chemicals, and mining sectors (Salter and Weinhold, 1980, p. 4). Accordingly, the question of monopoly was not applicable in most cases, and the transformation of a near monopoly to an oligopoly by "merging for oligopoly" was more frequent (Stigler, 1950). While oligopoly provided a motive for many mergers, it was limited to no more than a small fraction of the mergers (Markham, 1955, p. 169). A large portion of mergers in the 1920s represented product extension mergers, as in the cases of IBM, General Foods, and Allied Chemical; market extension mergers in food retailing, department stores, and motion picture theaters; and vertical mergers in the mining and metals industries.

As for the motivational factors of these mergers, both Markham (1955) and Stocking (1955) emphasized major developments in transportation, communication, and merchandising. A new transportation system utilizing motor vehicles broke down small local markets by enabling sellers to extend their sales areas and by making consumers more mobile. Mergers in such industries as food processing and chemicals accompanied the rise of automobile transportation just as mergers in heavy industries in the previous merger movement accompanied the rise of railroad transportation. The development of home radios facilitated product differentiation through national-brand advertising. By the 1920s, mass distribution with low profit margins became a new method of merchandising. Both these developments caused an increase in the scale of operations and hence encouraged mergers. On the increase in vertical integration, Stocking noted that by the 1920s business had come to appreciate the advantages of integration. The advantages were related to technological economies such as the shortening of processes or elimination of waste motions in a mechanical sense, or the reliability of input supply.

THE CONGLOMERATE MERGERS OF THE 1960S

The Celler-Kefauver Act of 1950 amended Section 7 of the Clayton Act of 1914 to close the "asset-purchase" loophole and granted the federal government additional power to declare illegal those mergers that tended to increase concentration. (The Clayton Act had prohibited a corporation from acquiring the stock of another corporation if competition were to be substantially lessened. The act had referred only to acquisition of stock, not that of assets.) Thereafter, the relative importance of horizontal and vertical mergers declined in relation to conglomerate mergers. By 1967 to 1968 when the merger activity peaked, horizontal and vertical mergers declined to 17% of the total number of mergers. Among the conglomerate type of mergers, product extension mergers increased to 60% and market extension mergers became negligible in number. "Other" or pure conglomerates increased steadily to about 23% of all mergers (or 35% in terms of assets acquired). Merger activity reached its then historically highest level during the three-year period of 1967 through 1969. The period was also one of a booming economy. The number of mergers declined sharply as general economic activity slowed after 1969.

Most acquirers in the period that have subsequently been known as conglomerates were small or medium-sized firms that adopted a diversification strategy into business activities outside their traditional areas of interest. The acquired firms were also small or medium-sized and "operating in either fragmented industries or on the periphery of major industrial sectors" (Salter and Weinhold, 1980, p. 6). Based on an analysis of backgrounds and acquisition histories of the acquiring firms, Weston and Mansinghka (1971) suggested that the conglomerates were "diversifying defensively to avoid (1) sales and profit instability, (2) adverse growth developments, (3) adverse competitive shifts, (4) technological obsolescence, and (5) increased uncertainties associated with their industries" (Weston and Mansinghka, 1971, p. 928).

The largest single category of firms was the aerospace industry. This industry was subject to wide fluctuations in total market demand as well as abrupt and major shifts in its product mix. The Department of Defense (DOD) emphasized high technology weapons from 1945 through 1950. During the Korean War in the early 1950s, DOD procurement shifted to ammunition and ordinance. When Dwight Eisenhower became president in 1953, he quickly ended the Korean War, cut DOD spending substantially, and shifted to high tech weapons. These shifts created substantial demand uncertainty for defense firms. Reduced DOD spending caused excess capacity, aggravated by partial entry of firms from other industries.

The industrial machinery and auto parts companies were also subject to considerable instability in sales. Low growth prospects were associated with a major long-term decline in some markets. This was characteristic of the railway equipment industry, textiles, movie distribution (at an earlier period), and the tobacco industry.

Sometimes the conglomerate represented the personality of the chief executive, for example, Harold Geneen at ITT and Charles Bludhorn at Gulf & Western. Their successors sold off everything but a relatively focused core of activities. Some conglomerates were formed to imitate earlier conglomerates that appeared to have achieved high growth and high valuations. Many of the later conglomerates had no sound conceptual basis and were a substantial source of sell-offs in later years. Indeed, many writers view the merger activity of the 1980s as a correction to the unwise diversification of the 1960s (Shleifer and Vishny, 1990).

The rise of management theory that had begun in the 1950s led to the increased professionalization of business operations. The early success of the General Electric Company and Litton Industries in moving top executives from highly divergent types of business operations led some to generalize that "good managers can manage anything." This provided some intellectual underpinning for combining the unrelated activities in conglomerate firms.

Another influence was playing the differential price/earnings (P/E) game. When an acquiring firm with a high P/E ratio combines with a firm with a lower P/E ratio, the earnings per share (EPS) of the buyer will rise. Table 7.1 illustrates this generalization. The first three rows present assumed data for a buyer in column 1 and a seller in column 2 on P/E ratios, net income, and shares outstanding. Row 4 is calculated as net income divided by shares outstanding to obtain EPS. The final row is the indicated market value per share obtained by multiplying the P/E times EPS.

The results in column 3 for the combined firms are summarized briefly in column 4. The P/E ratio of the buyer is assumed to continue for the combined firm. The net income of $200 million is a simple addition. We postulate that the buyer pays a 20% premium for the seller, or $60 per share. Hence, the buyer pays the seller 0.6 of its $100 stock, so the buyer issues 12 million shares to replace the 20 million

Table 7.1 Playing the Relative P/E Game

	(1) Buyer	(2) Seller	(3) Combined	(4) Explanation for column 3
Price Earnings Ratio (P/E)	20	10	20	Assumed
Net Income	$100 million	$100 million	$200 million	(1) + (2)
Shares Outstanding	20 million	20 million	32 million	(1) + 0.6(20 million)
Earnings per Share (EPS)	$5	$5	$6.25	$200 / 32
Market Value per Share	$100	$50	$125	20 × $6.25

Table 7.2   Effects on Buyers and Sellers

	Buyer		Seller	
	Premerger	**Postmerger**	**Premerger**	**Postmerger**
Earnings per Share	$5	$6.25	$5	$3.75
Market Price per Share	$100	$125	$50	$75
Total Market Value	$2 billion	$2.5 billion	$1 billion	$1.5 billion

of the seller. The total shares in the combined column are 32 million. Dividing this number into the combined net income of $200 million gives $6.25 as the new EPS. Applying the P/E of 20 gives a market price per share of $125.

In Table 7.2, the effects on buyers and sellers are summarized. The postmerger EPS for the buyer increases by $1.25, or 25%. Its market price per share also increases by 25% to $125. The EPS of the seller is 0.6 of the postmerger price of $6.25, which is $3.75. It suffers dilution in EPS. But the seller now owns 0.6 share of stock worth $125. So postmerger, for each share the seller owned premerger, the seller holds a value of $75. This represents an increase in market value of 50%. This is the nature of P/E magic.

The key assumption in the above is that the P/E ratio of the buyer will carry over to the combined firm. Since the buyer could announce that its earnings per share had increased by 25%, its actual postmerger P/E ratio was likely to increase even further. While P/E magic works in the short run, in the longer run it is likely to come apart. The lower P/E ratio of the seller company must reflect either lower growth and/or higher risk. In the longer term, the lower growth of the seller will depress the earnings growth of the buyer. The higher risk implies the occurrence of unfavorable events, also depressing earnings. So P/E magic works only if the new acquisitions are sufficient to offset the depressing influences of the older acquisitions.

In 1968, Congress began to move against conglomerate firms in both the antitrust and tax arenas. The Department of Justice (DOJ) began to file suits against conglomerate firms. Congressional hearings were held on the frightening increase in size and power of the big conglomerate firms. These actions adversely affected conglomerate prices. The Tax Reform Act of 1969 limited the use of convertible debt to finance acquisitions. The use of convertible debt had magnified P/E magic. The prospect of large future capital gains made it possible to sell convertible debt with low coupons, so the conglomerate firms obtained cash inflows from the sale of debt at low after-tax cost, which contributed to their growth in EPS and market prices. The act also provided that EPS would have to be calculated on a fully diluted basis, as if the debt had been converted into common stock.

The hostile public policy environment depressed the stock prices of conglomerate firms. In addition, the general stock market declined. The Dow Jones Industrial Average peaked in 1967 at slightly over 1,000, then declined to 631 by mid-1971. Thus, hostile antitrust policies, punitive tax laws, and declining stock prices brought the conglomerate merger movement to an end.

Table 7.3   Largest Transactions Announced in the 1980s

Buyer	Seller	Industry	Deal Value (Billions)	Year Announced
Kohlberg Kravis Roberts	RJR Nabisco	Food, tobacco	$27.5	1988
Beecham Group PLC	SmithKline Beecham	Drugs	$16.1	1989
Chevron Corp.	Gulf Corp.	Oil	$13.2	1984
Phillip Morris	Kraft Inc.	Food, tobacco	$13.1	1988
Bristol-Myers	Squibb	Drugs	$12.0	1989
Time Inc.	Warner Communications	Media	$11.7	1989
Texaco Inc.	Getty Oil	Oil	$10.1	1984
DuPont Co.	Conoco	Oil	$8.0	1981
British Petroleum	Standard Oil (Ohio)	Oil	$7.8	1987
U.S. Steel	Marathon Oil	Oil	$6.6	1981
			Total $126.1	

Source: *Mergerstat Review*, 1981–1989.

THE DEAL DECADE, 1981 TO 1989

The fourth merger movement during 1981 to 1989 excited the interest of the general public. The pace of activity exceeded even the conglomerate activity of the 1960s. There was a confluence of forces. The economy and the stock market began to surge upward in mid-1982. International competition was increasing, impacting mature industries such as steel and autos. As noted, the conglomerates began to be streamlined. New technologies and managerial innovations brought new industries into existence and affected the old. Computers and microwave communication systems impacted the communication and entertainment industries.

This was the decade of big deals as illustrated by Table 7.3. All of the 10 largest transactions of the 1980s exceeded $6 billion each. Five of the 10 involved oil companies, reflecting the increased price instability resulting from OPEC actions. The two drug mergers reflected the increased pressure to reduce drug prices because of the high proportion of spending by the rising proportion of the population represented by older people. Two of the remaining three reflected efforts by tobacco companies to diversify into the food industry.

The ability to undertake transactions was facilitated by the financial innovations of the 1980s. Michael Milken, through the Drexel Burnham investment banking firm, was able to underwrite the sale of large volumes of below investment grade (high yield junk bonds) debt securities. The concept was that yields on portfolios of junk bonds net of defaults would provide a differential over less risky portfolios commensurate with the risk differentials. The creation of a broad market for risky debt provided financing for aggressive acquirers who came to be known as raiders. Holderness and Sheehan (1985) studied the activities of six "controversial investors." They found that their stock purchases resulted in positive event returns as well as positive returns to shareholders net of benchmarks for the subsequent two years. This evidence appeared consistent with two hypotheses: (1) The six investors were able to identify underpriced stocks; (2) they influenced the improvement in the management of the target firms.

The 1980s also witnessed the rise of financial buyers such as Kohlberg Kravis Roberts (KKR) (Table 7.3). The financial buyers arranged going-private transactions, referred to as *leveraged buyouts* (LBOs). The LBO concept was to purchase a public company with substantial use of debt, provide managers with large equity interest for strong incentives, improve operations, reduce debt from operating cash flows, and harvest the investment by taking the firm public again within a 3- to 5-year holding period (LBOs are discussed in greater detail in chapter 16).

Often the financial buyers bought segments of diversified firms. Thus almost one-half of the annual acquisitions during the 1980s represented divestitures of selling firms. This was part of the process of unwinding the conglomerates, as firms sought to focus on their core capabilities.

Another process by which diversification was unwound was by the use of "bustup acquisitions." Corporate buyers and others would seek firms whose parts as separate entities were worth more than the whole. After the acquisition, segments would be divested. Proceeds of such sales were often used to reduce the debt incurred to finance the transaction.

The combined impact of raiders, financial buyers, and bustup merger activity was to put pressure on business firms, large or small, to defend against takeovers. Sophisticated acquisition activities began to be matched by the rise of a wide range of defensive measures (discussed in chapter 19). So the increased use of hostile takeovers financed by debt gave rise to the increased use of defensive measures.

With growing reports of insider trading during the 1980s and concern about the general impact of mergers on the economy, government actions became restrictive. A number of well-publicized insider trading cases cast doubt on the integrity and soundness of merger activity. The 1980s began to be referred to as the decade of greed. In a highly publicized case, Dennis Levine, who had joined Drexel in 1984 after experience with other investment banking firms, pleaded guilty in mid-1986 to charges of insider trading. He also implicated Ivan Boesky, a prominent arbitrageur on mergers. In a deal with prosecutor Rudolph Giuliani to lighten his sentence, Boesky implicated Michael Milken, who was indicted in 1989. Giuliani invoked the use of RICO, which would have enabled him to seize the assets of the defendant to pressure Milken. Milken argued his innocence and did not implicate others. Ultimately, Milken pleaded guilty to six of the 98 charges. He was originally sentenced to 10 years in prison, but in 1992 the sentence was reduced to 24 months. Milken was also required to pay $1 billion to settle various other charges.

With the indictment of Michael Milken and the subsequent bankruptcy of Drexel on February 13, 1990, the junk bond market was severely wounded. Some major LBO deals could not be financed. The weakness in the junk bond market was exacerbated by the passage in 1989 of the Financial Institutions Reform, Recovery, and Enforcement Act (FIRREA). This law essentially required financial institutions to mark their junk bond holdings down to market. The effect was to force massive sales of junk bonds by financial institutions, which further devastated the junk bond market.

The economic recession associated with the war against Iraq also put a damper on M&A activity. The development of powerful takeover defenses, state antitakeover laws, the weakness in the junk bond market, and the economic downturn all combined to bring the deal decade to an end. Some predicted that these forces would reduce future merger activity as well.

STRATEGIC MERGERS, 1992 TO ??

By 1992, another merger movement began to get under way. The Gulf War was over, and economic recovery was strong. The stock market resumed its upward course. Other investment banking firms moved into the junk bond market, which recovered to levels above its 1988 peak. The period of strategic mergers was under way to bring levels of activity higher than ever before experienced. The major forces were (1) technology, (2) globalization, (3) deregulation, (4) the economic environment, (5) the method of payment, (6) share repurchases, and (7) stock options.

Technological change has occurred at an explosive pace. Computer and software applications have impacted all aspects of business. Microwave systems and fiber optics have transformed the telecommunications industry. The Internet explosion has created new industries and firms, changing the forms and nature of competitive relationships. Acquisitions by firms in all segments of the Internet economy have been used to augment critical capabilities and to gain economies of scale and scope.

The globalization of markets matured in the 1990s. Competition can come from distant places. Europe and other regions continued to move toward common markets. The transcontinental railroads had made the United States a common market at the end of the 1800s. Technological developments in transportation and communications are making the world a common market at the beginning of the new millennium.

The intensification of competition brought on by technological change and globalization led to deregulation in major industries. These include financial services, telecommunications, energy in all its forms, airlines, trucking, etc. Increased competition forced deregulation, which in turn causes further massive reorganization of industries. M&As played a major role in the readjustment processes necessitated by deregulation.

M&A activities of all forms that have resulted from the preceding three forces have been facilitated by a favorable economic environment. Stock prices have been rising. Price-earning ratios have been moving upwards. Interest rate levels have been relatively low and financing available.

Many megamergers have been made possible by stock-for-stock transactions. Deals of over $500 million have been predominantly stock-for-stock. Compared with the high debt transactions of the 1980s, this places less time pressure for achieving improvements in cash flows, permitting longer term strategies to be executed.

Successful firms with superior revenue growth and favorable cost structures have used programs of share repurchases to signal their favorable future prospects. The combination of strong performance and credible signals of future success have produced impressive returns to shareholders.

Rising stock prices have made the use of stock options a powerful tool in competing in the managerial labor market. High tech firms have added stock options as an important component of compensation to attract innovative, experienced executives. Some firms have extended the use of stock options as a form of compensation widely throughout the organization. Stock options increase the number of shares outstanding; share repurchases provide a counterbalance. Both have been widely used by firms in the "New Economy" sectors.

These seven major factors defined the strategic mergers of the 1990s. The megamergers of the 1990s reflect the pervasive strength of the seven influences listed at the beginning of this section. The top 10 transactions of all time are listed in Table 1.2 of Chapter 1. All of these transactions occurred in 1998 and 1999. The top 10 transactions of the 1990s totaled about $700 billion, compared with $126 billion for the decade of the 1980s. The RJR Nabisco transaction was number 1 in the 1980s; it would rank 23rd in the 1990s.

Another measure of the impact of the 1990s is the size of M&As in relation to the level of economic activity as measured by gross domestic product (GDP). This is shown in Table 7.4. We calculated the annual average for four time segments. During the deal decade of the 1980s, M&As represented less than 4% of GDP. For the period 1993 through 1999, M&As became about 12% of GDP. In 1999, the number was 15%. For perspective, the largest previous merger movement was at the turn of the century, when M&A activity was about 10% of the size of the economy.

TIMING OF MERGER ACTIVITY

The foregoing summary of the major merger movements in U.S. history suggests that somewhat different forces were operating in different historical economic and financial environments. The data show merger waves in the sense that in some groups of years merger activity increases sharply. But the evidence does not support merger waves in the sense of regular patterns of periodic rises and declines of merger activity.

Two broad generalizations can be made. One is that each of the major merger movements reflected some underlying economic or technological factors. The early twentieth century movement was triggered by the completion of the transnational railroads, which made the United States the first large common market. This was the major force behind the horizontal mergers that consolidated regional firms into national firms. The automobile and radio had an impact on distribution systems, stimulating the vertical mergers of the 1920s (some articles have disputed whether vertical mergers were predominant—our judgment of the evidence is that they were). The conglomerate mergers of the 1960s reflected the view that good managers could manage unrelated activities. The use of differential price earnings ratios to augment earnings growth in the near term produced spectacular stock price movements for major conglomerates such as ITT and Litton Industries. The deal decade of the 1980s was fueled by unwinding diversification and innovations in financing. The strategic mergers of the 1990s were produced by the combination of seven factors described earlier. In some respects, therefore, each major merger movement was associated with strong economic and technological factors. But the strength and nature of these factors were different for each of the five major merger movements.

A second generalization is also possible. Some common economic factors are associated with different levels of merger activity. Rising stock prices, low interest

Table 7.4   M&As in Relation to the Size of the Economy

Year	(1) Dollar Amount of M&As (Billions)	(2) GDP in Current Dollars (Billions)	(3) M&As as Percent of GDP
1970	16.4	1,015.5	1.6%
1971	12.6	1,102.7	1.1%
1972	16.7	1,212.8	1.4%
1973	16.7	1,359.3	1.2%
1974	12.4	1,472.8	0.8%
1975	11.8	1,598.4	0.7%
1976	20.0	1,782.8	1.1%
1977	21.9	1,990.5	1.1%
1978	34.2	2,249.7	1.5%
1979	43.5	2,508.2	1.7%
1980	44.3	2,732.0	1.6%
1981	82.6	3,052.6	2.7%
1982	53.8	3,166.0	1.7%
1983	73.1	3,405.7	2.1%
1984	122.2	3,772.2	3.2%
1985	179.6	4,014.9	4.5%
1986	173.1	4,240.3	4.1%
1987	163.7	4,526.7	3.6%
1988	246.9	4,880.6	5.1%
1989	221.1	5,200.8	4.3%
1990	108.2	5,463.6	2.0%
1991	71.2	5,632.5	1.3%
1992	96.7	6,020.2	1.6%
1993	176.4	6,343.3	2.8%
1994	226.7	6,738.2	3.4%
1995	356.0	7,245.8	4.9%
1996	495.0	7,574.2	6.5%
1997	657.1	8,300.7	7.9%
1998	1,191.9	8,760.0	13.6%
1999	1,426.9	9,278.0	15.4%
Annual Average			
1970–1980	22.8	1,729.5	1.3%
1981–1989	146.2	4,028.9	3.6%
1990–1992	92.0	5,705.4	1.6%
1993–1999	647.1	7,748.6	8.4%

Sources: Column 1: Houlihan Lokey Howard & Zukin, *Mergerstat Review, 1999,* Los Angeles, CA; column 2: *Economic Report of the President,* various issues; *Economic Indicators.*

rates, favorable term structures of interest rates in the form of low short rates in relation to long rates, narrow risk premiums in the form of small differentials between treasury bonds and medium to low rated corporate bonds are all favorable to higher levels of merger activity (Weston, 1953; Nelson, 1959; Melicher, Ledolter, and D'Antonio, 1983; Shughart and Tollison, 1984).

INTERNATIONAL PERSPECTIVES

The data on M&A activities in other countries are not as complete as those for the United States. But the evidence is clear that the increased M&A and restructuring activity is not unique to the United States. In all of the developed countries of the world, M&A activity in recent decades has paralleled the patterns in the United States. The underlying major force has been the internationalization of markets and the globalization of competition.

Industries and firms in countries throughout the world have experienced the pressures of the increased intensity of competitive forces. Some have argued that relaxed government policies in the early 1980s stimulated an M&A wave in the United States. But clearly antimerger laws and regulations were increased in the United Kingdom in the 1980s. Also, the policies of the European Economic Community were to tighten antimerger regulations since the 1980s. Nevertheless, M&A activity increased in the United Kingdom and in all of Europe in the face of tighter legal restraints. This again suggests that M&A activity is determined primarily by underlying economic and financial forces.

SUMMARY

To place merger activity in perspective, we have traced the major merger movements since the turn of the twentieth century. All of the merger movements coincided with sustained growth of the economy and with significant changes in business environments. The horizontal merger movement in the 1890s was associated with the completion of national transportation systems and made the United States the first broad common market. Mergers in the 1920s were represented by both forward and backward vertical integration. They appeared to represent responses to radio, which made national advertising feasible, and to the automobile, which facilitated national distribution systems. The conglomerate merger movement of the 1960s appeared to reflect the philosophy of management technology that had developed in the 1950s. The mergers of the 1980s were associated with innovations in financing and the reversal of the diversification of the 1960s. The strategic mergers of the 1990s were propelled by favorable economic environments and by new forces of technology, globalization, and deregulation.

Fluctuations in merger activity over the years stimulated a number of attempts to explain the determinants of merger timing. These studies have demonstrated an association between merger activity and various macroeconomic variables. The main macroeconomic forces are rising stock prices, low interest rates, and favorable conditions of financing availability.

QUESTIONS

7.1 Describe each of the major merger movements that have occurred in the United States, indicating the major forces involved.

7.2 What percentage of gross domestic product is represented by M&A activity?

7.3 Discuss the effect of the following variables on merger activity:
 a. The growth rate of GDP.
 b. Interest rate levels.
 c. Interest rate risk premiums.
 d. Monetary stringency.

REFERENCES

Dewing, Arthur Stone, *The Financial Policy of Corporations,* Vol. 2, New York: The Ronald Press Company, 1953.

Golbe, Devra L., and Lawrence J. White, "A Time-Series Analysis of Mergers and Acquisitions in the U.S. Economy," chapter 9 in Alan J. Auerbach, ed., *Corporate Takeover: Causes and Consequences,* Chicago: The University of Chicago Press, 1988, pp. 265–309.

Holderness, Clifford G., and Dennis P. Sheehan, "Raiders or Saviors?: The Evidence on Six Controversial Investors," *Journal of Financial Economics,* 14, 1985, pp. 555–579.

Livermore, Shaw, "The Success of Industrial Mergers," *Quarterly Journal of Economics,* 50, November 1935, pp. 68–96.

Markham, Jesse W., "Survey of Evidence and Findings on Mergers," *Business Concentration and Price Policy,* National Bureau of Economic Research, Princeton, NJ: Princeton University Press, 1955.

Melicher, R. W., J. Ledolter, and L. D'Antonio, "A Time Series Analysis of Aggregate Merger Activity," *The Review of Economics and Statistics,* 65, August 1983, pp. 423–430.

Moody, John, *The Truth About the Trusts,* New York: Moody Publishing Company, 1904.

Nelson, R. L., *Merger Movements in American Industry, 1895–1956,* Princeton, NJ: Princeton University Press, 1959.

Salter, Malcolm S., and Wolf A. Weinhold, *Diversification Through Acquisition,* New York: The Free Press, 1979.

———, "Merger Trends and Prospects for the 1980s," U.S. Department of Commerce, Harvard University, December 1980.

Shleifer, Andrei, and Robert W. Vishny, "The Takeover Wave of the 1980s," *Science,* 249, August 1990, pp. 745–749.

Shughart, W. F., II, and R. O. Tollison, " The Random Character of Merger Activity," *Rand Journal of Economics,* 15, Winter 1984, pp. 500–509.

Stigler, George J., "Monopoly and Oligopoly by Merger," *American Economic Review,* 40, May 1950, pp. 23–34.

Stocking, G. W., "Commentary on Markham, 'Survey of Evidence and Findings on Mergers,' " in *Business Concentration and Price Policy,* Princeton, NJ: Princeton University Press, 1955, pp. 191–212.

Weston, J. F., *The Role of Mergers in the Growth of Large Firms,* Berkeley and Los Angeles: University of California Press, 1953, chapter 5.

———, and Surenda K. Mansinghka, "Tests of the Efficiency Performance of Conglomerate Firms," *Journal of Finance,* 26, September 1971, pp. 919–936.

Empirical Tests of M&A Performance

Previous chapters have discussed alternative theories of why mergers and tender offers occur. This chapter reviews the relevant empirical tests. We begin with some central issues to give us a brief reference framework for a discussion of empirical tests of M&A performance.

ISSUES IN EMPIRICAL STUDIES

There are a number of issues and questions that empirical studies of M&A performance may potentially elucidate. First and foremost, the goal is to provide tests of alternative theories. Another important objective from a public policy standpoint is to determine whether or not social value is enhanced by mergers. If, for example, the basic driving force for mergers is improved efficiency, the improvement represents a social gain regardless of the theory that explains how it is achieved.

Do value increases represent social gains or merely redistribution? The first issue then is: Is true social value increased?

If value is increased by mergers or tender offers, is it maintained? Is value maintained in the short term only for a period of six months or less? Or should the tests cover a subsequent period of five to ten years? A second basic issue is: Does the restructuring result in operating performance improvements that can be measured for subsequent years?

A third basic issue relates to industry effects. To what degree are restructuring activities related to fundamental technological, economic, regulatory, and other forces taking place in individual industries? Another important issue is: How do we analyze the effects of restructuring by one firm on other firms in the same industry?

These three major issues are tested by a large number of studies. We organize them into the following topics: returns in successful mergers and takeovers, unsuccessful takeovers, methods of payment and managerial resistance, positive total returns versus negative total returns, effects of regulation, single bids versus multiple bids, runup versus markup returns, efficiency versus market power, post-merger performance, industry influences on M&A activity, and patterns of takeover activity.

In chapter 7 we noted a difference between the deal decade of the 1980s and the strategic mergers of the 1990s. Hence, we will summarize the results on merger performance for each of the two periods.

MERGER PERFORMANCE DURING THE 1980S

Most of the leading studies of merger performance cover the 1980s time period or earlier. For example, in their comprehensive summary article, Jensen and Ruback (1983) reviewed 13 studies with sample data ending mostly in the late 1970s. Six of the studies were on mergers and seven on tender offers. Bradley, Desai, and Kim (1988) covered tender offer contests completed between 1963 and 1984. Schwert (1996) covered the years 1975 through 1991, using a sample of 1,814 companies. Sirower (1997) covered 168 transactions during the period 1979 to 1990.

Successful Transactions

The patterns of event returns for the 1980s suggested by a myriad of studies, including those just cited, are shown in Table 8.1. Clearly, targets always gained substantially. Mergers were more likely to be friendly negotiations. Tender offers during the 1980s were more frequently hostile. The big difference was that the method of payment was more likely to be cash in tender offers, compared with stock in merger deals. As we noted in earlier chapters, stock-for-stock deals are more likely to be nontaxable and to use pooling accounting. Cash deals are likely to be taxable and to use purchase accounting.

The evidence shows that the returns to target firms increased over the decades as government regulation increased and as sophisticated defensive tactics were developed by targets. The excess returns to bidding firms decreased over the decades because of the same influences operating in the reverse direction. But even for the 1980s it appears that the total wealth increase from M&A activity is positive.

These conclusions are also supported by the frequency distribution analysis of You, Caves, Smith, and Henry (1986). The mean return to target companies for 133 mergers during the period 1975 through June 1984 was about 20%. The excess returns to shareholders of bidder companies were a negative 1%. In addition to mean returns, You et al. presented frequency distributions. For target companies, 82% had positive excess returns. In fact, 20% of the companies had positive excess returns exceeding 40%. But 18% of the target companies had negative returns. For bidder com-

Table 8.1   Pattern of Event Returns for the 1980s

	Mergers	**Tender Offers**
Targets	Positive 20–25%	Positive 30–40%
Buyers	Positive 1–2%	Negative 1–2%

panies, about 47% had positive returns and about 53% had negative returns. However, most positive returns for bidder firms were modest in size. Twenty-five percent of the bidder companies had positive returns between 0 and 5%. This is also true for the bidders that experienced negative returns—28% had excess returns between 0 and −5%.

Thus, the mean returns cover up the wide diversity in experience for both target and bidder companies. Although bidder companies experience negative returns for some time period, there are always a substantial fraction of the bidder companies that experience positive returns. This may provide motivation for bidder firms to continue to engage in M&A activity even though average results may be unfavorable. Each firm, based on the evidence, may formulate the judgment that its own results can be positive.

Unsuccessful Takeovers

In discussing a sample of 112 unsuccessful takeovers, Bradley, Desai, and Kim (1983) divided the targets into three groups. Firms in the first group (58% of the sample) were subsequently taken over within 60 trading days after the announcement date (day zero). The cumulative abnormal return (CAR) was almost 50% during the two-day period [−1, 0] and rose to over 66% by the end of the 60 trading days. Those in a second group (19% of the sample) were taken over more than 60 days after the announcement but within five years. Their CAR for the two-day period [−1, 0] was about 23%. By day +60, their CAR rose to over 55%. So they did almost as well as the first group, but the market did not react until later, when the probability of a subsequent bid increased. For the third group (23% of the sample), which were not taken over within the five-year period, the CAR, which was initially about the same as for the second group, became negative after two years and drifted between a range of a negative 5% to 10% during the subsequent three years.

In discussing unsuccessful bidders, Bradley, Desai, and Kim divided their sample into two groups. Group 1 bidders lost out to a rival bidder by the end of 180 trading days after the announcement date. Their CAR was a negative 8% by the end of the 180 days. For group 2 bidders, no rival bidder had succeeded within the 180 days subsequent to the initial announcement. At the end of 180 days, these bidders experienced a small positive, but not significant, CAR.

The results for the unsuccessful acquiring firms are of interest because of the impact on total value. As observed previously, if the returns to acquiring firms are sufficiently negative, this could cause the total activity to be a negative net present value activity rather than one that created positive values.

Bradley, Desai, and Kim (1983) found that for the period 1963 through 1980, the unsuccessful bidders in the multiple-bidder contests on average lost 8% of their preoffer value. They observed that the gains to successful bidders in multiple-bidder contests during the same period were not significantly different from zero. They concluded that it is better to win than to lose in a multiple-bidding contest. But this conclusion did not hold for the 1981 to 1984 period, during which successful bidders in multiple-bidder contests lost 5.1% (highly significant) (Bradley, Desai, and Kim, 1988).

For a larger sample of tender offers, Opler (1988) found that for the period 1981 to 1986 unsuccessful bidders earned a positive 0.68%, marginally significant. The results for unsuccessful acquiring firms depended on a number of other variables, however. The cumulative average abnormal return was a positive 10% 18 months after termination if a later takeover had occurred. However, when no later takeover occurred, the cumulative average abnormal return was negative by about 5%.

The results also depended on whether the unsuccessful acquiring firms experienced positive CARs for the announcement period (the day before through the day after the announcement date). For the subsample of bidders that had positive announcement CARs and made a later takeover during the subsequent 18 months, the cumulative abnormal return by the end of the 18 months was 20%. For unsuccessful bidders with initial positive returns that made no later takeover, the cumulative average abnormal return was only slightly above zero.

For unsuccessful acquiring firms with negative initial event returns that made a later takeover within the 18 months after the announcement date, the cumulative return was positive for most of the 18-month period average but returned to approximately zero by the end of the 18 months. For those unsuccessful acquiring firms that made no subsequent takeover, the CARs declined sharply to about −18% by the twelfth month following the announcement date and then recovered to about a −10% CAR by the end of the 18 months.

These data and related patterns show that the experiences of unsuccessful acquiring firms were quite different depending on the initial response in the announcement period and also on whether or not the acquiring firm made a later takeover. However, no inference on causality appears possible, because the better performance of unsuccessful bidders making later takeovers may not be the result of such a takeover but simply due to a selection bias (that is, better performance led to takeovers).

Methods of Payment and Managerial Resistance

A study by Huang and Walkling (1987) combined the analysis of method of payment with acquisition form and managerial resistance. Whereas previous studies found higher abnormal returns (30% to 35%) for tender offers than for mergers (15% to 20%) for target shareholders, such studies did not consider the effect of payment method and target management resistance. Huang and Walkling found that when method of payment and degree of resistance were taken into account statistically, abnormal returns were no higher in tender offers than in mergers. Managerial resistance carried somewhat higher abnormal returns, but the results were not statistically significant. These results were not affected after controlling for form of payment and form of acquisition. The most powerful influence they found was the method of payment. After controlling for type of acquisition and for managerial resistance, cash offers had much higher abnormal returns than stock offers. The average CAR for cash offers was 29.3% compared with 14.4% for stock offers. For mixed payments, the average abnormal return was 23.3%, which fell between the values reported for stock and cash offers.

Huang and Walkling subjected the results to regression analysis. This enabled them to take the effects of form of payment, managerial resistance, and form of acquisition into account, holding two of the influences constant while the third varied. The difference between the abnormal returns of tender offers and mergers disappeared when the influence of the form of payment and managerial resistance were taken into account. But the difference between cash and stock offers remained strong even after controlling for resistance and the form of acquisition—merger or tender offer.

Interval Between Announcement and Completion

Wansley, Lane, and Yang (1983) studied 203 acquisitions that took place between 1970 and 1978. They found that the average time interval between an acquisition's announcement and its completion date was 66 days. When segmented by method of payment, interval length differed substantially. Securities transactions took, on average, twice as long to complete as their cash counterparts. No significant differences in interval length were apparent when comparing companies that used all securities and those that used a combination of cash and securities. The empirical data that demonstrate longer intervals for securities transactions are not surprising. Securities transactions are required to receive approval from the Securities and Exchange Commission, a process that can take many months. Cash transactions are less restrictive and often entail only "cooling-off" periods.

A lengthy acquisition interval may have disadvantages. A longer interval allows the target company more time to prepare defenses. It also allows other suitors to evaluate the target and potentially enter the bidding. A competitive situation often leads to a higher price and lower returns for the eventual acquirer. When managers evaluate a potential acquisition, they need to predict target reactions and potential competitor bids. If the acquisition is extremely time-critical, a cash transaction would have advantages. In addition, to forestall potential competitive bidders, the cash bid may be higher as a preemptive bid.

In summary, returns to targets in a merger transaction are in the 20% to 25% range, compared with a 30% to 40% range for tender offers. However, the method of payment in tender offers is usually cash whereas in mergers it is stock. So it is the use of cash that may result in higher returns to targets rather than whether the transaction is a merger or a tender offer. There are four possible reasons why the use of cash results in higher returns to target companies:

1. Cash transactions are taxable to target shareholders, so the higher premiums paid compensate for taxes paid.
2. The information effect suggests that the bidder uses stock when it is overvalued, so more of it has to be used to compensate the target; this would be a counter-effect.
3. The signaling effect may be that the use of cash by the bidder indicates that the bidder will be able to exploit the investment opportunities represented by the target; if so, the target is worth more and a higher premium may be paid.
4. The time interval to complete the transaction is shorter when cash is used because securities transactions may involve regulatory approval and much more documentation. A short interval reduces the time for targets to mount defenses such as turning to additional bidders. However, preemptive cash bids could be even higher.

Bad Bidders Become Good Targets

Mitchell and Lehn (ML) (1990) studied stock price reactions to acquisitions during the period 1982 to 1986. One sample was composed of firms that became targets of takeovers after they had made acquisitions. A control group consisted of acquiring firms that did not subsequently become targets of takeover bids. The stock prices of acquirers that became targets declined significantly when they announced acquisitions. The stock prices of acquiring firms that did not become subsequent targets increased significantly when they announced acquisitions.

Furthermore, ML found that for the entire sample of acquisitions, those that were subsequently divested had significantly negative event returns. Acquisitions that were not subsequently divested had significantly positive event returns. This suggests that when companies announce acquisitions, the event returns forecast the likelihood that the assets will ultimately be divested. Mitchell and Lehn point out that in the aggregate the returns to acquiring firms were approximately zero. But when acquiring firms experienced negative event returns, they were subsequently likely to become takeover targets. Bidders that experienced positive event returns were less likely to become targets. Event returns were able to discriminate between "bad" bidders and "good" bidders.

Positive Total Returns Versus Negative Total Returns

Of critical importance is whether the total event returns are positive or negative—whether value is created or destroyed. Berkovitch and Narayanan (1993) tested alternative theories of takeovers by grouping the results for positive total returns versus negative returns. Of their sample of 330 transactions, 250, or 76%, achieved positive total gains. The correlation between target returns and total returns is positive and highly significant. The correlation between target gains and bidder gains, however, is not statistically significant. Berkovitch and Narayanan suggest that hubris may be weakening the generally positive correlation in expected gains between bidders and targets.

For the sample of negative total gains, the correlation between target gains and total gains was negative and significant. This could result because target gains are always positive so that when total gains are negative, target gains would be negatively correlated with the nonpositive total gains. When target gains were related to bidder gains for the negative total gains sample, the correlation was again negative and highly significant. This implies that agency problems cause total gains to be negative and hubris still provides positive gains to targets, which implies that bidders will have negative returns.

Berkovitch and Narayanan also analyzed the influence of competition among bidders as reflected in multiple-bid contests. For positive total gains, the correlation between target returns and total gains was strongly positive. It appears that the synergy influence was reinforced. When total gains were negative, however, the correlation between target returns and total gains was negative. Multiple bidding appears to aggravate the agency problem and to stimulate hubris as well.

Berkovitch and Narayanan conclude that total gains are mostly positive and that synergy appears to be the dominant driving force in mergers and takeovers. They suggest that the empirical data convey that agency and hubris play some role as well. They observe that in more than three-fourths of the cases in the sample they employed, total gains are positive. It is likely, therefore, that value is created by M&As. This reinforces the conclusions of other studies as well.

Houston and Ryngaert (1994) studied gains from large bank mergers using a sample of 131 completed mergers and 22 uncompleted for the period 1985 to

1991. They focused on the total return measured by the return to a value-weighted portfolio of the bidder and target. The average total return to a completed bank merger was slightly positive but not significantly different from zero. However, in the later years covered by their sample, the total merger returns were positive and significant.

Bidding banks were more profitable than target banks, but the differences in profitability did not explain the size of total abnormal returns. However, total abnormal returns were significantly higher when acquiring banks had been more profitable. Banks with good track records were considered more likely to engage in value-increasing acquisitions.

Houston and Ryngaert point out that most bank takeover bids are financed with stock. When a bidding bank announces an acquisition, this may be interpreted as a signal that its stock is overvalued. This may partially account for the negative returns to bidder banks. Houston and Ryngaert find that the market responds most favorably when acquisition announcements are made by bidders that have a historical record of superior operating performance. Bank merger transactions in which there is a high degree of market overlap earn higher positive returns, presumably because of a greater potential for cost savings.

Effects of Regulation

The Bradley, Desai, and Kim (BDK) (1988) study updated much of the earlier work. Their primary database was a sample of 921 tender offers during the period October 1958 to December 1984. The average duration between the announcement date and the execution of a tender offer was three to four weeks. The average percent of shares purchased was about 60%. In 66% of the tender offers, there had been no toeholds or previous purchases of target stock by the bidders.

They present two measures of premium. One is the standard cumulative abnormal return (CAR) using market model parameter estimates based on the period 300 to 60 trading days before the announcement date. They observe that studies using monthly data find a positive alpha or abnormal return for acquiring firms for periods preceding the announcement date. Their second measure is a blended premium (BP). The BP for their sample for the period 1981 to 1984 was 43%; the CAR for the corresponding period was 35%. Their regression of the CAR on the BP had a zero intercept and a .8 regression coefficient. They give two reasons why the CAR is lower: One, the CAR is net of market movements. Two, the CAR is a simple arithmetic sum; the BP is a continuously compounded return. This would explain a difference, but generally a continuously compounded return is lower than an arithmetic average return.

Bradley, Desai, and Kim found that value was created in that the CAR was positive for the target and for the target and bidder combined for all subperiods and for the total period. Premiums to targets increased after 1968, the year of the adoption of the Williams Act, which provided for a 20-day waiting period. For acquirers, the CAR was positive and significant for 1963 to 1968; it had a small positive value but was insignificant for 1968 to 1980; it was negative and insignificant for the period 1981 to 1984. The combination of the Williams Act and increased competition as well as target defenses reduced the returns to bidders.

Single Bids versus Multiple Bids

The 1988 BDK study is also representative of the effects of multiple bidders. In multiple-bidder contests, the CAR for targets rose to 26% on the announcement day (AD) and continued to rise to over 45% by 80 trading days after the AD. For their single-bidder subsample, the CAR was about the same on the announcement date but rose no further by 80 days after the AD. For single bidders, the CAR was a positive 2% to 3%. In multiple bids, the bidder CAR was essentially zero. Late bidder acquirers (white knights) lost 2.38%, statistically significant. The authors concluded that white knights on average "pay too much" (BDK; 1988, p. 30).

We have summarized the pattern of returns with single bidders versus multiple bidders for target firms in Figure 8.1 and for acquiring firms in Figure 8.2. These figures seek to reflect patterns found in BDK (1988) and other studies of single-bidder versus multiple-bidder acquisitions. In Figure 8.1, the returns to target firms begin to rise about 20 days before the announcement date. On the announcement date, a further increase moves the abnormal returns of single-bidder

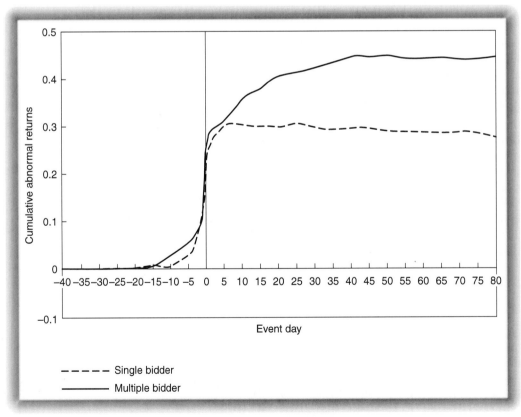

Figure 8.1 Cumulative Abnormal Returns of Target Firms

target firms to about 30%. Shortly after the announcement date, the returns to target firms drift down slightly. In multiple-bidder contests, the event returns to targets continue to rise after the announcement date. As subsequent bids take place, the event returns continue to rise. About 40 days after the announcement date for the first bidder, the event returns to the target firms level off at about 45%.

In Figure 8.2, we see that the event returns for acquiring firms that are single bidders rise to over 2% at the announcement date. Subsequently, the event returns drift down but only slightly. For acquiring firms that are competing in multiple-bidder contests, the event returns are slightly positive. But shortly after the announcement date, as new bidders come onto the scene, the event returns drop to negative levels.

These relationships are confirmed by a detailed regression analysis in BDK (1988). The regression analysis found that the premium to targets was higher when the fraction of target shares purchased was higher. The authors observe that this finding is consistent with the positive supply curve for target shares.

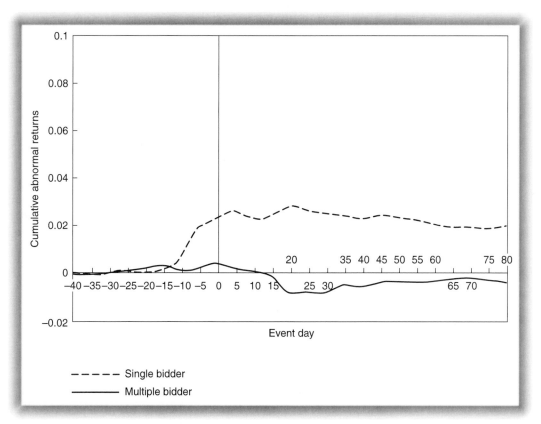

Figure 8.2   Cumulative Abnormal Returns of Acquiring Firms

Runup versus Markup Returns

An in-depth study was made of the relationship between the CAR for the preannouncement period and the CAR for the postannouncement period (Schwert, 1996). The central finding was that the preannouncement CAR (the runup) and the postannouncement CAR (the markup) were not correlated. The study concluded that because little substitution takes place between the runup and the markup, the runup is an added cost to the bidder. The role of private information versus public information and the interpretation of the runup price increases raise important issues that are not fully resolved. Schwert observes that his subsample that involved subsequent insider trading litigation resulted in higher runups. The gains to the insiders were only a fraction of the increased costs imposed on the bidders.

The Schwert study is of great value in updating empirical data on M&A activity. His empirical analysis uses the comprehensive database developed by Robert Comment covering all mergers and tender offers for NYSE and AMEX target firms from 1975 to 1991. A usable sample of 1,523 was the main basis for analysis. On average, for 1,174 successful deals, the runup and markup were about the same at 15% each. In the 564 tender offers, the runup was about 16% and the markup about 20%, approximating the 35% gain to targets in tender offers found in previous studies. In the 959 mergers, their runup was 12% and the markup 5%. The total premium of 17% was slightly below the average 20% found in earlier studies. In 173 MBOs, the runup and markup averages were approximately 10% each, totaling 20%.

In the subsample of 229 poison pills, the runup averaged 12%, the markup about 18%. In the 312-MBO subsample involving competitive bidding, the runup averaged 13%, the markup 18%, a total premium only slightly above the 30% for successful single-bid transactions on average.

In the 135 transactions in which an insider trading case was brought, the runup was 18.3%, significantly higher than the 13.3% for the full sample. The markup was 21.2%, almost double the markup of 10.5% for the main sample. The Schwert study provided a valuable updating of the earlier empirical studies of target returns as well as extending the coverage of issues treated.

With regard to returns to acquirers, Schwert found, as did earlier studies, that in establishing parameters for measuring CARs, the market model had a positive slope during the preannouncement test period. Schwert calculated the market model regression for the trading days -253 to -127 in relation to the announcement date. Like earlier studies, Schwert found that bidder firms had unusual stock price increases prior to their decisions to make takeover bids. Schwert sought to adjust for this by setting the intercepts of the market model regressions to zero. The consequence is that the negative CAR for bidders found in other studies that did not make such adjustments becomes zero. Our interpretation is that the abnormal returns to bidders on average are zero. This is consistent with a takeover market that is highly competitive so that bidders earn only normal returns on average.

Schwert (1996) examined share trading volume related to announcements of M&A activity. He found that across the main sample of 1,506 firms for which delisting occurred within one year of the first bid (the transaction was completed), the average volume runup from days -42 through $+126$ relative to the announcement date was 127.8%. The average volume runup was higher before tender offers and especially for transactions that involved subsequent insider trading prosecutions.

Postmerger Performance

The seminal study of postmerger performance is that of Healy, Palepu, and Ruback (HPR) (1992). They studied the postacquisition performance of the 50 largest U.S. mergers between 1979 and 1984. They used accounting data primarily but tested their results by using market valuation measures as well. They analyzed both operating characteristics and investment characteristics. The first two measures of operating characteristics are the cash flow margin on sales and asset turnover. When these two measures are multiplied, they obtain the margin on the market value of assets.

Their third variable measures the effect of the merger on employment. They calculate the change in the number of employees during a given year as a percentage of the number of employees in the previous year. This is to test the hypothesis that gains in mergers are achieved by downsizing and reducing the number of employees.

Their fourth measure is pension expense per employee. Again, this is to test whether gains from mergers come at the expense of reducing pension protection for employees.

Next, HPR consider a number of effects on investment. Here they are testing whether gains may come from underinvesting for the future, from selling off assets, or from reducing research and development activities.

They looked at the results for the firms themselves and then made a further adjustment. They made an industry adjustment to test whether the changes in the variables occurred because of industry effects as distinguished from the effects of the mergers on the individual firms. For example, the merged firms may have reduced employment. But if employment reduction in nonmerging firms in the same industry was even greater, then industry-adjusted employment in the merged firms would have increased.

Their data show that industry-adjusted employment decreased. This implies that the merging firms did more restructuring and reorganization than other firms in the industry. But the cash flow margin on sales did not significantly change. However, asset turnover significantly improved. The return on the market value of assets also improved significantly. However, the fact that the cash flow margin on sales had not changed implies that the improvement in the return on assets did not come from the reduction of employment costs, which would have increased the cash flow margin on sales. It was better asset management that increased the return on assets. Pension expense per employee was reduced somewhat but not by a statistically significant degree, none of the investment characteristics were significantly changed on the basis of industry-adjusted performance, except asset sales measured at book value.

These results imply that industry-adjusted performance of the merging firms had improved. The improvement came not at the expense of labor income but by improving the management of assets. The investments in capital equipment and investments in research and development were not significantly changed.

One of the important findings in the HPR study related to the event returns calculated as described in connection with the previous studies summarized in this chapter: The event returns for the firms are significantly correlated with the subsequent accounting returns during the postmerger period. This is evidence that on average, for their sample, event returns correctly forecast postmerger performance.

Agrawal, Jaffe, and Mandelker (AJM) (1992) also studied postmerger performance. They developed a larger sample of 937 mergers and 227 tender offers. Their sample included firms smaller than those of the HPR study, which focused on the 50 largest mergers. They adjusted for size effect and for beta-weighted market returns. They found that shareholders of acquiring firms experienced a wealth loss of about 10% over the five years following the merger completion.

This finding has some interesting implications. First, it represents an anomaly in the sense that it provides an opportunity for a positive abnormal investment return. If acquiring firms always lose after a merger, this suggests that investors short the acquiring firm on a long-term basis at the time of a merger announcement. Of course, over time this anomaly should be wiped out.

Another implication may be explored. Healy, Palepu, and Ruback (1992) found that industry-adjusted postmerger performance was positive. Agrawal, Jaffe, and Mandelker (1992) found that marketwide or economy-wide adjustments result in negative returns. These two results together imply that merger activity took place mainly in industries where performance was subpar compared to the market or the economy as a whole.

Franks, Harris, and Titman (FHT) (1991) found that postmerger share price performance is sensitive to the benchmark employed. Using an equally weighted index, their findings confirmed earlier studies that found negative postmerger performance. However, the use of a value-weighted benchmark results in positive postmerger performance. When various multiportfolio benchmarks are employed, no statistically significant abnormal performance is found.

Langetieg (1978) found that when the adjustment is made by use of matched control firms in the same industry, postmerger abnormal performance is not significantly changed. In another pair of studies, Magenheim and Mueller (1988) found underperformance, but using the same sample with a different methodology, Bradley and Jarrell (1988) did not find significant underperformance in the three years following acquisitions.

Loughran and Vijh (1997) studied 947 acquisitions during the period 1970 to 1989. Their overall sample had an average five-year buy-and-hold return of 88.2% compared to 94.7% for their matching firms. The difference had a t-statistic of 0.96, which was not significant. The compound annual return was 13.5% for their sample and 14.2% for the matching firms. Over the 20-year time period covered by their study, the Standard & Poor's 500 experienced a compound annual return of 6.15%—less than one-half the returns for their two samples. The returns to acquirers in cash tender offers for the five-year period was 145.6%, compared with 83.9% for their matching firm sample—statistically significant. For cash mergers, the difference was not statistically significant. In stock-for-stock mergers, the acquisition sample underperformed the matching firms; they also underperformed in tender offers, but the sample size was only eight observations over the 20-year period.

When we consider these findings and counterfindings and the many variables discussed at the beginning of this chapter that influence event returns as well as postmerger performance, it is clear that results are sensitive to sample selection and measurement methodology. Some mergers perform well; others do not. Also, it is probable that industry conditions influence merger results. This leads to the next section of this chapter, which considers industry influences and their implications.

Industry Influences on M&A Activity

This chapter began with a review of some central issues in evaluating merger performance from the standpoint of the individual firm. In assessing broad economic forces that explain merger activity, the causal factors are formulated somewhat differently. One broad influence cited is the incentive to improve management. A second view is that mergers of the 1980s sought to reverse prior paid acquisitions and to focus a firm's activities on core industries. A third view states that merger activity facilitates an efficient adaptation of existing industry structure that has become suboptimal because of relatively broad changes in the economy. The hostile takeovers of the 1980s "affected industries in decline or sharp change" (Shleifer and Vishny, 1990). The leverage-increasing transactions of the 1980s were said to have been most numerous in industries with relatively poor investment opportunities and high capital costs (Blair and Schary, 1993).

In an in-depth analysis of industry effects, Mitchell and Mulherin (1996) studied industry-level patterns of takeover and restructuring activity during the 1982 to 1989 period. They found that in their sample of 1,064 firms, 57% were the object of a takeover attempt or experienced a major restructuring during the 1980s. Of the firms involved in takeovers or restructuring, 40% were hostile takeover targets. Somewhat more, 47% of the firms, were targets of friendly takeovers. The remaining 13% of the firms engaged in defensive asset restructuring or financial recapitalization.

Among their 51 sample industries, they found significant differences in the rate of M&A activity as well as in the timing of the activity. Most of the M&A activity occurred in relatively few industries owing to identifiable major shocks defined as factors causing a marked change in overall industry structure and corporate control activity. One major force was deregulation, which had a major impact on the air transport, broadcasting, entertainment, natural gas, and trucking industries.

A second major factor was the oil price shocks that occurred in 1973 and 1979. These shocks affected not only the oil industry but also the structure of industries in which energy represented 10% or more of input costs. The industries most directly affected were integrated petroleum, natural gas, air transport, coal, and trucking.

A third major factor was foreign competition. This is measured by changes in the import penetration ratio, the ratio of imports to total industry supply. The industries with the largest change in import penetration ratios were shoes, machine tools, apparel, construction equipment, office equipment and supplies, autos and auto parts, tires and rubber, and steel.

A fourth major influence was innovations. The ability to use public markets for leveraged financing increased both the rate of takeovers and the size of takeover targets.

Mitchell and Mulherin conclude that the interindustry patterns in takeovers and restructuring reflect the relative economic shocks to the industries. Their results support the view that a major influence on the takeover activity of the 1980s was a combination of broad underlying economic and financial forces.

Andrade and Stafford (1999) extend the Mitchell and Mulherin results. Their dataset is based on Value Line companies and industry groupings covering the period 1970 to 1994. Their evidence supports an impact of industry shocks. Their broader framework also measures the role of other influences—synergy, diversification, agency costs, and market power. Their basic economic finding is that mergers, like internal investment, are a response to favorable growth potentials. They find a dual role in that own-industry mergers are used in industries with excess capacity to achieve consolidation. In contracting industries, acquiring firms appear to be those with better performance, lower capacity utilization, and lower leverage. The asset re-allocation results in improved efficiency.

MERGER PERFORMANCE DURING THE 1990s

We studied a sample of 364 transactions that accounted for almost half of the total M&A values between 1992 and mid-1998 (Weston and Johnson, 1999). Our information was obtained from the *Mergerstat* database, supplemented by proxy statements to share-holders soliciting approval of transactions. We summarized deal structure patterns and calculated event returns. Our results reflect large transactions whose patterns are different from those of smaller transactions; the event return results could differ also.

Our selection criteria began with all M&As in which the price paid for the target exceeded $500 million. By 1997, this annual number became so large we raised our cutoff to $1 billion or more. Our study ended with transactions announced through June 1998. The stock market adjustment that began in July 1998 dampened new M&A deal announcements. For completed transactions, however, the third quarter of 1998 was still high because of deals initiated earlier. The stock market began to recover in mid-October and was associated with a resumption in an active M&A market, with 11 major deals totaling $65 billion announced on "Merger Monday," November 23, 1998. Thus, our study captures a distinctive cycle of M&A activity. Our sample accounted for about 40% to 45% of total deal value in most years, increasing to almost 69% for the first half of 1998. The exploding number of blockbuster transactions is consistent with our data.

Pooling versus Purchase Accounting

Transactions that use purchase accounting involve a larger firm buying a smaller firm. Since one of the 12 requirements for pooling accounting is that the firms be of approximately equal size, the acquisition of smaller firms by larger firms would have to receive the accounting treatment of a purchase transaction. Our sample of the 364 largest transactions between 1992 and June 30, 1998 accounted for 44% of total transaction value over the entire period and 69% for the first half of 1998. The number of total transactions in 1998 was 9,149 in the *M&A Almanac* and 7,759 for *Mergerstat*. Thus, most of the 8,000 to 9,000 annual transactions in the broader compilations represent purchase accounting.

For our sample of 364 transactions, pooling accounted for slightly more than 52% of the transactions, as shown in Table 8.2. However, 75 of the 364 transactions (20.6%) involved banks. For banks, as shown by Table 8.2, 80% of the transactions were pooling, only 20% purchase. For our non-bank sample, purchases predominated at 55% of the total. The data indicate that banks had a very strong preference for pooling. One possible explanation is that the banks are strongly averse to the negative impact of goodwill write-offs on reported net income. In contrast, in non-bank transactions, the strong avoidance of non-pooling transactions does not manifest itself. One possible explanation is that in general the economies or synergies in the

Table 8.2   Accounting Treatment, 1992 to 1998

Method	Bank		Non-Bank		Combined	
	Number	Percent	Number	Percent	Number	Percent
Pooling	60	80.0%	130	45.0%	190	52.2%
Purchase	15	20.0%	159	55.0%	174	47.8%
Total	75	100.0%	289	100.0%	364	100.0%

Table 8.3   Method of Payment in Largest Mergers, 1992 to 1998

Method	Bank		Non-Bank		Combined	
	Number	Percent	Number	Percent	Number	Percent
Cash	7	9.3%	72	24.9%	79	21.7%
Stock	61	81.3%	159	55.0%	220	60.4%
Cash and stock	7	9.3%	57	19.7%	64	17.6%
Debt	0	0.0%	1	0.3%	1	0.3%
Total	75	100.0%	289	100.0%	364	100.0%

non-banking transactions are sufficiently strong that the negative effect of the good-will write-off is overcome by the increase in earnings that the new combined firm will be able to achieve. Firms in highly synergistic transactions would be less averse to the negative impact of the goodwill write-off because the increase in earnings of the combination would more than offset the negative effects. This also leads to the prediction that highly synergistic mergers will not be deterred after 2000 when the use of pooling accounting may no longer be available in merger transactions.

Method of Payment

The 1980s are referred to as the decade of mergers propelled by junk bond financing. The debt sold raised cash that was used in takeovers, often hostile. Data compilations showed these deals as cash transactions, but the underlying source was debt. Our data show that in the 364 largest deals during the 1990s, summarized in Table 8.3, stock accounted for 60% of the number of transactions, with combinations of stock and cash moving the proportion up to 80%. Stock-for-stock transactions are generally nontaxable. In bank mergers, stock is involved in over 90% of the deals. In non-bank mergers, the proportion drops to about 75%.

In large compilations of transactions, most would be smaller deals. These smaller transactions are typically made for cash. Thus, in broader compilations we

Table 8.4   Taxability, 1992 to 1998

Method	Bank		Non-Bank		Combined	
	Number	**Percent**	**Number**	**Percent**	**Number**	**Percent**
Taxable	6	8.0%	85	29.4%	91	25.0%
Nontaxable	64	85.3%	174	60.2%	238	65.4%
Election	5	6.7%	30	10.4%	35	9.6%
Total	75	100.0%	289	100.0%	364	100.0%

Table 8.5   Purchase Accounting and Taxability, 1992 to 1998

Method	Bank		Non-Bank		Combined	
	Number	**Percent**	**Number**	**Percent**	**Number**	**Percent**
Taxable	6	40.0%	85	53.5%	91	52.3%
Nontaxable	4	26.7%	44	27.7%	48	27.6%
Election	5	33.3%	30	18.9%	35	20.1%
Total	15	100.0%	159	100.0%	174	100.0%

find that stock is involved in about one-third of the transactions. A brief generalization is that big deals in the 1990s were mainly stock-for-stock. In the smaller deals, the seller was likely to be paid off in cash.

Taxability

Table 8.4 shows that for non-bank transactions in 1992 to 1998, 60% were nontaxable. Table 8.2 showed that 45% of non-bank deals in this period were accorded pooling of interests accounting treatment. Pooling deals are generally not taxable. Hence the additional 15% of nontaxable, non-bank transactions used purchase accounting but still qualified for nontaxable treatment. The reason for this is that some stock-for-stock transactions may not have met all of the 12 rules required to qualify for pooling of interests accounting. For example, if one of the participants in a merger had engaged in stock buybacks during the two years preceding the year of the deal, it would fail to qualify for pooling of interests treatment. However, since it was a stock-for-stock transaction, it could still qualify for nontaxability.

Table 8.5 shows that about 54% of all non-bank transactions in which purchase accounting was used were taxable transactions. In another 19%, taxability depended on whether the seller chose to take cash or stock when this election option was provided by the buyer.

Table 8.6   30-Day Percent Premium

Accounting Method	Tax Treatment	Bank		Non-Bank		Combined	
		Mean	Median	Mean	Median	Mean	Median
Pooling	Nontaxable	44%	35%	40%	33%	41%	34%
Purchase	Total purchase	36%	34%	41%	37%	40%	37%
	Taxable	23%	12%	42%	37%	41%	37%
	Nontaxable	48%	41%	34%	36%	35%	36%
	Election	34%	45%	52%	49%	47%	46%

Over 85% of bank transactions are nontaxable. This reflects the predominance of pooling in bank deals. If we add the 6.7% of bank deals in which the buyer offers the seller the option to take cash or stock, we find that probably over 90% of the bank deals qualified for nontaxability.

Premiums Paid

We next consider the premiums paid by sellers. We measured the premium based on the market price of the seller stock 30 days before the public announcement of the deal. We did this to try to avoid the runup in price of the seller stock in response to the leaks that occur predominantly in the 5 to 10 days before the formal public announcement date.

As shown in Table 8.6, the 30-day premium was about 40% for the seller in non-bank transactions when an arithmetic mean is used to average over the deals. In an arithmetic average, the larger numbers receive a higher implicit weighting. To avoid this we also used as a measure of the average the median firm (half the sample is above and half below the median). This gives less weight to the larger numbers, so the median falls to 33% for pooling transactions and 37% for purchase transactions.

When the purchase accounting non-bank transactions are grouped by taxability, the target received a 42% premium, compared with a 34% premium in nontaxable transactions. This implies that the buyer pays more when the seller is in a taxable transaction.

As a general guideline, for the big deals the pattern has been that premiums paid over the seller market price 30 days before the formal announcement date ranged from about 33% to 40% for nontaxable, non-bank deals. For taxable non-bank deals, the premiums to sellers appear to jump by three to four percentage points.

Analysis of Event Returns

Empirical studies have found that the initial market reactions to merger announcements are good predictors of subsequent performance (Healy, Palepu, and Ruback, 1992). We calculated positive and negative gains for our sample. Stock price data were not available for all transactions, so for this analysis our sample size dropped

Table 8.7 Percentage of Positive and Negative Total Gains

		Buyer		Seller		Combined	
		Number	**Percent**	**Number**	**Percent**	**Number**	**Percent**
Banks	Positive	27	38.0%	63	88.7%	41	57.7%
	Negative	44	62.0%	8	11.3%	30	42.3%
Non-Banks	Positive	124	52.1%	213	89.5%	161	67.6%
	Negative	114	47.9%	25	10.5%	77	32.4%
Total sample	Positive	151	48.9%	276	89.3%	202	65.4%
	Negative	158	51.1%	33	10.7%	107	34.6%

from 364 to 309. We multiplied the positive or negative net percentage gains or losses times the market value of equity for the acquirer and the target 20 trading days before through 10 trading days after the announcement date, $[-20, +10]$. The results can therefore be presented in absolute dollar terms. The dollar returns to targets, measured over the 30-day window, are almost always positive. The event returns for the acquiring firm will be positive or negative depending on the market's judgment of whether the premium paid to the seller by the buyer will be recovered in the subsequent performance of the combined firm.

Table 8.7 presents the overall results for our event return analysis. For the total sample, about two-thirds of the deals had positive returns. This provides one measure of whether M&As are successful in some sense. Our results suggest that two out of three large mergers are likely to add value to shareholders. Looking at the bank subsample alone, the percentage of predicted success drops somewhat. Without banks, the success ratio is slightly higher.

In Table 8.8, we look at the absolute dollar amounts involved. In the non-bank sample, when we add the dollar amount of increases in the market cap of the buyer over the 30-day window of 20 days before to 10 days after the formal announcement date, the positive gains of $130 billion exceed the deals in which the buyer suffered stock price losses of $82 billion, for a net gain to buyers of $48 billion. The stock market response for sellers is usually positive. So the total of plus event returns of market cap increases of $109 billion for sellers less negatives of $10 billion leaves a net of plus $99 billion for sellers. Bank buyers had net losses of $15 billion, while bank sellers had net gains of $22 billion. So even for bank transactions the gains of sellers did not simply represent a shift based on the loss in market value of the buyers.

We also analyzed stock market gains and losses stratified by method of accounting, taxability, etc. However, the differences are not statistically significant. Our judgment is that, based on the 1990s, the business soundness of the deal determines how the stock market will react. If the market judges that the deal will work out well in the future, the initial market response is likely to be favorable. If the market judges the deal to be misconceived and to not have a sound business foundation, it will react negatively. Whether the deal is soundly conceived or not determines whether the

Table 8.8   Summation of Positive and Negative Total Gains

		($ Millions)		
		Buyer	**Seller**	**Combined**
Banks	Positive	12,782	26,006	26,812
	Negative	(28,191)	(3,946)	(20,162)
	Sum	(15,409)	22,060	6,650
Non-Banks	Positive	129,675	108,880	213,947
	Negative	(81,641)	(9,723)	(66,756)
	Sum	48,034	99,157	147,191
Total sample	Positive	142,457	134,886	240,759
	Negative	(109,832)	(13,669)	(86,918)
	Sum	32,625	121,217	153,841

stock prices of the sellers and/or buyers will increase. The method of accounting used and taxability are of secondary importance. The important lesson is that good deals will assuredly increase market prices for the sellers and even for the buyers despite some initial shorting by risk arbitrage traders. Bad deals will be bad news for shareholders, both for the acquiring firms and ultimately for the selling firms.

Returns for Unrelated Acquisitions

Anslinger and Copeland (1996) studied returns to shareholders covering the 1985 to 1994 period for seemingly unrelated acquisitions. They studied in depth 21 successful acquirers of two types: diversified corporate acquirers and financial buyers such as leveraged buyout firms. These companies made a total of 829 acquisitions.

Anslinger and Copeland were consultants at McKinsey and Company at the time of their study. Their findings are in contrast to widely cited earlier studies for the 1970s and 1980s attributed to McKinsey and Company, which found that two-thirds of all mergers and takeovers were failures in that they did not earn their cost of capital. In this later study, merger performance was subjected to a particularly challenging test, because the sample covered only unrelated mergers. The Anslinger and Copeland study found that 80% of the 829 transactions (611) earned their cost of capital. Indeed, the corporate acquirers averaged more than 18% per year in total returns to shareholders over a 10-year period, exceeding the Standard & Poor's 500 benchmark by a substantial margin. The financial buyers estimated that they averaged returns of 35% per year over a corresponding period.

Anslinger and Copeland note that although many of the acquisitions seem to be unrelated in some respects, successful acquirers focused on a common theme. Clayton, Dubilier & Rice stockpiled management capabilities used to make turn-arounds. Another financial buyer, Desai Capital Management, focused on retail-related industries. Emerson Electric Company looked for companies with a core competence in component manufacturing to exploit cost control capabilities. Sara Lee used branding and retailing as its common thread.

Merger Performance in the 1990s

Schwert's (1996) data on bidder stock prices suggest that on average the abnormal returns to bidders for the period 1975 to 1991 were not significantly different from zero. The highly competitive nature of the takeover market continued through 1996, suggesting that the abnormal returns to bidders continued at levels not significantly different from zero. Although the abnormal returns to bidders were approximately zero from 1985 through 1996, the total wealth change continued to be positive through 1996, because the abnormal returns to targets were in the 35% to 40% range.

The preliminary evidence on merger performance in the 1990s suggests that large buyers increased their ability to make value-increasing mergers. Studies of individual companies in the high tech sector reveal spectacular successes. Cisco Systems grew in considerable measure by acquisitions. Their return to shareholders was remarkable. The Internet companies made considerable use of acquisitions to expand their customer coverage; their shareholder returns were high. Mergers continue to be high risk investments. Bad mergers and failures will continue to occur. But the odds for success in the 1990s appear to have significantly improved over those of the previous two decades.

EFFICIENCY VERSUS MARKET POWER

Empirical studies find that total value is increased by mergers and takeovers. The evidence is also strong that the shareholders of acquired firms gain. However, whether the shareholders of acquiring firms gain depends on the premiums paid versus the synergies achieved. On balance, total value appears to be increased by M&As. The possibility remains that the value gains result from increases in market power, however, rather than from increases in efficiency. A number of studies are relevant to these issues.

Ellert (1975, 1976) studied these issues at great length. He analyzed the data for 205 defendants in antimerger complaints for the period 1950 to 1972. He found that for four years before the filing of the complaint, the residual performance was positive and statistically significant for the defendants. As expected, the residuals became negative upon the filing of a complaint. However, the negative residuals were relatively small. Ellert observed that the record of effective asset management in the years preceding merger activity by acquiring firms may result in complaints by their rivals to antitrust authorities. Ellert termed such legal actions a "harassment" hypothesis. He indicated that incentives exist for complaining rivals to follow this course. The government agencies bear the costs of prosecution, and if successful the complaining firms' actions will handicap their rivals. The complaining parties may then file private treble damage suits. The harassment hypothesis is clearly the opposite of a monopoly explanation of merger activity. In addition, if a doubt exists about whether the acquiring firms obtain gains from the merger, this doubt itself is inconsistent with the monopoly theory. If the monopoly theory is valid, both parties should gain from the merger.

The monopoly theory was pursued even further in studies by Stillman (1983) and Eckbo (1981), who looked at the residuals of the rivals of firms participating in mergers. The problem is complex because at the theoretical level a number of alternative hypotheses can be formulated as illustrated in Table 8.9.

Table 8.9   Alternative Hypotheses of Merger Effects

	Participating Firms	**Rival Firms**
I. Announcement of Merger		
Collusion	+ Higher profits from colluding	+ Are part of the collusion
Efficiency	+ External investment with large positive NPV	+ Demonstrate how to achieve greater efficiency
		− Tougher competition
		0 Competition in marketplace unaffected by purchase of undervalued firm
II. Announcement of Challenge		
Collusion	− Collusion prevented	− Collusion prevented
Efficiency	− Prevents a positive NPV investment, also litigation costs	+ Threat of more efficient rivals reduced
		− Also prevented from mergers for efficiency
	0 Could do same thing internally.	0 Can do internally
III. Announcement of Decision		
Collusion	− Collusion definitely prevented	− Collusion prevented
		+ Defendants prevented from being more efficient
	0 (1) Negative impact already, at challenge date	0 (1) Negative impact already, at challenge date
	(2) Leakage of likely judicial decision during trial	(2) Leakage of likely judicial decision during trial
	(3) Underlying economics of the industry not affected	(3) Underlying economics of the industry not affected
Efficiency	+ Increased efficiency	+ Can now legally merge for efficiency
		− Tougher competition
		0 Could have accomplished the same thing internally

Note: The +, −, 0 signs denote the predicted positive, negative, and zero impacts, respectively, on the firms' values.

The studies appear to support the efficiency basis for mergers. Ellert emphasized that acquiring firms had positive residuals in prior years and acquired firms had negative residuals. Stillman's evidence showed that rival firms did not benefit from the announcement of proposed mergers, which is inconsistent with the concentration–collusion hypothesis. Eckbo found positive residuals on the merger announcement but no negative effects on rivals when it appeared that the merger would be blocked by the antitrust authorities. He interpreted this pattern of relationships as indicating that the main effect of the merger is to signal the possibility of achieving economies for the merging firms and to provide information to rivals that such economies may also be available to them.

EFFECTS ON CONCENTRATION

Impact on Macroconcentration

The high rate of divestitures is one of the reasons merger activity in recent years has not greatly affected aggregate concentration in the economy. The share of assets of the 200 largest U.S. corporations to the share of assets of all nonfinancial corporations was about 38% in 1970. Their share declined to 36% by 1980 and to 34% by 1984 (Golbe and White, 1988, p. 277). Our studies show that this share remained stable at about 35% through 1996. These data give a view that is biased upward in that the 200 largest firms are the ones that rank highest in each year of measurement, but the individual firms in the list change. If the same group of 200 firms were followed over a period such as 1970 to 1984, their share of assets or sales of all nonfinancial corporations would decline more substantially. The significance of the changing composition of the 200 largest firms from an economic point of view is that it reflects the vigor of competitive forces in the economy. Over time, some firms increase in relative size while others decline, depending on their relative success in the marketplace.

A *Business Week* article of April 29, 1996, raised concerns about "a dangerous concentration" (Mandel, 1996). The measure used was the market value of the top 50 companies in relation to the market value of the *Business Week* 1,000 companies based on first quarter data for each year. The measure rose from 35% in 1986 to almost 37% in 1987, dropping slightly in 1988. The measure reached almost 41% in 1991, dropped to 36% in 1994, and rose to 39% in 1996. These results are all within a range surprisingly small given the volatility of equity prices. The peak year was 1991, the year of the lowest M&A activity for the time period covered by the article.

International competition also needs to be taken into account. If aggregate concentration were measured in global terms, the share of the top 200 would be smaller. These data have not been compiled because of the difficulty of obtaining data for the denominator (all financial firms) on a world basis.

Impact on Microconcentration

Concentration measures have also been calculated for individual industries. These are called measures of microconcentration. Historically, the most widely used measure has been the share of the four largest firms of industry sales, assets, employment, or the value added in manufacturing, with the last receiving most emphasis. When the four-firm concentration ratio exceeds 40%, one view holds that competition in the industry may be diminished to some degree. But this view has also been disputed on both theoretical and empirical grounds. The degree of concentration varies widely among individual industries. When measured by value added, the weighted average level of concentration in individual industries stayed relatively constant at about 40% over the decades of the 1960s and 1970s (Scherer, 1980).

However, the published microconcentration measures are based on U.S. domestic data, without taking international factors into account. This impact can be conveyed by measures of concentration for individual markets. In an earlier study, for example, we found that the share of the four largest U.S. firms in steel production in the United States was 52%. The share of the four largest steel companies (two were non-U.S.) of world steel production for the same year was 14% (Weston, 1982). More generally, we found that 75 manufacturing industries could be identified as having international markets. The four-firm concentration ratio (the ratio of sales or value added of the four largest firms to the industry total) for these 75 industries averaged 50%, somewhat higher than the 40% average concentration ratio for all manufacturing industries (about 450 in total). However, when adjustments are made for the international nature of the 75 markets, the average four-firm concentration ratio for these industries declines from 50% to 25% (Weston, 1982).

SUMMARY

The empirical literature appears to support the notion that value is created by M&A activities. The gains to acquiring firms around the announcement date are generally close to zero, which is the appropriate excess return in perfectly competitive markets for corporate control. The gains to target firms are more substantial. Returns to targets in merger transactions are in the 20% to 25% range, while in tender offers the gains are in the 30% to 40% range, where the upper limits of return ranges involve multiple-bidder contests. The difference in the returns between tender offers and mergers could be explained by the method of payment for the acquisition. Mergers usually involve stock transactions whereas tender offers are usually for cash. Securities transactions entail a longer period for the takeover to be completed because they require approval from the regulatory agencies. This allows target companies to prepare defenses and permits other bidders to enter the contest. In contrast, cash transactions have fewer restrictions. Higher cash bids involve information and signaling effects and can pre-empt potential competitive bidders.

If the takeover is unsuccessful, cumulative abnormal returns for both bidder and target firms are generally negative but modest in size. This may indicate that the market slightly penalizes the firms for the forgone value-creating opportunity. For unsuccessful bidders with negative event returns for their bids, the market seems to identify these as "bad bidders" and therefore as likely to become takeover targets.

Target firms depict a general upward trend in the pattern of their cumulative abnormal returns. A more pronounced rise is observed in multiple-bids contest, drifting upward as each subsequent bid takes place. There is little correlation between the runup returns (preannouncement period) and the markup returns (postannouncement period). The respective pattern for bidders is a slight positive announcement date rise with a subsequent slight drift downward, trending to negative levels in the case of multiple bidders. Acquiring companies have unusual increases in their stock price prior to the announcement of a takeover bid.

The evidence for the total gains in M&A activity confirms that they are mainly positive and synergy appears to be the dominant driving force. In mergers with negative total gains, agency problems and hubris are involved. The total value increase by M&A activity could be attributable to increases in market power and not to increases in efficiency, but empirical studies do not support the monopoly theory.

The gains from M&A activity seem to persist in the period following the merger. The industry-adjusted postmerger performance of merging firms shows improvement. The source of this improvement is mainly the better management of the assets and not reductions in labor costs, capital investment, or research and development (R&D) expenditures. There is evidence that mergers are mainly concentrated in industries where performance was subpar compared with the economy as a whole. Factors that cause major adjustments in individual industries seem to drive the rate and timing of M&A activity.

The odds for success for the strategic mergers of the 1990s appear to have been improved relative to the mergers of previous decades. But all of the empirical studies for the earlier decades show high absolute and percentage positive returns for targets. In competitive markets for mergers, returns to bidders would be expected to be close to zero. The empirical studies show that even when returns to bidders are negative the gains to mergers from combining the returns of targets and bidders are substantially positive.

QUESTIONS

8.1 If residual analysis indicates positive abnormal returns to merging firms, what theory (or theories) of mergers is supported? If residual analysis indicates negative abnormal returns, what theory (or theories) is supported?

8.2 How do abnormal returns vary for acquiring and acquired firms during the period well before any merger announcement? What do these returns imply?

8.3 How do state and federal regulation affect returns to merging firms?

8.4 a. What do the following merger theories predict about the correlation between abnormal returns of buyer and seller returns in mergers:
   Managerialism
   Inefficient management
   Synergy/efficiency

   b. Discuss the empirical results of tests of the correlation between buyer and seller returns.

8.5 How should the returns to rivals of the merging firms be affected under the market power (monopoly) and efficiency theories?

8.6 What is likely to be the ratio of stock-for-stock versus cash acquisitions for the largest firms as compared with total acquisitions?

8.7 Compare the accounting treatment in large firm transactions between 1992 and 1998.

8.8 Contrast the taxability of bank versus non-bank mergers.

8.9 In non-bank mergers, using pooling, what was the median premium paid in relation to the stock price 30 days before the merger announcement? Compare this with the median premium for purchases.

8.10 Answer the previous question for large bank mergers.

8.11 What were total gains in non-bank mergers? Discuss.

REFERENCES

Agrawal, Anup, Jeffrey F. Jaffe, and Gershon N. Mandelker, "The Post-Merger Performance of Acquiring Firms: A Re-examination of an Anomaly," *Journal of Finance,* 47, September 1992, pp. 1605–1621.

Andrade, Gregor, and Erik Stafford, "Investigating the Economic Role of Mergers," working paper, August 1999.

Anslinger, Patricia L., and Thomas E. Copeland, "Growth Through Acquisitions: A Fresh Look," *Harvard Business Review,* 74, January-February 1996, pp. 126–135.

Berkovitch, Elazar, and M. P. Narayanan, "Motives for Takeovers: An Empirical Investigation," *Journal of Financial and Quantitative Analysis,* 28, September 1993, pp. 347–362.

Blair, Margaret M., and Martha A. Schary, "Industry-Level Pressures to Restructure," in Margaret M. Blair, ed., *The Deal Decade,* Washington, D.C.: Brookings Institution, 1993, pp. 149–191.

Bradley, Michael, Anand Desai, and E. Han Kim, "The Rationale Behind Interfirm Tender Offers: Information or Synergy?" *Journal of Financial Economics,* 11, 1983, pp. 183–206.

———, "Synergistic Gains from Corporate Acquisitions and their Division Between the Stockholders of Target and Acquiring Firms," *Journal of Financial Economics,* 21, 1988, pp. 3–40.

Bradley, Michael, and Gregg Jarrell, "Comment," chapter 15 in John Coffee, Jr., Louis Lowenstein, and Susan Rose-Ackerman, eds., *Knights, Raiders and Targets,* Oxford, England: Oxford University Press, 1988, pp. 283–310.

Eckbo, B. E., "Examining the Anti-Competitive Significance of Large Horizontal Mergers," unpublished Ph.D. dissertation, University of Rochester, 1981.

Ellert, J. C., "Antitrust Enforcement and the Behavior of Stock Prices," doctoral dissertation, University of Chicago, June 1975.

———, "Mergers, Antitrust Law Enforcement, and Stockholder Returns," *Journal of Finance,* 31, May 1976, pp. 715–732.

Franks, Julian R., Robert S. Harris, and Sheridan Titman, "The Postmerger Share-Price Performance of Acquiring Firms," *Journal of Financial Economics,* 29, 1991, pp. 81–96.

Golbe, Devra L., and Lawrence J. White, "A Time-Series Analysis of Mergers and Acquisitions in the U.S. Economy," chapter 9 in Alan J. Auerbach, ed., *Corporate Takeovers: Causes and Consequences,* Chicago: The University of Chicago Press, 1988, pp. 265–309.

Healy, Paul M., Krishna G. Palepu, and Richard S. Ruback, "Does Corporate Performance Improve After Mergers?" *Journal of Financial Economics,* 31, 1992, pp. 135–175.

Houston, Joel F., and Michael D. Ryngaert, "The Overall Gains from Large Bank Mergers," *Journal of Banking & Finance,* 18, December 1994, pp. 1155–1176.

Huang, Yen-Sheng, and Ralph A. Walkling, "Target Abnormal Returns Associated with Acquisition Announcements," *Journal of Financial Economics,* 19, 1987, pp. 329–349.

Jarrell, G. A., J. A. Brickley, and J. M. Netter, "The Market for Corporate Control: The Empirical Evidence Since 1980," *Journal of Economic Perspectives,* 2, Winter 1988, pp. 49–68.

Jensen, M. C., and R. S. Ruback, "The Market for Corporate Control: The Scientific Evidence," *Journal of Financial Economics,* 11, 1983, pp. 5–50.

Langetieg, T. C., "An Application of a Three-Factor Performance Index to Measure Stockholder Gains from Merger," *Journal of Financial Economics,* 6, December 1978, pp. 365–384.

Loughran, Tim, and Anand M. Vijh, "Do Long-Term Shareholders Benefit from Corporate Acquisitions?" *Journal of Finance,* 52, December 1997, pp. 1765–1790.

Magenheim, Ellen B., and Dennis C. Mueller, "Are Acquiring Firm Shareholders Better Off after an Acquisition?," chapter 11 in John Coffee, Jr., Louis Lowenstein, and

Susan Rose-Ackerman, eds., *Knights, Raiders and Targets,* Oxford, England: Oxford University Press, 1988, pp. 171–193.

Mandel, Michael J., "A Dangerous Concentration?," *Business Week,* April 29, 1996, pp. 96–97.

Mitchell, Mark L., and Kenneth Lehn, "Do Bad Bidders Become Good Targets?" *Journal of Political Economy,* 98, 1990, pp. 372–398.

Mitchell, Mark L., and J. Harold Mulherin, "The Impact of Industry Shocks on Takeover and Restructuring Activity," *Journal of Financial Economics,* 41, June 1996, pp. 193–229.

Opler, Tim C., "The Information Content of Corporate Takeover Announcements: Issues and Evidence," ms., The Anderson School at UCLA, October 1988.

Scherer, F. M., *Industrial Market Structure and Economic Performance,* Chicago: Rand McNally College Publishing Company, 1980.

Schwert, G. William, "Markup Pricing in Mergers and Acquisitions," *Journal of Financial Economics,* 41, 1996, pp. 153–192.

Shleifer, Andrei, and Robert W. Vishny, "The Takeover Wave of the 1980s," *Science,* 249, August 1990, pp. 745–749.

Sirower, Mark L., *The Synergy Trap,* New York: The Free Press, 1997.

Stillman, R. S., "Examining Antitrust Policy towards Horizontal Mergers," *Journal of Financial Economics,* 11, April 1983, pp. 225–240.

Wansley, James W., William R. Lane, and Ho C. Yang, "Abnormal Returns to Acquired Firms by Type of Acquisition and Method of Payment," *Financial Management,* 12, Autumn 1983, pp. 16–22.

Weston, J. Fred, "Domestic Concentration and International Markets," chapter 7 in J. Fred Weston and Michael E. Granfield, eds., *Corporate Enterprise in a New Environment,* New York: KCG Productions, Inc., 1982, pp. 173–188.

———, and Brian Johnson, "What It Takes for a Deal to Win Stock Market Approval," *Mergers & Acquisitions,* 34, September/October 1999, pp. 43–48.

You, Victor, Richard Caves, Michael Smith, and James Henry, "Mergers and Bidders' Wealth: Managerial and Strategic Factors," chapter 9 in Lacy Glenn Thomas, III, ed., *The Economics of Strategic Planning,* Lexington, MA: Lexington Books, 1986, pp. 201–220.

Alternative Approaches to Valuation

This chapter discusses valuation in relation to merger and acquisition activity. This subject is critical for the study of M&As because a major cause of acquisition failures is that the bidder pays too much. Sometimes a bidder makes a tender offer, which may stimulate competing bidders. The securities laws provide for a 20-day waiting period to give shareholders the opportunity to evaluate the proposal. This also gives other potential bidders time to evaluate the situation, to determine whether a competitive bid will be made. In a bidding contest, the winner is the firm with the highest estimates of the target's value. A framework is essential to discipline valuation estimates.

The leading methods used in the valuation of a firm for merger analysis are the comparable companies or comparable transactions approach, the spreadsheet approach, and the formula approach. In this chapter we explain and illustrate the logic or theory behind each of these three approaches. In chapter 10 we develop further the implementation of the leading valuation methods.

COMPARABLE COMPANIES OR COMPARABLE TRANSACTIONS APPROACHES

In the comparable companies or comparable transactions approach, key relationships are calculated for a group of similar companies or similar transactions as a basis for the valuation of companies involved in a merger or takeover. This approach is widely used, especially by investment bankers and in legal cases. The theory is not complicated. Marketplace transactions are used. It is a commonsense approach that says that similar companies should sell for similar prices. This straightforward approach appeals to businesspersons, to their financial advisors, and to the judges in courts of law called upon to give decisions on the relative values of companies in litigation. For a full elaboration of this approach, emanating from considerable application in court cases, see Cornell (1993).

First, a basic idea is illustrated in a simple setting, followed by applications to actual companies in an M&A setting. In Table 9.1, the comparable companies approach is illustrated. We are seeking to place a value on company W. We find three companies that are comparable. To test for comparability we consider size, similarity of products, age of company, and recent trends, among other variables.

Table 9.1 Comparable Companies Ratios
(Company W Is Compared with Companies A, B, and C)

Ratio	Company A	Company B	Company C	Average
Market*/sales	1.2	1.0	0.8	1.0
Market/book	1.3	1.2	2.0	1.5
Market/net income				
≡ price/earnings ratio	20	15	25	20

"Market" refers to the market value of equity.

Assume that companies A, B, and C meet most of our comparability requirements. We then calculate the ratio of the market value of shareholders' equity to sales, the ratio of the market value of equity to the book value of equity, and the price/earnings ratio for the individual companies. The resulting ratios are given in Table 9.1. These ratios are then averaged, and the average ratios are applied to the absolute data for company W. For the averages to be meaningful, it is important that the ratios we calculate for each company be relatively close in value. If they are greatly different, which implies that the dispersion around the average is substantial, the average (a measure of central tendency) would not be very meaningful. In the example given, the ratios for the three comparable companies do not vary widely. Hence, it makes some sense to apply the averages.

We postulate that for a relevant recent time period, company W had sales of $100 million, a book value of $60 million, and a net income of $5 million as shown in Table 9.2. We next apply the average market ratios from Table 9.1 to obtain the indicated value of equity for company W. We have three estimates of the indicated equity value of W based on the ratio of market value to sales, to book, and to net income. The results are close enough to be meaningful. When we average them, we obtain $97 million for the indicated market value of equity for company W.

One of the advantages of the comparable companies approach is that it can be used to establish valuation relationships for a company that is not publicly traded.

Table 9.2 Application of Valuation Ratios to Company W

Actual Recent Data for Company W		Average Market Ratio	Indicated Value of Equity
Sales	= $100	1.0	$100
Book value of equity =	60	1.5	90
Net income	= 5	20	100
			Average = $ 97

Table 9.3   Comparable Transaction Ratios
(Company W Is Compared with Companies TA, TB, and TC)

Ratio	Company TA	Company TB	Company TC	Average
Market*/sales	1.4	1.2	1.0	1.2
Market/book	1.5	1.4	2.2	1.7
Market/net income				
≡ price/earnings ratio	25	20	27	24

"Market" refers to the market value of equity.

This is a method of predicting what its publicly traded price is likely to be. The methodology is applicable in testing for the soundness of valuations in mergers also. Both the buyer and the seller in a merger seek confirmation that the price is fair to the values placed on other companies. For public companies, the courts will require such a demonstration if a suit is filed by an aggrieved shareholder.

The data in Table 9.1 can be reinterpreted to illustrate the comparable transactions approach. The data would then represent companies involved in the same kind of merger transactions as company W. In connection with merger transactions, a clarification should be made. When the term *market* is used, it does not refer to the prevailing market price of the companies' common stock before the merger announcement. In this context, "market" refers to the transaction price in a deal recently completed. Typically, merger transactions involve a premium as high as 30% to 40% over the prevailing market price (before news of the merger transaction has leaked out). The relevant valuation for a subsequent merger transaction would be the transaction prices for comparable deals.

Now let us reinterpret Table 9.1 as shown in Table 9.3, which covers comparable transactions. We postulate that the premiums over market that were paid caused the multiples (ratios) to be increased. We now view the companies as targets in acquisitions. The market values are now interpreted as the transaction market prices that were paid when these companies were acquired. Before a merger transaction, the prevailing market prices of companies include some probability that they will be acquired. But when they are actually acquired, the transaction price reflects the actual takeover event. Because takeover bids typically involve a premium over prevailing market prices, we accordingly illustrate this in the multiples reflected in Table 9.4. We now observe that the average transaction ratios for the comparable transactions have moved up. The indicated market value of company W is now $114, compared with $97, reflecting a premium of 17.5% over general market valuation relationships.

The practical implication of this is that if company W was going to be purchased and no comparable transactions had taken place, we would take the comparable companies approach as illustrated in Tables 9.1 and 9.2. But this would be only a starting point. There would then be some merger negotiations and probably some premium paid over prevailing market prices for the comparable companies.

Table 9.4   Application of Valuation Ratios to Company W

Actual Recent Data for Company W		Average Transaction Multiple	Indicated Value of Equity
Sales	= $100	1.2×	$120
Book value of equity =	60	1.7×	102
Net income	= 5	24×	120
			Average = $114

In Tables 9.1 through 9.4, we have illustrated the comparable companies and comparable transactions approaches using the ratios of market value of equity to book value, market value to sales, and market value to net income of the company. In some situations, other ratios might be employed in the comparable companies or comparable transactions approach. Additional ratios could include sales or revenue per employee, net income per employee, or assets needed to produce $1 of sales or revenue. Note that market values are not included in the ratios just listed. The additional ratios provide information on supplementary aspects of performance of the companies. This additional information could be used for interpreting or adjusting the average multiples obtained by using the comparable companies or comparable transactions approaches. Our experience has been that in actual merger or takeover transactions, investment bankers employ both the comparable companies approach and the comparable transactions approach and develop additional comparative performance measures as well.

THE SPREADSHEET APPROACH TO VALUATION AND MERGERS

The spreadsheet approach makes projections of the relevant cash flows. It begins with presentations of historical data for each element of the balance sheet, the income statement, and the cash flow statement. This provides the basis for a detailed financial ratio analysis to discover the financial patterns of the company. The detailed financial analysis covers data for the previous 7 to 10 years. For detailed and comprehensive illustrations of this approach, see Copeland, Koller, and Murrin (1994); see also chapter 17 in Weston and Copeland (1992). In addition to a review of the historical financial data on a company involved in a merger or takeover, the analysts compile considerable material on the business economics of the industry in which the company operates, the company's competitive position historically and prospectively into the future, and an assessment of financial patterns, strategies, and actions of its competitors—comparable companies.

Whereas in practice the spreadsheet approach involves many items of the balance sheets, income statements, and cash flow statements, the basic underlying logic builds on a basic capital budgeting analysis.

Capital Budgeting Decisions

Capital budgeting represents the process of planning expenditures whose returns extend over a period of time. Examples of capital outlays for tangible or physical items are expenditures for land, building, and equipment. Outlays for research and development, advertising, or promotional efforts may also be regarded as investment outlays when their benefits extend over a period of years. Whereas capital budgeting criteria are generally discussed in relation to investment in fixed assets, the concepts are equally applicable to investments in cash, receivables, or inventory as well as to M&As and other restructuring activities.

Several methods for evaluating projects have been developed. The net present value methodology is widely agreed to be the superior method for evaluation and ranking of investment proposals. The net present value (NPV) is the present value of all future cash flows discounted at the cost of capital, minus the cost of the investments made over time compounded at the opportunity cost of funds.

All of the formal models widely used in practice reflect the basic capital budgeting net present value analysis. We begin by illustrating the idea of the spreadsheet approach by relating it to a basic capital budgeting NPV approach. An acquiring firm (A) has the opportunity to buy a target company (T). The target company can be purchased for $180 million. The relevant net cash flows that will be received from the investment in the target company will be $40 million for the next 10 years, after which no cash flows will be forthcoming. The relevant cost of capital for analyzing the purchase of the target is 14%. Does this acquisition represent a positive NPV project? The applicable formula for calculating the NPV is

$$NPV = \sum_{t=1}^{n} \frac{CF_t}{(1+k)^t} - I_0$$

$$NPV = \sum_{t=1}^{10} \frac{\$40}{(1.14)^t} - \$180$$

where

NPV = net present value

$PVIFA$ = present value interest factor for an annuity

CF_t = net cash flows in year t (after taxes) = $40 million

k = marginal cost of capital = 14%

n = number of years, investment horizon = 10

I_0 = investment outlay in year zero = $180

We can now calculate the NPV of the acquisition.

$$
\begin{aligned}
NPV &= \$40 \, [PVIFA \, (14\%, 10 \text{ yr})] - \$180 \\
&= \$40 \, (5.2161 - \$180) \\
&= \$208.644 - \$180 \\
NPV &= GPV - I_0 \\
&= \$28.644 \text{ million}
\end{aligned}
$$

The present value of the cash inflows is the gross present value of the acquisition (GPV). From the GPV, the present value of the investment outlays (I_0) is deducted to obtain the NPV of the acquisition.

With this simple illustration of the analysis of an acquisition in the framework of capital budgeting principles, we can illustrate a very significant principle. Even acquisitions that achieve synergies will be unsound if the buyer (bidder, acquirer) pays too much. For example, if the bidder paid $250 million for the target company, the NPV of the acquisition would then become a negative $41.4 million.

$$NPV = \$208,644 - \$250,000$$
$$= -\$41.356 \text{ million}$$

The underlying concept that an acquisition is fundamentally a capital budgeting problem should be kept in mind even when the transactions involve great complications. Some mergers among firms have been called "marriages made in heaven." They make considerable sense from the business standpoint. The two companies blend beautifully. But if the acquirer (A) pays too much, it is a negative NPV investment and the value of the bidder will decline. The market recognizes this, and the event return for A will be negative. The financial press will report, "A acquired T and as a consequence the market value of A fell by $4 billion. A paid too much."

Spreadsheet Projections

The basic idea of the spreadsheet approach can be conveyed in a somewhat more detailed capital budgeting analysis. Company A is considering the purchase of a target company T. A detailed spreadsheet analysis of the financial statements of the target has been made. On the basis of that analysis and of all aspects of the business economics of the target's industry, the acquiring firm has made the spreadsheet projections exhibited in Table 9.5.

The first row of Table 9.5 is projected revenues. They start at $1,000 and are expected to grow at a 20% rate. Row 2 is total costs related to the sales levels shown in row 1. From the historical patterns and the economic outlook, the investment bankers make the spreadsheet projections that net operating income will be 20% of sales. The net operating income is projected in row 3. Corporate taxes of 40% are postulated and shown in row 4. Deducting taxes paid, we obtain net operating income after taxes, shown in line 5. Total capital requirements consist of net working capital plus net property, plant, and equipment. Net working capital is 4% of revenues, and net property, plant, and equipment are 6% of revenues. So for the target company a total capital investment of 10 cents is required for each dollar of revenues. This represents a capital turnover of 10, so that row 8 is 10% of the figures in row 1. Company T represents an investment opportunity in which revenues will grow at 20% for three years, after which they will level off at $1,728 as shown in the right-hand columns. In rows 6 to 8, the annual investment requirements are shown. *Investment* is defined as the addition to total capital made in a given year to have the total capital required to support sales in that year.

Table 9.5   Spreadsheet Projections of Company T

				Year		
	Percent of Revenue	**0**	**1**	**2**	**3**	**4 to ∞**
1. Revenues (R_t)	100%	$1,000	$1,200	$1,440	$1,728	$1,728
2. Costs	80%		960	1152	1382	1382
3. Net operating Income (X_t)	20%		240	288	346	346
4. Taxes (T)	40%		96	115	138	138
5. Net operating income after taxes [$X_t(1 - T)$]	12%		144	173	207	207
Investment Requirements						
6. Net working capital (I_{wt})	4%		$48	$58	$69	$0
7. Net property, plant, and Equipment (I_{ft})	6%		72	86	104	0
8. Total (I_t)	10%		120	144	173	0
9. Free cash flows [$X_t(1 - T) - I_t$]			$24	$29	$35	$207

The reader will recognize that the column values for each row in Table 9.5 grow at a 20% per annum rate through year 3. These assumptions were made for the convenience of simplicity. One of the advantages of the spreadsheet approach is that the growth rates for the items listed in the rows could be different from one another and from year to year. The spreadsheet approach provides great flexibility in the projections. However, it is equally important to recognize that when one is presented with a set of projections, as in the spreadsheet approach, it is useful to raise the question: What underlying growth patterns are illustrated by these projections? Further questions should be pursued. Are the growth rates in the projections consistent with the forecasts for the economy? For the industry? For market share in relation to competitors? And so on. Although the numbers shown in Table 9.5 are quite simplified, the basic principles that are illustrated are equally valid no matter how complicated the numbers turn out to be in real-life applications of the spreadsheet methodology.

Given the projections in the spreadsheets reflected in Table 9.5, we can illustrate the calculation of a value for the target that is the maximum the acquiring firm can pay if it is to earn its 10% cost of capital. Alternatively, we could say that if an acquirer pays more for the target than the value we calculate in Table 9.6, it will be making a negative net present value investment.

Table 9.6 is a worksheet to explain how free cash flows are measured. Each row is expressed in symbols that will be used throughout the book. Row 1 is before-tax cash flows (X_t) taken from row 3 of Table 9.5. In row 2, the 40% tax rate (T) is applied. Row 3 is after-tax cash flows [$X_t(1-T)$]. Annual investment outlays (I_t) are shown in row 4. Row 5 represents the free cash flows. When we discount the free cash

Table 9.6   Valuation of the Target

| | | | YEAR | |
| | | | | **3** | |
	1	**2**	**Beginning**	**End**
1. Before-tax cash flow (X_t)	240	288	346	346
2. Taxes at 40% (T)	96	115	138	138
3. After-tax cash flow [$X_t(1-T)$]	144	173	207	207
4. Investment (I_t)	120	144	173	0
5. Free cash flow [$X_t(1-T) - I_t$]	24	29	35	207.4
6. Discount factor	$(I+k)$	$(I+k)^2$	$(I+k)^3$	$k(I+k)^3$
a. Discount factor	1/1.10	1/1.21	1/1.331	10/1.331
7. Present value	$21.82	$23.97	$26.30	$1,558.23

flows at the applicable cost of capital (k), we obtain the NPV of the acquisition because the investment outlays have been deducted year by year.

We can now develop a spreadsheet valuation of the target company by discounting the free cash flows in Table 9.6 at the applicable cost of capital of 10%. The discount factor is $(1+k)$ to the first power for the cash flow in year 1, to the second power for the cash flow in year 2, and to the third power in the cash flow in year 3.

At the beginning of the fourth year, the after-tax (free) cash flow is $207.4, which remains constant to infinity. Since there is no further growth, the net new investment required to support growth is also zero. So the after-tax cash flows from the end of year 3 (the beginning of year 4) are the free cash flows to be discounted back to the beginning of year 4. The value of these constant cash flows is obtained by dividing by the discount factor of 10%. This gives us the so-called exit value of the target firm as of the end of the third year. This value of $2,074 is discounted back for three years under the general principle that we begin discounting with next year's cash flow. This timing of the discounting of the constant cash flows to infinity is followed in the widely used formulas employed by investment bankers and consulting firms in actual applications.

So the $2,074 is discounted back to the present by dividing by $(1+k)^3$ or $(1.10)^3$ in our example. This gives a present value of the exit value of $1,558.23. The value of the firm V_0 is

Present value of the discounted cash flow in year 1	$ 21.82
Present value of the discounted cash flow in year 2	$ 23.97
Present value of the discounted cash flow in year 3	$ 26.30
Present value of the discounted terminal value or exit value	$1,558.23
Total value of the target	$1,630.32

Thus the value of the target firm that would enable the acquiring firm to earn its cost of capital would be $1,630.32. If the acquiring firm is able to obtain the target for something less than $1,630.32, and if the projections are fulfilled, this would be a positive net present value investment. If the acquiring firm pays more than $1,630.32, it will be making a negative net present value investment, and its own market value will decline.

Brief Evaluation of the Spreadsheet Approach

An advantage of the spreadsheet approach is that it is expressed in financial statements familiar to businesspersons. A second major advantage is that the data are year by year with any desired detail of individual balance sheet or income statement accounts. Judgment and flexibility can be reflected in formulating the projections.

The spreadsheet approach also has some pitfalls. The specific numbers used in the projections may create the illusion that they are the actual or correct numbers. This is misleading. Projections are subject to error. Sometimes the bases for the projections may be obscured. A clear link is not always established between the projected numbers and the economic or business logic by which they were determined. Another limitation is that the spreadsheet may become highly complex. The advantage of including many details is also subject to the risk that the detail obscures the forces that are really important in making the projections. This is why in our initial explanation of the spreadsheet approach we employed a very simple numerical example. More complex applications are developed in chapter 10 when applications are made to actual companies.

FORMULA APPROACH

In this section we focus on the formula approach to valuation. There is no real distinction between the spreadsheet approach and the formula approach. Both use a discounted cash flow (DCF) analysis. The spreadsheet approach is expressed in the form of financial statements over a period of years. The formula approach summarizes the same data in more compact expressions. Both give the same numerical results, as we shall illustrate.

Valuation formulas appear in many different shapes, sizes, and expressions. The four basic formulas are shown in Table 9.7 (derivations in Appendix B). The concepts follow from basic finance materials. They will be illustrated in the case examples we subsequently present on valuations in acquisitions in this chapter and in Chapter 10. The leading practitioners in valuation employ these basic expressions in various forms.

The Basic Formula

In this section we set forth the formula for valuing free cash flows growing at a supernormal rate for a period of years followed by no growth. We use the data from

Table 9.7   Formulas for Valuation of a Firm/Discounted Cash Flow

No growth:

$$V_0 = \frac{R_0[m(1-T)]}{k} \qquad \text{for } k > 0 \tag{9.1}$$

Constant growth:

$$V_0 = \frac{R_0(1+g)[m(1-T)-I]}{k-g} \qquad \text{for } k > g \tag{9.2}$$

Temporary supernormal growth, then no growth:

$$V_0 = R_0[m(1-T)-I] \sum_{t=1}^{n} \frac{(1+g)^t}{(1+k)^t} + \frac{R_0(1+g)^n[m(1-T)]}{k(1+k)^n} \tag{9.3}$$

Temporary supernormal growth, then constant growth:

$$V_0 = R_0[m(1-T)-I_s] \sum_{t=1}^{n} \frac{(1+g_s)^t}{(1+k)^t} + \frac{R_0(1+g_s)^n[m(1-T)-I_c]}{(1+k)^n} \cdot \left(\frac{1+g_c}{k-g_c}\right) \tag{9.4}$$

where

R_0 = initial revenues
m = net operating income margin
T = tax rate
I = investment as a percentage of revenues
g = growth rate of revenues
k = cost of capital
n = number of years of supernormal growth

In equation (9.4), the subscript s indicates that I or g is for the supernormal growth period; the subscript c indicates that I or g is for the period of constant growth.

Table 9.6, which illustrated the spreadsheet approach. We evaluate the same data using the equation (9.3) formula to demonstrate that we obtain exactly the same numerical result. The widely used equation (9.3) for free cash flows has a period of supernormal growth followed by no growth as shown in Table 9.7.

$$V_0 = R_0[m(1-T)-I] \sum_{t=1}^{n} \frac{(1+g)^t}{(1+k)^t} + \frac{R_0(1+g)^n[m(1-T)]}{k(1+k)^n} \tag{9.3}$$

Using $1+h = (1+g)/(1+k)$, equation (9.3) becomes

$$V_0 = R_0[m(1-T)-I](1+h)\left[\frac{(1+h)^n-1}{h}\right] + \frac{R_0 m(1-T)}{k}(1+h)^n \tag{9.3a}$$

We use the numbers from Table 9.6 to obtain equation (9.3b):

R_0 = initial revenues = \$1,000
m = net operating income margin = 20%
T = tax rate = 40%
I = investment as a percentage of revenues = 10%
g = growth rate of revenues = 20%
k = cost of capital = 10%
n = number of years of supernormal growth = 3
$1 + h$ = calculation relationship $(1 + g)/(1 + k) = 1.09091$

$$V_0 = \$1,000[0.2\,(0.6) - 0.1](1.09091)\left[\frac{(1.09091)^3 - 1}{0.0909}\right] + \frac{1,000\,(0.2)\,(0.6)}{0.1}(1.09091)^3$$

$$= (20)\,(1.09091)\,(3.28) + \left(\frac{120}{0.1}\right)(1.09091)^3 \qquad\qquad \textbf{(9.3b)}$$

$$= 72 + 1558$$

$$= \$1,630$$

The final result approximates the period-by-period calculations in Table 9.6. This demonstrates that the DCF spreadsheet method and the DCF formula method are conceptually the same and give the same numerical result. The two approaches are complementary. The spreadsheet approach allows flexibility in making projections on a year-by-year basis. The formula approach helps us focus on the underlying elements or drivers that determine value.

Sensitivity Analysis

With the use of equation (9.3) we are able to do a sensitivity analysis of the impact of the size of the value drivers on the valuation. The results are shown in Table 9.8. In our initial case shown in line 1, the valuation was \$1,630. In line 2, we reduce the growth rate in revenues. Predictably, the valuation declines. In line 3, we go back to the initial case but increase the investment requirement percentage to 15%. Again, valuation declines because free cash flows are reduced by the higher investment requirements.

In line 4, we return to the initial case but now lower the operating profit margin. Clearly, valuation would decline sharply, indicating that the profitability rate is a powerful value driver. In line 5, we return to the initial case but reduce the cost of capital. Valuation increases substantially, showing that the cost of capital is another powerful influence. Line 6 indicates that an increased cost of capital has a strong negative influence on valuation. The impact of the number of periods of supernormal growth or period of comparative advantage or variations in the tax rate operate in predictable directions, as shown in lines 7 through 10.

Table 9.8   Sensitivity Analysis of Varying the Value Drivers*

	k	g	I	m	n	T	Valuation	2nd term as percent of total
Initial case								
1.	10%	20%	10%	20%	3	40%	$1,630	96%
Change g, I, and m:								
2.	10%	15%	10%	20%	3	40%	$1,437	95%
3.	10%	20%	15%	20%	3	40%	$1,451	107%
4.	10%	20%	10%	15%	3	40%	$1,133	103%
Back to initial case, but vary k:								
5.	9%	20%	10%	20%	3	40%	$1,852	96%
6.	11%	20%	10%	20%	3	40%	$1,449	95%
Back to initial case, but vary n:								
7.	10%	20%	10%	20%	2	40%	$1,474	97%
8.	10%	20%	10%	20%	5	40%	$1,985	93%
Back to initial case, but vary T:								
9.	10%	20%	10%	20%	3	35%	$1,795	94%
10.	10%	20%	10%	20%	3	45%	$1,464	98%

For meaning of column heads, see text

In Table 9.8, the second term (the present value of the terminal value) in the valuation model represents the higher proportion of the valuation. This is true in many practical cases. This should alert those who are performing the valuation to be quite careful as to the assumptions made about the factors that affect so-called exit or terminal values.

Our experience has been that executives knowledgeable in the industry and firm for which the analysis is being made are likely to be interested in having a sensitivity analysis. They are aware of the many influences that could alter the size of the value drivers, so they are interested in checking the impact of a range of alternative possibilities.

The sensitivity analysis performs another valuable function. It provides a framework for planning and control. By improving performance on one or more of the value drivers, the valuation of the firm can be increased. Tangible incentives are thereby created to stimulate improvements, particularly in areas where managers have responsibility.

In the valuation calculations to this point we have explained the measurement of all the value drivers except *k*, the cost of capital. This we do next in the context of a case study of ConAgra Inc.

CASE STUDY OF THE VALUATION OF CONAGRA INC.

ConAgra is the second largest food processor in the United States. It has three major product lines: grocery products, refrigerated foods, and food inputs such as crop protection chemicals and fertilizers, grain and bean processing, and specialty food ingredients. We studied the food industry and the competitors to ConAgra in some depth as a background to this analysis (Weston and Chiu, 1996).

In Table 9.9, we present a valuation of ConAgra based on a study of prospective revenue growth and cost structures. The future revenue growth estimate of 14% in Table 9.9 was developed from a study of the growth prospects in the major segments of its business activities. Other analysts have suggested revenue and earnings growth rates for ConAgra in the 10% to 15% per annum range.

The cost structure and investment requirement relationships in Table 9.9 were developed from the data in Table 9.10. The first three columns of data in Table 9.10 present calculations of annual growth rates for the decades beginning 1979 and 1989 and for the combined period. This was done for the major income statement and balance sheet items. ConAgra had growth rates for the first decade in the 25% to 30% range. For the second decade beginning in 1989, these rates dropped to the 8% to 10% range. We forecast some improvement for the decade beginning in 1999.

The second part of the table consists of developing relationships between revenues and other income statement and balance sheet categories. We focus on the coefficient column that represents the relationship between changes in revenues and changes in cost of goods sold, developed by regression analysis. The statistical tests demonstrate that the percentages of all the income statement and balance sheet items are stable and correct with probability levels over 99%. These close statistical relationships are also depicted in Figure 9.1.

We have a firm basis for all of the revenue, cost, and investment requirement relationships based on Table 9.10 and Figure 9.1. The final relationship we need to develop is the discount factor used in Table 9.9. Several steps are involved: (1) Estimate the cost of equity capital, (2) calculate the cost of debt, (3) formulate the applicable financial structure or financial proportions for the firm, and (4) apply the applicable financial proportions to the cost of equity capital and to the cost of debt; the result is the weighted cost of capital. This procedure provides us with a weighted marginal cost of capital. The first step is the cost of equity capital. We need first to discuss some broader economic issues.

COST OF EQUITY CAPITAL—ECONOMIC ISSUES

This section provides some general background for calculating the cost of equity capital—a key part of estimating the applicable discount factor in valuation. Although we will also discuss other approaches, the most widely employed is the Capital Asset Pricing Model (CAPM). The logic of CAPM is unassailable. The required return on equity is a risk-free return plus a risk component. For the economy as a whole, the risk-free rate would be related to the returns on U.S. government bonds. Because the discount factor used in valuation involves relatively long periods, the rates on relatively long term bonds would be employed. The analysis generally gives heavy weight

Table 9.9 Spreadsheet DCF Valuation, ConAgra ($ in millions)

	Rel	% of Rev	Forecast Year 1	2	3	4	5	6	7	8	9
Incremental Free Cash Flow	14.0%										
1. Revenues		100%	$23,840	$27,178	$30,982	$35,320	$40,265	$45,902	$52,328	$59,654	$68,006
2. Cost of Goods Sold (excl. Depr.)		83.0%	19,787	22,557	25,715	29,316	33,420	38,099	43,432	49,513	56,445
3. Selling, General, & Administrative		10.0%	2,384	2,718	3,098	3,532	4,026	4,590	5,233	5,965	6,801
4. Depreciation (tax)		2.0%	477	544	620	706	805	918	1,047	1,193	1,360
5. Merger economies		0.0%	—	—	—	—	—	—	—	—	—
6. Pretax Operating Income (NOI)		5.0%	1,192	1,359	1,549	1,766	2,013	2,295	2,616	2,983	3,400
7. After-Tax Operating Income: $(NOI)(1-T)$ Income tax rate = 40%; $(1-T)=60\%$			715	815	929	1,060	1,208	1,377	1,570	1,790	2,040
8. Net investment in working capital	Tbl A		$ (117)	$ (134)	$ (152)	$ (174)	$ (198)	$ (225)	$ (257)	$ (293)	$ (334)
9. Net investment in fixed assets	Tbl A		(351)	(401)	(457)	(521)	(593)	(676)	(771)	(879)	(1,002)
10. Free Cash Flow (FCF)			$ 247	$ 281	$ 321	$ 366	$ 417	$ 475	$ 542	$ 617	$ 704
Valuation		% Rates									
11. Discounted FCF Cost of Capital (k)		9.0%	$ 226	$ 237	$ 248	$ 259	$ 271	$ 283	$ 296	$ 310	$ 324
12. Total present value of FCF			$ 2,454								
			PVTV								TV

238

	Case A	Case B
13. Terminal Value Rate Assumptions		
a. Post-terminal year growth rate (g)	0%	5%
b. Reinvestment rate (z)	0%	40%
14. Terminal Value (TV)	22,669	32,133
15. Present Value of FCF	$ 2,454	$ 2,454
16. Present Value of TV (PVTV)	10,437	14,795
17. Total Present Value	$12,891	$17,249
18. Plus: Marketable Securities		
19. Total Value of the Firm	12,891	17,249
20. Less: Total Interest-Bearing Debt	3,400	3,400
21. Equity Value	$ 9,491	$13,849
22. Number of Shares (millions)	480	480
23. Value per Share	$ 19.77	$ 28.85

Table A—Investment	% of ΔRev	Year								
		1	2	3	4	5	6	7	8	9
A1. Revenues (14.0% growth)		$23,840	$27,178	$30,982	$35,320	$40,265	$45,902	$52,328	$59,654	$68,006
A2. Δ Revenues		2,928	3,338	3,805	4,338	4,945	5,637	6,426	7,326	8,352
A3. Net investment in working capital	4.0%	117	134	152	174	198	225	257	293	334
A4. Net investment in fixed assets	12.0%	351	401	457	521	593	676	771	879	1,002
A5. Δ Total Capital = Investment		$ 468	$ 534	$ 609	$ 694	$ 791	$ 902	$ 1,028	$ 1,172	$ 1,336

Table 9.10 Growth Rates and Value Driver Relations, ConAgra Inc., 1979 to 1998

	Annual Growth Rate			Regression Against Revenues 1979–1998			
	1979–1989	1989–1998	1979–1998	Intercept	t-Stat*	Coefficient	t-Stat*
Revenues	30.0%	6.9%	19.8%	—	—	—	—
Cost of Goods Sold	29.9%	6.4%	19.5%	133.261	1.666	0.841	163.101
SG&A	33.6%	8.3%	21.4%	−39.870	−1.149	0.095	42.271
Depreciation	29.5%	16.1%	23.9%	−37.169	−2.127	0.017	14.748
Interest Expense	21.3%	6.9%	19.1%	−12.240	−1.024	0.014	18.674
EBITDA	27.3%	12.6%	21.4%	−93.392	−1.739	0.065	18.647
NOI	26.8%	11.7%	20.7%	−56.223	−1.418	0.048	18.763
EBIT	25.3%	9.8%	19.4%	−30.286	−0.591	0.046	13.951
EBT	27.3%	10.9%	19.6%	−18.046	−0.358	0.032	9.771
Net Income (Loss)	25.3%	9.6%	18.2%	−3.714	−0.106	0.018	8.031
Net Income + $(1-T)$(Interest Expense)	23.9%	9.1%	18.6%	−11.641	−0.324	0.027	11.839
Average tax rate used	31.6%	36.0%	35.2%				
Cash and Short-Term Investments	39.0%	−25.4%	14.8%	68.042	0.771	0.012	2.171
Receivables—Total	26.0%	2.9%	16.2%	116.505	2.529	0.059	19.930
Inventories—Total	28.3%	10.5%	20.3%	−98.410	−1.067	0.131	22.113
Current Assets—Total	28.3%	6.0%	18.9%	44.172	0.554	0.217	42.179

Property, Plant, and Equipment—Total (net)	26.2%	14.1%	21.9%	−216.130	−1.873	**16.553**
Assets—Total	28.1%	9.9%	21.7%	−652.193	−2.361	**26.953**
Debt in Current Liabilities	34.1%	3.4%	31.9%	−68.301	−0.897	**5.828**
Accounts Payable	27.0%	2.6%	14.4%	300.910	2.834	**9.690**
Current Liabilities—Total	30.0%	6.5%	21.0%	−128.462	−1.150	**28.381**
Long-Term Debt—Total	25.5%	14.3%	22.6%	−212.568	−2.089	**15.825**
Liabilities—Total	29.3%	9.9%	22.6%	−581.192	−2.618	**25.859**
Stockholders' Equity—Total	25.2%	9.6%	19.3%	−71.001	−0.854	**20.486**
Net Working Capital	22.7%	8.8%	14.9%	77.753	*1.210*	**8.877**
Total Capital	24.7%	12.2%	19.4%	−138.378	−0.891	**15.963**
Price—Average high-low (adjusted)	24.9%	13.2%	18.9%			
Price—Close (adjusted)	23.8%	12.3%	18.7%			

*t-Stats in bold font are significant at the 1 % level.

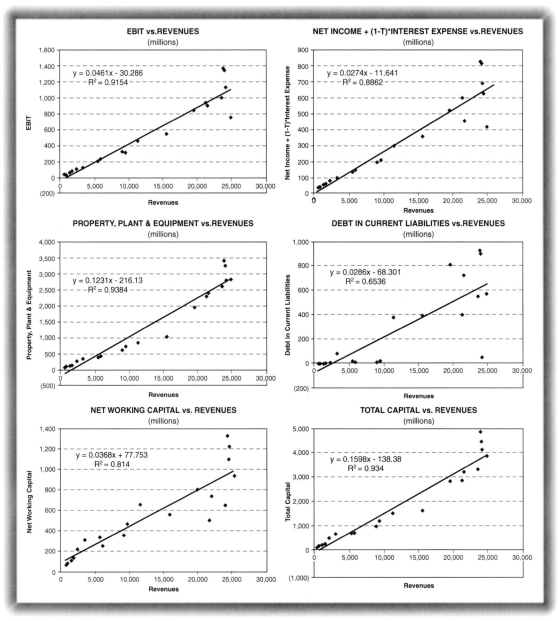

Figure 9.1 Graphs of Selected Value Driver Relations, ConAgra Inc., 1979–1998

to interest rate levels in the current economic environment. For the United States in the summer of 1999, the yields on long-term treasuries were about 6%.

In the CAPM, the risk adjustment is the required market-determined differential between equity yields and government bonds. To illustrate we use 5% as a starting point for the market price of risk. The 5% is multiplied by the firm's beta to obtain an estimate of the risk adjustment for an individual firm. The beta of a firm is a measure of how the return on its common stock varies with returns on the market as a whole. Returns on the market as a whole have been conveniently measured by use of the S&P 500, all stocks on the New York Stock Exchange, or other broad groupings. Thus, if the return on the market increased by 10%, a firm with a beta of 1.2 would experience a rise in its returns of 12% (and, conversely, a decrease of 12% if the market fell by 10%). Thus, high beta stocks exhibit higher volatility than low beta stocks in response to changes in market returns.

The beta for the market as a whole must necessarily be 1, by definition. With a risk-free rate of 6% and a market price of risk of 5%, we can write an equation for the expected return on the market:

$$\text{Return on the market} = 6\% + 5\%\ (1) = 11\%$$

From this relationship, we can generalize to individual firms.

$$\text{Return on equity of a firm} = 6\% + 5\%\ (\text{beta})$$

If the beta of the firm is 1.2, its expected return would be 12%. If the beta of the firm is 0.8, its expected return would be 10%, according to CAPM.

For many years, based on patterns of the long-term relationships between returns on long- and short-term government bonds, on long- and short-term corporate bonds, and on equity groups such as large caps, small caps, high techs, etc., the market equity premium appeared to be in the range of 6.5% to 7.5%. But by the mid-1990s, a new paradigm for a new economy began to emerge. Analysts moved toward using 4% to 5% as the market price of risk.

A number of arguments have been offered to justify a lower market risk premium in the New Economy. The U.S. economy experienced a period of sustained economic growth for almost two decades. Price inflation was reduced to the 1% to 2.5% levels. Unemployment was low, yet wage costs were relatively flat into mid-1999. High rates of productivity from the new technologies also helped keep costs low. The restructurings of the 1980s made U.S. firms more cost-efficient. These are the kinds of factors used to support the argument that the economy as a whole had become one of relatively stable, attractive growth, with lower risks of severe reverses.

As a practical matter, it would be difficult to develop quantitative relationships to explain the relatively high levels of stock prices without discount factors derived from lower levels of the market price of risk. Hence the broad shift to the use of 4% to 5% as the equity risk premium (ERP).

We next illustrate how the levels of the market price of risk influence the discount factors employed in the valuation of individual firms. With a risk-free rate of 6%, a firm with a beta of 1.2 in a world of a 7.5% ERP would have an expected cost of equity of 15%. In a world of a 4% ERP, it would have an expected cost of equity of 10.8%. This difference can have a vast impact on company valuations. With this economic background, we calculate the cost of capital for ConAgra (as of August 1999).

COST OF CAPITAL

We are now ready to present the methodology for calculating the cost of capital applicable for enterprise evaluation. Since the concepts are somewhat abstract, it is useful to use our case study of ConAgra as a vehicle for explaining how to calculate the cost of capital. We begin with the calculation of the cost of equity capital for ConAgra.

Cost of Equity Capital

We present three methods for calculating the cost of equity capital.

Capital Asset Pricing Model (CAPM)

$$\text{Required equity return for ConAgra} = R_f + \text{ERP} \times \text{beta}$$

1. For the risk-free rate, R_f, it is appropriate to use the yield on long-term U.S. government bonds. We use 6% as discussed above.
2. The Value Line Investor Survey gives a beta of 0.85 for ConAgra.
3. We use an ERP of 5%.
4. Required equity return for ConAgra equals $0.06 + 0.05 (0.85) = 0.06 + 0.0425 = 10.25\%$.

This is our first approximation to the cost of equity for ConAgra.

The Dividend Growth Model

The dividend growth model states that the value of equity is equal to the expected dividend divided by the cost of equity minus the growth rate of dividends in perpetuity. Solving this expression for the cost of equity for a firm gives

$$\text{Cost of equity} = \text{Expected dividend yield} + \text{Expected growth rate}$$

$$\text{Cost of equity of ConAgra} = 2.6\% + 8\% = 10.6\%$$

The expected dividend yield of 2.6% is taken from the Value Line projection of the ConAgra dividend yield for 2001 to 2003. The 8% expected long-term growth rate in dividends is based on the growth patterns presented in Table 9.10. The resulting 10.6% is consistent with the CAPM result.

Bond Yield Plus Equity Risk Adjustment

A third approach provides a check on the previous two. The yield on a firm's equity should be greater than the yield on its bonds, because equity claims are junior to the prior claims of creditors. The first type of ERP we discussed in the previous section was the required return on equity of a firm in relation to the equity return on the market. Here, the firm's equity risk adjustment is in relation to the yield on its bonds. ConAgra's long-term bonds were generally rated Baa in August 1999, and the yield on Baa bonds was in the 7.5% range. Historical data on the equity returns to ConAgra shareholders suggests a spread over its bond yields of 2.5% to 4%. Using the low point of the range in the then current market environment, we add 2.5% to the 7.5% bond yield to obtain 10%.

Cost of Debt

The cost of debt should be on an after-tax basis because interest payments are tax-deductible. Therefore, the cost of debt capital is calculated as follows:

$$k_b(1-T) = \text{After-tax cost of debt}$$

Here T is the corporate tax rate used previously. Thus, if the before-tax cost of debt were 9% and the firm's effective corporate tax rate were 35%, the after-tax cost of debt would be 5.85%.

We start with the firm's before-tax cost of debt and multiply it by the factor $(1-T)$ to obtain the relevant after-tax cost. How do we obtain the before-tax cost of debt in practice for an actual firm? Two main procedures may be used: (1) We can look in any investment manual to determine the rating of the firm's outstanding publicly held bonds. Various government agencies and investment banking firms periodically publish promised yields to maturity of debt issues by rating categories. (2) We can take a weighted average of the yield to maturity for all the firm's publicly traded bonds.

We use an estimate of 7.5% for the before-tax cost of debt for ConAgra based on the Baa rating of its long-term debt. Its after-tax cost of debt, using a tax rate of 35%, would be 4.9%.

All three of our estimates on the required return on equity of ConAgra are close to 10%. We estimated the after tax cost of debt to be 4.9%. The discount factor used in the valuations is the firm's weighted cost of capital, which is discussed next.

Weighted Cost of Capital

To calculate the marginal weighted cost of capital, we first calculate financing proportions at book values and at market values.

Financial Proportions at Book Value (millions)

Interest-Bearing Debt	$2,500	47%
Shareholders' Equity	$2,800	53%
Total	$5,300	

Financial Proportions at Market Value (millions)

Interest-Bearing Debt*	$2,500	16%
Shareholders' Equity* ($25 × 510.3)	$12,758	84%
Total	$15,258	

*The market value of shareholders' equity is calculated as the number of shares outstanding as of the end of 1998 times the average market price of the common stock during 1998. The market value of debt is assumed to be the same as its book value.

Taking these financial proportions as a guide, we use a financial structure consisting of 30% debt and 70% equity to calculate the weighted-average cost of capital for ConAgra as

$$0.10(0.70) + 0.049(0.30) = 0.07 + 0.0147 = 0.0847$$

We could then perform a sensitivity analysis with different proportions of debt and equity to obtain a range of cost of capital estimates for ConAgra. As a starting point, we can use the above estimate in the valuation of ConAgra as shown in Table 9.11.

The use of the 8.47% discount factor in the spreadsheet DCF valuation of ConAgra results in a base case market price of ConAgra of about $22. This lifts the indicated market value of ConAgra closer to its August 1999 price level than the somewhat under $20 price from Table 9.9. It is useful, therefore, to investigate the impact of variations in the levels of the key value drivers.

Sensitivity Analysis of the ConAgra Valuations

In Table 9.12 we calculate the sensitivity of the indicated market price per share to the level of its value drivers. We use four estimates of the levels of the following value drivers: growth rate of revenues, the levels of the cost of goods sold with

Table 9.11 Spreadsheet DCF Valuation, ConAgra ($ in millions)

	Rel	% of Rev					Forecast Year				
			1	2	3	4	5	6	7	8	9
Incremental Free Cash Flow											
1. Revenues	14.0%	100%	$23,840	$27,178	$30,982	$35,320	$40,265	$45,902	$52,328	$59,654	$68,006
2. Cost of Goods Sold (excl. Depr.)		83.0%	19,787	22,557	25,715	29,316	33,420	38,099	43,432	49,513	56,445
3. Selling, General, & Administrative		10.0%	2,384	2,718	3,098	3,532	4,026	4,590	5,233	5,965	6,801
4. Depreciation (tax)		2.0%	477	544	620	706	805	918	1,047	1,193	1,360
5. Merger economies		0.0%	—	—	—	—	—	—	—	—	—
6. Pretax Operating Income (NOI)		5.0%	1,192	1,359	1,549	1,766	2,013	2,295	2,616	2,983	3,400
7. After-Tax Operating Income: (NOI)(1 − T) Income tax rate = 40%; (1 − T) = 60%			715	815	929	1,060	1,208	1,377	1,570	1,790	2,040
8. Net investment in working capital	Tbl A		$ (117)	$ (134)	$ (152)	$ (174)	$ (198)	$ (225)	$ (257)	$ (293)	$ (334)
9. Net investment in fixed assets	Tbl A		(351)	(401)	(457)	(521)	(593)	(676)	(771)	(879)	(1,002)
10. Free Cash Flow (FCF)			$ 247	$ 281	$ 321	$ 366	$ 417	$ 475	$ 542	$ 617	$ 704
Valuation		**% Rates**									
11. Discounted FCF Cost of Capital (k)		8.47%	$ 227	$ 239	$ 251	$ 264	$ 278	$ 292	$ 307	$ 322	$ 339
12. Total present value of FCF			$ 2,519								
				PVTV							TV

246

	Case A	Case B
13. Terminal Value Rate Assumptions		
a. Post-terminal year growth rate (g)	0%	5%
b. Reinvestment rate (z)	0%	40%
14. Terminal Value (TV)	24,087	37,041
15. Present Value of FCF	$ 2,519	$ 2,519
16. Present Value of TV (PVTV)	11,588	17,819
17. Total Present Value	$14,106	$20,338
18. Plus: Marketable Securities		
19. Total Value of the firm	14,106	20,338
20. Less: Total Interest-Bearing Debt	3,400	3,400
21. Equity Value	$10,706	$16,938
22. Number of Shares (millions)	480	480
23. Value per Share	$ 22.30	$ 35.29

Table A—Investment	% of ΔRev	Year								
		1	2	3	4	5	6	7	8	9
A1. Revenues (14.0% growth)		$23,840	$27,178	$30,982	$35,320	$40,265	$45,902	$52,328	$59,654	$68,006
A2. Δ Revenues		2,928	3,338	3,805	4,338	4,945	5,637	6,426	7,326	8,352
A3. Net investment in working capital	4.0%	117	134	152	174	198	225	257	293	334
A4. Net investment in fixed assets	12.0%	351	401	457	521	593	676	771	879	1,002
A5. Δ Total Capital = Investment		$ 468	$ 534	$ 609	$ 694	$ 791	$ 902	$ 1,028	$ 1,172	$ 1,336

Table 9.12   Sensitivity of Market Price per Share to the Value Drivers

g_{rev}	Price	Cost of Goods Sold	Price	Net Operating Income	Price	Cost of Capital	Price	Fixed Asset	Price
Case A Post-terminal growth rate of zero									
10.0%	17.80	80.0%	45.91	2.0%	−1.30	8.5%	22.15	10.0%	23.55
12.0%	19.91	82.0%	30.17	4.0%	14.44	9.5%	17.68	12.0%	22.30
14.0%	22.30	84.0%	14.44	6.0%	30.17	10.0%	15.82	14.0%	21.06
16.0%	25.00	86.0%	−1.30	8.0%	45.91	10.5%	14.16	16.0%	19.81
Case B Post-terminal growth rate of 5% per annum to infinity									
10.0%	27.55	80.0%	66.69	2.0%	3.89	8.5%	34.87	10.0%	36.53
12.0%	31.18	82.0%	45.75	4.0%	24.82	9.5%	24.20	12.0%	35.29
14.0%	35.29	84.0%	24.82	6.0%	45.75	10.0%	20.50	14.0%	34.04
16.0%	39.92	86.0%	3.89	8.0%	66.69	10.5%	17.50	16.0%	32.80

associated net operating income percentages, the cost of capital, and fixed asset investment requirements.

The resulting impacts on indicated valuations per share of ConAgra are shown in Table 9.12. They are also depicted graphically in Figure 9.2. The indicated valuations are mostly within a relatively narrow range. These patterns provide the basis for our concluding observations.

Analysis of Merger Premiums

The ultimate objective of the foregoing analysis of DCF valuation methodology is its application for merger analysis. We seek to analyze the impact of the size of premiums paid and the relative size of the acquired firm on equity values under alternative levels of savings achieved by the merged firms. Our base case will use a cost of capital of 9% to avoid the impression that this analysis is dependent on the particular cost of capital we calculated for ConAgra. ConAgra acquires a firm of equal size with the same cost and income patterns and the same market price per share. No premium is paid in a stock-for-stock transaction. We predict no impact on equity values per share for either firm. This is confirmed by the data in Table 9.13.

Table 9.14 presents the analysis when ConAgra pays a 50% premium in a stock-for-stock transaction. The new market price per share is $15.82. In the bottom segment of Table 9.14, we perform a dilution analysis. For each share held by ConAgra shareholders, one share is still held. The acquired firm shareholders hold 1.5 to 1. For each original share there are now 2.5, so ConAgra shareholders own 40% of the combined company and the acquired firm shareholders hold 60%. It is sometimes said that in a stock-for-stock deal the number of shares paid doesn't matter because it is just paper for paper. This case study demonstrates that the premium paid establishes the percentage of the combined ownership each party to the merger will control. This was a merger between equals, but because of the premium paid the shareholders of the acquired firm became majority holders.

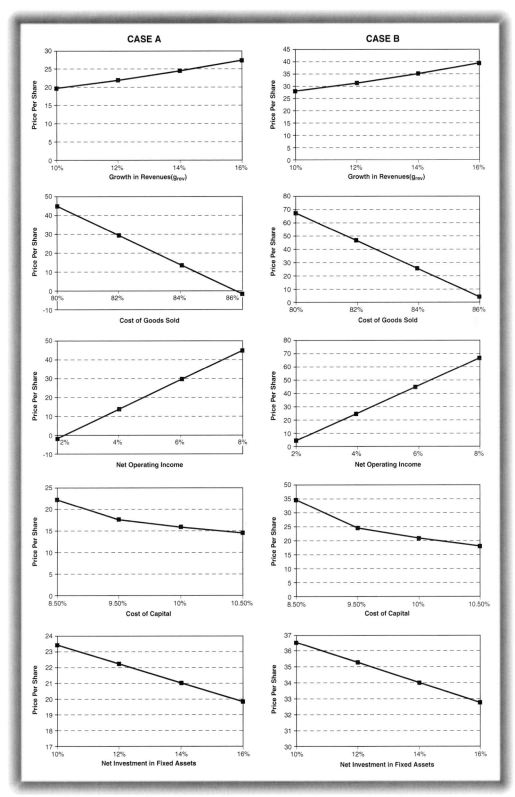

Figure 9.2 Sensitivity of Market Price per Share to the Value Drivers

Table 9.13 Spreadsheet DCF Valuation, ConAgra Equal Merger ($ in millions)

	Rel	% of Rev	1	2	3	4	5	6	7	8	9
							Forecast Year				
Incremental Free Cash Flow											
1. Revenues	14.0%	100%	$47,680	$54,355	$61,965	$70,640	$80,530	$91,804	$104,656	$119,308	$136,011
2. Cost of Goods Sold (excl. Depr.)		83.0%	39,574	45,115	51,431	58,631	66,840	76,197	86,865	99,026	112,889
3. Selling, General, & Administrative		10.0%	4,768	5,436	6,196	7,064	8,053	9,180	10,466	11,931	13,601
4. Depreciation (tax)		2.0%	954	1,087	1,239	1,413	1,611	1,836	2,093	2,386	2,720
5. Merger economies		0.0%	—	—	—	—	—	—	—	—	—
6. Pretax Operating Income (NOI)		5.0%	2,384	2,718	3,098	3,532	4,026	4,590	5,233	5,965	6,801
7. After-Tax Operating Income: $(NOI)(1-T)$ Income tax rate = 40%; $(1-T) = 60\%$			1,430	1,631	1,859	2,119	2,416	2,754	3,140	3,579	4,080
8. Net investment in working capital		Tbl A	$ (234)	$ (267)	$ (304)	$ (347)	$ (396)	$ (451)	$ (514)	$ (586)	$ (668)
9. Net investment in fixed assets		Tbl A	(703)	(801)	(913)	(1,041)	(1,187)	(1,353)	(1,542)	(1,758)	(2,004)
10. Free Cash Flow (FCF)			$ 494	$ 563	$ 641	$ 731	$ 834	$ 950	$ 1,083	$ 1,235	$ 1,408

Valuation % Rates

		1	2	3	4	5	6	7	8	9
11. Discounted FCF Cost of Capital (k)	9.0%	$ 453	$ 474	$ 495	$ 518	$ 542	$ 567	$ 593	$ 620	$ 648
12. Total present value of FCF		$ 4,909								

PVTV

TV

250

	Case A	Case B
13. Terminal Value Rate Assumptions		
a. Post-terminal year growth rate (g)	0%	5%
b. Reinvestment rate (z)	0%	40%
14. Terminal Value (TV)	45,337	64,265
15. Present Value of FCF	$ 4,909	$ 4,909
16. Present Value of TV (PVTV)	20,874	29,590
17. Total Present Value	$25,783	$34,498
18. Plus: Marketable Securities		
19. Total Value of the firm	25,783	34,498
20. Less: Total Interest Bearing Debt	6,800	6,800
21. Equity Value	$18,983	$27,698
22. Number of Shares (millions)	960	960
23. Value per Share	$ 19.77	$ 28.85

	% of ΔRev	\multicolumn{9}{c}{Year}
Table A—Investment		1	2	3	4	5	6	7	8	9
A1. Revenues (14.0% growth)		$47,680	$54,355	$61,965	$70,640	$80,530	$91,804	$104,656	$119,308	$136,011
A2. Δ Revenues		5,855	6,675	7,610	8,675	9,890	11,274	12,853	14,652	16,703
A3. Net investment in working capital	4.0%	234	267	304	347	396	451	514	586	668
A4. Net investment in fixed assets	12.0%	703	801	913	1,041	1,187	1,353	1,542	1,758	2,004
A5. Δ Total Capital = Investment		$ 937	$ 1,068	$ 1,218	$ 1,388	$ 1,582	$ 1,804	$ 2,056	$ 2,344	$ 2,673

Table 9.14 Spreadsheet DCF Valuation, ConAgra, No Savings ($ in millions)

	Rel	% of Rev					Forecast Year				
			1	2	3	4	5	6	7	8	9
Incremental Free Cash Flow											
1. Revenues	14.0%	100%	$47,680	$54,355	$61,965	$70,640	$80,530	$91,804	$104,656	$119,308	$136,011
2. Cost of Goods Sold (excl. Depr.)		83.0%	39,574	45,115	51,431	58,631	66,840	76,197	86,865	99,026	112,889
3. Selling, General, & Administrative		10.0%	4,768	5,436	6,196	7,064	8,053	9,180	10,466	11,931	13,601
4. Depreciation (tax)		2.0%	954	1,087	1,239	1,413	1,611	1,836	2,093	2,386	2,720
5. Merger economies		0.0%	—	—	—	—	—	—	—	—	—
6. Pretax Operating Income (NOI)		5.0%	2,384	2,718	3,098	3,532	4,026	4,590	5,233	5,965	6,801
7. After-Tax Operating Income: (NOI)(1 − T)											
a. Income tax rate = 40%; (1 − T) = 60%			1,430	1,631	1,859	2,119	2,416	2,754	3,140	3,579	4,080
8. Net investment in working capital	Tbl A		$ (234)	$ (267)	$ (304)	$ (347)	$ (396)	$ (451)	$ (514)	$ (586)	$ (668)
9. Net investment in fixed assets	Tbl A		(703)	(801)	(913)	(1,041)	(1,187)	(1,353)	(1,542)	(1,758)	(2,004)
10. Free Cash Flow (FCF)			$ 494	$ 563	$ 641	$ 731	$ 834	$ 950	$ 1,083	$ 1,235	$ 1,408
Valuation		**% Rates**									
11. Discounted FCF Cost of Capital (k)		9.0%	$ 453	$ 474	$ 495	$ 518	$ 542	$ 567	$ 593	$ 620	$ 648
											TV
12. Total present value of FCF			$ 4,909								
			PVTV								TV

	Case A	Case B
13. Terminal Value Rate Assumptions		
a. Post-terminal year growth rate (g)	0%	5%
b. Reinvestment rate (z)	0%	40%
14. Terminal Value (TV)	45,337	64,265
15. Present Value of FCF	$ 4,909	$ 4,909
16. Present Value of TV (PVTV)	20,874	29,590
17. Total Present Value	$25,783	$34,498
18. Plus: Marketable Securities		
19. Total Value of the firm	25,783	34,498
20. Less: Total Interest-Bearing Debt	6,800	6,800
21. Equity Value	$18,983	$27,698
22. Number of Shares (millions)	1,200	1,200
23. Value per Share	$ 15.82	$ 23.08

Table A—Investment	% of ΔRev	Year								
		1	2	3	4	5	6	7	8	9
A1. Revenues (14.0% growth)		$47,680	$54,355	$61,965	$70,640	$80,530	$91,804	$104,656	$119,308	$136,011
A2. Δ Revenues		5,855	6,675	7,610	8,675	9,890	11,274	12,853	14,652	16,703
A3. Net investment in working capital	4.0%	234	267	304	347	396	451	514	586	668
A4. Net investment in fixed assets	12.0%	703	801	913	1,041	1,187	1,353	1,542	1,758	2,004
A5. Δ Total Capital = Investment		$ 937	$ 1,068	$ 1,218	$ 1,388	$ 1,582	$ 1,804	$ 2,056	$ 2,344	$ 2,673

Table B—Dilution Analysis	Shares	% Ownership	Original Price	New Price	Accretion (Dilution)	% Increase (Decrease)
B1. ConAgra	1.0/1	40%	$19.77	$15.82	($3.95)	(20)%
B2. Acquired	1.5/1	60%	$19.77	$23.73	$3.96	20%

The third column in the dilution analysis at the bottom of Table 9.14 shows the original price, which was $19.77. The fourth column shows the new price of $15.82, which is the new price per share for ConAgra shareholders. The acquired firm's shareholders own 1.5 shares for each share they held originally. Multiplying the $15.82 by 1.5 gives a new effective price of $23.73 for the shares held by the acquired firm's shareholders. This represents a dilution of 20% per share value for ConAgra shareholders and a 20% market price appreciation for shareholders of the acquired firm.

We next consider the possibility of merger economies. These could result from synergies, cost savings, etc. In Table 9.15, we illustrate the impact of merger economies of 1% of revenues. This modest improvement in pretax operating income makes the deal accretive for shareholders of both companies. The new price is $21.67 per share, which for ConAgra represents a 10% accretion over the original price of $19.77. Multiplying the new price of $21.67 by 1.5 for the acquired firm gives a new price of $32.50 per original share. The acquired firm's shareholders achieve earnings accretion of 64%.

The one percentage point reduction in costs or increase in revenues is relatively modest in size; the absolute dollar amount is less than $0.5 billion. Well-conceived mergers between firms with combined revenues of almost $50 billion and combined market caps of $26 billion frequently estimate savings in the $2 billion to $3 billion range. This case study demonstrates that even a $0.5 billion savings can have powerful effects.

Our results differ dramatically from the widely expressed view that premiums of 40% to 50% are doomed to cause dilution in market value for the acquiring firm. The pessimistic view is based on relating the required savings to the revenues or costs of the acquired firm. The argument is made that the required percentage increase in revenues or reduction in costs would be impossible to achieve in a competitive market. But this orientation is misleading. Well-conceived mergers are designed to be synergistic and therefore improve the revenue–cost relationships for the acquiring firm. Examples are frequently cited in which the acquiring firm paid a large premium that produced a large negative stock price impact for the acquiring firm. In such cases investors did not expect the synergies to recover the premiums paid by the acquiring firms. In our own study of the 364 largest mergers since 1992, we found that for non-bank mergers the combined initial total stock market gains were positive in more than two-thirds of the cases. For the buyers, the initial stock market impact was positive in 52.1% of the cases. The average premium paid in these transactions was 40%. The data demonstrate that even with large average premiums, in more than half of the transactions the stock market predicted that the premiums would be more than recovered by revenue increases and cost reductions.

In the next set of tables we analyze the relationship between premiums paid and savings required for buyers and sellers of unequal size. For simplicity, we choose a seller of half the size of the acquiring firm, with the same 50% premium. These results are presented in Tables 9.16 through 9.18. The generalization that can be drawn is that, as shown by Table 9.18, when the seller is one-half the size of the buyer, the required economies to recover the 50% premium drop to $358 million.

SUMMARY

Valuation uses historical data as a starting point to establish first approximation patterns. Valuations depend on forecasts. The reliability of the forecasts depends heavily on a thorough analysis of the industry, on how it is impacted by evolving changes in the economies of the world as well as by competitive strategies and tactics. Valuation requires a thorough understanding of the business economics and financial characteristics of the industry.

Precision is not possible nor is it required. Recognizing that forecasts are subject to revision has positive aspects as well as challenges. It can be a valuable planning framework for guiding the firm to sound strategies and improved efficiencies. Valuation depends on identifying the critical factors that influence the levels of the value drivers. The DCF valuation approach provides a valuable framework to help identify what is really important to the future value of the firm.

Sensitivity analysis helps identify the really critical factors for the future. Such an analysis helps develop a business model for the firm with expectations of continuous reviews based on an effective information feedback system in the firm. It supports a flexible long-range planning process as a basis for short-term and medium-term budgets. It requires in-depth understanding of the industry, its environment, and its competitors to guide strategies, policies, and decisions.

QUESTIONS

9.1 How are mergers and acquisitions related to capital budgeting?

9.2 List four methods of valuation and briefly set forth the advantages and limitations of each.

9.3 What is the difference between gross basis and net basis cash flows?

9.4 The basic DCF sales growth model can be expressed in spreadsheets or in a formula, illustrated by equation (9.3) from the text shown below

$$V_0 = R_0 \left[m(1-T) - I \right] \sum_{t=1}^{n} \frac{(1+g)^t}{(1+k)^t} + \frac{R_0 (1+g)^n \left[m(1-T) \right]}{k(1+k)^n}$$

We will use the same symbols, definitions, and data inputs given below equation (9.3a) in the text except that we will change the number of years of supernormal growth (competitive advantage) to 10. Using a hand calculator, calculate the value beyond which you could not pay a target company with the characteristics illustrated, if you, as the buyer firm, are to earn the applicable cost of capital for the acquisition.

9.5 Some practitioners use an incremental profit rate instead of an average profit rate and normalize investment by dividing it by after-tax net operating income, defined as $X_t(1-T)$. This expression, $I_t/X_t(1-T)$, is defined as b. The new formula is equation (9C.12) repeated below.

$$V_0 = X_0 (1-T)(1-b) \sum_{t=1}^{n} \frac{(1+g)^t}{(1+k)^t} + \frac{X_0 (1-T)(1+g)^n}{k(1+k)^n}$$

(Question 9.5 continued on p. 264)

Table 9.15 Spreadsheet DCF Valuation, ConAgra Pays 50% Premium, 1% Savings ($ in millions)

	Rel	% of Rev	1	2	3	4	5	6	7	8	9
							Forecast Year				
Incremental Free Cash Flow											
1. Revenues	14.0%	100%	$47,680	$54,355	$61,965	$70,640	$80,530	$91,804	$104,656	$119,308	$136,011
2. Cost of Goods Sold (excl. Depr.)		83.0%	39,574	45,115	51,431	58,631	66,840	76,197	86,865	99,026	112,889
3. Selling, General, & Administrative		10.0%	4,768	5,436	6,196	7,064	8,053	9,180	10,466	11,931	13,601
4. Depreciation (tax)		2.0%	954	1,087	1,239	1,413	1,611	1,836	2,093	2,386	2,720
5. Merger economies		1.0%	477	544	620	706	805	918	1,047	1,193	1,360
6. Pretax Operating Income (NOI)		6.0%	2,861	3,261	3,718	4,238	4,832	5,508	6,279	7,158	8,161
7. After-Tax Operating Income: $(NOI)(1 - T)$ a. Income tax rate = 40%; $(1 - T) = 60\%$			1,716	1,957	2,231	2,543	2,899	3,305	3,768	4,295	4,896
8. Net investment in working capital	Tbl A		$ (234)	$ (267)	$ (304)	$ (347)	$ (396)	$ (451)	$ (514)	$ (586)	$ (668)
9. Net investment in fixed assets	Tbl A		(703)	(801)	(913)	(1,041)	(1,187)	(1,353)	(1,542)	(1,758)	(2,004)
10. Free Cash Flow (FCF)			$ 780	$ 889	$ 1,013	$ 1,155	$ 1,317	$ 1,501	$ 1,711	$ 1,951	$ 2,224
Valuation		% Rates									
11. Discounted FCF Cost of Capital (k)		9.0%	$ 715	$ 748	$ 782	$ 818	$ 856	$ 895	$ 936	$ 979	$ 1,024
12. Total present value of FCF			$ 7,754								
			PVTV								TV

	Case A	Case B
13. Terminal Value Rate Assumptions		
a. Post-terminal year growth rate (g)	0%	5%
b. Reinvestment rate (z)	0%	40%
14. Terminal Value (TV)	54,405	77,118
15. Present Value of FCF	$ 7,754	$ 7,754
16. Present Value of TV (PVTV)	25,049	35,507
17. Total Present Value	$32,803	$43,261
18. Plus: Marketable Securities		
19. Total Value of the firm	32,803	43,261
20. Less: Total Interest-Bearing Debt	6,800	6,800
21. Equity Value	$26,003	$36,461
22. Number of Shares (millions)	1,200	1,200
23. Value per Share	$ 21.67	$ 30.38

Table A—Investment

	% of Δ Rev	1	2	3	4	5	6	7	8	9
						Year				
A1. Revenues (14.0% growth)		$47,680	$54,355	$61,965	$70,640	$80,530	$91,804	$104,656	$119,308	$136,011
A2. Δ Revenues		5,855	6,675	7,610	8,675	9,890	11,274	12,853	14,652	16,703
A3. Net investment in working capital	4.0%	234	267	304	347	396	451	514	586	668
A4. Net investment in fixed assets	12.0%	703	801	913	1,041	1,187	1,353	1,542	1,758	2,004
A5. Δ Total Capital = Investment		$ 937	$ 1,068	$ 1,218	$ 1,388	$ 1,582	$ 1,804	$ 2,056	$ 2,344	$ 2,673

Table B—Dilution Analysis

	Original Price	New Price	Accretion (Dilution)	% Increase (Decrease)
B1. ConAgra	$19.77	$21.67	$1.90	10%
B2. Acquired	$19.77	$32.50	$12.73	64%

Table 9.16 Spreadsheet DCF Valuation, ConAgra Pays 0 Premium, Acquired 1/2 Size ($ in millions)

	Rel	% of Rev	Forecast Year								
			1	2	3	4	5	6	7	8	9
Incremental Free Cash Flow											
1. Revenues	14.0%	100%	$35,760	$40,766	$46,474	$52,980	$60,397	$68,853	$78,492	$89,481	$102,008
2. Cost of Goods Sold (excl. Depr.)		83.0%	29,681	33,836	38,573	43,973	50,130	57,148	65,149	74,269	84,667
3. Selling, General, & Administrative		10.0%	3,576	4,077	4,647	5,298	6,040	6,885	7,849	8,948	10,201
4. Depreciation (tax)		2.0%	715	815	929	1,060	1,208	1,377	1,570	1,790	2,040
5. Merger economies		0.0%	—	—	—	—	—	—	—	—	—
6. Pretax Operating Income (NOI)		5.0%	1,788	2,038	2,324	2,649	3,020	3,443	3,925	4,474	5,100
7. After-Tax Operating Income: (NOI)(1 – T); Income tax rate = 40%; (1 – T) = 60%			1,073	1,223	1,394	1,589	1,812	2,066	2,355	2,684	3,060
8. Net investment in working capital		Tbl A	$ (176)	$ (200)	$ (228)	$ (260)	$ (297)	$ (338)	$ (386)	$ (440)	$ (501)
9. Net investment in fixed assets		Tbl A	(527)	(601)	(685)	(781)	(890)	(1,015)	(1,157)	(1,319)	(1,503)
10. Free Cash Flow (FCF)			$ 370	$ 422	$ 481	$ 548	$ 625	$ 713	$ 812	$ 926	$ 1,056
Valuation		% Rate									
11. Discounted FCF Cost of Capital (k)		9.0%	$ 340	$ 355	$ 371	$ 388	$ 406	$ 425	$ 444	$ 465	$ 486
12. Total present value of FCF			$ 3,681								TV
			PVTV								

	Case A	Case B
13. Terminal Value Rate Assumptions		
a. Post-terminal year growth rate (g)	0%	5%
b. Reinvestment rate (z)	0%	40%
14. Terminal Value (TV)	34,003	48,199
15. Present Value of FCF	$ 3,681	$ 3,681
16. Present Value of TV (PVTV)	15,656	22,192
17. Total Present Value	$19,337	$25,874
18. Plus: Marketable Securities		
19. Total Value of the firm	19,337	25,874
20. Less: Total Interest-Bearing Debt	5,100	5,100
21. Equity Value	$14,237	$20,774
22. Number of Shares (millions)	720	720
23. Value per Share	$ 19.77	$ 28.85

Table A—Investment	% of Δ Rev	Year								
		1	2	3	4	5	6	7	8	9
A1. Revenues (14.0% growth)		$35,760	$40,766	$46,474	$52,980	$60,397	$68,853	$78,492	$89,481	$102,008
A2. Δ Revenues		4,392	5,006	5,707	6,506	7,417	8,456	9,639	10,989	12,527
A3. Net investment in working capital	4.0%	176	200	228	260	297	338	386	440	501
A4. Net investment in fixed assets	12.0%	527	601	685	781	890	1,015	1,157	1,319	1,503
A5. Δ Total Capital = Investment		$ 703	$ 801	$ 913	$ 1,041	$ 1,187	$ 1,353	$ 1,542	$ 1,758	$ 2,004

Table 9.17 Spreadsheet DCF Valuation, ConAgra Pays 50% Premium, Acquired One-Half Size ($ in millions)

	Rel	% of Rev	Forecast Year								
			1	2	3	4	5	6	7	8	9
Incremental Free Cash Flow											
1. Revenues	14.0%	100%	$35,760	$40,766	$46,474	$52,980	$60,397	$68,853	$78,492	$89,481	$102,008
2. Cost of Goods Sold (excl. Depr.)		83.0%	29,681	33,836	38,573	43,973	50,130	57,148	65,149	74,269	84,667
3. Selling, General, & Administrative		10.0%	3,576	4,077	4,647	5,298	6,040	6,885	7,849	8,948	10,201
4. Depreciation (tax)		2.0%	715	815	929	1,060	1,208	1,377	1,570	1,790	2,040
5. Merger economies		0.0%	—	—	—	—	—	—	—	—	—
6. Pretax Operating Income (NOI)		5.0%	1,788	2,038	2,324	2,649	3,020	3,443	3,925	4,474	5,100
7. After-Tax Operating Income: $(NOI)(1-T)$ Income tax rate = 40%; $(1-T)=60\%$			1,073	1,223	1,394	1,589	1,812	2,066	2,355	2,684	3,060
8. Net investment in working capital	Tbl A		$ (176)	$ (200)	$ (228)	$ (260)	$ (297)	$ (338)	$ (386)	$ (440)	$ (501)
9. Net investment in fixed assets	Tbl A		(527)	(601)	(685)	(781)	(890)	(1,015)	(1,157)	(1,319)	(1,503)
10. Free Cash Flow (FCF)			$ 370	$ 422	$ 481	$ 548	$ 625	$ 713	$ 812	$ 926	$ 1,056
Valuation		% Rate									
11. Discounted FCF Cost of Capital (k)		9.0%	$ 340	$ 355	$ 371	$ 388	$ 406	$ 425	$ 444	$ 465	$ 486
12. Total present value of FCF			$ 3,681								TV
			PVTV								

	Case A	Case B
13. Terminal Value Rate Assumptions		
a. Post-terminal year growth rate (g)	0%	5%
b. Reinvestment rate (z)	0%	40%
14. Terminal Value (TV)	34,003	48,199
15. Present Value of FCF	$ 3,681	$ 3,681
16. Present Value of TV (PVTV)	15,656	22,192
17. Total Present Value	$19,337	$25,874
18. Plus: Marketable Securities		
19. Total Value of the firm	19,337	25,874
20. Less: Total Interest-Bearing Debt	5,100	5,100
21. Equity Value	$14,237	$20,774
22. Number of Shares (millions)	840	840
23. Value per Share	$ 16.95	$ 24.73

Table A—Investment

	% of ΔRev					Year				
		1	2	3	4	5	6	7	8	9
A1. Revenues (14.0% growth)		$35,760	$40,766	$46,474	$52,980	$60,397	$68,853	$78,492	$89,481	$102,008
A2. Δ Revenues		4,392	5,006	5,707	6,506	7,417	8,456	9,639	10,989	12,527
A3. Net investment in working capital	4.0%	176	200	228	260	297	338	386	440	501
A4. Net investment in fixed assets	12.0%	527	601	685	781	890	1,015	1,157	1,319	1,503
A5. Δ Total Capital = Investment		$ 703	$ 801	$ 913	$ 1,041	$ 1,187	$ 1,353	$ 1,542	$ 1,758	$ 2,004

Table B—Dilution Analysis

	Shares	% Ownership	Original Price	New Price	Accretion (Dilution)	% Increase (Decrease)
B1. ConAgra	1.0/1	57%	$19.77	$16.95	($2.82)	(14)%
B2. Acquired	1.5/1	43%	$19.77	$25.42	$5.65	29%

261

Table 9.18 Spreadsheet DCF Valuation, ConAgra Pays 50% Premium, 1% Savings, Acquired 1/2 Size ($ in millions)

	Rel	% of Rev	Forecast Year 1	2	3	4	5	6	7	8	9
Incremental Free Cash Flow											
1. Revenues	14.0%	100%	$35,760	$40,766	$46,474	$52,980	$60,397	$68,853	$78,492	$89,481	$102,008
2. Cost of Goods Sold (excl. Depr.)		83.0%	29,681	33,836	38,573	43,973	50,130	57,148	65,149	74,269	84,667
3. Selling, General, & Administrative		10.0%	3,576	4,077	4,647	5,298	6,040	6,885	7,849	8,948	10,201
4. Depreciation (tax)		2.0%	715	815	929	1,060	1,208	1,377	1,570	1,790	2,040
5. Merger economies		1.0%	358	408	465	530	604	689	785	895	1,020
6. Pretax Operating Income (NOI)		6.0%	2,146	2,446	2,788	3,179	3,624	4,131	4,710	5,369	6,121
7. After-Tax Operating Income: $(NOI)(1-T)$ Income tax rate = 40%; $(1-T)$ = 60%			1,287	1,468	1,673	1,907	2,174	2,479	2,826	3,221	3,672
8. Net investment in working capital		Tbl A	$ (176)	$ (200)	$ (228)	$ (260)	$ (297)	$ (338)	$ (386)	$ (440)	$ (501)
9. Net investment in fixed assets		Tbl A	(527)	(601)	(685)	(781)	(890)	(1,015)	(1,157)	(1,319)	(1,503)
10. Free Cash Flow (FCF)			$ 585	$ 667	$ 760	$ 866	$ 988	$ 1,126	$ 1,283	$ 1,463	$ 1,668
Valuation		% Rate									
11. Discounted FCF Cost of Capital (k)		9.0%	$ 536	$ 561	$ 587	$ 614	$ 642	$ 671	$ 702	$ 734	$ 768
12. Total present value of FCF			$ 5,815								
			PVTV								TV

		Case A	Case B
13. Terminal Value Rate Assumptions			
a. Post-terminal year growth rate (g)		0%	5%
b. Reinvestment rate (z)		0%	40%
14. Terminal Value (TV)		40,803	57,839
15. Present Value of FCF		$ 5,815	$ 5,815
16. Present Value of TV (PVTV)		18,787	26,631
17. Total Present Value		$24,602	$32,446
18. Plus: Marketable Securities			
19. Total Value of the firm		24,602	32,446
20. Less: Total Interest Bearing Debt		5,100	5,100
21. Equity Value		$19,502	$27,346
22. Number of Shares (millions)		840	840
23. Value per Share		$ 23.22	$ 32.55

	% of	Year								
Table A—Investment	Δ Rev	1	2	3	4	5	6	7	8	9
A1. Revenues (14.0% growth)		$35,760	$40,766	$46,474	$52,980	$60,397	$68,853	$78,492	$89,481	$102,008
A2. Δ Revenues		4,392	5,006	5,707	6,506	7,417	8,456	9,639	10,989	12,527
A3. Net investment in working capital	4.0%	176	200	228	260	297	338	386	440	501
A4. Net investment in fixed assets	12.0%	527	601	685	781	890	1,015	1,157	1,319	1,503
A5. Δ Total Capital = Investment		$ 703	$ 801	$ 913	$ 1,041	$ 1,187	$ 1,353	$ 1,542	$ 1,758	$ 2,004

Table B—Dilution Analysis	Original Price	New Price	Accretion (Dilution)	% Increase (Decrease)
B1. ConAgra	$19.77	$23.22	$3.45	17%
B2. Acquired	$19.77	$34.83	$15.06	76%

QUESTIONS *(continued)*

Use this new expression to repeat the calculation in question 9.4. How does your answer compare to your answer in question 9.4?

9.6 In Rappaport (1998) our equation (9.3) is modified slightly. Investment is expressed as a ratio of the change in sales. So the first part of the first term in equation 3 will read:

$$R_0[m(1 - T) - g \text{ "I"}]$$

If "I" is 50%, how does the new value compare with what you obtained in the previous two questions?

9.7 How are the following valuation parameters related to each other? How do they affect the general free cash flow valuation model?
Revenues
Investment
Net operating income
Profitability rate
Growth rate

REFERENCES

Copeland, Tom, Tim Koller, and Jack Murrin, *Valuation: Measuring and Managing the Value of Companies,* 2nd ed., New York: John Wiley & Sons, 1994.

Cornell, Bradford, *Corporate Valuation,* Homewood, IL: Business One Irwin, 1993.

Weston, J. Fred, and Susan Chiu, "Growth Strategies in the Food Industry," *Business Economics,* 31, January 1996, pp. 21–27.

Weston, J. Fred, and Thomas E. Copeland, *Managerial Finance,* 9th ed., Fort Worth, TX: The Dryden Press, 1992.

Foundations of DCF Spreadsheet Valuation

OVERVIEW

The value of the firm equals the present value of all future cash flows. If we could know each period's cash flows from the present time to the time when the firm ceases to exist and the right discount rate to reflect the riskiness of the firm's cash flows in the future, we could compute the "true" value of the firm. However, both the future cash flows and their applicable discount rates cannot be known with certainty. Both can only be estimated. We offer some guidelines for using cash flow and discount rate estimates to achieve useful valuation analysis.

In practice, we find that a firm's cash flows exhibit different patterns. Over the years they could be rising, falling, constant, or combinations of the three. We observe that a successful firm gains a competitive advantage during times in which its cash flows are growing, but competition will ultimately erode the competitive advantage and the cash flow growth rates. Of course, a firm will battle back against the competition. Various combinations of cash flow patterns will reflect the ebb and flow of strategic and competitive struggles.

With rapid technological changes, the globalization of markets, and the increased intensity of competition, it is difficult to predict the future cash flows of an individual firm. However, the study of individual industries and the firms in it enables careful analysts to make some useful judgments. Future cash flow patterns could represent different combinations of high growth, medium growth, low growth, no growth, and various rates of negative growth. Obviously, alternative possible patterns are virtually infinite in number. The pattern most widely used by practitioners and consultants is a period of growth or supergrowth followed by no growth. The economic support for this standard approach is that a firm can have supergrowth only if it has a competitive advantage. Unless the firm can revitalize or find new sources of competitive advantage, its growth will be eroded.

This presentation begins with the standard pattern of future cash flows that exhibit supergrowth followed by no growth. The implementation requires a number of decision steps that provide an outline of the topics that need to be covered: the rate of supergrowth, the size of the discount rate to be applied to these cash flows, the length of the supergrowth period, the nature of the terminal value analysis, the date at which the constant growth period begins, the discount rate applicable to this second period, and how the forecasts are made. We illustrate the methodology with a succession of illustrative case examples.

Table 9A.1 Spreadsheet DCF Valuation, Gross PP&E Using NOI ($ in millions)

		Forecast Year							
	1	2	3	4	5	6	7	8	9
Incremental Free Cash Flow									
1. Revenues	$10,000	$12,000	$14,400	$17,280	$20,736	$24,883	$29,860	$35,832	$42,998
2. Cost of Goods Sold (excl. Depr.)	8,000	9,600	11,520	13,824	16,589	19,907	23,888	28,665	34,399
3. Selling, General, & Administrative	1,000	1,200	1,440	1,728	2,074	2,488	2,986	3,583	4,300
4. Depreciation (tax)	300	360	432	518	622	746	896	1,075	1,290
5. Merger economies	—	—	—	—	—	—	—	—	—
6. Pretax Operating Income (NOI)	700	840	1,008	1,210	1,452	1,742	2,090	2,508	3,010
7. After-Tax Operating Income: (NOI)(1 − T)	420	504	605	726	871	1,045	1,254	1,505	1,806
a. Income tax rate = 40%; (1 − T) = 60%									
8. Gross Cash Flows	720	864	1,037	1,244	1,493	1,792	2,150	2,580	3,096
a. NOI × (1 − T) + depreciation; (7) + (4)									
9. Net investment in working capital (see Table A)	$ (97)	$ (116)	$ (139)	$ (167)	$ (200)	$ (241)	$ (289)	$ (346)	$ (416)
10. Capital expenditures (see Table A)	(542)	(650)	(780)	(936)	(1,123)	(1,348)	(1,617)	(1,941)	(2,329)
11. Free Cash Flows (FCF)	$ 82	$ 98	$ 118	$ 141	$ 169	$ 203	$ 244	$ 293	$ 351

Valuation — % Rate

		1	2	3	4	5	6	7	8	9
12. Discounted FCF Cost of Capital (k)	10%	$ 74	$ 81	$ 88	$ 96	$ 105	$ 115	$ 125	$ 137	$ 149
13. Total present value of FCF		$ 970								

PVTV

TV

	Case A	Case B
14. Terminal Value Rate Assumptions		
a. Post-terminal year growth rate (g)	0%	5%
b. Reinvestment rate (z)	0%	40%
15. Terminal Value (TV)	18,059	22,755
16. Present Value of FCF	$ 970	$ 970
17. Present Value of TV (PVTV)	7,659	9,650
18. Total Present Value	$ 8,629	$10,621
19. Plus: Marketable Securities	500	500
20. Total Value of the firm	9,129	11,121
21. Less: Total Interest-Bearing Debt	2,000	2,000
22. Equity Value	$ 7,129	$ 9,121
23. Number of Shares (millions)	400	400
24. Value per Share	$ 17.82	$ 22.80

					Year				
Table A—Investment	1	2	3	4	5	6	7	8	9
A1. Revenues	$10,000	$12,000	$14,400	$17,280	20,736	$24,883	$29,860	$35,832	$42,998
A2. Δ Revenues	1,667	2,000	2,400	2,880	3,456	4,147	4,977	5,972	7,166
A3. Net investment in working capital	97	116	139	167	200	241	289	346	416
A4. Capital expenditures	542	650	780	936	1,123	1,348	1,617	1,941	2,329
A5. Δ Total Capital = Investment	$ 638	$ 766	$ 919	$ 1,103	$ 1,324	$ 1,588	$ 1,906	$ 2,287	$ 2,745

THE BASIC DCF SPREADSHEET MODEL

Table 9A.1 is used to illustrate the basic discounted cash flow (DCF) spreadsheet model. The numbers in Table 9A.1 represent a forecast for years 1 through 9. These forecasts are the basis for illustrating the DCF valuation procedure. In a later section we discuss how forecasts of this type are made. The forecast in Table 9A.1 extracts income statement and balance sheet data items required for performing the valuation analysis.

Line 1 in Table 9A.1 is revenues. This illustrates the underlying business logic that it is revenues and revenue growth that constitute the basic driver of a firm's value. Often in comparing the values of firms in the same industry, investment bankers will calculate market value-to-revenue multiples. This has been the main approach to valuing Internet stocks, although there are disagreements about the appropriate valuation-to-revenue multiples.

Lines 2 through 4 are forecasts of cost of goods sold; selling, general and administrative expenses; and the depreciation expenses defined by tax regulations. Because this analysis is for merger valuation purposes, line 5 permits consideration of merger economies or synergies.

Line 6 is pretax operating income, which is revenues less all operating costs plus estimates of merger economies. Line 7 is after-tax operating income. A 40% income tax rate is used. When depreciation is added to the after-tax cash flows, we obtain gross cash flows for use in the valuation analysis. We demonstrate later that this figure is also equal to net income plus after-tax interest expense plus depreciation. From the gross cash flows, we deduct the net investment in working capital and capital expenditures for each year. The resulting line 11 is the free cash flows.

We now have the basis for beginning our valuation computations. The free cash flows in line 11 are discounted at the applicable cost of capital. In this example, 10% is used. Later we discuss how the cost of capital is estimated. The sum of the discounted free cash flows for the competitive advantage period of nine years is shown in line 13.

CALCULATING TERMINAL VALUES

The second component of the value of the firm is to discount the free cash flows subsequent to the initial period of competitive advantage or above-average growth. This is generally referred to as the terminal value. A widely accepted general expression for calculating terminal values is given in equation (9A.1)

$$PVTV = \frac{FCF_n(1-z)(1+g_c)}{(k-g_c)(1+k)^n} \qquad \textbf{(9A.1)}$$

where

$PVTV$ = the present value of the terminal value
FCF_n = free cash flows at the end of the period of above-average growth
z = investment required to support future growth
k = the applicable cost of capital or discount rate
g_c = the constant growth rate of future free cash flows
n = the number of years of above-average growth.

This formula is perfectly general. If the firm does not retain any competitive advantage after the period of above-average growth, then its future growth will drop to zero. When g becomes zero, z also becomes zero, because there is no future growth that requires investment support. Equation (9A.1) simplifies to

$$PVTV = \frac{FCF_n}{k(1-k)^n} \tag{9A.2}$$

The meaning of the two formulas is illustrated by Table 9A.1. In case A, the post-terminal growth rate is zero. The reinvestment rate is also zero, as shown in line 14 of the table. The terminal value in case A is obtained by placing numbers in equation (9A.2) for the no-growth case, $TV = \$1,806/0.1 = \$18,060$. This is the figure in Table 9A.1, line 15, case A (it differs by 1, due to computer rounding).

The present value of terminal value, shown in line 17, is

$$\$18,060/2.3579 = \$7,659, \qquad \text{where } 2.3579 = (1.10)^9$$

The present value of free cash flows for the period of above-average growth is given by line 16. The sum of lines 16 and 17 gives us the total present value of the firm's future cash flows, shown as \$8,629 in line 18.

Because we are valuing the operations of the firm, we did not include the income from marketable securities in the analysis. The value of the firm's marketable securities at the valuation date, \$500, is added to obtain line 20, the total value of the firm. From the total value of the firm, we deduct total interest-bearing debt of \$2,000 to obtain the indicated market value of equity of \$7,129. In line 23, we divide by the total number of common shares of stock outstanding, or 400 million, to obtain an indicated market value per share of \$17.82.

An alternative approach to calculating the terminal value is case B, also presented in Table 9A.1. In case B, the forecast projects continued growth for the company at a constant level to perpetuity. Clearly, we predict this will result in a higher value than the no-growth case A. We employ equation (9A.1), inserting the data from Table 9A.1. The terminal value in case B would be

$$TV = \$1,806(1 - 0.4)(1 + 0.05)/(0.10 - 0.05) = 1,137.8/0.05 = \$22,756$$

This shows how the terminal value in line 15b is calculated (the difference of 1 is due to computer rounding). The present value of the terminal value shown in line 17 of Table 9A.1 is calculated as $\$22,756/2.3579 = \$9,651$. As predicted, this amount is higher than the \$7,659 in case A. The remainder of the analysis proceeds as before, giving a value per share of \$22.80.

What is the economic or financial meaning of the market value per share figure we have arrived at? The market value per share figure we have arrived at represents a first approximation to the intrinsic or economic value of the firm. This result will be influenced by the accuracy of our forecast and the reliability of the discount factor we employed. It will also depend on our handling of whichever terminal value approach we take.

The business logic for using the no-growth case for calculating terminal value is that competitive advantage is unlikely to be maintained forever. Unless the firm is able to follow superior product with competitive advantage, growth will level off. The business logic behind case B is that the firm has a portfolio of superior products with competitive advantage and in the long run it is unlikely that all of them will be able to overcome imitation and the development of competing firms and industries.

So, clearly, valuation is an art that involves experience and judgment. Valuation calculations can be performed with a calculator or a computer, but the valuation formulation and the forecasts require analysis and judgment. We next (1) describe some alternative formats for doing the valuation analysis, (2) discuss the calculation of the applicable cost of capital, (3) present some actual firm examples, and (4) discuss forecast methodologies.

THE NET INVESTMENT FORMAT

In Table 9A.1 we performed the calculations including depreciation in the gross cash flow measure and, using annual changes in the gross Property, Plant, and Equipment account (capital expenditures), we calculated gross fixed asset requirements. Implicitly, depreciation is included in the gross cash flow figure and also in the changes in gross fixed assets that have to be financed. The resulting free cash flow figure would be unchanged if we took depreciation out of cash flows (cash inflows) and financing requirements (cash outflows).

Table 9A.2 illustrates the validity of the net capital expenditure approach. The gross cash flow figures in line 8 are the same as line 7 because depreciation is not added. Line 10, the change in net fixed assets (net investment), reflects gross capital expenditures reduced by the amount of annual depreciation. As predicted, the free cash flows in line 11 of Table 9A.2 are exactly the same as in Table 9A.1. However, if there were substantial retirements of fixed assets in a given year, the results would be different. For this reason, we prefer the use of the Table 9A.1 format theoretically. From a practical standpoint, it is sometimes difficult to obtain capital expenditure data on individual firms from public database sources. Also, in the computer formula approaches that a number of practitioners and consultants have developed, the net investment approach is employed for convenience. The resulting computer programs or formulas are much more compact, permitting the analyst to focus on the underlying factors that determine value rather than deal with nonessential details. As demonstrated, numerical results are not likely to be greatly different.

THE VALUE DRIVER METHOD

A number of consultants have developed computer programs using key income statement and balance sheet items to focus on the main factors that drive values and value changes. This method is illustrated in Table 9A.3. We added two columns in front of columns 1 to 9, the forecast years. The column that precedes forecast year 1 expresses key income statement data as a percentage of revenues. For example, line 2 presents the cost of goods sold, excluding depreciation expense, as a percentage of revenues. Including depreciation from line 4, cost of goods sold would be 83% of revenues. Thus, the gross margin would be 20% of 83%, or 17%. Deducting selling, general, and administrative expenses gives line 6, the pretax net operating income.

These are significant relationships for analyzing a firm's policies and efficiency. For example, Harvard professor Clayton Christensen was quoted as saying, "I calculated that Amazon.com Inc. could equal the return on investment capital that a brick-and-mortar bookseller achieved if Amazon had only 5% gross margins, vs. 30% for a traditional retailer" (*Business Week,* June 28, 1999, p. 84).

Thus, one of the reasons for using a value driver approach is to sharpen the analysis. It helps focus on the relationships among a firm's strategies, policies, cost controls, and efficiency of operations. Valuations should not be a mechanical exercise. The valuation process provides an opportunity for placing the major strategic and operating policies and decisions in an integrated total framework.

In Table 9A.3, we illustrate a set of revenue and cost relationships. In addition, in the first column under the heading Rel (for relationships) the revenues of the firm are projected to grow about 20% per annum. Using the revenue growth projection, the cost and profit percentages of revenues shown in the top part of Table 9A.3, and investment requirements as a percentage of changes in revenues shown below that in Table A, we can generate the spreadsheets for the forecast years.

Table 9A.3 follows the format used by Alfred Rappaport in his book *Creating Shareholder Value* (The Free Press, 1996). It would be more logically consistent to express each value driver as a ratio or percentage of changes in revenues. This is equivalent to using a linear regression relationship. However, since valuation depends on forecasts of future revenues and forecasts of the value drivers in relation to future revenues, historical relationships, whether average or incremental, provide only a basis for judgments with respect to future relationships. The underlying economics of the industry and the firm will have the most important influence on the soundness of the projections used in the valuation analysis. For this reason, practitioners most generally express the value driver relationships as a percentage of sales. This is illustrated in a security analyst's valuation of MCI WorldCom presented in the final section of this appendix.

One of the powers of this approach (in addition to focusing the planning processes) is that we can construct a wide range of sensitivity scenarios. The effect of changing the revenue growth projection, any of the cost elements, any of the investment requirement relationships, or the size of the discount factor can be portrayed in tables and charts. What initially might appear as a set of mechanical relationships is actually a powerful quantitative expression of the firm's business model. It provides a framework for testing and retesting alternative strategies, policies, and decisions and their valuation consequences.

INCLUDING OTHER INCOME IN THE ANALYSIS

Table 9A.4 illustrates another slight variation employed by analysts, consultants, and other practitioners. This approach follows from the mathematical equality

Earnings before interest and taxes $\times$ $(1 - T)$ = Net income + $(1 - T)$ $\times$ Interest expense

We can illustrate this relationship with Table 9A.4, year 1. EBIT in line 6 is $750. Multiplying by $(1 - T)$, we obtain $450. Net income is $330 from line 10, year 1. Interest expense, from line 7, year 1 is $200. Multiply by $(1 - T)$ to obtain $120, which is the tax shield provided by interest expense. So net income of $330 plus the interest tax shield of $120 is $450, which is also equal to $EBIT \times (1 - T)$. There is some subtlety involved here because $EBIT \times (1 - T)$ does not appear to take account of the interest expense. But it actually does, because $EBIT$ of $750 contains net income of $330 plus taxes of $220 plus interest expense of $200.

Table 9A.2 Spreadsheet DCF Valuation, Net PP&E using NOI ($ in millions)

				Forecast Years					
	1	2	3	4	5	6	7	8	9
Incremental Free Cash Flow									
1. Revenues	$10,000	$12,000	$14,400	$17,280	$20,736	$24,883	$29,860	$35,832	$42,998
2. Cost of Goods Sold (excl. Depr.)	8,000	9,600	11,520	13,824	16,589	19,907	23,888	28,665	34,399
3. Selling, General, & Administrative	1,000	1,200	1,440	1,728	2,074	2,488	2,986	3,583	4,300
4. Depreciation (tax)	300	360	432	518	622	746	896	1,075	1,290
5. Merger economies	—	—	—	—	—	—	—	—	—
6. Pretax Operating Income (NOI)	700	840	1,008	1,210	1,452	1,742	2,090	2,508	3,010
7. After-Tax Operating Income: (NOI)(1 − T)	420	504	605	726	871	1,045	1,254	1,505	1,806
a. Income tax rate = 40%; (1 − T) = 60%									
8. Gross Cash Flows	420	504	605	726	871	1,045	1,254	1,505	1,806
a. (NOI) (1 − T); line 7									
9. Net investment in working capital (see Table A)	$ (97)	$ (116)	$ (139)	$ (167)	$ (200)	$ (241)	$ (289)	$ (346)	$ (416)
10. Net investment in fixed assets (see Table A)	(242)	(290)	(348)	(418)	(501)	(601)	(722)	(866)	(1,039)
11. Free Cash Flows (FCF)	$ 82	$ 98	$ 118	$ 141	$ 169	$ 203	$ 244	$ 293	$ 351

Valuation

% Rate

		1	2	3	4	5	6	7	8	9
12. Discounted FCF Cost of Capital (k)	10%	$ 74	$ 81	$ 88	$ 96	$ 105	$ 115	$ 125	$ 137	$ 149
13. Total present value of FCF		$ 970								

PVTV   TV

	Case A	Case B
14. Terminal Value Rate Assumptions		
a. Post-terminal year growth rate (g)	0%	5%
b. Reinvestment rate (z)	0%	40%
15. Terminal Value (TV)	18,059	22,755
16. Present Value of FCF	$ 970	$ 970
17. Present Value of TV (PVTV)	7,659	9,650
18. Total Present Value	$ 8,629	$10,621
19. Plus: Marketable Securities	500	500
20. Total Value of the firm	9,129	11,121
21. Less: Total Interest-Bearing Debt	2,000	2,000
22. Equity Value	$ 7,129	$ 9,121
23. Number of Shares (millions)	400	400
24. Value per Share	$ 17.82	$ 22.80

Table A—Investment

	Year								
	1	2	3	4	5	6	7	8	9
A1. Revenues	$10,000	$12,000	$14,400	$17,280	20,736	$24,883	$29,860	$35,832	$42,998
A2. Δ Revenues	1,667	2,000	2,400	2,880	3,456	4,147	4,977	5,972	7,166
A3. Net investment in working capital	97	116	139	167	200	241	289	346	416
A4. Net investment in fixed assets	242	290	348	418	501	601	722	866	1,039
A5. Δ Total Capital = Investment	$ 338	$ 406	$ 487	$ 585	$ 702	$ 842	$ 1,010	$ 1,212	$ 1,455

Table 9A.3 Spreadsheet DCF Valuation, Value Driver Method with NOI ($ in millions)

	Rel	% of Rev	Forecast Year								
			1	2	3	4	5	6	7	8	9
	20.0%										
Incremental Free Cash Flow											
1. Revenues		100%	$10,000	$12,000	$14,400	$17,280	$20,736	$24,883	$29,860	$35,832	$42,998
2. Cost of Goods Sold (excl. Depr.)		80.0%	8,000	9,600	11,520	13,824	16,589	19,907	23,888	28,665	34,399
3. Selling, General, & Administrative		10.0%	1,000	1,200	1,440	1,728	2,074	2,488	2,986	3,583	4,300
4. Depreciation (tax)		3.0%	300	360	432	518	622	746	896	1,075	1,290
5. Merger economies		0.0%	—	—	—	—	—	—	—	—	—
6. Pretax Operating Income (NOI)		7.0%	700	840	1,008	1,210	1,452	1,742	2,090	2,508	3,010
7. After-Tax Operating Income: $(NOI)(1 − T)$											
a. Income tax rate = 40%; $(1 − T) = 60\%$			420	504	605	726	871	1,045	1,254	1,505	1,806
8. Net investment in working capital	TblA		$ (97)	$ (116)	$ (139)	$ (167)	$ (200)	$ (241)	$ (289)	$ (346)	$ (416)
9. Net investment in fixed assets	Tbl A		(242)	(290)	(348)	(418)	(501)	(601)	(722)	(866)	(1,039)
10. Free Cash Flows (FCF)			$ 82	$ 98	$ 118	$ 141	$ 169	$ 203	$ 244	$ 293	$ 351
Valuation		% Rate									
11. Discounted FCF Cost of Capital (k)		10%	$ 74	$ 81	$ 88	$ 96	$ 105	$ 115	$ 125	$ 137	$ 149
12. Total present value of FCF			$ 970								

PVTV   TV

	Case A	Case B
13. Terminal Value Rate Assumptions		
a. Post-terminal year growth rate (g)	0%	5%
b. Reinvestment rate (z)	0%	40%
14. Terminal Value (TV)	18,059	22,755
15. Present Value of FCF	$ 970	$ 970
16. Present Value of TV (PVTV)	7,659	9,650
17. Total Present Value	$ 8,629	$10,621
18. Plus: Marketable Securities	500	500
19. Total Value of the firm	9,129	11,121
20. Less: Total Interest-Bearing Debt	2,000	2,000
21. Equity Value	$ 7,129	$ 9,121
22. Number of Shares (millions)	400	400
23. Value per Share	$ 17.82	$ 22.80

Table A—Investment	% of Δ Rev	Year								
		1	2	3	4	5	6	7	8	9
A1. Revenues (20.0% growth)		$10,000	$12,000	$14,400	$17,280	20,736	$24,883	$29,860	$35,832	$42,998
A2. Δ Revenues		1,667	2,000	2,400	2,880	3,456	4,147	4,977	5,972	7,166
A3. Net investment in working capital	5.8%	97	116	139	167	200	241	289	346	416
A4. Net investment in fixed assets	14.5%	242	290	348	418	501	601	722	866	1,039
A5. Δ Total Capital = Investment		$ 338	$ 406	$ 487	$ 585	$ 702	$ 842	$ 1,010	$ 1,212	$ 1,455

Table 9A.4 Spreadsheet DCF Valuation, Value Driver Method with EBIT ($ in millions)

	Rel	% of Rev				Forecast Year					
			1	2	3	4	5	6	7	8	9
Incremental Free Cash Flow											
1. Revenues	20.0%	100%	$10,000	$12,000	$14,400	$17,280	$20,736	$24,883	$29,860	$35,832	$42,998
2. Cost of Goods Sold		80.0%	8,000	9,600	11,520	13,824	16,589	19,907	23,888	28,665	34,399
3. Selling, General, & Administrative		10.0%	1,000	1,200	1,440	1,728	2,074	2,488	2,986	3,583	4,300
4. Depreciation (tax)		3.0%	300	360	432	518	622	746	896	1,075	1,290
5. Other income	10%		50	55	61	67	73	81	89	97	107
6. Earnings Before Interest and Taxes		7.0%	750	895	1,069	1,276	1,525	1,822	2,179	2,606	3,117
7. Interest Expense		2.0%	200	240	288	346	415	498	597	717	860
8. Income Before Taxes (EBT)			550	655	781	931	1,110	1,325	1,582	1,889	2,257
9. Income taxes	40%		220	262	312	372	444	530	633	756	903
10. Net income (NI)			330	393	468	558	666	795	949	1,133	1,354
11. Tax Shield: $(1 - T) \times (7)$			120	144	173	207	249	299	358	430	516
12. Cash Flow After Taxes			450	537	641	766	915	1,093	1,307	1,563	1,870
13. Net investment in working capital	Tbl A		$ (97)	$ (116)	$ (139)	$ (167)	$ (200)	$ (241)	$ (289)	$ (346)	$ (416)
14. Net investment in fixed assets	Tbl A		(242)	(290)	(348)	(418)	(501)	(601)	(722)	(866)	(1,039)
15. Free Cash Flows (FCF)			$ 122	$ 131	$ 154	$ 181	$ 213	$ 252	$ 297	$ 351	$ 415
Valuation		% Rate									
16. Discounted FCF Cost of Capital (k)		10%	$ 102	$ 108	$ 116	$ 124	$ 132	$ 142	$ 152	$ 164	$ 176
17. Total Present Value of FCF			$ 1,216								

PVTV

TV

276

	Case A	Case B
18. Terminal Value Rate Assumptions		
a. Post-terminal year growth rate (g)	0%	5%
b. Reinvestment rate (z)	0%	40%
19. Terminal Value (TV)	18,702	23,565
20. Present Value of FCF	$ 1,216	$ 1,216
21. Present Value of TV (PVTV)	7,932	9,994
22. Total Present Value	$ 9,147	$11,210
23. Plus: Marketable Securities	—	—
24. Less: Total Interest-Bearing Debt	2,000	2,000
25. Equity Value	$ 7,147	$ 9,210
26. Number of Shares (millions)	360	360
27. Value per Share	$ 19.85	$ 25.58

Table A—Investment	% of ΔRev	Year 1	2	3	4	5	6	7	8	9
A1. Revenues (20.0% growth)		$10,000	$12,000	$14,400	$17,280	20,736	$24,883	$29,860	$35,832	$42,998
A2. Δ Revenues		1,667	2,000	2,400	2,880	3,456	4,147	4,977	5,972	7,166
A3. Net investment in working capital	5.8%	97	116	139	167	200	241	289	346	416
A4. Net investment in fixed assets	14.5%	242	290	348	418	501	601	722	866	1,039
A5. Δ Total Capital = Investment		$ 338	$ 406	$ 487	$ 585	$ 702	$ 842	$ 1,010	$ 1,212	$ 1,455

In practice, some analysts find it more informative to build up to EBIT starting from the bottom line net income figure. However, EBIT includes other income, which can be royalty income and interest income from marketable securities. If royalty income is included in revenues, then other income will be mainly interest from marketable securities. In this approach, we would not add the value of marketable securities in calculating the value of the firm, so line 23 in Table 9A.4 has a value of zero.

MCI WORLDCOM VALUATION

The use of net income plus after-tax interest expense as a measure of free cash flows is illustrated by a Salomon Smith Barney valuation of MCI WorldCom, made on August 13, 1998. The free cash flow figure in Table 9A.5, line 8, starts with net income in line 3. Interest expense times $(1-T)$ is added. Depreciation and amortization are added, and capital spending is deducted. The forecasts assume no significant increases in working capital. Line 8 is discounted at an interest factor of 13%.

The terminal value is calculated next. The approach assumes zero future growth to perpetuity. Three alternative future interest rates or discount factors are analyzed. Three future value/EBITDA multiples are considered. EBITDA is EBIT plus depreciation expense. Although EBITDA is not used directly in calculating the free cash flows for the years 1998 to 2007, it is the figure used in the projection to infinity because with no growth there are no capital expenditure requirements.

We can now explain how line 15, the present value of perpetual cash flows, was calculated. The inverse of the multiples assumed in line 11 represent discount factors. For example, the multiple of 10 in alternative 3 represents a 10% discount factor for the perpetuity period. Note that this is lower than the 13% used for the period of above-average growth. The multiple of 8 for alternative 1 would be a discount factor of 0.125, or 12.5%.

We use the alternative 3 assumption of a multiple of 10. This multiple of 10 times the 2007 EBITDA of $47,284 = $472,840. The present value factor for 13% over the 10-year above-average growth period is 0.294588. This is multiplied by the $472,840 to obtain the line 15 present value of the perpetual cash flow of $139,292 in the alternative 3 column. The other figures for calculating the theoretical value per share of MCI WorldCom follow exactly the pattern we presented in Tables 9A.1 to 9A.4. This chapter was written on August 13, 1999, exactly one year after Table 9A.5 was published. The market price of MCI WorldCom during the latter part of the intervening year fluctuated mostly within the range of the values in columns 2 and 3, line 21.

This MCI WorldCom valuation illustrates the real-world use of the DCF spreadsheet methodologies we illustrated in Tables 9A.1 to 9A.4. As in our example, the forecast made by the analyst for MCI WorldCom in Table 9A.5 after the first two years exhibits steady growth in revenues approximating 19% per annum compounded. The revenue forecasts are based on market share estimates for MCI WorldCom in the segments of the communications industry in which it operates. The cost and net income projections are based on patterns for its businesses in a relatively early stage of the industry life cycle. The DCF spreadsheet valuation formulas summarized in Table 9.7 in the main body of this chapter are widely used by financial analysts, as illustrated by this MCI WorldCom example.

Table 9A.5 WorldCom Communications—Discounted Cash Flow Analysis 1998 to 2007

	1998*	1999	2000	2001	2002	2003	2004	2005	2006	2007
Part 1. Annual Free Cash Flow Projections										
1. Revenues	$10,849	$37,739	$44,809	$52,763	$61,891	$71,969	$83,397	$96,766	$112,593	$131,343
2. EBITDA	3,410	11,699	14,787	18,467	22,281	25,909	30,023	34,836	40,533	47,284
3. Net Income	948	3,673	5,674	7,826	10,182	12,211	14,510	17,254	20,555	24,451
Plus:										
4. Interest Expense After Taxes	$267	$790	$581	$493	$444	$343	$240	$241	$241	$241
5. Depreciation and Amortization	1,300	4,083	4,375	4,935	5,252	5,823	6,453	7,117	7,860	8,577
6. Less: Capital Spending	(3,400)	(7,000)	(7,500)	(7,750)	(8,000)	(8,365)	(9,125)	(9,995)	(11,000)	(13,000)
7. Less Working Capital Increase	0	0	0	0	0	0	0	0	0	0
8. Free Cash Flow	(884)	1,546	3,130	5,504	7,878	10,011	12,077	14,617	17,656	20,269
9. Discounted Free Cash Flow	($782)	$1,211	$2,170	$3,376	$4,276	$4,809	$5,134	$5,498	$5,878	$5,971

	Alternative		
	1	2	3
Perpetuity Value Calculation			
10. Discount Rate	13.0%	13.0%	13.0%
11. Assumed 2007 FV/EBITDA Multiple	8.0	9.0	10.0
12. Implied 2007 P/E Multiple	14.6	16.5	18.7
Part 2. Calculation of Theoretical Value per Share			
13. Discount Rate (%)	13.0%	30.0%	13.0%
14. Sum of Discounted Cash Flow (1998–2007)	$37,539	$37,539	$37,539
15. Present Value of Perpetual Cash Flow	111,434	125,363	139,292
16. Value of Debt Plus Equity	148,973	162,902	176,831
17. Less: Market Value of Debt	(21,000)	(21,000)	(21,000)
18. Plus: Market Value of Cash	100	100	100
19. Theoretical Value	128,073	142,002	155,931
20. Fully Diluted Shares Outstanding	1,876.7	1,876.7	1,876.7
21. Theoretical Value per Share	$68.24	$75.67	$83.09
22. Implied Trading Value (15%–20% discount included)	$56.30	$62.42	$68.55

*1998 does not include MCI.
Source: Smith Barney Inc./Salomon Brothers

Appendix B

Derivation of Revenue Growth Valuation Formulas

We present a derivation of the free cash flow basis for valuation. It has its roots in a generalization of the basic capital budgeting equation. We develop four basic models, but we could easily derive many other variants reflecting any range of assumptions postulated for analysis. The four basic models are

1. No growth.
2. Constant growth.
3. Supernormal growth followed by no growth.
4. Supernormal growth followed by constant growth.

We start with equation (9B.1).

$$V_0 = \frac{R_1[m(1-T)-I_1]}{(1+k)} + \frac{R_2[m(1-T)-I_2]}{(1+k)^2} + \ldots + \frac{R_n[m(1-T)-I_n]}{(1+k)^n} \quad \textbf{(9B.1)}$$

Equation (9B.1) is a general capital budgeting expression. The symbols have all been defined in the main text of this chapter. The initial revenue, R_0, grows at some rate g, which can be positive, negative, or zero. We can replace R_t values in (9B.1) by $R_0(1+g)^t$. We also assume that investment remains at a constant percentage of revenues so I_0 becomes I. We can rewrite equation (9B.1) as

$$V_0 = \frac{R_0(1+g)[m(1-T)-I]}{(1+k)} + \frac{R_0(1+g)^2[m(1-T)-I]}{(1+k)^2} + \ldots$$

$$+ \frac{R_0(1+g)^n[m(1-T)-I]}{(1+k)^n} \quad \textbf{(9B.2)}$$

We factor from each term in equation (9B.2) a common expression,

$$\frac{R_0(1+g)[m(1-T)-I]}{1+k}$$

This gives the equation

$$V_0 = \frac{R_0(1+g)[m(1-T)-I]}{1+k}\left[1 + \frac{1+g}{1+k} + \frac{(1+g)^2}{(1+k)^2} + \ldots + \frac{(1+g)^{n-1}}{(1+k)^{n-1}}\right] \quad \textbf{(9B.3)}$$

The series inside the large brackets can be written as a summation expression; giving

$$V_0 = \frac{R_0(1+g)[m(1-T)-I]}{1+k}\sum_{t=1}^{n}\frac{(1+g)^{t-1}}{(1+k)^{t-1}} \quad \textbf{(9B.3a)}$$

We can move the first $(1 + g)/(1 + k)$ term into the summation expression to obtain the equation

$$V_0 = R_0[m(1 - T) - I]\sum_{t=1}^{n}\frac{(1+g)^t}{(1+k)^t} \qquad \textbf{(9B.3b)}$$

From the valuation equation (9B.3), (9B.3a), or (9B.3b), we can obtain all the valuation expressions by specifying how g, the growth rate, behaves.

THE NO-GROWTH CASE

First assume that $g = 0$. If $g = 0$, then the firm requires no investment, so $I_0 = I_t = 0$ as well. Equation (9B.3) becomes

$$V_0 = \frac{R_0[m(1 - T)]}{1 + k}\left[1 + \frac{1}{1+k} + \left(\frac{1}{1+k}\right)^2 + \ldots + \left(\frac{1}{1+k}\right)^{n-1}\right] \qquad \textbf{(9B.4)}$$

The term in front of the large brackets has parameters that are all constants. The terms inside the large brackets form a geometrical progression that starts with the constant term 1 and increases by the ratio $1/(1 + k)$. A geometric progression can be written as follows:

$$a + ar + ar^2 + ar^3 + \ldots + ar^{n-1} = a[1 + r + r^2 + r^3 + \ldots + r^{n-1}]$$

Note that the constant term, a, can be factored out, and the form of the standard geometric progression is exactly as in equation (9B.4). When there are a finite number of terms, n, the sum of these terms is

$$S^n = \frac{a(r^n - 1)}{r - 1}$$

When n goes to infinity, the sum of this geometric progression is equal to $S^\infty = a/(1-r)$ when $r < 1$.

We can write equation (9B.4) (when $k > 0$, $r < 1$, and n goes to infinity) as

$$V_0 = \frac{R_0[m(1 - T)]}{1 + k}\left[\frac{1}{1 - 1/(1 + k)}\right]$$

$$= \frac{R_0[m(1 - T)]}{1 + k}\left[\frac{1}{(1 + k - 1)/(1 + k)}\right]$$

$$= \frac{R_0[m(1 - T)]}{1 + k}\left(\frac{1 + k}{k}\right)$$

Cancel the $1 + k$ in the numerator and denominator to obtain equation (9.1) of Table 9.7,

$$V_0 = \frac{R_0[m(1 - T)]}{k} \quad \text{for } k > 0 \qquad \textbf{(9.1)}$$

The result in equation (9.1) (see Table 9.7) is the familiar formula for the valuation of a stream of receipts or cash flows that continues at a constant level to infinity. This is the standard valuation expression for a perpetuity or bond that has no maturity, often called a consol.

CONSTANT GROWTH

For the second basic case, assume that g is not zero but a constant. We return to equation (9B.3). The constant ratio is equal to $(1 + g)/(1 + k)$. We again use the expression for the summation of a geometric progression that continues to infinity, which is $a/(1 - r)$, where $r = (1 + g)/(1 + k) < 1$. Equation (9B.3) can be written as

$$V_0 = \frac{R_0(1+g)\left[m(1-T)-I\right]}{(1+k)}\left[\frac{1}{1-(1+g)/(1+k)}\right]$$

$$V_0 = \frac{R_0(1+g)\left[m(1-T)-I\right]}{1+k}\left(\frac{1+k}{k-g}\right)$$

Simplifying, we obtain equation (9.2) of Table 9.7:

$$V_0 = \frac{R_0(1+g)\left[m(1-T)-I\right]}{k-g} \quad \text{for } k > g \qquad \textbf{(9.2)}$$

Equation (9.2) is the valuation expression (when k is larger than g) for cash flows that grow at a constant rate, g, to perpetuity.

SUPERNORMAL GROWTH FOLLOWED BY NO GROWTH

The third basic case is temporary supernormal growth followed by no growth. The valuation formula consists of two terms:

$$V_0 = V_1 + V_2 \qquad \textbf{(9B.5)}$$

In the first term, the V_1 component of total value, V_0, the firm experiences temporary supernormal growth for n periods. The V_2 component of value shown for the second term has no further growth in revenues from $n + 1$ to infinity.

Equation (9B.3b) becomes the first term in equation (9B.5), which gives us

$$V_1 = R_0[m(1-T)-I]\sum_{t=1}^{n}\frac{(1+g)^t}{(1+k)^t} \qquad \textbf{(9B.6)}$$

At the end of the first term, the revenues are $R_0(1+g)^n$. Since there is no further growth, the same level of revenues is expected forever with no additional investment requirements. The free cash flows will remain constant at:

$$FCF = R_0(1+g)^n[m(1-T)]$$

The present value of the cash streams in the second term is

$$V_2 = \frac{FCF}{(1+k)^{n+1}} + \frac{FCF}{(1+k)^{n+2}} + \frac{FCF}{(1+k)^{n+3}} + \ldots + \frac{FCF}{(1+k)^{\infty}}$$

$$= \frac{FCF}{(1+k)^n}\left(\frac{1}{1+k}\right)\left[1 + \frac{1}{(1+k)} + \frac{1}{(1+k)^2} + \ldots + \frac{1}{(1+k)^{\infty}}\right]$$

Using the property of the sum of a geometric progression,

$$V_2 = \frac{FCF}{(1+k)^n}\left(\frac{1}{1+k}\right)\left(\frac{1+k}{k}\right) = \frac{R_0(1+g)^n[m(1-T)]}{k(1+k)^n}$$

the formula for our third case of temporary supernormal growth followed by zero growth reduces to

$$V_0 = R_0[m(1-T)-I]\sum_{t=1}^{n}\frac{(1+g)^t}{(1+k)^t} + \frac{R_o(1+g)^n[m(1-T)]}{k(1+k)^n} \tag{9.3}$$

SUPERNORMAL GROWTH FOLLOWED BY CONSTANT GROWTH

By the same logic, we can develop the expression for the fourth case. The first term on the right in equation (9B.5) is given by equation (9B.6). Revenues grow at a supernormal rate, g_s, with an investment requirement, I_s, for the first n periods, so

$$V_1 = R_0[m(1-T)-I_s]\sum_{t=1}^{n}\frac{(1+g_s)^t}{(1+k)^t} \tag{9B.7}$$

At the end of the first term, the revenues are $R_0(1+g_s)^n$, and they will increase from then on at a constant rate, g_c, to perpetuity. If the investment requirement during the second term is I_c, we can think of a level of free cash flow,

$$FCF = R_0(1+g_s)^n[m(1-T)-I_c]$$

growing at a rate g_c to perpetuity. The present value of the cash streams is

$$V_2 = \frac{FCF(1+g_c)}{(1+k)^{n+1}} + \frac{FCF(1+g_c)^2}{(1+k)^{n+2}} + \frac{FCF(1+g_c)^3}{(1+k)^{n+3}} + \ldots + \frac{FCF(1+g_c)^\infty}{(1+k)^\infty}$$

$$= \frac{FCF}{(1+k)^n}\left(\frac{1+g_c}{1+k}\right)\left[1 + \frac{(1+g_c)}{(1+k)} + \frac{(1+g_c)^2}{(1+k)^2} + \ldots + \frac{(1+g_c)^\infty}{(1+k)^\infty}\right]$$

which reduces to

$$V_2 = \frac{FCF}{(1+k)^n}\left(\frac{1+g_c}{1+k}\right)\left(\frac{1+k}{k-g_c}\right)$$

$$= \frac{R_0(1+g_s)^n[m(1-T)-I_c]}{(1+k)^n}\left(\frac{1+g_c}{k-g_c}\right)$$

The formula for our fourth case of temporary supernormal growth followed by constant growth becomes

$$V_0 = R_0[m(1-T)-I_s]\sum_{t=1}^{n}\frac{(1+g_s)^t}{(1+k)^t} + \frac{R_0(1+g_s)^n[m(1-T)-I_c]}{(1+k)^n}\left(\frac{1+g_c}{k-g_c}\right) \tag{9.4}$$

Thus from a general capital budgeting equation, valuation expressions for four patterns of growth have been derived. The formulas for the four free cash flow patterns are summarized in Table 9.7 of the main text.

Derivation of Investment Opportunity Valuation Formulas

In the main body of this chapter, we used the DCF valuation method in which the value drivers are expressed in relation to revenues. Another valuation formulation widely used by practitioners is to define investment as $b = I_t / X_t(1 - T)$. This represents the dollar amount of investment normalized by after-tax cash flows. Profitability (r) is defined as

$$\frac{X_{t+1}(1 - T) - X_t(1 - T)}{I_t}$$

which is the incremental after-tax cash flows related to the new investment for the period. We can start with a general expression for value similar to that used in Appendix B, shown here as equation (9C.1):

$$V_0 = \frac{X_1(1 - T) - I_1}{(1 + k)} + \frac{X_2(1 - T) - I_2}{(1 + k)^2} + \ldots + \frac{X_n(1 - T) - I_n}{(1 + k)^n} \qquad \textbf{(9C.1)}$$

where

X = the earnings before interest and taxes (EBIT) or net operating income (NOI)
T = the actual cash tax rate
b = investment per period normalized by (divided by) the after-tax EBIT
r = marginal profitability rate measured by the change in after-tax profits divided by investments

$$r = (X_n - X_0)(1 - T) / \sum_{t=1}^{n} I_t$$

g = the growth rate in after-tax cash flows
n = the number of periods of supernormal growth
k = the applicable marginal weighted cost of capital

Because $b = I_t / X_t(1 - T)$, we can write $I_t = bX_t(1 - T)$. We substitute this expression into (9C.1) to obtain

$$V_0 = \frac{X_1(1 - T) - bX_1(1 - T)}{1 + k} + \frac{X_2(1 - T) - bX_2(1 - T)}{(1 + k)^2}$$

$$+ \ldots + \frac{X_n(1 - T) - bX_n(1 - T)}{(1 + k)^n} \qquad \textbf{(9C.2)}$$

The initial X_0 grows at some rate, g, which can be positive, negative, or zero. We replace the $X_t(1-T)$ values in equation (9C.2) by $X_0(1-T)(1+g)^t$ to obtain

$$V_0 = \frac{X_0(1-T)(1+g) - bX_0(1-T)(1+g)}{1+k} + \frac{X_0(1-T)(1+g)^2 - bX_0(1-T)(1+g)^2}{(1+k)^2}$$
$$+ \ldots + \frac{X_0(1-T)(1+g)^n - bX_0(1-T)(1+g)^n}{(1+k)^n} \tag{9C.3}$$

We factor the common expression $X_0(1-T)(1+g)^t$ from each term in the numerator to obtain a $(1-b)$ term.

$$V_0 = \frac{X_0(1-T)(1+g)(1-b)}{1+k} + \frac{X_0(1-T)(1+g)^2(1-b)}{(1+k)^2}$$
$$+ \ldots + \frac{X_0(1-T)(1+g)^n(1-b)}{(1+k)^n} \tag{9C.4}$$

We factor from each term in equation (9C.4) the common expression

$$X_0(1-T)(1+g)(1-b)/(1+k)$$

This gives the equation

$$V_0 = \frac{X_0(1-T)(1-b)(1+g)}{1+k}\left[1 + \frac{(1+g)}{(1+k)} + \frac{(1+g)^2}{(1+k)^2} + \ldots + \frac{(1+g)^{n-1}}{(1+k)^{n-1}}\right] \tag{9C.5}$$

From expression (9C.5), we can obtain all the valuation expressions by specifying how g, the growth rate, behaves.

THE NO-GROWTH CASE

First assume that $g = 0$. If $g = 0$, the firm requires no investment, so $b = 0$ as well. Equation (9C.5) becomes

$$V_0 = \frac{X_0(1-T)}{1+k}\left[1 + \left(\frac{1}{1+k}\right) + \left(\frac{1}{1+k}\right)^2 + \ldots + \left(\frac{1}{1+k}\right)^{n-1}\right] \tag{9C.6}$$

The term in front of the brackets has parameters that are all constants. The terms inside the brackets form a geometrical progression that starts with the constant term 1 and increases by the ratio $1/(1+k)$. A geometric progression can be written as follows:

$$a + ar + ar^2 + ar^3 + \ldots + ar^{n-1} = a[1 + r + r^2 + r^3 + \ldots + r^{n-1}]$$

Note that the constant term, a, can be factored out and the form of the standard geometric progression is exactly as in equation (9C.6). When there are a finite number of terms, n, the sum of these terms is

$$S^n = a(r^n - 1)/(r - 1)$$

When n goes to infinity the sum of this geometric progression is equal to $S^\infty = a/(1-r)$ when $r < 1$. We use both of these summation formulas.

We can write equation (9C.6) (when $k > 0$, $r < 1$, and n goes to infinity) as

$$V_0 = \frac{X_0(1-T)}{1+k}\left[\frac{1}{1-1/(1+k)}\right]$$

$$= \frac{X_0(1-T)}{1+k}\left[\frac{1}{(1+k-1)/(1+k)}\right]$$

$$= \frac{X_0(1-T)(1+k)}{k(1+k)}$$

Cancel the $(1+k)$ terms in the numerator and denominator to obtain the equation

$$V_0 = \frac{X_0(1-T)}{k} \quad \text{for } k > 0 \tag{9C.7}$$

The result in equation (9C.7) is the familiar formula for the valuation of a stream of receipts or cash flows that continues at a constant level to infinity.

CONSTANT GROWTH

For the second basic case, assume that g is not zero but a constant. We return to equation (9C.5). The constant ratio is equal to $(1+g)/(1+k)$. Here we use the expression for the summation of a geometric progression that continues to infinity, which is $a/(1-r)$, where $r = (1+g)/(1+k) < 1$. Equation (9C.5) can be written as

$$V_0 = \frac{X_0(1-T)(1-b)(1+g)}{1+k}\left(\frac{1}{1-(1+g)/(1+k)}\right)$$

Simplifying, we obtain the equation

$$V_0 = \frac{X_0(1-T)(1-b)(1+g)}{k-g} \quad \text{for } g < k \tag{9C.8}$$

Equation (9C.8) is the valuation expression (when k is larger than g) for cash flows that grow at a constant rate, g, to perpetuity.

SUPERNORMAL GROWTH FOLLOWED BY NO GROWTH

The third basic case is temporary supernormal growth followed by no growth. The fourth will be constant growth during the second phase. We develop an expression for the first term of temporary supernormal growth to which we add a second term that represents either no growth or constant growth. Equation (9C.5) becomes the first term set equal to S^n in the equation

$$S^n = \frac{X_0(1-T)(1-b)(1+g)}{1+k}\left[1+\frac{1+g}{1+k}+\frac{(1+g)^2}{(1+k)^2}+\dots+\frac{(1+g)^{n-1}}{(1+k)^{n-1}}\right] \tag{9C.9}$$

The series inside the brackets of (9C.9) can be written as a summation expression:

$$S^n = \frac{X_0(1-T)(1-b)(1+g)}{1+k} \sum_{t=1}^{n} \frac{(1+g)^{t-1}}{(1+k)^{t-1}} \tag{9C.10}$$

We can move the first $(1+g)/(1+k)$ term into the summation expression to obtain the equation

$$S^n = X_0(1-T)(1-b)\sum_{t=1}^{n}\frac{(1+g)^t}{(1+k)^t} \tag{9C.11}$$

The formula for our third case, temporary supernormal growth followed by zero growth, combines equations (9C.10) and (9C.7):

$$V_0 = X_0(1-T)(1-b)\sum_{t=1}^{n}\frac{(1+g)^t}{(1+k)^t} + \frac{X_0(1-T)(1+g)^n}{k(1+k)^n} \tag{9C.12}$$

In the second term on the right of equation (9C.12), we grow $X_0(1-T)$ at g for n periods and capitalize it at k to obtain its value at the end of n periods. We then discount it back to the present by $1/(1+k)^n$ to obtain the present value of the second term, which is added to equation (9C.11) to obtain the formula in (9C.12).

SUPERNORMAL GROWTH FOLLOWED BY CONSTANT GROWTH

By the same logic, we can develop the expression for the fourth case. The first term on the right is the value of S^n from equation (9C.10), and the second term is based on equation (9C.8).

$$V_0 = X_0(1-T)(1-b_s)\sum_{t=1}^{n}\frac{(1+g_s)^t}{(1+k)^t}$$
$$+ \frac{X_0(1-T)(1-b_c)(1+g_c)}{k-g_c} \times \frac{(1+g_s)^n}{(1+k)^n} \tag{9C.13}$$

In the second term, X_0 grows at the supernormal rate g_s for n periods, after which it grows at a constant rate, g_c, to perpetuity. The investment rate for the constant growth period is b_c. The numerator of the second term is capitalized at $k-g_c$. This capitalized value is discounted back to the present by $1/(1+k)^n$.

The formulas for the investment opportunities model are summarized in Table 9C.1.

We have developed equations for a valuation model in which b is defined as the dollar amount of investment requirements scaled by after-tax operating income. This alternative valuation approach also defines profitability as the change in after-tax operating income related to investment. It can then be shown that g, the growth rate in operating income, is equal to b times r. In symbols, b is the investment per period normalized by (divided by) the after-tax EBIT or NOI, or $b = I_t/[X_t(1-T)]$. Also, r is the marginal profitability rate measured by the change in after-tax profits divided by

Table 9C.1 Formulas for Free Cash Flow Valuation of a Firm

No growth:

$$V_0 = \frac{X_0(1-T)}{k} \tag{9C.7}$$

Constant growth:

$$V_0 = \frac{X_0(1-T)(1-b)(1+g)}{k-g} \tag{9C.8}$$

Temporary supernormal growth, then no growth:

$$V_0 = X_0(1-T)(1-b) \sum_{t=1}^{n} \frac{(1+g)^t}{(1+k)^t} + \frac{X_0(1-T)(1+g)^n}{k(1+k)^n} \tag{9C.12}$$

Temporary supernormal growth, then constant growth:

$$V_0 = X_0(1-T)(1-b_s) \sum_{t=1}^{n} \frac{(1+g_s)^t}{(1+k)^t} + \frac{X_0(1-T)(1-b_c)(1+g_c)}{(k-g_c)} \frac{(1+g_s)^n}{(1+k)^n} \tag{9C.13}$$

where:

X = the earnings before interest and taxes (EBIT) or net operating income (NOI)
T = the actual cash tax rate
b = investment per period normalized by (divided by) the after-tax EBIT
b_s = investment rate during supernormal growth period
b_c = investment rate during constant growth period
g = the growth rate in after-tax cash flows
g_a = growth rate during supernormal growth period
g_c = growth rate during constant growth period
n = the number of periods of supernormal growth
k = the applicable marginal weighted cost of capital

investments, or $r = [X_{t+1}(1-T) - X_t(1-T)]/I_t$. In this model, g is the growth rate in after-tax cash flows, or $g = [(X_{t+1} - X_t)(1-T)]/X_t(1-T)$. Multiply by I_t/I_t to obtain

$$\left(\frac{(X_{t+1} - X_t)(1-T)}{X_t(1-T)} \right)\left(\frac{I_t}{I_t} \right) = \left(\frac{(X_{t+1} - X_t)(1-T)}{I_t} \right)\left(\frac{I_t}{X_t(1-T)} \right) = rb = g$$

In this model if b, the investment requirements, is increased and r is unchanged, g will increase. If g increases, value will increase. In this model, investment requirements are growth opportunities. If b is greater than 1, the first term on the right in equations (9C.12) and (9C.13) may become negative, but the higher g makes the terminal cash flows larger and therefore the valuation higher.

In Table 9C.2, the widely used textbook constant dividend growth model is derived from equation (9C.8).

Table 9C.2   Constant Dividend Growth Valuation Model

Start with equation (9C.8):

$$V_0 = \frac{X_0 (1-T) (1-b) (1+g)}{k-g} \tag{9C.8}$$

If no debt: $V_0 = S_0$, the market value of shareholders' equity, k is the cost of equity k_s, so we have

$$S_0 = \frac{X_0 (1-T) (1-b) (1+g)}{k_s - g}$$

Substitute NI_0 for $X_0(1 - T)$, where NI = net income.

$$S_0 = \frac{NI_0 (1-b) (1+g)}{k_s - g} \tag{9C.14}$$

where

$\qquad b$ = retention rate or ratio of investment to net income

$$b = \frac{NI - Div}{NI}$$

$\qquad Div$ = dividends.

Divide through by NI, and subtract each side from 1.

$$1 - b = 1 - \left(1 - \frac{Div}{NI}\right)$$

Rearrange and remove parentheses.

$$(1-b) = \frac{Div}{NI} = Payout\ ratio$$

Multiply both sides by NI.

$$NI(1-b) = NI\left(\frac{Div}{NI}\right) = Div$$

Substitute into (9C.14)

$$S_0 = \frac{Div_0 (1+g)}{k_s - g} = \frac{D_1}{k_s - g} \qquad \text{Equation (9C.14) in dividend form} \tag{9C.15}$$

$$P_0 = \frac{d_1}{k_s - g} \qquad \text{Equation (9C.15) on a per share basis} \tag{9C.16}$$

where

P_0 = price per share
d_1 = next period dividend per share

Chapter 10

Increasing the Value of the Organization

In chapter 9, we described and illustrated three approaches to valuation that would be useful in merger analysis: comparable companies or comparable transactions, the spreadsheet approach, and the formula approach. We discussed their strengths and weaknesses, and we concluded that each approach has something to offer. We recommended that in an acquisition analysis all three be used for the guidance they can provide. In addition, other supplementary tests can be employed to judge the valuations in M&A transactions. We emphasize that whether the merger or takeover makes business sense and whether the premium involved is justified by a realistic assessment of potential synergies are critical to the analysis.

In this chapter we demonstrate how the three can be used in actual practice. Valuation must be related to the economic and strategic factors affecting business firms. To facilitate consideration of these broader influences that are involved in making valuations, it is necessary to focus on the industry in which the acquisition transaction takes place. We choose the oil industry because it is one of the three largest in the U.S. economy and has much economic as well as political and military importance.

In the second edition of this book, we focused on the acquisition in 1984 of Gulf Oil by the Chevron Corporation (at that time called the Standard Oil Company of California, SOCAL). This was a transaction of considerable importance for the oil industry as well as for the economy as a whole. It is also representative of the considerable amount of M&A activity and restructuring activities in the oil industry in the 1980s (for an in-depth study of M&A and restructuring activities in the oil industry, see Siu and Weston, 1996).

To illustrate the methodologies explained in chapter 9, we first summarize the materials on mergers in the oil industry in the 1980s, exemplified by Chevron and Gulf. Second, we discuss the oil mergers of the 1990s, centering on Exxon and Mobil. Third, we turn to a broader view of merger valuation over a wide range of industries using the stages in the life cycle of firms as a predictor of the behavior of the key value drivers. Fourth, we demonstrate that the DCF valuation model is relevant for gaining perspectives on the spectacular valuations observed in Internet industries.

THE OIL MERGERS OF THE EARLY 1980S

In response to a takeover attempt by a group led by T. Boone Pickens, Gulf Oil held an auction. Chevron won the auction in March 1984 with an $80 per share bid. The market price of Gulf before share purchases by Pickens was $39 per share. The premium paid by Chevron was $41, or 105%. Gulf had 165.3 million shares of common stock outstanding; at the purchase price of $80 a share the total paid was $13.2 billion, representing a gain to Gulf shareholders of about $6.8 billion.

The event returns for Chevron are more difficult to measure because the Federal Trade Commission delayed the consummation of the merger until Chevron sold off some specified assets. The *Wall Street Journal* reported on March 1, 1983 that Gulf had been talking with several oil companies including Chevron as a possible buyer. But final completion of the merger was delayed until May 1984. During the four months from February 1984 through May 1984, Chevron experienced a positive event return of $2 billion. Gulf's shareholders gained the difference between the $13.2 billion paid by Chevron and its $6.45 billion value before it was put in play. The event return to Gulf shareholders was about $6.8 billion. So the combined event return was about $8.8 billion. Thus, the market judged the merger to be value-increasing—that real synergistic gains would be achieved. The empirical studies discussed in chapter 8 demonstrate that the event returns are good predictors of the subsequent performance in M&A transactions. The subsequent analysis in this chapter confirms that Chevron's acquisition of Gulf was a positive net present value (NPV) investment.

We analyze the price paid by Chevron from a number of other perspectives, including the approaches we described in the preceding chapter. We begin with the comparable transactions approach.

Comparable Transactions Analysis of the Gulf Purchase

Table 10.1 presents the information needed for making a comparable transactions analysis of the $13.2 billion paid by Chevron for Gulf. The upper part of the table summarizes key information on five transactions similar to the Gulf transaction. The prices paid range from about $4 billion to $8 billion. While none is as large as the Gulf purchase, they are all multibillion-dollar transactions. After presenting data on the price paid, we present data for the acquired firm or seller for the latest period before the transaction took place. The four measures we use are widely employed by investment bankers: revenues, which represent the market position and profit potential; the earnings before interest, taxes, depreciation, and amortization (EBITDA); book equity, which represents shareholders' investment as shown on the balance sheet; and market equity, which is the market value of shareholders' equity.

In the bottom half of the table, for each of the five transactions comparable to the Chevron–Gulf purchase we present the multiple of the price paid to revenues, EBITDA, book equity, and market equity. We calculate both an unweighted mean and a weighted average of each of the four multiples for the five comparable transactions. Because the unweighted mean gives undue weight to outliers of multiples, we apply the average weighted multiple to the Gulf figures for 1983 to obtain the indicated value of Gulf. Based on the ratio of the price paid to the preacquisition market value in the other five transactions, Chevron should have paid $9.4 billion for

Table 10.1 Comparable Transactions Analysis of Gulf Purchase (dollars in millions)

| | | | Price | | Acquired or Seller | | |
Year	Buyer	Seller	Offered	Revenues	EBITDA*	Book Equity	Market Equity
1984	Chevron Corp.	Gulf Corp.	$ 13,205.5	$ 26,581	$ 3,717	$ 10,128	$ 7,027
1981	E.I. du Pont de Nemours & Co.	Conoco Inc.	8,039.8	18,326	4,048	4,585	7,049
1981	U.S. Steel Corp.	Marathon Oil Corp.	6,618.5	8,754	3,162	1,923	4,257
1984	Mobil Corp.	Superior Oil Co.	5,725.8	1,793	849	2,468	4,628
1981	Societe Nationale Elf Aquitaine-France	Texasgulf Inc.	4,293.7	1,090	440	1,168	1,972
1982	Occidental Petroleum Corp.	Cities Services Co.	4,115.6	8,546	954	2,107	3,572

| | | | Multiple | | | |
Year	Buyer	Seller	Revenues	EBITDA	Book Equity	Market Equity
1981	E.I. du Pont de Nemours & Co.	Conoco Inc.	0.44	1.99	1.75	1.14
1981	U.S. Steel Corp.	Marathon Oil Corp.	0.76	2.09	3.44	1.55
1984	Mobil Corp.	Superior Oil Co.	3.19	6.74	2.32	1.24
1981	Societe Nationale Elf Aquitaine-France	Texasgulf Inc.	3.94	9.76	3.68	2.18
1982	Occidental Petroleum Corp.	Cities Service Co.	0.48	4.31	1.95	1.15
	Unweighted mean		1.76	4.98	2.63	1.45
	Weighted average		0.75	3.05	2.35	1.34
	Value of Gulf (using weighted average)		$ 19,875	$ 11,322	$ 23,803	$ 9,420

*Earnings before interest, taxes, depreciation, and amortization.

293

Gulf. Based on the ratio of price paid to EBITDA, the indicated price for Gulf would have been $11.3 billion. Based on revenues, the value of Gulf would have been $19.9 billion. Based on the multiple of price paid to book equity, the price could have been $23.8 billion. The price paid by Chevron falls between two high estimates and two somewhat lower indicated values. One should generally give greater weight to the multiples related to EBITDA and to the market equity.

The Value of Gulf, 1983

We shall employ a number of methodologies to estimate the value of Gulf in 1983. Our purpose is to test whether the price of $13.2 billion paid by Chevron was a reasonable one.

The EBIT of Gulf had been flat at $2.99 billion for the previous 10 years. Hence, the applicable valuation methodology is to value Gulf as a no-growth company. We need to calculate a cost of capital for Gulf to use in the no-growth valuation formula. We estimate a cost of capital of 13% for Gulf, drawing on materials in a Harvard Business School case on the Gulf acquisition (Case No. 285-053). The CAPM is used to calculate the cost of equity. Reflecting the financial market conditions in the early 1980s, the risk-free rate is 8%, the market price of risk is 7.5%, and the required yield to maturity on Gulf's AA-rated debt is 10%. The target leverage ratio is 30%. These data yield the cost of capital calculation shown below:

$$
\begin{aligned}
k_s &= 0.08 + 0.075(1.15) \\
&= 0.08 + 0.08625 \\
&= 0.16625 \\
k_b &= 0.10(1 - 0.5) \\
&= 0.05 \\
k &= 0.70(0.16625) + 0.30(0.05) \\
&= 0.1164 + 0.015 \\
&= 0.1314
\end{aligned}
$$

Valuing Gulf as a no-growth company, we have

$$
V_0 = \frac{X_0(1 - T)}{k} = \frac{2{,}990 \times 0.50}{0.13} = \frac{1{,}495}{0.13} = \$11.5 \text{ billion}
$$

The resulting $11.5 billion value is below the $13.2 billion paid by Chevron. But Chevron has a number of ways to improve the earning power of Gulf, particularly a reduction in finding costs, which we next discuss.

Finding Cost Analysis

The approach taken in the Harvard Business School (HBS) case on the Gulf takeover (Case No. 285-053) calculates the negative returns from Gulf's exploration and development (E&D) programs. It then calculates the losses that could be avoided by curtailing or shutting down the unprofitable E&D activity of Gulf. A summary outline of the HBS analysis is shown in Table 10.2.

Table 10.2 Returns from E&D Programs in the Oil Industry, Early 1980s

1. Time lag in reserve use = reserves/annual production = 2,313 bbl/290 bbl = 8 years
2. Finding costs (FC) = $(E\&D)_{t-1}$/(reserve additions)$_t$ = \$2,671/336.5 = \$7.94/bbl
   Expensed in 1 year (E1%) 26%; expensed in 8 years (E8%) 74%
3. Tax shelter = (FC)(E1)(T)(1/cc) + (FC)(E8)(T)[1/cc^8]; T = tax rate; cc = (1 + k)
   (\$7.94)(0.26)(0.5)(1/1.17) + (\$7.94)(0.74)(0.5)[1/(1.17)^8] = \$0.88 + \$0.84 = \$1.72/bbl
4. Operating profit = (Op. revs. \$22.42 − direct operating costs \$7.08) times (1 − T) = \$7.67/bbl
   a. Present value = Op. profit (1 + p)^8[1/(1 + cc)^8] = \$7.67(1.05)^8[1/(1.17)^8] = \$3.25/bbl
5. Net present value of company E&D programs
   a. P.V. of Op. profit \$3.25 + P.V. of E&D tax shelters \$1.72 − P.V. of finding costs
      \$7.94 = \$(2.97)/bbl
   b. Total = Amt./bbl (\$2.97) times reserve additions 336.5 = (\$999)
   c. Capitalized value of perpetuity: \$(999)/(0.17 − 0.05) = \$(8,325)
   d. \$(8,325) ÷ # of Gulf shares = \$(8,325 million) ÷ 165.3 million = \$50.36/share

Source: Developed by the authors from information in Harvard Business School, "Gulf Oil Corporation—Takeover," Case No. 285-053, November 7, 1984; revised 1992.

The time lag in reserve use is obtained by dividing reserves by annual production to obtain eight years. This is a critical number, because it means that finding costs in a given year are not recovered in the sale of crude (if the E&D efforts are successful) until some years later. As a consequence, accounting profit and loss statements that do not take the time value of money into account are likely to overstate returns because of the substantial time lag between outlays incurred and revenues received.

In line 2, finding costs per barrel are obtained by dividing the outlays by the reserve additions with which they are associated. Using the Gulf financial data, finding costs were \$7.94 per barrel in the early 1980s; 26% was expensed in year 1 and 74% in year 8. In line 3, the actual dollar amount of tax shelter is calculated from the above relationships. The present value of tax shelter is calculated as \$1.72 per barrel. This analysis uses a projected inflation rate for oil prices (p) of 5%, one for direct operating costs (q) of 5%, and a weighted average cost of capital (k) of 17%.

In line 4, the operating profit per barrel after taxes is calculated. Operating revenues less direct operating costs times (1 − T) is found to be \$7.67 per barrel. In line 4a, this operating profit is compounded at the inflation rate for oil prices for eight years and then discounted back for eight years at the applicable cost of capital. The result is \$3.25 per barrel as the present value of after-tax operating profits per barrel.

We now have all of the results needed to calculate the net present value of Gulf's E&D programs as shown in lines 5a through 5d. The present value of operating profit (\$3.25) plus the present value of the E&D tax shelters (\$1.72) less the present value of finding cost (\$7.94) is a negative \$2.97 per barrel, as shown in line 5a of the table. In line 5b, the amount per barrel is multiplied by the related reserve additions to obtain the total negative net present value of \$999 million. The HBS case analysis postulated a continuation of this annual loss to perpetuity. It capitalizes the perpetuity at 12%, the applicable cost of capital (17%) less the inflation rate for oil prices (5%). The result is a total loss of $8.3 billion. Dividing by the number of Gulf shares (165.3 million) gives a loss of $50.36 per share. Thus, it was argued that a firm buying Gulf could avoid a destruction to shareholder value of $50.36 per share by simply shutting down Gulf's E&D programs. The HBS case concluded that adding this savings of $50.36 per share to the existing $39 price of Gulf would give a value of $89 per share, justifying the $80 per share actually paid by Chevron.

The Harvard Case analysis used a cost of capital of 17% for Gulf. This was based on the temporarily high interest rate levels during part of 1983. We had calculated a lower estimate of 13% for the cost of capital for Gulf. Our lower estimate was based on a longer term view of interest rate levels. Using the same pattern as in Table 10.2 with a cost of capital of 13% results in a loss per barrel of $42.10 from Gulf's E&D programs. When the existing $39 market price of Gulf is added, the result is $81 per share. The $80 purchase would still return SOCAL's cost of capital on the Gulf purchase.

Other Approaches to the Valuation of Gulf

Another approach would be to value the proved reserves obtained in the purchase. Gulf's total reserves were 2.313 billion barrels equivalent. The price of oil in the early 1980s had fluctuated in a range between $31.75 down to $10 per barrel. Using the $10 per barrel price, Chevron was obtaining a value of $23.13 billion. This was far in excess of the $13.2 billion paid.

In actual practice, after the acquisition Chevron cut back on its exploration and development programs. But it simply did not shut down all of Gulf's exploration activities. It made a full review of all exploration programs of the combined company. It reduced or shut down the least promising and continued with the most attractive whether of Gulf or Chevron heritage. Other cost savings and synergies were achieved.

VALUATION AND MERGER ANALYSIS

The circumstances of the Chevron–Gulf combination were somewhat special. We now turn to a more general framework for analyzing mergers. The analysis should include at least five major components: (1) the nature of the industry, (2) how industry characteristics drive mergers and potential synergies, (3) financial projections of the value drivers, (4) regulatory aspects, and (5) implementation. The merger between Exxon and Mobil is used to illustrate our analysis. We begin with a review of the nature of the oil industry.

The Characteristics of the Oil Industry

The oil industry, like other industries, has been affected by the massive change forces of technological change, globalization, industry transformations, and entrepreneurial innovations. The oil industry has some special characteristics as well. (1) Oil is a global market with 53% of volume internationally traded. It accounts for about 10% of world trade, more than any other commodity. (2) Oil continues to be strategically important for industrial, political, and military reasons. (3) Environmental legislation and regulation standards and requirements involve large costs. During the 1990s, these costs could aggregate as much as $67 billion (Finizza, 1996, p. 10).

Table 10.3   Spot Prices of Crude Oil—West Texas Intermediate

	Jan.	Feb.	Mar.	Apr.	May	Jun.	Jul.	Aug.	Sep.	Oct.	Nov.	Dec.
	(Dollars per Barrel)											
1995	18.03	18.59	18.54	19.90	19.70	18.45	17.33	18.02	18.23	17.43	17.99	19.03
1996	18.85	19.09	21.33	23.50	21.17	20.42	21.27	21.90	23.97	24.88	23.70	25.23
1997	25.13	22.18	20.97	19.70	20.82	19.26	19.66	19.95	19.80	21.33	20.19	18.33
1998	16.72	16.06	15.12	15.35	14.91	13.72	14.17	13.47	15.03	14.46	13.00	11.35
1999	12.51	12.01	14.68	17.31	17.75	17.89	20.07	21.26	24.00	24.50	26.00	25.00

Source: U.S. Department of Energy.

The Impact of OPEC

A fourth characteristic is that the Organization of Oil Exporting Countries (OPEC) has a major influence. Because their production costs are low, the market power of the OPEC countries is substantial. The two major oil price shocks of 1973 and 1979 had major impacts. But significant cheating on production quotas has taken place periodically among the OPEC participants. Non-OPEC production has increased. The OPEC impact has been uneven over time.

Another characteristic of the oil industry is that it is relatively unique in the degree of price instability. The oil price shock of 1973 moved oil prices from under $3 per barrel to $9 by 1978. The 1979 shock moved prices up to the $37.75 level. The third oil price shock was in a downward direction. Saudi Arabia had been the buffer to absorb supply increases of other countries to keep overall OPEC quotas on target. In late 1985, Saudi Arabia announced that it would change this role and would seek to recover some of its lost market share. On November 20, 1985, the price of West Texas intermediate crude was $31.75 per barrel. The Saudi announcement was made on December 9, 1985. By early 1986, oil prices had dropped to $10 per barrel, reducing oil prices by 68.5%.

These factors of change and price instability have characterized the oil industry over the years. The oil industry has engaged in continuous efforts to deal with its turbulent environments.

The Setting for Oil Industry Mergers in 1997 to 1999

Oil prices near the end of 1996 had reached levels of over $25 a barrel as shown in Table 10.3. By early 1999, oil prices had dropped to below $11 a barrel, a decline of approximately 60%. By November 1999, oil prices had moved up to the $26 per barrel range.

As in other industries with cash flows in excess of positive NPV (related) investment opportunities, oil companies tried diversification (Jensen, 1986). These efforts resulted in declines in shareholder values, and the unrelated businesses were sold. The oil companies then engaged in restructuring and other efforts to reduce costs. They invested in improved technologies to increase oil field recovery by more than 50%. Data from the annual *Performance Profiles of Major Energy Producers 1997* (U.S. Energy Information Administration) shows that finding costs (in 1997 dollars)

Table 10.4   Return to Shareholders (Annual Returns Net of CRSP VW Index)

	1989–1998	1993–1998	1995–1998	1998 Revenues ($ Millions)
Exxon Corp.	0.71%	3.62%	5.59%	100,697
British Petroleum PLC	1.62%	5.84%	2.46%	57,073
Royal Dutch Petroleum Co.	2.88%	−1.06%	−5.53%	56,215
Mobil Corp.	1.17%	−2.63%	−5.60%	46,287
Texaco Inc.	−2.01%	−1.15%	−6.22%	30,910
Amoco Corp.	−3.69%	−5.93%	−5.73%	26,695
Chevron Corp.	0.07%	−1.99%	−3.83%	26,187
Phillips Petroleum Co.	−3.86%	−9.66%	−14.12%	11,545
Atlantic Richfield Co. (ARCO)	−8.04%	−9.20%	−11.16%	10,303
Sunoco Inc.	−11.30%	−14.04%	−4.26%	6,854
Occidental Petroleum Corp.	−10.69%	−14.17%	−22.93%	6,596
Amerada Hess Corp.	−12.02%	−18.91%	−22.90%	6,590
Unocal Corp.	−8.74%	−13.23%	−20.74%	5,003
Regression: Net Returns vs. Revenues				
Intercept	−8.63%	−13.06%	−16.39%	
t-stat	−5.982	−7.484	−6.750	
Coefficient	1.489E-06	2.234E-06	2.509E-06	
t-stat	4.195	5.198	4.197	
R-square	0.615	0.711	0.616	

for the 20 largest companies covered by the performance profiles dropped from over $20 per barrel of oil equivalent in 1979 to 1981 to less than $5 per barrel by 1993 to 1995 (U.S. Energy Information Administration, 1997, p. 69). Similarly, lifting costs including taxes had been reduced to $4.60 per barrel in 1997 for onshore activity and to $4.19 a barrel for foreign activity. Production costs, which were $7.20 in the mid-1980s, had been reduced to $4.10 per barrel by 1990.

Restructuring, investment in technology, and cost reduction had helped oil companies achieve profitability at oil prices in the $16 to $18 per barrel range. But the gains from these efforts began leveling off in the 1990s. During the first half of the 1990s, finding costs fell at half the rate achieved in the 1980s. After 1995, finding costs began to rise to a degree that erased the reductions of the early 1990s. For 1995 to 1997, compared to 1994 to 1996, worldwide finding costs rose 13% (U.S. Energy Information Administration, 1997, p. 69). Refined product margins since 1989 have been below $1.50 per barrel, and during 1991 to 1996 they were below $1 per barrel.

Despite the efforts to reduce costs, returns to shareholders (market adjusted) have been uneven across companies (Table 10.4). Over the previous 1989–1998 period, only BP and Shell had earned returns significantly higher than the market. The

Table 10.5   Return to Shareholders (Annual Returns Net of DJ Oil Majors Industry Group Index)

	1989–1998	1993–1998	1995–1998	1998 Revenues ($ Millions)
Exxon Corp.	6.99%	9.45%	11.32%	100,697
British Petroleum PLC	7.90%	11.66%	8.19%	57,073
Royal Dutch Petroleum Co.	9.16%	4.77%	0.20%	56,215
Mobil Corp.	7.45%	3.19%	0.13%	46,287
Texaco Inc.	4.28%	4.68%	−0.49%	30,910
Amoco Corp.	2.60%	−0.11%	0.01%	26,695
Chevron Corp.	6.35%	3.83%	1.90%	26.187
Phillips Petroleum Co.	2.42%	−3.84%	−8.39%	11,545
Atlantic Richfield Co. (ARCO)	−1.76%	−3.38%	−5.43%	10,303
Sunoco Inc.	−5.02%	−8.21%	1.48%	6,854
Occidental Petroleum Corp.	−4.41%	−8.35%	−17.19%	6,596
Amerada Hess Corp.	−5.74%	−13.09%	−17.17%	6,590
Unocal Corp.	−2.46%	−7.41%	−15.01%	5,003
Regression: Net Returns vs. Revenues				
Intercept	−2.34%	7.24%	−10.66%	
t-stat	−1.625	−4.149	−4.389	
Coefficient	1.489E-06	2.234E-06	2.509E-06	
t-stat	4.195	5.198	4.197	
R-square	0.615	0.711	0.616	

returns for Exxon, Mobil, and Chevron were slightly positive. Shareholder returns net of the market were negative for 8 of these 13 largest oil companies. For the 1993–1998 period, BP and Exxon had shareholder returns above the benchmark, while the other eleven companies had returns below, with most substantially underperforming the market benchmark. For the most recent three years, the situation was similar. Net shareholder returns were positive for BP and Exxon but negative for the other eleven companies. Amoco and ARCO, before their acquisition by BP, had experienced negative net returns to shareholders for all three time periods analyzed.

When the benchmark is the annual returns net of the Dow Jones Oil Majors Industry Group Index, the pattern of relationships tell the same story (Table 10.5). The adjusted returns for the individual companies with the oil industry group benchmark are improved. This is evidence that the oil group underperformed the broader market index. This implies that repeated negative surprises had an impact on the oil industry.

Tables 10.4 and 10.5 also contain data on regression relationships between the 1998 revenues and the returns to shareholders. The relationships are statistically significant, with high *t*-stats. The economic interpretation of the results is that the largest companies were the lowest cost producers. This suggests the source of the benefits in the oil industry mergers in which the larger firms acquired relatively smaller firms. The acquirers were extending their low cost exploration and operating skills to the assets of the acquired firms.

The M&A activities of the oil industry should be viewed in this broader perspective of the efforts by oil companies to increase efficiencies, to reduce costs, to invest in new technologies, and to seek new profitable investment opportunities. The M&A activities should be viewed as one of a number of efforts to achieve returns to shareholders higher than market benchmarks.

The Reasons for the Exxon–Mobil Merger

The motivations for the Exxon–Mobil combination reflect the industry pressures we have summarized. By combining complementary assets, Exxon Mobil would have a stronger presence in the regions of the world with the highest potential for future oil and gas discoveries and production. The combined company would also be in a stronger position to invest in programs involving large outlays with high prospective returns and risk. Exxon's experience in deepwater exploration in West Africa would combine with Mobil's production and exploration acreage in Nigeria and Equatorial Guinea. In the Caspian region, Exxon's strong presence in Azerbaijan will combine with Mobil's similar position in Kazakhstan, including its significant interest in the Tengiz field and its presence in Turkmenistan. Complementary exploration and production operations also exist in South America, Russia, and eastern Canada.

Near-term operating synergies from combining complementary operations in the amount of $2.8 billion were predicted. Two-thirds of the benefits would come from eliminating duplicate facilities and excess capacity. It was estimated that the combined general and administrative costs would be reduced. Additional synergy benefits would also come from applying each company's best business practices across their worldwide operations.

With this background, we next turn to a financial analysis of the transaction.

Valuation Analysis of the Exxon–Mobil Merger

The basic characteristics of the Exxon–Mobil deal are set forth in Table 10.6. Exxon had a market value, premerger, of $175 billion, compared with $59 billion for Mobil. Exxon commanded a P/E ratio of about 24 versus 18 for Mobil. Exxon paid 1.32 shares for each share of Mobil. Since Mobil had 780 million shares outstanding, Exxon paid 1,030 million shares, times the $72 share price of Exxon, for a total of slightly over $74 billion. This was a 26.3% premium over the $59 billion Mobil market cap.

Table 10.7 shows that premerger, the equity value of Exxon shares represented 75% of the combined market value. Postmerger, the premium paid to Mobil caused the proportion of ownership to drop to about 70% for Exxon and rise to 30% for Mobil. This demonstrates the fallacy of the statement sometimes made: "In a stock-for-stock transaction, the terms of the deal don't matter because you are only exchanging paper." The terms of the deal determine the proportionate ownership in the combined company.

Table 10.6   Exxon–Mobil Financial Relations

	Exxon	Mobil
Market Value (billions)[1]	$175.0	$58.7
Book Value (billions)[2]	$43.7	$19.0
Market Value/Book Value	4.0	3.1
LTM Net Income (millions)[3]	$7,410	$3,272
PE Ratio	23.6	17.9
Total Paid (billions)	$74.1	
Premium Over Market		
Amount (billions)	$15.4	
Percent	26.3%	
Premium Over Book		
Amount (billions)	$55.1	
Percent	290.2%	

[1]*Market value as of Nov. 20, 1998.*
[2]*Book Value as of Sept. 30, 1998; source 1998 3Q 10Q.*
[3]*LTM net income is through Sept. 30, 1998. LTM = last 12 months.*

Table 10.7   Exxon–Mobil Deal Terms

	Dollar Amounts			Percentage	
	Exxon	Mobil	Total	Exxon	Mobil
Premerger					
Share Price[1]	$72.00	$75.25			
Shares Outstanding (millions)[2]	2,431	780			
Total Market Value (billions)	$175.0	$58.7	$233.7	74.9%	25.1%
Exchange Terms	1.32	for	1		
Postmerger					
Number of shares (millions)	2,431	1,030	3,461	70.2%	29.8%

[1]*Share prices as of Nov. 20, 1998, a few days before runup in stock prices; announced Dec. 1, 1998.*
[2]*Shares outstanding are as of 1998 3Q 10Qs*

Cost of Capital for Exxon and Mobil

Because it is used throughout the analysis, we next make an estimate of the cost of capital for Exxon and Mobil using CAPM. Published sources such as Value Line estimate a beta of 0.85 for Exxon and 0.75 for Mobil. Beta estimates are, of course, subject to estimation error. However, there is a logic behind beta levels below 1 for oil companies. Oil company stocks are greatly influenced by the oil supply policies of the dominant OPEC oil-producing nations as well as returns on the market.

With long-term treasuries in the 6% range, we have a reasonable estimate of the risk-free rate. We next consider the market equity risk premium (ERP). For many years, based on patterns of the long-term relationship between stock and bond returns, the market equity premium appeared to be in the range of 6.5% to 7.5%. But by the mid-1990s, a new paradigm for a new economy began to emerge. Academics and practitioners have moved toward using 4% to 5% as the market price of risk (Welch, 1999).

For reasons discussed in the previous chapter, we use a risk-free rate of 6% and a market equity risk premium of 5%. Exxon, with a beta of 0.85, would have an estimated cost of equity capital of 10.25% using CAPM. Mobil, with a beta of 0.75, would have a cost of equity capital of 9.75%.

Exxon has a AAA bond rating, with yields to maturity at about 120 basis points above treasuries. This would give a before-tax cost of debt for Exxon of about 7.2%. Mobil has an AA bond rating, requiring an additional 20 to 30 basis points over the Exxon yield to maturity, giving a before-tax cost of debt for Mobil of about 7.5%. These pretax cost of debt estimates indicate a risk differential of about three percentage points between equity and debt costs for Exxon and somewhat less than that for Mobil, providing further plausibility support for our cost of equity estimates.

Theory calls for market weights to be used in assigning weights to the cost of equity and the cost of debt to obtain a firm's weighted cost of capital. We have analyzed the leverage policies of the oil companies in some detail (Siu and Weston, 1996). Exxon has had debt-to-total firm value ratios at book as high as 30% to 40% but moving toward 20% in recent years. However, during major acquisition or other investment programs, debt-to-book ratios have been at the higher 40% level. At market values, these ratios would be substantially reduced. A similar analysis would apply for Mobil. We believe it would be reasonable to use 30% and 70% proportions for the debt and equity weights. Effective cash tax rates have averaged 35% for Exxon and 40% for Mobil. Accordingly, the weighted cost of capital for the two companies would be

$$\text{Exxon} = 0.7\,(0.1025) + (0.3)\,(0.072)\,(0.65) = 8.6\%$$

$$\text{Mobil} = 0.7\,(0.0975) + (0.3)\,(0.075)\,(0.60) = 8.2\%$$

The mix of upstream and downstream activities of the two companies, and the combination of different geographic areas of operations would increase the stability of the combined cash flows. The larger size of the companies would enable them to take on larger and riskier investment programs than either could do independently. The critical mass size requirements for research and development efforts in all segments of the oil industry have been increasing, so the combination would be risk-reducing in that dimension as well. The cost of capital for the combined firms could be in the range of 8.3% to 8.5%. We use 8.4% as a base for further sensitivity analysis.

Premium Recovery

We analyze the effects of the merger in two ways. First, we calculate the value impacts of a range of synergy estimates. Second, we present a financial value driver framework for calculating the value gain or loss to Exxon Mobil shareholders.

Table 10.8 Market Price Change for Exxon Mobil

1. Synergies (millions)	$0	$1,000	$2,000	$3,000	$4,000	$5,000	$6,000
2. Addition to value:							
8.4% discount factor (billions)	$0	$12	$24	$36	$48	$60	$71
3. New market value (billions)	$233.7	$245.6	$257.5	$269.4	$281.3	$293.3	$305.2
4. New Exxon price per share	$67.54	$70.98	$74.42	$77.86	$81.30	$84.74	$88.18
5. Exxon % change in market price	−6.2%	−1.4%	3.4%	8.1%	12.9%	17.7%	22.5%
6. New Mobil price per share	$89.15	$93.69	$98.23	$102.77	$107.32	$111.86	$116.40
7. Mobil % change in market price	18.5%	24.5%	30.5%	36.6%	42.6%	48.6%	54.7%

Dilution/Accretion Analysis

In Table 10.8, we postulate a range of synergies. With no synergies, Mobil shareholders achieve 18.5% accretion in share price. Exxon shareholders suffer dilution of 6.2%. We explain this result to convey the logic of Table 10.8. With no synergies the total market value of the two companies is the sum of their premerger levels, $234 billion. We divide by the postmerger total shares of 3,461 million to obtain a postmerger price without synergies of $67.54. Mobil shareholders receive 1.32 shares times the $67.54 per share price, which gives $89.15, representing accretion of 18.5%. Exxon shareholders have a base of $72 so suffer a value dilution of 6.2%.

Analyst articles suggest synergies in the range of $3 billion to $6 billion per year. Treating these as constant cash flows, the applicable 8.4% cost of capital would yield value increases of $36 billion to $60 billion. These amounts can be translated into increases in per share values as above. Table 10.8 shows that at synergies somewhat under $2 billion Exxon begins to experience accretion in its postmerger market price.

Value Driver Analysis

We next perform the analysis using a DCF value driver model. Instead of relating investment as a constant percentage of sales, we relate investment to the change in sales. The basic valuation expression that we developed in chapter 9, equation (9.3), simplifies the derivation process. An argument can be made that investment requirements should be a function of the change in sales, because if sales declined, no investment would take place. By the same logic, it is the incremental profit from incremental investment rather than the average profit rate that is relevant for decision making. A firm might have a zero return on incremental investment, but its profit ratio could remain high. For example, a firm has revenues of $100,000. A growth in sales of 10% would be $10,000. If the operating margin on revenues is 12%, the firm has operating income of $12,000. If the firm earns a zero return on the incremental investment of $10,000, the operating margin on revenues would be the original operating income of $12,000 divided by sales of $110,000, which equals 10.91%. Clearly it is important to know that the incremental investment associated with the incremental

Table 10.9 Valuation of Exxon

Inputs	
REV_1 = Period 1 Revenues	150,000
g = Sales Growth	10.0%
COGS = Cost of Goods Sold Margin	83.0%
SGA = Selling, General, & Adm. Margin	6.4%
DEPR = Depr Margin	2.7%
NOI = Net Operating Income Margin	7.9%
T = Tax Rate	35.0%
k = Cost of Capital	8.6%
n = Number of Periods	15
WC = Net investment in working capital	4%
FIX = Net investment in fixed assets	10%
g_t = Post-terminal year growth rate	0%
Marketable Securities	—
Total Interest-Bearing Debt	8,700
Number of Shares (millions)	2,425
Value	
Present Value of FCF	$ 87,659
Present Value of TV	$ 98,670
Total Present Value	$186,329
Plus: Marketable Securities	—
Total Value of the firm	$186,329
Less: Total Interest-Bearing Debt	8,700
Equity Value	$177,629
Number of Shares (millions)	2,425
EPS	$ 3.18
Value per Share	$ 73.25

sales produces zero profits. The relatively small decline in the profitability-to-sales ratio could be misleading in the analysis of future investments. Hence, the valuation formula that we employ in this analysis measures profitability in relation to investment on an incremental basis and investment normalized by after-tax NOI. The resulting expression, similar in spirit to equation (9.3), is equation (10.1). The new term in the equation is b, defined as $b = I_t / [X_t(1 - T)]$.

$$V_0 = R_0[m(1 - T)(1 - b)]\sum_{t=1}^{n} \frac{(1 + g)^t}{(1 + k)^t} + \frac{R_0(1 + g)^n[m(1 - T)]}{k(1 + k)^n} \qquad (10.1)$$

The analysis can also be made using the standard DCF value driver model. We present the analysis for the companies first on a stand-alone basis and then com-

Table 10.10   Valuation of Mobil

Inputs	
REV_1 = Period 1 Revenues	75,000
g = Sales Growth	10.0%
COGS = Cost of Goods Sold Margin	85.0%
SGA = Selling, General, & Adm. Margin	6.4%
DEPR = Depr Margin	2.7%
NOI = Net Operating Income Margin	5.9%
T = Tax Rate	40.0%
k = Cost of Capital	8.2%
n = Number of Periods	15
WC = Net investment in working capital	4%
FIX = Net investment in fixed assets	10%
g_t = Post-terminal year growth rate	0%
Marketable Securities	—
Total Interest-Bearing Debt	7,700
Number of Shares (millions)	800
Value	
Present Value of FCF	$26,527
Present Value of TV	$37,700
Total Present Value	$64,227
Plus: Marketable Securities	—
Total Value of the firm	$64,227
Less: Total Interest-Bearing Debt	7,700
Equity Value	$56,527
Number of Shares (millions)	800
EPS	$ 3.32
Value per Share	$ 70.66

bined. We use an initial forecast of next year's revenues of $150 billion for Exxon and $75 billion for Mobil. Tables 10.9 and 10.10 indicate roughly similar cost structure patterns for Exxon and Mobil except for a higher net operating income margin of 7.9% for Exxon versus 5.9% for Mobil. We use the actual cash basis tax rates of 35% for Exxon and 40% for Mobil. We use 8.6% for the cost of capital for Exxon and 8.2% for the cost of capital for Mobil. Given the long planning cycles and methods of extending the life of highly productive discoveries, a competitive advantage period of 15 years is plausible for each company.

The valuation for Exxon in Table 10.9 is very close to its premerger price of $72. The indicated value per share for Mobil in Table 10.10 is $70.66. This is

Table 10.11 Valuation of Combined Exxon Mobil

Inputs	
REV_1 = Period 1 Revenues	225,000
g = Sales Growth	10.0%
COGS = Cost of Goods Sold Margin	82.8%
SGA = Selling, General, & Adm. Margin	6.4%
DEPR = Depr Margin	2.7%
NOI = Net Operating Income Margin	8.1%
T = Tax Rate	35.0%
k = Cost of Capital	8.4%
n = Number of Periods	15
WC = Net investment in working capital	4%
FIX = Net investment in fixed assets	10%
g_t = Post-terminal year growth rate	0%
Marketable Securities	—
Total Interest-Bearing Debt	16,400
Number of Shares (millions)	3,481
Value	
Present Value of FCF	$138,000
Present Value of TV	$159,720
Total Present Value	$297,720
Plus: Marketable Securities	—
Total Value of the firm	$297,720
Less: Total Interest-Bearing Debt	16,400
Equity Value	$281,320
Number of Shares (millions)	3,481
EPS	$ 3.40
Value per Share	$ 80.82

somewhat below its premerger share price of $75.25, which we believe contained some probability of a takeover at a premium.

In Table 10.11, we begin the analysis of the results for the combination. A weighted (by revenues) average of the net operating income margins gives 7.2%. A synergy estimate of $2 billion represents 0.9% of revenues. So the combined net operating margin could be 8.1%. This would result in a total combined equity value of $281 billion.

Many judgments are required in estimating the future behavior of the value drivers. A careful analysis of future industry developments and the relative positions of individual firms is required. To assess the impact of changes on the future behavior of the key value drivers, we perform a sensitivity analysis. In Table 10.12,

Table 10.12 Exxon–Mobil Combination

Sensitivity of Equity Value ($ billions) to the Value Drivers

% Change	REV₁	V	g	V	NOI	V	T	V	k	V	FIX	V	WC	V	N	V
Base	$225		10.00%		8.10%		35.00%		8.40%		10.00%		4.00%		15.00	
−20%	$180.0	$221.8	8.00%	$235.4	6.48%	$213.0	28.00%	$318.1	6.72%	$393.4	8.00%	$287.6	3.20%	$283.8	12.00	$244.4
−18%	$184.5	$227.7	8.20%	$239.6	6.64%	$219.8	28.70%	$314.4	6.89%	$379.4	8.20%	$287.0	3.28%	$283.6	12.30	$248.0
−16%	$189.0	$233.7	8.40%	$243.8	6.80%	$226.6	29.40%	$310.8	7.06%	$366.1	8.40%	$286.3	3.36%	$283.3	12.60	$251.6
−14%	$193.5	$239.6	8.60%	$248.2	6.97%	$233.5	30.10%	$307.1	7.22%	$353.5	8.60%	$285.7	3.44%	$283.1	12.90	$255.3
−12%	$198.0	$245.6	8.80%	$252.6	7.13%	$240.3	30.80%	$303.4	7.39%	$341.6	8.80%	$285.1	3.52%	$282.8	13.20	$259.0
−10%	$202.5	$251.5	9.00%	$257.2	7.29%	$247.1	31.50%	$299.7	7.56%	$330.3	9.00%	$284.5	3.60%	$282.6	13.50	$262.6
−8%	$207.0	$257.5	9.20%	$261.8	7.45%	$254.0	32.20%	$296.0	7.73%	$319.5	9.20%	$283.8	3.68%	$282.3	13.80	$266.3
−6%	$211.5	$263.5	9.40%	$266.5	7.61%	$260.8	32.90%	$292.4	7.90%	$309.3	9.40%	$283.2	3.76%	$282.1	14.10	$270.1
−4%	$216.0	$269.4	9.60%	$271.4	7.78%	$267.7	33.60%	$288.7	8.06%	$299.5	9.60%	$282.6	3.84%	$281.8	14.40	$273.8
−2%	$220.5	$275.4	9.80%	$276.3	7.94%	$274.5	34.30%	$285.0	8.23%	$290.2	9.80%	$281.9	3.92%	$281.6	14.70	$277.6
0%	$225.0	$281.3	10.00%	$281.3	8.10%	$281.3	35.00%	$281.3	8.40%	$281.3	10.00%	$281.3	4.00%	$281.3	15.00	$281.3
2%	$229.5	$287.3	10.20%	$286.5	8.26%	$288.2	35.70%	$277.6	8.57%	$272.8	10.20%	$280.7	4.08%	$281.1	15.30	$285.1
4%	$235.0	$293.2	10.40%	$291.7	8.42%	$295.0	36.40%	$274.0	8.74%	$264.7	10.40%	$280.1	4.16%	$280.8	15.60	$288.9
6%	$238.5	$299.2	10.60%	$297.1	8.59%	$301.8	37.10%	$270.3	8.90%	$257.0	10.60%	$279.4	4.24%	$280.6	15.90	$292.7
8%	$243.0	$305.1	10.80%	$302.6	8.75%	$308.7	37.80%	$266.6	9.07%	$249.6	10.80%	$278.8	4.32%	$280.3	16.20	$296.6
10%	$247.5	$311.1	11.00%	$308.2	8.91%	$315.5	38.50%	$262.9	9.24%	$242.5	11.00%	$278.2	4.40%	$280.1	16.50	$300.4
12%	$252.0	$317.0	11.20%	$313.9	9.07%	$322.3	39.20%	$259.2	9.41%	$235.6	11.20%	$277.5	4.48%	$279.8	16.80	$304.3
14%	$256.5	$323.0	11.40%	$319.7	9.23%	$329.2	39.90%	$255.6	9.58%	$229.1	11.40%	$276.9	4.56%	$279.6	17.10	$308.2
16%	$261.0	$329.0	11.60%	$325.7	9.40%	$336.0	40.60%	$251.9	9.74%	$222.9	11.60%	$276.3	4.64%	$279.3	17.40	$312.1
18%	$265.5	$334.9	11.80%	$331.8	9.56%	$342.8	41.30%	$248.2	9.91%	$216.8	11.80%	$275.7	4.72%	$279.1	17.70	$316.0
20%	$270.0	$340.9	12.00%	$338.0	9.72%	$349.7	42.00%	$244.5	10.08%	$211.1	12.00%	$275.0	4.80%	$278.8	18.00	$319.9
Elasticity																
+20%	1.058		1.007		1.215		−0.654		−1.249		−0.112		−0.045		0.686	
−20%	1.058		0.816		1.215		−0.654		−1.991		−0.112		−0.045		0.657	

we calculate the elasticities of the response in the value levels to upward and downward changes in each of the value drivers. The analysis holds constant the levels of the other value drivers while one is changed. The elasticities shown in the bottom part of Table 10.12 are based on the maximum percent changes calculated. The elasticities are positive for the initial level of revenues, the growth rate in revenues, the net operating income margin, and the period of competitive advantage. The elasticities are negative for tax rates, cost of capital, and investment requirements. The logic for taxes and the cost of capital are obvious. The negative elasticity for investment requirements results from the construction of the sales growth DCF spreadsheet model. In this model when the investment requirements ratio changes, the growth rate remains unchanged so the profitability ratio changes in the opposite direction. In other models, such as in the Miller and Modigliani (MM) (1961) dividend paper, growth is defined as the product of profitability and investment requirements, which would have a positive elasticity.

From a business economic standpoint, the sensitivity analysis shown in Table 10.12 enables the decision maker to identify the relative power of the value drivers in the valuation of the enterprise. In consequence, an information system for monitoring the future behavior of the critical levels of value drivers can be put in place. The analysis provides a planning framework for improving the performance of the firm. The relative influence of each of the value drivers is depicted graphically in Figure 10.1.

In Table 10.13, we illustrate how to test for increases in shareholder value by analysis of the combined operations. Table 10.13 begins with the respective premerger values. Postmerger, we start with the value of the combined companies at $281 billion from Table 10.11. We deduct the $74 billion paid to Mobil. This leaves a remainder of $207 billion. The premerger value of Exxon was $175 billion. Hence the gain from the merger was $32 billion. Since the original Exxon shareholders own 70% of the combined company, the acquisition adds $22.4 billion to the value of their shares. Mobil shareholders (the target or acquired firm) had already received a premium of $15 billion (Table 10.6), to which can now be added their $9.6 billion share to total $24.6 billion.

An alternative approach is to compare the premium paid with the expected improvement in the value of the target. An example is Rappaport's analysis of Gillette's acquisition of Duracell (Rappaport, 1998). His analysis calculates the value of Duracell as a stand-alone company and its change in value resulting from the combination. The four major operating synergies discussed involve global distribution, product developments, marketing relationships, and cost efficiencies. But all these potential synergies involve the interdependencies between the two operations. Hence, we would argue that the analysis should be made with reference to the combined companies rather than the target alone. The reason this is important is that for large premiums, the reduction in costs or the improvement of sales growth rates for the target alone sometimes appears impossibly large for the requisite value increases.

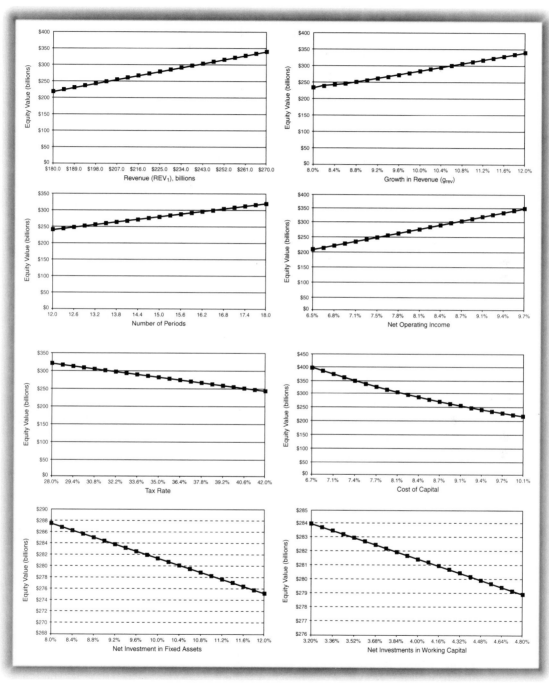

Figure 10.1 Exxon—Mobil Combination—Sensitivity of Equity Value to the Value Drivers

Table 10.13   Test of Merger Performance—
Exxon–Mobil Example

	($ in billions)	
Premerger		
	Market Caps	**Ownership Proportions**
Exxon	$175	74.5%
Mobil	$ 59	25.5%
Total	$234	100.0%
Postmerger		
Combined value	$281	
Paid to Mobil	$ 74	
Remainder	$207	
Exxon premerger	$175	
Gain from merger		$32.0
Portion to Exxon 70%		$22.4
Portion to Mobil 30%		$ 9.6

The plausibility of the foregoing analysis of value increases is supported by an event analysis of the announcement of the Exxon–Mobil combination. This is shown in Table 10.14 and Figure 10.2. Adjusted for the AMEX Oil Index, the cumulated return for the 10 trading days prior to the announcement date of December 1, 1998 was 16.2% for Mobil, and a positive return of almost 1% for Exxon. By the tenth trading day after the merger announcement, the cumulative adjusted returns for Mobil were 23.7% and for Exxon 6.3%. These event returns are consistent with the prior discussion of the reasons for the merger, the estimates of synergies, and the financial forecasts of the value drivers.

With the large fluctuations in oil prices, we recognize that the net operating income margin would fluctuate. We performed regressions of all income statement and balance sheet items (including the net operating margin) in relation to sales over the period 1979 through 1998 as well as for subsegments within that period. The relationships yielded t-statistics mostly significant at the 10% level or better. The operating margins used in the projections are based on levels that have prevailed over extended time periods. For short-term analysis, we could use different levels of operating margins.

In the joint Exxon–Mobil proxy to shareholders, dated April 5, 1999, the fairness opinions of JP Morgan for Exxon and Goldman Sachs for Mobil employed other valuation methodologies, including comparable companies, similar transactions, and other financial market relationships. Their results are consistent with the analysis we have presented.

Table 10.14 Exxon and Mobil Stock Returns

Date	XOI AMEX Oil Index	Return on AMEX Oil Index	Cumulative Actual Return	MOB	MOB Return	Cumulative Actual Return	Cumulative Adjusted Return	XON	XON Return	Cumulative Actual Return	Cumulative Adjusted Return
11/13/98	445.87			73.44				72.88			
11/16/98	442.63	-0.727%	-0.727%	72.63	-1.107%	-1.107%	-0.380%	71.44	-1.972%	-1.972%	-1.245%
11/17/98	436.80	-1.317%	-2.044%	71.94	-0.946%	-2.053%	-0.009%	70.56	-1.225%	-3.197%	-1.153%
11/18/98	438.53	0.396%	-1.648%	73.63	2.345%	0.292%	1.940%	70.69	0.177%	-3.020%	-1.372%
11/19/98	433.27	-1.199%	-2.847%	73.50	-0.170%	0.122%	2.969%	69.88	-1.150%	-4.170%	-1.322%
11/20/98	441.16	1.821%	-1.026%	75.25	2.381%	2.503%	3.529%	72.00	3.041%	-1.129%	-0.102%
11/23/98	441.51	0.079%	-0.947%	76.19	1.247%	3.750%	4.697%	71.88	-0.174%	-1.302%	-0.355%
11/24/98	437.63	-0.879%	-1.826%	74.94	-1.641%	2.108%	3.934%	72.75	1.217%	-0.085%	1.741%
11/25/98	438.11	0.110%	-1.716%	78.38	4.587%	6.696%	8.412%	72.69	-0.085%	-0.170%	1.546%
11/27/98	455.90	4.061%	2.345%	85.50	9.091%	15.786%	13.442%	74.38	2.321%	2.151%	-0.194%
11/30/98	443.34	-2.755%	-0.410%	86.00	0.585%	16.371%	16.782%	75.00	0.840%	2.991%	3.402%
12/1/98	434.17	-2.068%	-2.479%	83.75	-2.616%	13.755%	16.234%	71.63	-4.500%	-1.509%	0.970%
12/2/98	426.20	-1.836%	-4.314%	84.19	0.523%	14.278%	18.592%	71.25	-0.524%	-2.032%	2.282%
12/3/98	421.58	-1.084%	-5.398%	84.50	0.371%	14.649%	20.047%	70.56	-0.964%	-2.997%	2.402%
12/4/98	428.15	1.558%	-3.840%	86.00	1.775%	16.424%	20.264%	71.50	1.328%	-1.669%	2.171%
12/7/98	431.51	0.785%	-3.055%	87.38	1.599%	18.023%	21.078%	72.94	2.011%	0.343%	3.398%
12/8/98	428.34	-0.735%	-3.790%	87.94	0.644%	18.667%	22.457%	73.19	0.343%	0.685%	4.475%
12/9/98	436.35	1.870%	-1.920%	88.19	0.284%	18.951%	20.871%	73.94	1.025%	1.710%	3.630%
12/10/98	429.49	-1.572%	-3.492%	88.81	0.709%	19.660%	23.152%	74.56	0.845%	2.555%	6.047%
12/11/98	429.20	-0.068%	-3.559%	88.88	0.070%	19.730%	23.289%	74.63	0.083%	2.639%	6.198%
12/14/98	425.81	-0.790%	-4.349%	89.38	0.563%	20.292%	24.642%	74.44	-0.251%	2.388%	6.737%
12/15/98	425.29	-0.122%	-4.471%	88.44	-1.048%	19.244%	23.715%	74.00	-0.588%	1.800%	6.271%

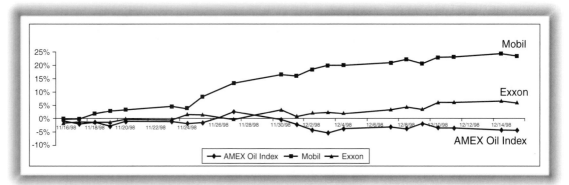

Figure 10.2 Cumulative Adjusted Returns

The use of historical data in valuation is only a starting point. The most valuable part of a valuation exercise is the business economics analysis of the industry dynamics and the firm's position in it. This provides a basis for the judgments on value driver levels. It also establishes a framework for strategic and competitive policy planning. The appropriate model for a synergistic merger requires analysis of its impact on the combined firm instead of the acquired firm alone. In the Exxon–Mobil transaction only a 25% premium was involved. We demonstrate that for a plausible valuation model only modest improvements in the value drivers are sufficient to recover the premium paid. For premiums in the 50% range the results would depend on the underlying business economics of the transaction.

Antitrust Issues

For large oil company mergers, antitrust issues are important. Antitrust agencies place great emphasis on market concentration, which we first address. As part of a broader study of the effects of M&A activity on industry concentration measures, we have collected data for the petroleum industry for selected years since 1975. These basic data were used to calculate concentration data using the Herfindahl–Hirschman Index (HHI or H index) adopted by the U.S. regulatory authorities in guidelines issued in 1982. Mergers in an industry with an H index below 1,000 are not considered to have anticompetitive consequences.

The H index measures are calculated for the petroleum industry in Table 10.15 for the years 1975 through 1996. In 1975, the H index started at about 410. It rose to 416 in 1979. In 1984, it dropped back to 377. In 1990, it declined again to 362, rising to 407 by 1995. In 1996, the index had moved to 415, about the same level as in 1979. It is clear that the H index for the petroleum industry has been well under the critical 1,000 level test in the guidelines employed by regulatory authorities. We updated the analysis for 1997 using data for 280 oil companies. The results are similar to those we report for 1975 through 1996.

In Table 10.16, the effects of a number of oil company mergers on the H index measures are shown. We begin with the merger of the two foreign oil firms, Total (SA) and Petrofina, using our 1997 data. For Total (SA) the initial H index was 4.93, for Petrofina, 1.90, summing to 6.83. Next we combine the revenues of $32,781 million for Total (SA) and $20,352 million for Petrofina to obtain $53,133. This sum is divided by the industry total revenues of $1,475,774 million to obtain a market share of 3.6%. This market share squared equals the new H index of 12.96 shown in Table 10.16. Thus, the industry H index is increased by 12.96 less 6.83 or 6.13 points. The oil industry H index in 1997 was 389.35; adding 6.13 gives the new H index of 395.48.

Total Fina's acquisition of Elf Aquitaine adds 22 points to the H index, increasing it to 417. The BP Amoco merger adds 29, resulting in an oil industry index of 447. The Exxon–Mobil merger would add another 83 points, bringing the index to 530. The BP Amoco–ARCO merger would add 51 points to bring the HHI for the industry up to 581. If a Chevron–Texaco merger took place, this would add another 18 points, so the new industry HHI would be 599. So with six mergers among the top 23 petroleum companies in the world, the HHI for the petroleum industry would rise from 389 points to 599 points, an increase of 210 points. The total HHI for the industry of 599 would still be well short of the 1,000 critical level specified in the regulatory guidelines.

The common sense of this is that although individual oil companies are large, they are in an industry that is also large, whether measured by revenues or by total assets. These are multibillion-dollar companies, but they are in a 1.5 trillion-dollar (revenues) industry. Thus, by the criteria of the U.S. regulatory authorities, the overall industry concentration measures are so far below the H index 1,000 threshold that from an aggregate industry standpoint antitrust concerns are not raised.

Emerging Competitive Forms

Preoccupation with measurement of concentration ratios misses the dynamism of the intensification of the new competitive patterns emerging in the oil and energy industries. Table 10.17 lists the diverse segments of the energy industry and the several forms of competitive strategies employed by illustrative firms. The integrated firms have long been in the traditional areas of oil and gas exploration and production, refining, and marketing. Less generally recognized is their significant penetration into the chemical industry, particularly petrochemicals. Table 10.18 shows that 10 petroleum companies occupy high ranking positions in U.S. chemical sales. The three U.S. megafirms occupy the ranks of 3, 11, and 13, with total chemical sales in 1998 of $19.1 billion.

The low cost advantages of the megafirms have now enabled them to be close to breakeven on oil prices as low as $15 per barrel. Improvements in technology and

Table 10.15 Petroleum Industry (Assets/Sales, in $ billion)

	1975 Assets	1975 H-Index	1979 Assets	1979 H-Index	1984 Sales	1984 H-Index	1990 Assets	1990 H-Index	1995 Assets	1995 H-Index	1996 Assets	1996 H-Index
1.	32.84	114.35	59.57	122.70	97.29	111.86	87.71	84.34	117.75	131.74	124.14	138.48
2.	28.35	85.22	49.49	84.69	77.12	70.29	60.34	39.92	91.30	79.20	95.53	82.01
3.	17.26	31.59	34.69	41.61	59.00	41.14	59.25	38.49	50.47	24.20	55.05	27.23
4.	15.05	24.02	27.51	26.17	47.10	26.22	51.87	29.50	49.43	23.21	47.14	19.97
5.	14.62	22.66	22.99	18.27	41.15	20.01	45.08	22.28	42.14	16.87	46.41	19.35
6.	12.90	17.64	19.73	13.46	29.49	10.28	42.31	19.63	40.50	15.58	39.75	14.20
7.	12.48	16.51	18.10	11.33	29.18	10.06	41.67	19.04	34.33	11.20	34.85	10.91
8.	12.43	16.38	17.26	10.30	28.89	9.86	35.09	13.50	31.98	9.72	33.74	10.23
9.	9.85	10.59	17.15	10.17	27.46	8.91	32.63	11.67	31.68	9.54	32.10	9.26
10.	8.60	7.84	16.13	9.00	25.02	7.40	32.21	11.37	29.85	8.47	30.20	8.20
11.	8.04	6.85	15.86	8.70	19.88	4.67	28.50	8.91	28.36	7.64	28.71	7.41
12.	7.36	5.74	14.29	7.06	18.19	3.91	25.98	7.40	27.60	7.24	28.06	7.08
13.	7.01	5.21	13.83	6.61	18.00	3.83	23.86	6.24	27.02	6.94	27.66	6.87
14.	6.77	4.86	13.09	5.92	16.76	3.32	22.10	5.35	25.69	6.27	26.96	6.53
15.	6.58	4.59	11.63	4.68	16.26	3.12	20.64	4.67	24.94	5.91	25.72	5.94
16.	5.56	3.28	11.03	4.21	16.20	3.10	19.74	4.27	24.00	5.47	25.45	5.82
17.	5.42	3.11	9.31	3.00	15.41	2.81	18.73	3.85	22.56	4.84	19.09	3.27
18.	5.18	2.84	9.21	2.93	15.33	2.78	17.63	3.41	17.92	3.05	19.00	3.24
19.	4.54	2.19	8.52	2.51	15.31	2.77	13.85	2.02	17.82	3.02	17.63	2.79
20.	4.38	2.03	7.46	1.92	13.25	2.07	12.65	1.75	16.95	2.73	17.63	2.79
21.	4.22	1.89	7.22	1.80	12.89	1.96	12.56	1.73	15.64	2.32	16.23	2.37
22.	4.14	1.82	7.00	1.69	12.87	1.96	12.31	1.66	14.61	2.03	16.14	2.34
23.	3.91	1.62	6.03	1.26	12.07	1.72	12.27	1.65	13.74	1.79	15.69	2.21
24.	3.78	1.51	6.01	1.25	11.30	1.51	12.13	1.61	13.51	1.73	13.79	1.71
25.	3.75	1.49	5.89	1.20	10.77	1.37	11.93	1.56	13.24	1.67	13.55	1.65
26.	3.64	1.40	5.56	1.07	10.77	1.37	11.83	1.53	12.09	1.39	12.08	1.31
27.	3.50	1.30	5.36	0.99	10.65	1.34	11.64	1.49	11.98	1.36	11.61	1.21
28.	3.24	1.11	5.09	0.90	9.81	1.14	11.53	1.46	11.57	1.27	11.61	1.21
29.	3.23	1.11	5.09	0.90	9.45	1.06	11.51	1.45	11.48	1.24	10.47	0.99
30.	3.21	1.09	4.90	0.83	9.27	1.02	9.85	1.06	10.66	1.08	10.15	0.93
31.	2.90	0.89	4.77	0.79	9.22	1.00	9.76	1.04	10.11	0.97	10.05	0.91
32.	2.48	0.65	4.32	0.65	8.42	0.84	9.23	0.93	9.89	0.93	9.12	0.75
33.	2.39	0.61	4.21	0.61	8.29	0.81	9.06	0.90	8.83	0.74	7.78	0.54

34.	2.15	0.49	3.98	0.55	8.26	0.81	8.44	0.78	7.76	0.57	7.68	0.53
35.	2.07	0.45	3.43	0.41	7.92	0.74	7.33	0.59	7.67	0.56	7.38	0.49
36.	2.01	0.43	3.37	0.39	7.83	0.72	6.20	0.42	7.20	0.49	7.27	0.47
37.	1.97	0.41	3.11	0.33	7.57	0.68	5.48	0.33	6.99	0.46	6.81	0.42
38.	1.75	0.32	3.02	0.32	7.24	0.62	5.26	0.30	6.06	0.35	6.10	0.33
39.	1.73	0.32	2.82	0.27	6.91	0.56	5.25	0.30	5.60	0.30	6.00	0.32
40.	1.70	0.31	2.81	0.27	6.78	0.54	5.12	0.29	5.42	0.28	5.74	0.30
41.	1.68	0.30	2.81	0.27	6.73	0.54	5.11	0.29	4.75	0.21	5.67	0.29
42.	1.62	0.28	2.74	0.26	6.65	0.52	5.01	0.28	4.53	0.19	4.68	0.20
43.	1.59	0.27	2.72	0.26	6.40	0.48	4.55	0.23	4.51	0.19	4.60	0.19
44.	1.56	0.26	2.68	0.25	6.20	0.45	4.47	0.22	4.49	0.19	4.41	0.17
45.	1.51	0.24	2.66	0.24	6.01	0.43	4.37	0.21	4.41	0.18	4.32	0.17
46.	1.39	0.20	2.63	0.24	5.77	0.39	4.29	0.20	4.31	0.18	4.29	0.17
47.	1.37	0.20	2.58	0.23	5.44	0.35	4.10	0.18	4.09	0.16	4.12	0.15
48.	1.35	0.19	2.41	0.20	5.40	0.34	3.69	0.15	3.90	0.14	3.79	0.13
49.	1.34	0.19	2.38	0.20	5.38	0.34	3.59	0.14	3.51	0.12	3.77	0.13
50.	1.29	0.18	2.34	0.19	5.24	0.32	3.53	0.14	3.38	0.11	3.77	0.13
51.	1.17	0.15	2.34	0.19	5.23	0.32	3.48	0.13	3.31	0.10	3.73	0.13
52.	1.16	0.14	2.29	0.18	5.12	0.31	3.47	0.13	3.23	0.10	3.65	0.12
53.	1.04	0.11	2.29	0.18	5.08	0.30	3.44	0.13	3.06	0.09	3.62	0.12
54.	1.02	0.11	2.18	0.16	5.00	0.30	3.36	0.12	3.01	0.09	3.43	0.11
55.	0.89	0.08	2.04	0.14	4.65	0.26	3.26	0.12	2.72	0.07	3.12	0.09
56.	0.89	0.08	2.03	0.14	4.39	0.23	3.20	0.11	2.68	0.07	2.86	0.07
57.	0.89	0.08	2.02	0.14	4.22	0.21	3.13	0.11	2.59	0.06	2.84	0.07
58.	0.80	0.07	1.97	0.13	4.17	0.21	2.97	0.10	2.49	0.06	2.74	0.07
59.	0.79	0.07	1.96	0.13	4.12	0.20	2.91	0.09	2.33	0.05	2.74	0.07
60.	0.77	0.06	1.88	0.12	4.08	0.20	2.85	0.09	2.27	0.05	2.70	0.07
Total	**307.11**		**537.79**		**919.86**		**955.04**		**1025.91**		**1054.92**	
Top 10 H-Index	84.6%		83.7%		83.9%		80.1%		81.1%		81.8%	
Top 20 H-Index	94.5%		95.1%		92.4%		93.3%		94.1%		94.3%	
Top 30 H-Index	98.0%		98.0%		96.3%		97.5%		98.0%		98.1%	
Top 10 H-Index	346.49		347.68		316.04		289.74		329.72		339.83	
Top 20 H-Index	387.21		395.23		348.42		337.62		382.83		391.59	
Top 30 H-Index	401.55		407.11		362.87		352.82		398.73		407.51	
HHI	**409.71**		**415.57**		**376.91**		**361.88**		**406.81**		**415.20**	

Table 10.16   Effects of Mergers on Oil Industry H-Index Measures

	Combined Revenues	Sum of Initial H Values	New H Index	Change in H Index	Cumulative Changes in Oil Industry H Index
Original H Index					389.35
Total–Petrofina	$53,133	6.83	12.96	6.13	395.48
TotalFina–Elf Aquitaine	$98,220	22.29	44.30	22.01	417.49
BP–Amoco	$123,871	41.27	70.45	29.18	446.67
Exxon–Mobil	$203,148	106.42	189.49	83.07	529.74
BP Amoco–ARCO	$143,143	42.98	94.08	51.10	580.84
Chevron–Texaco	$88,572	18.08	36.02	17.94	598.78

Table 10.17   Companies of the Oil and Gas Industry

Companies	Oil Exploration and Production	Gas Exploration and Production	Refining	Petro-chemicals	Oil Service	Marketing: Service Stations
Mega Integrated						
Exxon Mobil	X	X	X	X		X
BP Amoco	X	X	X	X		X
Royal Dutch Shell	X	X	X	X		X
Elf TotalFina	X	X	X	X		X
Large Integrated						
Texaco	X	X	X	X		X
Chevron	X	X	X	X		X
Phillips	X	X	X	X		X
Occidental	X	X		X		
Unocal	X	X		X		
Natural Gas						
Dynegy	X	X				
Petrochemical Specialists						
Huntsman				X		
Energy						
Enron	X	X				
AES						
MidAmerican Energy						
Specialists						
Apache	X	X				
Newfield	X	X				
Union Pac. Resources	X	X				
Ocean Energy	X	X				
Ultramar Diam. Sham.			X			X
Tosco			X			X
Schlumberger					X	
Halliburton					X	

cost structures also bring in substantial new supply quantities at prices in the $15 per barrel range. These developments place increased pressures on the other firms in the energy industry. They have reacted with new strategies drawing on increased use of relationships, alliances, joint ventures, focus, specialization, and mergers. The state-owned national oil companies (NOCs) are the dominant forces in OPEC with potentials and interests in expanding their roles, further dominating the publicly owned megafirms.

As shown in Table 10.17, the competitors to the megafirms occupy the broadest range of the activity grid. Traditionally, the petroleum industry has been characterized by a varied pattern of relationships among the majors, specialized firms, oil service firms, and the NOCs. Through alliances and joint ventures these relationships have been revitalized to respond to the new competitive dynamics of the industry. NOCs such as Saudi Arabia during 1998 began discussions about developing a gas business. Most of the firms

Stations with Food Marts	Energy Consultants	Basin Masters	Commodity Trading	Electricity Generation	Electricity Distribution	Gas Distribution
X				X		
X				X		
X				X		
X						
X						
X						
X						
				X		X
			X	X	X	X
	X			X	X	
				X	X	X
		X				
						X
X						
X						

Table 10.18   U.S. Chemical Sales of Petroleum Companies, 1998

Rank in U.S. Chemical Sales	Company Name	Chemical Sales ($ billions)
3	Exxon	10.5
11	BP Amoco	4.4
13	Shell Oil	4.2
15	Ashland Oil	4.0
19	Chevron	3.0
20	Occidental Petroleum	3.0
25	Phillips Petroleum	2.5
26	Mobil	2.4
29	Elf Atochem	2.2
35	Lubrizol	1.6

continue efforts to develop business with NOCs and OPEC nations. Many have knowledge and experience in exploration, drilling, and information technology to move toward systems for optimizing oil and gas production over the life cycle of a field. They also compete to develop new infrastructures in emerging markets. One focus is to develop a strong position geographically such as Unocal in Southeast Asia. Alliances and joint ventures help groups of firms in the development of long-term business relationships with NOCs and privatized entities. Another strategy is alliances and combinations between NOCs and some of the middle firms that could bring a broad range of expertise to the NOCs. This scenario is intriguing because, of the top 25 oil firms, 15 are at least partially state-owned. One of the large NOCs, such as Saudi Aramco, could conceivably become a megafirm by purchasing an operating company and broadening its interests.

Specialization is another important strategy. Tosco has expanded its position in refining and marketing. In this traditional low margin business it has developed management expertise to enable it to acquire refining assets from the majors and turn them into profitable activities. Similarly, Huntsman, a petrochemical firm, has profitably managed chemical units divested by petroleum companies. Oil field service firms such as Halliburton-Dresser and Schlumberger have been moving into creative resource management offerings.

Specialized firms as well as traditional operating companies have been leveraging their experience, reputations, and relationships to move into broader areas of the energy industry. New areas include basin masters, energy consultants, and the power businesses. Enron in particular has developed a broad vision of the energy industry. In addition to commodity trading, it has moved into electricity generation and distribution, gas distribution, and the world water market. It has articulated a strategic vision that a direct relationship with consumers will be critical for success in the energy industry.

Thus, the oil and energy industries are changing. Alliances, joint ventures, and other forms of relationships as well as merger activity have been competitive responses to the lower cost structures of the megafirms, the convergence of markets, deregulation, and the divestitures resulting from the tighter focus strategy pursued by some companies. Thus, the oil and energy industry competitive dynamism that resulted in HHI measures well below the critical 1,000 level has been invigorated rather than dampened by the M&A events that have been taking place.

Comments on the Exxon–Mobil Case Study

We have used the Exxon–Mobil merger to illustrate proposed methodology for analyzing mergers. The particulars of this case are less important than the approach utilized. The important generalization is that the merger must make sense in terms of the economics of the industry. The firm should also be sound from a social standpoint—it should intensify competition rather than dampen it. To further generalize, we next consider the analysis of M&A activity for firms in different industries at different stages in their life cycles.

VALUATION IN THE FRAMEWORK OF PRODUCT LIFE CYCLES

We begin with the widely used product life cycle construct, because it provides another key dimension of the dynamics of the firm. The usual depiction of the industry product life cycle is shown in Figure 10.3. The curve depicts growth at an increasing rate, an inflection point, growth at a decreasing rate, a maximum, and a decline. Figure 10.3 is for a product or industry, with the upper broken lines for a company. The individual firm seeks to avoid slow growth, maturity, and decline by adding new product life cycles, by improving products, adding new products, moving into new geographic markets, developing new capabilities and technologies. But beginning with the product life cycle we can identify the pressures that cause firms to repeatedly seek to superimpose new product life cycles. We identify seven segments: I, Strategic vision; II, innovation; III, super growth; IV, growth; V, maturity; VI, decline; and VII, renewal and restructuring.

Identifying seven segments is facilitated by additional considerations. The profit rate curve peaks near the inflection point of revenue growth. Peak profits stimulate substantial additions to capacity. As growth continues, unfavorable capacity-to-sales relationships cause profits to decline. As substitute products are introduced, the growth rate of revenues slows and begins to decline, causing profits to become negative. Free cash flows are likely to follow the profit curve at lower levels, reflecting investment requirements. As capacity-to-sales relationships deteriorate, investment requirements will drop sharply and become negative. Net external market financing requirements, the first segment, are negative, because initial financing is likely to be supplied by the entrepreneur and venture capital sources for plant and equipment, not leased. With initial sales, working capital requirements grow. At this stage additional plant and equipment investment and working capital requirements are financed by suppliers and commercial banks. For example, in the early stages, MCI's suppliers guaranteed its bank loans.

These relationships provide a basis for identification of the seven stages. In Table 10.19 we list the seven stages in the industry life cycle. In column 2 are listed industries that provide illustrative examples of each of these stages. As an initial basis

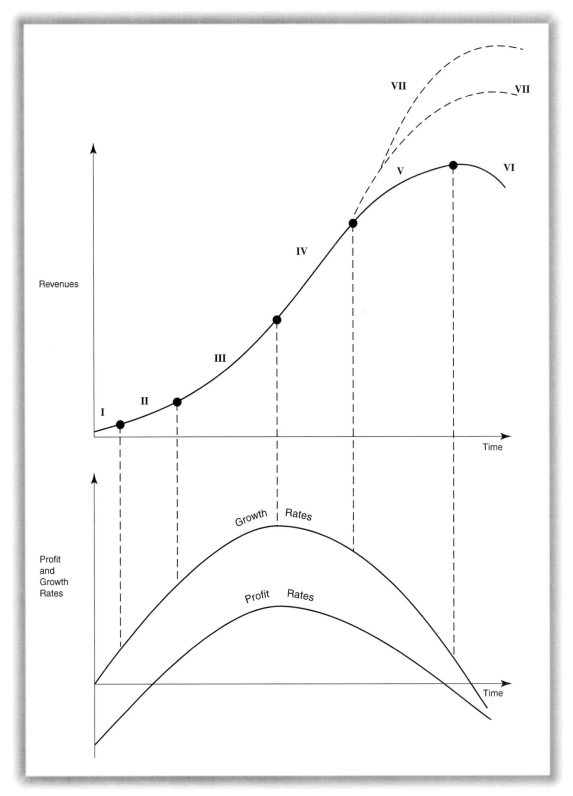

Figure 10.3 Product or Company Life Cycle

Table 10.19 Characteristics of Industry Stages

Stage	Industry Example	Revenue Characteristic	Profit Pattern	Type of Financing
I. Strategic vision	Internet	Beachhead revenues	Losses	Supplier financing
II. Innovation	Biotech	Accelerating revenue	Some net income	Increased external financing
III. Super growth	New telecommun	High levels of revenue	Strong profits	Ample external market financing
IV. Growth	Food	Revenue growth peaks	Profit margins level off	Most financing with internal cash flow
V. Maturity	Auto	Revenue growth slows	Profit margins narrow	Surplus cash
VI. Decline	Steel	Revenues flat or declining	Negative profit	Small cash flows
VII. Renewal	Oil	Revenue improves	Modest profit recovery	No external financing required

for distinguishing each stage, Table 10.19 also shows how the patterns of revenues, profits, and financing differ among the stages.

A quantitative basis for identifying the characteristics of each of the seven stages is set forth in Table 10.20. The key value drivers in a standard DCF spreadsheet valuation model have different patterns of relationships for each stage. We set revenues in period 1 at $1,000 to standardize for size. The resulting valuations, shown in line 10, can be expressed per dollar of revenue. Line 11 shows the value to cash flow multipliers for the different stages of the life cycle of an industry. Line 12 calculates another widely used relationship, the ratio of market to revenues. Clearly, this pattern shows that the market-to-revenue relationship can vary widely depending on the stage of the industry life cycle.

In line 2, the pattern of growth rates is shown to decline from a very high number for Internet companies to zero or negative for industries in decline. The NOI margin in line 3 is negative or small for the first stage. As an industry moves into a volume of revenues that demonstrates that an industry and its firms have a solid future, profit rates rise sharply. As the industry matures, profit rates decline. For an industry in decline, the NOI margin becomes zero or negative. Where numbers are zero or negative, we use 1% for convenience in computer computations. We do not vary tax rates across industry stages because so many variables would be involved. Also, by postulating tax neutrality across industry stages, we can focus on the underlying business and economic drivers.

Investment requirements are critical in the valuation analysis. In stage I, external investment requirements are low because of heavy reliance on supplier financing, as was indicated in Table 10.19. Internet companies are similar to patterns for earlier companies like MCI, which in its initial stage in the 1960s drew heavily on supplier financing and supplier guarantee of bank loans. This is particularly important because at very early stages accounting losses may be experienced. At the stage at which some firms in the industry are well launched, external financing requirements will be high, declining for subsequent stages.

n represents the number of years for which the firm will have a competitive advantage and therefore superior profit rates. The expected competitive advantage for firms with a sound strategic basis, launched in stage I, has the potential to be sustained for a long period of time. Optimistic expectations with respect to a potentially sustained period of competitive advantage leads to the high multiples depicted in line 11 for companies in attractive industries, such as Xerox as an early leader in copying in the 1960s and the early Internet companies and other high technology firms in the late 1990s.

The cost of capital is likely to be quite high because of high uncertainty associated with companies in the very early stages of an industry life cycle. Early leaders emerge, but thousands of imitators are likely to enter the industry, making the future uncertain for all. The cost of capital declines with each successive stage until uncertainty increases again as the stages of decline and renewal or restructuring are experienced.

In line 8 we introduce r, which is defined as the marginal profitability rate. It is the incremental after-tax cash flow related to the incremental amount of capital employed (investment). Implicit in any valuation formulation is the relationship between the rate earned on incremental investment and the firm's cost of capital. The larger the positive difference between r and k, the greater the ratio of the market value of an investment (the firm as a whole) and investment cost. This ratio is the market-to-book

Table 10.20 Value Driver Patterns for Industry Characteristics

	I Strategic Vision	II Innovation	III High Growth	IV Growth	V Maturity	VI Decline	VII Renewal/ Restructuring
Example:	Internet	Biotech	New Telecom	Food	Auto	Steel	Oil
1. Rev_1	$1,000	$1,000	$1,000	$1,000	$1,000	$1,000	$1,000
2. g	60%	40%	30%	14%	8%	0%	0%
3. NOI/Rev	1%	15%	10%	6%	4%	1%	4%
4. T	35%	35%	35%	35%	35%	35%	35%
5. n	40	20	15	10	5	0	0
6. k	25%	15%	13%	9%	9%	10%	10%
7. Inv. req.	2%	25%	20%	15%	14%	0%	0%
8. r	52%	55%	42%	30%	20%	—*	—*
9. b	115%	73%	71%	47%	40%	0%	0%
10. Value	$260,182	$28,962	$3,944	$828	$326	$65	$260
11. $V/NOI(1-T)$	40,028	297	61	21	13	10	10
12. Value/Rev	260.18	28.96	3.94	0.83	0.33	0.07	0.26
13. $r - k$	27%	40%	29%	21%	11%	0%	0%

*$r \leq k$.
Rev_1 = base year revenues
g = growth rate of revenues
NOI/Rev = net operating income margin
T = tax rate
n = number of supernormal growth years
k = cost of capital
Inv. req. = investment requirements
r = after-tax profitability rate
b = investment requirement rate.

ratio or in a proper context the q ratio. The spread by which r exceeds k, as shown by line 13 in Table 10.20, is 40 percentage points in stage II, declining in successive stages to 11% in stage V and becoming zero or negative as the stage of decline is reached.

In line 9 we express investment requirements (opportunities) normalized by after-tax cash flows. This gives a measure of the amount by which investment requirements will have to be financed from sources other than the cash flows of the current year. The ordering of line 9 is the same as the ordering of the investment requirements measured in relation to revenue growth, shown in line 5. The dimensions of the two are, of course, different. The product of r and b is always equal to g, as can be readily checked from the table. This is a useful property of the r and b terms, which are in spirit marginal profit rates and marginal investment requirements. The relationships between r and k are similarly a comparison between incremental measures: r is an incremental profit rate, and k should be properly defined and measured as the marginal weighted-average cost of capital. In some formulations of valuation equations, the $(r - k)$ term is explicitly set forth. Thus, the amount by which the marginal return on investment exceeds the rate at which the investment is financed multiplied times b, the investment opportunities rate, is the measure of incremental value creation. It is the net present value of investment formulation measured at the level of the firm. When r is greater than k, the higher the b, the higher the resulting value.

The stage of an industry's development will be a major influence on the value drivers of prospective merger partners, but it is not deterministic. Viewing industry stages as a first step provides perspective for understanding valuations in new industries such as the Internet as well as the general forces operating at each stage. But variations are found among firms in the same industry.

In Table 10.21 we present value driver relations based on regression analysis of historical accounting data (Compustat) for 1979 through 1998. Our sample consists of nine companies from the Value Line list of food companies. All percentages in the table are expressed in relation to revenues. Cost of Goods Sold percentages of revenues range from 35.1% for Kellogg to 85.6% for ADM. Selling, general, and administrative expense varies from 4.0% for ADM to 49.7% for Quaker. Depreciation and interest expense are low in absolute terms with a small range of variation. The net operating margin varies from under 5% to over 21%. Investment requirements (opportunities) also differ greatly.

The large variations could reflect differences in the product mix of these "food" companies. It could also reflect differences in management effectiveness. These differences highlight the role of valuation as a planning framework for dynamic financial management. Valuation provides a framework for the creation of business models central to the effective development of enterprise resource planning (ERP). This reformulation of valuation methodology also serves as a foundation for the analysis of individual mergers.

THE INTERNET AND ONLINE TECHNOLOGIES

Valuation of the Internet companies represents a new challenge. The Internet has resulted in a revolutionary distribution vehicle. It has grown from less than 5 million users in 1995 to over 100 million in 1999. The number of Internet service providers

Table 10.21 Value Driver Relations, 1979–1998

	Quaker Oats	ConAgra Sara Lee	ADM		Bestfoods	Campbell Soup	General Mills	Hershey	Kellogg
COGS	84.1%	85.6%	42.9%	42.4%	46.6%	46.0%	35.1%	37.9%	54.8%
SG&A	9.5%	4.0%	37.5%	32.1%	33.8%	34.0%	43.2%	49.7%	31.3%
DEPR	1.7%	3.6%	4.3%	3.8%	4.3%	4.3%	4.9%	3.4%	3.9%
INT EXP	1.4%	1.9%	1.9%	2.5%	1.3%	1.8%	1.4%	1.5%	1.5%
NOI	4.8%	6.8%	15.3%	21.7%	15.3%	15.8%	16.8%	9.0%	10.0%
NI	1.8%	4.1%	6.5%	9.7%	9.1%	8.0%	8.0%	5.0%	3.0%
TAX (Average rate)	35.2%	30.0%	36.7%	37.7%	37.6%	37.2%	36.8%	43.8%	37.0%

(ISPs) has grown from 1,200 in 1996 to 4,800 in 1999. The Internet market is global, with more than 150 countries having direct access to it. Two-thirds of users are from North America, and two-thirds of Internet hosts are in the United States.

As of mid-1999, there had been 107 Internet initial public offerings (IPOs) since the Netscape offering in August 1995. As of mid-1999, 80% of the offerings were up in price, 20% were down. Prices exhibited high volatility. For example, between April 13, 1999 and May 25, 1999, a sample of Internet stocks followed by Mary Meeker, an analyst with Dean Witter Morgan Stanley, dropped in price by 41%.

The market leaders among Internet companies at mid-1999 were as follows.

Market Segment	Leaders
Infrastructure	Cisco, MCI WorldCom, @Home
Software and Services	AOL, Netscape, Microsoft
Aggregators	AOL, Microsoft, Yahoo
Content Verticals	Intuit, CNET
Retail and Commerce	eBay, Amazon.com, Priceline.com, Dell, Intuit

Growth rates in the Internet market segments have been in the 40% to 60% per annum range. Individual companies have achieved even higher growth rates through improving market share in rapidly expanding segments. Different companies have illustrated different strategies. In the business-to-consumer market, Internet retailers with smaller brick-and-mortar investments in relation to incremental revenues can use supplier financing to reduce total investments. As a result, Internet retailers can earn returns on invested capital comparable to those of traditional retailers, with gross operating margins in the 5% to 10% range vs. 20% to 30%.

Some of the rapidly growing Internet companies have experienced losses in the early years. They have merchandised at large discounts to develop large market shares. The strategy is to create a large customer base. Consumers can benefit from superior product selection, efficient processing, and lower prices. To retain customer loyalty, however, will require effective execution of the Internet way.

Another dimension of Internet company growth strategy has involved the use of M&As. In its early stages, the Internet company sells a small percentage of its ownership shares (for example, 10%). Glamor and shortage run up the price. The high growth rates in Internet market segments both historical and projected have fostered optimism. With high prices relative to revenues, new Internet IPOs make a rapid series of acquisitions. The aim is to achieve critical mass, market leadership, and name recognition.

Valuation Approaches

In valuing Internet companies, we can begin with the traditional comparable companies approach. The ratio of market to EBITDA may not work because of low or negative EBITDAs. The ratio of market to book may be distorted, because losses depress the size of book values. The ratio most widely used is market to revenues.

We selected a group of Internet companies followed by Value Line. We compiled ratios of market to revenues, as shown in Table 10.22.

Column 1 is a list of companies. Column 2 is their market values as of the Value Line reports of September 3, 1999. Column 3 is 1998 revenues. Column 4 is 1999 rev-

Table 10.22   Characteristics of Value Line Internet Companies

(1)	(2)	(3)	(4)	(5)	(6)	(7)
	Market	**Revenues**			**Market to Revenue**	
	($ Billion)			**Implied**		
	9/3/99	**1998**	**1999**	**Growth Rate**	**1998**	**1999**
Yahoo	41.2	0.203	0.530	161%	203.0	77.7
Amazon	22.2	0.610	1.400	130%	36.4	15.9
America Online	113.4	2.600	4.777	84%	43.6	23.7
CNET	3.0	0.056	0.105	88%	53.6	28.6
Excite	10.5	0.048	0.410	754%	218.8	25.6
IDT	0.5	0.335	0.700	109%	1.5	0.7
Infoseek	2.0	0.051	0.135	165%	39.2	14.8
Lycos	2.9	0.056	0.130	132%	51.8	22.3
Mindspring	1.9	0.115	0.335	191%	16.5	5.7
			Average:	201%		

enues projected by Value Line. Column 5 presents the growth rates implied by the revenue projections. Columns 6 and 7 are the ratios of the market values to the 1998 and 1999 revenues, respectively. Of course, the market-to-revenues ratios drop substantially when we use the revenue estimates of 1999. The revenue growth rates are mostly above 50% and average 63% for the nine companies. It is these uniformly high expected growth rates that have stimulated the high multiples of market to revenues.

DCF Valuation

We can apply discounted cash flow (DCF) valuation to the Internet companies by recognizing multiple stages of growth. We bring together the market-to-revenue relationships with a DCF valuation model consisting of four stages. A review of data and analyst reports guides us to estimates of the value drivers we employ. In our initial case, as shown in Table 10.23, we identify four stages. Stage 1 is for the first five years of losses. Stage 2 lasts for 10 years after the company has matured sufficiently to achieve profitability. In stage 3, revenue growth decays until it reaches 3% per annum in the twentieth year. It remains at that constant growth rate thereafter. Our initial estimates of cost of capital are relatively high.

Revenue in period zero is $1,000 so that our model can be readily generalized to actual companies whose revenues are some multiple of our base. Because leverage ratios are relatively low, we assume no debt and therefore no interest expense. Investment is expressed as a simple ratio to revenues to simplify the analysis in view of the low investment requirements of Internet companies.

In Table 10.23, we identify four critical value drivers: revenue growth rate, operating margin, tax rate, and cost of capital. In the initial case, stage 1 is characterized by a revenue growth rate of 55.6%, an operating margin of −5%, a zero tax rate, and a 15% cost of capital. The relatively high cost of capital reflects the high betas

Table 10.23 Spreadsheet DCF Valuation, Value Driver Method ($ in millions)

Revenue Year 0 = $1,000

	Stage 1 Yr 1–5	Stage 2 Yr 6–15	Stage 3 Yr 16–20	Stage 4 Yr 21–∞
Revenue Growth Rate	55.6%	33.0%	==> 3.0%	0%, 3%
Operating Margin	−5.0%	30.0%	15.0%	10.0%
Tax Rate	0%	20%	40%	40%
Cost of Capital	15%	15%	15%	15%

						Year				
		1	2	3	4	5	6	7	8	9
Incremental Free Cash Flow	% Rev									
1. Revenue Growth Rate		55.6%	55.6%	55.6%	55.6%	55.6%	33.0%	33.0%	33.0%	33.0%
2. Revenues		$ 1,556	$2,421	$3,767	$5,862	$ 9,121	$12,131	$16,134	$21,459	$28,540
3. Cost of Goods Sold, SG&A, Depreciation		1,634	2,542	3,956	6,155	9,577	8,492	11,294	15,021	19,978
4. Pretax Operating Income (NOI)		(78)	(121)	(188)	(293)	(456)	3,639	4,840	6,438	8,562
5. Interest Expense	0.0%	—	—	—	—	—	—	—	—	—
6. Income Before Taxes (EBT)		(78)	(121)	(188)	(293)	(456)	3,639	4,840	6,438	8,562
7. Income Taxes		—	—	—	—	—	728	968	1,288	1,712
8. Net Income (NI)		(78)	(121)	(188)	(293)	(456)	2,911	3,872	5,150	6,850
9. Tax Shield: $(1-T) \times (5)$		—	—	—	—	—	—	—	—	—
10. NOPAT (8+9)		(78)	(121)	(188)	(293)	(456)	2,911	3,872	5,150	6,850
11. Investment	6.0%	(93)	(145)	(226)	(352)	(547)	(728)	(968)	(1,288)	(1,712)
12. Free Cash Flow (Cash Flow After Taxes, CFAT)		$ (171)	$ (266)	$ (414)	$ (645)	$(1,003)	$ 2,184	$ 2,904	$ 3,863	$ 5,137
Valuation										
13. Discounted CFAT*		$ (149)	$ (201)	$ (272)	$ (369)	$ (499)	$ 944	$ 1,092	$ 1,263	$ 1,460
14. Total Present Value of CFAT		$21,511								

	Case A	Case B
15. Terminal Value Rate Assumptions		
a. Post-terminal year growth rate (g)	0%	3%
b. Reinvestment rate (z)	0%	2%
16. Terminal Value (TV)**	125,365	158,179
17. PV of CFAT stage 1	$ (1,490)	$ (1,490)
18. PV of CFAT stage 2	19,788	19,788
19. PV of CFAT stage 3	3,213	3,213
20. Present Value of TV (PVTV)	7,660	9,665
21. Total Present Value	$ 29,170	$ 31,175
22. Plus: Marketable Securities	—	—
23. Less: Total Interest-Bearing Debt	—	—
24. Equity Value	$ 29,170	$ 31,175
25. PV NOPAT$_{20}$	$ 1,723	$ 1,723
26. Total PV/PV NOPAT$_{20}$	16.93	18.09
27. Total PV/Rev$_1$	18.75	20.04

*PV of $CFAT_t = CFAT_t/(1+k)^t$.

**Terminal value (TV) equals $(NOPAT_{21})(1-z)/(k-g_c)$. Its present value is $TV/(1+k)^{20}$.

	Year									
10	11	12	13	14	15	16	17	18	19	20
33.0%	33.0%	33.0%	33.0%	33.0%	33.0%	27.00%	21.00%	15.00%	9.00%	3.0%
$37,958	$50,484	$67,144	$89,302	$118,772	$157,966	$200,617	$242,747	$279,159	$304,283	$313,412
26,571	35,339	47,001	62,511	83,140	110,576	170,525	206,335	237,285	258,641	266,400
11,387	15,145	20,143	26,791	35,631	47,390	30,093	36,412	41,874	45,642	47,012
—	—	—	—	—	—	—	—	—	—	—
11,387	15,145	20,143	26,791	35,631	47,390	30,093	36,412	41,874	45,642	47,012
2,277	3,029	4,029	5,358	7,126	9,478	12,037	14,565	16,750	18,257	18,805
9,110	12,116	16,115	21,432	28,505	37,912	18,056	21,847	25,124	27,385	28,207
—	—	—	—	—	—	—	—	—	—	—
9,110	12,116	16,115	21,432	28,505	37,912	18,056	21,847	25,124	27,385	28,207
(2,277)	(3,029)	(4,029)	(5,358)	(7,126)	(9,478)	(12,037)	(14,565)	(16,750)	(18,257)	(18,805)
$ 6,832	$ 9,087	$12,086	$16,074	$ 21,379	$ 28,434	$ 6,019	$ 7,282	$ 8,375	$ 9,128	$ 9,402
$ 1,689	$ 1,953	$ 2,259	$ 2,613	$ 3,021	$ 3,494	$ 643	$ 677	$ 677	$ 641	$ 574

of Internet companies. Stage 2 is defined as reaching profitability on the basis of an established customer base and the completion of initial startup costs, including buying customers by extending large price discounts. Operating margins rise to 30%. The tax rate is 20%, reflecting the benefit of the carryforward of tax losses from stage 1. The cost of capital is assumed to continue to reflect high betas. After 10 years of very favorable growth and high margins, we have the Internet industry following the life cycle pattern depicted in Figure 10.3. In stage 3, the revenue growth rate decays over the five-year period by six percentage points each year until it reaches 3% by year 20, the end of stage 3. Operating margins decline to 15%. The cost of capital remains at 15%.

Stage 4 represents the beginning of the terminal period. The revenue growth rate reflects our standard no-growth and constant growth models of previous discussions, with calculations made under the columns Case A and Case B. The operating margin declines still further to 10%. The tax rate and cost of capital remain unchanged from stage 3.

The first 10 rows of the resulting spreadsheet are defined by the levels of the value drivers defined above. Line 4, the pretax operating income, reflects the operating margins described. Income taxes are deducted at line 7. We do not use the lines involved in interest expense because of the zero leverage assumption, but we have preserved the format to accommodate a leverage sensitivity analysis. In line 10, we have the net operating profit after taxes (NOPAT). This also represents gross cash flows before reductions for investment requirements. One of the characteristics of Internet companies is low investment requirements. We use 6% of revenues to convey this.[1]

The resulting entity values are then related to the initial year revenues. We obtain a market-to-revenue ratio in the range of 18 to 20 times. This falls in about the midrange of the data observed for our sample Internet companies, shown in Table 10.22. We can make some plausible variations in the value drivers to illustrate the implicit value drivers for companies with higher market-to-revenue ratios.

In Table 10.24, we reflect the higher profit margins observed in some Internet companies. This moves the market-to-revenue multiple into the 30 to 33 times

---

[1]We would prefer to define profit rates and investment on an incremental basis conceptually. However, as a practical matter, the volatility of the relationships swamps such technical differences. Also, during any growth stage, there is a simple transformation between average and marginal relationships. This can be illustrated by reference to Rappaport's basic model (1998,p. 34). Investment requirements are defined as 25% of the change in sales. His sales growth rate is assumed to be a constant 19% per annum. Investment would therefore represent a constant 5.263% of sales. For our example above, during the 10-year period when revenue growth is a constant 33%, investment would be 18% of the amount of sales growth.

range. In Table 10.25, we lower the operating margins but also lower the cost of capital to 10% for stages 2 to 4. The multiple rises to the 34 to 40 times range. Finally, in Table 10.26, we use high operating margins and the 10% cost of capital for stages 2 to 4. The resulting market-to-revenue ratios move to the high numbers for the sample of Internet companies shown in Table 10.22.

The above examples demonstrate that standard DCF methodology with multiple stages can explain the valuation relationships observed for Internet companies. We provide two case examples of DCF valuations of Internet companies. On August 9, 1999, Bear Stearns issued a report on Digital Island (ISLD), a provider of global networks for businesses to enable them to leverage the Internet for applications such as content, commerce, and communications. On the date of the forecast, the market price of ISLD was $15. A 10-year revenue forecast of 70% per annum, a gross margin of 36%, a cost of capital of 16%, and a terminal multiple of 12 times EBITDA was the basis for an 18-month $45 price target. On December 30, 1999, ISLD closed at $97.

On August 9, 1999, Wasserstein Perella issued a report on Level 3 Communications (LVLT) when its price was $54, with a 12-month target of $80. A DCF spreadsheet was used with starting total revenues of $476 million. A 10-year projection of total revenues used a 50% compound annual growth rate. A four-stage spreadsheet similar to ours was used with a negative EBITDA margin of about 50% in the first three years. A margin of a positive 15% in FY2002, rising to 35% in FY2003, rising to 45% for the next five years. A discount rate of 13% was employed. A capital expenditure rate of 8% of total revenues was used for FY2008. The terminal value was based on an EBITDA multiple of 12.5. LVLT closed at $81 on December 30, 1999.

These and other examples demonstrate that with value drivers of 50% or more for revenues, with operating margins in the 35% to 45% range, with a cost of capital in the 13% to 16% range, target prices were achieved within a three-month period. Despite the very high value driver estimates, the projections were conservative in terms of actual price performance (in a booming market for Internet stocks). The record as of the end of 1999 demonstrates that the DCF methodology has been useful even for the Internets. The high multiples of market to revenues observed reflect the high growth and high profit margins achievable in the early stages of new industries. These patterns have also exhibited high degrees of volatility. Expectations about the relative success and growth rates in free cash flows have fluctuated widely. Ultimately, Internets are valued on the basis of the business economics of their industry and their competitive position in it. New industries always attract an excess supply of companies; the strong survive and become stronger. The weak fail and are acquired or liquidated.

Table 10.24 Spreadsheet DCF Valuation, Value Driver Method ($ in millions)

Revenue Year 0 = $1,000

	Stage 1 Yr 1–5	Stage 2 Yr 6–15	Stage 3 Yr 16–20	Stage 4 Yr 21–∞
Revenue Growth Rate	55.6%	33.0%	==> 3.0%	0%, 3%
Operating Margin	−5.0%	30.0%	25.0%	25.0%
Tax Rate	0%	20%	40%	40%
Cost of Capital	15%	15%	15%	15%

		Year								
		1	2	3	4	5	6	7	8	9
Incremental Free Cash Flow	% Rev									
1. Revenues Growth Rate		55.6%	55.6%	55.6%	55.6%	55.6%	33.0%	33.0%	33.0%	33.0%
2. Revenues		$ 1,556	$2,421	$3,767	$5,862	$ 9,121	$12,131	$16,134	$21,459	$28,540
3. Cost of Goods Sold, SG&A, Depreciation		1,634	2,542	3,956	6,155	9,577	8,492	11,294	15,021	19,978
4. Pretax Operating Income (NOI)		(78)	(121)	(188)	(293)	(456)	3,639	4,840	6,438	8,562
5. Interest Expense	0.0%	—	—	—	—	—	—	—	—	—
6. Income Before Taxes (EBT)		(78)	(121)	(188)	(293)	(456)	3,639	4,840	6,438	8,562
7. Income Taxes		—	—	—	—	—	728	968	1,288	1,712
8. Net Income (NI)		(78)	(121)	(188)	(293)	(456)	2,911	3,872	5,150	6,850
9. Tax Shield: $(1-T) \times (5)$		—	—	—	—	—	—	—	—	—
10. NOPAT (8+9)		(78)	(121)	(188)	(293)	(456)	2,911	3,872	5,150	6,850
11. Investment	6.0%	(93)	(145)	(226)	(352)	(547)	(728)	(968)	(1,288)	(1,712)
12. Free Cash Flow (Cash Flow After Taxes, CFAT)		$ (171)	$ (266)	$ (414)	$ (645)	$(1,003)	$ 2,184	$ 2,904	$ 3,863	$ 5,137

Valuation										
13. Discounted CFAT*		$ (149)	$ (201)	$ (272)	$ (369)	$ (499)	$ 944	$ 1,092	$ 1,263	$ 1,460
14. Total Present Value of CFAT		$27,936								

	Case A	Case B
15. Terminal Value Rate Assumptions		
a. Post-terminal year growth rate (g)	0%	3%
b. Reinvestment rate (z)	0%	2%
16. Terminal Value (TV)**	313,412	395,447
17. PV of CFAT stage 1	$ (1,490)	$ (1,490)
18. PV of CFAT stage 2	19,788	19,788
19. PV of CFAT stage 3	9,638	9,638
20. Present Value of TV (PVTV)	19,150	24,162
21. Total Present Value	$ 47,085	$ 52,098
22. Plus: Marketable Securities	—	—
23. Less: Total Interest-Bearing Debt	—	—
24. Equity Value	$ 47,085	$ 52,098
25. PV NOPAT$_{20}$	$ 2,872	$ 2,872
26. Total PV/PV NOPAT$_{20}$	16.39	18.14
27. Total PV/Rev$_1$	30.26	33.48

*PV of $CFAT_t = CFAT_t/(1+k)^t$

**Terminal value (TV) equals $(NOPAT_{21})(1-z)/(k-g_r)$. Its present value is $TV/(1+k)^{20}$

	Year									
10	11	12	13	14	15	16	17	18	19	20
33.0%	33.0%	33.0%	33.0%	33.0%	33.0%	27.00%	21.00%	15.00%	9.00%	3.0%
$37,958	$50,484	$67,144	$89,302	$118,772	$157,966	$200,617	$242,747	$279,159	$304,283	$313,412
26,571	35,339	47,001	62,511	83,140	110,576	150,463	182,060	209,369	228,212	235,059
11,387	15,145	20,143	26,791	35,631	47,390	50,154	60,687	69,790	76,071	78,353
—	—	—	—	—	—	—	—	—	—	—
11,387	15,145	20,143	26,791	35,631	47,390	50,154	60,687	69,790	76,071	78,353
2,277	3,029	4,029	5,358	7,126	9,478	20,062	24,275	27,916	30,428	31,341
9,110	12,116	16,115	21,432	28,505	37,912	30,093	36,412	41,874	45,642	47,012
—	—	—	—	—	—	—	—	—	—	—
9,110	12,116	16,115	21,432	28,505	37,912	30,093	36,412	41,874	45,642	47,012
(2,277)	(3,029)	(4,029)	(5,358)	(7,126)	(9,478)	(12,037)	(14,565)	(16,750)	(18,257)	(18,805)
$ 6,832	$ 9,087	$12,086	$16,074	$ 21,379	$ 28,434	$ 18,056	$ 21,847	$ 25,124	$ 27,385	$ 28,207
$ 1,689	$ 1,953	$ 2,259	$ 2,613	$ 3,021	$ 3,494	$ 1,930	$ 2,030	$ 2,030	$ 1,924	$ 1,723

Table 10.25 Spreadsheet DCF Valuation, Value Driver Method ($ in millions)

Revenue Year 0 = $1,000

	Stage 1 Yr 1–5	Stage 2 Yr 6–15	Stage 3 Yr 16–20	Stage 4 Yr 21–∞
Revenue Growth Rate	55.6%	33.0%	==> 3.0%	0%, 3%
Operating Margin	−5.0%	30.0%	15.0%	10.0%
Tax Rate	0%	20%	40%	40%
Cost of Capital	15%	10%	10%	10%

						Year				
		1	2	3	4	5	6	7	8	9
Incremental Free Cash Flow	% Rev									
1. Revenues Growth Rate		55.6%	55.6%	55.6%	55.6%	55.6%	33.0%	33.0%	33.0%	33.0%
2. Revenues		$1,556	$2,421	$3,767	$5,862	$ 9,121	$12,131	$16,134	$21,459	$28,540
3. Cost of Goods Sold, SG&A, Depreciation		1,634	2,542	3,956	6,155	9,577	8,492	11,294	15,021	19,978
4. Pretax Operating Income (NOI)		(78)	(121)	(188)	(293)	(456)	3,639	4,840	6,438	8,562
5. Interest Expense	0.0%	—	—	—	—	—	—	—	—	—
6. Income Before Taxes (EBT)		(78)	(121)	(188)	(293)	(456)	3,639	4,840	6,438	8,562
7. Income Taxes		—	—	—	—	—	728	968	1,288	1,712
8. Net Income (NI)		(78)	(121)	(188)	(293)	(456)	2,911	3,872	5,150	6,850
9. Tax Shield: $(1-T) \times (5)$		—	—	—	—	—	—	—	—	—
10. NOPAT (8+9)		(78)	(121)	(188)	(293)	(456)	2,911	3,872	5,150	6,850
11. Investment	6.0%	(93)	(145)	(226)	(352)	(547)	(728)	(968)	(1,288)	(1,712)
12. Free Cash Flow (Cash Flow After Taxes, CFAT)		$ (171)	$ (266)	$ (414)	$ (645)	$(1,003)	$ 2,184	$ 2,904	$ 3,863	$ 5,137
Valuation										
13. Discounted CFAT*		$ (149)	$ (201)	$ (272)	$ (369)	$ (499)	$ 987	$ 1,193	$ 1,443	$ 1,944
14. Total Present Value of CFAT		$31,029								

	Case A	Case B
15. Terminal Value Rate Assumptions		
a. Post-terminal year growth rate (g)	0%	3%
b. Reinvestment rate (z)	0%	2%
16. Terminal Value (TV)**	188,047	271,164
17. PV of CFAT stage 1	$ (1,490)	$ (1,490)
18. PV of CFAT stage 2	26,797	26,797
19. PV of CFAT stage 3	5,723	5,723
20. Present Value of TV (PVTV)	22,381	32,274
21. Total Present Value	$ 53,411	$ 63,303
22. Plus: Marketable Securities	—	—
23. Less: Total Interest-Bearing Debt	—	—
24. Equity Value	$ 53,411	$ 63,303
25. PV NOPAT$_{20}$	$ 3,357	$ 3,357
26. Total PV/PV NOPAT$_{20}$	15.91	18.86
27. Total PV/Rev$_1$	34.33	40.68

*PV of $CFAT_t = CFAT_t/(1+k)^t$

**Terminal value (TV) equals $(NOPAT_{21})(1-z)/(k-g_c)$. Its present value is $TV/(1+k)^{20}$.

	Year										
	10	**11**	**12**	**13**	**14**	**15**	**16**	**17**	**18**	**19**	**20**
	33.0%	33.0%	33.0%	33.0%	33.0%	33.0%	27.00%	21.00%	15.00%	9.00%	3.0%
	$37,958	$50,484	$67,144	$89,302	$118,772	$157,966	$200,617	$242,747	$279,159	$304,283	$313,412
	26,571	35,339	47,001	62,511	83,140	110,576	170,525	206,335	237,285	258,641	266,400
	11,387	15,145	20,143	26,791	35,631	47,390	30,093	36,412	41,874	45,642	47,012
	—	—	—	—	—	—	—	—	—	—	—
	11,387	15,145	20,143	26,791	35,631	47,390	30,093	36,412	41,874	45,642	47,012
	2,277	3,029	4,029	5,358	7,126	9,478	12,037	14,565	16,750	18,257	18,805
	9,110	12,116	16,115	21,432	28,505	37,912	18,056	21,847	25,124	27,385	28,207
	—	—	—	—	—	—	—	—	—	—	—
	9,110	12,116	16,115	21,432	28,505	37,912	18,056	21,847	25,124	27,385	28,207
	(2,277)	(3,029)	(4,029)	(5,358)	(7,126)	(9,478)	(12,037)	(14,565)	(16,750)	(18,257)	(18,805)
	$ 6,832	$ 9,087	$12,086	$16,074	$ 21,379	$ 28,434	$ 6,019	$ 7,282	$ 8,375	$ 9,128	$ 9,402
	$ 2,109	$ 2,550	$ 3,084	$ 3,728	$ 4,508	$ 5,450	$ 1,049	$ 1,154	$ 1,206	$ 1,195	$ 1,119

Table 10.26 Spreadsheet DCF Valuation, Value Driver Method ($ in millions)

Revenue Year 0 = $1,000

	Stage 1 Yr 1–5	Stage 2 Yr 6–15	Stage 3 Yr 16–20	Stage 4 Yr 21–∞
Revenue Growth Rate	55.6%	33.0% ==>	3.0%	0%, 3%
Operating Margin	−5.0%	30.0%	25.0%	25.0%
Tax Rate	0%	20%	40%	40%
Cost of Capital	15%	10%	10%	10%

						Year				
		1	2	3	4	5	6	7	8	9
Incremental Free Cash Flow	% Rev									
1. Revenue Growth Rate		55.6%	55.6%	55.6%	55.6%	55.6%	33.0%	33.0%	33.0%	33.0%
2. Revenues		$1,556	$2,421	$3,767	$5,862	$ 9,121	$12,131	$16,134	$21,459	$28,540
3. Cost of Goods Sold, SG&A, Depreciation		1,634	2,542	3,956	6,155	9,577	8,492	11,294	15,021	19,978
4. Pretax Operating Income (NOI)		(78)	(121)	(188)	(293)	(456)	3,639	4,840	6,438	8,562
5. Interest Expense	0.0%	—	—	—	—	—	—	—	—	—
6. Income Before Taxes (EBT)		(78)	(121)	(188)	(293)	(456)	3,639	4,840	6,438	8,562
7. Income Taxes		—	—	—	—	—	728	968	1,288	1,712
8. Net Income (NI)		(78)	(121)	(188)	(293)	(456)	2,911	3,872	5,150	6,850
9. Tax Shield: $(1-T)\times(5)$		—	—	—	—	—				
10. NOPAT (8+9)		(78)	(121)	(188)	(293)	(456)	2,911	3,872	5,150	6,850
11. Investment	6.0%	(93)	(145)	(226)	(352)	(547)	(728)	(968)	(1,288)	(1,712)
12. Free Cash Flow (Cash Flow After Taxes, CFAT)		$ (171)	$ (266)	$ (414)	$ (645)	$(1,003)	$ 2,184	$ 2,904	$ 3,863	$ 5,137
Valuation										
13. Discounted CFAT*		$ (149)	$ (201)	$ (272)	$ (369)	$ (499)	$ 987	$ 1,193	$ 1,443	$ 1,744
14. Total Present Value of CFAT		$42,475								

	Case A	Case B
15. Terminal Value Rate Assumptions		
a. Post-terminal year growth rate (g)	0%	3%
b. Reinvestment rate (z)	0%	2%
16. Terminal Value (TV)**	470,117	677,909
17. PV of CFAT stage 1	$ (1,490)	$ (1,490)
18. PV of CFAT stage 2	26,797	26,797
19. PV of CFAT stage 3	17,168	17,168
20. Present Value of TV (PVTV)	55,953	80,635
21. Total Present Value	$ 98,428	$123,160
22. Plus: Marketable Securities	—	—
23. Less: Total Interest-Bearing Debt	—	—
24. Equity Value	$ 98,428	$123,160
25. PV NOPAT$_{20}$	$ 5,595	$ 5,595
26. Total PV/PV NOPAT$_{20}$	17.59	22.01
27. Total PV/Rev$_1$	63.26	79.15

*PV of $CFAT_t = CFAT_t/(1+k)^t$.

**Terminal value (TV) equals $(NOPAT_{21})(1-z)/(k-g_r)$. Its present value is $TV/(1+k)^{20}$.

336

					Year					
10	11	12	13	14	15	16	17	18	19	20
33.0%	33.0%	33.0%	33.0%	33.0%	33.0%	27.00%	21.00%	15.00%	9.00%	3.0%
$37,958	$50,484	$67,144	$89,302	$118,772	$157,966	$200,617	$242,747	$279,159	$304,283	$313,412
26,571	35,339	47,001	62,511	83,140	110,576	150,463	182,060	209,369	228,212	235,059
11,387	15,145	20,143	26,791	35,631	47,390	50,154	60,687	69,790	76,071	78,353
—	—	—	—	—	—	—	—	—	—	—
11,387	15,145	20,143	26,791	35,631	47,390	50,154	60,687	69,790	76,071	78,353
2,277	3,029	4,029	5,358	7,126	9,478	20,062	24,275	27,916	30,428	31,341
9,110	12,116	16,115	21,432	28,505	37,912	30,093	36,412	41,874	45,642	47,012
—	—	—	—	—	—	—	—	—	—	—
9,110	12,116	16,115	21,432	28,505	37,912	30,093	36,412	41,874	45,642	47,012
(2,277)	(3,029)	(4,029)	(5,358)	(7,126)	(9,478)	(12,037)	(14,565)	(16,750)	(18,257)	(18,805)
$ 6,832	$ 9,087	$12,086	$16,074	$ 21,379	$ 28,434	$ 18,056	$ 21,847	$ 25,124	$ 27,385	$ 28,207
$ 2,109	$ 2,550	$ 3,084	$ 3,728	$ 4,508	$ 5,450	$ 3,146	$ 3,461	$ 3,618	$ 3,585	$ 3,357

SUMMARY

The goal of valuation analysis is to provide a disciplined approach to analyzing acquisition premiums and their recovery. This chapter illustrates alternative approaches to achieving this basic objective. In the analysis of Chevron's acquisition of Gulf, we first used the comparable transactions approach. Second, finding cost analysis was employed. In the early 1980s, the price of oil had risen to about $33 per barrel due to restrictions on supply by the OPEC cartel. This stimulated expansion of exploration and development programs by the major oil companies. Production in excess of quotas by the cartel members resulted in a collapse of oil prices down to $10 per barrel. But finding costs were at about $13 per barrel. As a consequence, the stock prices of oil companies fell and made them takeover targets. Value increases could be achieved simply by curtailing exploration and development programs. In addition, the crude reserves of the companies acquired, even at the depressed $10 price levels, were worth more than the market values of companies. It was cheaper to acquire oil on Wall Street than in the oil fields.

The valuation approach to oil companies changed in later time periods. By the late 1990s, oil companies had substantially reduced finding costs and production costs. By 1998, oil prices had fallen to about $9 per barrel. Profit margins were squeezed. The goal of oil company mergers was to further reduce costs and to increase size to make the firm less vulnerable to losses on the high risk projects, especially in international activities. The Exxon–Mobil merger analysis presented illustrates a general framework for analyzing mergers.

First the underlying economics of the industry must be understood. This provides the basis for the second step, which is to understand the potential benefits and synergies from the merger. Third is the application of the DCF valuation procedures, which quantifies potential synergies and permits a comparison of whether the value increases will recover the premiums paid by the acquiring firm. This analysis is based on financial projections of the value drivers. Fourth, all aspects of potential regulatory factors need to be taken into account. Fifth, the competitive reactions of rival firms and the changes in industry dynamics need to be taken into account. These five major financial factors must be related to the challenges of combining two organizations' cultures and achieving effective implementation of the merger plans.

We place the analysis in a dynamic framework by analyzing how the key value drivers behave for firms at different stages of their life cycles. The key value drivers identified were: the growth rate in revenues, the net operating income-to-revenue margin, working capital requirements in relation to revenue growth, plant and equipment expenditures in relation to revenue growth, applicable tax rates, applicable cost of capital, and the years of competitive advantage producing above-average growth and profitability.

We used this dynamic framework in assessing valuation patterns in Internet companies. We presented a four-stage DCF valuation model to show the relationship between the value drivers and the resulting revenue valuation relationships.

Key valuation relationships are used in some industries. For example, cable companies were bought at $5,000 to $8,000 per subscriber (or "pop"). In the high tech area, the price paid for a company could be $2 million to $4 million per engineer, depending upon the nature of their capabilities in relation to the acquiring firm's needs.

QUESTIONS

10.1 Discuss methods of calculating the cost of equity capital.

10.2 The Alcindor Company is very similar to and is in the same industry as the Walton Company. Both Alcindor Co. and Walton Co. have a cost of equity of 12%, cost of debt of 8%, and 30% debt. If Walton has revenues (R_0) of $1,000, operating margin (m) of 15%, investment (I) of 8%, growth rate (g) of 18%, 5 years of supernormal growth (n), and 40% tax rate (T), what value should Alcindor Co. be willing to pay for Walton Co.?

10.3 Suppose Alcindor Co. is instead interested in the Elway Company, a firm in a completely unrelated (and riskier) industry. Elway Co. has the same parameters as Walton Co. (question 10.2), except Elway Co. has a cost of equity of 15%, a cost of debt of 10%, and 20% debt. What value should Alcindor Co. be willing to pay for Elway Co.?

10.4 Kubrick Company decides to buy Hitchcock Company. Both firms have the same characteristics as Walton Co. (question 10.2), except Kubrick Co. has a beta of 1.2, and Hitchcock Co. has a beta of 1.4. Both firms have 30% debt, and a cost of debt of 8%. Because of the nature of the synergies anticipated in the acquisition, the combined firm is expected to have a beta of 1.1.

a. If the risk free rate is 6% and the equity risk premium is 5%, calculate the cost of capital for the two firms and the combined firm.

b. Assuming the value drivers remain constant (and revenues are simply combined), what would be the value of the individual firms and combined company?

10.5 Vonnegut Company and Heller Company are two identical firms that agree to merge. Both have revenues (R_0) of $1,500, operating margin (m) of 15%, investment (I) of 10%, growth rate (g) of 11%, 5 years of supernormal growth (n), 40% tax rate (T), and a 9% cost of capital (k).

a. What are the values of the firms as standalone companies?

b. If the combined firm increases its operating margin by 2%, revenues are combined, and the other value drivers remain unchanged, what is the value of the combined firm?

REFERENCES

Finizza, Anthony J., "The Future of Oil," *Business Economics,* 31(4), October 1996, pp. 7–11.

Harvard Business School, "Gulf Oil Corporation—Takeover," Case No. 285-053, November 7, 1984; revised 1992.

Jensen, Michael C., "Agency Costs of Free Cash Flow, Corporate Finance, and Takeovers," *American Economic Review,* 76, 1986, 323–329.

Miller, Merton H., and Franco Modigliani, "Dividend Policy, Growth, and the Valuation of Shares," *Journal of Business,* 34, October 1961, pp. 411–433.

Rappaport, Alfred, *Creating Shareholder Value,* New York: The Free Press, 1998.

Siu, J. A., and J. F. Weston, "Restructuring in the U.S. Oil Industry," *Journal of Energy Finance & Development,* 1, 1996, pp. 113–131.

U.S. Energy Information Administration, *Performance Profiles of Major Energy Producers 1997,* Washington, D.C, January 1999.

Welch, Ivo, Views of Financial Economists on the Equity Premium and Other Issues, Unpublished working paper, June 1999, The Anderson School, UCLA.

Calculating
Growth Rates

Growth rates play a crucial role in many areas of financial analysis. This appendix describes three ways to calculate the growth rate of a particular variable, such as net operating income (NOI) or stock price for example, over a series of time. The data in Table A10.1 represent net operating income (NOI) for a company that has grown at a steady annual rate of 20%.

The first method calculates a **discrete compound annual growth rate,** d, as discussed in the text. It is a geometric average based on the end points of the time series, and is found by dividing the final year by the initial year, then taking, for this example, the tenth root. This is done below:

$$(61.9/10.0)^{(1/10)} = 1.20 = 1 + d$$

Thus, the discrete growth rate is 20%. Note that these data plot as a curved line (concave from above) on arithmetic graph paper and as a straight line on semilog paper (Figures A10.1 and A10.2).

Table A10.1   Data to Illustrate
Growth at 20%

Time Period	NOI
1	$10.0
2	12.0
3	14.4
4	17.3
5	20.7
6	24.9
7	29.9
8	35.8
9	43.0
10	51.6
11	61.9

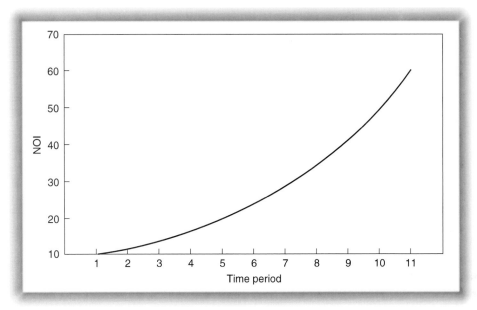

Figure A10.1   Constant Growth Rate, 20%

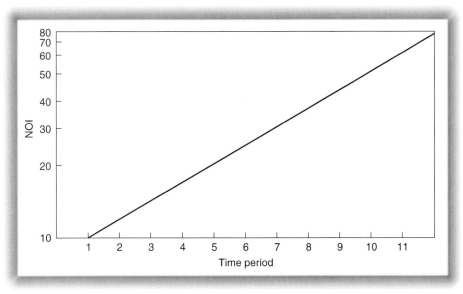

Figure A10.2   Constant Growth Rate (20%) Graphed on Semilog Paper

The second method calculates a **continuously compounded growth rate,** c, as shown in Table A10.2. It is found as the slope of the regression line where the natural logarithm of NOI (in this case) is the dependent variable, and the year (designated as 1, 2, 3, . . . rather than as the actual year number such as 1996) is the independent variable. This is

Table A10.2 Regression Method of Calculating Growth Rate—
Constant Growth

Time Period	NOI	ln (NOI)	Regression Output	
1	10.0	2.302585	Constant	2.120411
2	12.0	2.484906	Std. err. of Y est.	0.000909
3	14.4	2.667228	R squared	0.999997
4	17.3	2.850706	No. of observations	11
5	20.7	3.030133	Degrees of freedom	9
6	24.9	3.214867		
7	29.9	3.397858	X coefficient(s)	0.182302
8	35.8	3.577947	Std. err. of coef.	0.000086
9	43.0	3.761200		
10	51.6	3.943521		
11	61.9	4.125520		

easily accomplished on a personal computer using Excel or other software packages, and even on some handheld calculators. For our data, the slope of the regression equation tells us that the continuously compounded growth rate is 18.23%.

Because of the nature of the data, the only difference in the growth rates is caused by the compounding assumption in each case. The regression method results in a continuously compounded growth rate, while the end-points method implicitly assumes annual compounding. This is illustrated using the standard formula relating discrete and compound growth rates: $d = e^c - 1$. We first solve the equation for d, the discrete rate, using the continuously compounded growth rate we obtained in the regression.

$$d = e^{0.182302} - 1 = 1.20 - 1 = 20\%$$

Alternatively, we can solve for c, using the d we obtained in the end-point method:

$$0.20 = e^c - 1$$
$$1.20 = e^c$$

Taking the natural logarithm of both sides of the equation we have

$$\ln (1.20) = \ln (e^c)$$

Because the natural logarithm of (e^x) is simply x, we have

$$\ln (1.20) = c = 0.1823$$

These results obtain only for the special case we have illustrated in which the discrete growth rate has no fluctuations. Now consider a case where the NOI does fluctuate, while still exhibiting overall growth, as depicted in Table A10.3.

Table A10.3   Data to Illustrate
Fluctuating
Growth Rates

Time Period	NOI ($)
1	1,000
2	1,400
3	1,250
4	1,600
5	1,250
6	2,000
7	3,300
8	2,800
9	2,600
10	3,000
11	3,700

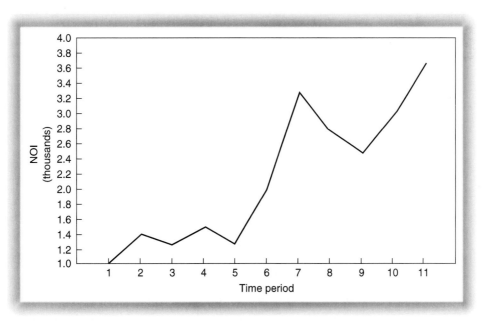

Figure A10.3   Fluctuating Growth Rates

Table A10.4 Regression Method of Calculating Growth Rate— Fluctuating Growth

Time Period	NOI	ln (NOI)	Regression Output	
1	1000	6.907755	Constant	6.835528
2	1400	7.244227	Std. err. of Y est.	0.189571
3	1250	7.130898	R squared	0.844064
4	1600	7.377758	No. of observations	11
5	1250	7.130898	Degrees of freedom	9
6	2000	7.600902		
7	3300	8.101677	X coefficient(s)	0.126157
8	2800	7.937374	Std. err. of coef.	0.018074
9	2600	7.863266		
10	3000	8.006367		
11	3700	8.216088		

Figure A10.3 portrays the greater variability. The discrete growth rate, d, using end points, is calculated as:

$$(3,700/1,000)^{(1/10)} = 1.1397 = 1 + d$$

Thus, $d = 14\%$.

Using the regression method, the continuously compounded growth rate, c, is 12.6% as shown in Table A10.4. As before, the continuously compounded growth rate is lower than the discrete rate. In this example, the difference is not due solely to the compounding method, but also because the regression method considers the fluctuations. If we again use the standard relationship between d and c, we obtain the discrete rate. Solving for d, using c, we have

$$d = e^{0.126157} - 1 = 1.13446 - 1 = 13.45\%,$$

which is below the end-point result of $d = 14\%$.

Alternatively, the annual compounding 14% result found by the end-points method can be converted into a continuously compounding rate:

$$0.14 = e^c - 1$$
$$1.14 = e^c$$
$$\ln (1.14) = c = .1310 = 13.1\%$$

This is above the 12.6% continuously compounded rate found using the regression method. The end-points method is a useful rough method of calculating growth rates. But the end-points method may be seriously flawed if the end values are not representative. The regression method takes into account all data points.

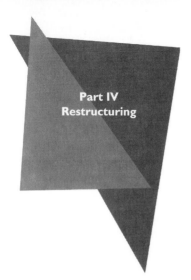

Part IV
Restructuring

Restructuring and Divestitures

This chapter discusses the broad strategies of corporate restructuring and reorganization. These take many forms.

CORPORATE RESTRUCTURING STRATEGIES

To place the subject matter in perspective, Table 11.1 provides a general framework for asset management, ownership organizations, reorganizing financial claims including recontracting, and other strategies.

Table 11.1   General Framework for Corporate Restructuring and Reorganization

1. Reorganization of assets (chapter 11)
   a. Acquisitions
   b. Sell-offs or divestitures
2. Creating new ownership relationships (chapter 12)
   a. Spin-offs
   b. Split-ups
   c. Equity carve-outs
3. Reorganizing financial claims (chapter 13)
   a. Exchange offers
   b. Dual-class recapitalizations
   c. Leveraged recapitalizations
   d. Financial reorganization (bankruptcy)
   e. Liquidation
4. Other strategies
   a. Joint ventures (chapter 14)
   b. ESOPs and MLPs (chapter 15)
   c. Going-private transactions (LBOs) (chapter 16)
   d. Using international markets (chapter 17)
   e. Share repurchase programs (chapter 18)

Table 11.1 suggests a broad framework within which to review the major strategic decisions of the firm. In previous chapters, we have shown that the firm operates in economic, social, and competitive environments with considerable turbulence. The future is difficult to assess. The firm must have a grand plan and a strategic framework. These are useful, broad guides for developing policies and decisions. But even broad strategic plans are subject to revision and augmentation both in anticipation of and in reaction to dynamic changes. Firms, like individuals, must continuously engage in sequential learning and in adjusting and improving. The product mix and scope of a firm's activities are continuously reviewed and modified on the basis of external changes and new knowledge and understanding.

Table 11.1 conveys the wide range of types of adjustments that the firm may employ in the effort to survive and grow to yield benefits in a balanced way to each class of its stakeholders. Section 1 topics in Table 11.1 are covered in the present chapter. The remaining topics are discussed in the next seven chapters.

Some Basic Forces

The restructuring of business firms stems from a number of forces. One of the most basic is the need to meet global competition. One objective addresses the agency problem of conflict of interest between managers and shareholders. A central purpose of restructuring is to better align the interests of managers and shareholders. A second function of restructuring is to move assets to owners who can utilize them more effectively. This helps the economic system move assets to their highest valued uses.

A third general reason given for the restructuring of the 1980s was to reverse the conglomerate merger movement of the 1960s. Some argue that it was unsound to combine many diverse activities into conglomerates as occurred in the 1960s. Conglomeration appeared to be the result of management theories that held that at the level of general management functions particularly, executives could effectively manage a wide range of business types. Another factor involved in conglomeration was that firms in industries with depleting resources such as forestry and a range of mining industries, or industries with narrow or specialized product lines or with uncertain outlooks such as defense industries, sought defensive diversification. In addition, horizontal and vertical mergers were effectively prohibited by the administration of the antitrust laws in the United States. Also the stock market appeared to prefer "pure-play" securities.

Some ascribe the restructuring to the need to break up conglomerates as a consequence of the intensification of competition in the U.S. economy, particularly increased international competition. Others view deconglomeration as a result of an emphasis on developing new core businesses with more favorable outlooks or better suited to the capabilities possessed by the managements of the firms. Voluntary liquidations and "bust-up" takeovers reflect the judgment that the sale of individual parts of some firms could realize greater values than the combination of the parts in one corporate enterprise. Thus, the subject matter of this chapter deals with a fundamental new force in the economy—the restructuring of corporate America.

Definitions and Examples

Most studies have focused on divestitures and spin-offs as a means of eliminating or separating a product line, division, or subsidiary. Divestitures represent the sale of a segment of a company to a third party. Assets, product lines, subsidiaries, or divisions are sold for cash or securities or some combination thereof. The compensation received, net of capital gains taxation, may be used however the seller's management sees fit. The assets are revalued by the sale for purposes of future depreciation by the buyer. Dun and Bradstreet's 1983 sale of its television stations is an example of a divestiture. Divestitures are related to merger and acquisition (M&A) transactions in that in the 1980s about 40% of acquisition activities represented divestitures by other firms. Divestitures in the 1990s ran at about 35% of the dollar value of transactions (*Mergerstat Review*, 2000).

Spin-offs are more often associated with controlled subsidiaries. In a spin-off, a company distributes on a pro rata basis all the shares it owns in a subsidiary to its own shareholders. Two separate public corporations with (initially) the same proportional equity ownership now exist where only one existed before. No money changes hands, and the subsidiary's assets are not revalued. The transaction is treated as a stock dividend and a tax-free exchange. AT&T's court-ordered reorganization in 1984 represented a massive (albeit involuntary) spin-off of its operating subsidiaries.

Examples of spin-offs abound. The *Mergers & Acquisitions* magazine in its annual almanac issue lists major spin-offs of the year. It listed 27 for 1999. We describe a few: Olin Corp., a producer of copper alloys, ammunition, and some chemicals, spun-off Arch Chemicals Inc. in the specialty chemical business on a basis of one share of the spin-off for each two shares of Olin stock. Harris Corporation, to focus on the communications equipment market, divested its semiconductor business and did a spin-off of Lanier Worldwide Inc., whose business is office equipment distribution, on a one-for-one basis. Nabisco Group Holdings spun-off RJR Tobacco Holdings Inc. on a one-for-three basis. Allegheny Teledyne Inc., in steel and several other businesses, did a spin-off of Water Pik Technologies Inc., whose product is dental irrigation equipment, on a one-for-twenty basis.

Spin-offs sometimes follow as the second stage following an equity carve-out, in which some of a subsidiary's shares are offered for sale to the general public, bringing an infusion of cash to the parent firm without loss of control. In 1983 Trans World Corporation initially sold 15% to 20% of its stock in TWA (its airline subsidiary) to the general public in an equity carve-out. (This transaction was followed by a spin-off in which the remaining controlling interest in TWA was spun-off, that is, distributed on a pro rata basis to Trans World Corporation's shareholders.) A notable equity carve-out IPO in 1999 was made by Hewlett-Packard Inc. of Agilent Technologies Inc. to separate the electronic test and measurement equipment from the computer business.

In a split-up, two or more new companies come into being in place of the original company. Split-ups are usually accomplished by spin-offs. We describe the recent reorganizations of AT&T and of ITT before its acquisition by Starwood Hotels and Resorts.

In this chapter, we discuss aspects of diverstitures. In chapter 12, we discuss the rationale for spin-offs, split-ups, tracking stocks, and equity carve-outs and include case studies. In chapter 13, we discuss exchange offers, dual-class recapitalizations, leveraged recapitalizations, financial reorganization (bankruptcy), and liquidation.

DIVESTITURES

We first discuss divestitures because of the major role they perform in M&A activity. Among the top divestitures of 1999 was the sale by Volvo AB of its worldwide passenger vehicle business to Ford Motor Company for $6.5 billion. The second largest was the purchase by AT&T of the global network operations of IBM Corp. for $5 billion. The Long Term Credit Bank of Japan sold its U.S. loan assets portfolio business to the General Electric Capital Corp. for $4 billion. Hoechst AG sold its Herberts Paints division to the Du Pont Co. for $2 billion. Like M&A activity in general, the explanations for divestitures are multiple and diverse.

Background Materials on Divestitures

Both acquisition and divestiture activity may represent efforts by business firms to adjust to their changing economic environments. After the post–World War II adjustments appeared to have been made, the war in Korea caused new shifts in the U.S. economy. Major post–Korean War adjustments took place in the latter half of the 1950s. These abrupt changes stimulated the development of the literature on long-range planning and corporate strategy. The 1960s included the involvement in the war in Vietnam. This was the period of the conglomerate merger movement in which about half the firms actively involved were from the defense industry or natural resource industries with depleting resources. The decade of the 1970s marked a change in international currency standards, floating exchange rates, oil shocks, and relatively high rates of inflation throughout the world. The 1980s were initiated by tight monetary policy in the United States followed by an easing, in part to control the debt service costs of the huge indebtedness incurred by many of the less developed nations. It was a period of deregulation in a number of major industries in the United States.

Merger and acquisition activity as well as divestitures represented one set among strategies followed by business firms attempting to adjust to these successive changes in their economic and political environments. Some firms succeeded better than others in these efforts.

In the effort to deal with the changing economic environments discussed earlier, many firms used M&As as well as internal start-ups to probe opportunities in other product market areas. Some firms sought to make use of the strengths in their existing product market areas to combine with new capabilities in new environments. [The strategy literature urged them to attempt to do so; see the pioneering book by Ansoff (1965).] A related strategy was to seek at least a toehold in new product market areas. The hope was that initial entry could be a beachhead for further growth and development. Much M&A activity involved moving from industries with unfavorable outlooks to industries with more favorable opportunities. Sometimes firms did not have the capabilities to effectively exploit the possible opportunities. Divestitures enabled selling firms to salvage a portion of their investments by selling to other firms that could exploit the opportunities more effectively (Loh and Rathinasamy, 1997).

The pressures for overcoming a firm's strategic planning gap or aligning more effectively with the changing environments have varied from industry to industry and during different time periods. The motives for divestiture activity are many and diverse.

Motives for Divestitures

1. **Dismantling conglomerates.** The 1960s marked the height of conglomerate merger activity. In part it stemmed from "defensive" diversification out of the aerospace and natural resource industries. In part it represented the philosophy that general managerial capabilities could be profitably transferred to diverse busi-

nesses. Many such conglomerates have proven to be inefficient combinations over time. Divestitures have been used to reduce the number and diversity of activities that had been assembled in firms such as Gulf & Western (Paramount) and ITT.

2. **Abandoning the core business.** The sale by a company of its original business cannot be attributed to a diversification mistake but to changing opportunities or circumstances. In 1987 Greyhound sold its bus business. In 1988 DuPont divested its original commercial explosives business, Wurlitzer sold its basic piano and electric keyboard business (to Baldwin Piano), and B. F. Goodrich Co. sold its remaining stake in the tire business.

3. **Changing strategies or restructuring.** A change in strategic focus may reflect mistakes, learning, or realignment with the firm's changing environments. In 1983 Warner-Lambert sold its successful bakery unit, Entenmann's, to General Foods. In 1982 General Dynamics divested its telecommunications switching business to concentrate on defense business. In 1987 and 1988 Allegis Corp. sold its hotel and car rental units to become UAL Corp. and concentrate on operating United Air Lines, a reversal of a previous strategic plan. Alco Standard Corp. sold off distribution businesses and most manufacturing units after 1987 to focus on paper distribution, office products, and food service equipment. Between 1985 and 1988, TRW divested about $1 billion worth of lower technology businesses in favor of the high technology segments of aerospace and defense, automotive components, and information systems and services. Household International sold its manufacturing units to concentrate on financial services. IBM sold Rolm's manufacturing and development operations to Siemens AG, with whom a joint venture was formed for U.S. sales and service operations for Rolm's switchboard business.

4. **Adding value by selling into a better fit.** Dow Jones divested its textbook business to concentrate on business publishing and regional newspapers by selling its Richard D. Irwin unit to Times Mirror, a newspaper company that was seeking to expand into textbook and professional publishing. In 1986 IBM sold 81 IBM Products Centers, its U.S. retailing operations, to NYNEX, one of the regional telephone companies created in the AT&T court-directed divestiture. In 1988 IBM sold most of its U.S. copier business to Eastman Kodak. Such sales may reflect different capabilities, different strategic philosophies, or different expectations.

5. **Large additional investment required.** Sometimes remaining in a business requires additional investments that a firm is unable or unwilling to make. Thus, in 1988 Eaton sold its defense electronics business, including the B-1B electronics system, to focus on two other major business areas. For similar reasons, Gould sold its antisubmarine warfare business to Westinghouse Electric.

6. **Harvesting past successes.** Some divestitures represent the harvesting of successful investments, often stimulated by favorable market conditions. Here the purpose is to make financial and managerial resources available for developing other opportunities. Such divestitures represent successes rather than failures (or mistakes). Hanson PLC is said to make a business of this activity. Other examples are hotel sales by Hilton and Marriott.

7. **Discarding unwanted businesses from prior acquisitions.** Some divestitures of the type that involved selling to a value-increasing buyer were planned at the time of prior M&A activity. Such divestitures may have been preplanned because they represented a poor fit with the acquiring firm. Sometimes such divestitures

could be turned at a profit; sometimes they involved a loss that was offset by the good segments retained. Examples are Pullman's sales of Bruning Hydraulics and Waterman Hydraulics to Parker Hannifin in 1988 following its acquisition of Clevite Industries in 1987.

8. **Financing prior acquisitions.** A number of divestitures also regularly follow major acquisitions or LBOs for financing reasons. Campeau Corp., which acquired Allied Stores in 1986, stated that it would sell 16 Allied divisions to pay down bank debt. Similarly, after its $6.5 billion acquisition of Federated Department Stores, Campeau engaged in a program of divestitures beginning in late 1988. Other similar patterns followed Beazer PLC's acquisition of Koppers Co. and Maxwell Communications' takeover of Macmillan Inc. Earlier, DuPont, which acquired Conoco in 1981, had sold off $2 billion of Conoco's assets by 1984.

9. **Warding off takeovers.** Divestitures have functioned as a takeover defense by removing the "crown jewel" that attracted the takeover threat. A clear example was the sale by Brunswick Corp. of its medical division in 1982 to American Home Products when facing a takeover threat from Whittaker. The proceeds to Brunswick from the sale of the division were $100 million more than Whittaker had offered for the entire company. Ironically, faced with a similar threat in 1989, Whittaker sold its chemical and technology operations.

10. **Meeting government requirements.** Divestments are a common requirement for obtaining government approval of a combination. Baker Hughes was required to divest its Reed Tool Co. subsidiary to comply with the Justice Department conditions for approval of its merger. Similarly, in 1988 Santa Fe Southern Pacific Corp. was required by the ICC to sell one of its railroads. In general, the government may require divestitures as a condition for approval when a combination includes segments with competing products. This holds for LBOs as well. KKR was required to sell off some RJR Nabisco product segments that overlapped with KKR's prior holdings.

11. **Selling businesses to their managers.** Corporate sales of divisions or business units to operating management are increasing in both number and size. Leveraged buyouts and other going-private transactions have averaged a consistent 11% of total corporate divestitures.

12. **Sell unrelated businesses.** In late 1997, Xerox sold the fifth of the seven insurance units it originally owned. Xerox appeared to be exiting the insurance business (McLeod, 1997).

13. **Sell low margin product lines.** In late 1998, it was announced that the Royal Dutch/Shell Group was planning to divest 40% of its chemicals assets. The divestitures involved seven chemicals operations with combined assets worth $5 billion. The reason given was to improve margins to improve profitability. Shell would continue to produce products in 13 chemical businesses.

14. **Taking a position in another firm.** Divestitures may be used to finance an investment in another firm. An example is the sale in 1989 by Emerson Electric of five units for $149 million to BSR International PLC for a 45% stake in the U.K. firm.

15. **Reversing mistakes.** Exxon's acquisition of Reliance Electric and Mobil's purchase of Montgomery Ward are widely cited as failed attempts at diversification. Both sales were management buyouts.

16. **Learning.** Successful companies may divest businesses after learning more about them. Merck & Co., whose growth had been mainly internal, divested Baltimore Aircoil Co. and part of a Calgon Corp. acquisition after its experience and review process indicated that the businesses "no longer fit its basic long-range strategy" (Horan, 1987). ARA Services, which grew principally by acquisition, eventually divested a construction management business because of lack of fit. Also, it divested a management consulting firm because it found that the business depended on key individuals while ARA was built on systems and controls.

Porter (1987, p. 49) gives a number of examples of how divestiture can perform a very valuable role in the strategic activities of a firm: "Once the results of the one-time improvement are clear, the diversified company no longer adds value to offset the inevitable costs imposed on the unit. It is best to sell the unit and free up corporate resources."

The preceding are examples of the useful functions that divestitures may perform in a company's evolving planning process.

Another general observation is that the use of acquisitions to achieve diversification was severely restricted during the period 1950 through 1980 by government antitrust policies. The 1950 Celler-Kefauver Amendment to the 1914 Clayton Act effectively gave the government the power to stop horizontal and vertical mergers or acquisitions, and the government vigorously exercised its expanded powers. The legal and regulatory environment caused most large mergers during 1950 to 1980 to be the conglomerate form.

However, Matsusaka (1996) observes that antitrust restrictions did not motivate or cause corporate diversification during the 1960s. In a sample of 549 acquisitions, diversification was equally common in large and small mergers. Antitrust barriers would have caused diversification to occur more frequently when large firms merged than when small firms merged. He also cites evidence that diversification movements were also taking place in other developed nations where antitrust enforcement was not tough.

With this background on the economic and political setting of acquisition and divestiture activity, we now examine the evidence on the results.

FINANCIAL EFFECTS OF DIVESTITURES

Studies on divestitures have found significant positive abnormal two-day announcement period returns of between 1% and 2% for selling firm shareholders. The announcement effects on returns to buyers did not appear to be statistically significant (Alexander, Benson, and Kampmeyer, 1984; Jain, 1985; Linn and Rozeff, 1984). A later study by Klein (1986) looked at divestitures in greater depth. Klein analyzed the announcement date effects according to whether the selling firms initially announced the price of the sell-off or whether no price was initially announced. When no price was announced, there was no statistically significant effect on share price for the seller. When firms initially announced the price, the size of effects depended on the percentage of the firm being sold as measured by the announced price of the sell-off divided by the market value of the equity on the last day of the month prior to the announcement period.

There was no significant price effect when the percentage of the equity sold was less than 10%. When the percentage of equity sold was between 10% and 50%, the abnormal returns to the seller averaged a positive 2.53%. When the percentage of the equity sold was greater than 50%, the percentage abnormal return was 8.09%.

When the abnormal gains to sellers from divestitures are aggregated, the totals represent substantial dollar amounts. Black and Grundfest (1988) estimate that for the period 1981 to 1986, the abnormal value increases to sellers in corporate divestitures could be conservatively placed at $27.6 billion.

Lang, Poulsen, and Stulz (LPS) (1995) studied a sample of 93 significant asset sales during the period 1984 to 1989. The firms were divided into a payout sample (40 sales) and a reinvest sample (53 sales). The event return analysis showed that the payout firms had positive abnormal returns of about 2% from day −1 to day zero. The reinvest sample had negative event returns of about 0.5% over the same window. The payout sample firms, on average, had poorer prior performance and higher leverage. Managerial ownership as a fraction of total equity was about 17% for the payout sample compared with 11% for the reinvest sample.

Lang, Poulsen, and Stulz concluded that the positive stock price reaction to asset sales was significantly positive only for firms that planned to pay out the proceeds. The reinvest firms did not have positive event returns because the market is concerned with the agency costs of managerial discretion in the use of the funds. One concern is that managers will use the retained funds to engage in ill-advised diversification. The authors judge their evidence to be inconsistent with the hypothesis that the positive returns associated with asset sales lead to more efficient redeployment of assets and that the selling firm captures some of the gains from increased efficiency.

Kaplan and Weisbach (KW) (1992) provide an insightful analysis of divestiture results. Their study covered a sample of 271 acquisitions between 1971 and 1982 of at least 100 million 1982 dollars. By 1989, 119 had been divested after a median holding period of seven years. Almost 60% of the acquisitions in which the acquirer and target were not highly related had been divested. Fewer than 20% of the highly related acquisitions were divested over the same time period. Only 44% of the acquirers who reported an accounting result for the divestiture reported a loss on sale. The remaining 56% reported a gain or no loss.

When they could compare sales prices to purchase prices for divested units, KW found that most units were sold for more than they cost. Deflated by the S&P 500, the average sale price of these divested units was 90% of the purchase price—a small return but not the failure suggested by previous work. The sale price (deflated by the S&P 500) averaged 143% of the target's pretakeover market value. Targets appear to have been worth less than the bidders pay but more than the target was worth before the takeover occurred. Acquirer returns and total (acquirer and target) returns at the acquisition announcement were significantly lower for divestitures KW classify as unsuccessful than the corresponding returns for divestitures they do not classify as unsuccessful and for acquisitions that were not divested. This last result has two implications. First, in a setting where the nature of the news being revealed is not initially obvious, results suggest that stock market prices do react to fundamentals. Second, it suggests that acquisitions that ultimately prove unsuccessful are considered poor investments by the market when they are made.

We can simplify their findings by setting the pretakeover value (PTV) of the acquisition subsequently divested as 100%. Their data show that the sale price was 171.6% in relation to the PTV of 100%. During the average seven-year holding period, the Standard & Poor's 500 stock index rose by 20%. When we divide the sale price by 1.2, we obtain a deflated sale price equal to 143% of PTV. They state that the deflated sale price was 0.9 of the purchase price. The purchase price, therefore, must have been 159.9% of PTV.

Thus, the story on this large-sample study is that the purchase price was about 60% higher than the pretakeover value. The sale price was about 72% higher. Deflated, the sale price is only 43% higher than PTV. Thus, compared with the original pretakeover value, the predeflated sale price represented a very substantial increase in value. Even after deflation, the sale price represents a 43% gain over the pretakeover value. However, the purchase price was 60% higher than the pretakeover value. So although value was added, the acquirer paid too much in the sense that the deflated value of the sale price was only 90% of the purchase price. If the acquisition price had been roughly 10% lower, the acquirers would have earned the 20% rise in the S&P 500 over the average seven-year holding period. Because these data are on acquisitions that were subsequently divested, we may infer that the acquisitions not subsequently divested performed even better.

The data on divestiture and acquisition rates portray a continued healthy dynamism among U.S. firms. Divestitures perform vital economic functions. Resources, on average, are being moved from less valued uses to higher valued uses. Whether or not sell-offs by one firm to another may sometimes represent efforts to correct previous mistakes, they are evidence that the market system is working. Irrespective of their implications for individual company strategies, divestitures contribute to the resource mobility essential to the effective operation of an enterprise economy.

CASE STUDIES OF DIVESTITURES

The purpose of these case examples is to illustrate the nature of divestiture transactions. The divestiture by the seller represents a movement toward a narrower central core of activities. The acquisition by the buying firm helps it strengthen its strategic programs.

Federal-Mogul–Cooper Automotive

The auto parts industry experienced rapid consolidation in past years. Cost-cutting pressure from vehicle makers is forcing auto parts manufacturers to buy and sell businesses in order to be able to manufacture and deliver complete systems of parts rather than individual items. Major suppliers are staking out specific auto parts segments in which they seek to acquire smaller or strategic competitors.

Cooper Industries announced in April 1998 its intention to separate its auto parts business, Cooper Automotive. The auto parts unit, which includes brand names such as Champion spark plugs, Anco windshield wipers, and Moog steering and suspensions, did not complement its other segments, which include electrical products and tools and hardware. Cooper Automotive's total sales were $1.9 billion in 1997.

On August 18, 1998, Federal-Mogul agreed to acquire Cooper Industries' automotive unit for $1.9 billion. The acquisition was part of the strategic plan of Federal-Mogul's chairman and CEO, Richard A. Snell. Mr. Snell wants Federal-Mogul to become one of the biggest suppliers in auto component systems and replacement parts. To fulfill his plan, Federal-Mogul has been on a five-year strategic acquisition program that will culminate when the company reaches $10 billion in revenues by

2002. Cooper Automotive was the sixth acquisition or joint venture in 1998. Through acquisitions, including the planned Cooper deal, Federal-Mogul quadrupled its annual revenue from $1.8 billion in 1997 to $7 billion in 1998.

Even though Federal-Mogul's main strategy was to acquire businesses that allow it to manufacture complete engine systems for auto makers, Mr. Snell also wanted Federal-Mogul to become the major supplier for brake components. The crown jewel of the Cooper deal is Cooper's brake and friction product business, which is its biggest segment, with 29% of the unit's sales.

The announcement of the deal on August 18, 1998 boosted Federal-Mogul's stock by $7.625 to $63.125, a 14% jump, as investors signaled their approval of Mr. Snell's strategy. Shares of Cooper Industries closed up $1.625 at $48.1875.

Stryker Corp.–Howmedica

Pfizer's strategy in 1998 was to focus on its highly profitable core pharmaceutical business by selling off its medical product divisions. On June 16, 1998, Pfizer announced it would sell Schneider Worldwide to Boston Scientific Corp. for $2.1 billion. On July 22, 1998, it sold its American Medical Systems business to the investment firm E. M. Warburg Pincus & Co. for $130 million. The final piece of Pfizer's strategy was announced on August 14, 1998, when it sold its orthopedic product division, Howmedica, to Stryker Corp. for $1.9 billion.

Stryker is a manufacturer of orthopedic instruments. It has revenues of about $980 million. The acquisition of Howmedica, with estimated sales of more than $800 million, would create the No. 1 or No. 2 firm in the medical products industry. Stryker's acquisition appears to have a strategic fit both by product and by geography. The combined company would have 15% of the worldwide orthopedic market and more than 20% of the reconstructive device market.

The medical product business has experienced rapid consolidation, driven by cost-cutting efforts by hospitals, a fragmented industry, and the desire to concentrate on higher margin businesses. On May 25, 1998, Tyco International Ltd. announced a $3.3 billion acquisition of U.S. Surgical Corp., and Johnson & Johnson announced on July 21, 1998, its plans to expand its own orthopedic business by acquiring DePuy Inc. for $3.5 billion. Stryker's strategic acquisition would almost double its size, allowing it to become a formidable contender in the competitive orthopedics industry.

On the announcement date of 8/14/98, shares of Stryker fell $5.75 (14%) to $36. The shares dipped because the cost of the acquisition would slow down the company's earnings growth. In addition, the transaction would require a sharp increase in debt for a company that had virtually no debt on its books. Pfizer dropped 81.25 cents to $101.1875.

Quaker Oats–Snapple

Quaker Oats acquired Snapple on November 2, 1994, for $1.7 billion. Quaker's chairman, William D. Smithburg, stated that the combination of Snapple fruit and tea drinks with Quaker's Gatorade sports drinks would create the country's third largest beverage company. However, by the end of 1995, Snapple's sales were down 9% with a loss of $100 million. In 1996, sales dropped another 8% instead of rising the predicted 20%.

Quaker has a strong and profitable business in oatmeal, cereals, rice cakes, and sports drinks. It is an expert in warehouse-based business, but it was not prepared for the distribution system of the soft drink industry. There were several missteps in Quaker's approach to Snapple's business:

➤ Quaker forged ahead with the acquisition deal even with the knowledge that Snapple's earnings report would be much worse than anticipated and that sales would continue with a weak trend.

➤ Quaker signed long-term agreements with bottlers that guaranteed them payments even if the demand did not keep up with anticipated production.

➤ Quaker alienated its distributors by trying to change the distribution system in a manner that benefited Quaker and Gatorade but hurt the distributors.

➤ Quaker was unprepared for the onslaught from Coca-Cola Co. and PepsiCo, Inc. in creating and promoting new products to compete with Snapple. It responded with an ineffective ad campaign for more than a year. Finally, Quaker resorted to a giant Snapple giveaway campaign in August 1996, but it made no difference as sales continued to drop.

A divestiture was rumored beginning in November 1996. Some acquirers would consider Snapple only if they could also get Gatorade, Quaker's crown jewel. Although Quaker agreed to bundle Snapple and Gatorade and to consider bids of $3 billion or more, the high price, antitrust concerns, and Snapple's problems scared off potential buyers. It was expected that Snapple alone could be sold at an amount at least equal to its annual sales. However, on March 27, 1997, Quaker announced the signing of a definitive agreement to sell Snapple to Triarc Co. for $300 million, an amount just over half of Snapple's sales of $550 million in 1996. Triarc is a holding company that includes Royal Crown Cola, Mistic drinks, and Arby's restaurants. The market responded with a 25 cent rise in Quaker's stock, to $37.75, on a day when the overall market was sharply down. Triarc's shares went from $15.75 to $17.375.

A *Wall Street Journal* story of December 14, 1998, reported that after 18 months of managing Snapple, Triarc had given Snapple back its "buzz." The double-digit declines that Quaker had been suffering with Snapple had been reversed with a 7% increase in sales volume through the first nine months of 1998. Relationships with distributors were improved. Many new products were introduced. The first was Wendy's Tropical Inspiration, which received national media attention. By August 1997, Snapple introduced a line of exotic teas, such as ginseng, orange jasmine, and green tea. In December 1997 they came out with Snapple Farms, a line of 100% juices, in response to requests from distributors for a product that could be an entrée to schools. A crowning achievement was the introduction in April 1998 of Whipper Snapple, a fruit juice drink with a dairy base, to compete with the growth of juice bars selling "smoothie" fruit shakes.

A *Forbes* article of December 27, 1999, described Quaker's recovery after the divestiture of Snapple. A new chairman, Robert Morrison, was recruited from Philip Morris, where he had been head of the Kraft Foods division. After his arrival in October 1997, Chairman Morrison reorganized Quaker into nine groups, placing younger managers in charge as president of each group. The president of the hot cereals division, which includes the leader, Quaker Oats, added flavors such as Baked Apple and French Vanilla. Dinosaur Eggs instant oatmeal requires only boiling water to change sugary eggs in the oatmeal into baby Triceratops. Sea Adventures is an instant mix that makes sharks and treasure chests appear and turns the water blue. This creativity increased oatmeal sales by 10% in 1999.

Previously, the Gatorade business, which accounts for 40% of Quaker's revenues and operating income, had been sold through independent brokers, with only 15% of Gatorade's grocery customers visited by a Quaker-employed salesperson. More Quaker salespersons were used. This helped to revive the slumping snacks division, because the Gatorade salespeople, who now covered 85% of their grocery customers, could stock convenience stores with Quaker's new lines of snacks such as crispy rice.

Gatorade had achieved an 80% share of a narrowly defined "sports drink" market. Redefining the market to include soft drinks, juice, and bottled water, Gatorade had only 7% of the broader market, so creative new products were introduced. A smoother tasting Frost brand and a sweeter, more intense version of Gatorade, Fierce, quickly exceeded $100 million in sales. Another new product is a "fitness water" called Propel, which contains vitamins and carbohydrates and is aimed at women, who have been slow to use Gatorade. Quaker identified 100,000 new sites where Gatorade might be sold and hired over 200 new college graduates to develop new accounts through cold calls. Within two years, their efforts accounted for 25% of the 1999 growth in Gatorade's top line, exceeding $100 million in sales.

Following the divestiture of Snapple, Robert Morrison revitalized Quaker. This was achieved through cost cutting in addition to building on Quaker's strengths. At the time of Morrison's appointment in October 1997, Quaker stock was $46. By the end of 1999, Quaker stock had risen to $65. This is said to represent the best performance among the big companies in the food industry during that time period. The moral of the story is that a major divestiture can trigger a major renewal at a corporation.

Dillingham

Hite and Owers (1984) describe the Dillingham case, which is a virtual textbook illustration of restructuring. Over the period 1978 to 1983, Dillingham was involved in divestitures, a spin-off, partial liquidations and suspended operations, proxy contests, antitakeover amendments, a tender offer buyback from small shareholders, a premium buyback with standstill agreement to thwart a takeover, and finally a leveraged buyout to take the company private. Although a few of these moves had immediate adverse effects, over a four-year period Dillingham's shareholders experienced abnormal positive returns of 185%, over 85% of which occurred before the LBO announcement. These returns may not be typical, but they do illustrate the potential for gains from restructuring in a dynamic setting.

Entenmann's Bakery

Linn and Rozeff (1984) analyze the specific returns in two divestitures. In 1983 Warner-Lambert sold its Entenmann's Bakery subsidiary to General Foods. The general rationale for gains was discussed earlier; here we look at the numbers involved. The sale price for Entenmann's was $315 million. Upon announcement of the sale, the value of Warner-Lambert stock increased by $101 million and the value of General Foods stock increased by about $44 million (both adjusted for marked effects). Both parties benefited from the transaction. From the point of view of Warner-Lambert shareholders, we have

Sale price of Entenmann's received	$315 million
Less: Stock value increase	101 million
Implied value of Entenmann's as part of Warner-Lambert	$214 million

From the point of view of General Foods shareholders, we have

Purchase price of Entenmann's paid	$315 million
Plus: Stock value increase	44 million
Implied value of Entenmann's as part of General Foods	$359 million

Warner-Lambert's shareholders received a premium over what they perceived to be the value of Entenmann's to them. General Foods' shareholders could expect that they would receive benefits from Entenmann's in excess of costs. The total value increase as a result of the divestiture amounted to $145 million, distributed approximately 70–30 between seller and buyer. That the seller received the larger proportion of the gain is not inconsistent with merger studies.

Hospital Affiliates International

Another case involved the sale of Hospital Affiliates International (HAI) by INA Corporation to Hospital Corporation of America (HCA) for $650 million in 1981. INA was primarily in the insurance business, and the economic rationale for the divestiture seemed to have been that while HAI was a "poor fit" with INA's other operations, HCA would be able to realize operating economies as a result of the acquisition. INA shareholders realized a $75 million abnormal gain upon announcement of the sale, and shareholders of HCA realized $126 million. In this case the total value increase was $201 million, divided approximately 40–60 between seller and buyer, respectively.

RATIONALE FOR DIVESTITURES

It has been observed that targets gain from takeovers and that a commonly observed post-takeover initiative is divestiture (Boot, 1992). If gains from takeovers reflect at least in part the anticipation of such divestitures, why didn't the target firm's management divest earlier? Boot concludes that a manager may choose to avoid a value-improving divestiture because it would represent an admission of an earlier unwise decision that could adversely affect the manager's reputation.

A later study (Cho and Cohen, 1997) seeks to explain why managers may ultimately sell losers. If the firm has other operating units that are performing well, this may partially hide the poor performance of other units. When the firm's other units begin to underperform relative to their industry peers, this triggers the sale of the poorly performing units. (See also Kang and Shivdasani, 1997).

Another aspect has been developed based on the size of the diversification discount or value losses in relation to imputed stand-alone values (Berger and Ofek, 1996). Firms with the largest diversification discounts or losses are more likely to become takeover targets and be bought by financial buyers. The extent of post-takeover bustup sales activity is positively associated with the size of the diversification discount. In the post-takeover bustups, the divested divisions are generally purchased and become part of a focused, stand-alone firm.

Linn and Rozeff (1984) analyze the various motives given for divestitures. Among the reasons given for selling assets are the need to raise working capital and to pay off debt. However, these are financial decisions and can potentially be accomplished by actions that do not include divestitures. Furthermore, financing as such should not be expected to significantly increase the seller's share price (Smith, 1986a, 1986b).

Linn and Rozeff (1984) argue that there are only two valid reasons for divestitures:

1. The assets are worth more as part of the buyer's organization than as part of the seller's.
2. The assets are actively interfering with other profitable operations of the seller.

For example, it is sometimes said that the reason for a divestiture is that the subsidiary is losing money. However, the present value of the subsidiary's future cash flows is already reflected in the seller's stock price. Unless the subsidiary is sold for more than this present value (that is, it is worth more to the buyer), no gain will result from the divestiture. However, if the subsidiary is actually preventing other operations from realizing their potentials, then the removal of this negative synergy could cause a positive price impact even if no more than the present value of the subsidiary were received.

The fact that gains to divestitures (1% to 2%) are on average smaller than for spin-offs (3% to 5%) may reflect poor performance prior to the divestiture. Information about worse-than-expected performance may be revealed to the market simultaneously with the divestiture announcement, offsetting to some extent any positive price effect that might otherwise occur. The seller may have to dispose of assets quickly to avert a liquidity crisis and may not be able to wait for a "fair price" (Linn and Rozeff rejected this rationale).

The smaller gains from divestitures may reflect their smaller relative scale. On average, divestitures may be smaller in relative magnitude than spin-offs. The managerial incentive factor may also play a role. Spun-off subsidiaries become free-standing independent firms with their own common stock. But divested operations may become segments of another company.

John and Ofek (1995) studied the motives and effects of divestitures. They found that value gains resulted from improved management of the assets remaining after divestiture. This, in turn, was attributed to increased focus measured by an increase in the Herfindahl Hirschman Index and a decrease in the number of reported lines of business. Also they found that 75% of the divested divisions are unrelated to the core activities of the seller.

They observed that some of their findings supported the hypothesis that a better fit between the buyer and the divested division accounts for some of the value gains. For example, seller returns were higher when the buyer was an LBO group, which is likely to improve operating performance due to the organizational changes and strengthening of incentive systems.

SUMMARY

Because divestitures are voluntary decisions by management, we would expect them to represent positive NPV strategies toward the goal of maximizing shareholder wealth. Several principles form the basis for the value increase observed in sell-offs. In some cases the underlying cause is clear; in others it may be impossible to distinguish between two or more possible sources. We summarize some explanations.

A general reason for the sale of a segment is that it is a poor fit with the firm's other activities. There are at least two factors involved. The parent firm's management may lack the expertise to manage dissimilar assets. The assets may be creating negative synergy, that is, actively interfering with other profitable operations of the parent. The high incidence of sell-offs after a period of acquisitions and rapid growth may reflect this motive.

Another possibility is that the sell-off reflects new information about the value of the segment to another firm. In divestitures, the transaction is generally initiated by the seller, who has discovered a higher valued use for a subset of business assets elsewhere. However, gains that take place at the time of the sell-off announcement dissipate if the sell-off is canceled. This may indicate that no new information has been uncovered. Alternatively, it is possible that the new information cannot be exploited in canceled sell-offs. It is possible that another organization is required to have the knowledge or capabilities to develop the potential of the business segment involved.

Still other reasons for divestitures relate to providing a sharper management focus on strategic business units. One theory holds that a more homogeneous organization may be managed more effectively and evaluated more accurately by financial analysts. In addition, managers may receive incentives and rewards more closely related to actual performance than when the quality of performance may be obscured in consolidated financial statements or monitored by superiors unfamiliar with the unique problems of a disparate segment.

Divestitures (sell-offs) represent mistakes in a sense because previous investment decisions are altered. However, they may also represent the harvesting of sound investments made earlier. Some sell-offs were planned at the time of earlier acquisitions, sometimes to help finance the larger transactions. Sell-offs may also reflect organizational learning or the reorientation of business strategies. To some degree at least, divestitures represent the movement of business resources to higher valued uses.

QUESTIONS

11.1 What are the gains in divestitures and why?

11.2 What are pure-play securities, and what is their role in the information and managerial efficiency hypothesis of divestitures?

11.3 According to Linn and Rozeff, what are the only two valid reasons for divestitures?

11.4 How do tax and/or regulatory factors affect returns to divestitures?

11.5 What is the magnitude of divestiture activity in relation to M&A activity generally?

REFERENCES

Alexander, Gordon J., P. George Benson, and Joan M. Kampmeyer, "Investigating the Valuation Effects of Announcements of Voluntary Corporate Selloffs," *Journal of Finance*, 39, June 1984, pp. 503–517.

Ansoff, H. Igor, *Corporate Strategy*, New York: McGraw-Hill, 1965.

Berger, Philip G., and Eli Ofek, "Bustup Takeover of Value-Destroying Diversified Firms," *Journal of Finance*, 51, September 1996, pp. 1175–1200.

Black, Bernard S., and Joseph A. Grundfest, "Shareholder Gains from Takeovers and Restructurings Between 1981 and 1986: $162 Billion Is a Lot of Money," *Journal of Applied Corporate Finance*, 1, Spring 1988, pp. 5–15.

Boot, Arnoud W. A. "Why Hang On To Losers? Divestitures and Takeovers," Journal of Finance, 1992, v47(4), 1401–1424.

Cho, Myeong-Hyeon, and Mark A. Cohen, "The Economic Causes and Consequences of Corporate Divestiture," *Managerial & Decision Economics*, 18, August 1997, pp. 367–374.

Hite, Gailen, and James E. Owers, "The Restructuring of Corporate America: An Overview," *Midland Corporate Finance Journal*, 2, Summer 1984, pp. 6–16.

Horan, John J., "Merck & Co.: Study in Internal Growth," chapter 8 in Milton L. Rock, ed., *The Mergers & Acquisitions Handbook*, New York: McGraw-Hill Book Company, 1987.

Jain, Prem C., "The Effect of Voluntary Sell-Off Announcements on Shareholder Wealth," *Journal of Finance*, 40, March 1985, pp. 209–224.

John, Kose, and Eli Ofek, "Asset Sales and Increase in Focus," *Journal of Financial Economics*, 37(1), January 1995, pp. 105–126.

Kang, Jun-Koo, and Anil Shivdasani, "Corporate Restructuring During Performance Declines in Japan," *Journal of Financial Economics*, 46, October 1997, pp. 29–65.

Kaplan, Steven N., and Michael S. Weisbach, "The Success of Acquisitions: Evidence from Divestitures," *Journal of Finance*, 47(1), March 1992, pp. 107–138.

Klein, A., "The Timing and Substance of Divestiture Announcements: Individual, Simultaneous and Cumulative Effects," *Journal of Finance*, 41, 1986, pp. 685–697.

Lang, Larry, Annette Poulsen, and René Stulz, "Asset Sales, Firm Performance, and the Agency Costs of Managerial Discretion," *Journal of Financial Economics*, 37(1), January 1995, pp. 3–37.

Linn, Scott C., and Michael S. Rozeff, "The Corporate Sell-off," *Midland Corporate Finance Journal*, 2, Summer 1984, pp. 17–26.

Loh, Charmen, and R. S. Rathinasamy, "The Impact of Antitakeover Devices on the Valuation Consequences of Voluntary Corporate Selloffs," *Financial Review*, 32, November 1997, pp. 691–707.

Matsusaka, John G., "Did Tough Antitrust Enforcement Cause the Diversification of American Corporations?" *Journal of Financial and Quantitative Analysis*, 31(2), June 1996, pp. 283–294.

McLeod, Douglas, "Resolution Sale Furthers Xerox Plan to Exit Insurance," *Business Insurance*, 31(37), September 15, 1997, p. 75.

Milmo, Sean, "Shell Slashes Chemical Assets Valued at $5 Billion," *Chemical Market Reporter*, 254(25), December 21, 1998, p. 33.

Porter, Michael E., "From Competitive Advantage to Corporate Strategy," *Harvard Business Review*, 65, May–June 1987, pp. 43–59.

Smith, Clifford W., Jr., "Investment Banking and the Capital Acquisition Process," *Journal of Financial Economics*, 15, January/February 1986a, pp. 3–29.

————, "Raising Capital: Theory and Evidence," *Midland Corporate Finance Journal*, 4, Spring 1986b, pp. 6–22.

Restructuring Organization and Ownership Relationships

In this chapter we continue the analysis of several forms of restructuring. Here we focus on restructuring organization and ownership relationships: spin-offs, equity carve-outs, tracking stock, and split-ups. The presentation pattern is to describe briefly each form of restructuring, summarize studies of the immediate stock market reaction as measured by event returns, and summarize longer term performance results. The business and economic reasons for the methods are discussed as a group. This is because they all represent methods by which diversified companies become less diversified, moving toward more focused activities.

SPIN-OFFS

In a spin-off, a company owns or creates a subsidiary whose shares are distributed on a pro rata basis to the shareholders of the parent company. The subsidiary now becomes a publicly owned corporation. The number of shares in the spin-off in relation to the parent's shares varies. The parent company will often retain from 10% to under 20% of the shares in the new subsidiary. Often the spin-off follows the initial sale of under 20% of the shares in an initial public offering (IPO). This transaction is called an equity carve-out and is discussed in the following section.

In its March–April almanac issue, *Mergers & Acquisitions* magazine generally lists major spin-offs for the year. Notable spin-offs in 1993 included the spin-off by Sears of the Dean Witter Discover operation, whose initial value was $530 million. The spin-off by Eastman Kodak of Eastman Chemical represented a $3.7 billion initial valuation. Later spin-offs by well-known parent companies included Dole Food, General Mills, Host Marriott, ITT, Kimberly Clark, Hanson PLC, and US West.

In 1998, examples included the spin-off by Ralston Purina of its animal feeds business into Agribrands International Inc., granting stockholders one share in Agribrands per 10 shares of Ralston Purina. Alleghany Corporation did a spin-off of a title insurance business, Chicago Title Corp. on a 1-to-3 ratio. Qualcomm Inc.

placed its cellular phone service business into Leap Wireless International on a 1-to-4 ratio. Hilton Hotels Corporation split off its casinos business into Park Place Entertainment Corp 1-to-1.

Event Return Studies of Spin-Offs

Schipper and Smith (1983) found a positive 2.84% abnormal return to the parent (statistically significant) on the spin-off announcement date. The size of the announcement effect is positively related to the size of the spin-off relative to parent size (the average size of the spin-off is about 20% of the original parent). Spin-offs motivated by avoidance of regulation experienced an abnormal return of 5.07% compared to 2.29% for the remainder of the sample. Examples of regulation avoidance include separating a regulated utility subsidiary from nonutility businesses and spinning off a foreign subsidiary to avoid restrictions by the U.S. Congress.

Hite and Owers (1983) found abnormal returns of 3.8%, somewhat higher than for the full sample of Schipper and Smith. They also found a positive relation between the relative size of the spin-off and the announcement effect. Neither study found an adverse effect on bondholders.

The Copeland, Lemgruber, and Mayers (1987) study extended the earlier studies in a number of dimensions. Particularly, they tested for postselection bias. In their first sample, they did this by including announced spin-offs that were not completed (11% of the sample). This led them to examine the effects of successive announcements. A second expanded sample, subject to postselection bias, confirmed the impact of successive announcements. They also studied ex-date effects, which they also found to have positive abnormal performance. They conclude that taxable spin-offs did not have positive abnormal returns, whereas nontaxable spin-offs did. However, when they controlled for the size of the spin-off, the difference between the two tax categories disappeared.

For their small sample with no postselection bias, the two-day abnormal return from the first announcement was 2.49%; for the larger sample it was 3.03%. Both results are highly significant from a statistical standpoint. Thus, avoiding the postselection bias makes a difference; the return is lower for the sample that includes firms with announced spin-offs that were never consummated. For the eight firms with announced spin-offs that were never made, the two-day average return was a negative (but insignificant) 0.15%.

Copeland, Lemgruber, and Mayers (1987) also calculated the effects of announcements subsequent to the first (most firms had at least three or four announcements; one had 13). They found that, excluding the ex-date from the estimate, the abnormal return for a firm that actually completed the spin-off was 5.02%. They concluded that the first announcement return is not a good estimate of the effect of a completed spin-off because not all spin-offs are completed and earlier studies had underestimated the wealth effect of a completed spin-off.

In terms of dollar value, overall company gains were roughly equal to the value of the subsidiary spun off. The parent's value was virtually unchanged by the restructuring, while the subsidiary had a new independent market value of its own. For example, if the original firm before the spin-off has a value of 5, and the subsidiary's value becomes 1, then the post-spin-off value of the parent remains at 5. Thus, the total value would be 6.

A study by Cusatis, Miles, and Woolridge (CMW) (1993) covered returns for a sample of 146 spin-offs for the 1965 to 1988 period. They measured the market performance of spin-offs and their parent firms for periods of up to three years after the distribution. For the 146 spin-offs, unadjusted returns were significantly positive for each of the time segments subsequent to the distribution—one-half year, one year, two years, and three years. The mean return for the three-year period following the spin-off was 76%. They also calculated the adjusted returns net of the contemporaneous returns to firms matched on the basis of market value and industry classification. The returns remained significantly positive for the two- and three-year holding periods but not significant for the shorter holding periods. These findings differ from the results for samples of initial public offerings (IPOs), which achieved high initial returns but over the longer term, such as three years, underperformed the market and matched firms. In contrast, CMW found positive long-term abnormal returns for spin-offs.

Similarly, the raw returns of the parent firms of 146 spin-offs achieved positive and significant abnormal returns for each of the four time segments. For example, the raw mean return over a three-year period was 67.2%. The matched firm adjusted returns remained positive for all of the time periods but only marginally significant for the three-year holding period.

CMW (1993) also found that both the spin-offs and their parents were more frequently involved in takeovers than comparable firms in their control groups. One-third of the spin-off–parent combinations became involved in takeover activity within three years of the spin-off. For parent firms, most of the takeovers took place within the first two years following the spin-off, the years during which the stock returns of the parent firms were the highest. For the spin-offs, most of the takeovers occurred in years 2 and 3, which are the years of their strongest stock performance. Interestingly, when the firms involved in takeovers are removed from their sample, the adjusted returns remain positive but not significantly different from zero for most intervals. This implies that parent firms and their spin-offs that engage in no further restructuring activity earn only normal returns during the subsequent three-year period of time. It is the parent firms and their spin-offs that engage in further restructuring through takeovers that account for the positive abnormal returns during the subsequent three-year period.

In addition to the academic studies of the event returns from spin-offs, several papers have measured the performance of spin-offs. These studies cover different time segments for different sample groups. The average stock performance of the parent and spin-off is compared to returns on the S&P 500. Illustrative is the study by Anslinger, Klepper, and Subramanian (1999). The entire sample outperformed the S&P 500. However, a few spectacular performances dominate the results. Generally, as high as 50% of the spin-off sample companies underperformed the S&P 500 or other broad benchmark. Our own analysis of spin-off groups reported in *Mergers & Acquisitions* magazine suggests that spin-offs that take place in industries with excess capacity or low sales growth underperform a broad index. Spin-offs should be grouped and related to comparable non-spin-off companies to take into account differences in the economic developments of different industries.

Tax Aspects of Spin-Offs

To qualify for tax-exempt status on a spin-off, the parent company must own 80% of a voting subsidiary stock. But companies have been spinning off firms with two classes of stock. The parent sells a nonvoting class of stock in a public offering and then spins off the voting stock tax-free. The company can do an equity carve-out of 20% of the voting stock and spin off the remainder, and the entire spin-off transaction is tax-free. But the company is able to raise substantial sums of money through the sale of the nonvoting stock associated with the spin-off.

Another thing companies have been doing with spin-offs is to form a new subsidiary. Peoplesoft created a subsidiary called Momentum Business Applications. Momentum has two classes of shares. Peoplesoft owns all the B shares, which are essentially the ones with voting rights. The A shares were distributed to Peoplesoft shareholders. Momentum, which shares office space with Peoplesoft, has little more than a former Peoplesoft executive and $250 million of Peoplesoft's cash. Momentum will work on research to develop software programs for Peoplesoft. Momentum will pay for the software development from the $250 million cash fund, from which it will also pay an extra 5% or more to cover Peoplesoft's administrative costs. Momentum will own any new software it develops; Peoplesoft has an option to buy licenses for the products or to buy back the proportion of Momentum's stock it does not now own. Nothing requires Peoplesoft to buy back the shares or to put any more money into Momentum. Peoplesoft has said that the $250 million should cover research for about three or four years. But there is no requirement to pay Momentum any more money. So when the cash runs out, the Momentum shares may be worthless.

The Peoplesoft arrangement was copied from a practice used earlier by biotechnology and pharmaceutical companies such as Allergan Inc. and Alza Corporation. Alza set up a subsidiary called Crescendo. In the Peoplesoft deal, Merrill Lynch received a $2.5 million fee for setting up the transaction and for its written opinion that the deal was fair to shareholders. Peoplesoft says that Momentum allows it to separate the risk of research from its core operations. This allows shareholders to decide whether to increase or decrease their own risk.

EQUITY CARVE-OUTS

An equity carve-out is the IPO of some portion of the common stock of a wholly owned subsidiary. Equity carve-outs are also referred to as "split-off IPOs." An IPO of the equity of a subsidiary resembles a seasoned equity offering of the parent in that cash is received from a public sale of equity securities. However, there are also differences. The IPO of the common stock of the subsidiary initiates public trading in a new and distinct set of equity claims on the assets of the subsidiary.

Other changes often take place as well when the subsidiary equity is "carved out" from the consolidated entity of the parent. The management system for operating the assets is likely to be restructured in this new public entity. A public market value for the operations of the subsidiary becomes established. Financial reports are issued on the subsidiary operations and are studied by financial analysts as reports of a separate entity. Ongoing public information on the value of the subsidiary may have a positive influence on performance in the subsidiary. In addition, as an entity now separate from the parent, evaluation of performance may be facilitated. Incentives may be strengthened by relating the compensation of the executives in the subsidiary to the performance of the publicly traded stock. If the parent should decide to sell the subsidiary, having established a public market for the stock may facilitate reaching an agreement with a buyer on a sales price.

An equity carve-out or split-off IPO is similar to a voluntary spin-off in that both result in subsidiary's equity claims that are traded separately from the equity claims on the parent entity. The equity carve-out differs from a spin-off in two respects. In a spin-off a distribution is made pro rata to the shareholders of the parent firm as a dividend—a form of noncash payment to the shareholders. In an equity carve-out, the stock of the subsidiary is sold in the public markets for cash that is received by the parent. A second distinction is that in a spin-off the parent firm no longer has control over the subsidiary assets. In a carve-out, the parent generally sells only a minority interest in the subsidiary and maintains control over subsidiary assets and operations.

Spin-Offs, Carve-Outs, Split-Ups

Equity carve-outs can be used by a firm to raise equity funds directly related to the operation of a particular segment or subsidiary. But equity carve-outs are also used as the first step in a spin-off and split-up. To clarify, we now present some examples.

The GM–Delphi Carve-Out and Spin-Off

Overview of Delphi

Delphi was able to gain a full understanding of the design, engineering, manufacture, and operation of all aspects of the automotive vehicle by serving as the principal supplier of automotive parts to GM. It has both technical expertise in many product lines and strong systems integration skills, which allow it to supply its customers with comprehensive systems-based solutions. In the early 1990s Delphi began to transform its business from a captive component supplier to General Motors to a supplier of components, integrated systems, and modules to every major manufacturer of light vehicles in the world. From 1993 to 1998, Delphi's sales to customers other than GM grew from 13.3% to 21.4% of total sales.

By 1999 Delphi had become the world's largest and most diversified supplier of automotive parts, with a network of manufacturing sites, technical centers, sales offices, and joint ventures located in every major region of the world. Primarily a "tier 1" supplier (a supplier that provides products directly to automotive vehicle manufacturers), Delphi also sells its products to the worldwide aftermarket and to non-vehicle manufacturers. Delphi operates in three major product sectors: electronics and mobile communications; safety, thermal, and electrical architecture; and dynamics and propulsion.

Background of Delphi Separation

Prior to 1991 General Motors had acquired many separate automotive parts operations. In 1991 GM organized these separate businesses into the Automotive Components Group with the intent to improve competitiveness and then penetrate new markets. GM wanted the group to establish a separate identity in the automotive parts industry, so the group was renamed Delphi Automotive Systems in 1995. In 1997 Delco Electronics became part of the Delphi Automotive Systems business sector. After several years of comprehensive review, the GM board of directors determined in August 1998 that it would be in the best interests of all involved to separate Delphi from GM. The board of directors believed that Delphi would not be able to reach its full business potential with other original equipment manufacturers as long as it remained part of GM. Therefore, Delphi was incorporated in September 1998 in Delaware.

On January 1, 1999, GM supplied Delphi with those assets and liabilities that were part of the Delphi Automotive Systems business sector of GM. The following month, Delphi completed its initial public offering of 100,000,000 shares of common stock (17.7% equity carveout) while GM held the remaining 465,000,000 (82.3%) of Delphi's outstanding stock. Then in April the board of directors approved the spin-off of 452,565,000 of GM's shares (80.1%) through a dividend of 0.7 share of Delphi per share of GM common stock. The remaining 12,435,000 of GM's shares (2.2%) were contributed to the General Motors welfare benefit trust. Based on the closing price of Delphi and the number of shares of GM common stock outstanding, the Delphi spin-off had a value of $13.62 per share of GM common stock.

Upon completion of the spin-off, executives of GM serving on Delphi's board resigned their positions. Delphi became a fully independent, publicly traded company after the spin-off and the contribution to the GM benefit trust.

Dividends on GM Common Stock

In April 1999 the GM board of directors also indicated its intention to maintain a $0.50 quarterly dividend on GM common stock. This provides holders of GM common stock with an effective dividend increase, because Delphi intends to pay quarterly dividends of $0.07 per share of Delphi common stock. Holders of GM common stock will benefit from an increased overall dividend payment of about $0.20 per year.

Tax Aspects

General Motors received a private letter ruling from the IRS that the spin-off would be tax-free. GM common stockholders would not recognize a gain or loss for receiving the Delphi shares, and GM would not realize a gain or loss from the spin-off. The tax basis of the Delphi stock would be based on the investor's tax basis in the GM stock.

Delphi's Future with GM

Delphi and General Motors will continue to have significant ongoing relationships following the spin-off in April 1999. GM is Delphi's largest customer, and Delphi is GM's largest automotive parts supplier. They have entered into a supply agreement that will provide Delphi with a substantial base of business with GM well into the next decade. The supply agreement between GM and Delphi provides that all existing contracts between them as of January 1, 1999 will generally remain in effect, including the pricing, duration, and purchase order terms and conditions. Delphi has the right to provide on competitive terms the first replacement cycle of all products programs in the United States and Canada that Delphi was providing GM as of January 1, 1999 if Delphi is competitive in terms of design, quality, price, service, and technology.

This case study of the GM–Delphi separation illustrates that a carve-out, spin-off, and split-up were involved. GM first did a 17.7% equity carve-out. This was followed by a spin-off of 0.7 share of Delphi for 1 share of GM common stock. The result was to split Delphi off from General Motors. Thus, in interpreting the stock market reaction and subsequent performance, the three aspects of the process need to be kept in mind. The GM–Delphi case is a pure form of equity carve-out followed by a spin-off in which shareholders received Delphi shares as a dividend on their GM stock. The DuPont–Conoco case, next described, involved a share exchange.

DuPont's Spin-Off of Conoco

In 1981 after a bidding war with other companies, DuPont bought Conoco for $7.41 billion. Over the entire period of the bidding war, between June 19, 1981 and August 5, 1981, DuPont had negative abnormal returns of 9.9% for a loss in equity value of $789 million. On May 12, 1998, DuPont announced that it would divest 20% of its Conoco oil subsidiary and subsequently spin off the remainder. For the full year of 1997, Conoco had sales of $21.41 billion, with after-tax operating income of $1.07 billion. The initial market reaction was a rise of $5.44 in the value of DuPont's shares, or 7.3% on top of the 30% rise in DuPont's shares that had taken place earlier in the year.

In the initial IPO, DuPont sold 150 million A shares, which carried one vote, at $23, raising $3.45 billion. This established a price of the Conoco class A common stock that ranged from a low of $19 to a high of $27 between the time of the IPO and July 8, 1999. Prior to the share exchange, described in a proxy statement to shareholders on July 12, 1999, Conoco raised $9.22 billion in debt, which was used to repay intercompany indebtedness to DuPont.

The spin-off of the remainder of Conoco was accomplished by a share exchange in which for each share of DuPont stock the holder could receive 2.95 shares of class B stock of Conoco. The class B stock was identical to the class A stock except that each share carried 5 votes. The price relationships between DuPont and Conoco at the time of the exchange enabled DuPont shareholders to acquire Conoco at a price of $23.26 when the market price of the class A stock was $27.37, representing a discount of 15%. The proxy to shareholders of July 12, 1999 showed an increase in the net worth account of DuPont of $12.596 billion. This represented receiving 148 million DuPont shares with a market value of $11.95 billion plus cash paid for 8 million DuPont shares at $646 million held by foreigners who could not participate in the exchange offer. So the total received by DuPont was the $3.45 billion in the IPO plus $11.95 billion share value turned in plus the debt repayment of $9.22 billion, totaling $24.62 billion on an after-tax basis.

By using the share exchange method, DuPont enabled its shareholders to choose whether they wanted to invest in the chemical industry versus the petroleum industry. A spin-off of Conoco shares to DuPont shareholders would have resulted in sales of the Conoco shares by holders who preferred not to invest in the petroleum industry. This would have depressed the price of the Conoco shares.

DuPont stated that it would use the proceeds of the Conoco transaction to invest in its program to make chemicals out of agricultural commodities rather than oil. On January 11, 2000, the *Wall Street Journal* carried a story announcing that

Cargill and Dow Chemical were planning full-scale commercial production of plastic made from plants such as corn or wheat instead of petroleum. This appears to support the feasibility of DuPont's strategic shift.

Instead of a dividend, the DuPont–Conoco spin-off required the DuPont shareholders to exchange or give up their DuPont shares to obtain the Conoco shares. This contrasts with the GM–Delphi situation, where the Delphi shares were a form of dividend.

Carve-Out Event Returns

A split-off IPO is similar to a divestiture in that cash is received. But a divestiture is usually to another company. Hence, control over the assets sold is relinquished by the parent-seller, and the trading of subsidiary stock is not initiated.

Spin-offs generally result in abnormal returns to the parent firm of 2% to 3% on average. Divestitures result in gains of 1% to 2% to selling firms on average. New seasoned equity issues are associated with announcement period negative residuals of about 2% to 3%. Because equity carve-outs have characteristics in common with each of the three types of transactions, it is not readily predictable what the announcement period market reactions will be.

Schipper and Smith (1986) studied the performance of a usable sample of 81 equity carve-outs announced between 1965 and 1983. Underwritten offerings represented about 73% of the sample. This is lower than the 93% underwriting used in common stock issues of exchange-listed firms for the period 1971 to 1975 reported by Smith (1977). In 81% of the cases, less than 50% of the subsidiary shares were sold. The parent took a minority position in about 9% of the issues, and data were not available on the other 10%. The dollar amount sold ranged widely, from $300,000 to as high as $112 million. About 30% were below $10 million in size, but 26% were over $30 million. The proceeds represented a relatively small percentage of parent common equity value measured at the end of the month preceding the carve-out announcement. Data were not available on 20% of the sample. Of the 65 offerings for which data were available, 62% represented an amount less than 10% of the size of the parent common equity. Another 15% were in the 10% to under 15% range.

The initial percentage return on the stock of the new subsidiaries was calculated (Schipper and Smith, 1986) by relating the closing bid price on the first day of trading for which a price could be obtained (within 10 trading days of the offering) to the offering price. The average initial return was 4.9%, whereas the median was 2.1%. When an outlier is removed, the average initial return drops to 1.7%. These returns are much lower than those observed in studies of public offerings generally. Ibbotson (1975) found average initial returns of 11.4% for 120 IPOs for the period 1960 to 1969. For the period 1977 to 1982, Ritter (1984) observed average initial returns of 26.5% for 1,028 initial public offerings, but these results were greatly influenced by the high initial returns on natural resource stocks during 1980 to 1981, probably related to OPEC's oil price increases in 1979.

Although the large initial returns on IPOs generally were not matched by these split-off IPOs, substantial returns were observed in a small sample reported by *Corporate Restructuring* (1988) for the period between 1986 and the first half of 1988, which includes the major market decline of October 1987. The postoffering performance of the IPOs was related to the trends of the industries in which the firms were situated. The best performance was achieved by three split-off IPOs in the chemical industry. During the period of the study, profits in this segment of the industry had risen because of increased demand for their output while raw materials prices remained stable. USX Corporation in late 1986 took public an entity named Aristech Chemical Corp. Its offering price of 17 3/4 on November 26, 1987 rose to 35 1/4 by July 6, 1988, a gain of almost 100%. Similar gains were achieved by Borden Chemicals & Plastics, which was taken public by its parent, Borden Inc., on November 20, 1987, and by IMC Fertilizer Group, which was taken public by International Minerals & Chemicals on January 26, 1988. Five other companies achieved large positive gains that averaged 38%. The stock prices of two were unchanged. Three carve-outs by firms in financial services declined an average of 32%. The latter firms were greatly affected by the decline in public trading following the market drop in October 1987. The other split-off IPOs provided excellent returns for that difficult time period.

Equity carve-outs on average are associated with positive abnormal returns of almost 2% over a five-day announcement period (Schipper and Smith, 1986). This is in contrast to findings of significant negative returns of about 2% to 3% when parent companies publicly offer additional shares of their own (as opposed to their subsidiary's) stock (Smith, 1986a, 1986b).

Michaely and Shaw (MS) (1995) compared the performance aspects of spin-offs with equity carve-outs. Unlike early studies, this one covered a special set of spin-offs and equity carve-outs in which the organization form is master limited partnerships (MLPs), which, like other partnerships, do not pay tax on entity income. The tax is paid by each shareholder on the pro rata share of MLP income. Dividends received by partnership shareholders are not taxed, avoiding the double taxation borne by corporate shareholders. These tax benefits were augmented by the Tax Reform Act of 1986, under which the marginal and average tax rates paid by individuals were lower than for corporations.

Although the shares of MLPs are publicly traded on major stock exchanges, the shares are nonvoting. The sponsoring corporation or one of its units functions as the general partner and has sole control over all of the decisions of the MLP. One of the reasons for the creation of an equity carve-out or spin-off is to formulate compensation schemes that will strengthen management incentives and motivation. However, with control completely held by the general partner, the discretionary power of management may be circumscribed.

The special characteristics of MLPs may affect their empirical results. For example, Michaely and Shaw found that for a two-year period the parents of carve-outs experienced a 27.3% increase in stock prices compared with 23% for a control group; the parents of spin-offs had a 70% reduction in equity values compared with a 22% decline for their control group. The shares of both the carve-out and spin-off MLPs underperformed a similar group of existing firms. The authors acknowledge that their results for spin-off firms differed from those of Cusatis, Miles, and Woolridge (1993), who found that both the parents and the new entities experience positive abnormal stock price performance. The value increases are associated with the firms that subsequently engaged in takeover activity.

However, with regard to event returns, MS found a positive reaction to both spin-off and carve-out announcements. Over a four-day window, the event returns to spin-off parents were about 4.5%, but for the carve-out parents they were only 0.4%. The market appeared to respond more favorably to spin-offs than to equity carve-outs for their sample. They also found that the larger, less leveraged, and more profitable parent firms more often chose to use equity carve-outs. Only the spin-off parents decreased debt levels at the time of the transaction, probably transferring debt into the spun-off firm.

MS acknowledge that over half their spin-off sample was from the oil and gas industry, which had very poor performance during the 1980s, the time period of their study. Because they used control-matched samples, they feel that industry characteristics do not explain their results. However, it is our experience that MLPs are at least sometimes formed to give the control group, the general partner, protection while the firm works through some performance problems. MLPs may also involve adverse selection or timing the market. The Boston Celtics basketball team was converted from private ownership to publicly traded MLPs just before the retirement of key players, resulting in the loss of its premier position.

Klein, Rosenfeld, and Beranek (KRB) (1991) found that carve-outs were the first stage of a two-stage process. In their sample of 52 carve-outs between 1966 and 1983, KRB found that 44 had been either sold off or reacquired by the parent firm. None of the reacquisitions occurred in the first year following the carve-out, suggesting that carve-outs are used to showcase subsidiaries to prospective buyers. Because carve-outs involve two events, KRB analyzed the returns for both the carve-out announcements and the second event announcement. They found a 2.75% cumulative abnormal return during the five-day window from day -4 through day 0 for the announcement of the initial carve-out. The five-day cumulative abnormal return for the second event is 1.98% for parents, with those firms engaging in sell-offs at 3.67% versus 0.81% for reacquisitions. Subsidiaries had highly positive returns for second events, 11.4% for sell-offs, and 13.3% for reacquisitions. However, these positive returns are largely offset by negative abnormal returns over the preceding trading period. The positive returns to parents over both announcements suggest that carve-outs serve as a positive alternative to a one-stage sell-off.

Allen and McConnell (1998) suggest that managers tend to undertake equity carve-outs only when other capital options are constrained. Firms that are less financially stable have more difficulty obtaining financing from conventional sources such as debt or new stock issues. Consequently, carve-outs provide an effective alternative. Consistent with this hypothesis, Allen and McConnell found that firms that undertake equity carve-outs have higher leverage ratios, lower interest coverage ratios, and lower profit ratios than their industry peers. The market also reacts positively when firms explicitly state that the proceeds of a carve-out will be used to pay down debt. Such a statement results in an average excess stock return of 6.63%. This is much greater than the -0.01% average excess stock return to firms that plan to use funds for internal investment purposes.

Slovin, Sushka, and Ferraro (SSF) (1995) extended the study of equity carve-outs, spin-offs, and asset sell-offs to the firms' rivals. Their motivation was to test the effects on the relevant subsidiary. However, because the subsidiary does not have stock price data at the time of the restructuring announcement, the rivals of the subsidiary are used as proxies. The authors found a negative valuation effect of -1% on rivals of carved out subsidiaries. Because a carve-out is a form of an IPO of common stock, they measured the effects on rival firms of the announcements of conventional IPOs; they found similar negative returns.

However, for spin-offs, rivals of subsidiaries have positive share price effects. For asset sales, rivals experience normal returns. SSF confirmed that parent firms earn positive returns from carve-outs, spin-offs, and asset sales; the rivals of parent firms earn normal returns. They concluded that managers try to time equity carve-outs or conventional IPOs for when outside investors are likely to overvalue these new equity issues. They cite previous models of decisions on going public based on informational advantages of managers over outside investors.

SSF also found that the aggregate loss in shareholder wealth for industry rivals over a two-day window is $2.5 billion, representing 39% of the gross proceeds of the carve-out, spin-off, or asset sale. They contrast this to the finding by Hertzel (1991) that the rivals of firms announcing stock repurchases experience normal returns.

They also found that decisions by the parent to sell noncore assets result in positive returns for the parent. In addition, the event returns are significantly positive but small (0.55%) for rivals. This suggests that greater focus by one firm increases the likelihood that its rivals will imitate this behavior.

SSF cite the Healy and Palepu (1990) study that found that firms that make seasoned equity issues experience postissue increases in market risk. This is consistent with the hypothesis that managers raise additional equity funds to reduce financial leverage when they forecast an increase in business risk. SSF tested this by calculating the betas of rivals to firms engaged in equity increasing transactions. They found the equity betas for industry rivals to be stable for the relevant period. They concluded that the negative effects on rivals (of equity carve-outs and conventional IPOs) do not result from new information about changes in industry systematic risk.

Performance Studies

Vijh (1999) studied a sample of 628 carve-outs that occurred from 1981 to 1995. He found that carve-outs do not underperform benchmarks over a three-year period following the execution of the carve-outs. Benchmarks used include CRSP value-weighted market returns, book-to-market ratios among CRSP firms within 70% to 130% of firm size, comparison with closest sized firm within two-digit industry code, earnings-to-price ratios among 70% to 130% of firm size, comparison with parent firm. Carve-outs earned an annual raw return of 14.3% during the first three years. Vijh found that this contrasts with the poor performance of initial public offerings (IPOs), which have an annual return of only 3.4%. He calculated that the average initial listing-day returns for carve-outs was 6.2%, with a median of 2.5%. This is much smaller than the 15.4% for IPOs.

Vijh offers several possible explanations for the performance of the carve-outs. The parent firms tend to be relatively unfocused, making a carve-out an opportunity to improve focus. Subsidiaries gain partial freedom to pursue their own activities, but the parents generally maintain a monitoring position. Vijh tested whether the performance of the subsidiary stock was related to the number of business segments of the parent. Because the relationship was not always significant, he concluded that the subsidiary stock probably performs up to benchmarks because the market was reacting efficiently to quality performance.

Allen (1998) looked at the performance of equity carve-outs at Thermo Electron, a manufacturer of biomedical, recycling, and environmental monitoring equipment. George Hatsopoulos, CEO of Thermo Electron, incorporated the firm in 1956. It went public in 1967 and was listed on the NYSE in 1980. Through the early 1980s, the stock performance was poor. In 1983, Hatsopoulos implemented a new strategy with the carve-out of Thermedics. The carve-out helped raise capital to fund research on a heart-assist pump that the unit was developing. It also allowed the subsidiary to retain the developer of the product, who received options in Thermedics. Although the performance of the carved-out unit was poor, it became the basis for Thermo Electron's structure.

As of mid-1997, Thermo Electron had carved out seven divisions, and those divisions had carved out another 15 units. Thermo Electron maintains majority stakes in its carve-outs, and the carve-out subsidiaries do the same in their own carve-outs. Thermo Electron provides centralized legal, banking, taxation, and other services for about 1% of each unit's revenues. The decentralized structure allows fledgling ideas to have the backing of a large firm's resources. Thermo Electron is also able to combat agency problems with its managers, because it grants options in both the parent company and the specific subsidiary. This allows the market to price each unit. Thermo Electron has performed remarkably well since implementing its program. One hundred dollars invested in the firm in 1983 would have appreciated to $1,667 by the end of 1995. This is in contrast to an industry index, which grew to $524, and the S&P 500, which grew to $381.

Other firms have given serious consideration to pursuing a structural arrangement similar to Thermo Electron's. Companies like The Limited (a clothes retailer) and Acer (a computer manufacturer) have worked toward splitting into more carve-outs. 3M has actively sought to follow a similar strategy but has found it difficult to achieve "critical mass" in many markets. As a result, it has had to abandon some markets, such as audio and video tapes. IBM also considered a restructuring along the lines of the Thermo Electron model before John Akers lost his CEO post. We argue that Thermo Electron's success is not simply a result of its structure. Structure alone cannot mandate the success or failure of a firm. Thermo Electron has hired good people and has been able to achieve success in attractive new growth businesses.

The performance of equity carve-outs is related to industry growth prospects. *Mergers & Acquisitions* magazine (1999, pp. 27–28) observed that six of the seven best-performing (from issue date in 1998 to the end of the year) carve-outs had Internet and/or computer connections. The largest price increases were achieved by two Internet stocks: uBid, an Internet auction firm, increased 611%, and Ticketmaster Online-City Search, provider of ticketing and community information, rose 300%. But there also were some losers: Caliber Learning Systems by 70%, ONIX Systems by 56%, and Vysis by 55%.

TRACKING STOCK

Tracking stocks are separate classes of the common stock of the parent corporation. They were first issued in 1984, when GM used a tracking stock in connection with its acquisition of EDS. This class of GM's common stock was identified as E stock and was called letter stock at the time. In 1985, GM acquired Hughes aircraft and assigned it the letter H.

Other Examples

When the same type of stock was used later by U.S. Steel, it was called target stock. In recent years, all of these types of stocks have become referred to as tracking stocks. Although they differ in some details, their basic characteristics are similar. In May 1991 USX distributed U.S. Steel stock to its existing shareholders and redesignated the USX common stock as USX-Marathon stock. In September 1992 USX created a third tracking stock when it sold shares of the USX-Delhi group stock in an initial public offering. Thus, the quarterly 10Q report for the period ending September 30, 1995 for the USX Corporation presents financial information for (1) the consolidated corporation, (2) the Marathon group (oil), (3) the U.S. Steel group (steel), and (4) the Delhi group (natural gas). The 10Q shows common stock outstanding on September 30, 1995 of 287 million shares for the USX-Marathon group, 83 million shares for the USX-U.S. Steel group, and 9 million shares for the USX-Delhi group. Each tracking stock is regarded as common stock of the consolidated company for voting purposes.

Quantum Corp. believed that investors were overlooking the progress the firm had made in its digital tape storage division, which had revenues that grew tenfold in five years. The firm felt that the poor performance of its disk drive division was holding down the price of the firm as a whole. As a solution, the firm decided to separate the two stocks. For each share of Quantum stock, investors received one share of the storage system stock and one-half share of the disk drive stock, distributed as a dividend.

The tracking stock company is usually assigned its own distinctive name. For example: DLJ calls its tracking stock DLJdirect, Sprint Corp. formed a PCS group subsidiary, Georgia Pacific created Timber Co., Ziff-Davis formed ZDNet. The special characteristics of Internet companies have stimulated the use of tracking stocks. Internet companies trade at high valuations, which makes it difficult for "Old Economy" companies to compete with or to acquire such rivals. This has led a number of them to establish or acquire interests in separately traded entities for their e-commerce businesses. Examples are Barnes & Noble/Bertelsmann/barnesandnoble.com, Disney/Infoseek, and AT&T/Excite@Home.

Comparisons

From the foregoing description, it can be seen that tracking stock has similarities to both dual-class stock and spin-offs. In dual-class stocks, class A generally has one vote per share whereas class B shareholders have five or more votes per share. Class A stock has higher allocations of dividends. In contrast, holders of tracking stock usually have the same voting rights as shareholders who hold stock in the parent company.

Tracking stock is similar to a spin-off in that the financial results of the parent and the subsidiary are reported separately. However, a spin-off is a separate entity with its own board of directors and shareholders who can vote for the board of their separate company but not for the parent. In a spin-off the initial assignment of assets and other relationships are defined, but thereafter they are independent entities. In the tracking stock relationship, the board of the parent continues to control the activities of the tracking segment. So tracking stocks do not represent an ownership interest. They trade separately, so dividends paid to shareholders can be based on the cash flow of the tracking company. Compensation of managers can be based on financial results and the stock price behavior of the tracking stock.

Although 80% of firms issuing tracking stocks use a dividend process, some firms use the issuance of tracking stock as a source of cash. DLJ raised $138 million from the sale of DLJdirect and gave the proceeds to DLJdirect. Ziff-Davis raised over $200 million in its ZDNet IPO but used over 85% to pay down debt on the parent's balance sheet. This raises one of the major criticisms of tracking stocks. The subsidiary is generally subject to the will of the parent.

Benefits and Limitations

Tracking stocks have advantages and limitations. The benefits of creating separate public equities in the form of tracking stocks have been described in the literature (Logue, Seward, and Walsh, 1996; Barr, 1999). (1) Stock issuance is tax-free. (2) The financial markets can value different businesses on the basis of their own performance. (3) Analysts' coverage is likely to be improved. (4) Stock-based management incentive programs can be related to each targeted business unit. (5) Investors are provided with quasi-pure-play opportunities. (6) Tracking stock increases flexibility in raising equity capital. (7) Tracking stock provides alternative types of acquisition currency.

The limitations have also been widely noted (1) The parent retains influence and latent control over the tracking stock company. (2) Potential conflicts of interest may arise over cost allocations or other internal transfer transactions. Such conflicts would have unfavorable consequences in the market price behavior of both the parent and the subsidiary. (3) In contrast to spin-offs, which may become attractive acquisition targets, the tracking stock subsidiary may command less takeover interest because of the blurred relationship with the parent.

The stock price performance of tracking stocks has been uneven. The main determinant is the economic characteristics of the businesses in which the tracking stock subsidiaries have been established. With few exceptions, the combined parent–tracking stock performance has been superior to the performance of their peer groups.

SPLIT-UPS

In recent years, there have been dramatic examples of restructuring in which companies split themselves into two or more parts. This has usually been accomplished by initial carve-outs and spin-offs of individual parts from one or more core activities. The rationale for split-ups is conveyed by three case studies.

Hewlett-Packard and Agilent

On November 18, 1999, Hewlett-Packard Company (HP) completed a $2.2 billion initial public offering of its test and measurement equipment subsidiary, Agilent Technologies. The IPO was the largest in Silicon Valley history and was the first stage of a split-up of HP. HP had decided to move in a new direction. The company's roots were in test and measurement equipment. Bill Hewlett and David Packard started out making such equipment in their garage. HP's decision to split the equipment segment out of the company was a dramatic change. Agilent's stock opened at $45.50, 52% above the $30 offering price. HP initially retained 85% of Agilent's stock, with the intention of distributing it to shareholders in mid-2000.

Hewlett-Packard announced the decision to spin off Agilent in March 1999. HP had experienced growth near 20% for much of the mid-1990s as it focused on producing computers. Many observers felt that HP was being held back by Agilent's test and measurement business, which makes medical products, semiconductor components, and devices used to test cable TV and phone networks. The Asian economic crisis of the late 1990s hurt the instrumentation business and contributed to the desire to spin it off from the more promising computer business. During 1998 and 1999, HP experienced low sales growth and came under fire for being in too many businesses. Analysts were critical of the overlap of capabilities between the computer business and the instrumentation business.

The spin-off of Agilent was well regarded because it could bring more focus back to HP. Some analysts felt that HP should have spun its printer division off from the computer division as well. However, many insiders felt that spinning off the measurement division was already too great a departure from the history of HP. Bill Hewlett and David Packard had started the company making such devices. Breaking this function out of HP was seen as blasphemous by some.

AT&T Restructuring

On September 20, 1995, Chairman Robert E. Allen announced that at a special meeting that morning the board of AT&T had approved plans for a strategic restructuring that would split AT&T into three publicly traded global companies. Under the plan, AT&T shareholders would receive shares in two other companies. A fourth business, AT&T Capital Corp., would be sold. Note that this restructuring in the form of a split-up is accomplished by means of spin-offs of two additional companies.

The AT&T name would continue for the Communications Services group with revenues of about $50 billion. This would include AT&T Wireless (formerly McCaw Cellular Communications), AT&T's long distance business, and Universal Card operations, a credit card business. About 15% of Bell Laboratories employees would also be retained. It would also include a newly established AT&T Solutions consulting and systems integration organization.

The second company would be an equipment company called Communications Systems (later renamed Lucent Technologies). Its production would encompass public network switches, transmission systems, wire and cable, and wireless equipment whose total revenue in 1994 was somewhat over $10 billion. Communications products include business phone systems and services, consumer phones, and phone rentals, totaling about $6.5 billion. Microelectronics consisting of chips and circuit boards represented another $1.5 billion of revenues. The equipment company would also include an AT&T Laboratories unit around the core (85%) of Bell Laboratories for research and development in communications services. The equipment company would have 20,000 of the Bell Lab employees, with about 6,000 remaining with the long distance company.

Splitting off the equipment business from long distance was motivated by the need to split AT&T's roles as supplier and competitor. AT&T's biggest equipment customers were typically the seven regional Bell companies (the "Baby Bells"). But the Bell companies and the long distance carriers are competitors, each seeking to invade the others' telephone services markets.

The third company would be Global Information Solutions (GIS) (later renamed back to NCR). It was further announced that NCR would halt the manufacture of personal computers. It would continue to offer customers personal computers as a part of total solutions but would use outside suppliers. NCR would continue to support and service all of its current hardware and software installations and would market its capabilities to all industries, particularly the three key segments where it has a strong market position—financial, retail, and communications. NCR, with 43,000 people in more than 120 countries, announced major cost-cutting initiatives that would eliminate more than 8,500 jobs.

NCR would be a remnant of AT&T's efforts to be an effective competitor in the computer business. AT&T had long had a vision of a presence in the computer business because central stations switching equipment units are simply large-scale specialized computers. AT&T long felt that it could be a presence in the computer business, but for many years it was prevented from achieving that goal by a consent decree, entered into with the Department of Justice in 1956. A part of the divestiture decree of 1984 gave AT&T increased freedom to compete in other businesses, including computers. But AT&T had the disadvantage of starting far behind the established computer companies. The purchase of NCR in 1991 was an effort to catch up. However, the computer industry itself went through such major dynamic changes that even the former leader, IBM, was unable to keep up. The acquisition of NCR did not help AT&T realize its aspirations in the computer business.

The main reasons for the AT&T split-up can be briefly summarized. The equipment business was spun off in the effort to avoid conflicts with its main customers, with which the phone service activities were in competition. It was hoped that selling off the computer business would improve the valuation multiples for the core AT&T long distance and other telephone services. The taint of poor performance in the computer business would thereby be removed from the main AT&T operation.

The success of the split-up is apparent from the market values of the firms. Before the announcement of the restructuring, AT&T's market value was $75 billion. By January 1998, just slightly more than a year after the restructuring went into effect, the separately trading AT&T, Lucent, and NCR had a combined market capitalization of $159 billion. In January 2000, following numerous acquisitions, AT&T stood at $175 billion, Lucent at $168 billion, and NCR at $3.3 billion, a total of $376 billion.

The division that benefited the most from the restructuring was the equipment division, which became Lucent Technologies. Lucent was able to become a supplier for firms that had been reluctant to buy from AT&T, a competitor. In addition, Wall Street began to recognize Lucent as an attractive high tech stock. Lucent's role as a supplier of networking equipment helped investors recognize it as a major Internet player. Although the market did not give Lucent as much attention as its competitor, Cisco Systems, Lucent stock still had risen more than 900% by the end of 1999.

The least successful division was the computer division, which was divested under the NCR name. When the company was spun off at the end of 1996, it was disclosed that AT&T had contributed over $2 billion to keep the poorly performing division running. NCR continued to struggle even after being separated from AT&T. By the end of 1999, its stock was priced virtually the same as it had been at the time of the spin-off.

The new AT&T proved to be agile enough to change its corporate focus. Under C. Michael Armstrong, who became CEO in October 1997, AT&T has changed from focusing almost entirely on long distance to becoming the leading cable TV provider in the United States. Becoming more focused helped AT&T adjust to the effects of increasing competition in the long distance market. AT&T pursued cable with a vision of providing television, high speed Internet access, and local and long distance telephone service through one AT&T-controlled pipeline.

AT&T's foray into cable began on June 24, 1998 with the announcement of a merger agreement with TCI. The initial market reaction was extremely negative. AT&T shares lost $5.375 (8.2%) from $65.375 on the day of the announcement. This represented a loss of nearly $9 billion. In the following days, AT&T continued to suffer, falling as low as $54.875 on July 2, only a week after the announcement. Analysts criticized the feasibility of utilizing TCI's somewhat archaic cable system. They also felt that the technology AT&T proposed to use would be too expensive to make the merger pay off.

AT&T furthered its cable strategy with a hostile bid for MediaOne on April 22, 1999. MediaOne had already entered into a deal with Comcast, but AT&T was not deterred. Rumors began to circulate that Comcast would seek a partner, such as AOL or Microsoft, to defeat AT&T. To avoid a protracted bidding war, Comcast agreed to drop its offer in exchange for an opportunity to buy up to 2 million cable subscribers from AT&T. AT&T also struck a deal with Microsoft, which invested $5 billion in AT&T in exchange for the opportunity to provide software for AT&T's forthcoming cable boxes.

While the ultimate success or failure of this cable venture is not yet evident, it is important to recognize that AT&T was able to implement a massive strategic shift, primarily through the use of acquisitions. Because of a major change in the technology for long distance, microwave systems and fiber optics, AT&T faced competition from new competitors whose investment costs were much lower than those of the old AT&T long distance lines.

The Telecommunications Act of 1996 recognized new competitive forces, made local phone service more open to competition, and allowed local phone operators to offer long distance provided they could demonstrate competition in their markets. Thus, AT&T would have the opportunity to be a local phone provider but would also face a serious challenge to its long distance dominance. By the end of 1999, WorldCom's planned acquisition of Sprint had created a competitor of comparable size to AT&T. Also, Bell Atlantic had gained approval to offer long distance service to its local customers in New York. These and other competitors have contributed to the great reduction in long distance rates, which is what prompted AT&T to seek an alternative revenue source, cable.

ITT

The ITT Corporation had a long and interesting history. When Harold Geneen became head of ITT in 1959, it was drifting. It was heavily dependent on running telephone companies in countries outside the United States, often in less developed countries subject to a high degree of political and social risk. Geneen determined to reduce this vulnerability of ITT to political instability abroad. Under his direction, ITT embarked on a vast acquisition of a wide variety of products.

Subsequently, Geneen was succeeded by Rand V. Araskog as the head of ITT in 1979. In the 15-year period through 1994, Araskog sold off 250 of ITT's business units. A December 26, 1994 article in *Barron's* observed that during the 15-year period the price of ITT shares had lagged the S&P 500 Index by 43% and the S&P conglomerate group by 11% with a stock price of $84 near year-end 1994. The article observed that accounting changes made at ITT in late 1994 effectively split the company into three parts: insurance, manufacturing, and leisure. The aim was to improve the share price performance of ITT. The article noted that if ITT sold in three parts, their combined stock market value could be as high as $130 per share, representing a 55% increase over the $84. In the restructuring, the umbrella company for the hotels, casinos, and entertainment companies would be ITT Holdings, which would be headed by Araskog. It was reported that Araskog was seeking to add a broadcast TV network to this group and had tried to buy CBS and General Electric's NBC network. The market was pleased that ITT failed to acquire a network. The view was that ITT did not have the experience or capability to successfully run a network.

In March 1994 ITT had completed the spin-off of its forest products business, ITT Rayonier. In late August 1994 ITT announced its intention of buying the famed Madison Square Garden along with its MSG Cable Network, the New York Knicks, and the New York Rangers. The purchase price was to invest $1.1 billion in an equal partnership with Cablevision Systems, then the nation's fourth largest cable TV firm. During the week in late August 1995 when the agreement to buy the Garden was announced, the ITT shares dropped from $86 to $79. The completion of the deal was delayed by the U.S. Department of Justice so that it could conduct a study of the deal's antitrust implications.

In the meantime, in mid-December 1994, ITT announced it would buy Caesar's World, which owned gambling operations in Las Vegas, Lake Tahoe, and Atlantic City, for approximately $2 billion. The market saw synergy with Sheraton's chain of hotels and casinos, including the Desert Inn in Nevada. The stock rose 3% to $84 on the Friday before Christmas 1994.

In addition to ITT Holdings, which would manage hotels, casinos, and entertainment companies, there would be two other major parts of ITT. One would be ITT Insurance and Finance, which would represent 52% of ITT's 1993 revenues of $23 billion. This group included ITT Hartford, a life insurance as well as property and casualty insurance company. Hartford was strong in the life insurance segment as an underwriter in variable annuities.

The third area would be ITT Industries, which, along with about 3% miscellaneous activities, accounted for 30% of ITT revenues. This segment included the automotive business, where ITT had been a leader in antilock brake systems. ITT fluid technology would also be in this group, with favorable prospects as the nation's largest pump maker and a major producer of valves, heat exchangers, and fluid management systems.

There was talk that further divestment might occur in insurance and finance, accounting for over 50% of ITT revenues. ITT's emphasis appeared to be aimed at the leisure and entertainment segment, accounting for about 18% of 1993 revenues. This is the area where apparently ITT management felt that stock market multiples would be most favorable. Nevertheless, the risks of concentrating on leisure and entertainment appeared to be substantial. These risks included the usual one of overpaying for acquisitions in areas of intense competition, where future growth depended on the ability to successfully extrapolate future social trends and spending patterns.

ITT Holdings became a takeover target in early 1997. Starwood Lodging's acquisition of ITT stemmed from a failed takeover attempt by Hilton Hotels. The takeover battle lasted 10 months, beginning in January 1997.

Hilton's Initial Offer

After ITT rejected several informal offers from Hilton for a friendly combination, Hilton decided to pursue a hostile bid. On January 27, 1997, Hilton announced its offer to purchase 50.1% of ITT's outstanding shares for $55 per share. The remaining ITT shareholders would receive $55 of Hilton stock in a back-end merger offer. ITT had about 117.9 million shares outstanding at the time of the announcement. At $55 a share, the Hilton offer gave ITT a market equity value of about $6.5 billion ($55 × 117.9 million shares). Although the bid represented a 26% premium over ITT's previous close of $43.75, many on Wall Street felt that the bid was too low. The announcement sent the ITT stock price up to $58.50. Many analysts believed that the true value of ITT was closer to $63.00 to $71.00 per share if the $130 million in estimated synergies associated with the deal were believable.

ITT's board of directors immediately rejected Hilton's bid as inadequate and retained Goldman, Sachs and Lazard Freres to advise on a takeover defense. On February 12, 1997, ITT announced its plan to divest $3 billion of assets unrelated to the company's lodging and gaming business. Shortly thereafter, ITT sold its ownership interest in Madison Square Garden for $650 million and liquidated its equity ownership in the French communications concern Alcatel for $830 million.

On July 16, 1997, ITT announced a broad restructuring and recapitalization plan. ITT would split into three separate publicly trade companies: ITT Destinations (lodging and gaming), ITT Corporation (ITT World Directories), and ITT Educational Service. ITT Corporation would undertake a $70 self-tender offer for 30 million of its outstanding shares (about $2.1 billion total). The Clayton, Dubilier & Rice investment firm would then acquire a 32.9% interest in the new ITT Corporation for $225 million in cash.

ITT's otherwise well-structured defense did not include a vote of its shareholders. Based on this, Hilton filed suit in U.S. Federal Court seeking an injunction requiring shareholder approval of the restructuring plan. On August 15, 1997, Hilton raised its bid to $70 cash for 50.1% of ITT's stock and $70 in Hilton stock for the remaining shares. This new offer raised ITT's market equity value to about $8.3 billion ($70 × 117.9 million shares). On September 29, 1997, the court ruled in favor of Hilton, ordering ITT to hold a shareholder vote by November 14, 1997.

Starwood Lodging

ITT found a white knight in Starwood Hotels & Resorts Trust, a fast-growing real estate investment trust (REIT). Starwood offered ITT shareholders $82 per share: $15 in cash and $67 in Starwood stock. This offer gave ITT a market equity value of about $9.7 billion ($82 × 117.9 million shares).

Starwood was able to offer such a high price largely because of special tax treatment given to "paired share" REITs. Starwood consists of a trust, which owns the hotel assets, and a corporation, which operates the hotels. Under this structure, substantially all of the earnings of the operating company are paid to the trust as tax-free rent, thereby avoiding corporate income taxation. As a REIT, the trust is a pass-through entity for tax purposes and must distribute 95% of its earnings to shareholders to avoid taxation as a corporation. The trust and the operating company are publicly held; and the common shares of each are "paired" together on a one-for-one basis and can only be owned and transferred as such.

Under the REIT qualifications of the IRS Code of 1986, REITs must generally lease their hotels to third party lessee/operators. The "paired share" structure circumvents this requirement. It allows shareholders to retain the economic benefits of both the lease payments received by the trust and the operating profits realized by the corporation while maintaining the tax benefits of the REIT. The IRS prohibited paired shares between REITs and an operating company in 1983, but Starwood was grandfathered. Starwood's tax structure as a paired share REIT would allow it to offset the amortization of goodwill resulting from the purchase.

Proxy Fight

On November 5, 1997, Hilton raised its offer to $80 per share in cash for 55% of ITT's stock and $61.63 in Hilton stock in the back-end merger. This bid valued ITT's market equity at about $8.5 billion [(55% × 117.9 million shares × $80) + (45% × 117.9 million shares × $61.63)] Hilton's increased offer prompted ITT's board to exercise the "fiduciary out" provision of the Starwood agreement. The company announced that it would auction itself to the highest bidder. In response to this announcement, Starwood raised its offer to $85 per share, valuing ITT's market equity at about $10 billion (117.9 million shares × $85). The offer required ITT shareholders to choose to take the $85 entirely in cash or in stock. However, if over 60% of the shareholders elected cash, then the cash payout would be capped at $25.50 per share.

On November 12, 1997, ITT shareholders voted to reelect the board of directors. Hilton lost the proxy fight and formally terminated its offer the following day.

Post-Merger Developments

On November 13, 1997, the first full trading day after the proxy vote, Hilton stock closed at $31.00. Compared to its stock price on January 24, the last trading day before its original offer, Hilton stock had gained $5.25, or 20%. With about 249.2 million shares outstanding, its market value had increased by about $1.3 billion, from $6.4 billion to $7.7 billion. Starwood Lodging's stock remained virtually the same throughout its involvement in the takeover battle. On November 13, it closed at $56.13, compared to a close of $56.50 on October 17. This was a drop of less than 1% of its value.

ITT stockholders initially appeared to benefit from the merger. The final purchase price of $85 per share represented a 94% gain over ITT's January 24, 1997, price of $43.75. With about 117.9 million shares outstanding, ITT's market equity value increased by about $4.8 billion, from $5.2 billion to $10 billion. With Starwood Lodging's stock price remaining virtually the same, ITT's increase appeared to be a favorable market response to the deal.

However, as noted by Rappaport and Sirower (1999), the long-term benefits to ITT shareholders were not so clear-cut. Even though ITT's board chose the highest offer, it had a large stock component. Meanwhile, ITT shareholders had a strong preference for a cash exchange. Over 75% of ITT shareholders elected to take cash instead of Starwood stock, triggering the $25.50 cap, with the remainder paid in Starwood stock. As a result, ITT shareholders ended up owning 67% of the combined company's shares. Starwood stock turned out to be a risky investment. Although it held steady around $55 during the proxy contest with Hilton, Starwood's stock price dropped to $32 a year after the deal was completed. This reduced the value of the offer from $85 to $64 for ITT shareholders who took cash. Those who took stock received $49. Thus, ITT shareholders in the long term were forced to pay for Starwood's struggles.

The original Starwood Lodging split into two separate companies since the merger was completed. There are now Starwood Lodging and Hotels and Starwood Capital, the REIT. As of August 10, 1998, the closing prices of Starwood Hotels and Hilton common stock were $43.625 and $25.813, respectively. At these prices, Starwood Hotel and Resorts had a market capitalization of $8.25 billion (189.1 million shares × $43.625) and Hilton had a market capitalization of $6.37 billion (246.9 million shares × $25.813).

Starwood moved quickly to integrate the two companies after the deal was closed in February 1998. In order to reduce the $5.6 billion in debt it assumed to purchase ITT, Starwood divested non-core assets. It sold ITT World Directories, a yellow pages business, for $2.1 billion and spun off 60% of ITT Educational Services for about $275 million. One of the interesting developments in the aftermath of the takeover contest for ITT was that Starwood ended up selling ITT's gaming division to Park Place Entertainment, a Hilton spin-off. The casino operations of ITT, led by Caesar's, were one of the main reasons for Hilton's interest in the firm. Some analysts estimated that Starwood lost up to $500 million on ITT's gaming operations. It was said that buying the casinos from Starwood proved that Hilton avoided doing a deal at the wrong price.

RATIONALE FOR GAINS TO SELL-OFFS AND SPLIT-UPS

A number of hypotheses have been advanced to explain the positive returns found in spin-offs, carve-outs, split-ups, and tracking stock.

Information

The information hypothesis holds that the true value of subsidiary assets is obscured by the complexity of the business structure in which they are embedded. The supposed stock market preference for "pure-play" or single-industry securities is cited in support of this hypothesis. Given the disclosure requirements of public corporations and the nature and extent of the securities analysis industry, it might seem unlikely that parts of a firm would be undervalued. But security analysts tend to specialize. An oil industry analyst may undervalue an oil company's chemical and real estate businesses because he or she does not follow those industries. Also, to the extent that spin-offs and equity carve-outs enhance the incentive to gather and analyze a greater amount of publicly available information through their creation of new publicly traded securities, the information effect may explain at least part of the gains.

Managerial Efficiency

The managerial efficiency hypothesis suggests that the preference (if any) for pure-play securities stems not from lack of confidence in the market's ability to value complex organizations but from the perceived inability of managers to manage them effectively. Even the best management team may reach a point of diminishing returns as the size and diversity of assets under their control increases. Part of the problem is that top management may be unaware of the unique problems and opportunities of a subsidiary in a different line of business. An announced motive in many sell-offs is to sharpen the corporate focus by spinning off (or divesting) units that are a poor fit (anergy) with the remainder of the parent company's operations. Writers on corporate strategy have long emphasized the principle of relatedness to guide business planning. Equity carve-outs are often preceded by asset regroupings in the effort to achieve greater efficiency (and are often followed by spin-offs or divestitures). Warner-Lambert's sale of its Entenmann's subsidiary to General Foods is an example of the efficiency source of sell-off gains.

Both Entenmann's and Warner-Lambert stood to benefit from the transaction: Warner-Lambert management could now focus attention on their area of comparative advantage, pharmaceuticals; and Entenmann's would be controlled by managers more experienced with a food company's operations. The managerial efficiency hypothesis is supported by evidence of acquisition activity in the pre-spin-off period as well as dissimilarities between the business lines of the parent firms and spun-off subsidiaries.

Management Incentives

The issues of management incentives and accountability are related to management efficiency. Bureaucratization of management and consolidation of financial statements can stifle entrepreneurial spirit and result in good performance going unrewarded (or bad performance unpunished). The problem is compounded when the subsidiary's outlook and objectives are not the same as the parent's, for example, a high growth subsidiary of a parent in a mature industry or a regulated subsidiary of a nonregulated parent. Incentive compensation plans tied to parent company stock options may be meaningless or even counterproductive. A spun-off subsidiary has the advantage of an independent stock price that directly reflects the market's response to management actions and more closely links compensation to performance.

Tax and/or Regulatory Factors

Another important source of gains available in some sell-offs is tax and/or regulatory advantages. Subsamples of spin-offs citing these motives exhibit higher abnormal returns than the more inclusive samples. Tax advantages can be achieved by the creation and spin-off of subsidiaries into natural resource royalty trusts or real estate investment trusts. As long as these entities pay out 90% of their income to their shareholders, they pay no income tax. Thus, the parent company can shelter income from taxes and benefit the spun-off subsidiary's shareholders, who are the same (initially) as the parent's shareholders.

Regulated subsidiaries are sometimes penalized by their association with profitable parents if regulators look to parent company earnings when considering rate increases. The spun-off subsidiary might have a greater chance of being granted rate increases, and the nonregulated operations of the parent would be freed from regulatory scrutiny. Some parent firms have spun off foreign subsidiaries so that they would not be subject to the laws and regulations of the home country of the parent.

Bondholder Expropriation

Agency costs are involved in the hypothesis that the gains to shareholders are the result of bondholder expropriation. A spin-off reduces (and a divestiture changes the nature of) the collateral initially relied on by bondholders. However, this argument assumes that sell-offs are unanticipated (and unanticipatable) events. In fact, most, if not all, bond covenants contain dividend restrictions (limiting stock dividends, including spin-offs) and restrictions on asset disposition (limiting divestitures).

Furthermore, many subsidiaries already have their own debt, and many are assigned a pro rata share of parent debt when they are spun off. Bondholders may actually benefit if hitherto junior claims on the parent become senior claims on the spun-off subsidiary. Studies by Hite and Owers (1983) and Schipper and Smith (1983) found little evidence of decline in bond prices or ratings to support the bondholder expropriation hypothesis.

Changing Economic Environment

Yet another rationale advanced for the positive price effects is that there has been a major shift in the economic environment affecting the firm. Thus, the opportunity sets of both parent and subsidiaries may be altered. Although joint operations may have been optimal in the past, separate operations may have become more appropriate.

Avoiding Conflicts with Customers

A strong motive in the AT&T split-up was to separate the equipment, manufacturing, and sales activities from the core telephone business of AT&T. The regional Bell operating companies are the biggest customers for the equipment that AT&T sells. Yet the "Baby Bells" are seeking to invade the long distance markets of AT&T. AT&T is considering a number of ways of competing with their offspring, operating companies in their local markets. It was hoped that by spinning off the equipment company AT&T would lessen the irritation to the regional operating companies stemming from AT&T competition.

Provide Investors with Pure Winners

When some segments of a firm are losing money or sell products that are in disrepute in some markets, the valuation multiple for the overall company may be lowered. Thus, pressure caused RJR Nabisco to separate its tobacco and food businesses. AT&T put its computer activities in a separate company so that its core long distance and related phone operations would command a better valuation multiple.

Option Creation

A more esoteric explanation of value creation is based on options theory and the state preference model. The idea is that since incorporating limits the stockholders' liability, spin-offs multiply the protection. If common stock is viewed as an option on the underlying technologies of the firm, then a spin-off creates two options on the same assets. Two options will be more valuable than only one (Sarig, 1985).

Increase Market Spanning

Another theoretical benefit of sell-offs is related to financial market spanning or whether financial markets are complete. [For further explanation see Copeland and Weston (1988), chapter 5.] John Lintner (1971) made a similar argument for conglomerate mergers. To the extent that financial markets may be incomplete, spin-offs increase the number of securities for a given number of possible states of the world. In addition, the opportunities for investment of the parent and its divisions will be expanded. Also, the parent and the spun-off subsidiaries may provide investors with a wider range of investment policies and financial policies. The parent and the new entities may package dividends, retained earnings, and capital gains possibilities in different proportions to appeal to different investor clienteles.

Enable More Focused Mergers

Spin-offs are also used to facilitate mergers when the bidder is interested in only a subset of the target's operations. That is, there may be some segments of the target that the bidder does not want to acquire. If for some reason the target/parent firm does not want to sell these segments outright before the merger (for instance, for tax reasons), a future spin-off may be included in the merger planning. At the time of the spin-off, the acquiring (bidder) firm is the parent of the subsidiary. Abnormal positive returns at the spin-off announcement may represent the market realization to the parent's (acquiring firm's) shareholders of the increased value reflected in the premium paid earlier to the target shareholders.

Thus, a wide range of plausible reasons may account for the positive gains from sell-offs. Any one factor could contribute to the positive gains to shareholders when a spin-off or carve-out takes place.

THE CHOICE OF RESTRUCTURING METHODS

After making a decision to restructure, a firm must still determine what type of restructuring it will pursue. Spin-offs are best when a parent's potential to create value through skills, systems, or synergies is weak. In some cases, parents and subsidiaries may have conflicts of interest. This could include conflicting products or different stances on regulatory issues. In such situations, a spin-off allows the parent and subsidiary to go their separate ways.

Equity carve-outs are most helpful to firms that can easily separate subsidiaries. In particular, a subsidiary with a high margin and high growth compared to its competitors could benefit from the added attention given to carve-outs. Capital gained in a carve-out can be used in acquisitions. Carve-outs allow companies to have better access to capital. Subsidiaries can take advantage of the parent's debt rating. Firms can more easily fund projects that would depress earnings if the subsidiary were not carved out. In addition, carve-outs allow division managers to take primary responsibility for financial and investment decisions. Managers can go to capital markets for money rather than trying to overstate budgeting needs to the parent.

Tracking stocks share many advantages of carve-outs. They can provide capital for acquisition or other investment programs. Also, tracking stocks can bring attention to subsidiaries with high growth or margins. Tracking stock subsidiaries can take advantage of the capital structure of the parent. Parent firms may issue tracking stock as a means of reducing taxes. If a parent or subsidiary has net operating losses, those losses can be used to reduce overall corporate taxes. Tracking stocks are particularly useful for firms with divisions that share significant synergies. Because it is impractical to try to carve out or spin off divisions with such a relationship, a tracking stock is an attractive option for raising capital.

SUMMARY

In a spin-off, a company creates a subsidiary whose shares are distributed on a pro rata basis to the shareholders of the parent company. A new publicly owned corporation results. In a split-up, a company engages in restructuring to create two or more separate entities. An equity carve-out is the initial public offering (IPO) of a portion of the common stock of a previously wholly owned subsidiary. The parent generally retains majority control. When a company creates tracking stock, it splits its business operations into two or more common equity claims. However, the businesses remain wholly owned segments of a single parent.

The stock market response to these four types of restructuring is positive. The strength of the positive response depends on industry and company circumstances. The factors that influence the size of the market event returns are related to the motives and effects of these restructuring activities, which include (1) tax effects, (2) regulatory effects, (3) separate market prices for the entities, (4) avoidance of a confusing mix of activities with favorable and unfavorable prospects, (5) improvement in the ability of security analysts to understand and evaluate each separate entity, (6) a better match between the activities of the segments and the capabilities of managers, (7) more accurate evaluation of managerial performance, (8) more effective formulation of compensation contracts with managers, and (9) stronger managerial incentive systems.

QUESTIONS

12.1 What is tracking stock, and what are the reasons for creating it?

12.2 Summarize the case study of the creation of "targeted" stock by USX.

12.3 What are the gains in spin-offs, split-ups, equity carve-outs, and tracking stock?

12.4 What role does the information hypothesis have in explaining the gains that result from spin-offs?

12.5 How do tax and/or regulatory factors affect returns to spin-offs, split-ups, equity carve-outs, and tracking stock?

12.6 Summarize the 1994–1995 ITT split-up, and evaluate its soundness.

12.7 How did the split-up affect the subsequent history of ITT?

12.8 Summarize the 1995 AT&T split-up, and discuss its reasons.

12.9 Summarize the Hewlett-Packard split-up, and discuss the reasons for it.

12.10 What are the advantages and limitations of spin-offs, carve-outs, and tracking stock?

Case 12.1 Sears, Roebuck and Co. Restructuring[1]

On November 10, 1994, Sears, Roebuck and Co. announced that it intended to spin off its 80.1% stake in the Allstate Corporation, the nation's largest publicly held property and casualty insurance company. This divestiture would amount to Sears's final major step in its plan to return exclusively to its core retailing operations established in 1886.

The 1980s witnessed Sears's declining market share in retailing as discount stores such as Wal-Mart and Kmart, and specialty stores such as The Gap and The Limited captured a large portion of the retailing market from Sears. Many analysts contend that Sears's diversification into the real estate and financial services markets as well as its hefty investment in the insurance industry precipitated this decline.

Recognizing that Sears's future success depended on successful retail operations, management announced in September 1992 that it had developed a strategy to refocus its resources almost exclusively on the Sears retail operations. Over the next two years this included

1. Spinning off securities broker Dean Witter Reynolds, Inc. and its associated Discover Credit Card operation, the largest issuer of general-purpose credit cards.
2. Selling 19.9% interest in Allstate in the largest initial public offering in U.S. history up to that date.
3. Selling 100% of Coldwell Banker Residential Services, which had earned record profits in 1991 and which analysts considered one of Sears's most valuable assets.

These actions raised $4.2 billion in cash and eliminated $19 billion in debt.

Between the time of the September 1992 announcement and November 10, 1994, the day of the Allstate spin-off announcement, Sears dramatically improved its position in both the retail market and the stock market. Sears outpaced its major rivals in the first three quarters of 1994 as operating profit for its merchandise group increased 26% and revenues increased 9.4%. In addition, since September 1992 shareholder returns had amounted to 66% and the market value of the corporation had increased by more than $8 billion as the price of Sears stock rose from $41.375 to $51.625 per share. According to one analyst, Sears management had recognized and begun to benefit from the theory that often "the sum of the parts is worth more than the whole."

The spin-off of Allstate, which occurred in mid-1995, was intended to continue the positive momentum. Under the agreement, Sears's 80.1% (approximately 360 million) shares were to be distributed to Sears shareholders in the form of a tax-free dividend at an expected rate of 0.95 Allstate shares per Sears share. The spin-off was expected to be valued at $9 billion, making it one of the largest spin-offs in U.S. history. Analysts believed that this action would increase the value of the retailing operations. They cited the fact that the improved retail results had not been fully reflected in the price of Sears stock primarily because of the way insurance stocks were valued. Analysts' expectations were reflected on Wall Street as the price of

[1]This case was prepared with Scott Miller, a Research Associate in the Research Program in Competition and Business Policy, The Anderson School at UCLA.

Sears stock rose by $2.75 per share (5.6%) to $51.625 immediately following the announcement.

Edward A. Brennan, chief executive officer and chairman, who had previously resisted attempts to break up the Sears–Allstate relationship, explained the rationale behind the divestiture: "It's the right time, Sears and Allstate are ready, and the economic environment is right." As independent concerns, Sears and Allstate "will have greater flexibility to pursue their own growth strategies." In addition, Sears's management cited eroding marketing synergies as a reason for the breakup. Whereas Allstate agents previously relied heavily on Sears by working directly out of their department stores, Allstate's sales force presently consists of a network of neighborhood sales offices. Also, the split provided stronger incentives to employees of both corporations because they knew that their actions would more directly affect the value of the stock they owned. Finally, al-

though Allstate would lose some tax advantages of being consolidated, Brennan expected that the loss would amount only to a modest 5 to 10 cents per share loss on Allstate stock in 1995.

Upon completion of this divestiture and the anticipated sale of Homart Development Co., a leading regional mall and community center developer, Sears would be left with approximately 800 department stores, 1,200 specialty stores, 61% of Sears Canada, and 75% of Sears Mexico. This would leave Sears virtually debt-free and allow the new Sears to commit all of its debt to support a high quality credit card receivables portfolio.

QUESTIONS

1. Summarize the restructuring of Sears initiated in November 1994.
2. Evaluate the reasons for the spin-offs.
3. Compare the stock market performances of Sears and the spin-offs.

Case 12.2 GM Spin-Off of EDS

The spin-off of EDS by GM announced on August 7, 1995, appeared to be part of a pattern in which General Motors had been selling off its nonautomotive operations. In June 1995 GM sold its national car rental unit. After the spin-off of EDS, GM would have one nonautomotive unit, Hughes Electronics. GM stated that it had no plans to dispose of Hughes because of the technological capabilities as a strategic asset.

EDS performs a wide range of information-processing activities for government agencies and other companies. It is regarded

as the inventor of "outsourcing," representing the farming out of computer operations to third-party specialist companies. EDS sells a wide range of telecommunications, systems integration, and computer services. GM accounts for about 35% of its business. Some big customers include Xerox Corporation, with which it has a 10-year, $3.2 billion contract. It also provides services to the Internal Revenue Department of Great Britain. EDS-NET is the company's global digital network. It processes about 43 million transactions a day, linking 411,000 personal computers, and its storage capacity is 45 times the size of the Library of Congress. EDS also has capabilities in the emerging global health care information technology.

EDS has an interesting history:

- 1962: Company founded by Ross Perot with $1,000 of his wife's savings.
- 1966: EDS becomes active in Medicare and Medicaid transactions processing.
- 1968: EDS goes public priced at $16.50 per share.
- 1979: Ross Perot sends an EDS squad to free two company employees who are being held prisoners in Iran.
- October 1984: GM acquires EDS for $2.5 billion. Perot receives approximately $1 billion in cash plus a substantial number of shares of GM preferred stock. GM holds 100% of the capital stock of EDS, issuing a new class of GM stock called class E, 70% owned by the public and 30% by GM's Hourly Worker Pension Fund. The class E stock receives the EDS dividend stream as well as one-eighth of a liquidation right in GM's net assets relative to a holder of GM stock. Another provision specifies that if GM sells more than half of the capital stock of EDS, it must buy out class E shareholders at a 20% premium over the market, using GM common stock.
- Fall 1984: Ross Perot joins the GM board and begins public criticism of company management.
- Fall 1986: GM holds talks with AT&T to sell part or all of EDS, but no agreement is reached.
- December 1986: Les Alberthal, an executive of EDS, becomes president and chief executive of EDS as Perot and three other top officials depart. GM pays $743 million to Mr. Perot for his preferred stock plus a premium on his 12 million class E shares. Mr. Perot agrees to resign from the GM board.

- Spring 1993: EDS and British Telecommunications PLC hold talks about a sale of 25% of class E shares. No agreement is reached.
- June 1994: EDS seeks to separate from GM through a spin-off and subsequent merger with Sprint Corp. Sprint is unwilling to accept the EDS asking price.
- March 1995: GM contributes 173 million class E shares valued at $6.3 billion to a GM pension fund.
- June 1995: EDS buys the A. T. Kearney consulting firm for $300 million.
- August 7, 1995: GM announces that it will spin off EDS through an exchange of EDS stock for shares of GM class E stock with a market value of about $22 billion, almost 10 times the price GM paid for EDS in 1984. The spin-off is subject to an appropriate tax ruling from the Internal Revenue Service.

The announced reason for the spin-off was to enable EDS to adjust more flexibly to the rapidly changing competitive environment in which it operates. The news reports also suggested that EDS was seeking participation in multimedia and on-line services. An independent EDS would have greater flexibility for mergers with a telecommunications company as a part of the general trend toward vertical integration in the emerging information age.

It appeared also that the original reasons for the acquisition of EDS by GM were no longer considered valid. Roger B. Smith, the chairman of GM in 1984, viewed EDS as a strategy for achieving high tech diversification to offset cyclical fluctuations in automotive sales. It was also hoped that EDS could revolutionize factory automation, but this was not achieved. It was also recognized that GM did not need to own EDS to buy its computer services.

Thus, the GM–EDS story represents a strategic move that did not achieve its original objectives. However, the rise in the market value of the company from $2.5 billion to $22 billion over a 10-year period represents a value gain as well as a learning experience for GM management. As a competitive environment changes, company strategies are adjusted, and spin-offs represent one method of restructuring a company.

QUESTIONS

1. Summarize the reasons for the original acquisition of EDS by GM.
2. What were the reasons for the spin-off?
3. Were the EDS acquisition and subsequent spin-off a success or failure for GM? For EDS?

REFERENCES

Allen, Jeffrey W., "Capital Markets and Corporate Structure: The Equity Carve-Outs of Thermo Electron," *Journal of Financial Economics*, 48, 1998, pp. 99–124.

Allen, Jeffrey W., and John J. McConnell, "Equity Carve-Outs and Managerial Discretion," *Journal of Finance*, 53, February 1998, pp. 163–186.

Anslinger, Patricia L., Steven J. Klepper, and Somu Subramaniam, "Breaking Up Is Good To Do," *The McKinsey Quarterly*, 1999(1), pp. 16–27.

Barr, Stephen, "On the Right Track?" *CFO*, November 1999, pp. 105–109.

Bary, Andrew, "Corporate Castaways," *Barron's*, January 10, 1994, pp. 19–20.

Copeland, Thomas E., and J. Fred Weston, *Financial Theory and Corporate Policy*, 3rd ed., Reading, MA: Addison-Wesley Publishing Company, 1988.

Copeland, Thomas E., E. F. Lemgruber, and D. Mayers, "Corporate Spinoffs: Multiple Announcement and Ex-Date Abnormal Performance," chapter 7 in T. E. Copeland, ed., *Modern Finance and Industrial Economics*, New York: Basil Blackwell, 1987.

Corporate Restructuring, Mergers & Acquisitions, August 1988.

Cusatis, Patrick J., James A. Miles, and J. Randall Woolridge, "Restructuring Through Spinoffs," *Journal of Financial Economics*, 33, 1993, pp. 293–311.

Healy, Paul, and Krishna Palepu, "Earnings and Risk Changes Surrounding Primary Stock Offers," *Journal of Accounting Research*, 28, 1990, pp. 25–48.

Hertzel, Michael, "The Effects of Stock Repurchases on Rival Firms," *Journal of Finance*, 46, 1991, pp. 707–716.

Hite, Gailen, and James E. Owers, "Security Price Reactions Around Corporate Spin-Off Announcements," *Journal of Financial Economics*, 12, 1983, pp. 409–436.

Ibbotson, R., "Price Performance of Common Stock New Issues," *Journal of Financial Economics*, 2, September 1975, pp. 235–272.

Klein, April, James Rosenfeld, and William Beranek, "The Two Stages of an Equity Carve-Out and the Price Response of Parent and Subsidiary Stock," *Managerial and Decision Economics*, 12, 1991, pp. 449–460.

Lintner, John, "Expectations, Mergers and Equilibrium in Purely Competitive Securities Markets," *American Economic Review*, 61, May 1971, pp. 101–111.

Logue, Dennis E., James K. Seward, and James P. Walsh, "Rearranging Residual Claims: A Case for Targeted Stock," *Financial Management*, 25(1), Spring 1996, pp. 43–61.

Mergers & Acquisitions, 30, March/April 1996, pp. 27–29.

Michaely, Roni, and Wayne H. Shaw, "The Choice of Going Public: Spin-Offs vs. Carve-Outs," *Financial Management*, 24(3), Autumn 1995, pp. 5–21.

Rappaport, Alfred and Mark L. Sirower, "Stock or Cash? The Trade-Offs for Buyers and Sellers in Mergers and Acquisitions," *Harvard Business Review*, November–December 1999, pp. 147–158.

Ritter, J., "The 'Hot Issue Market' of 1980," *Journal of Business*, 57, 1984, pp. 215–240.

Sarig, Oded H., "On Mergers, Divestments, and Options: A Note," *Journal of Financial and Quantitative Analysis,* 20, September 1985, pp. 385–389.

Schipper, Katherine, and Abbie Smith, "Effects of Recontracting on Shareholder Wealth," *Journal of Financial Economics,* 12, 1983, pp. 437–467.

———, "A Comparison of Equity Carve-Outs and Equity Offerings: Share Price Effects and Corporate Restructuring," *Journal of Financial Economics,* 15, 1986, pp. 153–186.

Slovin, Myron B., Marie E. Sushka, and Steven R. Ferraro, "A Comparison of the Information Conveyed by Equity Carve-Outs, Spin-Offs, and Asset Sell-Offs," *Journal of Financial Economics,* 37(1), January 1995, pp. 89–104.

Smith, Clifford W., Jr., "Alternative Methods for Raising Capital: Rights Versus Underwritten Offerings," *Journal of Financial Economics,* 5, December 1977, pp. 273–307.

———, "Investment Banking and the Capital Acquisition Process," *Journal of Financial Economics,* 15, January/February 1986a, pp. 3–29.

———, "Raising Capital: Theory and Evidence," *Midland Corporate Finance Journal,* 4, Spring 1986b, pp. 6–22.

Vijh, Anand M., "Long-Term Returns from Equity Carveouts," *Journal of Financial Economics,* 51, 1999, pp. 273–308.

Ward, Sandra, "Giving Gifts," *Barron's,* December 26, 1994, pp. 21–24.

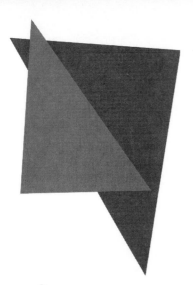

Financial Restructuring

We emphasize throughout this book that M&A policies should take place within the framework of the strategic planning processes of the firm. Equally important, M&A decisions are not separate compartments. It is impossible to separate internal programs for growth and the use of external M&A markets. Financial and M&A decisions also interact. In this chapter we illustrate the implementation of these generalizations, particularly in some of the areas of traditional financial management. We include the following topics: leverage and leveraged recapitalizations, dual-class stock recapitalizations, exchange offers, reorganization processes, financial engineering, and liquidations and takeover bust-ups.

UNLOCKING THE VALUE IN THE FIRM

As an overview we utilize the relationships depicted in Figure 13.1, which presents some major factors affecting the value of the firm. First is the value of a firm when it is all equity-financed. To this can be added the present value of tax shields. A third source of value growth is the present value of other benefits of leverage such as pressures for efficiency to meet debt obligations (Jensen, 1986; Wruck, 1990, pp. 430–433).

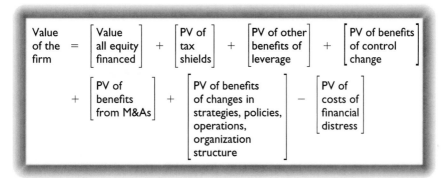

Figure 13.1   Sources of Value Increases

A fourth group of benefits involves top management changes and changing roles of other control groups such as banks, insurance companies, and pension funds. Fifth, M&As can perform a constructive role in augmenting the capabilities and product–market spans of firms.

Sixth, in taking positive actions for growth and improvement, such as expansion, M&As, leverage changes, and dealing with financial distress, performance improvement is essential. The present value of benefits of changes in strategies, policies, and operations, as well as organizational structure and processes, can be substantial (Wruck, 1990, pp. 434–435). A demonstration of a leveraged recap plus efficiency improvements is to be found in a case study of the Sealed Air Corporation developed by Wruck (1994). Finally, the present value of the costs of financial distress would reduce the value of the firm. Figure 13.1, therefore, summarizes major factors that influence the success of the individual restructuring efforts we now describe.

LEVERAGE AND LEVERAGED RECAPITALIZATIONS

Capital structure and leverage decisions are often involved in mergers and takeovers. A firm with zero leverage may be vulnerable to takeover by a firm seeking to capture the tax benefits of debt. Capital structure and leverage decisions represent potentials for value enhancement, for acquiring other firms, or for defending against acquisition by others. We start with a simple example that provides a foundation for more complex financial recapitalizations.

Table 13.1 presents the initial input-values for the analysis. Table 13.2 presents a series of balance sheets to illustrate the effects of increasing leverage. Before the financial recapitalization, the firm has no debt. The next two columns illustrate taking on debt equal to 20% or 40% of the market value of the firm before adding leverage. Table 13.2 depicts $600 of debt or $1,200 of debt. Table 13.3 presents the effects of tax shields on share prices. The present value of tax shields is calculated by multiplying the amount of debt by the tax rate of the firm, which was given in Table 13.1 as 40%. This is a simplified version of the tax effects, but the qualifications would not change the central principles we are illustrating (DeAngelo and DeAngelo, 1996; Mitchell and Mitchell, 1996). Line 4 of Table 13.3 shows that the market value of the firm has been increased by the present value of the tax shields.

Table 13.1   Initial Input Values

1. Operating income (millions)	$300
2. Shares outstanding (millions)	100
3. Management ownership	20%
4. Market value per share	$30
5. Market value of the firm (millions)	$3,000
6. Tax rate	40%

Table 13.2   Balance Sheets with Increasing Leverage

	Before Recap	20% Debt	40% Debt
1. Cash	$ 10	$ 10	$ 10
2. Other current assets	100	100	100
3. Long-term assets, net	90	90	90
4. Total assets	$200	$200	$ 200
5. Debt	$ 0	$600	$1,200
6. Equity at book	200	−400	−1,000
7. Total claims	$200	$200	$ 200

Table 13.3   Effect of Tax Shields on Share Prices

	Before Recap	20% Debt	40% Debt
1. Debt as percent of original firm value	0%	20%	40%
2. Amount of debt	$0	$600	$1,200
3. Present value of tax shields	$0	$240	$480
4. Market value of the firm	$3,000	$3,240	$3,480

Table 13.4 illustrates other effects of increasing leverage. We start with the total market value of the firm from Table 13.3. In line 2, the amount of debt is deducted to obtain the market value of equity. The values shown in lines 3 to 5 are calculated simultaneously because the shares repurchased and the share price must be determined simultaneously. For example, with 20% debt, we would have the following expression for the new share price, P.

$$P = \frac{2,640}{100 - 600/P} \tag{13.1}$$

In words, the expression says

$$\text{New Share Price} = \frac{\text{Market Value of Equity}}{\text{Previous Shares Outstanding} - \text{Shares Purchased}}$$

Solving equation (13.1), we obtain $32.40 for the share price. The second term in the denominator of (13.1) represents shares repurchased with the debt proceeds and equals 18.52. When this number is subtracted from the previous shares outstanding of 100, we obtain the new shares outstanding with 20% debt of 81.48. The amounts for lines 3 to 5 with 40% debt are calculated in the same way.

Table 13.4   Leverage Ratios and Interest Coverage

	Before Recap	**20% Debt**	**40% Debt**
1. Market value of the firm	$3,000	$3,240	$3,480
2. Market equity	$3,000	$2,640	$2,280
3. Shares repurchased with debt proceeds	0.00	18.52	34.48
4. Shares outstanding	100.00	81.48	65.52
5. Share price	$30.00	$32.40	$34.80
6. Book equity	$200	−$400	−$1,000
7. Debt-to-market equity ratio	0.00	0.23	0.53
8. Pretax cost of debt	8.0%	9.5%	11.5%
9. Interest expense	$0.0	$57.0	$138.0
10. Operating income	$300	$300	$300
11. Interest coverage	—	5.3	2.2

In the remainder of Table 13.4 we calculate some ratios and coverages. Line 6 is developed by using the data in Table 13.2 on the balance sheets. For example, in Table 13.2 the total assets remain the same after $600 of debt is incurred. This is because the proceeds of debt were used to retire equity shares outstanding. Because total assets and total claims remain at $200, equity at book, which had been $200, must be a negative $400 for total claims to continue to equal assets of $200. Book equity becomes negative. This is what is observed in actual cases of leveraged recapitalizations. Whereas book equity becomes negative, the debt to market equity ratio is positive because market equity is positive.

In lines 8 through 11 we calculate the interest coverage. Some plausible levels of the pretax cost of debt are shown in line 8. When these percentages are multiplied by the level of debt outstanding, we obtain the amount of interest expense. Operating income was given in Table 13.1 at $300. The ratio of operating income to interest expense gives the interest coverage shown in line 11.

In this base case example of increasing leverage, we can draw a number of generalizations. Using the original Modigliani–Miller measure of the tax shield benefits of debt, we have demonstrated that management has increased the value of the firm by adding leverage where there was none before. Other measures of tax benefits might produce different levels of value increases for the firm. However, adding leverage where there had been none before is likely to move the firm away from a suboptimal (zero) level of debt.

Table 13.5 illustrates the impact of a leveraged recapitalization on the percentage of control by the management of the firm. In the previous examples, the funds were used to repurchase shares. Table 13.5 illustrates the effects of using the funds from selling debt to pay a cash dividend to nonmanagement shareholders, who are assumed to hold 80% of the outstanding shares. The funds raised from selling debt are divided by 80 to obtain dividends of $7.50 per share when the funds raised by debt are $600 and $15 per share for the $1,200 level of debt, as shown in line 3. Recall that before debt was sold, the value per share of stock was $30. Therefore, for manage-

Table 13.5   Leveraged Recapitalization: Alternative I

	20% Debt	40% Debt
1. Amount of debt	$600	$1,200
2. Shares held by nonmanagement shareholders	80	80
3. Dividend per share	$7.50	$15.0
4. Fraction of shares received by management	0.25	0.50
5. Original number of management shares in total	20	20
6. Additional number of management shares	5	10
7. New total number of management shares	25	30

	Ownership %				
	Before Recap		After Recap		
Shareholders	80.0%	80	76.2%	80	72.7%
Managers	20.0%	25	23.8%	30	27.3%
		105		110	

ment to receive the equivalent in shares of stock, they would receive 0.25 share of stock for each share held. When the dividend per share is $15, the share fraction due management is 0.50. Taking into account the original number of management shares, as shown in line 5, the new total number of management shares would be 25 and 30, as shown in line 7.

As shown in Table 13.5, it is straightforward to see that the share of ownership by management would rise as high as 27.3% when the amount of debt sold is $1,200. If higher levels of debt were incurred and paid out as a dividend, the patterns in Table 13.5 would become even more pronounced.

Table 13.6 goes through an analysis in which the interest-bearing debt becomes 77.5% of the pre-recap market value of equity. In this example, each shareholder receives all the funds raised not only by selling new debt, (add $176 new debt to $10 old debt; multiply $24 market value per share times 10 equals 240; then 186 divided by 240 equals 77.5) but also by drawing down $40 of available cash, a total of $216. The accounting entry is to credit cash $216 and debit "equity" $216. So equity after recap becomes a negative $16. The example illustrates the case where the shareholders receive in cash the full pre-recap market value of the equity. In addition, it is assumed that the market value of share per stock falls to $4 and that the nonmanagement shareholders receive in exchange for their old shares one share of the new equity stub. The common equity is referred to as a *stub* when a financial recap results in the decline of its market value to 25% or less of its previous market value. Management receives no cash but instead receives seven equity stubs for each equity share to obtain the same value received by each nonmanagement share. As a result, as shown in section D of Table 13.6, the ownership proportion held by managers rises from 10% to 44%. Thus, the higher the percentage of original equity raised in debt form and distributed to nonmanagement, the larger the increase in management's share of ownership.

Table 13.6   Recap to Increase Management Control

A. Basic Data Inputs

Market value of equity per share		$24
Net operating income (NOI), millions		$30
Shares outstanding, millions		10
Shares owned by management, millions		1
Each shareholder share (SH) receives		
Cash		$24.00
Stub	1 @ $4	$ 4.00
		$28.00
Each management share receives		
Stub	7 @ $4	$28.00

B. Sources and Uses of Cash

Sources of cash		Uses of cash	
Cash on books	$ 40	Cash offer per SH	$24.00
Short-term interest-bearing debt	0	Number of stubs for SH	× 9
Senior long-term debt	100		$ 216
Subordinated debt	76		
	$216		

C. Balance Sheets

	Before Recap	After Recap
Cash	$ 50	$ 10
Other current assets	100	100
Long-term assets, net	120	120
Total assets	$270	$230
Non-interest-bearing ST debt	$ 60	$ 60
Short-term interest-bearing debt @ 10%	10	10
Senior long-term debt @ 12%	0	100
Subordinated debt @ 15%	0	76
Equity	200	−16
Total liabilities and shareholders' equity (SHE)	$270	$230
Difference	0	0

D. Ownership Proportions

Total number of shares (millions)	Before Recap	After Recap
Owned by shareholders	9 (90%)	9 (56%)
Owned by managers	1 (10%)	7 (44%)
	10	16

E. Interest Coverage

	Before Recap	After Recap
Net operating income (NOI)	$30	$30
Interest expense		
Short-term interest-bearing debt (STIBD)	$1.0	$ 1.0
Senior long-term debt	0.0	12.0
Subordinated debt	0.0	11.4
	$1.0	$24.4
NOI/interest expense ratio	30.0	1.2

The Effects of the Use of Leveraged Recaps

In the preceding section, we presented models of leveraged recaps (LRs). In this section, we discuss the rationale for their use. From the preceding examples, we see that a leveraged recap involves (1) a relatively large issue of debt, (2) the payment of a relatively large cash dividend to nonmanagement shareholders, and (3) as an alternative to the cash dividend or combined with it, a repurchase of common shares.

A number of empirical studies show that book leverage measured by total debt to total capitalization increases from about 20% to about 70% (Gupta and Rosenthal, 1991; Handa and Radhakrishnan, 1991; Kleiman, 1988). The ownership share of management increases from 9% to 24% on average.

The market response to announcements of leveraged recaps depends on whether the action was defensive or proactive. In defensive LRs, the actions are taken in response to actual takeovers or indications of a likely takeover bid. Proactive LRs are part of a longer term program of improving the performance of the firm. Event returns in a proactive LR experience a cumulative abnormal return of about 30%, similar to the level in tender offers (Gupta and Rosenthal, 1991; Handa and Radhakrishnan, 1991; Kleiman, 1988). Surprisingly, in such LRs the event returns to bond shareholders have been a positive 5% even though leverage has been substantially increased.

For defensive LRs, the abnormal returns include negative as well as positive values. The range is so wide as to make generalization difficult (Kleiman, 1988). Gupta and Rosenthal (1991), however, show cumulative abnormal returns of 48% over a window beginning 30 days before the start of the takeover and ending 150 days after the completion of the leveraged recapitalization and a positive 5% to bondholders.

Subsequent Performance

A defensive LR may succeed by returning cash to shareholders that is close to or more than the takeover offer. In addition, share owners continue to hold the equity stubs received. The substantial increases in leverage may also discourage the outside bidders. The high leverage ratios may represent a form of scorched earth policy. Prospective bidders may be reluctant to face the task of returning the firm to leverage ratios closer to historical industry patterns. Although LRs are used as a takeover defense, a high percentage of firms that adopt them are subsequently acquired.

One study (Denis and Denis, 1995) found that 31% of their 29-firm sample completing LRs between 1985 and 1988 encountered financial distress. The high rate of financial distress, however, resulted mainly from unexpected and adverse macroeconomic and regulatory developments. The main factors influencing subsequent performance appear to have been (1) industry conditions, (2) whether the LRs were defensive or proactive, and (3) whether operating improvements were achieved.

Critical to the performance of the firm following an LR (proactive or defensive) is whether other operating improvements are made. This has been demonstrated in a number of case studies (Healy and Palepu, 1995; Mitchell and Mitchell, 1996; Stewart, 1991; Wruck 1994). The evidence is also consistent with a positive disciplinary role of debt (Dann, 1993; Gupta and Rosenthal, 1991). The large overhang of debt stimulates management to improve operations to generate sufficient cash flows to pay down the debt.

A leveraged recapitalization is likely to achieve the best results if it is part of a strategic plan to improve the performance of a firm in relation to its changing environments. In addition to the financial restructuring, the success of an LR depends heavily on programs to improve operating performance.

We now present a series of mini case studies to illustrate the proposition that organizational restructuring can produce more basic improvements than financial engineering.

The Sealed Air Corporation illustrates the policy changes required as a result of moving from a position of competitive advantage from strong patent positions in the early 1960s to increased competition by the late 1980s after the expiration of its major patents (Wruck, 1994). During the period of patent protection, its profit margins were high and its cash flows were high, with little pressure to control costs. With the expiration of its patents, new firms entered its product line. Price pressures developed, which put Sealed Air at a competitive disadvantage because of its inefficient operations and high costs. In response, the management of Sealed Air initiated major policy changes. It increased financial incentives to focus on efficiency and cash flow. It developed capital budgeting procedures to improve investment decisions. It substantially increased leverage, which created pressures to develop cash flows to service the debt. But the increased leverage without the other policy changes to increase efficiency would have resulted in bankruptcy. The policy changes were successful in improving earnings performance and Sealed Air's stock price.

After years of dominance of the copier market, Xerox Corporation faced competition from an increasing number of competitors who produced cheaper and better copiers in the early 1980s. Xerox responded by a focus on improving the reliability of its products. It redefined its strategy, in a 1990 initiative called "Xerox 2000," from a maker of machines to a manager of documents. Its organizational restructuring involved moving from a classic functional form to an M-form of organization (recall our discussion of organization and strategy in chapter 5), providing increased decentralized decision making in nine strategic business units, each focusing on a distinct type of customer. Xerox also introduced a contingent executive compensation system. Bonuses and long-term incentives were determined by a combination of individual achievement, business unit success, and overall company performance. The increased efficiency resulted in a 10% cut in its workforce in October 1993; note that this downsizing was the result of major policy changes. The Xerox case illustrates that successful restructuring requires improvements in strategy and organizational structure, as well as new incentive compensation programs to motivate better performance. Downsizing alone is an indication of weakness.

In summary, the Sealed Air and Xerox examples illustrate that increased efficiency is critical in strategic programs to improve a firm's performance. If such a program is successful, a firm's vulnerability to a takeover offer will be reduced. On the positive side, restructuring can help the firm enhance long-run benefits for its stakeholders.

DUAL-CLASS STOCK RECAPITALIZATIONS

In dual-class recapitalizations (DCRs), firms have created a second class of common stock that has limited voting rights and usually a preferential claim to the firm's cash flows. Most firms create the new class by distributing limited voting shares pro rata to current shareholders. A typical DCR creates a class A type of shares with one vote per share but with a higher dividend rate than the other class. The class B shares can cast multiple votes such as three, five, or 10 per share; their dividend rate is lower than for the class A shares. As a result of a DCR, officers and directors as a group will usually have 55% to 65% of common stock voting rights (DeAngelo and DeAngelo, 1985; Partch, 1987). However, the officers and directors have a claim on about 25% of the total cash flows from common stock. In a substantial proportion of companies with dual classes of common stock, the control group represents founding families or their descendants (DeAngelo and DeAngelo, 1985). In one-third of a sample of firms, two or more of the top executives were related by either blood or marriage.

Reasons for Dual-Class Recapitalizations

A positive reason for DCRs is to enable top management to solidify its control so that long-term programs can be carried out. This avoids the pressure to show good results every quarter. This motive is particularly applicable if the operations of the firm are relatively complex so that it is difficult for acquirers to evaluate managerial performance.

A related rationale is that managers may develop firm-specific abilities that are fully compensated when long-range plans come to fruition. Before the longer term results are in, these managers would suffer the risk that their prospective rewards would be appropriated when outside shareholders responded favorably to an acquisition offer. Alternatively, it is also possible that managers who are not performing well may be motivated to entrench their positions against a takeover so that they will not be replaced.

Market Response to Dual-Class Recaps

One way to test the alternative motives for DCRs is to measure the market response. In such studies the 90-day period preceding the announcement of a DCR represents a period of positive abnormal returns of over 6% (Lease, McConnell, and Mikkelson, 1984; Partch, 1987). When the event return is measured over a narrow window of two or three days including the day of announcement of plans to create limited voting common stock, the market response is about a 1% significantly positive gain. When the average stock price reaction is cumulated over the time period from the announcement of the plan to the shareholder meeting at which it is approved, the response is negative but not significantly different from zero. The conclusion is that shareholder wealth is not adversely affected by the adoption of a DCR.

However, it was found that when a firm was taken over the holders of superior voting right shares received a differentially higher payment than the holders of inferior voting shares (DeAngelo and DeAngelo, 1985). Other studies found that few firms with dual-class stock have experienced takeover bids. A virtual laboratory test of this issue was provided when the Ontario Securities Commission, on March 2, 1984, adopted a policy that it would not approve a prospectus offering for inferior voting shares unless they were given coattails that would permit them to participate equally in any takeover bid for the superior shares. After some experience, the commission reversed this policy on October 12, 1984. The premium to superior shares was then increased again (Maynes, 1996). The consensus view appears to be that superior shares sell at a premium and mainly because they receive more in a takeover (Lease, McConnell, and Mikkelson, 1983).

Paradox of the Entrenchment

Shareholder approval is required for the adoption of a DCR. Why do DCRs continue to be approved if their purpose is management entrenchment? In some cases, the voting power of insiders will be sufficient to achieve shareholder approval, but this cannot explain all approvals. Ruback (1988) developed a model that explains shareholders' behavior in exchange offers in which shareholders are given the opportunity to exchange common stock for shares with limited voting rights but higher dividends. These offers induce shareholders to exchange their shares for limited voting rights shares carrying higher dividends, even though such shareholders are harmed by the exchange as a result of the decline in the share price. In these offers, the wealth of shareholders who retain the superior-vote shares is transferred to shareholders who elect the inferior-vote shares with higher dividends. Thus, all outside shareholders rationally choose the higher dividend. This leads to the approval of the exchange plan and in turn to the decline in their wealth. If collective action were possible, outside shareholders would collude to defeat the exchange offer in order to avoid the reduced probability of receiving a takeover bid caused by the recapitalization.

Lehn, Netter, and Poulsen (LNP) (1990) found DCRs to be comparable with leveraged buyouts, reasoning that both are forms of increasing ownership by management. However, they also found that DCRs experienced significantly higher growth rates in sales and number of employees than LBO firms. This is predictable, because during the period of their study, 1977 through 1987, LBOs were mainly in relatively mature industries with stable cash flows. The ratios of research and development expenditures to sales and of advertising expenditures to sales were higher for the DCR firms. The recap firm also had lower pretransaction tax liabilities.

With respect to performance after the transaction, LNP found that the dual-class firms use a higher percentage of their cash flows for capital expenditures than the LBO firms. A large proportion of the dual-class firms issue equity following the recapitalization. For the period studied, the LBOs were in more mature industries, whereas the dual-class firms were in industries with higher growth prospects. Significant increases in industry-adjusted operating income to sales ratios are achieved by dual-class firms. The LBO firms outperform dual-class firms in terms of size of improvement and performance, reflecting the turnarounds associated with managers with substantially increased equity stakes in LBOs. Insiders of dual-class firms already held 43.1% of the common equity before the transaction. In contrast to LBOs, which were often used as antitakeover transactions, takeover rumors or bids preceded recaps in only three of the 97 firms. Dual-class firms have relatively lower leverage policies and do not alter them as a consequence of the transaction.

All of the above findings on DCRs are consistent with the other studies. Insiders in DCR firms seek to consolidate their control so as to carry through their long-run plans. They are willing to sacrifice some current dividend income for the prospect of larger long-term capital gains.

Moyer, Rao, and Sisneros (MRS) (1992) examined the hypothesis that DCRs are accompanied by ways to decrease managerial control of the corporation—specifically by increasing leverage, dividends, and monitoring by security analysts and institutional investors. Their sample consisted of 114 firms that announced in the *Wall Street Journal* or in some SEC document (on a date that could be identified) DCRs during the 1979 to 1987 period. The average asset size per firm was $517.1 million. MRS show that the mean proportion of outside directors on the board changed from 53.7% to 59.1% over the two years preceding the announcement. Only the changes in debt ratio and the mean number of analysts following the firm showed significant change. Changes in dividend payout and changes in the number of institutions holding the stock after the recapitalization were statistically insignificant. For prior ownership levels of up to 7.5%, the change in debt ratio was significantly greater in the low prior ownership groups than in the high prior ownership groups. The mean number of analysts following the sample firms was 5.72 prior to announcement and 7.47 after the announcement. Thus a moderate increase in external control took place.

EXCHANGE OFFERS

An exchange offer provides one or more classes of securities the right or option to exchange part or all of their holdings for a different class of securities of the firm. Like a tender offer repurchase, an exchange offer is usually open for about one month. However, the offer is frequently extended. To induce the securities holders to make the exchange, the terms of exchange offered necessarily involve new securities of greater market value than the preexchange offer announcement market value. Exchange offers usually specify the maximum number of securities that may be exchanged. Also, many exchange offers are contingent upon acceptance by holders of a minimum number of the securities to be exchanged. Masulis (1980) reports that initial announcement dates precede the beginning of the exchange offer by, on average, nine weeks. He states that the average life of the offer is about seven weeks.

Tax Aspects of Exchange Offers

When a company sells bonds at a discount, this generally implies that the coupon interest rate is below the market rate of interest. If the amount of the discount is material, the discount for tax purposes must be amortized over the life of the debt instrument. The amount of the amortized discount is treated as an additional interest payment to make up for the low coupon. It is, therefore, a tax expense to the corporation. When a corporation sells a bond at a premium, this means that the coupon payment is higher than the market rate. The amortization of the premium is a reduction in the interest tax expense to the corporation.

When a firm redeems debt at a price below the issue price, the difference is treated as ordinary income. If debt is redeemed at a price above the issue price, the difference is treated as an ordinary loss to the corporation and a gain to the seller of debt (Masulis, 1980). When stock is tendered for debt, stockholders incur a capital gains tax liability just as if they had sold their stock for cash. Masulis (1980) therefore observes that an exchange of debt for common stock is likely to occur when stocks are selling at relatively low prices and most shareholders would incur little or no capital gains liability as a consequence.

Empirical Evidence on Exchange Offers

With some of the characteristics of exchange offers as a background, we next turn to the empirical data. Table 13.7 shows that an exchange of debt for common stock

Table 13.7 Exchange Offers with Positive Returns

P1. Debt for common stock (Masulis, 1983)	+14.0%
P2. Preferred for common stock (Masulis, 1983; Pinegar and Lease, 1986)	+ 8.2%
P3. Debt for preferred stock (Masulis, 1983)	+ 2.2%
P4. Income bonds for preferred stock (McConnell and Schlarbaum, 1981)	+ 2.2%

involves the largest positive returns to shareholders. It is 14%, about the order of magnitude of wealth effects observed in stock repurchase tender offers. The exchange of preferred stock for common also carries a large gain of over 8%. The exchange of debt or the exchange of income bonds for preferred stock carries small but significant positive returns.

Table 13.8 summarizes the results of exchange offers with negative returns. Why do some types of exchange offers result in negative returns while others achieve positive returns? A number of theories or explanations are possible. The effects appear to depend on whether the exchanges have one or more of the following consequences:

1. Leverage increasing or decreasing.
2. Implied increases or decreases in future cash flows.
3. Implied undervaluation or overvaluation of common stock.
4. Increases or decreases in management share ownership.
5. Increases or decreases in control of management use of cash.
6. Positive or negative signaling effects.

The exchange offers in Table 13.7 have positive returns. They appear to have in common a number of characteristics: They increase leverage, they imply an increase in future cash flows, and they imply undervaluation of common stock. In two of the four cases management share ownership is increased, and in three of the four cases the control over management's use of cash is decreased. It is difficult to judge whether the leverage effect is also a signaling effect or whether it is purely a tax effect. It could be argued that the exchange of preferred for common stock does not carry tax impli-

Table 13.8 Exchange Offers with Negative Returns

N1. Common stock for debt (Masulis, 1983)	−9.9%
N2. Private swaps of common for debt (Finnerty, 1985; Peavy and Scott, 1985)	−0.9%
N3. Preferred stock for debt (Masulis, 1983)	−7.7%
N4. Common for preferred stock (Masulis, 1983; Pinegar and Lease, 1986)	−2.6%
N5. Calls forcing debt conversion (Mikkelson, 1981)	−2.1%

cations for the corporation. On the other hand, because 80% of the dividends (85% before 1986) on preferred stock (for the period of these studies) could be excluded as income for a corporate investor, the incidence of this tax advantage accrued at least partially to the issuing corporation. Copeland and Lee (1991) judge the signaling effects to be most consistent with theory and empirical evidence.

Another curiosity in connection with the leverage-increasing exchange offers is noted by Vermaelen (1981). He points out that 30.1% of the leverage-increasing exchange offers in the sample developed by Masulis were announced during the period of dividend controls, roughly from mid-1971 through mid-1974. This suggests that they were by relatively smaller firms that were seeking to avoid the requirement that dividend increases could be no more than 4% per year. Of course, another strong external effect came about on the swaps that were stimulated by a tax law change in 1984 documented by Finnerty (1985). Because multiple explanations could account for the positive returns shown by Table 13.7, it is difficult to assign weights to each explanation.

Similarly, in Table 13.8, for exchange offers causing negative returns, it appears that the five explanations will run in the opposite direction. Swaps of common stock or preferred stock for debt carry about the same relatively large negative returns. However, private swaps of common stock for debt carry a small but significant return. Much more detailed studies would be required to attempt to assess the relative weight of each of the potential explanations for the pattern of abnormal returns observed.

One study introduces the q-ratio as an additional variable (Born and McWilliams, 1993). In a study of 127 equity-for-debt exchange offers, firms with q-ratios less than 1 experienced significantly negative abnormal returns on announcement. This confirms the studies reported above. However, firms with q-ratios greater than 1 did not experience a significant event response. These findings suggest that the equity-for-debt exchanges with low q values may be used to rescue the firm from pressures resulting from the inability to service debt obligations.

Distressed exchanges have been widely used in recent years by firms that issued high yield "junk" bonds and tried to work out what they felt was a short-term problem caused by overleveraging a basically sound operating company. Exchanges usually involve either a total exchange of preferred and/or common equity for the old debt or a combination of some equity and some new, but extended, debt for the old debt.

The classic distressed exchange involves a firm whose operating and financial condition has deteriorated due to both chronic and cyclical problems. It attempts to restructure both its assets and its liabilities. For example, International Harvester Corporation, a large farm equipment, truck, and bus manufacturer, was on the verge of total collapse in 1980 to 1982. The firm first exchanged preferred stock for its interest payment obligations to banks and extended both its interest payments to creditors and payables to suppliers. Next, it converted its short-term bank debt (1 to 3 years) to longer term "junk" bonds (10 to 12 years). Finally, it exchanged common equity in its newly named entity, Navistar International, for the "old" junk bonds. These distressed restructuring strategies helped the firm improve its operations; it eventually paid its short- and long-term creditors in full (Chen, Weston, and Altman, 1995).

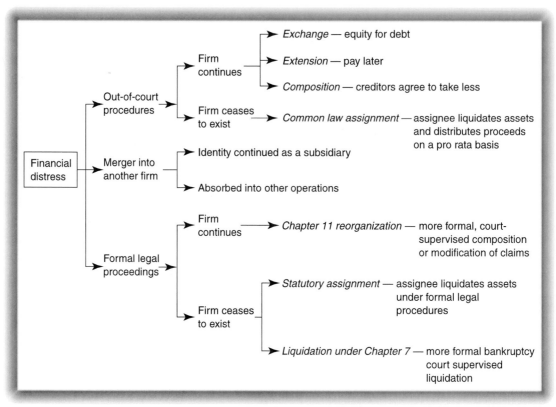

Figure 13.2   Alternative Adjustments to Financial Distress

REORGANIZATION PROCESSES

Several forms of financial restructuring may take place when a firm experiences financial distress. Financial distress is defined here as the condition in which the liquidation value of the firm's assets is less than the total face value of creditor claims.

Out-of-Court Procedures

Figure 13.2 provides an overview of alternative adjustments that a firm may make to relieve financial distress. The three main alternatives are informal procedures, merger, and legal proceedings. In out-of-court procedures, the firm can either continue or be liquidated. If the firm continues, (1) a residual or equity claim can be substituted for a debt priority claim or (2) the maturity of the debt can be postponed. A third alternative is to scale down the obligation. All three procedures are based on the idea that if the distressed firm is given some breathing room to improve operations, the creditors will ultimately receive more than they would otherwise.

Merger into Another Firm

Mergers can also be used to rescue a floundering or failing firm. A study of 38 takeovers of distressed firms between 1981 and 1988 (Clark and Ofek, 1994) found that such combinations were more likely to involve firms in the same industry and less likely to be hostile takeovers than general patterns. In the sample of 38 restructuring efforts that used mergers, Clark and Ofek classified 20 as failures, nine as marginally successful, and nine as clearly successful. These evaluations were based on the use of five different measures to evaluate the postmerger performance of the combined and target firms: (1) ratio of earnings before interest, taxes, and depreciation (EBITD) to sales; (2) return to the bidder on its investment in the target; (3) beta excess return during the two years after completion of the merger; (4) the bidder's excess equity return over its industry three-digit SIC code median during the two years after merger completion; and (5) a qualitative variable that equals $+1$ if it was successful, 0 if marginal, and -1 if a failure.

Clark and Ofek also studied the relationship between the announcement period cumulative abnormal return (CAR) and each of their five performance variables. The bidder CAR was positively related to each of the five performance measures. This is another study that demonstrates the ability of market event returns to forecast postmerger results.

They found also that bidders overpay for the distressed targets. Much of the post-merger performance results appear to be dominated by industry factors. Takeovers of target firms that are financially distressed are more likely to be successfully restructured than those of target firms whose operating performance is poor. Distressed targets that are small compared to the bidder yield positive returns to the bidder. Clark and Ofek conclude that in the majority of cases takeovers do not successfully restructure a distressed target. They observe, however, that the effort to do so may appear to be the best alternative available at the time.

Formal Legal Proceedings

When an informal extension or scaling down of the obligations as well as the merger alternative do not appear to solve the problems of a distressed firm, more formal legal proceedings are required. The formal court proceedings follow the bankruptcy law adopted in 1978. Its five major provisions are (1) an automatic stay, (2) debtor in possession (DIP), (3) increased power of managers in the recontracting process, (4) new voting rules for creditors, and (5) some flexibility in applying absolute priority rules.

An automatic stay permits the firm to stop all payments of principal and interest, preventing secured creditors from taking possession of their collateral. This makes it easier for the firm to obtain additional financing. Debtor-in-possession financing makes it possible to issue new debt claims with priority over existing debt.

Managers retain considerable power after a firm has filed for bankruptcy. Managers are able to continue to make operating decisions, and, for 120 days after the Chapter 11 filing, managers have the exclusive right to propose a reorganization plan. The court often grants one or more extensions of this deadline. Management has 180 days from the filing date to obtain creditor and shareholder approval. If management fails to propose a plan or its plan is rejected, creditors can propose their own plan. To do so, they must provide proof of values for claims to be issued and assets to be retained or sold. This requires costly appraisals and hearings compared with a management plan that requires the bankruptcy judge to evaluate it as "fair and reasonable."

The 1978 Bankruptcy Code introduced new voting rules for approval by creditors of a reorganization plan. It specifies majority (in number) requirements for approval of the plan and provides that dissenters must accept the terms approved by the majority.[1] In this sense, each class of creditors behaves as one part in which minority creditors cannot hold out. The new voting rules facilitate renegotiation of the debt, so the potential for investment efficiency is improved by reducing bargaining costs.

The code also provides for absolute priority rules in establishing the order of claims under reorganization. Frequent but small (2.3% to 7.6%) deviations from absolute priority occur. Here are two possible explanations: (1) One or more classes of claimants may provide new or future financing as a basis for improving their position over what it would have been under absolute priority; (2) estimated market values are used as a basis for establishing priority positions. But market values depend on the success of the restructuring and the future performance of the firm. The value estimates are subject to negotiation among the claimants. Thus, deviations from absolute priority may facilitate approval of a plan earlier than would otherwise be possible.

The basic goal for the legal bankruptcy-restructuring process is to preserve organization value. By recontracting with claimants, the aim is to restore the firm to operating and financial health. Thus, there is a positive side to the procedures for restructuring financially distressed firms.

FINANCIAL ENGINEERING

Financial engineering involves the use of calls, puts, swaps, and forward and futures contracts to influence the payoffs from taking on various types of financial exposure. These instruments have helped to limit the financial exposures of business firms as well as other types of investors. This is a rich literature. We limit our discussion to one example of how financial engineering can facilitate a merger transaction (Mason et al., 1995; Tufano, 1996).

In 1991 in its strategic planning processes, Amoco, a major oil company, made a decision to dispose of its marginal oil and gas properties. It created a new organization, MW Petroleum Corporation, as an entity with interest in 9,500 wells in more than 300 producing fields. The Apache Corporation, a smaller independent oil and gas company, was interested in purchasing Amoco's unit. Apache's strategy was to

---

[1]If the reorganization is proposed in an out-of-court distressed restructuring, i.e., not under Chapter 11, then a virtually unanimous acceptance by those creditors who are impaired must be received. This explains the relatively recent phenomenon known as a "prepackaged Chapter 11," whereby the required (but not necessarily unanimous) proportion of accepting creditor votes is assembled for a plan *prior to* the filing of the petition for relief (which initiates the bankruptcy process). In most cases, the formal Chapter 11 reorganization that follows the prepack agreement is a relatively simple procedure. The actual time spent in the bankruptcy process has been as little as one month, and it generally averages only a few months. The money spent in a prepackaged bankruptcy is also typically less. See Altman (1993), Betker (1995), McConnell and Servantes (1991), and Salerno and Hansen (1991) for discussions of prepackaged plans and their recent experience. Betker analyzes 49 cases and concludes that although direct costs of prepacks are comparable to those of traditional Chapter 11's, gains come from the binding of holdouts and from favorable tax treatment on tax loss carryforwards.

acquire properties that others regarded as marginal and use its lower cost operations to achieve higher returns. The negotiations were taking place during the spring of 1991, just after Iraq's invasion of Kuwait had pushed up oil prices. Future oil prices were highly uncertain. Financial engineering provided a solution.

Amoco was willing to write Apache a guarantee that if oil prices fell below a specified level during the first two years after the sale, Amoco would make compensating payments to Apache. Apache, in turn, agreed to pay Amoco if oil prices exceeded a specified level over a 5- to 8-year period. Thus, the commodity risk of the transaction was shared. In financial engineering terms, Amoco and Apache had created a "collar"—a combination of a call option and a put option. Option pricing theory can price a collar.

After the merger was completed, each company was approached with an offer to purchase its option position. Thus the financial markets gave the companies the opportunity to monetize (sell) their options and thereby close their risk exposures if they so desired. The literature of financial engineering is rich with creative transactions. This example illustrates their implications for facilitating M&As.

LIQUIDATIONS AND TAKEOVER BUST-UPS

Corporate liquidations can be either involuntary or voluntary. Creditors force a firm to liquidate if it is worth more "dead" than "alive." In other words, attempting to operate an unsuccessful firm may cause values to deteriorate even further. Voluntary liquidations have a much more positive orientation. When a firm can be sold in parts or as a whole for an amount that exceeds the market value of the firm's securities, liquidation will realize more for the security holders. Managers may be encouraged to take such actions because of the threat that an acquirer will mount a proxy contest for control or launch a tender offer to buy the firm and then liquidate it. Even the threat of such "bust-up" takeovers is enough to stimulate voluntary liquidations. Corporate liquidations are often associated with bankruptcy proceedings, but they are usually involuntary.

Voluntary liquidations partake of the characteristics of divestitures and spin-offs. Diverstitures have the advantage of realizing gains by moving resources to other companies for whom the operations are worth more. In voluntary liquidations, the seller may have different types of activities for which larger gains could be achieved by selling to different types of buyers. This is superior to the alternative of a merger in which one buyer obtains three types of businesses and seeks to sell off the types that do not fit in to its own operations. The original owner can probably obtain more since it can justify more fully the value of the business. Liquidations may substitute for a spin-off when the key managers might have otherwise left the company to start up a competing operation.

An important tax advantage of liquidations was removed by the Tax Reform Act of 1986. Under the General Utilities Doctrine, the corporate capital gains to the selling firm were not taxable if it adopted a plan of complete liquidation and all liquidating dividends were paid to shareholders within 12 months after the plan was adopted. One effect of the repeal of the General Utilities Doctrine by the 1986 act was to eliminate the tax incentive for firms to liquidate voluntarily after partial sell-offs. The 1986 act also eliminated the preferential personal capital gains tax rate, which makes the deferral of realization in nontaxable mergers more attractive. It appears that the Tax Reform Act of 1986 reduced the tax advantages of liquidations compared with nontaxable mergers.

Empirical Studies

Skantz and Marchesini (1987) studied a sample of 37 firms that announced liquidation between 1970 and 1982. They found that the announcement-month average excess return was +21.4%. Interestingly, they found that their sample firms were "not highly dissimilar to their industry members" (p. 71) in profitability prior to the liquidation decision.

Of the possible reasons for the positive abnormal return, Skantz and Marchesini found only one to be applicable. Although divestitures had been generally subject to capital gains taxes, voluntary liquidations could be structured to qualify for preferential tax treatment on a major portion of the gains. This does not explain the much higher positive gains to liquidations (21.4% for the announcement with a cumulative average excess return of 41.3%) than for spin-offs, which are also treated as tax-free exchanges. The reason may be that spin-offs average only 20% of the original parent; if the abnormal returns found by Copeland, Lemgruber, and Mayers (1987) of 5.02% are multiplied by 5 for comparable sizing of investment, the gains are similar.

Hite, Owers, and Rogers (1987) included an analysis of total liquidations in their study of the market for interfirm asset sales. They analyzed 49 voluntary liquidations during the period 1963 to 1983. The median market value of equity was $41 million. The median book value of total assets was about $72 million. Although mergers were eliminated, they found that 21 of the 49 firms had been targets in earlier merger, tender offer, or leveraged buyout bids in the 24 months preceding the liquidation proposal. An additional three firms had been involved in proxy solicitation control contests.

Hite, Owers, and Rogers observed a two-day announcement period average abnormal return of 12.24% for total liquidations, and more than 80% of the sample observations were positive. They estimated that for the seven liquidating firms that had senior securities, an equally weighted portfolio yielded a two-day holding period average return of 8.57%. Their analysis of the source of the positive returns to both the shareholders and senior claimants is that assets are being moved to higher valued uses.

The study of voluntary liquidations by Kim and Schatzberg (1987, 1988) covered a sample of 73 liquidating firms over the period 1963 to 1981. They observed that their sample was composed of relatively small firms. The median market value of equity was $23 million. The median ratio of the market value of equity of the liquidating firm to the market value of equity of the acquiring firm was 0.28. Kim and Schatzberg found that the liquidation announcement was associated with an average three-day market adjusted return of 14% to the shareholders of liquidating firms. An additional 3% abnormal return took place at shareholder confirmation. Acquiring shareholders experienced a small positive return at a liquidation announcement and a small negative return at confirmation, but these returns were not statistically significant.

As in the Hite, Owers, and Rogers (1987) study, liquidation announcements were often associated with prior news related to mergers, tender offers, or partial sell-offs. At the time of the prior announcements, an abnormal return of 9% was realized. When Kim and Schatzberg took into consideration all public announcements, they obtained even higher returns. They measured the abnormal returns for shareholders from two days before the earliest announcement date until two days after the last announcement date, obtaining total gains of 30% for firms without prior announcements and 34% for firms with prior announcements. The average gain to the shareholders of acquiring firms was not statistically significant.

The Kim and Schatzberg (KS) (1987, 1988) papers confirm the beneficial effect on senior claimants found by Hite, Owers, and Rogers (1987). The majority of the firms in the KS sample retired debt that had a market value less than the face value. Kim and Schatzberg also analyzed the question of why liquidations increase market values. They observed that one advantage of liquidations is that there may be several purchasers, whereas in a merger there is likely to be only one. This enables the selling firm to move its assets to the individual purchasers from whom the greatest value can be realized.

Kim and Schatzberg also compared the tax effects of liquidations with those of nontaxable mergers, and they discuss the impact of the Tax Reform Act of 1986. In general, a nontaxable merger had the advantage of deferring the recognition of a gain to the stockholders of the selling firm until a subsequent sale of the securities involved. First, in a liquidation, the selling stockholders must recognize the gain immediately. Second, unused tax credits and losses belonging to either of the pre-merger firms are carried over in a nontaxable merger, but those of the selling firm are lost at liquidation. Third, a liquidation permits the acquiring firm to step up the tax basis of the assets acquired, but this cannot be done in a nontaxable merger.

Berger and Ofek (1996) found that between 1986 and 1991 the average diversified firm destroyed about 15% of the value its individual segments would have had if they had been operating as independent business units. For a sample of 100 large acquisitions, they found that half of the large diversified targets were broken up. The negative value of diversification that was recovered by the bust-up ranged from 21% to 37%. The large targets that were not broken up after they were taken over had a mean value effect of diversification of only 5%, implying that they were not broken up after the acquisition because not much could be gained by doing so. Berger and Ofek studied the buyers of the divested divisions in the bust-up group and found that 75% of the buyers were LBO associations (financial groups taking segments private in a leveraged buyout) or focused, related firms. This indicates that the bust-up was carried out to move the segments to firms with experience in related businesses.

A paper by Mehran, Nogler, and Schwartz (MNS) (1998) studies the influence of executive ownership and executive compensation incentives on voluntary liquidation decisions. They cover 30 firms for the period 1975 to 1986 related to a sample of control firms in the SIC 1000 to 3999 categories. They found that the probability of a voluntary liquidation increases as the percent ownership of the firm's shares by top executives increases. The greater the use of stock options and other executive compensation incentives, the higher the probability of voluntary liquidation. The median total asset size of the liquidating firm sample was $46 million; the control sample had a median size of $44 million.

The abnormal event returns for their sample of voluntary liquidations over an 11-day window beginning five days before the announcement were 15.5%, significant at the 1% level. So voluntary liquidation decisions increase value for shareholders. MNS note that their study generalizes the earlier Dial and Murphy (1995) case study of General Dynamics' partial liquidation in which the executive compensation plans motivated them to shrink the firm's assets, sometimes eliminating their own jobs.

Six firms in their sample had received takeover bids. The average gain to the shareholders measured by the discounted value of payments in liquidation was 10.3% higher than the average of the takeover bids. They found that 70% of the CEOs in the liquidating firms did not find another CEO position for at least three years.

SUMMARY

The firm's internal growth program is closely tied to the external market for corporate control. Capital structure and leverage decisions represent potentials for value enhancement, for acquiring other firms, or for defending against being acquired by others. These are illustrated in the financial restructuring transactions currently in use.

In leveraged recapitalizations, a relatively large issue of debt is used for the payment of a relatively large cash dividend to nonmanagement shareholders or for the repurchase of common shares, or a combination of the two. The end result is an increase in the ownership share of management. Leveraged recaps should be proactive as part of a long-run program to improve the performance of the firm rather than defensive in response to actual or possible takeovers.

In dual-class stock recapitalizations (DCRs), firms create a second class of common stock that has limited voting rights but usually has a preferential claim to the firm's cash flows. Top management may use DCRs as a way to solidify their control to pursue long-run improvement programs or, alternatively, to entrench their position against takeovers or against being replaced. As a result of a DCR, officers and directors will have, on average, from 55% to 65% of the common stock voting rights but a claim on only about 25% of the total cash flows.

An exchange offer provides the holders of one or more classes of securities the right or option to exchange part or all of their holdings for a different class of securities of the firm. Positive returns are associated with exchange offers that increase leverage, imply an increase in future cash flows, suggest undervaluation of common stock, increase management share ownership, and/or decrease management control over cash. These are illustrated by debt-for-common stock and preferred-for-common stock exchanges. In recent years, distressed exchanges have been widely used by firms in attempts to restructure both assets and liabilities.

Financial distress becomes a driving force for financial restructuring. There are many alternative adjustments that a distressed firm can make. Out-of-court procedures allow the firm's obligations to be restructured to give it some breathing room. Mergers may be used to rescue a floundering or failing firm. However, takeovers do not, in the majority of cases, successfully restructure a distressed target firm. Takeovers are more likely to be successful for financially distressed target firms than for target firms whose operating performance is poor. As a last resort, formal legal proceedings such as filing for a Chapter 11 reorganization or for bankruptcy may be employed.

Firms have used financial engineering to limit their financial exposure. Financial engineering has also been used to facilitate merger transactions. If the acquiring firm and the prospective target firm are able to share the risk exposures of their mutual transaction, then it is more likely that the deal will be completed.

If the firm is worth more "dead" than "alive," creditors will force the firm to liquidate. The firm can be sold in parts or as a whole for an amount that exceeds the preliquidation market values of its securities. Liquidation can also be voluntary when there is the threat of a "bust-up" takeover. Managers may prefer to liquidate if outsiders are likely to mount a proxy contest for control or launch a tender offer to buy the firm and conduct the liquidation themselves.

The case examples in the chapter illustrate that the best forms of restructuring involve strategy, structure, efficient operations, and compensation systems that provide the correct incentives. Xerox changed its organizational structure to decentralize decision making close to the customer to implement its strategy of quality, reliability, and meeting document management needs. Compensation systems that balance the performance of individuals, business units, and the corporation can help implement programs to reduce costs and improve quality. A solid foundation is thereby established for gaining the benefits of financial engineering.

QUESTIONS

13.1 What are the goals of a leveraged recapitalization?

13.2 What are the pros and cons of dual-class recapitalizations?

13.3 What types of exchange offers have positive event returns, and what types have negative event returns?

13.4 Discuss the relationship between financial reorganizations of various types, including a Chapter 11 reorganization.

13.5 How can financial engineering be used to facilitate M&As?

13.6 How do bust-up takeovers and subsequent liquidation of the parts increase the total value realized over the market price of the firm prior to its sale by parts?

Case 13.1 Management Assistance, Inc.

Liquidating for profit is discussed from the standpoint of case studies plus the analysis of what is going on. When a firm "liquidates," its economic resources have not necessarily been destroyed. Indeed, even though an individual firm may cease to exist, it typically sells some or most of its assets to other ongoing firms. In the hands of the buying companies, the assets may be put to a higher economic use than when they were held by the seller.

The case study of Management Assistance, Inc. (MAI) illustrates a number of the concepts involved in liquidating a company (Rosenberg, 1985). MAI had started as a company leasing punch card equipment and then in the late 1950s it became a computer leasing company. It was somewhat unique as a leasing company in that it emphasized the need for strong marketing and customer engineering organizations. In particular, it emphasized customer engineering as a method of assuring customers that the products it leased would receive prompt and effective attention to maintain their serviceability.

In the 1970s MAI was a leader in the development of personal computers with its Basic Four Information Systems. This enabled MAI to record a $19 million profit in 1979. With increased competition in personal computers, the company recorded a $17 million loss in fiscal 1984. The reported losses caused the price of its stock to decline substantially. MAI caught the attention of Asher Adelman early in his career in corporate takeovers. "But where others saw only red ink, Adelman discerned hidden value" (Rosenberg, 1985, p. 9). The customer engineering and service activity of MAI had been placed in a corporate subsidiary named Sorbus Service. Adelman says that he judged that this activity alone would sell for more than two times the then current market price of the common stock of MAI as a whole. The personal computer business of MAI had been placed in a corporate subsidiary with the name Basic Four Information Systems. The division was experiencing losses but Adelman saw potential in the strong marketing organization as a distribution operation, selling not only the products of MAI but the products of other companies as well. By January 1985 Adelman had won control of the board of directors and sold off Sorbus and Basic Four. In February 1985 MAI began to distribute liquidating dividends of about $26 a share to stockholders. It is said that Adelman made a profit of $11 million on his investment of $15 million, a gain of 73%.

QUESTIONS

1. Were the main assets of MAI destroyed?
2. What happened to Sorbus and Basic Four?
3. Why didn't the previous control group at MAI liquidate MAI?

REFERENCES

Altman, E. I., *Corporate Financial Distress and Bankruptcy,* 2nd ed., New York: John Wiley & Sons, 1993.

Berger, Philip G., and Eli Ofek, "Bustup Takeovers of Value-Destroying Diversified Firms," *Journal of Finance,* 51, September 1996, pp. 1175–1200.

Betker, B., "An Empirical Examination of Prepackaged Bankruptcy," *Financial Management,* Spring 1995, pp. 3–18.

Born, Jeffery A., and Victoria B. McWilliams, "Shareholder Responses to Equity-for-Debt Exchange Offers: A Free-Cash-Flow Interpretation," *Financial Management,* 22, Winter 1993, pp. 19–20.

Chen, Yehning, J. Fred Weston, and Edward I. Altman, "Financial Distress and Restructuring Models," *Financial Management,* 24, Summer 1995, pp. 57–75.

Clark, Kent, and Eli Ofek, "Mergers as a Means of Restructuring Distressed Firms: An Empirical Investigation," *Journal of Financial and Quantitative Analysis,* 29, December 1994, pp. 541–565.

Copeland, Thomas E., and Won Heum Lee, "Exchange Offers and Stock Swaps—New Evidence," *Financial Management,* 20, Autumn 1991, pp. 34–48.

Copeland, Thomas E., E. F. Lemgruber, and D. Mayers, "Corporate Spinoffs: Multiple Announcement and Ex-Date Abnormal Performance," chapter 7 in T. E. Copeland, ed., *Modern Finance and Industrial Economics,* New York: Basil Blackwell, 1987.

Dann, Larry Y., "Highly Leveraged Transactions and Managerial Discretion Over Investment Policy: An Overview,"

Journal of Accounting & Economics, 16, January–April–July 1993, pp. 237–240.

DeAngelo, Harry, and Linda DeAngelo, "Managerial Ownership of Voting Rights: A Study of Public Corporations with Dual Classes of Common Stock," *Journal of Financial Economics,* 14, 1985, pp. 33–69.

———, "Ancient Redwoods and the Politics of Finance: The Hostile Takeover of the Pacific Lumber Company," *Journal of Financial Economics,* 47, January 1998, pp. 3–53.

Denis, David J., and Diane K. Denis, "Causes of Financial Distress Following Leveraged Recapitalizations," *Journal of Financial Economics,* 37, February 1995, pp. 129–157.

Dial, J., and K. Murphy, "Incentives, Downsizing, and Value Creation at General Dynamics," *Journal of Financial Economics,* 37, 1995, pp. 261–314.

Finnerty, John D., "Stock-for-Debt Swaps and Shareholder Returns," *Financial Management,* 14, Autumn 1985, pp. 5–17.

Gupta, Atul, and Leonard Rosenthal, "Ownership Structure, Leverage, and Firm Value: The Case of Leveraged Recapitalizations," *Financial Management,* 20, Autumn 1991, pp. 69–83.

Handa, Puneet, and A. R. Radhakrishnan, "An Empirical Investigation of Leveraged Recapitalizations with Cash Payout as Takeover Defense," *Financial Management,* 20, Autumn 1991, pp. 58–68.

Healy, Paul M., and Krishna G. Palepu, "The Challenges of Investor Communication: The Case of CUC International, Inc.," *Journal of Financial Economics,* 38, 1995, pp. 111–140.

Hite, Gailen, James E. Owers, and R. C. Rogers, "The Market for Interfirm Asset Sales: Partial Sell-Offs and Total Liquidations," *Journal of Financial Economics,* 18, 1987, pp. 229–252.

Jensen, Michael C., "Agency Costs of Free Cash Flow, Corporate Finance and Takeovers," *American Economic Review,* 76, May 1986, pp. 323–329.

Kim, E. H., and J. D. Schatzberg, "Voluntary Corporate Liquidations," *Journal of Financial Economics,* 19, 1987, pp. 311–328.

———, "Voluntary Liquidations: Causes and Consequences," *Midland Corporate Finance Journal,* 5, Winter 1988, pp. 30–35.

Kleiman, R. T., "The Shareholder Gains from Leveraged Cashouts: Some Preliminary Evidence," *Journal of Applied Corporate Finance,* 1, Spring 1988, pp. 46–53.

Lease, R., J. McConnell, and W. Mikkelson, "The Market Value of Control in Publicly Traded Corporations," *Journal of Financial Economics,* 11, 1983, pp. 439–472.

———, "The Market Value of Differential Voting Rights in Closely Held Corporations," *Journal of Business,* 75, 1984, pp. 443–467.

Lehn, Kenneth, Jeffry Netter, and Annette Poulsen, "Consolidating Corporate Control: Dual-Class Recapitalizations Versus Leveraged Buyouts," *Journal of Financial Economics,* 27, October 1990, pp. 557–580.

Mason, Scott P., Robert C. Merton, André F. Perold, and Peter Tufano, *Cases in Financial Engineering: Applied Studies of Financial Innovation,* Upper Saddle River, NJ: Prentice-Hall, 1995.

Masulis, Ronald W., "Stock Repurchase by Tender Offer: An Analysis of the Causes of Common Stock Price Changes," *Journal of Finance,* 35, 1980, pp. 305–319.

———, "The Impact of Capital Structure Change on Firm Value: Some Estimates," *Journal of Finance,* 38, March 1983, pp. 107–126.

Maynes, Elizabeth, "Takeover Rights and the Value of Restricted Shares," *The Journal of Financial Research,* 19, Summer 1996, pp. 157–173.

McConnell, John J., and Gary G. Schlarbaum, "Evidence on the Impact of Exchange Offers on Security Prices: The Case of Income Bonds," *Journal of Business,* 54, 1981, pp. 65–85.

McConnell, J., and H. Servantes, "The Economics of Prepackaged Bankruptcy," *Journal of Applied Corporate Finance,* 4, Summer 1991, pp. 93–97.

Mehran, H., G. Nogler, and K. Schwartz, "CEO Incentive Plans and Corporate

Liquidation Policy," *Journal of Financial Economics,* 50, 1998, 319–349.

Mikkelson, W. H., "Convertible Security Calls and Security Returns," *Journal of Financial Economics,* 9, 1981, pp. 237–264.

Mitchell, Mark, and Janet Mitchell, "UST, Inc.," CaseNet, Boston, MA: South-Western College Publishing, 1996.

Moyer, R. C., Ramesh Rao, and P. M. Sisneros, "Substitutes for Voting Rights: Evidence from Dual Class Recapitalizations," *Financial Management,* 21, Autumn 1992, pp. 35–47.

Partch, M. Megan, "The Creation of a Class of Limited Voting Common Stock and Shareholder Wealth," *Journal of Financial Economics,* 18, 1987, pp. 313–339.

Peavy, J. W., and J. A. Scott, "A Closer Look at Stock-for-Debt Swaps," *Financial Analysts Journal,* May/June 1985, pp. 44–50.

Pinegar, J. Michael, and Ronald C. Lease, "The Impact of Preferred-for-Common Exchange Offers on Firm Value," *Journal of Finance,* 41, September 1986, pp. 795–814.

Rosenberg, Hilary, "Newest Kid on the Takeover Block," *Barron's,* March 11, 1985, pp. 8–9, 11.

Ruback, R. S., "Coercive Dual-Class Exchange Offers," *Journal of Financial Economics,* 20, January/March 1988, pp. 153–173.

Salerno, T., and C. Hansen, "A Prepackaged Bankruptcy Strategy," *Journal of Business Strategy,* 12, January/February 1991, pp. 36–41.

Sikora, Martin, ed., *Capturing the Untapped Value in Your Company,* Philadelphia, PA: MRL Publishing Company, 1990.

Skantz, Terrance R., and Roberto Marchesini, "The Effect of Voluntary Corporate Liquidation on Shareholder Wealth," *The Journal of Financial Research,* 10, Spring 1987, pp. 65–75.

Stewart, G. Bennett, *The Quest for Value,* New York: HarperBusiness, 1991.

Tufano, Peter, "How Financial Engineering Can Advance Corporate Strategy," *Harvard Business Review,* 74, January/February 1996, pp. 136–146.

Vermaelen, Theo, "Common Stock Repurchases and Market Signaling: An Empirical Study," *Journal of Financial Economics,* 9, 1981, pp. 139–183.

Wruck, Karen Hopper, "Financial Distress, Reorganization, and Organizational Efficiency," *Journal of Financial Economics,* 27, October 1990, pp. 419–444.

———, "Financial Policy, Internal Control, and Performance: Sealed Air Corporation's Leveraged Special Dividend," *Journal of Financial Economics,* 36, 1994, pp. 157–192.

Chapter 14

Joint Ventures and Alliances

Part V
M&A Strategies

Mergers and tender offers involve a complete fusion of two independent firms or other entities into a single decision-making unit. Other forms of relationships between firms include licensing or cross-licensing of particular technologies, joint bidding on an individual contract, and franchising or other forms of short-term or long-term relationships. Alliances, which range from informal understandings to loose arrangements to formal contracts, have been increasingly used. Firms active in e-commerce particularly have built up networks of relationships facilitated by the ease of communication via the Internet. Joint ventures represent another form of relationship between two or more business entities and are widely and increasingly used by business firms. A *Wall Street Journal* article of November 1, 1995 describes joint ventures among competing firms (Templin, 1995). Texas Instruments and Hitachi have engaged in joint efforts since 1988 to develop new memory chips. In 1995 they jointly founded a $500 million plant near Dallas to produce memory chips. Another example is joint activity between Compaq Computer Corp. and Intel Corp., a major supplier of microprocessors. The two companies have worked together to develop new products. Before the firms merged, Compaq had a joint venture with Digital Equipment Corp. to handle service and support for Compaq customers.

The value of combining different skills is demonstrated by the relationship between USX Corp., a large integrated steel producer, and Nucor Corp., the leading minimill steel producer. USX researchers developed a theory for a new process of making steel from iron carbide, eliminating blast furnaces and supporting coke batteries. If successful, the new process would cut steel production costs by as much as one-fourth. The two companies entered into an agreement to study the feasibility of the process. Nucor possessed considerable experience and expertise in constructing the types of plants that would be required. They would interact with the physicists at USX, who had formulated the new concepts.

Additional examples encompass several different industries. Since 1984 Hewlett-Packard has sold laser printers that use an engine made by Canon. These machines compete with Canon's own laser printers. In telecommunications, we find examples of companies competing in the United States but participating in international joint ventures. US West Inc. competed with Tele-Communications Inc. (TCI) (AT&T Cable Services), a leader in cable, in the U.S. market. The two formed a joint venture in Great Britain to sell phone and cable services on one network. But in the U.S. market, US West had a relationship with Time Warner to offer local service in the New York market of NYNEX (Bell Atlantic) Corp. US West and NYNEX were participants in a four-company enterprise to sell wireless personal communications—cellular phones. TCI also formed a joint venture with Sprint Corp., a competitor to US West and other telephone operating companies that were spun off from AT&T in 1984. Chrysler Corp. had a joint venture with Mitsubishi Motors Corp. for the purchase of as many as 200,000 vehicles a year.

Joint ventures have been used for many years—decades before the highly publicized activities of the 1980s. In an early study Bachman (1965) described the entry of oil and gas companies into chemicals, using joint ventures to a considerable degree. For the early 1960s, some illustrative joint ventures and the products they produced included

Alamo Polymer (Phillips Petroleum and National Distillers)—polypropylene

American Chemical (Richfield Oil and Stauffer)—vinyl chloride, ethylene

Ancon Chemical (Continental Oil and Ansul)—methyl chloride

Avisun (Sun Oil and American Viscose)—polypropylene resins

Goodrich-Gulf (Gulf Oil and Goodrich Rubber)—S-type rubber

Hawkeye Chemical (Skelly Oil and Swift)—ammonia

Jefferson Chemical (Texas Co. and American Cyanamid)—ethylene, propylene, and others

National Plastics Products (Enjay and J. P. Stevens)—polypropylene fiber

Sun Olin (Sun Oil and Olin)—urea, ethylene, and others

Witfield Chemical (Richfield Oil and Witco Chemical)—detergent alkylate

Joint venture participants continue to exist as separate firms with a joint venture representing a newly created business enterprise. The joint venture may be organized as a partnership, a corporation, or any other form of business organization the participating firms might choose to select.

In contract law, joint ventures are usually described as having the following characteristics:

1. Contribution by partners of money, property, effort, knowledge, skill, or other asset to a common undertaking.
2. Joint property interest in the subject matter of the venture.
3. Right of mutual control or management of the enterprise.
4. Expectation of profit, or presence of "adventure."
5. Right to share in the profit.
6. Usual limitation of the objective to a single undertaking or ad hoc enterprise.

Thus, joint ventures are of limited scope and duration. Typically they involve only a small fraction of each participant's total activities. Each partner must have something unique and important to offer the venture and simultaneously provide a source of gain to the other participants. However, the sharing of information and/or assets required to achieve the objective need not extend beyond the joint venture. Hence the participants' competitive relationship need not be affected by the joint venture arrangement. Sometimes the joint arrangement is relatively informal, involving only an exchange of ideas and information while the participants work on similar challenges. The term "strategic alliances" has been used to describe relationships among companies that are something short of establishing a joint venture entity.

It has been found that joint ventures and mergers display similar timing characteristics. The correlation between completed mergers and joint venture start-ups is over .95, highly significant from a statistical standpoint. Merger activity is also highly correlated with plant and equipment outlays. Both joint ventures and mergers are likely to be stimulated by factors that affect total investment activity generally.

JOINT VENTURES IN BUSINESS STRATEGY

A number of motives have stimulated joint ventures:

1. Share investment expenses or combine a large company that has cash to invest with a smaller company with a product or production idea but with insufficient funds to pursue the opportunity. Whereas outside investors may be reluctant to take high risks even on an equity basis, a business firm may be interested because it has more information on the project or has other projects that may benefit from the learning experience that may be gained from the joint venture.
2. A greater learning experience may be achieved.
3. Even for a large company, a joint venture is a method of reducing the investment outlay required and of sharing the risk.
4. Antitrust authorities may be more willing to permit joint ventures than to permit mergers (*Los Angeles Times,* 1984). While mergers result in a reduction in the number of firms, joint ventures increase the number of firms. The parents continue in operation, and another firm is created. Joint ventures in research and development areas are likely to receive endorsement from government agencies.

Joint ventures may be used to acquire complementary technological or management resources at lower cost or to benefit from economies of scale, critical mass, and the learning curve effect—all elements of strategic alliances. The "go together–split" strategy achieves these ends in the usual 50–50 or 60–40 joint venture of limited scope and duration, whereas the successive integration strategy uses joint venturing as a way of learning about prospective partners before full merger or acquisition.

Firms may also use joint venturing as an element of long-run strategic planning. The spider's web strategy is used to provide countervailing power among rivals in a product market and among rivals for a scarce resource. Thus, a small firm in a highly concentrated industry can negotiate joint ventures with several of the industry's dominant firms to form a self-protective network of counterbalancing forces. Indeed, it is reported that large companies such as General Electric are involved in over 100 joint ventures and that IBM, GM, AT&T, and Xerox participate in more than a dozen joint ventures. Companies of the type listed have both financial resources and managerial and technical competence to bring to a joint venture (*Business Week,* 1986). This strategy presupposes, of course, that the small firm has something unique to offer the industry leaders (Templin, November 7, 1995).

Joint Ventures and Complex Learning

The expressed purpose of 50% of all joint ventures is knowledge acquisition (Berg, Duncan, and Friedman, 1982). The complexity of the knowledge to be transferred is a key factor in determining the contractual relationship between the partners.

Where the knowledge to be transferred is complex or embedded in a complicated set of technological and organizational circumstances, learning by doing and teaching by doing may be the most appropriate means of transfer. Successive adaptations to changing internal and environmental events may be necessary to achieve efficiency in the process being taught. It may be very costly or even impossible to give training in complex production tasks in a classroom situation—the atmosphere (operations, machines, work group) may be essential. In addition, job incumbents, no matter how skilled, may be unable to describe job skills to trainees except in an operational context. The demands of the task may make joint venture the most appropriate vehicle for the knowledge transfer.

Tax Aspects of Joint Ventures

Tax advantages may be a significant factor in many joint ventures. If a corporation contributes a patent or licensable technology to a joint venture, the tax consequences may be less than on royalties earned through a licensing arrangement. For example, one partner contributes the technology, while another contributes depreciable facilities. The depreciation offsets the revenues accruing to the technology; the joint venture may be taxed at a lower rate than any of its partners; and the partners pay a later capital gains tax on the returns realized by the joint venture if and when it is sold. If the joint venture is organized as a corporation, only its assets are at risk; the partners are liable only to the extent of their investment. This is particularly important in hazardous industries where the risk of worker, product, or environmental liability is high.

A number of other more technical tax advantages may tip the scale toward the use of joint ventures in many circumstances. These include the limitation on operating loss carryover, the partnership status of unincorporated commercial joint ventures, the use of the equity method of incorporating the joint venture into the partners' financial statements, and the benefits of multiple surtax exemptions.

Joint Ventures and Restructuring

Joint ventures have begun to perform a useful role in assisting companies in the process of restructuring. A number of case studies have been described (Nanda and Williamson, 1995). In the late 1980s, Philips, a large Dutch electronics company, decided to divest its appliances division, whose revenues had been running at $1.55 billion. The division had a history of poor performance because of a number of problems. It was trying to sell nine different brands and lacked coordination in marketing efforts. Production was spread across 10 plants in five countries and needed large investments for modernization. Nevertheless, the division had strong capabilities in design and manufacturing skills.

Whirlpool was seeking to expand beyond its U.S. base and saw a potential for developing the appliance business of Philips into a global, coordinated production and sales activity. But there were many uncertainties about the investment required, the future relationship with dealers, and the ability to turn around the operations. In 1989 Philips proposed a joint venture in which Whirlpool would own 53% of the appliance operation for $381 million and would have an option to buy the remaining 47% within three years. For Whirlpool, the joint venture enabled it to gain knowledge about the appliance division before committing further funds. Whirlpool also benefited from Philips' continued participation in a number of ways. For a period of time, the products were double branded as Philips-Whirlpool appliances. The incentive for Philips to help was that it would receive more for the remaining 47%, which it sold to Whirlpool in 1991 for $610 million. It was estimated that by the use of the temporary joint venture, Philips received about $270 million more than if it had tried to complete the transaction before the start of the joint venture two years earlier.

This example illustrates how the buyer can use the joint venture experience to better determine the value of brands, distribution systems, and personnel. Through direct involvement with the business, the risk of making mistakes is reduced.

How costly mistakes can be made is illustrated by the method used by the Maytag Corporation when it sought to enter the European appliances market in 1989. It bought the Hoover appliances line from the Chicago Pacific Corporation. In seeking to penetrate the British market, the Hoover executives on behalf of Maytag sought to build on Hoover's historically strong relationships with small retailers in fragmented markets. But in Britain six major retailers accounted for most of the market. Because of the difficulties of penetrating this market, the Hoover executives mounted a special promotional campaign offering free airplane tickets with the purchase of a major appliance in Great Britain and Ireland. In the United States, discounted airline tickets are widely available, but in Europe airfares are regulated and higher. About one of every 300 people in Britain and Ireland bought an appliance to receive the free flights. The people who bought the appliances for the free tickets soon put the appliances into an active market in second-hand Hoover appliances. In honoring the commitments of its promotion, Hoover incurred a $50 million charge. Maytag became discouraged by this unfortunate experience and disposed of the European portion of the Hoover appliances line in June 1995, booking a $130 million loss.

Nanda and Williamson (1995) described how the Corning Company in 1985 used a joint venture to exit the U.S. medical diagnostics business. In that year, Ciba-Geigy was studying how to enter the U.S. pharmaceuticals market. The two companies formed a 50–50 joint venture called Ciba Corning with a payment of $75 million from Ciba-Geigy to Corning. The activity was operated as a joint venture until 1989. During the intervening years, Ciba-Geigy demonstrated its commitment to the new-product market area by making long-term investments. The business was integrated into the global operations of Ciba-Geigy. Customers, vendors, and employees remained loyal to the joint venture enterprise. Corning was able to demonstrate the value of the unit it was seeking to sell. In 1989 Ciba-Geigy purchased the remaining 50% portion of the joint venture at a price double the $75 million paid to establish Ciba Corning. This example illustrates the value of continuity, which retains the loyalty of stakeholders.

The time-phased aspect of the joint venture is also illustrated by the disposal of the Rolm Systems Division by IBM to Siemens of Germany. IBM had purchased Rolm with a view to exploiting some computer applications to PBX systems. These potentials were not realized, and IBM found it had no particular advantages in the thin-margin PBX market. Siemens was interested in broadening its position in the

U.S. telecommunications market. The transaction illustrates the differences in treatment of tangible and intangible assets. The manufacturing activities of the Rolm business were sold outright to Siemens, but a 50–50 joint venture was formed between IBM and Siemens to handle marketing distribution and service for the Rolm products. This provided continuity for customer relationships and gave Siemens a basis for judging the value of Rolm's brand franchise. After three years, the joint venture moved entirely to Siemens, which during the course of the joint venture had paid $1.1 billion. This was a good price from IBM's standpoint. For Siemens, it provided a controlled cost for wider penetration of the U.S. telecommunications market.

The above examples from Nanda and Williamson (1995) illustrate how, in a broad restructuring process, joint ventures can be used as a transitional mechanism. Several advantages have been illustrated by the examples: (1) The customers are moved to the buyer over a period of time in which both the seller and buyer continue to be involved. (2) The buyer builds experience with the new line of business. (3) The buyer receives managerial and technical advice and assistance from the seller during the transition period. (4) The experience and knowledge developed during the life of the joint venture enable the buyer to obtain a better understanding of the value of the acquisition. (5) Consequently, the seller is able to realize a larger value from the sale than it could have under an immediate, outright sale when the buyer must necessarily discount the purchase price because of lack of knowledge about the asset being purchased.

International Joint Ventures

Joint ventures can be used to reduce the risk of expanding into a foreign environment. In fact, there may even be a legal requirement of a local joint venturer in some foreign countries. The contribution of the local partner is likely to be in the form of specialized knowledge about local conditions, which may be essential to the success of the venture. This topic is developed more fully in chapter 17, which discusses the international aspects of M&As.

RATIONALE FOR JOINT VENTURES

The previous sections described examples of firms engaging in joint ventures. A survey of the literature indicates a number of general reasons, which can be summarized as follows:

1. To augment insufficient financial or technical ability to enter a particular line of business.
2. To share technology and/or generic management skills in organization, planning, and control.
3. To diversify risk.
4. To obtain distribution channels or raw materials supply.
5. To achieve economies of scale.
6. To extend activities with smaller investment than if done independently.
7. To take advantage of favorable tax treatment or political incentives (particularly in foreign ventures).

In view of the availability of alternative forms of business relationships, a basic issue is why the use of joint ventures versus other forms of contractual arrangements is justified. The literature suggests that the underlying theoretical justification for joint ventures lies in the transaction cost theory of the firm.

Every exchange between productive agents involves transaction costs. The benefits of interaction arise from using resources efficiently, but resources are used up by the organizing activity itself as it obtains information on exchange opportunities, negotiates and enforces contracts, and so on. The exchange and organizational patterns viewed in the marketplace are responses to varying levels of transaction costs, which affect the allocation of resources in society. According to the theory, resource misallocation cannot exist in the absence of transaction costs.

Complementary production refers to the joint use of assets or inputs to create products that cannot be unambiguously attributed to any single input. Nor can the inputs simply be summed to yield the total output of the process, that is, synergy. A complementary asset is one whose value in a production process depends on its combination with other assets or a specifically chosen technology. Difficulty arises when these inputs are owned by different firms.

In general, an asset's productivity increases with its specialization to other inputs used in the production process. However, specialization also increases the risk of loss to the owner of the complementary asset if the other inputs are withdrawn. Complementary or composite quasi-rent is the economic term for the investment cost of the complementary asset that is nonrecoverable if the other inputs with which it is used are withdrawn. Thus, the owners of the other inputs, by threatening to remove their inputs, can expropriate the owner of the complementary asset by taking a larger share of the return from the process (which, by definition, cannot be unambiguously attributed to any single input).

Input owners will choose the organizational form that minimizes transactions costs. Long-term explicit contracts and common ownership of the complementary assets are possible solutions to the problem. However, a flexible contract may result in litigation for interpretation. A comprehensive contract is costly both to write and to enforce. These costs may outweigh the benefits of the contract. Business complexity increases the number of contingencies that might arise, thus increasing the cost of enumerating contingencies, the risk of omitting to specify contingencies, and costs of monitoring in a contractual relationship.

Finally, the greater the frequency of exchange of inputs, the greater the likelihood of joint ownership. The prospect of recovering the investment cost of specialized assets increases with the frequency of the transaction. In a contractual relationship, repetitive activity would mean repetitive contracting and thus higher contracting costs. The specialized organizations required in common ownership are easier to justify for recurring transactions than for identical transactions that occur only occasionally.

In some cases, common ownership might extend to complete merger, but in general joint venture is appropriate where

1. Complementary production activity involves only a limited subset of the firms' assets.
2. Complementary assets have limited service life.
3. Complementary production has limited life.

Reasons for Failure

Joint ventures are a form of long-term contract. Like all contracts they are subject to difficulties. As circumstances change in the future, the contract may be too inflexible to permit the required adjustments to be made. There is also evidence that in many joint ventures, the participants early become enamored of the idea of the joint activity but do not spend sufficient time and effort to lay out a program for implementing the joint venture. *Business Week* (1986) refers to independent studies by McKinsey & Co. and Coopers & Lybrand that found that about 70% of joint ventures fell short of expectations or were disbanded. Other studies suggest that on average joint ventures do not last as long as one-half the term of years stated in the joint venture agreement (Berg, Duncan, and Friedman, 1982). We conducted an independent survey that uncovered many examples of joint ventures that came apart either before they started or early into the venture. Some of the reasons for the abortive lives of joint ventures are

1. The hoped-for technology never developed.
2. Preplanning for the joint venture was inadequate.
3. Agreements could not be reached on alternative approaches to solving the basic objectives of the joint venture.
4. Managers with expertise in one company refused to share knowledge with their counterparts in the joint venture.
5. Management difficulties may be compounded because the parent companies are unable to share control or compromise on difficult issues.

Some joint ventures raise critical issues of public policy and long-term strategies of individual business firms. The announcement of a joint venture between Boeing Co. and a group of Japanese companies touched off much controversy (Harris and Wysocki, 1986). Boeing is the world's largest airplane builder, accounting for 60% of the world production of jetliners. In early 1986 it was announced that Boeing had entered into an agreement to form a joint venture with three Japanese companies: Kawasaki Heavy Industries Ltd., Mitsubishi Heavy Industries Ltd., and Fuji Heavy Industries Ltd. The joint venture would build a new 150-passenger airplane that would be ready in the early 1990s. The Japanese would contribute $1 billion of the $4 billion or more expected development cost. In return they would receive a share of the profits and learn about the manufacturing, marketing, and servicing of jetliners through their association with Boeing.

Great concern was expressed by a number of Americans that the Japanese would learn the secrets of aircraft manufacturing from Boeing. Because some of the key Boeing civilian aircraft had developed from military versions, concern was also expressed that this would help Japan build up a military aircraft production capability. But the major concern was that the Japanese would become leaders in commercial aviation as they had in autos, electronics, steel, and construction by copying and improving on American methods.

Boeing officials said that they were aware of and concerned about such possibilities. But they pointed out that the Japanese companies had solicited joint venture proposals from other western companies including Airbus, McDonnell Douglas, and Fokker of the Netherlands. Hence, in part, the Boeing action to agree to form the joint venture was a defensive strategy. As the then president of Boeing, Frank

Shrontz, stated: "We'd rather work with them [the Japanese] than have somebody else work with them and against us" (Harris and Wysocki, 1986, p. 1).

Early in the negotiations, the usual problems with joint ventures began to crop up. The Japanese complained that Boeing assigned to the project too many young, inexperienced executives who did not understand Japanese business practices. Americans complained that the Japanese negotiators lacked technical knowledge.

JOINT VENTURES AND ANTITRUST POLICY

Legal challenges may be faced by joint ventures. Although we have distinguished joint ventures from mergers, they are often subject to the same regulatory scrutiny and challenge by rivals. For example, Chrysler raised an antitrust challenge to the Federal Trade Commission approval of the General Motors–Toyota joint venture discussed in Case 14.1. (The challenge was dropped before the case went to the courts.) Court actions have been brought under the Clayton Act (for real or potential anticompetitive effects) and under the Sherman Act (for cartel behavior, boycotts, and exclusion of competitors). Three landmark cases illustrate legal actions against joint ventures in the past. The main objections raised are the threat of industrywide collusion, loss of potential competition, and restraints on distribution.

A number of factors led to the antitrust decision in the 1950 *U.S. v. Minnesota Mining and Manufacturing Co. et al.* These included the implied market dominance of the joint venture partners, the existence of a joint sales agency, and concern of spillover of joint venture cooperation into collusion. The venture was formed in 1929 to export coated abrasives for its nine partners. The partners could not export except through the joint venture; however, they could, and did, set up foreign manufacturing subsidiaries to supply foreign buyers. The courts ruled that this joint venture represented an illegal conspiracy and further suggested that the joint venturers would compete less vigorously in the American market as well.

In 1964 the main issue in *U.S. v. Penn-Olin* was the loss of potential competition. An Oregon firm, Pennsalt, wanted to penetrate the southeastern U.S. market for sodium chlorate, a bleaching agent used in paper pulp processing. The southeastern region accounted for 50% of all U.S. sales of sodium chlorate; however, two firms already dominated this area with a combined market share of 91.3% in 1960. Pennsalt's first step was to form a sales arrangement with Olin-Mathieson, a firm that did not manufacture sodium chlorate but had a marketing presence in the southeast. The success of this arrangement and projections of future capacity shortages in the area led to the formation of a 50–50 joint venture in 1960. A local manufacturing plant was operated by Pennsalt, while Olin continued to market the output.

The court's decision focused on whether the firms would have entered the market independently in the absence of the joint venture. That is, say Pennsalt entered the market independently; would Pennsalt and the other firms in the market view Olin as a threatening potential entrant? Would Olin view itself as a potential entrant, or would it drop out of the race, abandoning the idea of entering the market? If both firms could have seriously considered entering independently, then the joint venture would have decreased potential competition (by adding only one new productive entity to the market instead of potentially two). The final decision permitted the joint venture.

Independent entry by both firms was judged to be improbable due to the low expected rate of return (as a result of the high cost to a single firm of building an optimum-size plant) and due to possible excess capacity if two optimum-size plants were constructed.

The decision against the joint venture in *Yamaha v. FTC* (1981) was based on many factors (loss of potential competition, high industry concentration, spillover collusion, potential permanence of the joint venture). However, the distinguishing feature in terms of this discussion involves the collateral agreements between the venture partners. In 1972, Brunswick and Yamaha formed a joint venture to produce and sell outboard motors; the joint venture was to have a ten-year life with automatic three-year extensions. The same motor produced by the venture would be sold through Yamaha dealers as a Yamaha and through Brunswick dealers as a Mariner. (Brunswick had been selling motors worldwide since 1961, and Mariner was to be its second line.) Collateral agreements restricted distribution by assigning exclusive rights to sell the joint venture motor in certain parts of the world. Brunswick had North America, Australia, and New Zealand; Yamaha had exclusivity in Japan, and the rest of the world was open to competition. Other collateral agreements restricted competition beyond the joint venture. Yamaha could not make or distribute any motor similar to the joint venture's, and Brunswick was prohibited from making any products then produced by Yamaha (except snowmobiles).

The court determined that the joint venture eliminated Yamaha as a potential entrant (prior to the joint venture Yamaha had twice attempted unsuccessfully to penetrate the U.S. market) and that such independent entry would have reduced concentration in an industry becoming increasingly highly concentrated due to firm exits. It was felt that Brunswick would not allow the joint venture motor to compete with its other line, and therefore the joint venture could not be treated as a new entrant. The court found no efficiencies inherent in the collateral agreements restricting distribution and production. They were judged to be anticompetitive and thus potentially collusive.

Some industry conditions make collusion more likely. Other industry conditions make collusion difficult and probably impossible. These characteristics are summarized in Table 14.1. Any one condition in the second column, conditions that make collusion difficult, is enough to deny the validity of the structural approach. Contemplation of the characteristics of most actual industries in the United States would indicate characteristics that make collusion difficult. These would include heterogeneous products; inequality of costs; rapid and unstable changes in demand, supply, and technology; dissimilarity in firm strategies and policies; substitutability among products on the demand side; and the likelihood of additions to the supply of products by other firms if one firm restricted supply. *Los Angeles Times* November 3, 1984.

OUTSOURCING

Outsourcing falls within the broader framework of the make-or-buy decision. Outsourcing involves the use of a subcontractor or supplier or outside firm to perform some percentage of the total production of a product. Outsourcing can be used to perform only a small fraction of the total production process for a product, such as making an individual part or component, or a very high percentage. An example of

Table 14.1   Industry Characteristics and Possibility of Collusion

Collusion Possible	Collusion Difficult
Product homogeneity	Heterogeneous products
Equality of costs across firms	Inequality of costs
Stability of demand, supply, and technology	Rapid and unstable changes in demand, supply, and technology
Difficulty of entry and expansion	Ease of entry and expansion
Similarity in firm strategies and policies	Dissimilarity in firm strategies and policies
Few firms	Many firms
Low costs of enforcing collusive agreement and of being detected relative to benefits	Difficulties in enforcing collusion; high risk and cost of being detected
Low price elasticity of demand	High price elasticity of demand

the latter is the TopsyTail Company (*The Economist,* 1995). Between 1991 and 1995, its cumulative volume of sales was approximately $100 million of hair-styling devices. It had virtually no permanent employees. The major functions of design, manufacturing, marketing, distribution, and packaging were performed by subcontractors. This heavy reliance on outsourcing was chosen as a strategy to facilitate rapid growth by the use of outside organizations, avoiding the need to build the required competencies within the company itself. Outsourcing has been identified as a modern version of the use of division of labor to increase efficiency.

Although outsourcing has advantages, it also has limitations. This is especially true when the outside supplier is in a foreign country. Companies have found it necessary to employ executive personnel to monitor outsourcing activities in the companies that perform the outside functions.

Another limitation of outsourcing is that as firms become more experienced and more successful in improving their manufacturing operations, they may be able to produce components at a lower cost than outside suppliers. Restructuring and other methods by which costs have been reduced may cause a company to switch from outsourcing to production in-house.

With experience, some companies have also changed their strategy with respect to how they conduct outsourcing. To improve communication and still retain the benefits of competition among suppliers, some companies limit the number of outsourcing firms they use. They still retain competition but also emphasize close monitoring by a management group.

One limitation of outsourcing relates to product quality. Some companies require daily quality data and product integrity audits and reviews. Even though some final product defects may be due to the work of individual outsourcing suppliers, the firm that sells the final product must take responsibility for the quality and performance of the products.

Trade unions often resist outsourcing because they view it as reducing employment, particularly for the workers in an affected union. In recent years, consumers have increasingly demanded variety and custom designs. Some companies have found that only by producing totally within the company can it achieve the flexibility and speed needed for building to order. In the evolution of manufacturing activities, the advantages of outsourcing may be more than matched by efficient use of resources owned by the firm that produces the final products.

Overall, outsourcing continues to grow in the U.S. and abroad. Outsourcing represents a different form of arm's-length alliances similar to joint ventures. As industries and firms evolve, however, the benefits versus the costs of this activity may shift. The make-or-buy decision may need to change as the relative efficiency of in-house operations versus outside suppliers changes over time. Doubtless, e-commerce will also have significant impacts.

EMPIRICAL TESTS OF THE ROLE OF JOINT VENTURES

Two major types of studies of joint ventures have been made. One is a business and economic analysis; the other is the use of event returns.

Business and Economic Patterns

One of the most comprehensive and most methodologically robust studies of joint venture activity is that of Berg, Duncan, and Friedman (BDF) (1982), reported in their book, *Joint Venture Strategies and Corporate Innovation*. They identify three primary incentives for joint venture participation: (1) risk avoidance, (2) knowledge acquisition, and (3) market power. To carry out a cross-firm and cross-industry analysis on a large sample of joint ventures from the period 1964 to 1973, they used multiple regression to evaluate the relationships between joint ventures and concentration, research and development (R&D), financial variables, and firm size.

They found that industry joint venture participation also rose with average firm size, average capital expenditure, and average profitability. Technologically oriented joint venture participation also rose with average R&D intensity. Within each industry, BDF attempted to distinguish the characteristics of those large firms that engaged in joint ventures from those that did not and found firm size to be the *only* pervasive influence across industries.

Cross-firm patterns indicated that joint ventures substitute for research and development in the chemical and engineering industries but not in resource-based industries, and BDF found that the long-term R&D substitution effect was stronger than the short-term substitution effect. Joint ventures were also found to have a significant negative impact on large firms' rates of return in chemicals and engineering in the short run, although the long-run effect on rate of return was not significant.

At the industry level, technologically oriented and nonhorizontal joint ventures showed strong positive effects on R&D intensity, indicating that joint ventures and R&D are complements at the industry level. These same types of joint ventures also have a significant negative impact on industry average rates of return, consistent with the reduced risk or reduced time lag that may result from technological or commercial knowledge acquisition joint ventures. The result is also consistent with using joint ventures as a vehicle for new market entry.

Event Returns

The most thorough study of the performance of joint ventures was conducted by Mc-Connell and Nantell (MN) (1985) using residual analysis. Their study covered a selection from all joint ventures reported in *Mergers and Acquisitions* for the period 1972 to 1979. Their sample consisted of 210 firms engaged in 136 joint ventures. The average size of the joint ventures was about $5 million. The two-day announcement period abnormal return was 0.73%, which was significant at the .01 level. The cumulative average residual (abnormal return) over the 62-day period ending on the event day (announcement day) was 2.15%, significant at the .10 level. The cumulative average residual remains at 2.15% after 60 days subsequent to the joint venture announcement, indicating no further valuation effect following the initial announcement.

McConnell and Nantell compared the size of the abnormal return with the results for companies involved in mergers using a representative study of mergers by Asquith (1983). Asquith found excess returns for the two days ending in the announcement to be 6.5% for the target firm and 0.3% for the bidding firm. Because joint ventures do not identify the acquiring and acquired firm, their results should fall between the two, which they do. Asquith found that over a 60-day period prior to the merger announcement the CAR increased by 11% for acquired firms and was unchanged for the acquiring companies. Again the CAR for joint ventures lay between the CARs for the individual firms.

Because real estate and entertainment joint ventures constituted 23% of their sample, MN also tested for overrepresentation by calculating results without this group. Their results were similar. They also eliminated firms for which other information was released near the joint venture announcement date. Again the results were unchanged.

McConnell and Nantell also studied the relative size effect. They noted that in mergers the dollar value of gains appears to be evenly divided between the two companies. But if the acquiring company is 20 times as large as the target that gains 10% in market value, the acquiring company will gain only 0.5% in stock value. Accordingly, the firms in their joint venture sample were divided into large and small groups based on the total market value of their common stock 61 trading days before the announcement of the joint venture. Information was available to do this for 65 joint ventures but not for 80 other companies that were placed into a third, "all other," category. The statistical tests were repeated for the three groups. The small firms gained 1.10%, the large firms gained 0.63%, and all others gained 0.57%—all of these statistically significant. The dollar gain to the small-firm sample was $4.538 million, and to the large-firm sample $6.651 million. Thus, as in mergers, the dollar gain was about evenly divided, but the percentage gains were much higher for the smaller firms.

When the dollar gains are scaled by the amounts invested in the joint venture, the average premium is 23% (after removing one outlier). This result lies in the range of premiums observed in mergers and tender offers. McConnell and Nantell observe that the gains in mergers and tender offers could be from either synergy or the displacement of less effective management. Because joint ventures do not change the managements of the parents, McConnell and Nantell (1985, p. 535) conclude that "we are inclined to interpret our results as supportive of the synergy hypothesis as the source of gains in other types of corporate combinations."

STRATEGIC ALLIANCES

Thus far in this text, we have discussed mergers or takeovers in which two or more total organizations are combined. We began this chapter with a discussion of joint ventures in which a new entity is created (partnership, corporation, whatever) cemented by a formal long-term contract of 8 to 12 years duration. In this section, we discuss strategic alliances.

Strategic alliances are informal or formal decisions or agreements between two or more firms to cooperate in some form of relationship. Rapid advances in technology, the globalization of markets, and deregulation have created economic turbulence. These change forces have stimulated the reorganization of capabilities, resources, and product market activities of business firms. Methods by which firms have responded to the increased pace of change have included mergers or takeovers, joint ventures, and strategic alliances. Mergers and joint ventures have been methods by which firms have increased the intensity of competition. Value chains have been altered, and product life cycles have been shortened. Industry boundaries have become blurred, with firms eyeing a wide range of other products and markets as potential new growth opportunities. This ambiguity in the nature of industries and the scope of firms has given rise to a new form of relationship—the strategic alliance.

Strategic alliances are created out of uncertainty and ambiguity and represent forms of relationships that are also uncertain and ambiguous. To convey the nature of strategic alliances, we begin with some examples. A March 2, 1999 *Wall Street Journal* article (p. B8) described a joint cooperation between AT&T, Lucent, and Motorola on a software language that would allow users to access the Internet by voice. The companies were seeking to establish a voice extensible markup language (VXML) as a standard for voice commands to the Internet.

A *New York Times* article of May 19, 1999 (p. C5) announced an alliance between Xerox and Microsoft aimed at bridging the worlds of paper documents and computers. The new relationship included Xerox licensing a Web surfing technology to Microsoft. Xerox would incorporate Microsoft's embedded NT operating system in a future generation of its high-end copying systems. Xerox stated that its relationship with Microsoft would have no impact on a similar arrangement Xerox had with Sun Microsystems.

Another *New York Times* article, dated June 22, 1999 (p. C6), described an investment by AOL in Hughes Electronics "as part of a wide-alliance" providing on-line service to achieve high speed Internet access using the Hughes satellite data delivery system. This was said to represent the broadening of a deal that had been announced by the companies a month earlier.

A *Wall Street Journal* article of July 28, 1999 (p. B8) reported "multi-million-dollar collaboration agreements" between Glaxo Wellcome and SmithKline Beecham to extend the therapeutic qualities of existing drugs. One objective was to develop a version of the antibiotic tetracycline that would be effective against drug-resistant bacteria. Other potential drug developments that could be furthered by the alliance were described. Apparently this kind of collaboration laid the groundwork for the announcement on January 17, 2000 of an agreement on a merger that the two companies were unable to achieve a year earlier.

A *Wall Street Journal* article of March 4, 1999 (p. B2) describes an alliance between Abbott Laboratories and Germany's Boehringer Ingelheim GmbH. Abbott acquires U.S. co-marketing rights to Mobic, a pain medication aimed at arthritis. The article described how the competitive landscape for this therapeutic drug class would be altered by adding Abbott's powerful marketing force to the German company's efforts in the U.S. market. Monsanto and Pfizer were already comarketing the drug Celebrex for arthritis pain relief with great success.

On March 2, 1999, the U.S. Postal Service (USPS) formed an alliance with DHL Worldwide Express to jointly offer a two-day delivery service between 18 major U.S. cities and 18 foreign countries (*Wall Street Journal*, p. A4). Customers could track the shipments by telephone or at the USPS Internet site. John F. Kelly, the head of packing services for USPS, stated that "a series of international alliances" would be used for further growth. The article also noted that spokespersons for FedEx and UPS stated that the alliance made it necessary for tighter controls on forays into private-sector competition by USPS, financed by its monopoly profits on first class mail.

It was widely announced on February 3, 1999 (*Wall Street Journal*, p. A3) that Goodyear Tire & Rubber had formed a "broad alliance" with Sumitomo Rubber Industries. Some cross investments would be made, and the two companies would combine research and purchasing activities in six joint ventures. A number of duplicate efforts would be combined, saving a total of more than $300 million per year in combined costs.

Other aspects of strategic alliances have been developed in the literature. One issue is whether interfirm alliances lead to mergers and acquisitions. This issue was addressed in an empirical study by Hagedorn and Sadowski (1999), who used two large data sets. A data set on over 6,000 strategic technology alliances was related to information on 16,000 M&As of the same group of nearly 3,000 firms. Only 2.6% of the alliances led to an M&A between the same partners. These findings were inconsistent with the encroachment hypothesis that larger firms use their strategic technology alliances to take over their smaller partners. It appears that the strategic alliances represent a form of exploratory learning. In high technology industries, where turbulence and change dominate, strategic alliances are used to scan market-entry possibilities, to monitor new technological developments, and to reduce the risks and costs of developing new products and processes. As industries mature, learning and flexibility become less important, so integration through M&As is more likely.

Another study predicts the success or failure of alliances depending on their characteristics (Bleeke and Ernst, 1995). Six types of alliances are discussed:

1. **Collisions between competitors.** The core businesses of two strong, direct competitors form an alliance. Because of competitive tensions, they are short-lived and fail to achieve their strategic and financial goals.
2. **Alliances of the weak.** Two weak companies join forces in the hope that they will improve. But the weak grow weaker, and the alliance fails.
3. **Disguised sales.** A weak company joins with a strong competitor. The alliance is short-lived and the weak is acquired by the strong.
4. **Bootstrap alliances.** By forming an alliance with a strong company, the weak company may be improved so that the partnership develops into an alliance of equals.

5. **Evolution to a sale.**   Two strong and initially compatible partners initiate an alliance. These alliances may succeed in meeting the initial objectives and exceed the seven-year average life span for alliances. When competitive tensions develop, one partner ultimately sells out to the other.

6. **Alliances of complementary equals.**   Complementarity and compatibility lead to mutually beneficial relationships likely to last more than the seven-year average.

Chan, Kensinger, Keown, and Martin (CKKM) (1997) investigated the stock price response to the formation of 345 strategic alliances in the period 1983 to 1992. On the announcement date, they found positive abnormal returns of 0.64%, significant at the .01 level. The magnitude of these returns is similar to the magnitude of those for the announcement of joint ventures as reported by McConnell and Nantell (1985). There is no evidence that the observed wealth effect is due to wealth transfer between the partners in the alliance. For a subsample of high tech firms, the abnormal returns were a highly significant 1.12%, while low tech firms had an insignificant 0.10% return.

Partitioning the sample by industry focus and presence of technological transfer reveals that horizontal alliances between firms in the same three-digit SIC class that involved the transfer or pooling of technology experienced the highest average abnormal return, 3.54%, significant at the .01 level. Nonhorizontal alliances whose main objective was to position or enter a new market encountered a significant 1.45% return. For the remaining cases, horizontal nontechnical and nonhorizontal technical alliances, the returns were positive but not significant.

Finally, CKKM found no evidence that firms enter into strategic alliances because of deteriorating past performance. In fact, in their sample, firms that entered into strategic alliances exhibited better operating performance than their industry peers over a five-year period around the formation of the alliance.

The samples of case studies and articles just summarized provide a basis for some generalizations on strategic alliances, which are outlined in Table 14.2.

From the foregoing, we can summarize the relationships among three major forms of interfirm relationships—acquisitions, joint ventures, and strategic alliances—as shown in Table 14.3.

Table 14.3 summarizes the leading characteristics of the three forms of relationships. Each form has distinctive contributions to make in achieving the objectives of the individual firms. Since each contributes different types of benefits, major firms use all three. For example, Microsoft reported that it had completed 90 transactions during 1999, valued at approximately $10 billion (*Wall Street Journal*, January 7, 2000, pp. C1, C17). Microsoft made 14 acquisitions, engaged in five joint ventures, and made 71 equity investments.

The many equity investments by Microsoft suggest the possibility of many kinds of relationships with other firms, each with different benefits and limitations. Equity

Table 14.2   Characteristics of Strategic Alliances

 1. The creation of a new entity is unnecessary.
 2. A contract need not be specified.
 3. The relative sizes of the firms may be highly unequal.
 4. The alliance may involve relations with competitors and complementor firms.
 5. There is synergistic value creation from combining different resources.
 6. Both companies may learn and internalize new knowledge and capabilities from the relationship.
 7. The alliance can add more value to the partnering firms by creating an organizational mechanism that better aligns decision authority with decision knowledge.
 8. The alliance can add value to the partnering firms through the organizational flexibility they provide.
 9. Partner firms pool resources and expertise rather than transferring the specialized knowledge, so the partners will have a continuing need for each other.
10. The relationship is an evolving one.
11. Adaptability and change are required over time.
12. There may be deliberate efforts to change the direction of at least one partner.
13. The alliance blurs corporate boundaries.
14. The alliance members can have multiple partners.
15. An alliance requires mutual trust.
16. The speed of change is increased.
17. Participating companies move to other alliances as attractive possibilities emerge.
18. An alliance can provide access to creative people who want to work with smaller firms, not giants. A strategic alliance with small firms enables the larger to attract and provide incentives to more creative people.

investments enable a firm to obtain financial gains from business activities in which it is not directly involved. Such equity investments are often guided by the knowledge developed about firms engaged in similar areas of activity. The monitoring and interactions may lead to direct entry by the investing firm.

Other relationships include serving in an advisory capacity or even as an observer of other companies. Knowledge about the changing boundaries of product market areas may be achieved by such interactions or even by networking at industry conferences and trade shows. Effective strategic planning includes continued surveillance of suppliers, competitors, and complementors (Grove, 1996, pp. 28–29).

Table 14.3 Acquisitions vs. Joint Ventures vs. Strategic Alliances

Acquisition	Joint Venture	Strategic Alliance
Allows 100% control	Firms intersect over narrow, well-defined segments	Useful for creation of complex systems among multiple firms
No need for interfirm consensus	Exploits distinctive or narrow opportunities	Blurs corporate boundaries
Less flexible	Generally involves only two firms	Partner is usually larger than in a joint venture (10/1 vs. 5/1)
Larger commitment of resources	Poses limited risk	Allows firms to focus on fewer core competencies
Risky	Enables joint production of single products	Difficult to measure contributions of participants and to measure or assign benefits
Often acquires more than is needed	Combines known resources	Difficult to anticipate consequences
May cause upheaval in corporate culture	Requires interaction of high level management	Gives firms access to people who would not otherwise work directly for them
May require accommodating different management systems	Rarely used in new markets or technologies	Often small resource commitment
Requires combining and harmonizing information systems	Can be used to reduce risk in a merger transaction	Limited time duration
Requires combining different corporate cultures	Often crosses borders	Must be managed actively by senior executives
Requires rapid, effective integration	Tensions: Your firm wants to learn as much as possible but not convey too much.	Likely to evolve in directions not initially planned
Remedy for strategic miscalculations		Requires adaptability to change and new knowledge for management over time
Affords the most cost-cutting possibilities		Especially useful across borders
Can have partial investments as an interim step		Replaces government-prohibited cross-border mergers
Can cross borders		

SUMMARY

Joint ventures are new enterprises owned by two or more participants. They are typically formed for special purposes for a limited duration. This brings the participants into what is essentially a medium- to long-term contract that is both specific and flexible. It is a contract to work together for a specified period of time. Each participant expects to gain from the activity but also must make a contribution.

To some degree the joint venture represents a relatively new thrust by each participant, so it is often called a strategic alliance. Probably the main motive for joint ventures is to share risks. This explains why joint ventures are frequently found in bidding on oil contracts and in drilling oil wells, in large real estate ventures, and in movies, plays, and television productions. The second most frequently cited aim in joint ventures is knowledge acquisition. One or more participants are seeking to learn more about a relatively new product market activity. This may concern all aspects of the activity or a limited segment such as R&D, production, marketing, or product servicing.

International joint ventures magnify the potential advantages and weaknesses of joint venture activity. The GM–Toyota joint venture in Case 14.1 illustrates the kind of potentials that may be achieved in a joint venture. GM hoped to gain new experience in the management techniques of the Japanese in building high quality, low cost compact and subcompact cars. Toyota was seeking to learn from the management traditions that had made GM the number one auto producer in the world and in addition to learn how to operate an auto company in the environment of the United States, dealing with contractors, suppliers, and workers. It appears that differences in cultures and management styles provide a valuable learning experience for both parties in this joint venture.

Other reasons for joint ventures are numerous. One frequently encountered is the small firm with a new product idea that involves high risk and requires relatively large amounts of investment capital. A larger firm may be able to carry the financial risk and be interested in becoming involved in a new business activity that promises growth and profitability. By investing in a large number of such ventures, the larger firm has limited risk in any one and the possibility of very high financial payoffs. In addition, the larger firm may thereby gain experience in a new area of activity that may represent the opportunity for a major new business thrust in the future. Case studies illustrate how joint ventures can facilitate different types of restructuring activities for either or both participant firms in the joint venture.

A basic tension is often found in joint ventures. Each participant hopes to gain as much as possible from the interaction but would like to limit the gains to the other participants. This is particularly true when the firms are competitors in other areas of their activities.

Antitrust authorities often view joint ventures with suspicion. One concern is that each of the participants might have entered the new area independently. Hence, they reason that absent the joint venture, multiple new competitors might have emerged. But it is also possible that the risk-to-reward outlook is so uncertain that absent the joint venture, no additional competitors would have emerged. In areas of research and development activities, the antitrust authorities are more favorably disposed. For one reason, R&D activity is recognized to be inherently risky. For another, if the R&D joint venture effort turns out to be successful, it may contribute to the economic and competitive strength of the nation as a whole in the world economy.

On balance, the most thorough study of the value effects of joint ventures finds that positive returns are achieved. Judged by the standard abnormal returns or residual analysis, joint ventures result in positive gains for the participants. When scaled to the size of investments, joint ventures appear to achieve returns about 23% higher than predicted by general capital market return–risk relationships. This may be biased somewhat upward, because only joint ventures that have actually been formed and been in operation for some time were included in the sample. The many joint ventures that never even reached the launching pad and those aborted shortly after takeoff could not be included in the sample.

Strategic alliances are formal or informal agreements between two or more firms to cooperate in some form of relationship. They allow firms to gain knowledge, expertise, and interfirm relationships without requiring the creation of a new entity. Strategic alliances are flexible and can be adapted to the individual situations of the participating firms. However, because alliances are dynamic, they require considerable interaction between firms. Often, an alliance can have unforeseen effects.

Studies have explored whether an alliance is a precursor to a merger. By establishing a bond between corporations, alliances open lines of communication that can lead to merger discussions. Because strategic alliances often involve competitors and firms in similar industries, it is logical that their interactions would lead to closer relationships including mergers.

QUESTIONS

14.1 How do joint ventures differ from merger activity? In what ways are they similar?

14.2 What are the advantages and disadvantages of joint ventures?

14.3 How does the concept of complex learning relate to joint ventures?

14.4 What is the primary difference between a joint venture and a strategic alliance?

14.5 How can joint ventures be affected by public policy on antitrust?

14.6 How do joint venture returns compare with returns in mergers and tender offers?

Case 14.1 GM–Toyota Joint Venture

This case study brings together a number of the theoretical arguments and legal issues involved in connection with evaluating joint ventures. The GM–Toyota joint venture provided for production of a subcompact car in a GM plant in Fremont, California that previously had been closed down. The plan was approved by a 3–2 majority of the Federal Trade Commission (FTC) in December 1983. After approval by the FTC, Chrysler brought suit to stop the joint venture. After a series of legal skirmishes, Chrysler withdrew its suit. The following discussion is from an extended analysis of the joint venture (Weston, 1984).

The business reasons underlying the GM–Toyota joint venture are straightforward. GM hoped to obtain hands-on experience in the advanced management technology of building small cars and to add this experience to other efforts under way to become more cost-efficient in producing a family of small cars.

For its part, Toyota aimed to test its production methods in a new setting with different labor and supplier relationships. Each firm was seeking to become more efficient to meet the tough competition in the automobile industry. Because the cars would be produced at an unused plant in Fremont, California, the new investment costs would be reduced. Hence, the risk/return prospects of the venture were better than those of alternative methods of achieving their objectives.

In contrast to earlier joint ventures that had been found illegal, this agreement expressed the intention of both parties to compete vigorously in all their markets for every product. This joint venture, as codified by the conditions of the FTC consent order, was quite circumscribed. It limited the annual volume of the one model the joint venture could produce for GM to 250,000. It limited the duration of the venture to a maximum of 12 years. It restricted the exchange of information between the parties. The order also required that records be kept of certain contacts between the parties and that both companies file annual compliance reports with the FTC.

The FTC majority weighed efficiency benefits against anticompetitive costs: "To the extent the Fremont venture can demonstrate successfully that the Japanese system can work in America, the Commission finds that this will lead to the development of a more efficient, more competitive U.S. automobile industry." The FTC determined that the GM–Toyota joint venture would achieve an important management technology transfer to the United States; it reinforced GM's strong commitment to the small-car market and provided incentives for other U.S. firms to do likewise.

QUESTIONS

1. What did GM hope to gain from the joint venture?
2. What did Toyota seek to gain?
3. In your judgment, was the joint venture procompetitive or anticompetitive?
4. Do you think that the Fremont joint venture influenced Toyota's subsequent decision to establish its own manufacturing operations in the United States while continuing the Fremont activity?

REFERENCES

Asquith, Paul, "Merger Bids, Uncertainty, and Stockholder Returns," *Journal of Financial Economics*, 11, 1983, pp. 51–83.

Bachman, Jules, "Joint Ventures in the Light of Recent Antitrust Developments," *Antitrust Bulletin*, 10, 1965, pp. 7–23.

Berg, Sanford V., Jerome Duncan, and Philip Friedman, *Joint Venture Strategies and Corporate Innovation*, Cambridge, MA: Oelgeschlager, Gunn & Hain, 1982.

Bleeke, Joel, and David Ernst, "Is Your Strategic Alliance Really a Sale?" *Harvard Business Review*, 73, January–February 1995, pp. 97–105.

Business Week, "Corporate Odd Couples," July 21, 1986, pp. 100–105.

Chan, Su Han, John W. Kensinger, Arthur J. Keown, and John D. Martin, "Do Strategic Alliances Create Value?" *Journal of Financial Economics*, 46, 1997, pp. 199–221.

Department of Justice, *Merger Guidelines*, 1982, 1984, 1992, 1996.

The Economist, "The Outing of Outsourcing," November 25, 1995, pp. 57–58.

Grove, Andrew S., *Only the Paranoid Survive,* New York: Doubleday, 1996.

Hagedorn, John, and Bert Sadowski, "The Transition from Strategic Technology Alliances to Mergers and Acquisitions: An Exploratory Study," *Journal of Management Studies,* 36, January 1999, pp. 87–107.

Harris, Roy J., Jr., and Bernard Wysocki, Jr., "Ready for Takeoff?: Venture with Boeing Is Likely to Give Japan Big Boost in Aerospace," *The Wall Street Journal,* January 14, 1986, pp. 1, 22.

Los Angeles Times, "Antitrust Chief Urges Ventures over Mergers," November 3, 1984, part IV, p. 1.

McConnell, John J., and Timothy J. Nantell, "Corporate Combinations and Common Stock Returns: The Case of Joint Ventures," *Journal of Finance,* 40, June 1985, pp. 519–536.

Nanda, Ashish, and Peter J. Williamson, "Use Joint Ventures to Ease the Pain of Restructuring," *Harvard Business Review,* 73, November–December 1995, pp. 119–128.

Templin, Neal, "More and More Firms Enter Joint Ventures with Big Competitors," *The Wall Street Journal,* November 1, 1995, pp. A1, A9.

Weston, J. Fred, "The GM–Toyota Vows: A Reply to the Critics," *Across the Board,* The Conference Board Magazine, 21, March 1984, pp. 3–6.

Yamaha v. FTC, 657 F 2d. 971, 1981.

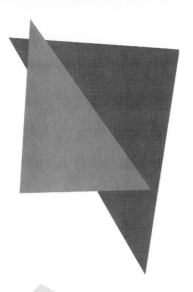

ESOPs and MLPs

An employee stock ownership plan (ESOP) is a type of stock bonus plan that invests primarily in the securities of the sponsoring employer firm. In a master limited partnership (MLP), the limited partnership interests are divided into units that trade as shares of common stock. Both ESOPs and MLPs have tax advantages, and both have been involved in takeover and takeover defense activities.

NATURE AND HISTORY OF ESOPS

To analyze the role that ESOPs perform it is necessary to understand their fundamental nature as an employee benefit plan and their relationship to other employee benefit plans. The employee benefit plans involved are pension plans. A pension plan is established by an organization to provide for payments to plan participants after retirement. Such plans are subject to federal government regulation established by the Employee Retirement Income Security Act (ERISA) of 1974.

Types of Pension Plans

ERISA divides employee pension plans into two major types: (1) defined benefit plans and (2) defined contribution plans. The **defined benefit plans** are what people usually have in mind when they think about a pension plan. It is the type used by most large corporations. According to a formula set in advance, these plans specify the amounts that participants will receive in retirement. A flat benefit formula is a fixed amount per year of service, such as $10 for each year of service. An employee with 30 years of service would receive a pension of $300 per month, subject to a maximum percentage (for example, 60%) of (average) final salary. Under a unit benefit formula, the participant receives a fixed percentage of earnings per year of service, such as 2% of the average of the last five years. An employee with 30 years of service would receive a monthly pension based on 60% of the average final salary. Plans must meet federal fiduciary standards to qualify for favorable tax treatment. They are subject to minimum funding standards and are guaranteed by the Pension Benefit Guarantee Corporation (PBGC).

   Defined contribution plans make no fixed commitment to a pension level. Only the contributions into the plan are specified, and participants receive over the period of their retirement what is in their accounts when they retire. Defined contribution plans can be of three kinds: stock bonus plans, profit-sharing plans, and money purchase plans. In a **stock bonus plan,** the firm contributes a specified number of shares of its common stock into the plan annually. The value of the contribution is based on the price of the stock at a recent date if it is traded; otherwise an appraisal is required. The other two forms of defined contribution plans provide for the payment of cash into the plan. Contributions to qualified **profit-sharing plans** are related to profitability rates, so they can vary in dollar amounts from year to year. Defined contribution plans are required by law to make "prudent" investments. They are not subject to minimum funding standards and are not covered by the PBGC.

ESOPs are defined contribution employee benefit pension plans that invest at least 50% of their assets in the common shares of the sponsoring corporation. Under ERISA, ESOPs are stock bonus plans or combined stock bonus plans and money purchase plans designed to invest primarily in qualifying employer securities. The plans may receive stock or cash, the latter being used by the plan managers to buy stock. A stock bonus plan can determine each year the amount to invest. A money purchase plan has a specific contribution schedule, such as 4% of ESOP salaries per year. ESOPs may also provide for employee contributions.

Since 1977, Treasury Department regulations have permitted ESOP contributions to represent a portion of a profit-sharing plan. But an ESOP is different from an employee stock purchase plan. Stock purchase plans are programs under which a firm enables employees to buy company stock at a discount. The Internal Revenue Code specifies that all or most employees must participate and that the shares must be sold at 85% or more of the prevailing market price of the shares.

ESOPs should also be differentiated from executive incentive programs. The latter are provided mainly to top management and other key employees. These programs are part of executive compensation packages aimed to align the interests of managers with those of the stockholders. Although many forms can be used, the tax laws since 1981 govern two types of plans: incentive stock options (ISOs) and stock appreciation rights (SARs). The exercise price of ISOs must be equal to or greater than the stock price at time of issue. The SARs can have an exercise price as low as 50% of the stock price. Both can have a maximum life of 10 years from date of issue.

Types of ESOPs

In its reports on ESOPs, the U.S. General Accounting Office (GAO) identified four main kinds: leveraged, leveragable, nonleveraged, and tax credit. Each of these is briefly described in U.S. General Accounting Office (1986). Leveraged ESOPs were recognized under ERISA in 1974. In a **leveraged ESOP,** the plan borrows funds to purchase securities of the employer firm. The employer firm makes contributions to the ESOP trust in an amount that meets the annual interest payments on the loan as well as repayments of the principal. It is well known that corporations can deduct interest as a tax expense but not principal. However, contributions by the corporations to ESOPs to cover both interest and principal (subject to some limitations) are fully deductible. Leveragable and nonleveraged ESOPs, also recognized under ERISA, are plans that have not used leveraging. In a **leveragable ESOP** the plan is authorized but is not required to borrow funds. The plan documents for nonleveraged ESOPs do not provide for borrowing. **Nonleveraged ESOPs** are essentially stock bonus plans that are required to invest primarily in the securities of the employer firm.

The Tax Reduction Act of 1975 provided for tax credit ESOPs. In addition to the regular investment credit in existence at that time, an additional investment credit of 1% of a qualified investment in plant and equipment could be earned by a contribution of that amount to an ESOP. The plans were called Tax Reduction Act ESOPs or TRASOPs. An additional 0.5% credit was added in 1976 for companies that matched contributions of their employees of the same amount to the TRASOP. In 1983 the basis for the credit was changed from plant and equipment investments to 0.5% of covered payroll. These types of plans were called payroll-based ESOPs or PAYSOPs. TRASOPs and PAYSOPs have been called tax credit ESOPs. The other three types of ESOPs are referred to as ERISA-type ESOPs.

THE USES OF ESOPS

During the period 1982 to 1987, the number of employees at companies with ESOPs increased by 66% to 9 million. During the following period, 1988 to 1993, the number increased by only 11% to 10 million (Bernstein, 1996). We estimate that about 11 million to 12 million employees are covered by ESOP plans in 2000.

Employee stock ownership plans have been used in a wide variety of corporate restructuring activities (Bruner, 1988; GAO, 1986). Fifty-nine percent of leveraged ESOPs were vehicles used to buy private companies from their owners. This enabled the owners to make their gains tax-free by investing the funds received into a portfolio of U.S. securities. ESOPs have also been used in buyouts of large private companies.

Thirty-seven percent of leveraged ESOPs were employed in divestitures. In a very substantial ESOP transaction, the Hospital Corporation of America sold over 100 of its 180 hospitals to Health Trust, a new corporation created and owned by an employee-leveraged ESOP.

Leveraged ESOPs have also been used as rescue operations. An ESOP was formed in 1983 to avoid the liquidation of Weirton Steel, which subsequently became a profitable company. ESOPs used in the attempt to prevent the failure of Rath Packing, McLean Trucking, and Hyatt Clark Industries were followed by subsequent bankruptcies.

A number of leveraged ESOPs were formed as a takeover defense to hostile tender offers. Early examples of ESOPs established as takeover defenses were those set up by Dan River in 1983, by Phillips Petroleum in 1985, and by Harcourt Brace Jovanovich in 1987.

Especially noteworthy was the use of an ESOP by Polaroid to defeat a takeover attempt in 1988 by Shamrock Holdings, the investment vehicle of Roy E. Disney. Shamrock Holdings had purchased a 6.9% stake in Polaroid with the expectation of making a tender offer for control. Polaroid created an ESOP that purchased 14% of its common stock. Polaroid was chartered in Delaware, whose antitakeover statute prevents a hostile acquirer from merging with the target for at least three years unless 85% of the target's voting shares are tendered. (This is generally referred to as the Delaware "freeze-out" law.) By creating its ESOP, Polaroid made it virtually impossible for Shamrock to obtain the necessary 85% in a tender offer. Shamrock

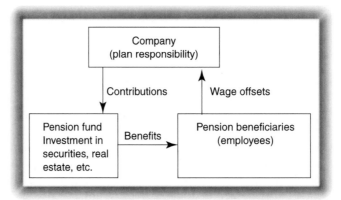

Figure 15.1   How a Pension Plan Operates

fought this ESOP defense by Polaroid in the courts but ultimately lost. After Polaroid, ESOPs became a widely used antitakeover weapon.

The Tax Reform Act of 1986 also permits excess pension assets to be shifted tax-free if they are placed into an ESOP. Ashland Oil reverted $200 million and Transco Energy Co. $120 million into new ESOPs.

Employee stock ownership plans represent one among a number of restructuring activities. They may be used as a substitute for or in connection with the purchase of private companies, divestiture activities, efforts to save failing companies, as a method of raising new capital, and as a takeover defense.

ESOPs as Pension Plans

It is helpful in understanding how ESOPs are used to continue to view them in the setting of a form of employee benefits, particularly as a pension plan. The basic relationships involved in a pension plan are shown in Figure 15.1. An individual corporation is responsible for setting up the pension fund. It makes dollar contributions in the form of either a defined benefit plan or a defined contribution plan, as discussed earlier. The pension fund uses the dollar contributions to make investments in a wide range of securities, real estate, and so on. The implication of ERISA is that prudence generally requires diversification of the pension fund investments. The benefits of the pension fund accrue to and are finally paid to the pension beneficiaries who are the employees of the company. It is presumed that, at least to some degree, wages are lower than they otherwise would be because of contributions by the company to the pension fund on behalf of its employees.

Contributions by a company to a qualified pension fund are tax-deductible expenses at the time of payment by the company. However, these dollar flows are not taxable to the recipient at the time the pension fund is set up. They are taxable to the recipient only when the benefits are actually received. Because the income of the employees would be expected to be lower after retirement, the employee has the benefit of a lower tax rate on the value of the contributions into the pension fund. In addition, of course, the pension fund earns income that augments the amount of

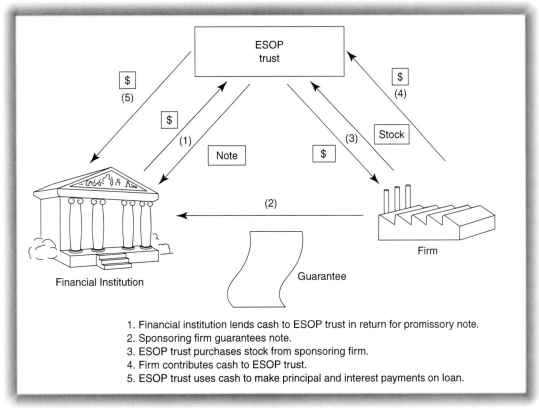

1. Financial institution lends cash to ESOP trust in return for promissory note.
2. Sponsoring firm guarantees note.
3. ESOP trust purchases stock from sponsoring firm.
4. Firm contributes cash to ESOP trust.
5. ESOP trust uses cash to make principal and interest payments on loan.

Figure 15.2   Illustration of a Leveraged ESOP

Source: United States General Accounting Office, *Employee Stock Ownership Plans: Benefits and Costs of ESOP Tax Incentives for Broadening Stock Ownership,* Washington, DC, December 1986, p. 49.

benefits payable to the employees in the future. Both the original payments by the employer into the pension fund and earnings thereon receive the benefit of tax deferral until received by employees.

Concept of a Leveraged ESOP

In an ESOP, the logic of the arrangement is the same as in Figure 15.1. The pension fund would be called an ESOP fund or trust. In a basic ESOP, the contribution by the company could be either cash or securities of the sponsoring company as described earlier. Like ordinary pension funds, ESOPs may also provide for employee contributions. Unlike the general pension fund, which is expected to diversify its investments widely for financial prudence, an ESOP is set up to invest in the securities of the sponsoring company. In practice, ESOPs are likely to use leverage to increase the tax benefits to the sponsoring company. The nature of a leveraged ESOP is shown in Figure 15.2.

We now have an additional element in the arrangement. This is the financial institution, which is the source of the borrowing by the ESOP. As shown in Figure 15.2, the lender transfers cash to the ESOP trust in return for a written obligation. The sponsoring firm generally guarantees the loan. The ESOP trust (ESOT) purchases securities from the sponsoring firm. Because the sponsoring firm has a contingent liability, it does not actually transfer the stock to the name of the ESOP trust until payments are made that reduce the principal that the firm has guaranteed. As portions of the principal are repaid, the firm then transfers stock to the name of the ESOP trust. The source of payment of both interest and principal to the financial institution is the cash contributed to the ESOP trust by the company. Both the interest and principal amounts transferred by the company are deductible expenses for tax purposes.

Examples of the Use of ESOPs

An example with numbers can illustrate the nature of a leveraged ESOP. John Jones is the president and 100% owner of Ace Company. His entire estate is represented by the value of Ace. His children are grown and have no interest in running the business. His attorney has recommended the sale of Ace because Jones does not have other investments. In the case of his death his estate would be unable to pay the required estate taxes and would be forced to sell the company under unfavorable conditions.

Jones has received an offer from Universal Company. It is to be a share-for-share stock exchange for each of the 300,000 Ace shares outstanding. Universal is trading at around $15 per share. Investment bankers have placed a value on Ace at around $20 per share. Because Jones is only 54 years old, he is reluctant to relinquish ownership and control of his company. Jones recognizes the need to increase his liquidity but does not want to sell the company at this time.

We can now illustrate how an ESOP could be helpful. An ESOP is established with all of the employees of Ace Company as beneficiaries. The ESOP borrows $2 million from a bank. These funds are used to purchase 100,000 shares of Ace Company stock from Jones. The loan from the bank to the ESOP is guaranteed by Ace Company and is secured by the 100,000 shares held in trust. Ace Company agrees to make ESOP contributions to cover both interest and repayment of principal. These are tax-deductible expenses for Ace Company. Note that at this point Jones has received $2 million in cash; presumably he will place this in a diversified portfolio with a relatively high degree of liquidity and/or marketability. As long as these funds are invested in other U.S. corporations within 12 months, the proceeds are not taxable to Jones at this time (see below for more detail).

As the ESOP repays the loan, the stock held in trust will be allocated to each individual employee's account. When the loan is completely paid off, the ESOP will have received and will own 100,000 shares of stock representing 33.3% of the outstanding stock of Ace Company. These relationships are illustrated in Figure 15.3.

Another example will sharpen the advantages of the use of an ESOP compared with a merger. It is similar to the previous illustration, which was streamlined to bring out the essential nature of a leveraged ESOP. In the present case study, more variables are considered in the analysis. Consider John Doe, the aging owner of 100% of the stock of Doeskin Textiles. Most of his personal wealth is tied to the firm's fortunes; he is thinking about retirement and worries about his relatively

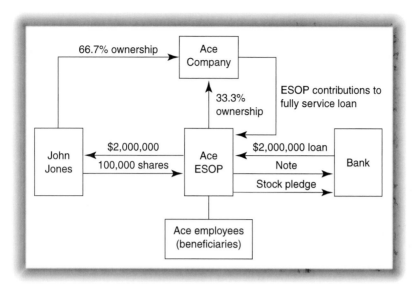

Figure 15.3   Leveraged ESOP Example

illiquid position as well as about having all his eggs in one basket. In addition, declining health has caused him to consider the effect of substantial estate taxes, which might necessitate a hasty sale of the firm by his heirs in the event of his death. All these factors led him to seriously consider a recent overture from Polyestech Corporation to acquire Doeskin in a tax-free exchange of securities for $8,000,000. The offer is acceptable in terms of price, although Doe is somewhat concerned that the value received would deteriorate if Polyestech's stock price declined. Also, Polyestech has a rather unsavory reputation in terms of labor relations and social responsibility. Doeskin has been the mainstay of the Minnesota community where it is located, and Doe feels quite paternalistic toward his employees and managers. He is uneasy about turning the firm over to outsiders and would like to find another solution. ESOPs offer such a solution.

Suppose Doe would like to withdraw $2,500,000 of Doeskin's $8,000,000 value to invest in a diversified portfolio of publicly traded corporate securities to provide both diversification and liquidity. He should take the following steps:

1. Doeskin should establish an ESOP.
2. The ESOP should borrow $2,500,000 from a bank, insurance company, or other lender. Doeskin would most likely be required to guarantee the ESOP loan.
3. Doe should sell 31.25% of his stock to the ESOP for $2,500,000.

As long as Doe invests the $2,500,000 in securities of other U.S. corporations within 12 months, he can defer any federal tax on the transaction. This tax-free rollover is allowable under the 1984 Deficit Reduction Act as long as the ESOP owns at least 30% of the firm's stock following the sale and neither the owner nor his family participates in the ESOP once it is formed. (If Doe sells less than 30%, he will have to pay capital gains tax on the sale, but he will be able to participate in the ESOP, reducing over time the extent of his ownership dilution.) Doeskin would make tax-deductible contributions to the ESOP sufficient to repay the loan principal and to pay interest. As the loan was repaid, the Doeskin shares belonging to the ESOP would be allocated to Doeskin employees participating in the plan. Thus, the owner of a privately held firm can achieve tax-free liquidity without selling his firm to outsiders and can even maintain control, depending on his need for cash and thus the proportion of stock sold to the ESOP.

Among the advantages and disadvantages of the ESOP versus the Polyestech offer are the following:

ESOP
1. Employee loyalty increases as a result of stock ownership through an ESOP.
2. Liquidity and diversification increase for Doe.
3. Dilution of ownership is not critical here because Doe maintains control.
4. The tax-free rollover is actually only a tax deferral until the replacement securities are sold.
5. The ESOP establishes a market value for Doeskin stock that may help in estate valuation. This may be a positive or negative effect.
6. An ESOP provides a market for Doeskin shares if heirs must sell shares to pay estate taxes. Avoids a "fire sale," and furthermore, 50% of the proceeds from the sale of stock to an ESOP may be excluded from the estate's value.

SALE TO POLYESTECH
1. Liquidity is not improved until Polyestech shares are sold.
2. Potential deterioration of value received.
3. Doe completely loses control over the firm.
4. The tax advantage in tax-free exchange of securities is one of timing only. Tax must be paid when securities are sold to achieve liquidity.
5. There is no diversification effect, because all eggs would still be in one basket, albeit a different and perhaps more marketable basket.

ESOPs in Lieu of Subsidiary Divestitures

Large corporations often have subsidiaries or plants that they wish to divest for one reason or another. The usual alternatives are to sell the subsidiary to another corporation (although it may be difficult to find a buyer at an acceptable price) or to liquidate the subsidiary's assets, which is disruptive for the subsidiary's employees and often for others as well. An ESOP can function well in this type of situation. The subsidiary's employees are likely to be willing purchasers (through an ESOP), because they have a great deal at stake and the alternatives are highly uncertain.

First, a shell corporation is established. The shell establishes an ESOP; the debt capacity of the shell and the ESOP (with the guarantees of the parent corporation) is used to arrange financing to purchase the subsidiary from the parent. The shell corporation (now no longer a shell) operates the former subsidiary while the ESOP holds the stock. If successful, enough income will be generated to make the most of allowable tax-deductible contributions to the ESOP, which will enable it to service its debt. As the debt is reduced, the ESOP will allocate shares to the employees' accounts, and over time the former subsidiary will come to be owned by its employees.

This entire transaction is, of course, predicated on the subsidiary's viability as an independent entity and its ability to generate sufficient income to cover its financing. In many cases, the original motivation for divestiture is that the subsidiary is in a dying industry or requires extensive modernization of inefficient facilities. If so, selling the subsidiary to the employees benefits neither them nor the economy as a whole in the long run even though short-term disruption might be kept to a minimum. In such cases, liquidation might be the preferred solution.

TAX ADVANTAGES

Scholes and Wolfson (1992) caution that many of the claimed tax advantages of ESOPs may be illusory. Expenses incurred by business firms to create pension benefits for its employees are generally tax-deductible. The full deductibility of payments to an ESOP for the amortization debt is claimed to have tax advantages because principal is being repaid as well as interest. However, Scholes and Wolfson point out that viewing such payments as pension benefits demonstrates that providing pension benefits directly would yield substantially the same tax benefits.

The Scholes and Wolfson argument may be illustrated by an example. Suppose a firm spends $100,000 in year X to add to its pension fund for employees. The total $100,000 would be a tax-deductible expense for that year. Alternatively, assume that the firm had borrowed an amount in an earlier year to set up an ESOP and that the tax deductible amount paid in year X to amortize the debt was $100,000. The amount of tax deduction for the firm with an ESOP is no different than if the same amount had been paid in to its pension fund.

Other studies have discussed tax benefits that may be associated with the use of ESOPs.

Interest Exclusion

Beatty (1995) describes tax provisions that appear to apply exclusively to leveraged ESOPs, making their tax treatment different from that of other retirement plans. A bank, insurance company, or investment company could exclude from taxable income 50% of the interest income earned on loans to ESOPs that own more than 50% of the employer's equity. Although the 50% interest exclusion is accorded to the lender, competitive markets would result in lower interest rates on ESOP loans than on non-ESOP loans. As part of the Small Business Job Protection Act of 1996, this loan interest exclusion provision of the Internal Revenue Code was repealed (P.L. 104-188, Section 1602(a)).

Dividend Deduction

Another possible tax benefit is that the employer can deduct the dividends paid on ESOP shares if they are allocated to employee accounts or used to repay ESOP debt. When dividends are used to repay ESOP debt, the value of the ESOP shares declines by the amount of the dividend. However, the employer can deduct the entire market value of the shares at the time they are placed in the ESOP. Beatty (1995) presents an example. On May 9, 1988, the Berry Wright Corporation (BWC) loaned $24 million to its new ESOP, which purchased 1.525 million newly issued BWC common shares at $15.75 each. On the same day, a dividend of $8 per share was announced with a record date of May 31, 1988. The ESOP shares received $12.2 million of dividends that were then used to repay about one-half the ESOP loan. The BWC shares dropped by exactly $8 a share on the ex-dividend date. Because the ESOP was not able to keep the dividend, it bought shares worth $7.75. The ESOP contribution, therefore, was worth $11.8 million, representing the balance of the ESOP loan that was repaid during 1988 by BWC. The corporation was permitted to deduct $24 million but made only an $11.8 million contribution to the ESOP. Beatty observes that this example illustrates the Chaplinsky and Niehaus (1990, 1994) position that dividends used to repay ESOP debt provide a distinctive tax benefit.

Deferment of Capital Gains Tax

As noted earlier in the Ace Company and Doeskin Textiles cases, an owner of a closely held firm can defer capital gains taxes resulting from the sale of his firm by selling at least 30% of the outstanding shares to an ESOP.

Tax Loss Carryforwards

The Tax Reform Act of 1986 placed a number of restrictions on the ability of a corporation to carry losses forward after a change in control unless an ESOP purchases at least 50% of the equity.

Excess Pension Asset Reversions

Also in 1986, an excise tax was placed on reversions of excess assets from a defined benefit plan. But if the excess pension assets are placed in an ESOP, the excise tax rate is lower.

Conclusions on Tax Benefits

In the opposite direction, the method of allocating ESOP assets to the accounts of employees results in a smaller expected present value tax deduction for leveraged ESOPs than other retirement plans. Shares purchased by a leveraged ESOP are initially placed in a temporary company account. The shares are allocated to employees on a percentage basis related to the repayment of principal and interest in each year of the loan. Other retirement plans provide for immediate allocation of assets to the employees. The value of the ESOP tax deduction is based on the market value of the shares when they were placed in the ESOP, but the deduction cannot be taken until the debt is repaid and the assets are allocated some years in the future. The present value factor is applied to the future value of the shares but on the generally lower value at the time they are placed into the suspense account.

Beatty (1995, p. 229) estimates that for ESOPs established in 1987 and later, the average net tax benefit was 0.3% of equity value. The General Accounting Office

(1986) estimated that for the period 1977 to 1983 the federal revenue losses from ESOPs were about $13 billion, an annual average of $1.9 billion. These net tax benefits would cause event returns from the announcement of ESOPs to be positive.

THE PERFORMANCE OF ESOPS

Five dimensions of the performance of ESOPs have been studied: (1) corporate control or antitakeover defense, (2) a method of financing, (3) comparison with profit sharing, (4) effects on productivity, and (5) economic consequences.

ESOPs as a Takeover Defense

Many individual case studies document how ESOPs have been used as a takeover defense. Beatty (1995) documents this evidence systematically from her sample of 145 ESOP announcements. Seventy-five percent of the transactions occurred in 1987 or later when both the interest exclusion for lenders and the dividend deduction used to repay ESOP debt became effective. This is consistent with her data for tax benefits discussed above. She notes also that 57% of the transactions took place in 1988 and 1989 after the Polaroid decision and the related Delaware "freeze-out" law that increased the effectiveness of ESOPs as a takeover defense.

Empirical studies generally find that when a firm is subject to a takeover attempt, the announcement of an ESOP has a negative effect on equity values (Beatty, 1995, and references cited therein). If the firm is not subject to a takeover attempt, the announcement of an ESOP is not associated with a change in equity values if the company was subject to the Delaware freeze-out law and the size of the ESOPs results in the establishment of an effective blocking percentage ownership.

ESOPs Versus Alternative Methods of Raising Funds

Bruner (1988) analyzes ESOPs as an alternative to other methods of raising funds. In one example, the outlays in a leveraged ESOP represented by interest expense and principal repayment represent a substitute for pension payments that otherwise would have been made. Another plausible assumption is that the interest rate charged by the lender will reflect all or some of the tax advantage that permits the financial institution to exclude from taxable income 50% of the income on loans to ESOPs. This would make the debt interest expense under a leveraged ESOP arrangement lower than under straight debt financing.

Another issue is control of the stock that is placed in the ESOP. Some people argue that management continues to control the ESOP, so the stock remains in friendly hands. On the other hand, technically the stock belongs to the individual employees, and with a strong union speaking on behalf of the employees there is always the risk that the employees and/or their union might vote the stock in a way that conflicts with the interests of management. The point was made in connection with Polaroid's establishment of an ESOP that the employees who wished to maintain the status quo and who did not want an outside firm to take over the company would be even more strongly opposed to the takeover than management. Typically, after a takeover, employment is reduced, and to protect their positions the employees are likely to be supporters of management when ESOPs are used as a takeover defense.

The view has been set forth that ESOP transactions represent economic dilution. Potentially they transfer shareholders' wealth to employees (Bruner, 1988). As we observed at the beginning of this chapter, ESOPs represent a form of an employee pension program. If the ESOP contribution is not offset by a reduction to some degree in other benefit plans or in the direct wages of workers, employees gain at the expense of shareholders. The argument has also been made that any borrowing by the ESOP uses some of the debt capacity of the firm (Bruner, 1988). It could also be argued that such borrowing substitutes for other forms of borrowing that the firm would otherwise use. To the extent that there is a valid belief that ESOP transactions represent economic dilution to the original shareholders, the price charged to the ESOP for the company stock transferred to it may be at a premium to compensate for economic dilution. The Department of Labor's reviews of such transactions may be a source of its disagreements about the fairness of the price charged by management to the ESOP.

The impact of moving equity shares into the ownership of the employees is apparently an important disadvantage of ESOPs despite their considerable tax advantage. Kaplan (1988, note 12) expresses this view in the following terms: "The infrequent use of ESOP loans in the sample analyzed in this paper (5 of 76 companies) suggests that the non-tax costs of using an ESOP are high. One such cost is the large equity stake that eventually goes to all contributing employees and significantly reduces the equity stake that can be given to managers and the buyout promoter." A potential advantage is that shares can be sold at higher prices over the years as the ESOP contributes to higher earnings through tax advantages and through the increased incentives and improved motivations of employees as a result of their stock ownership through the ESOP.

Comparison with Profit Sharing

A study by Professor Daniel Mitchell (1995) compares profit sharing with ESOPs. He notes that deferred profit-sharing plans are found in about 16% of all medium-sized and large establishments compared with only 3% for ESOPs. So, despite the tax subsidies to ESOPs, their coverage of workers is relatively small. Mitchell states that non-insured private pensions held $1.2 trillion in equity in 1991. Insured pensions account indirectly for additional equity holdings. Equity holdings by ESOPs for 1991 are estimated at only $47 billion. Thus, the worker coverage of ESOPs is relatively small compared with other pension plans in terms of its impact on helping workers achieve equity holdings.

Mitchell argues that profit sharing from an economic standpoint has advantages over ESOPs. Profit sharing introduces flexibility in worker compensation so it may improve the stability of employment desirable because of the macroeconomic aspects of stabilizing the economy. ESOPs do not have the same macroeconomic benefits. An ESOP involves a form of bonus to employees in the form of equity shares in their own firm. An ESOP does not add to pay flexibility.

Mitchell considers the ability of the firm to deduct the repayment of both interest and principal in payments to retire the debt of an ESOP as a tax subsidy. He reasons that in publicly held companies the principal repayment reflects the value of stock given to employees. If the valuation of the stock is accurate, the value of the stock represents a true cost to the employer and should be deductible just as wages are. But owners of closely held companies have the incentive to overvalue the stock assigned to employees, which according to Mitchell would represent a form of tax evasion. Mitchell accordingly argues that if tax subsidies are to be employed, they should be made to profit-sharing schemes that have macroeconomic benefits.

Effects on Company Productivity

Because one of the objectives expressed in the writings in support of the ESOP idea was to achieve "people's capitalism," it is of interest to consider the stock ownership and control of ESOPs. However, most studies indicate that ownership percentages have been relatively small—10% or less. Even when stock carries voting rights, the voting rights associated with the stock of ESOP accounts may be exercised by the plan trustees (usually the company management) without input by participants. This has given rise to the charge that ESOPs can be used by management to obtain tax benefits without sharing control with employees. This has been justified in the following terms (Hiltzik, 1984, p. 2).

> "Our programs are the antithesis of workplace democracy," says Joseph Schuchert, managing partner of Kelso & Co., the firm founded by Louis Kelso, which has installed about 800 ESOPs for companies since 1956 and has arranged 80 buy-outs with ESOP participation since 1970. "We've been criticized for not giving workers more participation, but we believe workers are natural shareholders, not natural managers."

There are interesting issues raised in connection with the preceding quote. Apparently the aim of ESOPs is to enable workers to participate in ownership for the purpose of augmenting their income from both dividends and capital gains. But ownership carries the ultimate control power in a corporation. If workers are not to participate in the decision-making process or to exercise ultimate control in their role as shareholders, some unresolved issues are posed.

With regard to productivity performance, the most exhaustive study was performed by the U.S. General Accounting Office (1987), which reviewed a number of prior studies on ESOPs and corporate performance. Few of these earlier studies found significant gains in either profitability or productivity. Only one of the studies reported a significant improvement in the growth rate of sales. No study reported a significant improvement in the growth rate of employment.

Later studies report mixed evidence. For example, Park and Song (1995) find that, on average, firms sponsoring ESOPs experience a permanent improvement in performance. But when they partition their sample between firms with large outside block-holders (block firms) and firms without them (nonblock firms), important differences are observed. The improvement in performance is limited to block firms. Their regression analysis finds a negative relation between the fraction of ownership held by the ESOPs and changes in performance for nonblock firms. But no systematic relationship is observed for block firms.

450 PART V M&A Strategies

Conte, Blasi, Kruse, and Jampani (CBKJ) (1996) find that the financial returns of public companies with ESOPs are significantly higher than those of comparable non-ESOP companies. Paradoxically, after companies adopt an ESOP their financial returns decline, indicating a negative incentive effect. CBKJ observe that these patterns are consistent with the proposition that most ESOPs in large publicly traded companies are adopted as takeover defenses.

Most systematic studies of the effects of ESOPs in the United States have not documented performance improvements. Considerable anecdotal evidence can be found that suggests that ESOPs have had positive effects on individual companies. Some positive effects of an ESOP adopted in July 1994 by United Airlines have been reported (Bernstein, 1996). Following the 1994 ESOP, operating revenue per employee increased, the number of employee grievances fell, the market share of United inched up, and pretax operating margins reached about 7.5%. Between June 30, 1994, and March 5, 1996, the stock price of United Airlines increased by almost 150%, compared with an increase of only about 50% over the same period for four other major airlines. The establishment of the United ESOP was associated with concessions representing an average of 15% in pay cuts for 55% of the employees and reduced wage costs overall by 7% in 1995. In part, at least, the improvements in reported profitability and stock prices reflect a reduction in costs resulting from the wage concessions. Thus, the employees who accepted wage cuts became equity holders in the company. The effects on profitability and stock prices are similar to those experienced at TWA earlier when Carl Icahn obtained control. The positive results were only temporary, and three years later TWA faced severe financial problems again. TWA has gone through Chapter 11 bankruptcy twice. While in its second bankruptcy in 1995, employees agreed to forgo wage increases and to reduce their equity ownership share from 45% to 30%.

The use of an ESOP at United has not been an unqualified success (Chandler, 1996). Flight attendants were unwilling to participate because they felt that the pay cuts were too large. With regard to individual measures of performance, United appears to still have problems. ESOPs in other individual companies have also encountered some problems and conflicts. Avis set up a 100% ESOP in 1987, but management has not granted employees board seats or voting rights. The stock price of the company dropped from $22 in 1992 to $12.50 in 1996.

Weirton Steel Corporation was formed in 1984 when workers bought 100% of the company to avoid a shutdown. In the following decade they had to accept successive wage and job reductions and sold 30% of their stock to pay for plant improvements and to reduce debt. In 1994 top management spent $550 million on plant modernization. To help finance this, the ESOP sold more stock, reducing its voting share to 49%.

One problem illustrated by these examples is that management has been unwilling to grant employees full shareholder rights when ESOPs are formed. Employees own an average of 13% of their companies at 562 public corporations, according to a *Business Week* article citing Professor Joseph R. Blasi of Rutgers University (Bernstein, 1996). Most of the 562 companies are unionized, and employees hold board seats in less than a dozen.

In contrast to the uneven experience with ESOPs in the United States, in a study of Japanese manufacturing companies for the period 1973 to 1988, Professors Derek C. Jones of Hamilton College and Takao Kato of Colgate University found positive results for ESOPs in Japan. They found that since 1973 the portion of publicly traded Japanese firms that had ESOPs jumped from 61% to more than 90%. By 1989 the average holdings per employee had reached about $14,000. Jones and Kato also found that in three to four years after setting up an ESOP, companies averaged a 4% to 5% increase in productivity. A 10% increase in employee bonuses relative to the bonuses of competitors resulted in a 1% increase in productivity in the next year (*Business Week,* 1995, p. 24).

These mixed results for ESOPs suggest that they have strong potentials but are not a panacea. It depends on how the ESOPs are utilized.

Economic Issues

ESOPs have been analyzed from an economic standpoint as a bargaining game with asymmetrical information. Ben-Ner and Jun (1996) postulate that management has information about the firm's future cash flows superior to that of employees. They formulate a model in which employees attempt to overcome this informational handicap by making simultaneous offers on wages and a purchase price for the firm. Their model predicts that owners of relatively unprofitable firms will establish ESOPs in lieu of paying higher wages. Owners of more profitable firms will prefer to pay higher wages rather than to dilute control by establishing an ESOP.

Of concern are the charges that ESOPs have been used by management not only as instruments for increasing their control, but also to conduct financial transactions in their own interests and to the detriment of the ESOPs and the workers they represent. Some of the court cases in which these issues were at least raised include the following. In Hall-Mark Electronics, employees owned one-third of the company stock through their retirement plan. The issue in the court case is the allegation that three Hall-Mark executives arranged to have the ESOP sell its shares back to the company at $4 per share shortly before they participated in the sale of the company for $100 per share (Hiltzik, 1986, p. 1).

Another example is the Chicago Pneumatic Tool Company, which established an ESOP in 1985. The controlling trustee was the chief executive of the company. In March 1986 the company became the target of a hostile takeover. To defeat the bid, it is alleged that the chief executive transferred 1 million shares from the company's treasury to the ESOP under his own voting control. The U.S. Department of Labor (which has responsibility for implementing the provisions of ERISA and of employee pension plans generally) stated that the cost of the transaction to the ESOP was $32.4 million for the shares, which were trading at about 30% over their historical average because of takeover speculation (Hiltzik, 1986, pp. 1, 6).

In 1985 the Department of Labor blocked an ESOP-financed $500 million leveraged buyout of Scott & Fetzer, the publisher of *The World Book Encyclopedia.* The department objected to the arrangement, which provided that the Scott & Fetzer ESOP would invest $182 million in borrowed funds to receive 41% of the company in the leveraged buyout. A group consisting of Scott & Fetzer's top management plus Kelso & Co. were to invest $15 million, for which they would receive 29% of the company. The General Electric Credit Corporation, which financed the $182 million ESOP loan and provided other financing, would receive the remaining 30%. The Department of Labor alleged that the ESOP was putting up more than 92% of the equity investment for only 41% of the company. The rebuttal view was that the ESOP investment represented a purchase of shares at market value (or takeover value), not an initial equity contribution. Another issue raised by this case is whether it was appropriate for Kelso & Co., a leading investment banking firm specializing in setting up ESOPs and formulating the terms of the deal, to have a substantial equity participation. There would appear to be the possibility of a conflict of interest.

The broader economic consequences of ESOPs have also been analyzed (Chen and Kensinger, 1988). If managements also control the ESOPs that are created, there is no increase in employee influence on the company. Although employees may receive stock that may be sold, the additions to their wealth may be relatively small. The amounts received may be insufficient to provide motivation for increased efforts by workers or to achieve harmonious relations between workers and management. On the other hand, if workers did receive substantial increases in control over the company through ESOPs, other harmful results might follow. Workers might use their increased ownership powers to redistribute wealth away from the original shareholders and other shareholders in the firm. The view has also been expressed that reliance can be placed on market forces to bring about employee ownership where it is appropriate, without the necessity of tax subsidies.

ESOP EVENT RETURNS

The event return effects of establishing an ESOP depend on the circumstances. Chang (1990) calculated the two-day abnormal portfolio returns for 165 announcements of employee stock ownership plans. The overall return was a positive 11.5%. But the announcement produces small positive event returns if the ESOP is used as a leveraged buyout (LBO) or as a form of wage concession. However, if the ESOP is established as a defense against a takeover, the event returns will be negative. Managers of such firms, on average, hold smaller ownership interest in their firms than do managers of comparable firms.

Sellers, Hagan, and Siegel (1994) sharpen the analysis of event returns to ESOPs. They eliminate from the sample those ESOPs that provide tax incentives. A positive market two-day return of 1.5% is consistent with other favorable effects of ESOPs such as improvements in employee productivity. Similarly, Chang and Mayers (1992) find non-tax influences on event returns from the establishment of ESOPs. The largest positive event returns were observed when officers and directors initially controlled between 10% and 20% of share ownership. The positive effects on shareholder wealth were smaller when the initial control was less than 10% or more than 20%. When officers and directors controlled 40% or more of total shares, a negative association was found between event returns and the fraction of shares added to the ESOP.

Event return studies of ESOPs have obtained different results reflecting the multiple motives for ESOPs. Anne Beatty published two empirical studies of ESOPs (1994, 1995). In the first study she examined three motivations for leveraged ESOPs: (1) as a takeover defense, (2) incentives to employees, and (3) tax savings. Her empirical study suggests that companies that adopt ESOPs are likely to have adopted other types of takeover defenses as well. But companies that adopt ESOPs are likely to have characteristics consistent also with tax and incentive effects.

In her 1995 study, Beatty analyzed a sample of 122 ESOP transaction announcements during the 1976 to 1989 period. She found an average 1% two-day cumulative positive return over the days −1 to 0. This increase in equity value reflects primarily tax effects. She also found some relationship between a positive share price reaction and the size of ESOP benefits and found that equity values decline for firms that are subject to takeovers. The latter again supports the view that ESOPs are used as a takeover defense.

Event returns were also calculated in the Chaplinsky, Niehaus, and Van de Gucht (1998) study. Market-adjusted returns for the three-day window covering the days before and after the announcement were 13.3% for ESOPs and 14.9% for management buyouts, with which their study made comparisons.

EVALUATION OF ESOPS

The role of ESOPs is further illuminated by a study of comparisons with management buyouts (MBOs). In chapter 16, we explain that in MBOs officers and directors, not workers, substantially increase their percentage ownership; in ESOPs workers do not effectively increase their control rights. Chaplinsky, Niehaus, and Van de Gucht (1998) first made comparisons prior to the buyout transaction. The transaction size for ESOPs, measured by the median, was $209 million, compared with $172 million for MBOs. ESOP firms had poorer stock price performance. Leverage measured by the ratio of long-term debt to total capitalization (defined as long-term debt plus market value of equity) was significantly lower for ESOPs, 12% versus 27%. ESOP firms were more likely to have experienced takeover threats. The ESOP firms had lower ratios of ownership by officers and directors.

Second, they analyzed the relationships after the transaction. Compensation to employees was reduced by 56% of the ESOPs but by only 2.6% of the MBOs. This suggests that ESOPs are used to reduce direct employment costs. The median post-buyout leverage rose for both ESOPs and MBOs. Including the effects of the reversion of excess pension fund assets, the median post-buyout leverage for ESOPs was about 80%, compared to about 75% for MBOs, statistically different. ESOP firms also used a higher proportion of bank debt, which was predictable based on the tax subsidy to institutional lenders. ESOP firms did not differ greatly from MBO firms with regard to post-buyout industry-adjusted employment growth over a three- to five-year period. They found also that employees failed to obtain substantial control rights through the formation of ESOPs.

ESOPs are not panaceas for productivity improvement. Their effect on the performance of the firm depends heavily on how they are employed. Some of the notable examples of the use of ESOPs have occurred in industries such as steel and airlines. These are industries where changed economic circumstances forced employees to give up a portion of their wages for a partial equity position in the firm. Even in these circumstances management continued to exercise major control over decision processes in the firm. Thus, even where ESOPs have been used in a major way, employees have not received full shareholder rights and ownership incentives have been severely diminished. Many ESOPs were established as takeover defenses. However, the proliferation of a broad arsenal of other takeover defenses has reduced the role of ESOPs in this area.

Finally, the supposed tax advantages have sometimes been confused with the tax deductibility of employee benefits. A major tax advantage for closely held corporations is the tax shelter for the owners, but there are no clear effects on employee incentives. Arguments have also been made that the tax subsidies involved with ESOPs might have perversely negative effects. Similar positive effects might also be achieved through alternative compensation arrangements.

MASTER LIMITED PARTNERSHIPS

The corporation has been the dominant form of business organization in the United States when measured by total assets. When measured by numbers, proprietorships and partnerships are the most numerous, applying mostly to relatively small businesses. A corporation has four major advantages in raising large sums of money.

1. It provides for limited liability of stockholders. Stockholders are not personally liable if the firm is unable to pay its debts.
2. The corporation has an unlimited life. Managers can come and go and owners may change, but this does not affect the continuity of the corporation.
3. The ownership shares carry the residual risk, but they are divided into many units. Hence, investors can limit their risk exposure in any one firm, and this facilitates diversification by investors across many firms.
4. The shares of common stock are freely bought and sold. This facilitates tradability and transferability of ownership interest in the firm.

The Nature of MLPs

The master limited partnership (MLP) is a type of limited partnership whose shares are publicly traded. The limited partnership interests are divided into units that trade as shares of common stock. In addition to tradability it has the advantages of limited liability for the limited partners. The tradability also provides for continuity of life. The MLP retains many of the advantages of a corporation, but it has an advantage over the corporation in that it eliminates the double taxation of corporate earnings. The MLP is not taxed as an entity; it is treated like any other partnership for which income is allocated pro rata to the partners. Unit holders reflect all income deductions and credits attributable to the partnership's operation in determining the unit holder's taxable income.

The Internal Revenue Service has focused on four characteristics in distinguishing between a corporation and a master limited partnership (MLP); unlimited life, limited liability, centralized management, and transferability. To avoid being taxed as a corporation, an MLP may have only two, and no more, of the four corporate characteristics, which are usually centralized management and transferability. Master limited partnerships typically specify a limited life of 100 years more or less. The general partner or manager of the partnership has unlimited liability even though the limited partners do not.

Probably in part because the general partner has unlimited liability, it also has virtually autocratic powers. Once a general partner and the formation of an MLP have been approved by the courts and have been reviewed at least by the Securities and Exchange Commission, it is very difficult to change the general partner in the absence of readily provable fraud or the equivalent. The probability of success of an MLP is increased if it is structured to achieve an alignment of interests between the general partner and the public unit holders. One way to do this is by using management incentive fees such as providing the general partner with a sharing rule of 4% to 6% of the distributable cash flows from the MLP. Alignment of incentives is also achieved because the management of the general partnership usually owns a significant number of the limited partnership units.

The Boston Celtics Case Example

The Boston Celtics case illustrates many aspects of MLPs, including important tax changes in 1987 and 1997. In October 1986, the Boston Celtics MLP was formed. A hoped-for offering price of $20 per unit had to be reduced to $18 for the public offering. For the second edition of this book, we obtained a quotation from the New York Stock Exchange composite list for March 26, 1997. The 52-week range in price for the units was a high of 25¼ and a low of 20⅛. Based on dividend payments of $2.50 during the previous 52 weeks, the units were yielding 11.05%.

The Revenue Act of 1987 provided that publicly traded limited partnerships (MLPs or PTPs) would become taxed as corporations for federal income tax purposes, except for partnerships involving oil and gas, timber and real estate. However, other PTPs existing on December 17, 1987 would be "grandfathered" until their first taxable year beginning after December 31, 1997. In August 1997, Congress passed the Taxpayer Relief Act of 1997, which permitted PTPs to elect, as an alternative to taxation as a corporation, to pay a federal tax at a rate of 3.5% of gross income from the active conduct of trades or businesses ("Toll Tax") in taxable years beginning after December 31, 1997. Accordingly, the Boston Celtics Limited Partnership (BCLP) would have become taxable as a corporation during its taxable year beginning July 1, 1998 if it remained a PTP, unless it elected to pay the Toll Tax. As a result of the two major tax changes, the BCLP was reorganized on April 13, 1998. The reorganization created multiple corporations and limited partnerships with cross-ownership relationships, described in the 10K—Annual Report of the BCLP filed 9/17/99.

The BCLP's most significant operating asset is its indirect investment in Celtics Basketball, which owns and operates the Boston Celtics. The following summarizes the performance of the Boston Celtics during the past 15 basketball seasons:

Season	Regular Season Record	Finish in Division	Playoff Results	Stock Price*
1999–2000	35–47	5	—	10.00
1998–99	19–31	5	—	12.06—NBA Lockout
1997–98	36–46	6	—	20.00—MLP reorganization
1996–97	15–67	7	—	25.00
1995–96	33–49	5	—	23.50
1994–95	35–47	3	Lost in 1st round	21.00
1993–94	32–50	5	—	19.63
1992–93	48–34	2	Lost in 1st round	16.63
1991–92	51–31	1	Lost in 2nd round	20.50
1990–91	56–26	1	Lost in 2nd round	16.75
1989–90	52–30	2	Lost in 1st round	16.88
1988–89	42–40	3	Lost in 1st round	13.88
1987–88	57–25	1	Lost in 3rd round	12.25
1986–87	59–23	1	Lost in finals	14.38
1985–86	67–15	1	NBA Champions	Stock offered in Oct. 1986 at $18

*We chose the last day in April to present the latest price for 2000.

Reflecting the declining fortunes of the basketball operations, the quotation on the BCLP on 4/19/00 was slightly under $10.

Needless to say, the tax law changes have discouraged the formation of new MLPs and have caused existing MLPs to reorganize in various forms. For example, Plum Creek Timber, which had been a successful MLP, converted into a real estate investment trust (REIT) on July 1, 1999.

Advantages of MLPs

A strong motivation for the formation of an MLP is the tax advantage. The MLP is taxed as a partnership and therefore avoids the double taxation to which corporate dividends are subject. The nature of the advantage to the use of an MLP is shown by Table 15.1. The marginal corporate rate of 40% is below the marginal personal rate of 45%. For company income of $100, the investor would receive $55 under the MLP, compared with $33 under the corporation. This is 67% more income.

Initial Pricing of MLPs

Muscarella (1988) analyzed the price performance of MLP units. His sample consisted of all initial public offerings of MLP units from January 1983 to July 1987. He analyzed the price performance of the MLPs for the 20 days following the initial public offerings. He found no significant underpricing or overpricing for his total sample or any subsample except for a slight overpricing of oil and gas and hotel/motel limited partnerships. This contrasts with substantial underpricing of initial public offerings (IPOs)

Table 15.1   Tax Benefits of MLPs

	Corporation	MLP
Company income	$100	$100
Company tax (federal 35%, state 5%)	40	0
After-tax income	60	100
Retained income	0	0
Payout	60	100
Personal tax (federal plus state @ 45%)	27	45
Investor after-tax income	$ 33	$ 55

of corporate securities. Ritter (1984), for example, reported initial average returns of 26.5% for 1,028 IPOs from 1977 to 1982. Chalk and Peavy (1987) reported 22% initial returns for 649 firms from 1975 to 1982. Muscarella and Vetsuypens (1988) had found an initial return of 7.61% for 1,184 firms for the period 1983 to June 1987. All of these studies indicated substantial underpricing. Theoretical models of IPO underpricing argue that the level of IPO underpricing is related to the degree of uncertainty about the market value of the common stock of the issuing firm. The study of initial price performance of MLP units implies much less uncertainty in the valuation of MLP units. Muscarella was unable to provide an explanation as to why there should be relatively little uncertainty about the valuation of MLP units.

Moore, Christensen, and Roenfeldt (1989) found a two-day return $[-1, 0]$ of 4.61% (significant) and some evidence of anticipation of the MLP announcement. The reasons they give for the positive market reaction include (1) tax advantages, (2) reduced information asymmetry, (3) improved asset management, and (4) information signaling.

SUMMARY

Employee stock ownership plans were designed ostensibly to promote employee stock ownership and to facilitate the raising of capital by employers. They have a number of shortcomings in the performance of both functions. Nevertheless, ESOPs may be quite valuable in a number of circumstances, particularly for privately held companies engaged in ownership transfer or for firms near the limit of their debt capacity.

The argument for employee stock ownership holds that employees who own stock in their employer are more productive, because as part owners they have a greater stake in the firm's profitability. However, ESOPs provide a good deal less than direct stock ownership. Participants typically do not receive any distribution of securities from the plan until they separate from service. Dividends and voting rights are passed through only with respect to shares actually allocated to participants' accounts. But most participants are not allowed to sell even those shares that have been allocated to them and thus cannot achieve a level of diversification in their benefit plans. (ERISA excludes ESOPs from the requirement to diversify.) A 1987 report by the U.S. General Accounting Office (GAO) concluded that although ESOPs do broaden stock ownership within participating firms, given the limited number of ESOPs within the economy as a whole the effect is modest overall. Perhaps more important, it found little evidence of improved performance in terms of either profitability or productivity.

As a financing tool, ESOPs provide benefits midway between those of debt financing and equity financing. They can bring additional debt capacity to highly leveraged firms or provide a market for equity financing for closely held firms. They are very useful devices for transferring ownership. The same 1987 GAO report indicated that the use of ESOPs in corporate finance had not lived up to its potential—most leveraged ESOP funds were being used to buy back stock from existing shareholders (for instance, retiring major shareholders) and not for capital expansion by the sponsoring firms. Thus ESOP contributions to corporate finance had been limited.

The MLP is an organizational form that offers investors the structure and tax attributes of more traditional partnerships but differs in one key respect. MLPs offer investors liquidity via an organized secondary market for the trading of partnership interests.

Tax advantages were an important motivating factor in the early development of MLPs. However, some of these advantages have been eroded. The Tax Reform Act of 1986 (TRA 86) eliminated an important tax benefit of corporate–MLP conversions with its repeal of the General Utilities doctrine. Before TRA 86, in a liquidation MLP the corporate sponsor would contribute assets to the MLP in exchange for units in a roll-out transaction.

The units would then be distributed to the corporate sponsor's shareholders in a complete liquidation of the corporation. This transaction would be completely tax free. However, with the repeal of the General Utilities doctrine, this was no longer the case. The general rule had been that corporate gains from the sale of appreciated assets were taxed at the corporate level at the time of the sale and at the shareholder level when this income was distributed as dividends. Under the General Utilities doctrine, a significant portion of the assets involved in a corporate MLP conversion would escape corporate taxation at the time of conversion. But TRA 86 eliminated this exception and taxed at the corporate level the entire difference between the adjusted basis of the assets and their fair market value. In addition, the shareholders at time of conversion after TRA 86 continued to be taxed on the difference between their basis in the common stock and the market value of the MLP units at conversion.

The main tax advantages of MLPs were the result of the status of MLPs as nontaxable entities. All profits and losses of an MLP flow through to individual investors, to be taxed at lower personal rates while avoiding the double taxation at both the corporate and personal levels of corporate dividend distributions to shareholders. However, these tax advantages are highly sensitive to an MLP's need to retain earnings, because MLP earnings are taxable to investors whether they are distributed or not. Thus, the liquidity advantages of MLPs assume even greater importance. Siciliano (1987, p. 1) suggested that this aspect of MLPs had led to "a distinctly different investment and marketing thesis," appealing to investors to view MLP units as simply another component of their equity securities portfolio rather than "as a long-term method of sheltering income from taxes."

QUESTIONS

15.1 What are the advantages and limitations of ESOPs?

15.2 How successful have ESOPs been in achieving their goals of increasing employee stock ownership and facilitating capital raising by employers?

15.3 Explain the differences between leveraged and nonleveraged ESOPs. Compare the EPS and control dilution under equity financing versus financing through an ESOP.

15.4 How do MLPs differ from ordinary limited partnerships?

15.5 What are the advantages and limitations of MLPs?

15.6 How are MLPs similar to corporations? How do they differ?

15.7 What were the significant tax changes involving MLPs?

Case 15.1 Pan Petroleum MLP

Most of the literature on MLPs has emphasized tax aspects. This case study of the Pan Petroleum MLP, whose formation was reviewed by the courts on April 26, 1989, illustrates the underlying business and economic rationales as well. The 1989 transaction involved a consolidation of a group of 45 oil and gas limited partnerships with Pan Petroleum MLP, a publicly traded master limited partnership. The consolidated partnership had approximately 4,300 limited partners. It was predicted that as a result of the consolidation, general and administrative expenses would be reduced by as much as $300,000 per year. These savings would result from several types of economies of scale resulting from the consolidation. The savings in general and administrative expenses became possible because of the need for only one set of financial records rather than 46, one annual appraisal of mineral properties, the maintenance of one legal entity, and one partnership tax return.

Many of the limited partners in the constituent partnerships consolidating with Pan Petroleum MLP were limited partners in more than one partnership. This made possible further cost savings with respect to record keeping and participant reporting. Many of the constituent partnerships owned interests in the same mineral properties. Duplicate accounting and record keeping could be eliminated as a result of the consolidation. The constituent partnerships participated mainly in wells drilled by two different major exploration companies. The consolidation provided Pan Petroleum MLP with a majority of the working interest in many of the properties. This enabled the MLP to conduct negotiations with the two large exploration companies on a more effective basis.

The basis for the consolidation appeared to be efficient and equitable. Engineering surveys established the proved reserves in developed producing properties as well as nonproducing or undeveloped properties. From the estimates of proved reserves of oil and gas, the amounts of cash flows and their duration were projected. Similar projections were made for the nonproducing or undeveloped properties. The cash flows for this latter group were reduced by 30% as an uncertainty factor. The resulting cash flows both for the developed producing properties and for the nonproducing or undeveloped properties were discounted at a 10% rate over the expected future economic producing lives of each of the properties. The MLP into which the other constituent partnerships were consolidated had its future cash flows discounted into a value figure on the same basis. For each constituent limited partnership and the Pan Petroleum MLP, the value of other assets and liabilities were also taken into account to arrive at a total "formula value." These were summed to arrive at a total figure of approximately $23 million. Of this amount, something over $11 million represented the "formula value" of Pan Petroleum MLP, 49.2% of the total. Pan Petroleum MLP had 2,571,670 limited partnership units already outstanding. Using these as the reference factor, a total of 5,226,191 MLP units were issued, of which Pan Petroleum accounted for 49.21%. The other constituent partnerships received MLP units representing the same percentage of the total MLP units issued that their formula value represented in relation to the total formula value. Inherently, forecasts and projections were required, but the methodology appears to have represented a rational and equitable basis for making the apportionment of ownership and income rights.

Clearly one of the major advantages to the owners of the constituent limited partnerships is that they would now have ownership rights that could be freely traded, bought, and sold. A number of the constituent limited partnerships would have had to be liquidated and would have ceased to exist except for the consolidation with Pan Petroleum MLP. In addition, by exchanging their limited partnership units for units in the Pan Petroleum MLP, the limited partners now have pro rata ownership rights in an efficient business operation.

QUESTIONS

1. What were the economics in grouping 45 oil and gas limited partnerships into one MLP?
2. What were some advantages to the owners of the constituent limited partnerships of the formation of the MLP?

◻REFERENCES

Beatty, Anne, "An Empirical Analysis of the Corporate Control, Tax and Incentive Motivations for Adopting Leveraged Employee Stock Ownership Plans," *Managerial and Decision Economics*, 15, 1994, pp. 299–315.

———, "The Cash Flow and Informational Effects of Employee Stock Ownership Plans," *Journal of Financial Economics*, 38, June 1995, pp. 211–240.

Ben-Ner, Avner, and Byoung Jun, "Employee Buyout in a Bargaining Game with Asymmetric Information," *American Economic Review*, 86, June 1996, pp. 502–523.

Bernstein, Aaron, "Why ESOP Deals Have Slowed to a Crawl," *Business Week*, March 18, 1996, pp. 101–102.

Bruner, Robert F., "Leveraged ESOPs and Corporate Restructuring," *Journal of Applied Corporate Finance*, 1, Spring 1988, pp. 54–66.

Business Week, "How Japan Perks Up Productivity." August 28, 1995, p. 24.

Chalk, A. J., and J. W. Peavy III, "Initial Public Offerings: Daily Returns, Offering Types, and the Price Effect," *Financial Analysts Journal*, 43, September/October 1987, pp. 65–69.

Chandler, Susan, "United We Own." *Business Week*, March 18, 1996, pp. 96–100.

Chang, Saeyoung, "Employee Stock Ownership Plans and Shareholder Wealth: An Empirical Investigation," *Financial Management*, 19, Spring 1990, pp. 48–58.

———, and David Mayers, "Managerial Vote Ownership and Shareholder Wealth,"

Journal of Financial Economics, 32, August 1992, pp. 103–131.

Chaplinsky, Susan, and Greg Niehaus, "The Tax and Distributional Effects of Leveraged ESOPs, " *Financial Management,* 19(1), 1990, pp. 29–38.

———, "The Role of ESOPs in Takeover Contests," *Journal of Finance,* 49, September 1994, pp. 1451–1470.

Chaplinsky, Susan, Greg Niehaus, and Linda Van de Gucht, "Employee Buyouts: Causes, Structure, and Consequences," *Journal of Financial Economics,* 48, 1998, pp. 283–332.

Chen, A. H., and J. W. Kensinger, "Beyond the Tax Effects of ESOP Financing," *Journal of Applied Corporate Finance,* 1, Spring 1988, pp. 67–75.

Conte, Michael A., Joseph Blasi, Douglas Kruse, and Rama Jampani, "Financial Returns of Public ESOP Companies: Investor Effects vs. Manager Effects," *Financial Analysts Journal,* 52, July/August 1996, pp. 51–61.

Hiltzik, Michael A., "ESOPs Now a Boon for Management," *The Wall Street Journal,* December 30, 1984, pp. 1–2.

———, "Do ESOPs Aid Workers or Managers?" *Los Angeles Times,* May 25, 1986, Part IV, pp. 1, 6.

Kaplan, Steven, "A Summary of Sources of Value in Management Buyouts," Presentation at the Conference on Management Buyouts, Graduate School of Business Administration, New York University, Salomon Brothers Center for the Study of Financial Institutions, May 20, 1988.

Mentz, J. Roger, Department of the Treasury, Statement on June 30, 1987 in *Master Limited Partnerships,* Hearings Before the Subcommittee on Select Revenue Measures of the Committee on Ways and Means, House of Representatives, 100th Congress, First Session, Serial 100-39.

Mitchell, Daniel J. B., "Profit Sharing and Employee Ownership: Policy Implications," *Contemporary Economic Policy,* 13, April 1995, pp. 16–25.

Moore, W. T., D. G. Christensen, and R. L. Roenfeldt, "Equity Valuation Effects of Forming Master Limited Partnerships," *Journal of Financial Economics,* 24, 1989, pp. 107–124.

Muscarella, C. J., "Price Performance of Initial Public Offerings of Master Limited Partnership Units," *The Financial Review,* 23, November 1988, pp. 513–521.

———, and M. R. Vetsuypens, "Initial Public Offerings and Information Asymmetry," Working Paper, Southern Methodist University, 1988.

Pan Petroleum MLP, Proposal, March 8, 1989.

Park, Sangsoo, and Moon H. Song, "Employee Stock Ownership Plans, Firm Performance, and Monitoring by Outside Blockholders," *Financial Management,* 24, Winter 1995, pp. 52–65.

Ritter, J. R., "The 'Hot' Issue Market of 1980," *Journal of Business,* 57, April 1984, pp. 215–240.

Scholes, Myron S., and Mark A. Wolfson, *Taxes and Business Strategy: A Planning Approach,* Englewood Cliffs, NJ: Prentice-Hall, 1992.

Schultz, Ellen, "All That Payout and Capital Gains Too," *Fortune,* 118, October 10, 1988, p. 28.

Sellers, Keith F., Joseph M. Hagan, and Philip H. Siegel, "Employee Stock Ownership Plans and Shareholder Wealth: An Examination of the Market Perceptions of the Non-Tax Effects," *Journal of Applied Business Research,* 10, Summer 1994, pp. 45–52.

Siciliano, John M., "Investment Banking Considerations," in Lionel M. Allan, *Master Limited Partnerships for Real Property Investments,* Berkeley, CA: California Continuing Education of the Bar, 1987, pp. 1–13.

U.S. General Accounting Office, *Employee Stock Ownership Plans: Benefits and Costs of ESOP Tax Incentives for Broadening Stock Ownership,* Washington, DC: December 1986.

———, *Employee Stock Ownership Plans: Little Evidence of Effects on Corporate Performance,* Washington, DC, October 1987.

Going Private and Leveraged Buyouts

"Going private" refers to the transformation of a public corporation into a privately held firm. A leveraged buyout (LBO) is the purchase of a company by a small group of investors using a high percentage of debt financing. Whether performed by an outside financial group or mainly by the managers or executives of the company (management buyout; MBO), an LBO results in a significant increase in the ownership of equity shares by the managers. A turnaround or improvement in performance is usually associated with the formation of an LBO.

The average performance of LBOs has been outstanding. We noted in chapter 8, in which we discussed empirical tests of M&A performance, that a sample of LBOs over the period 1985 to 1994 achieved average returns of 25% annually compared with a return of 14.3% on the S&P 500 for a comparable period (Anslinger and Copeland, 1996). Examples of financial buyers are Kohlberg, Kravis, Roberts & Company; E.M. Warburg, Pincus & Company; Thomas H. Lee Company; and Hicks, Muse, Tate & Furst. The financial buyers make acquisitions in many different industries that are unrelated to various degrees. They were described as "nonsynergistic acquisitions" by Anslinger and Copeland.

An example will illustrate how a financial buyer operates. In March 1993 Hicks, Muse, Tate & Furst purchased from DuPont for $370 million a small division that it then named Berg Electronics Inc. Hicks Muse replaced top management and bought six more related companies for $135 million. Berg moved from the seventh ranked electrical supplier in 1993 to number 4 by 1995, during which time earnings doubled to $113 million. In March 1996 Hicks Muse was able to make a public offering of Berg at $21 per share. By midyear it traded at $25 compared to the original purchase price of $4.11 per share paid by Hicks Muse.

The financial groups that have been major players in the LBO market represent a significant new form of business organization. They have played a major role in the restructuring of corporate America. We analyze their characteristics and performance in this chapter.

CHARACTERISTICS OF LEVERAGED BUYOUTS

Leveraged buyout activity reached its peak during the years 1986 to 1989. The largest was RJR Nabisco (in 1988), with a purchase price of $24.6 billion. The next largest

LBOs were the Beatrice Companies (in 1985) at $5.4 billion, the Safeway Stores (in 1986) at $4.2 billion, and the Borg Warner Corporation (in 1987) at $3.8 billion. The total purchase price of the 20 largest LBOs formed between 1983 and 1995 was $76.5 billion (*Mergerstat Review*, 1996, p. 43).

Incumbent management is usually included in the buying group. Sometimes an entire company is acquired. Sometimes only a segment, a division, or a subsidiary of a public corporation is acquired from the parent company. These are usually of relatively smaller size and key executives perform such an important role that these going-private transactions are called unit management buyouts (MBOs). Notable examples of unit management buyouts announced in 1995 include the Merck & Co. sale to a management group of its Medco Behavioral Care Corporation at a purchase price of $340 million. Another example is the sale by Torchmark Corporation of a unit involved in energy asset management (Torch Energy Advisors Inc.) for $115 million (*Mergerstat Review*, 1996, p. 34).

Especially when financial groups such as venture capital companies or other types of buyout specialists are involved, the LBO transaction is expected to be reversed with a public offering. The aim is to increase the profitability of the company taken private and thereby increase market value. The buyout firm seeks to harvest its gains within a three- to five-year period of time.

THREE MAJOR STAGES OF LEVERAGED BUYOUTS

Leveraged buyout activity may be placed into three distinct time periods: the 1980s, the early 1990s, and post-1992. Leveraged buyouts did not begin with the 1980s; they actually have a long history. Before 1980 they were often referred to as bootstrap transactions characterized by highly leveraged deals. During the 1980s the economic and financial environments that stimulated M&A activity were also fertile environments for LBOs.

Economic and legislative changes as well as some unsound patterns in LBO transactions of the late 1980s resulted in a correction period. From a peak of a total of $65.7 billion of LBO transactions in 1989, the volume declined to $7 billion in 1991. New developments in the nature of LBO transactions and market participants led to a revival in LBO transactions to a level of $62 billion in 1999.

The percentage relationships underscore the changing relative importance of LBOs, as shown in Table 16.1. For the years 1986 to 1989, LBOs accounted for more than one-fifth of the total dollar value of completed mergers. From 1990 to 1992, LBOs dropped to less than 7% of the total dollar value of merger activity. For the years 1996–1999, LBOs represented only 4.0% of total M&A activity. LBOs continue to perform an important role in improving the utilization of corporate resources. The rising absolute dollar amounts of LBO activity are consistent with the material we present later in the chapter that describes the well-articulated business logic of LBO transactions.

Table 16.2 sets forth the relative premiums paid during the three different time periods. For all acquisitions, the mean or median premium did not change greatly. However, the mean and median premium were substantially lower for LBOs in all three periods. The decline in the premiums paid in LBOs was relatively sharp during 1990 to 1992, but for 1993 to 1998, the premiums paid in LBOs were only slightly below the 1986 to 1989 levels.

Table 16.1   Value of LBO Transactions

Year	($ Billions)		
	Value of Total Completed Mergers	**Leveraged Buyouts**	**% of Total Mergers**
1982	60.7	3.5	5.8%
1983	52.7	4.5	8.5%
1984	126.1	18.7	14.8%
1985	145.5	19.7	13.5%
1986	204.9	45.2	22.1%
1987	178.3	36.2	20.3%
1988	238.5	47.0	19.7%
1989	323.9	65.7	20.3%
1990	207.5	15.2	7.3%
1991	141.2	7.0	5.0%
1992	124.9	9.6	7.7%
1993	178.2	11.0	6.2%
1994	276.9	13.0	4.7%
1995	384.8	20.9	5.4%
1996	560.2	29.0	5.2%
1997	768.9	28.7	3.7%
1998	1,323.3	41.0	3.1%
1999	1,393.9	62.0	4.4%
Yearly Averages			
1982–1985	96.3	11.6	12.1%
1986–1989	236.4	48.5	20.5%
1990–1992	157.9	10.6	6.7%
1993–1995	280.0	15.0	5.3%
1996–1999	1,011.6	40.2	4.0%

Source: *Mergers & Acquisitions,* almanac issues.

Table 16.2   Relative Premium Offered

Period	All Acquisitions		LBOs	
	Mean Premium	**Median Premium**	**Mean Premium**	**Median Premium**
1986–1989	39.9%	30.2%	33.9%	26.5%
1990–1992	39.4%	32.0%	27.6%	19.9%
1993–1998	39.7%	30.4%	33.5%	24.2%

Source: *Mergerstat Review,* 1999.

Table 16.3 Relative P/E Ratios

Period	S&P 500 Mean P/E	LBOs Mean P/E	LBOs Median P/E
1986–1989	15.3	20.5	17.8
1990–1992	19.3	14.6	12.3
1993–1998	21.4	23.8	18.8

Source: *Mergerstat Review*, 1999.

In Table 16.3, it is clear that both the mean and median price earnings ratios reflected in the purchase price of the LBOs established dropped sharply in the 1990 to 1992 period compared with 1986 to 1989. Price earnings ratios (P/Es) paid in 1986 to 1989 appeared to be higher for the LBO transactions than for the benchmark S&P 500 during the period. The P/Es in the LBO transactions in 1990 to 1992, however, were much lower than in the benchmark S&P 500 for the period.

For 1993 to 1998, the P/E ratio of the S&P 500 had risen to 21.4. For LBOs the mean P/E ratio rose even higher. However, the median LBO P/E ratio was only slightly higher than during 1986 to 1989. This indicates that a few high P/E ratio transactions during the 1993 to 1998 time period increased the arithmetic average.

It is clear from the foregoing data that distinct differences can be discerned in the LBOs of the three periods. Accordingly, we first describe the basic pattern of LBO and MBO activity during the 1980s. We next describe the factors that caused LBO activity to drop sharply in the early 1990s. The final section of the chapter describes the new developments associated with the revival of leveraged buyouts after 1992.

LBOS IN THE 1980S

In the traditional LBOs of the 1980s, debt financing typically represented more than 50% of the purchase price. Debt was secured by the assets of the acquired firm or based on the expected future cash flows. The cash flows were typically measured by earnings before depreciation and amortization, before interest and taxes (EBITDA, also called EBDIT). Debt was scheduled to be paid off either from the sale of assets or from future cash flows generated by operations. Following completion of the buyout, the acquired company became a privately held corporation. It was expected that the firm would go public again after a period of three to five years at a gain. Before developing in some detail the financial patterns in an illustrative LBO, we first discuss the general economic and financial factors that stimulated the LBOs in the 1980s.

General Economic and Financial Factors

In substantial measure the increase in the number and dollar volume of mergers and restructuring activities in the 1980s reflected underlying forces in the economic and financial environments. The same general forces that produced mergers and restructuring appear also to have stimulated increased use of leveraged buyouts and management buyouts. Indeed, sometimes an LBO or MBO is a defensive measure against an unwanted takeover. On the other hand, sometimes the announcement of a going-private plan, an LBO, or an MBO will stimulate competing bids by outsiders. Thus, there are interactions between takeover activity and LBO activity. We briefly summarize here materials on the factors that stimulated M&A and LBO activity in the 1980s.

One fundamental influence was the period of sustained economic growth between 1982 and 1990. A new peak in all categories of M&A activity was reached in this period of sustained business expansion, as all previous major merger waves were also observed in periods of expansionary environments. Total M&A transactions, divestitures, and leveraged buyouts of public companies and divisions all followed similar patterns in the 1980s; total M&A transactions and divestitures peaked in 1986 in terms of the number of transactions, while leveraged buyouts peaked in 1988 (*Mergerstat Review*, 1996).

Another pervasive influence was (somewhat unanticipated) persistent inflation, which began to accelerate in the late 1960s and continued through 1982. The gross national product implicit price deflator during the period 1968 to 1982 increased by no less than 5%. Measured by the Consumer Price Index on all items, double-digit inflation or very close to that level was experienced in six out of the 14 years. The persistence of a relatively high level of inflation had a number of consequences. One was to cause the q-ratio to decline sharply. The q-ratio is the ratio of the market value of a firm to the replacement cost of its assets. When this ratio is less than 1 it is cheaper to buy capacity in the financial markets than in the real asset markets. The q-ratio moved from a peak of 1.3 in 1965 to a low of 0.52 in 1981. It began to rise in 1982 with the rise in stock prices after mid-1982. When the q-ratio was as low as 0.52 in 1981 this meant that a firm could be purchased in the financial markets at almost half of what it would cost to replace the firm's assets in brick and mortar and inventories. This undoubtedly motivated some takeovers, although takeovers can also be stimulated by the value creation reflected in high q-ratios.

In addition, the persistent inflation provided opportunities to realize tax savings through recapitalization. Because coupon payments on existing debt were not adjusted for inflation, real debt obligations declined with rising price levels. Thus the real levels of debt-to-equity ratios declined over the period of persistent but largely unanticipated inflation. Thus, opportunities existed for greater interest tax shields by releveraging business firms. On the other hand, increased free cash flows reflecting inflation and fixed interest payments (on old debt) may have allowed managers to increase self-aggrandizing but unprofitable expenditures, as suggested by Jensen (1986). For these reasons, firms that lagged in increasing leverage became inviting targets to outsiders who were ready, willing, and able to bring about the restructuring (Shleifer and Vishny, 1988). This in turn stimulated new forms of debt financing such as the use of high yield bonds in the innovative financial markets. Developments in the financial markets were further stimulated by a succession of laws that deregulated financial institutions.

Other legislative factors also played a role. New tax laws stimulated restructuring and takeover activity. In particular, the Economic Recovery Tax Act (ERTA) enacted in 1981 permitted old assets to be stepped up on purchase. These newly established high values could then be depreciated on an accelerated basis. In the period of high inflation, the nominal value of corporate assets was increased above their historical cost, enabling a large step-up in basis. Depreciation recapture was relatively small. Also under the General Utilities doctrine, the sales of assets in the liquidation process (actual or under technical legal terms) were not subject to capital gains taxes at the corporate level. (The General Utilities doctrine was repealed in the 1986 tax reform.)

Another legislative change that encouraged MBOs involved employee stock ownership plans (ESOPs). Although these had been around for some years, the 1981 ERTA increased the ability of ESOPs to borrow from a bank to invest the funds in the firm's shares. The firm was able to treat as a deductible expense for tax purposes contributions to the ESOP sufficient to cover both the interest and the principal payments on the loan. In addition, in 1984 a further tax law change permitted banks to deduct half of their interest income on loans to ESOPs. This enabled the banks to make loans to ESOPs on relatively more favorable terms. This loan interest exclusion provision was repealed in 1996.

A new antitrust climate began in 1980. New appointees to the Federal Trade Commission and to the Department of Justice made it clear through public speeches and agency actions that the stringent prohibitions against horizontal and vertical mergers would no longer be supported. Efficiency considerations and a "new economic realism" were substituted for the older structural view that held that the effects on competition could be judged by market concentration ratios. At least three competing explanations for the change in the antitrust regulatory environment have been proffered. First, the new administration had different political views. Second, the culmination of more than a decade of new empirical research from the academic community provided support for a dynamic competition view of the interactions among large firms. Third, most significant U.S. industries had become subject to intense competition from foreign firms. Thus, competitive pressures provided the stimulus for restructuring, and the recognition of these pressures was the basis for changed public opinion and regulatory policy toward mergers, takeovers, and restructuring.

It was these forces that increased merger activity and restructuring in a wide range of forms. LBOs and MBOs were part of this general pattern. Sometimes LBOs and MBOs were responses to the increased threat of takeover, and their announcements often stimulated rival offers by outsiders.

Illustration of an LBO

A simplified example illustrates the nature of a leveraged buyout transaction during the 1980s. Wavell Corporation, a successful, publicly traded manufacturer of glassware, was purchased in the 1970s by Eastern Pacific (EP), a large conglomerate that during this period seemed bent on buying everything in sight. Eventually, however, Eastern Pacific began to focus its interests predominantly in the transportation, communications, and real estate industries. Wavell did not fit into the EP mold and languished for a number of years. In 1983, when a small group of disgruntled Wavell executives began to consider the possibility of a leveraged buyout, EP was more than willing to consider divestiture; Wavell's growth rates did not meet EP's objectives, and EP had never been comfortable with Wavell's product line. Although the glassware industry was not growing rapidly, there was a steady demand for Wavell's product. The company had very stable production costs and good contribution margins, which consistently resulted in a strong steady cash flow. The production equipment was old but in good condition, and its replacement cost far exceeded its book value. Up until the EP acquisition, Wavell had always been managed well, if conservatively, and had little debt.

Wavell's current sales were $7,000,000 with EBIT of $650,000 and net income of $400,000. Negotiations between Wavell management and EP settled on a purchase price of $2,000,000. Because of the high replacement cost of Wavell's assets, its strong cash flow, and its relatively unencumbered balance sheet, Wavell was able to take on a large amount of debt. Banks supplied $1,200,000 of senior debt at an interest rate of 13%; this debt was secured by the finished goods inventory and by net property, plant, and equipment and was to be amortized over a five-year period. An insurance company loan of $600,000 was also arranged in the form of subordinated debt, likewise to be amortized over a five-year period. The insurance company also took an equity position worth $100,000; Wavell was expected to repurchase this equity interest after five years for an amount that would provide the insurance company with a 40% annual yield. Finally, the Wavell management team put up $100,000 as their own equity position.

The following calculations illustrate the cash flow patterns that might be expected following the LBO. First, amortization tables are provided for the bank and insurance company loans:

Bank Loan*

Year	Interest	Principal	Balance
1	156,000	185,177	1,014,823
2	131,927	209,250	805,573
3	104,724	236,453	569,120
4	73,986	267,191	301,929
5	39,248	301,929	—

*$1,200,000 at 13%; annual payment = $341,177.

Insurance Company Loan*

Year	Interest	Principal	Balance
1	96,000	87,245	512,755
2	82,041	101,204	411,551
3	65,848	117,397	294,154
4	47,065	136,180	157,974
5	25,271	157,974	—

*$600,000 at 16%; annual payment = $183,245.

The following pro forma cash flow calculations are made on the basis of a number of conservative assumptions. First, no growth is assumed. The tax rate is assumed to be 40%. Depreciation is calculated on a straight-line basis over a period of 16.67 years (or 6%); accelerated depreciation would clearly enhance cash flows. Furthermore, it is unlikely that debt levels would decline to zero. As the original debt was repaid, it is likely that Wavell would take on additional debt, perhaps long-term debt, to augment the declining interest tax shelter.

Pro Forma Cash Flows

	Year 0	Year 1	Year 2	Year 3	Year 4	Year 5
EBIT	$650,000	$ 650,000	$ 650,000	$ 650,000	$ 650,000	$ 650,000
− Interest		252,000	213,968	170,572	121,051	64,519
EBT		398,000	436,032	479,428	528,949	585,481
− Taxes		159,200	174,413	191,771	211,580	234,192
NI		238,800	261,619	287,657	317,369	351,289
− Depreciation		120,000	120,000	120,000	120,000	120,000
CFBDR*		358,800	381,619	407,657	437,369	471,289
− Principal repaid		272,422	310,454	353,850	403,371	459,903
Cash flow cushion		86,378	71,165	53,807	33,998	11,386
Equity	200,000	438,800	700,419	988,076	1,305,445	1,656,734
Debt	1,800,000	1,527,578	1,217,124	863,274	459,903	—
Total assets	2,000,000	$1,966,378	$1,917,543	$1,851,350	$1,765,348	$1,656,734
% Debt	90%	78%	63%	47%	26%	0%

*CFBDR: Cash flow before debt repayment.

If we now assume that Wavell is sold at the end of year 5 for book value (again a very conservative assumption given the track record in the pro forma cash flows), we can calculate the annual compounded rate of return on equity as follows:

$$ROE = \left(\frac{1,656,734}{200,000}\right)^{1/5} - 1 = 53\% \text{ annual compounded rate of return}$$

Since Wavell is required to pay only 40% annually on the insurance company's equity interest, a payment of $537,824 would be sufficient to repurchase this equity. This would leave $1,118,910 for the management group, or an annual return of over 62% on their investment.

Elements of a Typical LBO Operation

The preceding analysis was a simplified example of an LBO operation. If we abstract from this example and many more real-world LBOs, the following picture emerges. The first stage of the operation consists of raising the cash required for the buyout and devising a management incentive system. Typically, about 10% of the cash is put up by the investor group headed by the company's top managers and/or buyout specialists. This becomes the equity base of the new firm. Outside investors provide the remainder of the equity. The managers also receive stock price–based incentive compensation in the form of stock options or warrants. Thus, the equity share of management (not including directors) will grow to a higher percentage, possibly to more than 30%. Frequently, managers are also provided with incentive compensation plans based on measures such as increases in share price values.

About 50% to 60% of the required cash is raised by borrowing against the company's assets in secured bank acquisition loans. The bank loan may be syndicated with several commercial banks. This portion of the debt can also be provided by an insurance company or limited partnership specializing in venture capital investments and leveraged buyouts. The rest of the cash is obtained by issuing senior and junior subordinated debt in a private placement (with pension funds, insurance companies, venture capital firms, and so on) or public offering as "high yield" notes or bonds (that is, junk bonds). Subordinated debt is often referred to as "mezzanine money" and may carry payment-in-kind provisions. If adverse surprises result in the inability to meet interest obligations on portions of mezzanine financing, the debt holders receive more of the same paper in lieu of cash interest payments.

In the second stage of the operation, the organizing sponsor group buys all the outstanding shares of the company and takes it private (in the stock purchase format) or purchases all the assets of the company (in the asset purchase format). In the latter case, the buying group forms a new, privately held corporation. To reduce the debt by paying off part of the bank loan, the new owners sell off some parts of the acquired firm.

In the third stage, the management strives to increase profits and cash flows by cutting operating costs and changing marketing strategies. It will consolidate or reorganize production facilities; improve inventory control and accounts receivables management; improve product quality, product mix, customer service, and pricing; trim employment; and try to extract better terms from suppliers. It may even lay off employees and cut spending on research and new plants and equipment as long as these are necessary to meet payment on the swollen debt. (However, in reviewing business plans, lenders would require that provisions for capital expenditures be adequate.)

In the fourth stage, the investor group may take the company public again if the "leaner and meaner" company emerges stronger and the goals of the group are achieved. This reverse LBO is effected through a public equity offering, referred to as a secondary initial public offering (SIPO). One purpose of this reconversion to public ownership is to create liquidity for existing stockholders. Aside from this, a study of 72 firms engaging in reverse LBOs over the period 1976 to 1987 reveals that 86% of the firms intended to use the SIPO proceeds to lower the company's leverage (Muscarella and Vetsuypens, 1990). Only eight out of 72 firms raised the funds for capital expenditures. The reverse LBOs are undertaken mostly by ex post successful LBO companies, and indeed the equity participants at the time of the LBO realized a median return of 1,965.6% on their equity investment, or a median annualized rate of return of 268.4% by the time of the SIPO. (The median length of time between the LBO and the SIPO was 29 months.)

Conditions and Circumstances of Going-Private Buyouts in the 1980s

For LBOs of the 1980s, typical targets included manufacturing firms in basic, nonregulated industries with at least predictable and/or low financing (capital expenditure) requirements. Stability and predictability of earnings were essential in the face of substantial interest payments and loan amortization. The financing needs of very high growth firms might put a strain on debt service capability. High tech firms were considered less appropriate because they generally have a shorter history of demonstrated profitability as well as greater business risk; they generally have fewer leveragable assets. Furthermore, they command high P/E multiples well above book value because of future growth opportunities.

These generalizations are supported by the empirical data developed by Lehn and Poulsen (1988), who studied a sample of 108 leveraged buyouts during the period 1980 to 1984. Almost half of the firms were in five industries: retailing, textiles, food processing, apparel, and bottled and canned soft drinks. Note that these are all consumer nondurable goods industries for which the income elasticity of demand would be relatively low. Hence, these industries would be least subject to fluctuations in sales as the level of gross national product fluctuated. Note also that all of these are mature industries with limited growth opportunities.

The success of an LBO in the 1980s was enhanced by a track record of capable management. The company should have a strong market position in its industry to enable it to withstand economic fluctuations and competitors' assaults. The balance sheet should be highly liquid; it should show a large, relatively unencumbered asset base for use as collateral, in particular a high proportion of tangible assets whose fair market value exceeds net book value.

The transaction required sufficient leverage to maximize return on equity but not so much as to drain funds needed to sustain growth. Lenders were attracted by interest rates three to five percentage points above the prime rate and by the characteristics of the company and its collateral. Borrowing capacity was favorably affected by large amounts of cash or cash equivalents, and undervalued assets (hidden equity) whose market value exceeded depreciated book value. Lenders may also look to subsidiaries of the LBO candidate whose liquidation would not impact ongoing operations. In addition, lenders such as venture capital and insurance companies, which also take an equity interest in the LBO, look to the high rate of return they expect on their equity participation. Last, but by no means least, lenders must have confidence in the management group spearheading the LBO, whether incumbent or external. The managers involved typically have a proven record as highly capable executives. They are betting their reputations on the success of the venture and are highly motivated by the potential for large personal wealth gains that might not be achievable in larger public corporations.

Among the sources of MBO targets are divestitures of unwanted divisions by public companies, privately owned businesses whose current growth rate is insufficient to provide opportunities for capable management or to attract corporate acquirers, and public companies whose shares are selling at low earnings multiples representing a substantial discount from book value.

Empirical Results of Going Private in the 1980s

The earliest comprehensive study of going-private transactions was by DeAngelo, DeAngelo, and Rice (1984). Their sample consisted of 72 firms that made 72 initial and nine subsequent (revived) going-private proposals during the period 1973 to 1980. The median market value of total equity was about $6 million for the sample of 45 pure going-private proposals (that is, without third-party equity participation in the private firm) and somewhat over $15 million for 23 leveraged buyout proposals. Thus, the firms were relatively small. In addition, management held a relatively large ownership position. In 72 going-private proposals, management's mean preoffer ownership fraction was 45%, with a median measure of 51%. For the 23 LBOs with third-party participation, the mean and median were 32% and 33%, respectively.

DeAngelo, DeAngelo, and Rice found that the average change in stockholder wealth at announcement was a positive 22%, which was highly significant from a statistical standpoint. The cumulative increase in stockholder wealth over the 40 days including the announcement date was over 30%. They note that public stockholder gains measured as the average premium above market (two months before the proposal) were over 56% in 57 sample proposals involving all payment in cash.

DeAngelo, DeAngelo, and Rice also tested for the effects of the announcement of a going-private withdrawal. Their sample was 18 firms for the period 1973 to 1980. The announcement effect was a negative change in stockholder wealth of almost 9%. However, since the cumulative prediction error for the 40 days up to the announcement date was almost 13%, the cumulative prediction error for the 40 days through the announcement date was +4%. During the subsequent 40 days the cumulative prediction error rose to about 8%. They note three potential explanations for the positive returns net of both proposal and withdrawal announcement effects. First, an information effect causes a permanent upward revaluation of the firm's prospects. Second, a positive probability may remain that managers will revive the going-private proposal at a future date. Third, the positive return may reflect the possibility that another party will offer to acquire the firm.

The Lehn and Poulsen study (1989) covered 284 going-private transactions for the period 1980 to 1987. The mean equity value for the Lehn and Poulsen sample was $191 million. The size of going-private transactions increased significantly during the period covered. In a separate study, Lehn and Poulsen (1988) reported that the average pre-LBO debt-to-equity ratio for a sample of 58 firms was about 46%. For the post-LBO period, the average debt-to-equity ratio rose to over 552%. Thus, substantial increases in leverage took place.

Lehn and Poulsen (1988) found that the average net-of-market stock price reaction to the announcement for 92 leveraged buyouts was slightly over 20%, measured over a period of 20 days before the announcement to 20 days after the announcement. The result was highly significant from a statistical standpoint. The average value of the premium paid in the LBO offer compared to the market price of the firm's common stock 20 trading days prior to the announcement was 41%, calculated for the 72 leveraged buyouts in the sample that were all cash offers. These results are somewhat lower than those found by DeAngelo, DeAngelo, and Rice. The Lehn and Poulsen sample represented larger firms for a later period. Also the Lehn and Poulsen study covered LBOs during 1980 to 1984, when the takeover and restructuring market was much more active. In addition, they measured the premium from a reference point 20 days prior to the announcement, whereas DeAngelo, DeAngelo, and Rice measured the premium from a reference point two months before the announcement.

Another empirical study was performed by Lowenstein (1985). His sample was 28 management buyout proposals made from 1979 to 1984; each was worth at least $100 million to the shareholders at the winning bid price. The percentage of shares owned by management for the Lowenstein sample was much smaller than for the

DeAngelo, DeAngelo, and Rice sample. It was only 3.8% when measured by the median and 6.5% measured by the mean. In 15 new companies formed as the result of going private, management shares increased to 10.4% measured by the median and to 24.3% measured by the mean.

Lowenstein also measured the premium of the winning bid over the market price 30 days before the first significant announcement. He found that on all bids the premium was 58% measured by the median and 56% measured by the mean. However, the size of the premium was higher the greater the number of bids involved in the going-private transactions. When three or more bids were received, the premium rose to 76% when measured by the median and 69% when measured by the mean. The premium of 11 successful third-party bids over the management bid was 8% (median) and 14% (mean). Lowenstein argued strongly for the creation of an auction that would ensure that multiple bids would be received. He acknowledged difficulties in implementing such a proposal. In addition, we would observe that the relatively small percentage increase in third-party bids over the management bids casts doubt on the need for such a proposal. Furthermore, the Lowenstein findings corroborate those of DeAngelo, DeAngelo, and Rice in observing premiums for public stockholders of 50% or more over their market price a month or two before the announcement. This would appear to be a very substantial reward to public shareholders. If they left nothing "on the table" for the entrepreneurs involved in the LBO activity, it would leave little incentive for the transactions to take place. The subsequent losses to the public shareholders would be much greater than the relatively small kicking up of the bid when third-party offers are involved. Besides, market competition ensures that if the entrepreneurs are taking too much, this will stimulate other nonmanagement outside offers. But in any event it is difficult to feel that a great injustice is done to the public shareholders or the subsequent minority shareholders, because they have received premiums exceeding 50%.

Later studies also found large premiums and abnormal announcement returns to prebuyout shareholders (Kaplan, 1989a; Muscarella and Vetsuypens 1990; Travlos and Cornett, 1993).

For divisional management buyouts, Hite and Vetsuypens (1989) found small but statistically significant wealth gains to parent company shareholders. The mean abnormal return during the two-day period surrounding the buyout announcement was 0.55% for their sample of 151 unit MBOs. Because the mean sale price of the divisions represented only 16.6% of the market value of equity of an average seller, the abnormal return would translate into 3.3% for a full LBO, which is much lower than the gains found for LBOs above. Hite and Vetsuypens suggest that divisional buyouts reallocate ownership of corporate assets to higher valued uses and that parent company shareholders share in the expected benefits of this change in ownership structure. For a sample of 45 divisional buyouts that subsequently went public (after an average period of 34 months), Muscarella and Vetsuypens (1990) reported a mean abnormal return of 1.98% to the seller in the two days (-1 and 0) around the announcement.

Harlow and Howe (1993) found that there was little insider trading before third-party LBOs. However, they found evidence that insider trading prior to management LBOs was associated with private managerial information. But the net buying by insiders resulted from decreased levels of insider sales of stock rather than from increased levels of purchases. In the MBO subsample, they found a positive correlation between the offer premium and the amount of abnormal net buying by insiders.

Most of the LBOs were highly leveraged transactions (HLTs). Andrade and Kaplan (1998) studied a sample of 136 HLTs completed between 1980 and 1989 that subsequently became distressed. As of December 1995, 31 of the 136 had defaulted, and an additional eight attempted to restructure debt because of problems in meeting debt payments. Of these 39 financially distressed firms, data were available on 31. The median EBITDA-to-interest expense ratio pre-HLT was 7.95. Post-HLT the median had dropped to 1.16, indicating that for over half of the sample the debt coverage was precarious.

All of the sample firms had positive operating margins in the distressed years, typically exceeding their industry median. So the firms were financially distressed but not economically distressed. Surprisingly, the sample firms experienced a small increase in value from pretransaction to distress resolution. The implication is that the HLTs overall earn significantly positive market adjusted returns. Thus, for this HLT sample, despite financial distress, performance was positive.

Another study looked at 41 leveraged buyout firms that made 134 divestments in response to financial distress (Easterwood, 1998). Most of the LBOs were formed during the years 1984 to 1988. The common stock in the companies was privately owned. Bond returns for their publicly traded debt were used to measure the wealth effects of the divestment announcement. The divestments on average are not associated with significant wealth effects for the total sample of firms. Firms that suffered financial distress experienced significant negative abnormal returns associated with the divestments. Firms that were not distressed experienced positive bond returns when the asset sales were announced.

Sources of Gains

The empirical evidence is consistent among studies in finding that the premiums paid are 40% or more of the market price of the stock a month or two before the announcement of the buyout. The standard residual analysis shows that these gains are substantially sustained in stock price performance after the completion of the change in ownership control. What are the sources of these large gains? A number of explanations have been offered: (1) taxes, (2) management incentives, (3) wealth transfer effects, (4) asymmetrical information and underpricing, and (5) efficiency considerations. Each is considered in turn.

Tax Benefits

The tax benefits are clearly there. The question is whether they are the only factor, the major factor, or simply a facilitating factor added to more fundamental business and economic forces. It is difficult to quantify the degree. Some students of the subject ascribe a major role to taxes. Lowenstein (1985), for example, argued that most of the premium paid is financed from tax savings. He stated that the new company can expect to operate tax-free for as long as five to six years. Of course, an LBO is often sold after about this period of time when its debt-to-equity ratio has been pulled down from about 10 to 1 or under.

The sources of the tax gain are standard and have been detailed in previous pages. They include the following. The high leverage provides the benefits of interest savings. Asset step-ups can provide higher asset values for depreciation expenses. This tax advantage became much more difficult under the Tax Reform Act of 1986. The accelerated depreciation provisions of the 1981 ERTA had enhanced this benefit. Lowenstein (1985, p. 760) pointed out that the extent of write-up of assets depended in part on the ability to assign larger value to items for which there is little recapture (inventory, film libraries, mineral resources, or real estate) than to items for which recapture may be substantial (equipment).

Tax benefits were further augmented by the Tax Reform Act of 1984, which broadened the benefits of the use of ESOPs. The ESOP purchases the shares using borrowed funds. The borrowings are secured by the employer's schedule of contributions to the fund. Both the interest and principal on the ESOP are deductible, and the lender could exclude one-half of the interest income from taxable income. These are substantial benefits indeed. These changes increased the use of ESOPs in management buyouts, representing tangible evidence that this particular tax factor was of importance. However, Kaplan (1989a) suggested that ESOP loans are infrequently used due to nontax costs. One such cost pointed out by Kaplan is that all contributing employees share in the equity, which will not leave an adequate equity stake to the managers and the buyout promoter.

Kaplan (1989b) also provided empirical evidence on the potential value of tax benefits. Although it is not difficult to estimate current tax savings on new buyout debt, valuation of these savings flows is dependent on, among other factors, whether the debt is permanent and the appropriate marginal tax rate applied to the interest deduction. Further, there is the argument that the interest rate on corporate debt is higher to compensate for higher personal taxation on interest income than on equity income, and thus the use of debt to obtain tax savings may have no value. When Kaplan assumed a marginal tax rate of 46% and permanent new debt, interest deductions were worth a median 1.297 times the premium. A 30% tax rate and a maturity of eight years for new debt implied a median value equal to 0.262 times the premium. In Kaplan's sample of 76 companies, 33 were known to have elected to step up the basis of their assets, and the median value was estimated at 0.304 times the premium.

These tax benefits appear large, but Kaplan argued that they are predictable and thus appropriable by the prebuyout shareholders. However, Kaplan found that only a portion of the tax benefits could be attributed to unused debt capacity or the inefficient use of tax benefits prior to buyout. This implies that a large portion of the tax benefits were the result of buyout and that the buyout structure may be necessary to realize those benefits. It turns out that the buyout companies eliminated their federal taxes in the first two years after the buyout.

In regression analyses, the excess return to prebuyout shareholders is significantly related to the potential tax benefits generated by the buyout, but the excess return to postbuyout shareholders is not. Kaplan interpreted this result as indicating that prebuyout shareholders capture most of the tax benefits. The premium paid to prebuyout shareholders is also found to be positively related to the pre-LBO tax liability-to-equity ratio by Lehn and Poulsen (1988). This is interpreted as evidence that tax benefits play a significant role in LBOs.

The preceding findings on strong tax benefits are at odds with the regression result of Travlos and Cornett (1993) that capital structure change-induced effects fail to explain the abnormal returns experienced at the announcement of buyouts. One reason for this result might be that both the dependent and independent variables only partly capture the full effects that they are supposed to measure. Travlos and Cornett (1993) defend their results by stating that increased leverage serves no long-term purpose but rather "functions primarily as a part of the mechanism to take the company private." The temporary nature of at least some portion of the new debt was also shown by Muscarella and Vetsuypens (1990). Their sample of 72 reverse LBO firms had an average debt-to-total value ratio of over 0.90 at the time of the LBO, and average debt-to-total asset ratios of 0.78 prior to the SIPO and 0.60 after the SIPO.

The preceding results indicate that tax factors can improve a deal but come into play only if some underlying positive business factors are also operating. This is where other factors come into consideration.

Management Incentives and Agency Cost Effects

It is argued that management's ownership stake is enhanced by the LBO or MBO so that their incentives are stronger for improved performance. Some profitable investment proposals call for disproportionate efforts on the part of managers, so they will be undertaken only if managers are given a correspondingly disproportionate share of the proposal's income (Easterbrook and Fischel, 1982). However, such managerial compensation contracts might be viewed as "overly generous" by outside shareholders. In this case, going-private buyouts facilitate compensation arrangements that induce managers to undertake those proposals (DeAngelo, DeAngelo, and Rice, 1984; Travlos and Cornett, 1993). This reasoning is similar to the argument that the threat of a hostile takeover decreases incentives for managers and employees to invest in firm-specific human capital (DeAngelo and DeAngelo, 1987, p. 107). Going-private buyouts can guarantee compensation for those investments.

When information on managerial performance is costly, incumbent management can be mistakenly replaced. Managers waste resources to defend their position to potential proxy contestants and to outside shareholders. They may undertake projects that are less profitable but have payoffs more easily observed by outsiders (DeAngelo and DeAngelo, 1985). Going private may eliminate these costs. In many buyouts, the promoters retain a large equity stake and serve on the board. Their equity stake and their desire to protect their reputation as efficient promoters give them the incentive to closely monitor postbuyout management. This will decrease the information asymmetry between the managers and shareholders. In this view, the concentrated ownership resulting from an LBO represents reunification of ownership and control, which must reduce agency costs.

Finally, free cash flows motivate managers to use them in self-aggrandizing expenditures rather than to pay them out as dividends. Increasing debt through leveraged buyouts commits the cash flows to debt payment, which is an effective substitute for dividend payment. Managers have less discretion over debt payments than over dividends. Thus, the increased debt reduces managerial discretion in the allocation of free cash flows; the agency costs of free cash flows will be decreased in LBOs (Jensen, 1986). If managers are risk-averse, the increased debt will also put pressure on them and give them an incentive to improve the firm's performance to prevent bankruptcy (because bankruptcy will cause a decline in their compensation and the value of human capital). The LBO thus represents a debt-bonding activity; it bonds (precommits) managers to meet newly set targets.

These agency cost arguments contrast with the notion that the internal controls of the firm already align managers' interests to those of the stockholders. The internal controls are compensation arrangements and settling up, stock options, bonuses based on performance, and surveillance by the board of directors. If internal controls do not take hold sufficiently, the market for corporate control and the threat of takeovers will ensure that managers operate to their full potential. However, a study by Baker, Jensen, and Murphy (1988) found that actual executive compensation contracts are insufficient to provide optimal incentives for managers and that most CEOs hold trivial fractions of their firms' stock, although stock ownership generally swamps incentives generated by compensation. The median fractional ownership of CEOs in their sample of 73 large manufacturing firms was only 0.16%, while the average was 1.2%. The CEO salary plus bonus changes by only two cents for every $1,000 change in equity value. Baker, Jensen, and Murphy ascribe the low ratio between pay and performance to pressures from other stakeholders and the public, including the media.

Roden and Lewellen (1995) analyzed capital structures of LBOs to test traditional theories of capital structure. Their sample covered 107 LBOs formed during 1981 to 1990, accounting for about two-thirds of the total dollar volume of LBO activity during that period. The postbuyout capital structure of their LBO sample resembled what they call "an inverted pyramid." At the top was senior secured debt financing by banks, representing just over 60% of total funds raised. The next layer was mezzanine financing, consisting of unsecured subordinated long-term debt securities (junk bonds), about 25%. Preferred stock was 4%, and common equity about 7%. These patterns were consistent with prior studies. Within these averages, cross-sectional variations were observed. Their econometric analysis suggested that the prospective cash flow profile of the firm greatly influenced the capital structure. They presented a balancing model of the capital structure decision process. Leverage-related benefits included the motivating and disciplining effects of debt on management and the tax shields provided by debt.

Empirical evidence consistent with the management incentive rationale is reported in other studies. First, ownership shares of management are increased substantially after MBOs. For a sample of 76 MBOs in 1980 to 1986, Kaplan (1989a) reported prebuyout and postbuyout equity ownership of management. The median prebuyout ownerships of the CEO, all managers, and all managers and directors were 1.4%, 5.88%, and 19.3%, respectively. (The corresponding mean values were 7.13%, 12.20%, and 22.89%.) The median postbuyout ownership fractions of the CEO and all managers were 6.40% and 22.63%, respectively. Thus, in terms of median values, management ownership increased by about three times the prebuyout levels. For a reverse LBO sample, Muscarella and Vetsuypens (1990) reported the before-SIPO (postbuyout) and after-SIPO management equity ownership fractions. The median before-SIPO fractions for the most highly paid officer, three most highly paid officers, and all officers and directors were 9.2%, 26.1%, and 61.6%, respectively. The management ownership remained high even after the firm went public through a SIPO. The median after-SIPO fractions were 6.5%, 18.8%, and 44.2%. Evidence on the concentration of ownership is provided by Smith (1990). The median post-MBO ownership share of all officers, outside directors, and other major holders was 95.26%. The corresponding pre-MBO ownership share was 75.45%.

The second set of evidence on management incentives was provided by Muscarella and Vetsuypens. They documented various management incentive plans in LBO firms. Almost all firms in their sample (69 out of 72) had implemented at least one type of incentive plan under private ownership, and about 75% of the sample firms had at least two separate incentive plans. Among the different types of incentive plans, stock option plans and stock appreciation rights were the most popular. The importance of incentive plans was also described in most anecdotes on individual LBOs. For example, see Anders (1988).

The third and most important item of evidence is the operating performance of LBO firms. However, it should be pointed out in advance that the following results on operating performance may be subject to a selection bias because the reverse LBO firms or firms with postbuyout data available might be only the more successful ones. Muscarella and Vetsuypens described the multiple restructuring activities under private ownership. Based on examination of the SIPO prospectuses of the firms that went public again after the LBO, they found that more than two-thirds of all firms (54 out of 72) disclosed at least one restructuring activity undertaken since the LBO. Among the activities were asset redeployment (reorganization of production facilities, divestitures, and so on); initiation of cost reduction programs; changes in marketing strategies involving product mix, product quality, and pricing; and customer service. Judging from the tone of the offering prospectuses, the authors suggested that these activities "represent a significant departure from pre-LBO strategies which would not have been implemented by the predecessor company" (p. 1390). As a result of these restructuring activities, the firms under private ownership realized substantial improvements in operating performance. In 35 cases for which data were available, total sales increased by 9.4% in real terms for the median firm between the LBO and SIPO (a median period of 29 months), and gross profits and operating profits increased 27.0% and 45.4%, respectively.

Kaplan (1989a) also provided evidence of improved operating performance following an LBO. The level of operating income in LBO firms increased more than in other firms in the same industry during the first two years after the LBO, but sales growth rates were lower. The results on operating income and sales suggested that the operating margins of LBO firms would improve relative to their industries. Statistical tests by Kaplan confirmed this proposition. One potential source of operating improvement was found to be in the area of working capital management as the inventory-to-sales ratio declined in the postbuyout years.

Similar results were obtained by Smith (1990). She found that both the profit or before-tax operating margin and the ratio of sales to operating assets or employees increased significantly relative to other firms in the same industry. Improvement in working capital management was evidenced by both a reduction in the inventory holding period and receivables collection period. There was little evidence that cutbacks in research and development, advertising, and maintenance were responsible for the increase in operating cash flows. Although the ratio of capital expenditures to sales was reduced after the MBO, this should not affect the short-run operating gains. Smith also provided regression results that suggested a positive relationship between the change in operating returns and the changes in financial leverage and percentage stockholdings by officers, outside directors, and other major stockholders. These results were consistent with the debt bonding effect, managerial incentive effect, and the improved monitoring (concentrated ownership) effect. Smith conducted various empirical analyses to provide evidence that the improved post-MBO performance was not attributable to the sample selection procedures in her study. Overall, the results did not tend to indicate selection bias. Smith also considered whether favorable inside information on future cash flows explained the observed increase in operating returns associated with MBOs and provided indirect evidence that the improved performance did not reflect the realization of gains privately anticipated by the buyout group.

Travlos and Cornett (1993) found a statistically significant negative correlation between the abnormal return to prebuyout shareholders and the P/E ratio of the firm relative to its industry. They interpreted this result as being consistent with the joint hypothesis that the more severe the agency problems of the going-private firms, the lower their P/E ratios; and that the lower this ratio, the greater the room for improvement and thus the greater the efficiency gains to be obtained by taking the firm private. But this interpretation may not be correct, because a low P/E ratio may simply mean lower growth opportunities. The Jensen hypothesis predicted that the LBO firms were mature firms with limited growth opportunities.

The theory of agency costs involving free cash flow also has empirical support. Lehn and Poulsen (1989) posit that a direct relationship between measures of cash flows and premiums paid to prebuyout shareholders was consistent with Jensen's hypothesis. Their data for 149 LBOs in the 1984 to 1987 period showed highly significant direct relationships between the undistributed cash flow-to-equity value ratio and the premium paid even after controlling for the effects of tax savings (by using the tax-to-equity variable). The likelihood of going private was also directly related to the cash flow-to-equity value ratio in their data for LBOs and matched control firms. Further evidence that appeared consistent with the free cash flow argument of Jensen included the findings that most LBOs took place in mature industries and that the growth rates and capital expenditures of LBO firms (without controlling for divestitures after the buyout) were lower than those of their industry control sample in both the pre- and postbuyout periods (Kaplan, 1989a; Lehn and Poulsen, 1989).

However, one potential difficulty of the free cash flow argument is that it does not directly predict the strengthened incentive compensation schemes after the buyout, which are evidenced in the study by Muscarella and Vetsuypens. They also found an elasticity of compensation (defined as salary plus bonus) to sales of 0.46 for the most highly paid officer in their sample, whereas Murphy (1985) reported that the typical elasticity appeared to be about 0.3. But it may be the case that going private enabled the firm to institute more incentive compensation plans, which may not be possible for public firms due to the political process (Baker, Jensen, and Murphy, 1988). Holthausen and Larcker (1996) argued that the performance and equity ownership incentive effects have not been fully demonstrated.

Wealth Transfer Effects

Critics of leveraged buyouts argue that the payment of premiums in these transactions may represent wealth transfers to shareholders from other stakeholders including bondholders, preferred stockholders, employees, and the government. Increased efficiency cannot automatically be inferred from the rise in the equity value. Because debt is increased in LBOs, at least part of the increased value can be offset by a reduction in the value of the firm's outstanding bonds and preferred stock. Many bond covenants do protect existing bondholders in the event of changes of control, debt issues, and so forth, but some do not. The newly issued debt may not be subordinated to the outstanding bonds and/or may have shorter duration than the outstanding bonds. Further, the "absolute priority rule" for a senior security may not be strictly adhered to in bankruptcy court decisions.

Empirical evidence on the change in the value of outstanding debt at the time of LBO announcement is mixed. While Lehn and Poulsen (1988) found no evidence that (nonconvertible) bondholders and preferred stockholders lose value, Travlos and Cornett reported statistically significant losses at the announcement of going-private proposals. However, the losses were small relative to the gains to the prebuyout shareholders, which implies that wealth transfer cannot be an economically significant factor in explaining the shareholder gain. Such anecdotes as the lawsuit filed against RJR Nabisco by large bondholders do suggest that bondholders can lose substantially in certain cases (Quigley, 1988, pp. 1, 5). In the Nabisco case, it was charged that its $5 billion in highly rated bonds had lost nearly 20% ($1 billion) in market value since the announcement of a management-led buyout proposal involving new borrowing of $16 billion (Greenwald, 1988, p. 69).

Warga and Welch (1993) demonstrated that the source of bond price data greatly influences the empirical results. Previous studies used exchange-based data such as the Standard & Poor's Bond Guide data. Warga and Welch used trader-quoted data from a major investment bank. They give an illustration of the role of the data source. In an earlier study, Asquith and Wizman (1990) found LBO risk-adjusted announcement bondholder returns of -3.2%. Warga and Welch found negative returns of about 7% in a set of overlapping bonds for which the Asquith and Wizman data show a -3.8% return. They note that when they "either properly aggregate returns among correlated bonds or if we exclude RJR Nabisco" the S&P data source suggests no significant loss of bondholder wealth. When they use their trader-quoted data, however, they find a risk-adjusted bondholder loss of about 6%. However, these losses in the value of debt were only 7% of the size of shareholder gains. Their conclusion is that while bondholders do suffer negative returns, their losses account for only a very small percentage of shareholder gains.

Wealth may also be transferred from current employees to the new investors in hostile takeovers (Shleifer and Summers, 1988). The hostile bidder can break implicit contracts between the firm and employees by reducing employment and lowering wages to expropriate quasi-rents accruing to their past firm-specific investments. Whether this argument can be extended to leveraged buyouts is an empirical question, although the supposed hostility against existing employees does not appear to be present in most LBOs. Management turnover in buyout firms is lower than in an average firm, although sometimes a new management team is brought in after the LBO (Muscarella and Vetsuypens, 1990). The number of employees grows more slowly in an LBO firm than in others in the same industry and sometimes even decreases, but this appears to be the result of postbuyout divestitures and more efficient use of labor (Kaplan, 1989a; Muscarella and Vetsuypens, 1990).

There is also the argument that the tax benefits in an LBO constitute a subsidy from the public and cause a loss in tax revenues of the government (Lowenstein, 1985). There is evidence that the premiums paid in LBOs are positively related to potential tax benefits at the corporate level. However, the net effect of an LBO on government tax revenues may be positive (Morrow, 1988). Shareholders pay ordinary income taxes on the capital gains realized on the sale of their stock in the LBO tender offer. Of course, these gains might be realized even without the LBO, but the shareholders could postpone the capital gains taxes to a later date or even eliminate them by bequeathing stocks in an estate. If the firm becomes stronger and goes public at a later date, which is suggested by the empirical evidence reviewed earlier, then the LBO investor group will pay capital gains taxes and the firm will pay more corporate taxes.

Asymmetrical Information and Underpricing

Large premiums paid by the buyout investors are also consistent with the argument that the managers or investors have more information on the value of the firm than the public shareholders. In this theory, a buyout proposal signals to the market that future operating income will be larger than previously expected or that the firm is less risky than perceived by the public.

A variant of this theory is that the investor group believes the new company is worth more than the purchase price and thus the prebuyout shareholders are receiving less than adequately informed shareholders would receive. This theory amounts to the claim that the MBO proposal cannot reveal much of the information and establish a competitive price for the target firm (despite the fact that a special committee of the board of directors who do not participate in the new company has to approve the proposal).

Kaplan (1989a) provided evidence that runs counter to these arguments. He found that informed persons (managers and directors) often do not participate in the buyout even though these nonparticipants typically hold large equity stakes in the buyout firm (a median share of 10% compared to 4.67% held by the management participants). Also, as indicated earlier, Smith (1990) provided indirect evidence that asymmetrical information cannot explain the improved performance of bought-out firms. For instance, MBO proposals that fail due to board/stockholder rejection, withdrawal, or a higher outside bid are not followed by any increase in operating returns among the involved firms.

Efficiency Considerations

The other arguments are related to efficiency considerations. The decision process can be more efficient under private ownership. Major new programs do not have to be justified by detailed studies and reports to the board of directors. Action can be taken more speedily, and sometimes getting a new investment program under way early is critical for its success. In addition, a public firm must publish information that may disclose vital and competitively sensitive information to rival firms. These arguments are difficult to evaluate, and empirical evidence on these has yet to appear. Stockholders' servicing costs and other related expenses do not appear to be a major factor in going private (Travlos and Cornett, 1993).

Evidence of Postbuyout Equity Value

We now turn to statistical evidence on how the investment in an LBO has fared and what has determined the rate of return. Muscarella and Vetsuypens (1990) first compared the total value of the firm at the time of the LBO (the purchase price paid plus the book value of debt assumed) to the value of the firm at the time of its SIPO (the book value of outstanding debt plus the market value of equity minus any proceeds from the SIPO used to retire existing debt). The median rate of change in firm value for the 41 companies that went public again was 89.0% for the entire period between an LBO and the subsequent SIPO. The mean rate was 169.7%. The median annualized rate of change was 36.6%.

The total shareholder wealth change was positively and statistically significantly correlated with the fraction of shares owned by officers and directors. Thus, larger shareholder gains under private ownership are associated with greater managerial stock ownership. Also, the correlation between the size-adjusted measure of salary and shareholder wealth was positive and statistically significant. This finding is consistent with the notion that well-compensated managers work harder to increase shareholder wealth. But the causality might be the reverse. The change in equity values was also associated with the improvements in accounting measures of performance. Thus, it is possible that the improved corporate performance led to both increased managerial compensation and higher equity value. Further, the improved corporate performance does not disprove that exploiting inside information alone can explain postbuyout shareholder gains.

Other interesting results were also obtained by Kaplan (1991). He first notes that returns on *leveraged* equity in a period of rising stock prices should be very large because interest payments are fixed. Thus, the really interesting comparison should be between the total return to all capital (debt and equity) invested in the buyout and the return on a stock index like the S&P 500. He found for his sample of 21 buyouts that the median excess return to postbuyout investors (both debt and equity) was 26.1% higher than the benchmark return on the S&P 500 (the length of time is not stated). He suggests that this excess return is close to the premium earned by prebuyout shareholders. This implies that the prebuyout shareholders actually share handsomely in the gains to the buyout. Because the 21 companies in the sample had publicly available valuation of their securities, the result may be subject to selection bias; that is, they may represent the more successful LBOs.

Finally, Kaplan's regression analysis shows that the excess return to postbuyout investors was significantly related to the change in operating income but not to the potential tax benefits. It is shown that the prebuyout shareholders capture most of the tax benefits that become publicly available information at the time of the LBO.

Degeorge and Zeckhauser (1993) analyzed a particular aspect of reverse LBO decisions. They found that on average reverse LBOs experienced an industry-adjusted rise in operating performance of 6.90% during the year before an initial public offering (IPO). In the year following an IPO, these same firms saw an industry-adjusted decline in operating performance of 2.59%.

Degeorge and Zeckhauser attribute the rise and fall of operating performance to information asymmetries and pure selection. More specifically, if management, and not the market, knew the expected profitability of the company, management would use this asymmetry and take the firm public only during exceptional years. Managers also have an incentive to quietly improve current performance at the expense of future profitability. The complementary theory of pure selection relies on the behavior, or perceived behavior, of IPO purchasers. Degeorge and Zeckhauser hypothesize that purchasers look at the strength of current performance and future growth. Subsequently, only strong companies have the ability to go public and experience normal mean reversion following the IPO.

Trends in operating performance do not translate into market inefficiencies. The market apparently understands the manager's incentive for performance manipulation and pure selection. Stock returns do not penalize the company for expected poor performance following the reverse LBO. In fact, reverse LBOs tend to outperform their peer group, although not significantly.

Mian and Rosenfeld (MR) (1993) also studied the long-run performance of reverse LBOs. They observe that their results were consistent with those of Muscarella and Vetsuypens (1990). They studied 85 firms that had reverse LBOs during the period 1983 to 1989. They measured stock price performance for a three-year period beginning one day after the firm went public. They found evidence of significant positive cumulative abnormal returns. They observe that this performance differed from the performance of IPOs as reported by Ritter (1991).

MR found that about 39% of their sample firms were taken over within three years after going public. The CARs using their comparable firm index for the first three years were 4.65%, 21.96%, and 21.05%. Most of the takeovers took place during the second year when the CARs were the highest. Firms that were taken over outperformed comparable investments by over 100%. For the sample of firms that were not taken over, the CAR was essentially zero. This suggests that the firms taken over had qualities attractive to the bidding firm. Mian and Rosenfeld also found that 79% of the acquired firms had gone private with an active investor. This suggests that the firm's interest in being taken over reflects the desire of the main investor to liquidate their ownership.

Holthausen and Larcker (1996) also studied the financial performance of reversed leveraged buyouts. They analyzed a sample of 90 LBOs that returned to public ownership between 1983 and 1988. They related changes in accounting performance to incentive variables. The firms outperformed their industries for the four years following the reverse LBO, with some weak evidence of a decline in accounting performance over the period. The firms increased capital expenditure subsequent to the public offering; working capital levels also increased. The authors observed that firm performance decreased with declines in levels of equity ownership by management and other insiders. They found no evidence that performance after the IPO was related to changes in leverage. The fact that capital expenditures increased after the LBO was consistent with these firms being cash constrained while they were LBOs. This would suggest that the high leverage during an LBO constrained investments but that the reduced leverage after the IPO facilitated efficient investments.

Holthausen and Larcker also found that for the firms that were still public three years after the IPO, a median decline in ownership by management insiders was 15% and by nonmanagement insiders 20%. They also found that board structure moves toward the standard patterns of non-LBO firms.

THE CORRECTION PERIOD 1991 TO 1992

We have seen from the previous materials on LBOs that the investors in the companies that were bought out received substantial premiums. The mean premiums were on the order of magnitude of 35%, similar to the premiums found in cash takeovers. The groups that formed the LBOs and MBOs, on average, made returns in excess of the S&P 500 over the holding period as private companies. Returns to shareholders in the LBOs that again went public (the SIPOs) outperformed comparable companies over a four-year period following the reverse LBO. These performance results had at least two forms of selection bias. LBOs that were able to return to the public markets were the relatively more successful ones. In addition, most published empirical studies to date cover LBOs formed mostly during the early part of the 1980s. LBOs formed in the latter half of the 1980s did not perform as well (Kaplan and Stein, 1993).

Opler (1992) found that LBOs in 1985 to 1989 were associated with operating improvements comparable to those in earlier transactions. Kaplan and Stein (1993) found similar results for the later LBOs. However, despite improvements in operating performance, many of the later buyouts experienced financial distress. The defects in the later LBO deals were due to the relatively high prices paid and weakened financial structures for the LBOs formed. In addition, management, investment bankers, and other deal promoters were able to take more cash up front, which also weakened the structure and incentives in the later deals (Kaplan and Stein, 1993).

Both general economic principles and factors more specific to LBO activity explained the deterioration in the quality of LBOs in the second half of the 1980s. In an enterprise system, high return segments of the economy attracted more financial resources. Investments flowed to areas of high prospective returns (Weston and Chen, 1994). This occurred with the LBOs. Many specialized LBO funds were formed. More banks and other financial intermediaries participated. The dollar volume of funds seeking to organize LBO deals began to exceed the number of good prospects available. The successful LBOs of the early 1980s were able to make purchases on very favorable terms; purchase prices were as low as three to four times prospective cash flows (EBITDA). However, in the late 1980s the quantity of funds exceeded the availability of good prospects. As a consequence, the price-to-expected cash flow multiples rose sharply. The difference between the winning price and the next highest bid was often very substantial. Winner's curse operated in the extreme.

Public high yield debt substituted for both private subordinated debt and "strip" financing in which subordinated debt holders also received equity stakes. This raised the cost of reorganizing companies that encountered financial difficulties.

Commercial banks took smaller positions. They sought to reduce their commitments and shorten maturities and required an accelerated program for required principal repayments. As a consequence, the coverage of debt service declined. In some cases, coverage ratios were less than 1. Sometimes the first interest payment in the buyout could be achieved only if asset sales were accomplished and substantial cost reductions were achieved. Some deals utilized high yield bonds with either zero coupons or interest payments consisting of more of the same securities, payment in kind (PIK). Cash requirements for debt service were postponed for several years after the formation of the LBO.

Consistent with the general economic principles about the flow of resources to high return areas, the leveraged buyout market began making some "corrections." Allen (1996, p. 22) observed that movement toward lower transactions prices, larger equity commitments, lower debt ratios, and lower up-front fees were under way. Despite the corrections under way, the rules of the game and the general economic environment were altered. Legislative and regulatory rule changes interacting with the economic downturn devastated the LBO market. The main legislative change was the S&L legislation in 1989, the Financial Institutions Reform, Recovery and Enforcement Act (FIRREA). Its major effect was to push masses of high yield debt from S&L portfolios onto the marketplace. The downward impact on the prices of high yield debt was predictable. Bank regulators put pressures on banks to reduce their exposures in highly leveraged transactions (HLTs). The recession of 1990 and 1991 brought to an end the rising levels of economic activity that supported the revenue growth and profitability of individual companies. Leveraged buyout activity in 1991 dropped to $7.0 billion, 10.7% of the $65.7 billion in 1989.

THE ROLE OF JUNK BONDS

Junk bonds are high yield bonds either rated below investment grade or unrated. Using Standard & Poor's ratings, junk bonds are defined at below BBB; using Moody's the level is below Baa3. Allegations have been made that junk bonds have contributed to excessive takeover activity and LBOs and have resulted in unsound levels of business leverage.

There have always been high yield bonds. But prior to 1977 high yield bonds were "fallen angels," bonds that had initially been rated investment grade but whose ratings had been subsequently lowered. The first issuer of bonds rated below investment grade from the start is said to have been Lehman Brothers in 1977. Drexel Burnham Lambert (Michael Milken) soon became the industry leader. Competition followed, but Drexel still had 45% of the market in 1986 and 43.2% of the market through mid-November 1987 (Frantz, 1987). However, as a result of its legal problems, Drexel's share of public underwritings of junk debt fell to only 16% in the first quarter of 1989 (Laing, 1989). Subsequently, Drexel declared bankruptcy and dropped from the market. By the early 1990s the volume of high yield bond financing had exceeded the peak levels of the 1980s. Other investment banks took over the market share previously held by Drexel.

Between 1970 and 1977 junk bonds represented on average about 3% to 4% of total public straight debt bonds. By 1985 this share had risen to 14.4%. These are shares of the totals of public straight bonds outstanding. As a percentage of yearly flows of new public bond issues by U.S. corporations, the straight junk bond shares had risen from 1.1% in 1977 to almost 20% by 1985. Clearly, junk bonds began to play a significant role.

The use of high yield bonds represented a financial innovation in opening public financing to less than investment grade credit firms. They were used to finance growing firms such as MCI. Junk bonds were also used in takeovers, making even the largest firms vulnerable to changes in ownership. Default rates for high yield bonds by 10 years after issuance had run as high as 20% to 30%. The average recovery rate for junk bonds after default had been about 40% of their original par value. Taking default rates and average recovery rates into account, the realized return spreads between high yield bonds and other investments had been calculated. Over most segments of the period 1978 to 1994, the promised yield spread between high yield bonds and 10-year Treasury bonds had been about 4.5%. The realized return spread had been somewhat over two percentage points (Altman, 1989, 1996).

A study by Professor Glenn Yago (1991) covered all public firms issuing junk bonds during the period 1980 to 1986. About one-fourth of the proceeds were used for acquisition financing, whereas about three-fourths of the proceeds were used to finance internal corporate growth. Although high yield bonds facilitated takeover activity, their significance was much broader. Junk bonds made financing available to high risk growth firms and helped them realize their potentials. A high percentage of employment growth in the economy had been accounted for by the growth of firms using high yield financing. These high yield firms had higher than average rates of sales growth, capital expenditures, and productivity improvements.

High yield financing was not the fundamental cause of the problems of the savings and loan (S&L) industry during the 1980s. Their basic problem was that the changing nature of financial markets removed the economic basis for the existence of the industry. By 1980, before the era of takeovers and high yield financing had started, the S&L industry had a negative net worth on a market value basis of over $100 billion. Ninety percent of the firms in the S&L industry were suffering losses in 1980 and 1981.

Investments in junk bonds in total represented 1% or less of their total assets. Some individual S&Ls had high ratios of junk bonds in their portfolios. Legislation enacted by Congress in 1989 essentially required S&Ls to liquidate the high yield bonds they currently held and prohibited them from further investing in high yield bonds. This artificial interference with normal supply and demand conditions in the high yield bond market caused temporary losses. However, by 1993 the junk bond market was achieving record high returns for investors and the size of the high yield bond market reached new highs, suggesting a sound fundamental economic basis for this financial innovation.

Much has been written on the role of Michael Milken, with opposing views reflected in two contrasting studies. The first was written by Ralph S. Saul (Saul, 1993), who served as a court-appointed member of the oversight committee to monitor the liquidation of Drexel; he later served as the chairman of its board in reorganization. From his close and long association in overseeing the liquidation of Drexel, Saul also reviewed closely the activities of Michael Milken. His detailed review of Milken and his activities can be summarized into three charges; that Milken engaged in (1) securities parking, (2) market stabilization, and (3) market monopolization.

Securities parking entails having an associate or cooperating firm or firms hold securities in their account names. Historically, this was a common practice used by investment banking firms to avoid technical violations of net equity or capital requirements in relation to assets held or obligations outstanding. The need to add to an investment banking firm's equity or net worth on a permanent basis was avoided by having other nominees hold temporary surges in asset holdings and related debt obligations incurred. But parking became a more serious violation when the Williams acts, initially enacted in 1968 and subsequently amended, made it illegal to engage in parking to avoid triggering the Rule 13(d) requirement of filing a report with the SEC when 5% ownership of the equity securities of a firm had been reached. The main evidence of the charge against Milken for parking was from the testimony of Ivan Boesky.

Saul placed heaviest emphasis on the market stabilization activities of Milken. He stated that Milken was able to develop underwriting and investment participation by other institutions by guaranteeing them against losses on their high yield bond investments during the time required for the markets to absorb them. In addition, Saul (1993, p. 44) states that Milken did not make "public disclosure in high-yield bond offering documents of the hundreds of millions in equities or warrants that he took as underwriting compensation." Furthermore, Saul pointed out, "In the most egregious cases, he made side payoffs, awarding interests in his investment partnerships to portfolio managers in return for investing institutional funds in his issues" (p. 43). Saul further stated that "such reprehensible conduct" helped Milken achieve his third crime of becoming the dominant firm or monopolist of the high yield bond market. He then described the advantages that Milken achieved as the innovator or first mover in developing the high yield bond market.

Saul then posed the question, "Why—in the fiercely competitive world of Wall Street, where a new financial product rarely has an edge for more than a few years at most—was no competitor able to challenge Milken?" (p. 42). The answer Saul gave was in three parts. First, they did not have Milken's network to be "highly confident" that it could successfully "place" or sell a high yield offering. "Second, and most important, no other firm on Wall Street was prepared to commit so much of its capital to inventory high-yield bonds in secondary market trading" (p. 42). Third, Milken over time developed close relationships with client issuers, institutional customers, and his employees.

A positive case for Milken was developed by Professor Daniel Fischel (1995), who was a consultant on the Milken case and other lawsuits in the 1980s. Fischel has also served as an expert witness on behalf of several government agencies. Fischel addressed the question, "Was Milken guilty?" His summary view is as follows. "Milken was a tough and formidable competitor. . . . His success made him the envy of many. . . . After the most thorough investigation, the government came up with nothing" (p. 158).

Fischel described the action against Milken as a part of the hysteria against the "excesses of the 1980s" and the ability of the government to invoke the Racketeer Influenced and Corrupt Organizations Act (RICO), which would have enabled the government to seize all of Milken's assets at the start of a trial. At the time of his decision to avoid the application of RICO by his guilty plea, so many other defendants had lost their court cases that it appeared that Milken simply could not win. But in 1991 the Second Circuit court reversed numerous convictions that the U.S. attorney's office had previously achieved in the lower courts (Fischel, p. 183). Fischel argued that these reversals supported his position that Milken was not, in fact, guilty of breaking any security law violations.

LBOS IN THE 1992–2000 PERIOD

After 1992 the economy experienced sustained economic growth, stock prices reached new highs, the size of the total market for high yield debt reached new highs, and the size of aggregate LBO transactions moved to $62.0 billion in 1999, almost 900% of the volume in 1991. This more favorable economic environment was a major factor in the resurgence of LBOs. In addition, the financial structure of the deals changed. Innovative approaches were developed by LBO sponsor companies, LBO sponsor specialists, investment banks, and commercial banks. Because of innovative approaches, LBOs were applied increasingly beyond mature slow-growing industries to high growth technology-driven industries.

The changed financial structure of the transactions after 1992 are first described. The price-to-EBITDA ratios paid moved down toward 5 to 6 from the 7–8–10 multiples of the late 1980s. The percentage of equity in the initial capital structure moved up to 20% to 30% compared with equity ratios as low as 5% to 10% in the late 1980s. Interest coverage ratios moved up. The ratio of EBITDA to interest and other financial requirements moved to a standard of 2. This contrasts with the deals in the late 1980s when asset sales and immediate improvements in profitability margins were required to cover interest and other financial outlays in the first year of the LBO.

A major restructuring of the intermediaries was also taking place. Milken and Drexel were no longer present to dominate LBO activity as in the 1980s. But the LBO resumed its growth through other investment banking houses, the larger commercial banks, the traditional LBO sponsors such as Kohlberg Kravis Roberts (KKR), and innovative approaches by investment banking-sponsoring firms. For example, Forstmann Little & Company emphasized using its own funds and participation in management over a period of time (Antilla, 1992, 1993). A general partner of Forstmann Little stated in a *New York Times* interview of December 27, 1992, "We're looking more and more to finance our deals without any bank debt—substituting what was once bank debt with more of our own capital." This represents a strategy of substituting sponsor equity for bank debt. Sometimes deals are structured so that principal repayments are not required until 10 years after the deal. This reduces the pressure for immediate performance improvement or asset sales.

Clayton, Dubilier & Rice Inc. (CD&R) has emphasized a partnership structure with members who have considerable previous managerial experience. It structures the transaction, owns the majority of the equity, controls the company it acquires, and establishes management incentives by linking compensation to performance. Detailed examples of CD&R activities are provided in a *Business*

Week story of November 15, 1993, pp. 70, 74. CD&R has emphasized buying undermanaged segments of larger companies to achieve a turnaround. Financial buyers may also develop joint deals with corporate strategic buyers to purchase companies on a leveraged basis.

The financial press provides numerous examples of innovative approaches by LBO sponsors. The increased participation by commercial banks is described in detail in a comprehensive survey by Allen (1996). He describes the increased use of syndication of HLT transactions to other banks and the development of a highly liquid secondary loan trading market. He emphasizes a continued close client-focused relationship by the commercial bank. This embraces not only LBO and M&A activity but the broad gamut of financial services the client company may require. He also describes a range of capital structure strategies tailored to the characteristics of the transaction. Similar innovative approaches have been developed by investment banking firms and other financial intermediaries.

Financial buyers (LBO sponsors, investment banks, commercial banks) have faced increased competition from corporate buyers. All have adopted new strategies. One is the leveraged buildup. The leveraged buildup identifies a fragmented industry characterized by relatively small firms. Buyout firms based on partners with industry expertise purchase a firm as a platform for further leveraged acquisitions in the same industry (Allen, 1996, p. 27). They seek to build firms with strong management, developing revenue growth while reducing costs, with the objectives of improved margins, increased cash flow, and increased valuations.

SUMMARY

The 1980s were characterized by LBOs focused on mature industries with stable cash flows. High leverage was used to provide owners and LBO sponsors with a high percentage of the equity. The cash flows were used to pay off the debt. In the standard case, debt was 90%, equity was 10% of total capital. When the debt was paid off, the equity holders became owners of 100% of the company. It could then be sold with strong management incentives. A turnaround could achieve substantial operating improvements. The value of the company when sold represented good returns to the equity holders.

In the late 1980s buyers paid too much, and leverage was excessive for realistic future cash flows. The deals were unsound from a strategic and financial structure standpoint. In 1990 to 1991 the LBO market had almost dried up.

The LBO market revived in 1992. The volume of high yield debt outstanding by 1995 was greater than it had ever been before. In addition, investments in the LBO market by sponsors' investment banks and commercial banks also increased. Innovative approaches augmented more traditional financial strategies. Financial structures have been related to the characteristics of the companies involved. Leveraged transactions have moved from mature industries to growth-oriented technology-driven industries. There is often greater equity participation by financial buyers. In addition, financial buyers increasingly offer management expertise and close interaction with or control of operating management. In short, LBO activity appears to have moved to an age of renewal.

QUESTIONS

16.1 Discuss the typical types of financing involved in LBOs and MBOs.

16.2 What were the characteristics of industries and firms in which LBOs and MBOs took place in the 1980s?

16.3 What are the advantages and disadvantages of LBOs and MBOs?

16.4 What were the magnitudes of abnormal returns for LBOs and MBOs during the early 1980s?

16.5 What were the sources of these gains?

16.6 What were the reasons for the increase in LBO activity during the early 1980s?

16.7 Why were LBO/MBOs able to use such high leverage ratios compared with other forms of business organizations?

16.8 What were some of the unsound developments in the LBO market that began to take place in the late 1980s?

16.9 How were these developments corrected during the resurgence of the LBO market after 1992?

Case 16.1 Sources of Value in LBOs

In the text, we use spreadsheets to convey how an LBO is set up and how cash flows can be used to pay down debt in a successful LBO. We can convey the same concepts more succinctly by use of the second type of valuation formulas developed in chapter 9.

Consider the following set of value drivers:

$X_0 =$	$1,000
$T =$	40.0%
$b =$	20.0%
$r =$	30.0%
$g =$	6.0%
$n =$	10
$k =$	11.0%
$(1 + h) = (1 + g)/(1 + k) =$	0.95

These value drivers reflect a firm with the characteristics of the usual LBO candidate in the 1980s. The investment opportunities rate, b, is a modest 20%. The marginal profitability rate, r, is 30%. The growth rate is only 6%. The initial EBIT is set at $1,000 so the results can be expressed in general

terms. We postulate a cost of capital of 11%. Here is the resulting valuation:

1st term: $X_0 (1 - T)(1 - b) \sum_{t=1}^{n}\left(\frac{1+g}{1+k}\right)^t =$ $3,758 (52.2%)

2nd term: $\frac{X_0(1-T)}{k}\left(\frac{1+g}{1+k}\right)^n =$ $3,440 (47.8%)

$7,198 (100.0%)

In an LBO, the high use of debt could reduce the tax rate to 30%. Because a turnaround situation is usually involved, the profitability rate rises to 40%. With the higher use of debt in the capital structure, the cost of capital drops to 10%.

QUESTIONS

1. With the new value drivers, what will be the new value of the LBO?
2. What other types of sensitivity analysis could be performed?

Case 16.2 RJR Nabisco LBO

Many studies set forth materials on the 1988 RJR Nabisco LBO. Two examples are Allen Michel and Israel Shaked, "RJR Nabisco: A Case Study of a Complex Leveraged Buyout," *Financial Analysts Journal,* September–October 1991, pp. 15–27; and Harvard Business School Case of RJR Nabisco. Both articles project the cash flows from 1989 through 1998. In competition with other bidders, KKR won with a bid of $109 per share.

From the spreadsheets in the two sources cited above, the following value drivers could be estimated.

$X_0 =$	$2,848
$T =$	40.0%
$b =$	30.0%
$r =$	46.7%

$g =$	14.0%
$n =$	10
$k =$	12.0%
$(1 + h) = (1 + g)/(1 + k) =$	1.02

Using these date, the total value of RJR Nabisco could be calculated. From the total value, the debt outstanding of $5.4 billion would be deducted to obtain the equity value. The number of shares outstanding was 223.5 million.

QUESTION

1. Compare the indicated value per share of RJR Nabisco using the given value drivers with the $109 per share paid by KKR.

REFERENCES

Allen, Jay R., "LBOs—The Evolution of Financial Structures and Strategies," *Journal of Applied Corporate Finance,* 8, Winter 1996, pp. 18–29.

Altman, Edward I., "Measuring Corporate Bond Mortality and Performance," *Journal of Finance,* 44, September 1989, pp. 909–922.

———, "The Investment Performance of Defaulted Bonds for 1987–1995 and Market Outlook," ms. with Anthony C. Morris, New York University Salomon Center, January 1996, pp. 1–23.

Anders, George, "Leaner and Meaner: Leveraged Buy-Outs Make Some Companies Tougher Competitors," *The Wall Street Journal,* September 15, 1988, pp. 1, 14.

Andrade, Gregor, and Steven N. Kaplan, "How Costly is Financial (Not Economic) Distress? Evidence from Highly Leveraged Transactions that Became Distressed," *Journal of Finance,* 53, October 1998, pp. 1443–1493.

Anslinger, Patricia L., and Thomas E. Copeland, "Growth Through Acquisitions: A Fresh Look," *Harvard Business Review,* 74, January–February 1996, pp. 126–135.

Antilla, Susan, "A Different Face on the L.B.O. Front," *New York Times,* December 27, 1992, Section 3, p. 13.

———, "Forstmann Turns Toward the Future," *New York Times,* November 14, 1993, Section 3, p. 13.

Asquith, P., and T. A. Wizman, "Event Risk, Covenants, and Bondholder Returns in Leveraged Buyouts," *Journal of Financial Economics,* 27, 1990, pp. 195–214.

Baker, G. P., M. C. Jensen, and K. J. Murphy, "Compensation and Incentives: Practice vs. Theory," *Journal of Finance,* 43, 1988, pp. 593–616.

DeAngelo, Harry, and Linda DeAngelo, "Management Buyouts of Publicly Traded Corporations," chapter 6 in Thomas E. Copeland, ed., *Modern Finance & Industrial Economics,* New York: Basil Blackwell Inc., 1987, pp. 92–113.

———, and Edward Rice, "Going Private: Minority Freezeouts and Stockholder Wealth," *Journal of Law and Economics,* 27, October 1984, pp. 367–401.

Degeorge, Francois, and Richard Zeckhauser, "The Reverse LBO Decision and Firm Performance: Theory and Evidence," *Journal of Finance,* 48, September 1993, pp. 1323–1348.

Easterbrook, F. H., and D. R. Fischel, "Corporate Control Transactions," *Yale Law Journal,* 92, 1982, pp. 698–711.

Easterwood, John C., "Divestments and Financial Distress in Leveraged Buyouts," *Journal of Banking & Finance,* 22, 1998, pp. 129–159.

Fischel, Daniel, *Payback,* New York: HarperCollins Publishers, 1995.

Frantz, Douglas, "Crash Hasn't Shaken Drexel's Faith in the Value of 'Junk Bonds,' " *Los Angeles Times,* November 19, 1987, Part IV, p. 1.

Greenwald, J., "Where's the Limit?" *Time,* December 5, 1988, pp. 66–70.

Harlow, W. V., and J. S. Howe, "Leverage Buyouts and Insider Nontrading," *Financial Management,* 22, Spring 1993, pp. 109–118.

Hite, G. L., and M. R. Vetsuypens, "Management Buyouts of Divisions and Shareholder Wealth," *Journal of Finance,* 44, 1989, pp. 953–970.

Holthausen, Robert W., and David F. Larcker, "The Financial Performance of Reverse Leveraged Buyouts," *Journal of Financial Economics,* 42, 1996, pp. 293–332.

Jensen, M. C., "Agency Costs of Free Cash Flow, Corporate Finance, and Takeovers," AEA Papers and Proceedings, May 1986, pp. 323–329.

Kaplan, Steven, "The Effects of Management Buyouts on Operating Performance and Value," *Journal of Financial Economics,* 24, 1989a, pp. 217–254.

———, "Management Buyouts: Evidence on Taxes as a Source of Value," *Journal of Finance,* 44, July 1989b, pp. 611–632.

———, "The Staying Power of Leveraged Buyouts," *Journal of Financial Economics,* 29, 1991, pp. 287–313.

———, and Jeremy C. Stein, "The Evolution of Buyout Pricing and Financial Structure (Or, What Went Wrong) in the 1980s," *Journal of Applied Corporate Finance,* 6, 1993, pp. 72–88.

Laing, J. R., "Up and Down Wall Street," *Barron's,* April 10, 1989, pp. 1, 49–50.

Lehn, Ken, and Annette Poulsen, "Leveraged Buyouts: Wealth Created or Wealth Redistributed?" chapter 4 in M. Weidenbaum and K. Chilton, eds., *Public Policy Towards Corporate Takeovers,* New Brunswick, NJ: Transaction Publishers, 1988.

———, "Free Cash Flow and Stockholder Gains in Going Private Transactions," *Journal of Finance,* 44, 1989, pp. 771–788.

Lowenstein, Louis, "Management Buyouts," *Columbia Law Review,* 85, 1985, pp. 730–784.

Mian, Shehzad, and James Rosenfeld, "Takeover Activity and the Long-Run Performance of Reverse Leveraged Buyouts," *Financial Management,* 22, Winter 1993, pp. 46–57.

Morrow, D. J., "Why the IRS Might Love Those LBOs," *Fortune,* December 5, 1988, pp. 145–146.

Murphy, K. J., "Corporate Performance and Managerial Remuneration: An Empirical Analysis," *Journal of Accounting and Economics,* 7, 1985, pp. 11–42.

Muscarella, C. J., and M. R. Vetsuypens, "Efficiency and Organizational Structure: A Study of Reverse LBOs," *Journal of Finance,* 45, December 1990, pp. 1389–1413.

Opler, Tim, "Operating Performance in Leveraged Buyouts: Evidence from 1985–1989," *Financial Management,* 21, Spring 1992, pp. 27–34.

Quigley, E. V., "Big Bondholders Launch Revolt Against Nabisco," *Los Angeles Times,* November 18, 1988, Part IV, pp. 1, 5.

Ritter, Jay R., "The Long-Run Performance of Initial Public Offerings," *Journal of Finance,* 46, March 1991, pp. 3–27.

Roden, Dianne M., and Wilbur G. Lewellen, "Corporate Capital Structure Decisions: Evidence from Leveraged Buyouts," *Financial Management,* 24, Summer 1995, pp. 76–87.

Saul, Ralph S., "DREXEL," *The Brookings Review,* 11, Spring 1993, pp. 41–45.

Shleifer, A., and L. H. Summers, "Breach of Trust in Hostile Takeovers," chapter 2 in A. J. Auerbach, ed., *Corporate Takeovers: Causes and Consequences,* Chicago: University of Chicago Press, 1988, pp. 33–56.

Shleifer, A., and R. W. Vishny, "Management Buyouts as a Response to Market Pressure,"

chapter 5 in A. J. Auerbach, ed., *Mergers and Acquisitions,* Chicago: University of Chicago Press, 1988.

Smith, Abbie, "Corporate Ownership Structure and Performance: The Case of Management Buyouts," *Journal of Financial Economics,* 27, September 1990, pp. 143–164.

Travlos, N. G., and M. M. Cornett, "Going Private Buyouts and Determinants of Shareholders' Returns," *Journal of Accounting, Auditing and Finance,* 8, 1993, pp. 1–25.

United States Government Printing Office, *Economic Report of the President,* Washington, DC, 1996.

Warga, Arthur, and Ivo Welch, "Bondholder Losses in Leveraged Buyouts," *Review of Financial Studies,* 6, 1993, pp. 959–982.

Weston, J. Fred, and Yehning Chen, "A Tale of Two Eras," *Business Economics,* 29, January 1994, pp. 27–33.

Yago, Glenn, *Junk Bonds: How High Yield Securities Restructured Corporate America,* New York: Oxford University Press, 1991.

International Takeovers and Restructuring*

The annual reports of individual business firms make increasing reference to international markets as sources of future growth. The world has truly become a global marketplace. A significant proportion of total takeover activity has an international dimension. United States firms are buying foreign firms, foreign firms are buying U.S. entities, and U.S. and foreign firms are buying one another.

HISTORICAL PATTERNS

Table 17.1 presents data on trends in foreign versus U.S. merger activity during the decade 1990–1999. M&A activity is grouped by the U.S. alone and by three categories of international deals. U.S. company acquisitions of non-U.S. companies are in the range of about 10% of total world M&A activity. Acquisitions by non-U.S. companies of U.S. companies have been in the 6% range. Deals not involving U.S. companies, including both cross-border and within border transactions, account for about 40% of total world M&A activity. So by dollar value, shown in Panel A of Table 17.1, international deals account for more than 50% of total world activity. Measured by number of deals, as shown in Panel B, the U.S. accounts for about one-third of M&A activity, with international deals accounting for the other two-thirds.

      The main reasons for the large levels of foreign M&A activity can be summarized briefly. Europe is moving toward becoming a common market, so it continues to experience the kind of M&A activity that took place in the United States when it first became a common market as a result of the completion of the transnational railroad systems in the late 1880s. Piled on that is globalization and the increased intensity of international competition, which has been impacting U.S. M&A activity as well. The impact of rapid technological change and the consolidation of major industries represent additional forces for increased M&A activity throughout the world.

---

*This chapter benefited from the presentations on Globalization and Corporate Strategy by José de la Torre to the Anderson School–UCLA biennial Merger Week Programs.

Table 17.1 Foreign vs U.S. Merger Activity, 1990–1999

Panel A. Dollar Volume

| | U.S. | | INTERNATIONAL DEALS | | | | | | | | Total |
| | U.S. Alone | | U.S. by Non-U.S. | | Non-U.S. by U.S. | | Deals outside U.S. | | Total International | | |
Year	$ in billions	% of Total	$ in billions	% of Total	$ in billions	% of Total	$ in billions	% of Total	$ in billions	% of Total	$ in billions
99	998	42.0%	247	10.4%	150	6.3%	979	41.3%	1,376	58.0%	2,373
98	1,005	48.1%	221	10.6%	117	5.6%	749	35.8%	1,086	51.9%	2,092
97	626	46.5%	86	6.4%	85	6.3%	550	40.8%	721	53.5%	1,348
96	516	48.1%	70	6.5%	61	5.7%	426	39.7%	557	51.9%	1,072
95	285	41.1%	54	7.8%	47	6.7%	308	44.3%	409	58.9%	694
94	205	44.8%	46	10.1%	24	5.1%	183	40.0%	253	55.2%	458
93	131	40.9%	22	6.8%	19	5.9%	149	46.4%	189	59.1%	320
92	95	32.3%	15	5.2%	15	5.2%	168	57.3%	199	67.7%	294
91	98	27.9%	31	8.8%	16	4.4%	205	58.8%	252	72.1%	349
90	101	24.9%	57	14.0%	21	5.3%	226	55.7%	304	75.1%	405

Panel B. Number of Deals

| | U.S. | | INTERNATIONAL DEALS | | | | | | | | Total |
| | U.S. Alone | | U.S. by Non-U.S. | | Non-U.S. by U.S. | | Deals outside U.S. | | Total International | | |
Year	# of Deals	% of Total	# of Deals	% of Total	# of Deals	% of Total	# of Deals	% of Total	# of Deals	% of Total	# of Deals
99	6,209	32.5%	1,034	5.4%	1,452	7.6%	10,413	54.5%	12,899	67.5%	19,108
98	7,584	39.1%	922	4.7%	1,586	8.2%	9,329	48.0%	11,837	60.9%	19,421
97	6,030	36.8%	777	4.7%	1,336	8.2%	8,227	50.3%	10,340	63.2%	16,370
96	5,453	37.0%	652	4.4%	1,127	7.6%	7,517	51.0%	9,296	63.0%	14,749
95	4,465	33.5%	597	4.5%	994	7.4%	7,291	54.6%	8,882	66.5%	13,347
94	3,748	33.8%	476	4.3%	765	6.9%	6,104	55.0%	7,345	66.2%	11,093
93	3,096	33.1%	385	4.1%	636	6.8%	5,250	56.0%	6,271	66.9%	9,367
92	2,807	29.6%	394	4.1%	552	5.8%	5,744	60.5%	6,690	70.4%	9,497
91	2,540	26.4%	532	5.5%	474	4.9%	6,090	63.2%	7,096	73.6%	9,636

Source: Mergers and Acquisitions Annual Almanac. Issues 1992–2000

LARGE CROSS-BORDER TRANSACTIONS

To give real-life content to the broad statistical compilations of these tables, we present tables listing the 25 largest cross-border transactions in history completed as of December 31, 1999 for three categories. Table 17.2 presents data for cross-border transactions in which U.S. firms were acquired. Both announcement dates and effective dates are given. The lag of effective dates behind announcement dates range mostly from 4 to 12 months. The table gives the target and buyer names plus a brief description of their business activities. With the exception of the acquisition by BAT Industries of the Farmers Group, the 25 transactions would be classified as horizontal mergers. The predominance of these mergers became effective in 1998 or 1999. Only seven took place before the 1990s. Acquiring firms were domiciled in eight different nations.

In Table 17.3, we present a similar analysis of the top 25 in which U.S. firms acquired foreign firms. All 25 of these are horizontal or consolidating mergers. The total of the top 25 largest cross-border acquisitions (U.S. acquirers) is $105.4 billion, only 34.5% of the value of the transactions in Table 17.2 in which U.S. firms were targets.

Table 17.4 lists the top 25 in history in which cross-border transactions took place without the involvement of U.S. firms. It can readily be seen that most of these transactions involve European firms. The Bermuda (BER) designation is somewhat ambiguous because some large firms are domiciled in that tax haven. Tyco International is a large U.S. diversified firm chartered in Bermuda; in our analysis, we would classify Tyco as a U.S. firm rather than a foreign firm to reflect practical realities.

The companies listed in Tables 17.2 through 17.4 can be placed in industry groups as shown in Table 17.5. We emphasize that the companies listed represent only the largest transactions in each category. For example, Appendix A to Chapter 6 on the chemical industry we present a list of companies with reasons for merging or divesting in Table 6.A.2. Similarly, we compiled an extended list of large M&As in the pharmaceutical industry, as shown in Table 17.6. The major reasons for the transactions listed in Table 17.6 were to combine complementary capabilities, to strengthen distribution networks, and to achieve the greater size required for the new approaches to R&D.

The industries represented in the combined company listing in Table 17.5 can be regrouped into eight categories. All have been greatly impacted by the broad forces of technological change and the globalization of markets. These in turn have produced deregulation, the blurring of industry boundaries, and unequal growth patterns among industries. These and other industries' specific influences have combined to produce some high takeover industries. The industry characteristics related to M&A pressures can be summarized as follows:

1. Telecommunications.   Technological change, deregulation in the United States and abroad (particularly Europe) have stimulated efforts to develop a global presence.
2. Media (movies, records, magazines, newspapers).   Technological changes have impacted the relationship between the content and delivery segments. Potential overlap in content of different media outlets. Attractive and glamorous industry (attracted Japanese beginning in late 1980s).

Table 17.2 Major Cross-Border Transactions Involving U.S. Targets

	Date Announced	Date Effective	Target Name	Target Business Description
1	01/18/1999	06/30/1999	Air Touch Communications	Mobile telecommunications
2	08/11/1998	12/31/1998	Amoco Corp	Oil and gas company
3	05/07/1998	11/12/1998	Chrysler Corp	Manufacture automobiles and trucks
4	12/07/1998	11/30/1999	PacifiCorp	Electric utility; telecomm svc
5	02/18/1999	07/21/1999	TransAmerica Corp	Insurance company
6	06/18/1998	08/31/1998	Bay Networks Inc	Mfr data networking prods
7	11/30/1998	06/04/1999	Bankers Trust New York Corp	Banking
8	03/31/1989	07/26/1989	SmithKline Beckman Corp	Mfr pharmaceutical products
9	03/26/1987	07/07/1987	Standard Oil Co of Ohio	Oil and gas company
10	03/08/1999	05/12/1999	RJ Reynolds International (RJR Nabisco Inc/RJR Nabisco Holdings)	Mfr tobacco products
11	05/10/1999	12/31/1999	Republic New York Corp	Bank holding company
12	09/24/1990	01/03/1991	MCA Inc	Motion picture production
13	02/28/1995	07/18/1995	Marion Merrell Dow Inc (Dow Chemical Co)	Manufacture pharmaceuticals
14	01/24/1988	06/24/1988	Federated Department Stores Inc	Department stores
15	06/15/1998	11/10/1998	Excel Communications Inc	Telephone communications services
16	03/22/1999	04/30/1999	United States Filter Corp	Mfr Water treatment equip
17	05/17/1999	11/12/1999	Case Corp	Agricultural equipment
18	06/05/1998	07/01/1998	Astra Merck Inc (Merck & Co Inc, Astra AB)	Manufacture pharmaceuticals
19	10/04/1988	01/10/1989	Pillsbury Co	Food and restaurant company
20	01/24/1984	06/07/1985	Shell Oil Co	Oil and gas company
21	05/02/1994	11/03/1994	Syntex Corp	Manufacture pharmaceuticals
22	01/13/1988	12/16/1988	Farmers Group Inc	Insurance holding company
23	06/26/1981	09/25/1981	Texasgulf Inc	Potash, phosphate mining
24	07/27/1998	01/05/2000	AT&T Corp-Segment	Telecommunications
25	06/26/1997	11/26/1997	Rhone-Poulenc Rorer Inc (Rhone-Poulenc SA/France)	Manufacture pharmaceuticals

Source: Thomson Financial Securities Data

Acquirer Name	Acquirer Business Description	Acquirer Nation	Value of Transaction ($ million)
Vodafone Group PLC	Mobile telecommunications	UK	60,287
British Petroleum Co PLC (BP)	Integrated oil and gas company	UK	48,174
Daimler-Benz AG	Manufacture automobiles and trucks	GER	40,467
Scottish Power PLC	Electric utility	UK	12,600
Aegon NV	Insurance holding company	NETH	10,814
Nortel Networks Corp	Mfr telecommunications equipment	CAN	9,269
Deutsche Bank AG	Banking	GER	9,082
Beecham Group PLC	Mfr pharmaceutical products	UK	7,922
BP America Inc (British Petroleum Co PLC)	Integrated oil and gas company	UK	7,858
Japan Tobacco Inc	Mfr tobacco products	JPN	7,832
HSBC Holdings PLC	Bank holding company	UK	7,703
Matsushita Electric Industrial Co Ltd	Mfr home audio, video products	JPN	7,406
Hoechst AG	Mfr. chemicals and fibers	GER	7,265
Campeau Corp	Commercial real estate	CAN	6,512
Teleglobe Inc	Telephone communications services	CAN	6,407
Vivendi SA	Water, elec utility; construction	FRA	6,318
New Holland NV (New Holland Holdings NV/Fiat SpA)	Agricultural equipment	NETH	6,236
Astra AB	Manufacture pharmaceuticals	SWE	6,090
Grand Metropolitan PLC	Produce milk, beer; own, op pubs	UK	5,758
Royal Dutch/Shell Group (Royal Dutch Petroleum, Shell Transport)	Integrated oil and gas company	NETH	5,670
Roche Holding AG	Manufacture pharmaceuticals	SWI	5,307
BATUS Inc (BAT Industries PLC)	Mfr tobacco products	UK	5,200
E A Dev Inc (Elf Aquitaine)	Oil production	FRA	5,100
British Telecommunications PLC-Segment	Telecommunications	UK	5,038
Rhone-Poulenc SA	Manufacture pharmaceuticals	FRA	4,832
		TOTAL =	305,144

Table 17.3 Major Cross-Border Transactions Involving U.S. Acquirers

	Date Announced	Date Effective	Target Name	Target Business Description
1	03/02/1998	08/19/1998	Energy Group PLC	Electric utility; coal mining
2	06/14/1999	08/20/1999	ASDA Group PLC	Op food, clothing superstores
3	08/21/1995	11/02/1995	Pharmacia AB	Manufacture pharmaceuticals
4	01/28/1999	05/11/1999	LucasVarity PLC	Provide engineering services
5	01/26/1999	03/05/1999	Japan Leasing Corp	Provide business credit svcs
6	01/28/1999	03/31/1999	Volvo AB-Worldwide Passenger Vehicle Business	Manufacture passenger vehicles
7	05/22/1995	02/15/1996	CarnaudMetalbox SA	Manufacture metal cans
8	04/13/1987	09/01/1988	Dome Petroleum Ltd	Oil and gas exploration, prodn
9	03/02/1998	04/30/1998	BTR PLC-Global Packaging & Materials Division	Manufacture packaging
10	01/26/1998	03/03/1998	Norcen Energy Resources Ltd	Oil and gas exploration, prodn
11	03/24/1999	06/01/1999	Bell Canada (BCE Inc)	Telecommunications services
12	10/27/1997	01/20/1998	TeleDanmark A/S (Denmark)	Telecommunications services
13	10/16/1998	01/31/1999	Telus Corp	Telecommunications equipment
14	01/28/1999	06/30/1999	JDS Fitel Inc (Furukawa Electric Co Ltd)	Fiberoptic components
15	08/18/1999	12/01/1999	National Power Drax Ltd (National Power PLC)	Electricity
16	04/15/1999	06/30/1999	Imperial Chemical Industries PLC (Polyurethane segment)	Chemicals
17	03/08/1999	11/15/1999	Newcourt Credit Group Inc	Financing, leasing services
18	10/11/1994	12/23/1994	Societe Francaise du Radiotelephone (Cofira/Cie Generale Eaux)	Cellular telecommunications
19	01/26/1989	04/13/1989	Consolidated-Bathurst Inc	Mfr paper products; lumber
20	11/06/1995	04/24/1996	Seeboard PLC	Electric utility
21	08/16/1999	11/19/1999	Poco Petroleums Ltd	Oil and gas exploration, prodn
22	05/06/1996	06/17/1996	Midlands Electricity PLC	Electric utility
23	02/24/1997	04/16/1987	Yorkshire Electricity Group PLC	Provide electrical services
24	10/24/1989	03/14/1990	Jaguar PLC	Manufacture automobiles
25	03/04/1999	06/01/1999	MetroNet Communications Corp	Telecommunications services

Source: Thomson Financial Securities Data

500

Target Nation	Acquirer Name	Acquirer Business Description	Value of Transaction ($ million)
UK	Texas Utilities Co	Electric and gas utility	10,947
UK	Wal-Mart Stores (UK) Ltd (Wal-Mart Stores Inc)	Investment holding company	10,805
SWE	Upjohn Co	Mnfr pharmaceutical prods	6,989
UK	TRW Inc	Equipment and credit reporting	6,827
JPN	General Electric Capital Corp (General Electric Capital Svcs/GE Co)	Financing services	6,566
SWE	Ford Motor Co	Mfr autos, trucks, auto parts	6,450
FRA	Crown Cork & Seal Co	Manufacture cans, crowns	4,982
CAN	Amoco Canada Petroleum Co Ltd (Amoco Corp)	Oil and gas exploration, prodn	3,616
AUS	Owens-Illinois Inc	Mfr glass, plastic containers	3,600
CAN	Union Pacific Resources Group Inc (Union Pacific Corp/CNW Corp)	Oil and gas exploration, prodn	3,449
CAN	Ameritech Corp	Telecommunications services	3,383
DEN	Ameritech Corp	Telecommunications services	3,160
CAN	BC Telecom Inc (Anglo-Canadian Telephone Co)	Telecommunications equipment	3,107
JPN	Uniphase Corp	Fiberoptic components	3,058
UK	AES Corp	Electricity	3,008
UK	Huntsman ICI Holdings LLC (Huntsman Corp)	Mfr polyurethane	2,750
CAN	CIT Group Inc	Financing, leasing services	2,690
FRA	Southwestern Bell Mobile Systems-Cellular Operations (SBC Commun)	Cellular telecommunications	2,645
CAN	Stone Container Corp	Mfr containerboard, paper prod	2,609
UK	Central & South West Corp	Electric utility holding co	2,543
CAN	Burlington Resources Inc	Oil and gas exploration, prodn	2,540
UK	Avon Energy Partners Holdings (General Public Utilities, CINergy Corp)	Electric utility	2,436
UK	Yorkshire Holdings PLC (American Electric Power Co, Public Service)	Electric utility	2,410
UK	Ford Motor Co	Manufacture automobiles and trucks	2,395
CAN	AT&T Canada Inc	Telecommunications services	2,394
		TOTAL =	105,357

Table 17.4 Major International Cross-Border Transactions (non U.S.)

	Date Announced	Date Effective	Target Name	Target Business Description
1	10/21/1999	01/12/2000	Orange PLC	Mobile telecommunications
2	11/16/1998	12/15/1999	Hoechst AG	Chemicals
3	10/13/1997	09/07/1998	BAT Industries PLC-Financial Services Operations	Insurance company
4	07/28/1999	10/01/1999	One2One (Cable & Wireless PLC, MediaOne Group Inc)	Telecommunications services
5	04/29/1999	06/24/1999	YPF SA	Oil and gas company
6	12/01/1998	06/09/1999	Petrofina SA	Oil and gas company
7	05/21/1998	12/04/1998	PolyGram NV (Philips Electronics)	Mfr prerecorded records
8	05/26/1997	03/05/1998	Corange Ltd	Manufacture pharmaceuticals
9	02/20/1999	06/15/1999	Ing C Olivetti & Co SpA-Telecommunications Interests	Telecommunications services
10	08/19/1999	12/08/1999	Cies Reunies Electrobel et Tractionel (TRACTEBEL SA) (Soc Generale de B)	Electric and gas utility
11	05/07/1997	07/08/1997	Quest International, National Starch and Chemical, Unichema, Crosfield (Unilever)	Manufacture flavoring extracts
12	01/11/1999	06/07/1999	Rothmans International BV (Cie Financiere Richemont AG, Rembrandt)	Mfr tobacco products
13	04/07/1998	06/26/1998	Societe Generale de Belgique SA (Suez Lyonnaise des Eaux)	Bank
14	04/10/1995	06/05/1995	MCA Inc (Matsushita Electric Industrial Co Ltd)	Motion pictures
15	02/01/1999	07/14/1999	Guardian Royal Exchange PLC (GRE)	Insurance company
16	01/18/1999	05/29/1999	Nissan Motor Co	Manufacture automobiles
17	11/17/1997	05/12/1998	Assurances Generales de France (AGF)	Insurance company
18	12/22/1997	07/09/1998	Aachener und Muenchener Beteiligungs-AG	Insurance company
19	06/02/1998	12/28/1998	Stora Kopparbergs Bergslags AB	Forestry services
20	10/09/1995	12/21/1995	CRA Ltd-Assets	Mining assets
21	09/17/1992	12/31/1992	Elsevier NV-Operations	Newspapers
22	11/27/1998	11/01/1999	KLM Royal Dutch Airlines-Passenger and Cargo Activities	Air transport services
23	11/11/1997	12/19/1997	Banque Bruxelles Lambert SA	Bank
24	10/13/1997	04/01/1998	Merita Oy	Investment bank
25	09/25/1998	12/18/1998	Castorama Dubois Investissements SCA	Own, operate hardware stores

Source: Thomson Financial Securities Data

Target Country	Acquirer Name	Acquirer Business Description	Acquirer Nation	Value of Transaction ($ million)
UK	Mannesmann AG	Mfr steel products; telecom	GER	32,595
GER	Rhone-Poulenc SA	Chemicals	FRA	21,918
UK	Zurich Versicherungs GmbH	Insurance company	SWI	18,355
UK	Deutsche Telekom AG	Telecommunications services	GER	13,629
ARG	Repsol SA	Oil and gas company	SPA	13,152
BEL	Total SA	Oil and gas company	FRA	12,769
NETH	Universal Studios Inc (Seagram Co Ltd)	Motion pictures	CAN	10,236
BER	Roche Holding AG	Manufacture pharmaceuticals	SWI	10,200
ITA	Mannesmann AG	Mfr steel products; telecom	GER	8,404
BEL	Suez Lyonnaise des Eaux SA	Water utility; construction co	FRA	8,179
NETH	Imperial Chemical Industries PLC (ICI)	Manufacture petrochemicals	UK	8,000
NETH	British American Tobacco PLC	Mfr tobacco products	UK	7,515
BEL	Suez Lyonnaise des Eaux SA	Water utility; construction co	FRA	5,939
JPN	Seagram Co Ltd	Produce wine, brandy, liquor	CAN	5,704
UK	Sun Life and Provincial Holdings PLC (AXA-UAP)	Insurance company	FRA	5,692
JPN	Regie Nationale des Usines Renault SA (Renault SA)	Manufacture automobiles	FRA	5,391
FRA	Allianz AG	Insurance company	GER	5,118
GER	Assicurazioni Generali SpA	Insurance company	ITA	5,075
SWE	Enso Oy	Mfr paper, lumber, chemicals	FIN	4,913
AUS	RTZ Corp PLC-Assets	Mining assets	UK	4,653
NETH	Reed International PLC-Operations	Publishing	UK	4,637
NETH	Alitalia Linee Aeree Italiane SpA-Passenger and Cargo Activities	Air transport services	ITA	4,547
BEL	ING Groep NV	Insurance company	NETH	4,516
FIN	Nordbanken (Fortvaltnings AB Venantius/Sweden)	Bank	SWE	4,292
FRA	B&Q PLC (Kingfisher PLC)	Retail DIY products	UK	4,149
			TOTAL =	229,577

Table 17.5 Industrial Classification of Selected Cross-Border Mergers

Telecommunications Vodafone–AirTouch Nortel–Bay Teleglobe–Excel Mannesmann–Orange Deutsche–One2One Mannesmann–Olivetti (some units)	**Oil** BP–Amoco Repsol—YPF Total–Petrofina Union Pacific Resources–Norcen
Media Seagram–Polygram	**Packaging** Crown Cork–CarnaudMetalbox BTR–Owens-Illinois
Financial Aeogon–TransAmerica Deutsche–BT HSBC–Republic New York Zurich Insurance–BAT (financial) GE Capital–Japan Leasing CIT Group–Newcourt	**Agricultural Machinery** New Holland–Case **Electric** Scottish Power–PacifiCorp Suez Lyonnaise–Tractebel Texas Utilities–Energy Group
Pharmaceuticals Hoechst–Marion Merrell Dow Rhone Poulenc–Hoechst Roche–Corange (medical diagnostics) Upjohn–Pharmacia	**Water** Vivendi–US Filter **Retail** Wal-Mart–ASDA
Chemical ICI–Unilever (specialty chemical)	**Timber** Weyerhaeuser–MacMillan Bloedel
Autos Daimler–Chrysler TRW–LucasVarity Ford–Volvo Ford–Jaguar Renault–Nissan	**Tobacco** Japan Tobacco–RJR Int'l BAT–Rothmans International

3. Financial (investment banks, commercial banks, insurance companies). Globalization of industries and firms requires financial services firms to go global to serve their clients.

4. Chemicals and pharmaceuticals. Both require high amounts of R&D but suffer rapid imitation. Chemicals become commodities. Pharmaceuticals enjoy a

Table 17.6   Largest Recent Drug M&As

Target (Country)	Acquirer (Country)	Date Announced	Deal Value ($ billions)
SmithKline Beecham (UK/US)	GlaxoWellcome (UK)	Jan. 17, 2000	$76
Warner-Lambert (US)	Pfizer (US)	Nov. 4, 1999	$70
Astra (SWE)	Zeneca (UK)	Dec. 9, 1998	$37
Ciba-Geigy (SWI)	Sandoz (SWI)	Mar. 7, 1996	$30
Pharmacia & Upjohn (US)	Monsanto (US)	Dec. 20, 1999	$23
Hoechst (GER)	Rhone-Poulenc (FRA)	Nov. 16, 1998	$22
Wellcome (UK)	Glaxo (UK)	Jan. 20, 1995	$14
Squibb (US)	Bristol-Myers (US)	July 27, 1989	$12
Synthelabo (FRA)	Sanofi (FRA)	Dec. 2, 1998	$11
Corange (GER)	Roche (SWI)	May 26, 1997	$10
American Cyanamid (US)	American Home (US)	Aug. 2, 1994	$10
SmithKline Beckman (US)	Beecham (UK)	Mar. 31, 1989	$8
Marion Merrell Dow (US)	Hoechst (GER)	Feb. 28, 1995	$7
Pharmacia (SWE)	Upjohn (US)	Aug. 21, 1995	$7
Marion Laboratories (US)	Dow (US)	July 17, 1989	$6

Source: Securities Data Corporation.

limited period of patent protection but are eroded by "me too" drugs and generics. Changes in the technology of basic research and increased risks due to competitive pressures have created the stimulus for larger firms through M&As.

5. Autos, oil and gas, and industrial machinery.   All face unique difficulties that give advantages to size, stimulating M&As to achieve critical mass. Autos face global excess capacity. Oil faces the uncertainty of price and supply instability due to actions of the OPEC cartel.

6. Utilities.   Deregulation has created opportunities for economies from enlarging geographic areas. New kinds of competitive forces have created the need to broaden managerial capabilities.

7. Food, retailing.   Hampered by slow growth. Food consumption will grow only at the rate of population growth. Expanding internationally offers opportunities to grow in new markets.

8. Mining, timber.   Sources of supply are being exhausted. There are problems of matching raw material supplies with manufacturing capacity.

CASE STUDIES OF CROSS-BORDER TRANSACTIONS

To convey further content and understanding of the forces operating in transnational M&As, we present summaries of some of the leading cross border transactions organized by the three types covered in Tables 17.2, 17.3, and 17.4.

Deutsche Telekom AG–One2One
Announced July 28, 1999; Effective Oct. 1, 1999; $13.629 billion

Deutsche Telekom (DT) acquired One2One, Britain's smallest mobile telephone business, which was jointly owned by London-based Cable & Wireless and MediaOne Group. The deal allowed DT to shore up its presence in the changing European telecommunications arena as it sought to expand beyond the very competitive German market into Britain and other high growth regions.

The acquisition came after DT had suffered a serious blow to its international strategy when it failed to merge with Italian phone giant Telecom Italia SpA, a setback that also damaged its partnership with France Telecom S.A. DT was pressured to revise its strategy when France Telecom agreed to invest $5.5 billion in British cable operator NTL Inc. to gain a major foothold in the British telecommunications market.

DT and other telecom giants were attracted to the British market not only for the possibility of huge demands for their services but also for the prospects of technological innovation. Both Britain and Japan were in line to be among the first countries to offer the next generations of voice and data mobile phone services. These cutting edge services would not be available for the next three or four years, but the British government planned to sell five licenses for such services by the end of 1999. By owning One2One, DT hoped to have an edge in acquiring one of those licenses.

Deutsche Bank AG–Bankers Trust New York Corp.
Announced Nov. 30, 1998; Effective June 4, 1999; $9.082 billion

Deutsche Bank's (DB) dominant position in Germany had eroded from increasing competition and from the big American investment banks taking over the lucrative work advising large European companies. DB needed to expand its investment banking business, which was badly battered by its ill-considered acquisition of Morgan Grenfell, and it needed to compete in the United States, the world's largest capital market.

The acquisition of Bankers Trust (BT) secured a foothold in the United States. BT had a middle-rank investment banking firm, BT Alex Brown, with a strong reputation in underwriting young high tech companies. BT also had a sizeable business issuing high yield bonds.

The deal created the world's largest financial services company. The firm became a global leader in leveraged finance and one of the largest issuers of high yield bonds. Its portfolio included one of the largest global custody and processing businesses as well as a huge asset management operation.

The new company could reap the benefits of an expanding European market for new stocks and high yield corporate bonds issues for smaller companies, especially as the advent of a common currency was expected to boost European securities issuance and trading volume. High yield bonds were also attracting new interest as more European companies underwent management buyouts.

CIT Group Inc.–Newcourt Credit Group Inc.
Announced Mar. 8, 1999; Effective Nov. 15, 1999; $2.69 billion

CIT Group's acquisition of the Canadian firm Newcourt Credit Group created the largest publicly owned commercial finance company and the second largest nonbank lender after GE Capital. CIT was a leading commercial and consumer lender aimed at large but slow-growing construction, rail, air transportation, and logging companies. Newcourt specialized in financing the fast-growing high tech firms.

The weakness in Newcourt's share price allowed CIT to pursue the acquisition. Newcourt relied on asset-backed securities to secure over half of its funding, but it had experienced a jump in its financing cost and a weakness in the asset-backed securities market. The deal allowed CIT access to high tech firm financing with a cheaper cost of funding due to its stronger credit rating.

Rhone-Poulenc SA–Hoechst AG
Announced Nov. 16, 1998; Effective Dec. 15, 1999; $21.918 billion

The merger created Aventis SA, the world's largest life sciences company. It became the No. 1 agrochemical company and one of the world's biggest pharmaceutical firms. By joining forces, the two companies could achieve the critical mass necessary to sustain an ambitious R&D program and the global marketing muscle to push new drugs. The projected annual cost savings of more than $1 billion would allow them to continue their profit growth until new promising drugs were in the pipeline. The size of the combined company could attract a U.S. partner on an equal footing if they decided to boost their presence in the American pharmaceuticals market.

Both companies were disposing of their industrial chemical operations in an attempt to narrow their strategic focus to life sciences. Hoechst planned to spin off its industrial chemical operation as a separate company named Celanese AG.

Daimler-Benz–Chrysler
Announced May 7, 1998; Effective Nov. 12, 1998; $40.467 billion

As the automobile industry entered a period of brutal competition, Daimler-Benz and Chrysler were trying to become a full-line global automobile company. The merger signified huge economies of scales in engineering and purchasing, broader complementary product lines, and a worldwide network of manufacturing and distribution.

They combined the famous Mercedes-Benz line of luxury sedans and limousines with Chrysler's mass market cars and light trucks, including pickups, minivans, and sport utility vehicles. Daimler was known for its engineering and technical know-how. Chrysler had design and production expertise. The combination gave Daimler a huge U.S. distribution network the company had lacked. Chrysler obtained a much stronger base in Europe, where it had 1% of the Western European market compared to the 12% each of GM and Ford. Substantial cost savings would come from combined purchasing operations, economies of scale in automobile components, and combined technical product developments.

Ford Motor Co.–Jaguar PLC
Announced Oct. 24, 1989; Effective Mar. 14, 1990; $2.395 billion

In mid-1989, Ford Motor Co. announced its interest in purchasing Jaguar PLC. Ford was the second largest auto maker, while Jaguar, a British company, specialized in high-end luxury cars. Ford and General Motors briefly engaged in a bidding war for Jaguar. However, GM was unwilling to buy more than a minority stake at the prices that were being discussed. Eventually, Ford managed to secure a deal on October 24, 1989, for $2.4 billion.

Ford's interest in Jaguar stemmed from its lack of a viable luxury car. The Ford name was synonymous with cars aimed at the middle class buyer. Jaguar offered a brand that was recognized for its "snob appeal." Meanwhile, Jaguar was in dire need of help. After surviving the intense competition of the early 1980s with the help of the British government, its profits and quality were very low in the late 1980s. It desired a minority partner to provide additional capital. As things worked out, Ford ended up providing the cash, engineering technology, and quality management that Jaguar needed to produce a successful luxury product.

Renault SA–Nissan Motor Co.
Announced Jan. 18, 1999; Effective May 29, 1999; $5.391 billion

In May 1999, Renault SA and Nissan Motor Co. reached an agreement in which Renault would invest $5.4 billion in Nissan for a 37% stake in the company. Renault won the stake in Nissan after a brief bidding war with DaimlerChrysler AG. The combination of Renault, a French auto maker, and Nissan, a Japanese auto maker, would form the fourth largest auto partnership in the world. Renault was allowed to purchase up to a 44% stake in Nissan, but the firm said it did not want to take majority control. However, in exchange for its considerable investment, Renault was allowed to exercise some control over Nissan.

Nissan's search for a partner began because of its weak financial position. Analysts said that Nissan had over $20 billion in debt, more than any other auto maker. If it were an American company, Nissan would have been forced into bankruptcy. In addition to the weak Asian market of the late 1990s due to the Asian financial crisis, Nissan's troubles were blamed on its botched management of the U.S. market. While Honda and Toyota profited from the Accord and Camry, Nissan never managed to put out a viable challenger. Instead, Nissan marketed the Altima as a low-end sedan and the Maxima as a high-end sedan. During the mid 1990s, these cars combined were selling fewer units than the Accord or Camry, and Nissan had to bear the costs of carrying two cars while Honda and Toyota each had one.

Renault decided to take on the burden of a stake in Nissan in hopes of enjoying synergies from engineering and design. The two firms have very little overlap in their product markets, with Renault being primarily focused on Europe and Nissan focused on Japan, Asia, and North America. However, Renault's decision to invest in Nissan apparently carried great risk. Renault was about half the size of Nissan, and it depended heavily on the very competitive European market.

British Petroleum Co. PLC–Amoco Corp.
Announced Aug. 11, 1998; Effective Dec. 31, 1998; $48.174 billion

The merger of BP and Amoco came at a time of low oil and chemical prices. Oil companies were struggling to boost their profits but were unable to increase production or find additional ways to cut costs. The merger added more oil reserves and assets from which to squeeze out costs.

BP got Amoco's large reserves of oil and gas, which would have taken BP an extraordinary amount of time and capital to accumulate. The two companies were quite complementary. Amoco had lots of gas, and BP had lots of oil. Amoco brought in its U.S. presence, and BP had extensive international assets. Amoco was the largest natural gas producer in North America and had a vast U.S. gasoline marketing network. BP had a huge worldwide exploration and production operation and a strong European retail network.

The two companies could do more together than they could as stand-alone firms and could do it more efficiently. There were plenty of possibilities for synergy: there would be cost reductions from the elimination of duplicate operations, BP could bring its expertise in deepwater exploration and production to Amoco's fields in the Gulf of Mexico, and BP could combine its cheaper finding cost with Amoco's lower development costs. The cost savings were projected to amount to $2 billion annually by the end of 2000.

The size of the new company made it comparable to Exxon and Royal Dutch. It could give BP even greater market clout, enabling it to finance more development, keep costs down, and help win more auctions of oil reserves.

Union Pacific Resources Group–Norcen Energy Resources Ltd.
Announced Jan. 26, 1998; Effective Mar. 3, 1998; $3.449 billion

Canada's weak currency had made acquisition opportunities much more attractive. In addition to the lower acquisition prices, Canada's energy businesses received much of their revenues in U.S. dollars while their expenses were in Canadian dollars.

Union Pacific Resources, an independent oil and gas company, acquired the Canadian oil producer Norcen Energy. Union Pacific Resources was trying to diversify its reserve portfolio. After its failed attempt to acquire Pennzoil, the weakness of the Canadian dollar allowed it greater leverage in its bid for Norcen. The deal gave Union extensive oil and natural gas reserves in western Canada, the Gulf of Mexico, and exploration acreage in Venezuela and Guatemala. This represented a doubling of its reserves, access to international operations, and a lessening of investor fear that Union's aggressive drilling and production strategy would deplete the capital needed to replace reserves over the long run.

Scottish Power PLC–PacifiCorp
Announced Dec. 7, 1998; Effective Nov. 30, 1999; $12.60 billion

The deal represented the first major foreign acquisition of a U.S. electric utility. It was driven by the global liberalization of electricity markets. Scottish Power became one of the world's 10 largest electricity and utility companies. The company had been looking to acquire a U.S. utility for some time. Its officials believed that the United States was four to five years behind the United Kingdom in deregulating its power markets and that the U.S. industry was ripe for consolidation. There was also deregulation activity in continental Europe, but Scottish Power regarded the U.S. market as having better potentials.

Texas Utilities Co.–Energy Group PLC
Announced Mar. 2, 1998; Effective Aug. 19, 1998; $10.947 billion

As the U.S. market continued to deregulate, U.S. electric utilities were trying to find new sources of revenues as they were forced to open their service area to competitors. U.S. electric utilities had been purchasing British utilities since the United Kingdom privatized the industry in 1990. They were looking for cash-rich utilities in a more relaxed regulatory environment with high growth prospects.

Texas Utilities decided to enter the U.K. market for the first time. The deal allowed it to become a major player in Britain, which opened its electricity market to full retail competition in late 1998. Texas Utilities was able to successfully bid over another American suitor, PacifiCorp. The acquisition doubled Texas Utilities' revenues and gave it the necessary marketing muscle to compete in Britain and a possible entry into other European markets.

Vivendi SA–United States Filter Corp.
Announced Mar. 22, 1999; Effective April 30, 1999; $6.317 billion

The trends toward privatization of municipal water systems and outsourcing of industrial water supplies opened opportunities in the water business in the United States and abroad. Vivendi acquired U.S. Filter, the largest U.S. water company, whose main operation was in managing municipal and industrial water treatment facilities.

Vivendi was one of France's largest conglomerates, with a range of businesses including utilities such as water and waste management, media and telecommunications, and construction. The acquisition allowed Vivendi to move early into the U.S. water supply and water treatment business, the world's largest, as changes in the law stirred competition in a sector almost entirely controlled by a large number of small public operators.

The deal gave Vivendi a strong foothold to build its presence in the United States. Vivendi was known for its long history of operating municipal water systems. With the acquisition, Vivendi became one of the world's largest water companies and allowed it to better compete against the French rival, Suez Lyonnaise des Eaux SA, which until now had been more aggressive in its international expansion.

Vivendi could expect to benefit from the projected wave of privatization and consolidation in the global water supply business. Many municipal agencies were seeking partnerships with well-capitalized water companies that were able to help finance infrastructure upgrades and to meet strict environmental laws.

Wal-Mart Stores Inc.–ASDA Group PLC
Announced June 14, 1999; Effective Aug. 20, 1999; $10.805 billion

Wal-Mart, the giant retailer, was trying to gain critical mass outside the United States. Wal-Mart had expanded to several countries but had not achieved a dominant position except in Mexico and Canada. The acquisition of the British supermarket chain

ASDA Group gave it a strong presence in Europe and fulfilled its longstanding goal of doubling its international business. Wal-Mart achieved immediate economies of scale and got a chain of stores with nearly identical operating strategy. The deal would shift European retailing to a more efficient, low-price, long-hours model that could allow Wal-Mart to dominate its competitors.

Weyerhaeuser Co.–MacMillan Bloedel Ltd.
Announced June 21, 1999; Effective Nov. 11, 1999; $2.349 billion

Weyerhaeuser Co. announced an acquisition of MacMillan Bloedel Ltd. on June 21, 1999. Weyerhaeuser, a forest products company based in the United States, offered MacMillan, a leading Canadian timber firm, $2.3 billion in a stock swap. The combined company became one of the largest forest product firms in the world, with over 39 million acres of timber and annual sales of over $13 billion.

There were many reasons for the deal. Unlike most international mergers, the two firms were geographically compatible. Weyerhaeuser, based in the state of Washington, operated in close proximity to MacMillan Bloedel, whose primary operations were in the neighboring Canadian province of British Columbia. The combination was part of a consolidation wave that was overcoming the industry. Timber firms were experiencing difficulties that were partially due to lower demand from the struggling Asian nations. In addition, Weyerhaeuser believed it could increase its production of building materials because MacMillan had ample mills.

FORCES DRIVING CROSS-BORDER MERGERS

The data and cases just presented provide a basis for identifying the major forces driving cross-border mergers. Some of the forces are similar to those for purely domestic transactions, whereas others apply more strongly to international M&As. We first outline 10 major forces to serve as a road map for the discussion that follows.

1. Growth
2. Technology
3. Advantages in differentiated products
4. Roll-ups
5. Consolidation
6. Government policy
7. Exchange rates
8. Political and economic stability
9. Following clients
10. Diversification

Growth

Growth is the most important motive for international mergers. Growth is vital to the well-being of any firm. Mergers provide instant growth, and merging internationally adds a whole new dimension to this instant growth. Both the size of a market and the growth rates of markets are relevant for achieving growth objectives. The United States has long been highly regarded by foreign firms for exports, direct investment, and M&As because of its large and attractive markets. Firms in the United States have looked abroad to countries in relatively earlier stages of their life cycles, characterized by industries with rates of growth higher than in the United States. This has been especially true of U.S. food companies.

Leading firms in the domestic market may have lower costs because of economies of scale. Overseas expansion may enable medium-sized firms to attain the size necessary to improve their ability to compete. Finally, even with the most efficient management and technology, the globalization of world markets requires a critical size level simply to be able to carry out worldwide operations. Size enables firms to achieve the economies of scale necessary for effective global competition. Most of the firms listed in Table 17.5 whose characteristics were conveyed in our summary descriptions were motivated by growth objectives in their international M&As.

Technology

Technological considerations impact international mergers in two ways: (1) a technologically superior firm may make acquisitions abroad to exploit its technological advantage, or (2) a technologically inferior firm may acquire a foreign target with superior technology to enhance its competitive position both at home and abroad. It is generally accepted that for an investment project (in this case, the acquisition of a foreign firm) to be acceptable, the present value of benefits must exceed the present value of costs. If an asset (the target firm) is correctly priced, the present value of benefits should equal the present value of costs. For positive net present values to occur, an acquiring firm must either be able to buy the target for less than the present value of its benefits (the target must be underpriced) or be able to increase the present value of future benefits. It is unlikely that target firms are systematically underpriced (even if they were, underpricing would be more difficult to detect in foreign firms in an unfamiliar market than in domestic firms). Hence, the acquiring firm must bring something to the target that will increase the present value of benefits, or the target firm must bring something to the acquirer that enables the combined benefits of the merged firm to be greater than the sum of what the individual firms could have achieved separately—it must exhibit synergy.

In domestic mergers, increased benefits often result when the superior management efficiency of the acquiring firm is applied to the target firm's assets. In international mergers, the acquiring firm may have an advantage in general management functions such as planning and control or research and development. But capabilities in specific management functions such as marketing or labor relations, for example, tend to be environment-specific and are not readily transferred to different surroundings. Such factors may help to explain the predominance of the United Kingdom and Canada as international merger partners of the United States; that is, the common language and heritage and similar business practices minimize the drawbacks, making such skills more transferable.

Technological superiority, on the other hand, is a far more portable advantage and can be exploited more easily without a lot of cultural baggage. The acquirer may deliberately select a technologically inferior target that, because of this inferiority, is losing market share and thus market value. By injecting technology into the acquired firm, the acquirer can improve its competitive position and profitability both at home and abroad. Most of the firms in our sample also were strongly motivated by technology considerations. Some sought to buy into foreign markets to exploit their technological knowledge advantage. The Wal-Mart–ASDA transaction is an example. By using its superior inventory technologies, Wal-Mart could achieve lower prices. This would be a basis for expansion into widening foreign markets.

A primary motive for cross-border transactions is to acquire new technologies. This was true of many of the chemical, pharmaceutical, oil, and auto mergers. Renault's investment in Nissan was motivated in part by the desire to learn some of Nissan's manufacturing techniques as well as to establish a presence in Japan.

Advantages in Differentiated Products

There is strong correlation between multinationalization and product differentiation (Caves, 1982). This may indicate an application of the parent's (acquirer's) good reputation. A firm that has developed a reputation for superior products in the domestic market may find acceptance for the products in foreign markets as well. In the 1920s, the early days of the U.S. automobile industry, cars were exported to Europe in large numbers. This was before the auto industry was developed in European countries. The advantage of the U.S. mass production facilities and know-how made the American cars cheaper despite the high foreign tariffs and motivated foreign direct investments. The tables were then turned. First Volkswagens came from Germany to the United States. Then cars from Japan came to have a strong acceptance in the United States. Later, manufacturing operations were established by foreign makers in the United States. In the other direction, Ford's acquisition of Jaguar brought modern assembly lines and other production systems to achieve improved design, quality, and costs to the Jaguar operations.

Roll-Ups

Roll-ups to combine firms in fragmented industries have been taking place within the United States as well as internationally. US Filter had achieved a roll-up of water improvement facilities in the United States, and Vivendi, a French conglomerate, sought to apply these concepts in the broader European market. Similar motives appear to be working out in the energy industry, as exemplified by Scottish Power's acquisition of PacifiCorp. The acquisition by Texas Utilities of the U.K. Energy Group in 1998 reflected deregulation of energy markets, which created opportunities for energy industry roll-ups abroad as well as in the United States.

Consolidation

The ultimate aim of consolidation M&As has been to reduce worldwide excess capacity. The Daimler–Chrysler merger is a prime example.

Government Policy

Government policy, regulation, tariffs, and quotas can affect international mergers and acquisitions in a number of ways. Exports are particularly vulnerable to tariffs and quotas erected to protect domestic industries. Even the threat of such restrictions can encourage international mergers, especially when the market to be protected is large. Japan's huge export surplus, which led to voluntary export restrictions coupled with threats of more binding restrictions, was a major factor in increased direct investment by Japan in the United States.

Environmental and other government regulations (such as zoning, for example) can greatly increase the time and cost required to build facilities abroad for de novo entry. The added cost of compliance with regulation amplifies other effects that may be operating. Thus, the rationale for acquiring a company with existing facilities in place is reinforced by regulation.

The Deutsche Telekom acquisition of One2One is an example of the many influences of government policy. Deutsche Telekom had been a monopoly protected by the German government. German deregulation created competition from both international and German firms. Similarly, Deutsche Telekom acquired One2One because of the possibility of purchasing a coveted mobile phone license from the British government. The influence of government policy is also reflected in the European Union's decision to open previously regulated industries such as electric utilities to competition.

Exchange Rates

Foreign exchange rates affect international mergers in a number of ways. The relative strength or weakness of the domestic versus foreign currency can have an impact on the effective price paid for an acquisition, its financing, production costs of running the acquired firm, and the value of repatriated profits to the parent. Accounting conventions can give rise to currency translation profits and losses. Managing exchange rate risk is an additional cost of doing business for a multinational firm. The acquisitions by Union Pacific Resources and the CIT Group (both U.S. companies) of Canadian firms were facilitated by the decline in the value of the Canadian dollar in 1998 and 1999.

Political and Economic Stability

The relative political and economic stability of the United States has been an important factor in attracting foreign buyers. Political and/or economic instability can greatly increase the risk of what is already a riskier situation than purely domestic investments or acquisitions. Acquiring firms must consider the frequency with which the government changes, how orderly the transfer of power is, and how much government policies differ from one administration to the next, including the degree of difference between the dominant political parties. They must assess the likelihood of government intervention on both the upside and the downside (for example, subsidies, tax breaks, loan guarantees, and so forth, on the one hand, all the way to outright expropriation on the other hand).

Desirable economic factors include low, or at least predictable, inflation. Labor relations are another important consideration in economic stability. Western European labor unions appear to have a greater voice in the management of companies than do American unions.

The United States excels in virtually every measure of economic and political stability (except exchange rate stability in recent years). It is also a superior target because of the size and homogeneity of the market and the sophistication of the infrastructure. Transportation and communications networks in the United States are among the best in the world; the depth and breadth of U.S. financial markets are attractive; there is little risk of expropriation. Indeed, most states offer inducements to investment, and the labor force is relatively skilled and tractable. The high levels of foreign acquisitions described in Table 17.2 provide many examples.

Following Clients

The importance of long-term financial relationships is a major factor in international mergers in the financial services industry. If enough of a financial firm's clients move abroad, it makes economic sense for the firm to expand abroad as well. Foreign firms abroad may wish to remain loyal to their longstanding, home country banks. However, if a financial firm does not have offices available for servicing its clients, it runs the risk of losing business to more convenient local financial firms.

For some time, foreign financial services firms operating in the United States actually had an advantage over U.S. firms, especially in interstate banking, in that they were allowed to have branches in more than one state (with restrictions), whereas this was denied to U.S. banks. Over the years the playing field has become more equal. Because of its weak presence in the United States, especially in investment banking, Deutsche Bank acquired Bankers Trust. Similarly, Owens-Illinois' foreign acquisitions were made in part to support their major industrial customers as they expanded their businesses worldwide.

Diversification

International mergers can provide diversification both geographically and by product line. To the extent that various economies are not perfectly correlated, merging internationally reduces the earnings risk inherent in being dependent on the health of a single domestic economy. Thus, international mergers can reduce systematic as well as nonsystematic risk. The cross-border oil mergers have provided geographic diversification as well as opportunities for reducing excess capacity, increasing efficiency to reduce costs, and achieving the larger size required by global operations.

PREMIUMS PAID

Academic studies as well as the *Mergerstat* data show that foreign bidders pay higher premiums to acquire U.S. companies than the average of premiums paid in total acquisitions. In the Harris and Ravenscraft (1991) study of a sample of companies between 1970 and 1987, foreign bidders paid higher premiums by 10 percentage points. They found also that high foreign currency values led to increased premiums. Their data show that when foreign firms buy U.S. firms, they concentrate on research and development (R&D)-intensive industries. They found that the R&D intensity of foreign acquisitions is 50% higher than in purely domestic transactions. The Harris and Ravenscraft study found also that U.S. bidders earn only normal returns in both domestic and cross-border acquisitions. These results are consistent with other studies of bidder and target returns.

In Table 17.7, we pick up with 1987, the final year of the Harris and Ravenscraft study. A simple average of the percentages in Table 17.7 shows that average premiums

Table 17.7   Mean Premium in Foreign vs. Total
Announcements, 1987–1998

Year	Foreign Acquisitions	All Acquisitions
1987	39.4%	38.3%
1988	56.2%	41.9%
1989	38.9%	41.0%
1990	48.1%	42.0%
1991	39.8%	35.1%
1992	54.1%	41.0%
1993	41.8%	38.7%
1994	46.2%	41.9%
1995	41.9%	44.7%
1996	47.8%	36.6%
1997	33.0%	35.7%
1998	45.2%	40.7%
1999	43.2%	43.3%
1987–1999 avg	44.3%	40.1%

Source: *Mergerstat Review,* 1999.

in foreign acquisitions exceeded the average of all acquisitions by about four percentage points. One reason offered as an explanation is that foreign buyers offer higher premiums to preempt potential domestic bidders. Another possible reason is that U.S. targets have less knowledge of foreign buyers and need a higher premium to resolve some uncertainty. A third possible influence is that prospective future exchange rate movements give an edge to the U.S. dollar. But in four years, the average premium in foreign acquisitions was lower. In 1999 the difference was insignificant.

EVENT RETURNS

An early study (Doukas and Travlos, 1988) found that the announcement of international acquisitions was associated with positive abnormal returns for U.S. multinational enterprises that previously had not been operating in the target firm's country. When American firms expand internationally for the first time, the event returns are positive but not significant. When the American firm has already been operating in the target firm's home country, the event returns are negative but not significant. Shareholders of multinational enterprises gain the greatest benefits from foreign acquisitions when there is simultaneous diversification across industry and geographically.

Harris and Ravenscraft (1991) investigated shareholder returns for 1,273 U.S. firms acquired during the period 1970 to 1987. They found that in 75% of cross-border transactions the buyer and seller were not in related industries and that the takeovers were more frequent than domestic transactions in R&D-intensive industries. The percentage gain to the U.S. targets of foreign buyers was significantly higher than to the targets of U.S. buyers. The cross-border effects were positively related to the weakness of the U.S. dollar, indicating an important role for exchange movements in foreign direct investment.

A study of Japanese takeovers of U.S. firms (Kang, 1993) found that significant wealth gains are created for both Japanese bidders and U.S. targets. Returns to Japanese bidders and to a portfolio of Japanese bidders and U.S. targets increased with the leverage of the bidder, bidder's ties to financial institutions, and the depreciation of the dollar in relation to the Japanese yen. A study that controlled for relative corporate wealth and levels of investment in different countries found no statistically significant relationship between exchange rate levels and foreign investment relative to domestic investment in the U.S. chemical and retail industries (Dewenter, 1995).

Eun, Kolodny, and Scheraga (1996) studied 225 foreign acquisitions of U.S. firms that occurred during the period 1979 to 1990. For an 11-day event window, $[-5, +5]$, the CAR was 37.02% for the whole sample of U.S. targets, significant at the 1% level. Those acquired by firms from countries other than Japan were very similar, with a CAR between 35% and 37%. Cakici, Hessel, and Tandon (1996) examined the wealth gains for 195 foreign firms that acquired U.S. target firms during the period 1983 to 1992 compared to a sample of 112 U.S. acquisitions of foreign firms during the same period. The foreign acquiring firms experienced positive CARs of 0.63% for a two-day period, $[0, +1]$, and 1.96% over a $[-10, +10]$ window, both significant at the 1% level. Meanwhile, the U.S. acquirers had negative CARs of -0.36% and -0.25%, respectively, neither being significant.

Doukas (1995) used a sample consisting of 234 U.S. bidding firms involved in 463 international acquisitions over the period 1975 to 1989 to study the relationship between bidders' shareholders' gains and their q-ratios. The sample was divided into value maximizers and overinvestors based on Tobin's q. The two-day $[-1, 0]$ CAR for firms with average q-ratios greater than 1 (value-maximizing firms) was 0.41%, significant at the 5% level. Bidders with average q-ratios less than 1 (overinvested firms) had a negative CAR of -0.18%, not significant. The difference was significant at the 1% level. The impact of exchange rates was consistent with Froot and Stein's (1991) hypothesis of a negative relationship between the dollar exchange rate and the level of foreign direct investment. The method of payment and industry relatedness did not appear to be significant.

Seth, Song, and Pettit (2000) studied a sample of 100 cross-border acquisitions of U.S. targets during 1981 to 1990. The average CAR of acquirers was 0.11% for an event window $[-10, +10]$, not statistically significant. For targets, the average CAR was 38.3%, significant at the 1% level. Hudgins and Seifert (1996) looked at the announcement gains and losses for a sample of 88 American acquirers and 72 American targets involved in cross-border transactions of financial firms during 1968 to 1989. Announcement effects for U.S. financial firms acquiring foreign firms were not significant and were not statistically different from the effects experienced by U.S. financial firms acquiring domestic firms. Target shareholders of foreign bids gained significant positive returns of 9.2%.

Markides and Oyon (1998) used a sample of 236 acquisitions made by U.S. companies in the period 1975 to 1988. The total sample consisted of 189 U.S. acquisitions in Europe and 47 U.S. acquisitions in Canada. Using standard event-study methodology, they found significant but small gains for the acquiring firms. For a two-day event window, $[-1, 0]$, the acquirers' CAR for the whole sample was 0.38%, significant at the 5% level. However, the gains came from continental European acquisitions, a CAR of 0.47%, significant at the 10% level. Canadian and British acquisitions created no significant value for the acquiring U.S. firms. Wider event windows, $[-5, +5]$ and $[-10, +10]$, yielded positive nonsignificant CARs for all cases.

Event studies involving U.S. buyers of foreign targets and foreign buyers of U.S. targets gave results very similar to those of domestic transactions. Targets received large abnormal returns regardless of the direction of the transactions. Buyers similarly earned nonsignificant percentage returns regardless of whether they were U.S. firms or foreign firms engaged in cross-border acquisitions.

INTERNATIONAL JOINT VENTURES

International joint ventures magnify both the potentials and the weaknesses of joint ventures. In general, joint ventures should involve complementary capabilities. The risks posed by different cultural systems among firms from different countries may increase the tensions normally found in joint ventures.

Despite the increased challenges of international joint ventures, the advantages of joint ventures may be expanded. Some of the particular benefits of international joint ventures may be noted (Zahra and Elhagrasey, 1994): (1) The joint venture may be the only feasible method for obtaining access to raw materials and overcoming government barriers to exporting key raw materials. (2) Different historical backgrounds and different managerial and technological skills may be associated with firms in different countries. International joint ventures, therefore, may involve different capabilities and link together complementary skills. (3) Having local partners may reduce the risks involved in operating in a foreign country. (4) The joint ventures may be necessary to overcome trade barriers. In addition, some of the advantages of domestic joint ventures may be enhanced. These include the achievement of economies of scale in providing a basis for a faster rate of corporate growth.

Management styles may be different for companies from different countries. However, it appears that over time there has been increasing convergence of western and Asian management styles (Swierczek and Hirsch, 1994). In the past, the basic values of western management emphasized the individual, legal rules, and confrontation. In contrast, the Asian approach emphasized the group, trust, and compromise. With regard to management style, the western approach was emphasized by rationality and structured relationships. The Asian approach involved relationships, consensus, flexibility, and adaptive behavior. Over time, however, a convergence of the different management styles has been taking place.

Because of the complexity of relationships of international joint ventures, some principles have been suggested for the management of successful collaborations (Shaughnessy, 1995). Because joint ventures are a temporary alliance for combining complementary capabilities, joint venture contracts should make it easy to terminate the relationship. The initial contract should take into account which firm will become the outright owner of the joint venture activity and formulate the terms under which one company can buy out the other. The control and ultimate decision makers should be specified in advance. The activities and information flows in the joint venture should be tied into normal communication structures.

Criteria for evaluation of performance should be part of the contractual relationship. Because of the inherent uncertainties of the future alternative outcomes, scenarios should be visualized as a basis for allocation of rewards and responsibilities under different types of outcomes. Finally, it is in the international area particularly that the knowledge acquisition potentials of joint ventures can be substantial. However, contractual differences may also put these potentials at considerable risk or failure of realization.

A study of 88 international joint venture announcements found statistically significant positive portfolio excess returns (Chen, Hu, and Shieh, 1991) when U.S. firms invested relatively small amounts in joint ventures that gained significantly positive excess returns. When firms made relatively large investments in the joint ventures, the positive excess returns were no longer significant.

An in-depth book-length study of joint ventures in the steel industry documents the diverse motives and effects (Mangum, Kim, and Tallman, 1996) (MKT). These authors place the steel industry in the setting of an industrial staircase that moves from the agrarian age to an industrial age and finally to the present information age. The steel industry is put in the setting of a basic intermediate product with a capital resource emphasis. Summary data are provided on the investments by 17 foreign steelmakers in U.S. joint ventures. The foreign partners are mainly from Japan. In-depth case studies of seven joint ventures in steel are presented. The initial motive was the availability of foreign capital for modernizing the U.S. steel industry. Another important objective was to transfer the superior process technologies of the Asian partners to American plants. Cross-cultural differences added to the tensions usually found in joint ventures. Nevertheless, MKT judge the joint ventures to be generally successful. The only joint venture that experienced great difficulties was the combination between NKK of Japan and the National Steel Corporation of the United States. NKK was Japan's second largest steel producer but accounted for only 15% of Japan's total output of finished steel, compared with 72% for number 1 Nippon Steel. National Steel had been formed in 1929 and was number 7 in the United States. In the fall of 1983, it reorganized itself as National Intergroup Inc. (NII), announcing that it would withdraw from the steel business and diversify into pharmaceuticals, aluminum, financial services, and computer services. Early in 1984 NII sold its Weirton works to its employees under an ESOP. It offered the remainder of its steelmaking facilities to USX. But the Department of Justice blocked the sale on antitrust grounds.

Among the alternatives, the joint venture with NKK seemed the least unpalatable. NKK considered itself to be a world leader in steel technology but was unable to exploit its capabilities fully because of domestic overcapacity and rising obstacles to international trade. The joint venture with NII was viewed as the first step in its broader globalization plans. Despite considerable progress, the economic downturn in the United States in 1989 and 1990 caused losses. National Steel made a public offering of common stock as a device for NII to sell its ownership to the public. NKK's ownership share moved from 50% to 75%. NII "bailed out" of the joint venture. NKK took over ownership in an effort to restore its profitability. For 1994 a net income of $168.5 million was achieved. MKT conclude that although the joint venture came asunder, National Steel survived under a new management team.

COST OF CAPITAL IN FOREIGN ACQUISITIONS AND INVESTMENTS

The calculation of the appropriate cost of capital to apply to the free cash flows of a foreign entity requires the use of the principles of international finance. Two main sets of concepts are involved. First are the fundamental international parity or equilibrium relationships. Second are the issues of whether the global capital markets are integrated or segmented. The first provides some insights for understanding the relationship between the cost of domestic debt and the cost of debt in foreign countries. The capital market integration issues relate to measuring the cost of equity capital in different countries.

Cost of Debt Relationships

International business transactions are conducted in many different currencies. However, a U.S. exporter selling to a foreigner generally expects to be paid in U.S. dollars. Conversely, a foreign importer buying from an American exporter may prefer to pay in his or her own currency. The existence of the foreign exchange markets allows buyers and sellers to deal in the currencies of their preference. The foreign exchange markets consist of individual brokers, the large international banks, and other commercial banks that facilitate transactions on behalf of their customers. Payments may be made in one currency by an importer and received in another by the exporter.

Exchange rates may be expressed in U.S. dollars per foreign unit or in foreign currency (FC) units per U.S. dollar. An exchange rate of $0.50 to FC 1 shows the value of one foreign currency unit in terms of the dollar. We shall use E_0 to indicate the spot rate, E_f to indicate the forward rate at the present time, and E_1 to indicate the actual future spot rate corresponding to E_f. An exchange rate of FC 2 to $1 shows the value of the dollar in terms of the number of foreign currency units it will purchase. We will use the symbol X with corresponding subscripts to refer to the exchange rate expressed as the number of foreign currency units per dollar. We follow these conventions in developing four fundamental equilibrium relationships of international finance.

The model of international parity relationships is based on the assumptions required for perfect markets: Financial markets are perfect; goods markets are perfect; the future is known with certainty; the markets are in equilibrium. We can then establish the following equilibrium relationships:

1. The interest rate parity theorem (IRPT).
2. The forward parity theorem (FPT).
3. The purchasing power parity theorem (PPPT).
4. The international Fisher relation (IFR).

The Interest Rate Parity Theorem (IRPT)

The interest rate parity theorem holds that the ratio of the forward and spot exchange rates will equal the ratio of foreign and domestic nominal interest rates. The formal statement of the IRPT may be expressed as follows:

$$\frac{X_f}{X_0} = \frac{1 + R_{f0}}{1 + R_{d0}} = \frac{E_0}{E_f}$$

Where:

X_f = current forward exchange rate expressed as FC units per \$1 = 10.75
E_f = current forward exchange rate expressed as dollars per FC unit = \$0.093
X_0 = current spot exchange rate expressed as FC units per \$1 = 9.52
E_0 = current spot exchange rate expressed as dollars per FC unit = \$0.105
R_{f0} = current foreign interest rate
R_{d0} = current domestic interest rate = 0.09

We now illustrate a practical way of developing numerical examples. We begin by looking at the foreign exchange rates and currency future prices in the *Wall Street Journal*. Suppose we find that the spot price for the Mexican peso is \$0.105 in dollars, which is 9.52 pesos per dollar. The one-year futures value of the peso is \$0.093; in pesos per dollar, this is 10.75. So it takes more pesos to buy a dollar in the futures market than in the spot market. We use a U.S. prime rate of 9% as an indication of the borrowing cost to a prime business customer in the United States. These are the values shown in the foregoing list explanation of symbols.

We now apply the interest rate parity theorem to obtain the current foreign interest rate. We have

$$\frac{10.75}{9.52} = \frac{x}{1.09}$$

Solving for *x*, we obtain 1.23 or a Mexican interest rate to a prime borrower in Mexico of 23%. We next set forth the forward parity theorem.

The Forward Parity Theorem (FPT)

Under the perfect and efficient market assumptions postulated, spot futures or forward exchange rates should be unbiased predictors of future spot rates. Hence, X_f should equal X_1, or the future spot rate (X_1) should equal the current forward rate. In our numerical example, the future spot rate should be 10.75 pesos to the dollar. We can now make use of the purchasing power parity theorem.

The Purchasing Power Parity Theorem (PPPT)

The purchasing power parity theorem is an expression of the law of one price: In competitive markets the exchange-adjusted prices of identical tradable goods and financial assets must be equal worldwide (taking account of information and transaction costs). PPPT deals with the rates at which domestic goods are exchanged for foreign goods. Thus, if *X* dollars buy a bushel of wheat in the United States, the *X* dollars should also buy a bushel of wheat in the United Kingdom. In formal terms the PPPT may be stated as:

$$\frac{X_1}{X_0} = \frac{T_f}{T_d}$$

Where:

T_f = 1 + foreign country inflation rate = ?
T_d = 1 + domestic inflation rate = 1.03

Using the data we have developed to this point, we have:

$$\frac{10.75}{9.52} = \frac{x}{1.03}$$

We can now calculate Mexico's expected inflation rate based on the parity relationships by solving for the unknown in the above, which is 16.3% per annum. We can now illustrate the international Fisher relation.

The International Fisher Relation (IFR)

The Fisher relation states that nominal interest rates reflect the anticipated rate of inflation. The Fisher relation can be stated in a number of forms. We shall use:

$$1 + R_n = (1 + r)(T)$$

Where:

T = 1 + rate of inflation
r = real rate of interest
R_n = nominal rate of interest

For Mexico, we have $1.23 = (1+r)(1.163)$, so $r = 0.058$; for the United States we have $1.09 = (1+r)(1.03)$, so again r = 0.058. The real rates are the same, but the nominal rates differ by the inflation factors.

We can now summarize what the four parity relationships tell us. Interest rate parity states that current interest rate relationships will be consistent with a country's ratio of forward exchange rates to current spot rates. The forward parity condition says that the current forward rate is a good predictor of the expected future spot rate. Purchasing power parity states that the ratios of inflation rates will be consistent with the ratio of the future spot rate to the current spot rate. Finally, the Fisher relationship states that if the other parity conditions hold, real rates of interest will be the same across countries and nominal interest rates will reflect different inflation rates.

There are many real-world frictions that cause departures from parity conditions in the short run. But these are the relationships toward which international financial markets are always moving. Experience and empirical evidence teach us that these parity conditions provide a useful guide for business executives. For an individual manager to believe that he can outguess the international financial markets, which reflect the judgments of many players, is hubris in the extreme. He puts his company at the peril of severe losses.

Standard textbooks in finance describe how the use of futures markets can be used to hedge foreign exchange risks. In addition, many strategies can be used in conjunction with the futures markets. These include borrowing in foreign markets for foreign projects, conducting manufacturing operations in multiple countries as a buffer for inflation and foreign exchange rate movements, and making sales in multiple countries to offset strong and weak currency buyers, among others. Details on such strategies are beyond the scope of this book. Our objective is to estimate the applicable cost of capital for foreign acquisitions or investments. Our discussion of the parity relationships provides a basis for understanding the applicable cost of capital for foreign acquisitions or investments.

Cost of Equity and Cost of Capital

We begin with the basic idea behind the capital asset pricing model (CAPM), which is widely used to calculate the cost of equity. CAPM states that the cost of equity capital is the risk-free return plus a risk adjustment that is the product of the return on the market as a whole multiplied by the beta risk measure of the individual firm or project. How the market is defined depends on whether the global capital market is integrated or segmented. If integrated, investments are made globally and systematic risk is measured relative to a world market index. If capital markets are segmented, investments are predominantly made in a particular segment or country and systematic risk is measured relative to a domestic index. With the rise of large financial institutions investing worldwide and mutual funds that facilitate international or foreign investments, the world is moving toward a globally integrated capital market. But we are not there yet because of the home bias phenomenon: Investors place only a relatively small part of their funds abroad. For recent data, see Hulbert (2000). The reasons are not fully understood. One possibility is there may be extra costs of obtaining and digesting information. Another possibility is the greater uncertainty associated with placing investments under the jurisdiction of another country whose authorities may change the rules of the game. If capital markets are not fully integrated, there are gains from international diversification. A multinational corporation (MNC) would apply to a foreign investment a lower cost of capital than a local (foreign) company would (see Chan, Karolyi, and Stulz, 1992; Stulz, 1995a, 1995b; Stulz and Wasserfallen, 1995; and Godfrey and Espinosa, 1996).

Let us continue with the Mexico example. A firm domiciled in Mexico will have a beta based on market returns for investments in Mexico. An MNC domiciled outside Mexico will have a cost of equity capital related to its beta measured with respect to the markets in which it operates. A world market index might be a reasonable approximation, but measurement problems and availability would be formidable. The examples we used in chapters 9 and 10 on valuation were firms like Exxon and Mobil, which participate in global oil markets. Their betas, calculated by Value Line and others, are based on the U.S. market. So the betas used for MNCs already reflect the benefits of their foreign activities. Since a part of their cash flow patterns reflect foreign market conditions, their total cash flow patterns in relation to the U.S. market are likely to have a smaller covariance or beta. Thus, the betas we used in chapters 9 and 10 for the Exxon–Mobil example were lower than if the firms had only domestic U.S. operations. The costs of equity capital used for Exxon was 10.25%, and for Mobil it was 9.75%. These are relatively low costs expressed in U.S. dollars.

If we calculated the cost of equity for an investment in Mexico in nominal peso terms, it would necessarily reflect a risk differential above the cost of debt borrowing in Mexico. If the cost of debt borrowing in Mexico is about 23% based on our prior analysis, then the cost of equity is likely to be four to seven percentage points higher. Assuming a leverage ratio of debt to equity at market of 50%, a cost of equity of 30%, and a tax rate of 40%, we can calculate the weighted cost as follows:

$$\text{WACC} = (0.23)(0.6)(0.5) + (0.30)(0.5) = 0.219$$

We could use this discount factor of approximately 22% in calculating the present value of an investment in Mexico. The cash flows expressed in pesos discounted by the peso cost of capital would give us a present value expressed in pesos. This

Table 17.8 Calculation of Expected Future Exchange Rates

Year	Relative Inflation Factors		X_t
0	X_0 = pesos per \$	=	9.50
1	$9.5(1.16/1.03)$	=	10.70
2	$9.5(1.16/1.03)^2$	=	12.05
3	$9.5(1.16/1.03)^3$	=	13.57
4	$9.5(1.16/1.03)^4$	=	15.28
5	$9.5(1.16/1.03)^5$	=	17.21

present value converted to dollars at the spot rate should give us the net present value of the investment in dollars.

We should get the same result by beginning with the cash flows in pesos, converting them to dollars over time, and discounting them by the WACC of the U.S. firm. We illustrate this second method. The project yields cash flows over a five-year period, at the end of which it hopefully can be sold to a local buyer for 10,000 pesos. First we calculate the expected foreign exchange rate expressed in the number of pesos per dollar.

We start with the spot rate of 9.5 pesos per dollar. From interest rate parity, for each subsequent year we multiply the 9.5 times $(1.16/1.03)^t$, the relative inflation rates, as shown in Table 17.8. These are inputs that we use in Table 17.9, the calculation of the present value of the firm or project expressed in dollars.

Line 1 of Table 17.9 represents the preliminary estimates of cash flows from the firm or project expressed in pesos. In line 2 we recognize that these projections are subject to error. We are particularly concerned that the foreign country may change the rules of the game. Political instability might bring a government with an anti-foreign business philosophy into power. Discriminatory taxes might be imposed. Restrictions on repatriation of funds might be enacted. Militant unions might raise wage costs, reducing net cash flows. We feel it is better to explicitly recognize these risk adjustments in the cash flows rather than fudge the discount factor. The discount factor should reflect systematic risk and not the idiosyncratic factors described.

Line 3 of Table 17.9 therefore represents the risk-adjusted expected peso cash flows. In line 4 we list the results from Table 17.8 where the expected future exchange rates were calculated. In line 5 the exchange rates are applied to the expected peso cash flows of line 3 to give us the expected cash flows expressed in dollars.

In line 6 we apply a discount factor. In the discussion of interest rate parity, we assumed a before-tax cost of debt for the U.S. firm of 9%. We postulate further a cost of equity, leverage, and tax rates to yield a WACC of 10%. Since we already covered these procedures in chapters 9 and 10, we can streamline this discussion to focus on the foreign investment issues. Line 7 presents the discounted dollar cash flows using the data in lines 5 and 6. In line 8 the present values from line 7 are summed to obtain the total present value of the firm or project of \$463 million. The U.S. firm could incur investment outlays with a present value of up to \$463 million to earn its cost of capital.

Table 17.9   Calculation of Present Value in Dollars

				Year			
	0	1	2	3	4	5	5*
1. Initial expected cash flows in pesos		1,000	1,100	1,200	1,400	1,600	10,000
2. Probability (risk) factors		0.9	0.9	0.8	0.8	0.6	0.5
3. Risk adjusted expected peso cash flow		900	990	960	1,120	960	5,000
4. Exchange rate in year t (X_t)		10.7	12.05	13.57	15.28	17.21	17.21
5. Expected dollar cash flows		$84	$82	$71	$73	$56	$291
6. Applicable discount factor @ 10%		1.10	1.21	1.33	1.46	1.61	1.61
7. Discounted dollar cash flows		$76.47	$67.90	$53.15	$50.06	$34.64	$180.40
8. Present value	$462.61						

*Sale of assets for 10,000 pesos in year 5.

We have illustrated a systematic methodology for valuing foreign acquisitions or making direct investments. The numbers used in the example were simplified to facilitate the exposition. The underlying principles and concepts would be the same if we were using a complex sophisticated computer program. The method is similar to the valuation of domestic investments. The complications are mainly foreign exchange risks and foreign country risks. The parity relationships provide useful guidelines for thinking about foreign exchange rates, relative inflation, and relative interest rates. In Table 17.9 we do not mean to imply that the risk factors applied in line 2 are to be approached passively. A company can use a wide range of strategies to minimize the unfavorable possibilities. A sound project or the purchase of a foreign firm can contribute to increased employment, productivity, and output in the foreign country. The technological and management practices the parent brings to the subsidiary may make its continued participation indispensable. Also, the foreign operation can be so organized that it could not function without the unique parts provided by the parent. Another possibility is that the investment is part of an international agency program to develop the infrastructure of the host country. Arbitrary changes in the rules of the game could injure the reputation and reduce future international support of a self-serving government.

As we noted at the beginning of this chapter, the number and magnitude of cross-border mergers are growing faster than that of U.S. mergers. Cross-border mergers involve international factors that need to be taken into account. Our aim has been to improve decision making in the area of international transactions.

SUMMARY

International mergers are subject to many of the same influences and motivations as domestic mergers. However, they also present unique threats and opportunities. The issue of mergers versus other means of achieving international business goals (such as import/export, licensing, joint ventures) builds on the fundamental issue in the theory of the firm: whether to transact across markets or to internalize transactions using managerial coordination within the firm.

When firms choose to merge internationally, it implies that they have concluded that this will result in lower costs or higher productivity than alternative contractual means of achieving international goals. In horizontal mergers, intangible assets play an important role in both domestic and international combinations. The exploitation of an intangible asset such as knowledge may require merger because of the "public good" nature of the asset. Attempts to exploit intangibles short of merger requires complex contracting, which is not only expensive but likely to be incomplete (especially when compounded by the problems of dealing with a foreign environment), possibly leading to dissipation of the owner's proprietary interest in the asset. Similarly, vertically integrated firms exist to internalize markets for intermediate products on both the domestic and international levels.

Among the special factors impacting international mergers more than domestic mergers are tariff barriers and exchange rate relationships. Operating within a tariff barrier may be the only means of obtaining competitive access to a large market, for example, the European Common Market. Exchange rates are also an important influence. A strong dollar makes U.S. products more expensive abroad but reduces the cost of acquiring foreign firms. The reverse holds when the dollar is weak, encouraging U.S. exports and foreign acquisitions of U.S. companies, all other factors held constant.

Although the risks of operating in a foreign environment are greater, they can be reduced through careful planning or by an incremental approach to entering the foreign market. Furthermore, to the extent that the foreign economy is imperfectly correlated with the domestic economy, the systematic risk to the company as a whole may be reduced by international diversification.

The increasing globalization of competition in product markets is extending rapidly into internationalization of the takeover market. The best method by which to achieve a firm's expansion goals may no longer be the takeover of a domestic firm but of a foreign one. International M&A activity has experienced substantial growth over the past 20 years, and this is likely to continue to increase into the future.

QUESTIONS

17.1 Why is M&A activity in Europe in recent years growing at a more rapid rate than in the United States?

17.2 Why is M&A activity increasing in Japan in recent years?

17.3 Why is M&A activity increasing in the People's Republic of China in recent years?

17.4 Why is M&A activity increasing in other Asian areas, such as Taiwan, Korea, and Malaysia?

17.5 Describe the two most important reasons behind each of the cross-border transactions discussed in the brief case studies in the text.

17.6 What has been driving the big pharmaceutical mergers in recent years?

17.7 Are there any forces driving cross-border mergers that operate more strongly than the reasons for transactions that take place within a given country's border?

17.8 How would you explain why foreign bidders pay higher premiums for U.S. targets than U.S. domestic bidders pay for U.S. targets?

17.9 Suppose you go to the web page of the Central Bank of Mexico and find that the inflation rate in Mexico during the last 5 years has been 12% per annum. You check a number of other research sources and find that this inflation rate is expected to continue for the next five years.

a. With a current spot rate of 9.5 Mexican pesos to the U.S. dollar and an expected inflation rate in the U.S. for the next five years at 3%, use PPPT to calculate the expected future spot rate in one year.

b. The forward parity theorem holds so that the spot futures or forward exchange rate is equal to the expected future spot rate. Use IRPT to calculate the current interest rate in Mexico when the comparable U.S. interest rate is 9%.

Case 17.1 The Saga of Gerber Products

The case study of Gerber Products is a more detailed analysis of the role of international markets in the growth of food companies. For years, Gerber saw the necessity of expanding abroad. But somehow Gerber was unable to implement its goals of expanding internationally. The M&A market accomplished what Gerber was unable to do on its own.

GERBER REBUFFS ANDERSON CLAYTON

In 1977 Gerber Products was approached by Anderson Clayton Company. Anderson Clayton was seeking to continue to expand its diversified operations, which had already included processing soy beans, coffee, and a life insurance company. Anderson Clayton's overtures were rebuffed by Gerber Products. Nevertheless, Anderson Clayton made a tender offer for Gerber Products at $40 a share.

Gerber management mounted a strong defense. Gerber Products filed suit against Anderson Clayton in a federal court in Grand Rapids, Michigan, relatively near the Gerber headquarters in Fremont, Michigan. Gerber charged that the acquisition by Anderson Clayton would represent a serious antitrust conflict. It charged that potential competition between the companies in the future would be stifled by the merger. Gerber argued that Anderson Clayton could develop a baby products business in the future. Gerber also stated that it had been considering entrance into the salad oil market, in which Anderson Clayton was already doing business. Gerber's lawsuit also charged that in its tender offer Anderson Clayton did not make adequate disclosure of $2.1 million in questionable payments it had made overseas. This charge obviously sought to embarrass Anderson Clayton by the adverse publicity that would be generated by raising this issue. Gerber also complained that Anderson Clayton had not made adequate disclosure of its financing arrangements in its tender offer filing. Under Michigan's antitakeover law, there is a requirement for a 60-day waiting period after a tender offer. Gerber Products used this time to seek out an acceptable white knight. Gerber began discussions with Unilever as a possible alternative purchaser. Anderson Clayton continued its friendly approaches to Gerber. In addition, Anderson Clayton secured a financing agreement from several New York banks to establish compliance with this requirement under Michigan's antitakeover law.

At its July 1977 annual meeting, Gerber reported that second-quarter earnings had dropped by one-third. Anderson Clayton indicated that Gerber was deliberately understating its earnings and lowered its offer from $40 to $37.

In the meantime, the Michigan courts issued a series of rulings, all favorable to Gerber. A trial on the securities charges was scheduled for September 1977. After this trial, there would be another in which the antitrust charges would be litigated. Faced with uncertain and expensive litigation and the possibility that over the extended period of time other bidders might force higher bids, Anderson Clayton withdrew its offer. In response to this announcement, the stock price of Gerber fell from $34.375 to $28.25.

GERBER'S STRATEGIC PROBLEMS

In the following years, Gerber sought to reduce its vulnerability to a takeover. Gerber attempted to diversify into other areas such as children's apparel, furniture, farming, day care centers, trucking, humidifiers, and life insurance. None of these appeared to have any real synergy with Gerber's baby food business.

Although Gerber held 70% of the U.S. baby food market, it was relatively weak abroad. Higher growth for Gerber would have meant increasing its sales in countries outside the United States, which annually account for 98% of births worldwide. Over the years, Gerber made some efforts to expand its overseas operations but hesitated to commit the funds that would have had a near-term negative impact on its profitability rates. Because it was an inexpensive way to go, Gerber often would license overseas manufacturers to make and distribute its baby food. Licensing has at least two drawbacks. First, the fees that can be charged for licensing are relatively small. Second, the licensee develops the critical capability and can always play one product off against another. Sometimes the licensing arrangements came to an end because the foreign manufacturer decided to shift to other products. As a consequence, increasingly Gerber was supplying Asia and the Middle East from its U.S. plants.

THE AUCTION OF GERBER

As a consequence of its weak performance abroad, Gerber's revenues stayed flat at about $1.2 billion from 1990 through 1994 (Gibson, 1994). Its net income for the years 1990 through 1994 averaged less than $100 million. Gerber had stock splits in 1982, 1984, 1989, and 1992. But adjusted for all splits, the Gerber stock stayed relatively flat in the range of $30 per share. Gerber realized it needed to go abroad but was reluctant to commit the resources that would have a negative impact on earnings. In early 1994 Gerber requested Goldman Sachs to explore a possible friendly buyout that would help Gerber become stronger in the overseas markets. Essentially, an auction was conducted. The winner was Sandoz AG, a Swiss company that bid $53 a share on May 23, 1994. When takeover speculation started, the price of Gerber shares moved up by 33% between early February 1994 and the period just before the Sandoz offer. After the Sandoz offer, Gerber shares increased another $15.50 to $50.125. The $53 price was high because it represented 30 times current earnings, 20 times after-tax cash flow, and three times sales.

For Sandoz, the acquisition would expand its position in the food business and in nutritional product sales. Sandoz already had a strong position in food sales in Europe and Asia, but only 14% of its food sales came from North America.

It was pointed out that the Sandoz bid would not include any form of stock option lockup. This followed from the court decision in the QVC takeover of Paramount. Paramount had granted Viacom, its preferred buyer, the right to buy 24 million Paramount shares for $69.14. When Paramount went to $80 a share, the option was worth $500 million to Viacom. Nevertheless, the Sandoz agreement involved a breakup fee. In a breakup fee arrangement, the original bidder receives a fee if it does not succeed in the takeover. Gerber agreed to pay $70 million to Sandoz if the Sandoz bid did not succeed.

Some writers argue that differences in tax laws made the acquisition more attractive to Sandoz than to a U.S. buyer (Sloan, 1994). The tangible net worth of Gerber was about $300 million. For a U.S. buyer, the difference between the $3.7 billion paid and the $300 million tangible net worth of Gerber would have represented goodwill. A U.S. company would have had to charge its after-tax profits, $85 million a year for 40 years, which was 75% of the $114 million net income of Gerber in its 1994 fiscal year. Sandoz, on the other hand, could charge the goodwill against its own net worth without affecting annual earnings. It was stated that the $114 million net income would represent a 38% return on the $300 million tangible assets Sandoz would add to its balance sheet (Sloan, 1994). In addition, there was also a possibility of a tax write-off by Sandoz in connection with the goodwill purchase and write-off.

QUESTIONS

1. Why was Gerber interested in expanding in international markets?
2. Why was Gerber unable to succeed on its own in developing international markets?
3. Why did Gerber reject the earlier efforts by Anderson Clayton to acquire it?
4. Why did Gerber request its investment banker to find a buyer who could develop Gerber's potential in international markets?
5. Why was Sandoz interested in Gerber?

Case 17.2 Ciba-Geigy Merger with Sandoz*

In Basel, Switzerland on March 7, 1996, Ciba-Geigy and Sandoz issued a joint statement by the chairmen of both companies that they would merge into one company with the new name Novartis (Olmos, 1996). The company would focus on its core businesses, which are pharmaceuticals, agribusiness, and nutrition. Each company would divest its divisions that do not relate to the core life sciences focus of the new company Novartis. This includes Ciba's division of specialty chemicals (Tanouye, Lipin, and Moore, 1996).

*Written by Erica Clark and J. F. Weston.

Ciba is well known for its New Vues disposable contact lens, Habitrol nicotine patches, Ritalin for hyperactive children, Sunkist vitamins, Maalox, Zantac, and Efidac, an over-the-counter cold medicine. Sandoz is known for its nutrition division, which includes Gerber baby foods, Ovaltine, and Wasa crispbreads.

The new name Novartis is partly due to the strategy that the merger is between two equals who wish to become innovators for the next century (Guyon, 1996). The new name was developed by London's Siegal & Gale consultants, who were hired to create a powerful new marketing strategy for the company. The word derives from the Latin *novo,* which means new, and *artis,* which means skill. The new name had to be tested in 180 countries to make sure that it did not have any negative connotations.

Ciba-Geigy is the world's ninth largest drugmaker, while Sandoz is the 14th. The merger would create a new company that would be the world's number one supplier in agricultural chemicals, a world leader in biotechnology, and a large presence in the nutrition products field. The new firm would still have only 4.4% of the global market. The new company would have the third largest pharmaceuticals revenue, with drug sales at $10.94 billion (1995 revenue).

On April 24, 1996, in Basel, Switzerland, the merger was put to a vote at the final Ciba annual general meeting. The meeting counted 6,896 people in attendance with 70% of share capital with voting privileges. The CEO of Ciba, Dr. Alex Krauer, told shareholders that the merger "will not only improve shareholder value, but also open a promising future for the majority of our employees." The merger was approved by 98.7% of the members present and 69.4% of the share capital. The Sandoz shareholders approved the merger on April 24, 1996. The next phase of merger approval would involve regulatory agencies of the European Union and to a lesser extent that of the United States.

Shareholders of Ciba stock received 1.067 shares of Novartis, and shareholders of Sandoz stock received one share of Novartis for each share they currently held. Sandoz shareholders hold 55% of the new company, whereas Ciba shareholders hold 45% of Novartis.

The merger took many analysts by surprise, but most agree that it is an excellent strategic move because it is a proactive reaction to the general consolidation of the industry. The bankers who negotiated the deal were also praised because it was structured as a share swap instead of an outright purchase. This will cause the deal to be virtually tax-free, and there will also be no write-down of "goodwill." Goodwill compensates for the difference between sale price and the book value of assets but can be a negative force because it reduces reported profits.

The news of the merger sent stock prices of the large pharmaceutical companies soaring. It also affected smaller companies that are seen as possible takeover targets for the large companies looking to compete with the new Novartis. Both companies are traded on the Swiss stock market, and reaction to the news was positive for both companies, Sandoz shares rising 20% and Ciba's rising 30%. This can also be attributed to the intended cut of 10% of the work force of the newly created company. The new company will have an estimated total market value of $60 billion.

STRATEGIC REASONS FOR THE CIBA–SANDOZ MERGER

The consolidation of these two large companies reflects a growing trend in the fiercely competitive pharmaceuticals industry (Kraul, 1996). This is partly attributable to the high cost of research and development that is specific to the industry. There have been an estimated $80 billion in mergers since 1993 in the pharmaceutical industry. However, the top 20 companies still make up only 50% of total sales worldwide (*Economist,* 1994).

Both companies are facing the fundamental challenges that most drug companies are encountering in the current highly competitive market. The challenge is to develop a continuing supply of significant new drugs. This constant push for innovation based on the research and development of new products causes the pharmaceutical business to be inherently risky, because research and development is extremely costly but does not guarantee a constant stream of new products. In addition, the creation of new products is also heavily dependent on the approval of regulatory agencies such as the U.S. Food and Drug Administration (FDA). Of every 10 drugs that pass the initial investigation stage, only one will ultimately receive approval of the FDA. Of the few products that ultimately do gain regulatory approval, only a fraction generate sufficient sales to earn the cost of capital for a drug company, even a modest 10% to 12%.

Another major challenge facing these companies is that the pharmaceutical industry seems to produce important scientific breakthroughs in cycles. There are periods of great productivity and periods when the foundations for new research are in the development stage. This causes incredible pressure on the pharmaceutical companies to produce, even when their research is in the slow development phase. This particular issue was of great concern to both Ciba and Sandoz. The companies viewed the merger as a way to create a more powerful research arsenal, which will help them into the important new research frontiers of the new century, such as biotechnology. Sandoz has invested heavily in gene research, but newly developed products are still years away (Taber, 1996).

Sandoz and Ciba have both experienced the cyclical effects of research innovation. Sandoz was a market leader in Cyclosporin, used in organ transplantation, an area where Sandoz holds an 80% market share, accounting for almost one-fourth of its drug revenues. This major product will soon end its patent protection period in the U.S. and other major markets. This patent protection ensures a virtual monopoly on the drug that Sandoz researched and produced. The end of patent protection will cause a significant drop in its income from Cyclosporin because it will now face competition from cheaper generic drugs. Another large income source for Sandoz is Clozaril, used in treating schizophrenia, which has lost patent protection. Powerful new competition for Clozaril has been developing.

The highly aggressive nature of the current industry trend of merge or be an acquisition target caused Ciba and Sandoz to make a decisive move toward consolidation. The merger can be attributed to the rapid pace of other mergers that have taken place in the industry. Cost containment efforts by governments and managed health care organizations have squeezed profits and forced industry restructuring. Through mergers, firms have sought to economize on research costs, combine product lines, and increase marketing effectiveness. The Glaxo–Wellcome merger in 1995 produced a company with almost $12 billion in 1995 pharmaceutical revenues, making it number one worldwide. Glaxo planned to reduce costs by closing plants and reducing employment by 7,500 out of the 62,000 workforce.

BACKGROUND ON COMPANIES

Ciba-Geigy and Sandoz share a long corporate relationship dating back to Basel in the 1850s. The Ciba company merged with the Geigy company in 1970. The Geigy company was founded in 1758 by Johann Geigy, who traded organic compounds such as spices and natural dyes. It had grown into a large company by the 1900s. Another Basel citizen started a synthetic dye trade around the turn of the century called Gesellschaft für Chemische industrie im Basle, which was later shortened to CIBA. Sandoz was founded in 1886 in Basel as Kern & Sandoz. After World War I, the German chemical cartel that had previously dominated was broken up and the Swiss chemical companies took its place. A new cartel was established between Ciba, Sandoz, and Geigy known as Basel AG.

In the 1970s Ciba-Geigy had several public setbacks, including the discovery of the way the company had tested the chemical Galecron. In 1976 they paid six Egyptian boys to stand in a field and have the chemical sprayed on them. The result was public outrage, and the company was forced to improve its tarnished image. Then in 1978 over 1,000 deaths in Japan were linked to a Ciba-Geigy diarrhea medication.

In the 1980s Ciba-Geigy decided to focus its operations in specialty chemicals and the health care products field. In 1988 Ciba sold its Ilford Group, a photographic products division, to International Paper. Subsequently, Ciba formed alliances with high technology companies, including a joint venture with a Carlsbad, California company, Isis Pharmaceuticals, and with Affymax of Palo Alto, California to study computer-aided screening of its products.

Sandoz spent the post–World War II era concentrating on product development based on internal research and development. In the 1950s and 1960s Sandoz expanded its production units across Europe and to Japan. In 1967 Sandoz acquired Dr. Wander A.G., which gave Sandoz a consumer products presence and strengthened its international holdings. In 1976 it continued to diversify its product scope by acquiring Northrup King & Co., one of the largest U.S. seed companies.

Crucial acquisitions occurred in 1980 and 1981 with the acquisitions of a French dye company, SA Cardoner, a U.S. seed company, McNair, and a U.S. pharmaceutical company, Ex-Lax. In the mid-1980s, Sandoz enjoyed a strong cash flow and was able to continue to strengthen itself with new investments and acquisitions, including Sodyeco, a division of Martin Marietta, and Zoecon Corporation from Occidental Petroleum.

In 1989 Sandoz had to reorganize due to harsher worldwide trading conditions. In 1990 a new structure was formed in which Sandoz Ltd. holds 100% of six operating companies: Sandoz Chemicals, Sandoz Pharma, Sandoz Agro, Sandoz Seeds, Sandoz Nutrition, and MBT Holdings.

QUESTIONS

1. What were the individual strengths and weaknesses of Sandoz and Ciba-Geigy?
2. How would the merger help each company?
3. What was the expected future strategic focus of Novartis, and why?

REFERENCES

Cakici, N., C. Hessel, and K. Tandon, "Foreign Acquisitions in the United States: Effect on Shareholder Wealth of Foreign Acquiring Firms," *Journal of Banking & Finance*, 20, 1996, pp. 307–329.

Caves, Richard E., *Multinational Enterprise and Economic Analysis*, Cambridge, MA: Cambridge University Press, 1982.

Chan, K. C., G. A. Karolyi, and R. M. Stulz, "Global Financial Markets and the Risk Premium on U.S. Equity," *Journal of Financial Economics*, 32, 1992, pp. 137–167.

Chen, Haiyang, Michael Y. Hu, and Joseph C. P. Shieh, "The Wealth Effect of International Joint Ventures: The Case of

U.S. Investment in China," *Financial Management,* 20, Winter 1991, pp. 31–41.

Dewenter, Kathryn L., "Do Exchange Rate Changes Drive Foreign Direct Investment?" *Journal of Business,* 68, July 1995, pp. 405–433.

Doukas, J., "Overinvesting, Tobin's q and Gains from Foreign Acquisitions," *Journal of Banking & Finance,* 19, 1995, pp. 1285–1303.

Doukas, John, and Nickolaos G. Travlos, "The Effect of Corporate Multinationalism on Shareholders' Wealth: Evidence from International Acquisitions," *Journal of Finance,* 43, December 1988, pp. 1161–1175.

The Economist, "Drug Mergers: Understanding the Pill Poppers," August 6, 1994, p. 53.

Eun, C. S., R. Kolodny, and C. Scheraga, "Cross-Border Acquisitions and Shareholder Wealth: Tests of the Synergy and Internationalization Hypotheses," *Journal of Banking & Finance,* 20, 1996, pp. 1559–1582.

Froot, K., and J. Stein, "Exchange Rates and Foreign Direct Investment: An Imperfect Capital Markets Approach, *The Quarterly Journal of Economics,* 106, 1991, pp. 1191–1217.

Gibson, Richard, "Gerber Missed the Boat in Quest to Go Global, So It Turned to Sandoz," *The Wall Street Journal,* May 24, 1994, pp. A1, A4.

Godfrey, Stephen, and Ramon Espinosa, "A Practical Approach to Calculating Costs of Equity for Investments in Emerging Markets," *Journal of Applied Corporate Finance,* 9, Fall 1996, pp. 80–89.

Guyon, Janet, "What Is Novartis?" *The Wall Street Journal,* March 11, 1996, p. B1.

Harris, Robert S., and David Ravenscraft, "The Role of Acquisitions in Foreign Direct Investment: Evidence from the U.S. Stock Market," *Journal of Finance,* 46, 1991, pp. 825–844.

Hudgins, S. C., and B. Seifert, "Stockholder Returns and International Acquisitions of Financial Firms: An Emphasis on Banking," *Journal of Financial Service Research,* 10, 1996, pp. 163–180.

Hulbert, Mark, "A Plan to Overcome Investors' Home Bias," *New York Times,* January 23, 2000, Sec. 3 p. 9.

Kang, Jun-Koo, "The International Market for Corporate Control: Mergers and Acquisitions of U.S. Firms by Japanese Firms," *Journal of Financial Economics,* 34, December 1993, pp. 345–371.

Kraul, Chris, "Pain-Relieving Compound: Ciba-Sandoz Plan Is Part of the Bigger Survival Picture," *Los Angeles Times,* March 8, 1996, p. D1.

Mangum, Garth L., Sae-Young Kim, and Stephen B. Tallman, *Transnational Marriages in the Steel Industry,* Westport, CT: Quorum Books, 1996.

Markides, C., and D. Oyon, "International Acquisitions: Do They Create Value for Shareholders?" *European Management Journal,* 16, 1998, pp. 125–135.

Olmos, David, "Two Swiss Drug Firms Agree to Merge in $27-Billion Deal," *Los Angeles Times,* March 8, 1996, p. A1.

Seth, A., K. P. Song, and R. Pettit, "Synergy, Managerialism or Hubris? An Empirical Examination of Motives for Foreign Acquisitions of U.S. Firms," *Journal of International Business Studies,* 2000.

Shaughnessy, Haydn, "International Joint Ventures: Managing Successful Collaborations," *Long Range Planning,* 28(3), June 1995, pp. 10–17.

Sloan, Allan, "As Swiss Sandoz Scoops Up the Gerber Baby, Blame U.S. Accounting Law," *Los Angeles Times,* June 5, 1994, p. D1.

Stulz, René M., "The Cost of Capital in Internationally Integrated Markets: The Case of Nestlé," *European Financial Management,* 1, March 1995a, pp. 11–22.

———, "Globalization of Capital Markets and the Cost of Capital: The Case of Nestlé," *Journal of Applied Corporate Finance,* 8, Fall 1995b, pp. 30–38.

———, and Walter Wasserfallen, "Foreign Equity Investment Restrictions, Capital Flight, and Shareholder Wealth

Maximization: Theory and Evidence," *The Review of Financial Studies,* 8, Winter 1995, pp. 1019–1057.

Swierczek, Frederic, and Georges Hirsch, "Joint Ventures in Asia and Multicultural Management," *European Management Journal,* 12(2), June 1994, pp. 197–209.

Taber, George, "Remaking an Industry," *Time,* September 4, 1996.

Tanouye, Elise, Steve Lipin, and Stephen D. Moore, "In Big Drug Merger Sandoz and Ciba-Geigy Plan to Join Forces," *The Wall Street Journal,* March 7, 1996, p. A1.

Zahra, Shaker, and Galal Elhagrasey, "Strategic Management of International Joint Ventures," *European Management Journal,* 12(1), March 1994, pp. 83–93.

**Part VI
Strategies for
Creating Value**

Share
Repurchase

The topics covered in this chapter represent areas of considerable practical significance to corporate managements. High level executives often face questions related to the subject of this chapter, such as, "We are contemplating repurchase of up to 20% of the outstanding shares of our common stock. What will be the effects on share price, and will our shareholders be happy or unhappy with this activity?"

Share repurchase generally deals with cash offers for outstanding shares of common stock. This repurchase has the effect of changing the firm's capital structure because if nothing else occurs, even if the amount of debt is not changed the amount of common stock is reduced, so the debt-to-equity ratio or leverage ratio is increased. In determining a firm's leverage ratio, the amount of cash and marketable securities in excess of its transaction needs should be deducted from its debt. The use of cash to extinguish common stock would magnify the leverage ratio because debt would no longer be reduced by the excess cash, and equity would be smaller. Thus, a share repurchase is almost equivalent to an exchange of debt for common stock. However, the two transactions have different characteristics.

THE USE OF SHARE REPURCHASES

Share repurchases have increased both in absolute terms and relative to the use of dividends in returning cash to shareholders. Table 18.1 shows that in 1980 share repurchases were a negligible percentage of cash dividend payouts. By 1998, share repurchases were about 85% of cash dividends. Between 1980 and 1998, cash dividends grew at a rate of about 9% a year. Share repurchases had grown at a compound annual rate of about 30% per year.

For the S&P 500, share repurchases exceeded cash dividends beginning in 1997 (Liang and Sharpe, 1999). In 1997 share repurchases were $120 billion, compared with cash dividends of $105 billion. In 1998 share repurchases were $145 billion versus $118 billion for cash dividends. The excess of share repurchases over cash dividends shows an upward movement: $15 billion in 1997, increasing to $27 billion in 1998.

Within these broad economy-wide relationships, the use of stock options by individual companies has been significant. For example, between January 31, 1995 and

Table 18.1 Share Repurchase vs. Cash Dividends, 1980–1998

Year	Dividends ($ Billion)	Share Repurchase ($ Billion)	% Share Repurchase to Dividends
1980	59.3	0.3	0.5%
1981	69.5	0.6	0.9%
1982	66.7	0.7	1.0%
1983	74.4	6.8	9.1%
1984	79.3	27.3	34.4%
1985	83.9	20.3	24.2%
1986	91.4	28.2	30.9%
1987	96.0	55.0	57.3%
1988	111.1	37.4	33.7%
1989	134.4	63.7	47.4%
1990	143.9	36.1	25.1%
1991	147.2	20.4	13.9%
1992	147.9	35.6	24.1%
1993	157.6	38.3	24.3%
1994	182.4	73.8	40.5%
1995	205.3	99.5	48.5%
1996	261.9	176.3	67.3%
1997	275.1	181.8	66.1%
1998	279.2	236.2	84.6%
Growth Rate 1980–1998	8.7%	29.9%	

Source: Department of Commerce, Bureau of Economic Analysis; Securities Data Company

April 28, 1998, IBM announced open market share repurchases totaling $24 billion. Over this same time period, the adjusted number of shares outstanding declined from 2,351 million to 1,832 million, representing a reduction of 22.08%. Thus, the number of shares of IBM stock over less than a four-year period had declined by over one-fifth. At the end of 1994, the adjusted price of IBM stock was $18.375; by the end of 1998, the adjusted year-end price close was $92.188. Thus, the stock price of IBM over this four-year period had grown at a compound annual rate of 49.7%, or roughly 50% per year. The numbers suggest an association between the supply of IBM shares and their price.

Similarly for Coca Cola—the number of shares outstanding declined from 3,258 million in 1982 to 2,464 million in 1998, a decrease of 24.4% over the period. The 1982 year-end price of Coca Cola common stock, adjusted for splits, was $2.167; by the end of 1998, Coke's price had risen to $67. The price of Coca Cola stock had risen between 1982 and 1998 by about 24% per year compounded. In 1999 and early 2000, the stock price of Coca Cola has been under some downward pressure; but that is another story.

Some Factors in the Growth of Share Repurchase

The overall data and some individual examples dramatize the growing use of share repurchases. We present 12 factors that may help explain the increased use of share repurchases.

1. *Tax savings.* Cash dividends to shareholders are subject to a maximum individual tax rate of 39.6%. The return of cash to shareholders in the form of share repurchases may qualify for the long-term capital gains rate of 20%. This represents a tax savings of potentially as much as 19.6 cents on each dollar received.

2. *Timing of taxes.* Shareholders can choose whether or not to participate in a stock buyback program. They can defer their tax payments to make their own selection of when to sell.

3. *Management incentives.* Share repurchases increase the percentage ownership of the firm for the nonsellers. Since officers and directors may hold a significant percentage of ownership of the firm, their nonparticipation in share repurchases will increase their proportionate ownership by an even greater degree. If the percentages are substantial, the incentives of officers and directors to think like owners of the firm will be strengthened. Agency problems will be reduced.

4. *Management responsibility.* When officers and directors return excess cash to shareholders through share repurchase programs, they may be acting in the best interest of shareholders (the owners). By not using the funds for unwise diversification or negative net present value investments in the firm's traditional lines of business activity, officers and directors may thereby increase the trust and confidence of the shareholders. This may have a positive influence on share prices.

5. *Undervaluation signal.* One reason that officers and directors usually do not sell into share repurchase programs at a premium price is that they may judge that the price of the stock is likely to increase in future years. Their nonparticipation may therefore serve as a signal that the stock is undervalued.

6. *Sharp price declines.* A special case of the undervaluation scenario is when a sharp decline in overall stock prices has taken place. Documentation of this point is provided by Table 18.1. When the stock market suffered a sharp decline in October 1987, many firms initiated substantial share repurchase programs in the subsequent weeks. Table 18.1 shows that the percent share repurchases to cash dividends rose from about 31% in 1986 to over 57% in 1987 and then decreased to 34% in 1988. The share repurchase programs of firms represented a statement by their managements that the overall market decline did not justify the sharp drops in the share prices of their individual firms.

7. *Greater flexibility.* Patterns of dividend behavior by individual firms and in the aggregate become established over time. The financial literature documents that corporate earnings rise with fluctuations, whereas dividends increase in a stair-step fashion and lag behind the growth in corporate cash flows. The market rewards a history of consistent increases in dividends. The market sharply punishes a company that announces a decline in dividends or failure to achieve historical patterns of annual percentage increases. With share repurchases the expectation is that cash will be returned to shareholders when funds are available in excess of needs to finance sound investment programs. Share repurchase programs thereby facilitate improved information exchange with shareholders.

Table 18.2   Accounting Model of Stock Buyback

Panel A

Net Income	$500 million
Shares Outstanding	500 million
P/E Ratio	30
Buyback	10%

Panel B

	Before Buyback	After Buyback*
Cash	$4,000	$2,500
Total Assets	$10,000	$8,500
Total Debt	$ 4,000	$4,000
Book Shareholders' Equity	$ 6,000	$4,500
Total Claims	$10,000	$8,500

Panel C

EPS	$1.00	$1.11
Market Price per Share	$30.00	$33.33
Book Value per Share	$12.00	$10.00
Market Capitalization (millions)	$15,000	$15,000
Return on Book Equity	8.33%	11.11%
Debt-to-Equity Ratio	41.67%	88.89%

Buy 50 shares @ $30 = $1,500.

8. *Accounting treatment.*   The basic accounting entry when shares are repurchased is to reduce (debit) shares outstanding and to reduce (credit) cash by the outlay required. Accounting principles permit the charge (debit) to the shareholders' equity account to be at cost or market. The common practice is for firms to charge the shareholders' equity account with the actual amount paid for the shares (at market). The results can best be made concrete by a simplified accounting model of a stock buyback, shown in Table 18.2. Panel A of the table postulates a firm with a net income of $500 million, shares outstanding of 500 million, a P/E multiple of 30 times, and a buyback of 10%. Panel B presents the balance sheet before and after the buyback. The relationships in panel C can be calculated. Before the buyback, earnings are $1 per share. The market price per share, applying the P/E multiple is $30. The book value per share is $6,000 divided by 500, which is $12 per share. Market cap is $30 times the 500 million shares outstanding, which gives $15,000 million. The return on book equity is the $500 million divided by $6,000 million, which is 8.33%. The debt to equity ratio is $4,000 debt less $1,500 excess cash equals $2,500 divided by $6,000, equals 41.67%.

We can now illustrate the accounting effects of the stock buyback. We postulate that in an open market share repurchase program, 10% of the shares are bought at $30, for a total of $1,500 million. This is the debit to the book shareholders' equity, which is reduced to $4,500 million. If the company maintains its net income at $500 million, earnings per share rise to $1.11. If the P/E ratio of 30 continues to hold, the resulting market price per share rises to $33.33. The book shareholders' equity per share is the $4,500 million divided by the 450 million shares remaining, or $10.00. Market cap remains at $15,000 million. The return on book equity rises to 11.11%.

   If the share repurchase program were 20% of shares outstanding, the results would be more dramatic. But the principles would be the same. The stock buyback, using generally accepted accounting principles (GAAP), would increase EPS, the market price per share, and the return on book equity. We do not claim that the market does not understand that accounting cosmetics have simply put a prettier face on the firm's financials. But neither will the accounting cosmetics hurt the firm in competing for market popularity and approval.

9. *Debt-to-equity ratio.*   If the share repurchase is financed through excess cash, as illustrated in Table 18.2, we can demonstrate the effects on the debt-to-equity ratio. Before the buyback, the total debt of $4,000 million less the excess cash of $1,500 million would be $2,500 million. The debt-to-equity ratio would therefore be 41.7%. After the buyback, as shown in Table 18.2, the debt-to-equity ratio becomes 88.9%, a substantial increase. Some firms finance share repurchases by debt issues. This would increase further the effect of increasing leverage.

   The moral of the debt-to-equity story is that a share repurchase increases the leverage ratio, whether measured at book or market. If the firm has been operating with less than the optimal debt leverage ratio, the share repurchase will move the firm toward that ratio. If so, it may lower the firm's cost of capital, with a resulting increase in share price and market cap.

10. *Offset stock options.*   Stock options have become increasingly used by firms in executive compensation programs and extended broadly to recruit or retain target employees. As stock options are exercised, the number of the firm's shares outstanding continuously increases. Conceivably, this could create downward pressure on the firm's stock prices. Share repurchases can be used to offset this potential dilutive effect. The examples of IBM and Coca Cola illustrate that share repurchases have been used to more than offset the effect of the exercise of stock options and may therefore have had an accretive effect on share prices.

11. *Takeover defense.*   The financial literature reports that share repurchases may be used as a takeover defense (Bagwell, 1992). Two possible influences may operate. One, the share repurchase price may be viewed more favorably than the takeover price. Two, when a firm tenders for 10% to 20% of its shares, the shareholders who offer their shares for sale are those with the lowest reservation prices. Those who do not tender have the higher reservation prices. Hence, for a takeover bidder to succeed with the remaining higher reservation price shareholders, the premium offered will have to be higher. The required higher premium may deter some potential acquirers from making bids. Whether this is good or bad for the firm is discussed subsequently.

12. *Restructuring factors.*   The financial literature also reports that share repurchases may be part of a more general restructuring program in which the firm is engaged (Nohel and Tarhan, 1998). If the firm has embarked on a general

program to improve its efficiency and performance and a share repurchase program is a part of that restructuring, the resulting influence on share prices is likely to be positive. But it is the restructuring that is the stronger causal force.

From these 12 factors that may generally cause share buybacks to have an upward impact on stock prices, it is clear that multiple forces may be operating. We can generalize to say that there may be several reasons why share repurchase programs could cause share prices to rise. A number of the reasons appear to be somewhat "iffy." So in reviewing empirical studies, we have to be careful in interpreting the results. The variables selected by the researchers may omit the truly strong influences whose impacts are reflected to an uncertain degree in the variables actually used in the study. We develop this theme further when we review the event and performance studies of share repurchases.

MAJOR TYPES OF SHARE REPURCHASE

We first briefly describe four major types of share repurchases. After this overview, we analyze in greater depth the nature and implications of each. The four major types are

1. Fixed-price tender offers (FPTs).
2. Dutch auctions (DAs).
3. Transferable put rights (TPRs).
4. Open-market repurchases (OMRs).

Fixed-Price Tender Offers (FPTs)

A firm offers to buy a specified fraction of shares within a given time period. The fixed tender price offered is usually higher than the prevailing market price of the stock at the time of the offer. Most fixed-price tender offers are at least fully subscribed. If the offer is oversubscribed—more shares are offered than are sought—the firm can buy the shares back on a pro rata basis. Alternatively, the firm may elect to buy back all shares (more than the original target number or fraction) at the tender offer price. If the tender offer is undersubscribed, the firm may extend the offer, hoping to have more shares tendered over time, or the firm may cancel the offer if it includes a minimum acceptance clause, or the firm may simply buy back whatever number or percentage of shares were actually tendered. In a fixed-price tender offer, the firm usually pays any transfer taxes involved and the shareholder pays no brokerage fees.

Dutch Auctions (DAs)

In a Dutch auction, the firm announces the number of shares it would buy in a specified time period and the price range in which shareholders may offer to tender. For example, the current price of the stock may be $14. The company may offer to buy 4 million shares at a price range of $15 to $19 a share. Typically, the price offers will be at intervals such as 10¢ or 25¢. At the offer price that results in 4 million shares being offered, all shares offered at or below that price will be purchased at that price. Thus, even though some shareholders may have offered to sell at $16, if $17 is the price at which the 4 million shares are offered, they will receive the $17 per share. Oversubscription is possible in a Dutch auction if the reservation prices of the shareholders are lower than the lower range price terms. Oversubscription may also occur from the lumpiness of bidding schedules. For example, if at $16.70 less than 4 million shares were offered but at $16.80, 4,100,000 shares were offered, the company might accept only a fraction of shares (4.0/4.1) of the amount tendered by each shareholder, or it might take the full 4.1 million shares at the $16.80.

Transferable Put Rights (TPRs)

A firm seeks to purchase 5% of its outstanding common shares. Each shareholder would receive one TPR for every 20 shares held. Thus, if a firm has 100 million shares outstanding and is seeking to repurchase 5 million shares or 5%, then 5 million TPRs will be issued, and for every 100 shares a shareholder will receive five TPRs. A secondary market develops in which TPRs are bought and sold. If the prevailing market price of the stock is $14 and the TPR gives the shareholder the right to put the stock to the company at $15.50, trading may take place in the TPRs. Shareholders who feel that the stock is worth less than $15.50 will be glad to have the opportunity to put the stock to the company at $15.50. These shareholders or other investors will be buyers of the TPRs. On the other hand, shareholders who feel that the stock is worth more than $15.50, for example $16 or even $18, will want to continue to hold their stock and sell their TPRs.

Open-Market Repurchases (OMRs)

A firm announces that it will repurchase some dollar amount (e.g., $5 billion or $10 billion) of its common stock from time to time in the open market. This is the most frequent type of share repurchase, outnumbering the other three methods by a factor of 10 to 1. However, open-market repurchases generally involve a smaller percentage of total shares outstanding than the other methods. OMRs probably average about 5% of shares outstanding versus around 16% for fixed-price tender offers.

The foregoing provides an overview of each of the four major types of share repurchases. Each one will be examined at greater depth in the attempt to understand the theory and practical decision making involved in choosing the form and terms of a share repurchase. We start the analysis with the fixed-price tender offers because they represent a convenient vehicle for developing the basic logic of share repurchases.

FIXED-PRICE TENDER OFFERS (FPTs)

In a cash tender offer the company usually sets forth the number of shares it is offering to purchase and the price at which it will repurchase them as well as the period of time during which the offer will be extended. The tender offer price is generally higher than the market price at the time of offer (by approximately 20% on average). The tender offer price is usually the net price received by the shareholders who tender their shares, because the tendering shareholders pay no brokerage fees and the company generally pays any transfer taxes that are levied.

The number of shares set forth in the tender offer typically represents the maximum number that the company seeks to repurchase. If the number of shares tendered exceeds this limit, the company may purchase all or a fraction of the shares tendered in excess of the amount initially set forth. The company also may reserve the right to extend the time period of the offer. If a company purchases less than all shares tendered, the purchases must be made on a pro rata basis from each of the tendering shareholders. The adoption of SEC Rule 13e-4 in September 1979 made mandatory the pro rata repurchase of shares when the number tendered exceeds the number the company purchases.

If fewer shares are tendered during the initial offer period than were targeted by management, the company may decide to extend the length of the offer period. If the offer period is lengthened, the company is likely to purchase all shares tendered before the first expiration date and then purchase shares offered during the extension period either pro rata or on the basis of the order in which the shares are offered.

Basic Stock Repurchase Model

To understand the implications of stock repurchasing and exchange offers, let us first set out some of the quantitative relationships involved. As is customary, it is necessary to set forth the assumptions of the model employed. The literature on the subject suggests a number of basic conditions involved in the equilibrium pricing of securities (Vermaelen, 1981):

1. The market is efficient in that at any time market prices reflect all publicly available information that influences the prices of securities.
2. This also implies that markets are informationally efficient, which specifies that information is costless and is received simultaneously by all individuals. In the economic literature these conditions are generally referred to as the condition of pure competition.
3. There is perfect competition in securities markets. This implies that individual investors are price takers and cannot influence the outcome of a stock repurchase offer.
4. Investors seek to maximize the value of their wealth, after taking into account taxes and transactions costs.
5. After the announcement date, investors have homogeneous expectations with respect to the change in value that will be caused by the share repurchase and with respect to the fraction of shares that will be tendered as well as the fraction of shares that will be purchased by the company.
6. Offers are maximum-limit offers. This means that if the offer is undersubscribed, the firm will buy all shares tendered. But if the offer is oversubscribed, the company will buy all shares tendered or will allocate shares pro rata—the company buys back the same fraction of the shares from every tendering shareholder.
7. The price changes analyzed in connection with share repurchase are after adjusting for marketwide price changes.

In the analysis that follows we employ a number of symbols:

$$P_0 = \text{the preannouncement share price}$$
$$P_T = \text{the tender price}$$
$$P_E = \text{the postexpiration share price}$$
$$N_0 = \text{the preannouncement number of shares outstanding}$$
$$N_E = \text{the number of shares outstanding after repurchase}$$
$$W = \text{the shareholder wealth effect caused by the share repurchase}$$
$$F_P = \text{the fraction of shares repurchased} = (N_0 - N_E)/N_0$$
$$1 - F_P = \text{the fraction of untendered shares} = N_E/N_0$$

The basic condition that must be met is set forth in the equation

$$P_E N_E = P_0 N_0 - P_T (N_0 - N_E) + W \qquad (18.1)$$

Equation (18.1) states that the value of the shares outstanding after expiration of the repurchase offer equals the value of the shares existing before the announcement of the repurchase offer less the value of the shares repurchased plus the change in shareholder wealth associated with the repurchase offer. The source of W, the shareholder wealth effect, will be analyzed subsequently. If we then divide equation (18.1) by N_0 and substitute for the definitions of fraction of shares repurchased and fraction of shares not repurchased, we obtain the equation

$$P_E (1 - F_P) = P_0 - P_T F_P + W/N_0 \qquad (18.2)$$

We next divide by P_0 and solve for the rate of increase in value or the rate of return created by the repurchase offer:

$$\frac{W}{N_0 P_0} = F_P \left(\frac{P_T - P_0}{P_0} \right) + (1 - F_P) \left(\frac{P_E - P_0}{P_0} \right) \qquad (18.3)$$

Equation (18.3) reveals the two components of rate of return associated with the repurchase offer. The first component is the rate of return received by the tendering shareholders weighted by the percentage of shares purchased. The second component is the rate of return received by nontendering shareholders weighted by the percentage of nontendered shares.

Dann (1981) found for his sample of open-market share repurchases totaling 143 observations over the period 1962 to 1976 that the fraction of shares repurchased averaged 20%. The shareholder wealth effect was 15%. The initial premium represented by the tender offer was 23%. From this information, using the equation (18.3) relation, we can solve for the relationship between the price premium (X) of the stock at expiration of the repurchase offer and the initial price, P_0:

$$15\% = (20\%)(23\%) + 80\% X \qquad (18.4)$$

The premium of the expiration price after the share repurchase is therefore 13% over the initial share price. Thus, as shown in equation (18.4a), of the 15% wealth effect associated with the share repurchase offer, 4.6% goes to the tendering shareholders and 10.4% goes to the nontendering shareholders.

$$15\% = 0.2(23\%) + 0.8(13\%)$$
$$15\% = 4.6\% + 10.4\% \qquad (18.4a)$$

The relationship is quite similar for the Vermaelen (1981) study, which covered 131 open-market share repurchases over the period 1962 to 1977. The initial premium was the same, 23%, but the fraction repurchased was 15%. The wealth effect was 16%. The relationships are shown in equation (18.5).

$$16\% = 15\%(23\%) + 85\% X$$
$$0.16 = 0.0345 + 0.85 X$$
$$X = 0.1476 = 14.76\% \qquad (18.5)$$
$$16\% = 0.15(23\%) + 0.85(14.76\%)$$
$$= 3.45\% + 12.5\%$$

The indicated postexpiration price is 14.76% over the initial price. Thus, using Vermaelen's data, the 16% wealth effect is composed of 3.45% to the tendering shareholders and 12.55% to the nontendering shareholders. Other studies of open-market share repurchases for sample periods prior to 1980 find similar results; these include Bradley and Wakeman (1983), Brickley (1983), Masulis (1980), and Vermaelen (1984).

The study by Comment and Jarrell (1991) covers the period 1984 to 1989. The median premium paid was 16%, with about 14% of the shares purchased. The postexpiration premium indicated by the event returns for a three-day window was about 11% for fixed price tender offers. The wealth effect equation would therefore be

$$11.7\% = 0.14(16\%) + 0.86(11\%)$$

The above equation treats the event returns as an approximation to the postexpiration percentage price increase over the price of the stock before the share repurchase announcement. It appears that the premiums offered during later fixed-price tender offer programs declined. This was associated with a decline in the event returns and in the postexpiration percentage price gain.

The still later study by Lie and McConnell (1998) extended the Comment and Jarrell sample through December 1994. The event returns for a three-day window were 7.9% mean and 6.8% median. The fraction of shares purchased and the premium offered were not significantly different from those of the earlier study. This suggests that the market expectation of future cash flow improvements was not as strong for later periods.

Rationale for the Postexpiration Price Changes

The earlier studies covering data prior to 1980 disagree on the sources of the postexpiration stock price increases associated with share repurchase programs. Masulis (1980) emphasizes the benefits of increased leverage. Vermaelen argues that while the leverage hypothesis may play a role, it is not the predominant explanation for the observed abnormal returns following the share repurchase offer. He argues that the more plausible explanation is the signaling or information effect. He reports that tender offers for share repurchase are associated with per share earnings of tendering firms that subsequently are above what would have been predicted by a time series model using preannouncement data.

Nohel and Tarhan (1998) also add to the Comment and Jarrell sample, covering the period 1978 through 1991 with a sample of 290 companies. Building on prior work by Lang and Litzenberger (1989), Howe, He, and Kao (1992), and Perfect, Petersen, and Petersen (1995), they divide the sample into low q-ratio firms and high q-ratio firms. They also focus their measurements on event returns of share repurchase firms in excess of a control group of non-share repurchase firms. They use monthly returns to compute event returns. They find that the share repurchase firms, net of the control group, have significantly positive event returns. However, the improvement comes entirely from the low q firms.

Nohel and Tarhan seek to explain the reasons the low q firms outperform the high q firms. They use five measures of operating performance and five measures of investment characteristics, similar to those employed in the study by Healy, Palepu, and Ruback (1992) described in our chapter 8 on merger performance. They find that the low q firms have higher asset turnover ratios relative to control firms, both before and after the repurchase. The difference widens following the repurchase. The improvement in asset turnover is associated with asset sales by the low q firms. They observe that successful repurchasing firms dispose of poorly performing assets as part of a corporate restructuring program.

The foregoing succession of studies illustrates the generalization we made after describing a list of 12 factors that could influence the stock price effects of share repurchase programs. All the studies agree that fixed-price tender offers result in postexpiration stock price increases on the order of magnitude of 8% to 10%. The studies disagree on the relative influence of the 12 potential factors that can affect the results of share repurchase programs. These conclusions are further reinforced by studies of Dutch auction repurchases, discussed next.

DUTCH AUCTION REPURCHASES

A fundamental difference between fixed-price tender offers and Dutch auction repurchases (DARs) is brought out by the description of the first firm to utilize the Dutch auction (Bagwell, 1992). In 1981 Todd Shipyards was planning a fixed-price tender offer at $28 for about 10% of its 5.5 million shares outstanding. Bear Stearns, the investment banker for Todd, suggested instead a Dutch auction repurchase at a range of prices not to exceed $28. The fee paid to Bear Stearns would be 30% of the savings if the clearing price was less than $28. Todd employed the Dutch auction. The clearing purchase price was $26.50.

This example illustrates one of the basic differences between the FPT and the DAR. In the FPT, the tender offer is made for one price. In the DAR, a range of prices is made available within which investors can choose a price at which their shares will be tendered. In the Bagwell (1992) study, data were obtained for 32 firms employing Dutch auctions between 1981 and 1988. These firms supplied schedules of the quantity of shares offered at each price within the specified range. Bagwell analyzed these data, setting the preannouncement price equal to $100, and expressed the price range as a percentage of the preannouncement price. She also calculated the percentage of total shares sought in the Dutch auction repurchase offer. Schedules were developed in which quantity is normalized to measure the cumulative percentage of outstanding shares tendered at or below each price within the price range. Bagwell presents supply curves for 17 firms that did not require confidentiality. We have directly contacted other firms conducting Dutch auctions to request supply schedules. These supply schedules are consistent with the data presented in Appendix II in the Bagwell study.

An important finding from the Dutch auction supply curves is evidence of shareholder heterogeneity (Bagwell, 1992). Consistently upward sloping supply curves are obtained from shareholders tendering responses in the Dutch auctions. An upward-sloping supply or valuation schedule is illustrated by the equation

$$V(r) = 80 + 0.04r \tag{18.6}$$

The meaning of equation (18.6) and the definition of the terms in it can be clarified with the help of Figure 18.1. The horizontal axis shows the number of

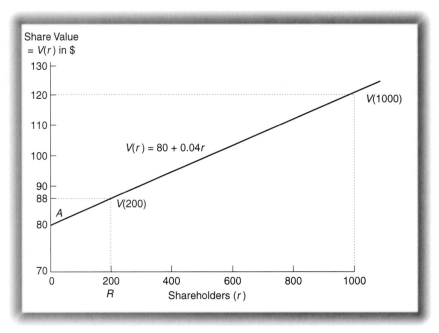

Figure 18.1   Valuation Schedule for Shareholder Reservation Prices

shareholders (r), and each point up through 1,000 is for an individual shareholder holding one share of stock. The total number of shares outstanding (N) is also equal to 1,000. Each rth shareholder has a reservation price $V(r)$. The reservation price $V(r)$ is the price at which the rth shareholder would be willing to sell the share of stock held. $V(r)$ means that the reservation price (or value) depends on which rth shareholder we are talking about. For example, the 1st shareholder has a reservation price of $80 + $0.04 (1), or $80.04. The 100th shareholder has a reservation price of $80 + $0.04 (100) = $84 and so on. Equation (18.6) and its graph in Figure 18.1 show the relationship between the rth shareholder and his or her associated reservation price $V(r)$. The vertical axis in Figure 18.1 depicts these reservation prices, $V(r)$, for the r shareholders. The intercept term, $V(r) = 80$, represents the prevailing market price of the stock. Shareholders with reservation prices at or below the prevailing market price of $80 would have already sold their shares.

We show what happens when the firm seeks to repurchase 200 shares (R) representing 20% of the shares outstanding. It offers to repurchase the shares at a range of prices between $84 and $90. If the reservation prices of the shareholders are depicted by the illustrative equation, $V(r) = 80 + 0.04r$, we would have the following result. The price that would elicit 200 shares in the Dutch auction would be $88. We can check this using equation (18.6).

$$V(r) = \$80 + 0.04(200) = \$88 \qquad \textbf{(18.6a)}$$

The gain to the tendering shareholders can be measured by triangle A:

$$0.5(88 - 80)200 = \$800$$

Because the prevailing market price of the stock before the tender offer was $80, the 200 shares had a market value of $16,000. The gain of $800, therefore, represents 5% of the pre-tender market value of the 200 shares ($80 × 200 = $16,000).

Let us next consider the situation of the nontendering shareholders (this analysis is based on Gay, Kale, and Noe, 1991). The nontendering shareholders now have a claim on the valuation curve less what was paid out to the tendering shareholders. The new upward-sloping supply curve for the nontendering shareholders is given for $V'(r)$ by the equation

$$V'(r) = (0.04r + 80)/0.8 - 88(200)/800 = 0.05r + 78 \qquad \textbf{(18.7)}$$

Thus, the new valuation schedule will have a lower implied intercept but a steeper slope.

The practical significance of the more steeply sloped valuation schedule is that the reservation prices of the remaining shareholders are higher than the reservation prices of the original valuation schedule. The role of share repurchase as a takeover defense is highlighted. The reservation price of the marginal shareholder after the share repurchase is something over $88 versus the original $80. In addition, the reservation price of the 1,000th shareholder is now $50 + $78 = $128. Therefore, to compete with the share repurchase alternative, a bidder would have to pay a higher premium than would have been required under the original supply schedule. In a fixed-price tender offer, the tender offer price probably would have been in excess of $88 to obtain 20% of the shares. The premium paid in the Dutch auction share repurchase is somewhat lower (Kamma, Kanatas, and Raymar, 1992).

Comment and Jarrell (1991) pushed the analysis still further. They investigated the influence of pro rata transactions and the role of the risk exposure of officers and directors. The logic of the necessity of prorationing is straightforward. If the reservation prices of the shareholders are so low that the tender offer stimulates a flood of tenders by shareholders, it is not likely that wealth effects will be high.

Comment and Jarrell (1991) also investigated the impact of whether officers and directors are exposed to a personal wealth loss if their signaling is not credible. Comment and Jarrell consider that officers and directors (OD) are at risk if two conditions hold. First, their collective proportionate ownership interest in their company's stock must increase as a result of the tender offer. Second, the premium in the tender offer is more than 2% above the market price of the stock four days before the offer is announced.

We summarize the empirical data for wealth effects that take into account the pro rata influence and the risk of officers and directors in Table 18.3. Average wealth effects in fixed-price tender offers are in the range of 12% to 13% as discussed previously. For Dutch auctions, the wealth effect is smaller, about 8%. This is plausible because the average premium paid in Dutch auctions is lower, as shareholder heterogeneity results in an upward-sloping supply schedule. If prorationing is involved, then shareholder reservation prices are low. Signaling of future value increases is less likely to be credible. With prorationing, the wealth effects are virtually zero for both fixed-price tender offers and for Dutch auctions. Where there is no prorationing, the reservation prices of shareholders are relatively high. They are more likely to view the premiums offered in the share repurchases as credible signals of future value increases. The wealth effects are relatively large.

Table 18.3 Wealth Effects

		Pro Rata		OD at Risk	
	Average	**Yes**	**No**	**Yes**	**No**
FPT	12–13%	0–5%	15%	16%	4%
DA	8%	0	8%	8%	0

Similarly, if officers and directors are at risk, the signaling will be credible and the wealth effects large. If officers and directors are not at risk, the wealth effects will be small or negligible.

After considering the kinds of evidence presented in Table 18.3, Comment and Jarrell (1991, pp. 1258–1259) conclude that Dutch auctions are favored by relatively large firms that are widely followed by security analysts and other informed investors. These are companies in which management owns a relatively low percentage of stock. Because their stock is widely followed and management stakes are relatively low, these firms are "ill-suited" to send strongly credible signals in premium repurchase offers. For such firms, Comment and Jarrell conclude that Dutch auctions are likely to be substitutes for open-market repurchases. They argue that the firms are not substituting Dutch auctions for fixed price tender offers but rather would have switched to open-market programs.

A further comparison of fixed-price versus Dutch auctions is made by Lie and McConnell (1998). Their study covered 130 fixed-price and 102 Dutch auction self-tender offers between 1981 and 1994. Dutch auctions started in 1981 and accounted for less than 10 transactions per year through 1987. For the peak years 1988 and 1989, the number of Dutch auction share repurchases moved up to slightly above 20 per year. In 1991 there were one fixed-price and two Dutch auctions. In 1993 there were six Dutch auctions, and in 1994 only four. Table 18.1 shows that total share repurchases in 1993 and 1994 were over $112 billion, so their sample covers a small fraction of total share repurchases. The dollar value of share repurchases grew 30% per year over the period of their study (1981 to 1994), so the sharp decline in the number of self-tenders in their sample after 1989 suggests that open-market share repurchases were substituting for both fixed-price and Dutch auction repurchases. Most of the fixed-price transactions in their sample were pre-1990. Thus, their findings may in part reflect the economic characteristics of the 1980s versus the 1990s.

Over a three-day window centered on the announcement date, the mean and median abnormal return for fixed-price tender offers were 7.9% and 6.8%, respectively, and for Dutch auctions they were 7.7% and 6.4%. Lie and McConnell note that Comment and Jarrell recognize that the excess returns for fixed-price tenders were higher than for Dutch auction tenders only when offers with coincident confounding news were excluded. The mean and median abnormal returns become 10.2% and 8.6%, respectively, for fixed-price versus 7.6% and 6.2% for Dutch auctions. This difference is significant at the 5% level.

The emphasis of the Lie and McConnell study is on a comparison of earnings patterns and on a refinement of the estimate of expected earnings developed by Barber and Lyon (1996). The Barber and Lyon methodology proposes that when firms in a sample exhibit abnormal (earnings) performance the benchmark should be firms with similarly abnormal performance. The logic is that performance may exhibit mean reversion, which means that over time firms with earnings higher than the mean will move down toward the mean, and conversely with firms with earnings below the mean. The deviation from the expected mean reversion is a measure of performance. Lie and McConnell find that their sample firms in both sets of tender offers exhibit superior performance during the year of the tender offer. They exhibit slower mean reversion in their operating performance than firms not undertaking tender offers. They observe that if there is an earnings signal in the two types of self-tenders under analysis it is that these firms continued to exhibit superior performance longer than what otherwise would have been expected. They emphasize, however, that there is no significant difference in the performance (as measured) between the fixed-price versus Dutch auction samples.

TRANSFERABLE PUT RIGHTS (TPRs)

As summarized earlier, transferable put rights (TPRs) represent options granted to shareholders in proportion to the number of shares owned. In our previous example, we noted that if a company sought to repurchase 20% of its shares using TPRs, it would issue 20 TPRs for every 100 shares held by stockholders. If the put price represents a substantial premium over the prevailing market price, the TPRs will have value and trading in them will take place. Because all shares put to the firm are repurchased, the possibility of prorationing that occurs in a fixed-price tender offer is avoided. This point is illustrated by the first company to use TPRs, which was Millicom, a small cellular telephone and electronic paging company (Kale, Noe, and Gay, 1989, p. 141). In April 1987 Millicom issued TPRs to its shareholders as a method of share repurchase. Millicom explained its choice of TPRs with reference to the prorationing problem. Under a fixed-price tender offer (FPT), because of the possibility of prorationing, shareholders cannot be sure what percentage of their tendered shares will actually be repurchased. Shareholders can avoid this risk by selling to arbitragers, who thereby achieve a strong bargaining position, particularly if a takeover or a control contest develops.

In their study, Kale, Noe, and Gay (1989) report the announcement by Vista Chemical Company in May 1989 of a plan to repurchase one-third of its 15 million shares outstanding at $70 a share through the issuance of TPRs. They also describe in some detail the use of TPRs by Gillette, the second company to initiate a share repurchase program with the use of TPRs. Gillette, the well-known maker of razor blades, pens, and other personal products, was subject to a series of hostile takeover attempts for various reasons. In 1986 Revlon's Ronald O. Perelman made a series of takeover bids that were fought off by a targeted share repurchase (greenmail) plus a standstill agreement.

In February 1988 Coniston Partners announced that it owned 6.8% of Gillette stock and was seeking four seats on Gillette's board. Gillette accelerated its open-market share repurchase program. In the proxy fight for control, Gillette defeated

Coniston by obtaining 52% of shareholder votes. Coniston filed a lawsuit claiming that Gillette had made false and misleading claims during the proxy contest. With the court contest under way, Gillette and Coniston reached a settlement, announced August 1, 1988, associated with the initiation of a stock repurchase through TPRs. Gillette, with 112 million shares outstanding, issued one put per seven shares, which would result in the repurchase of 16 million shares. Each TPR enabled the holder to sell back one share to the company at $45 (the prevailing market was about $39) by September 19, 1988. The TPRs were issued to shareholders of record as of August 12, 1988. Trading in the TPRs started on August 16, 1988 and took place through September 19, 1988. Over that period of time, the stock price of Gillette averaged about $35, with the TPR price fluctuating slightly above and below $10. Thus, one TPR plus one share of stock approximated the put price of $45. The average daily volume of trading during the period August 16 to September 19 was about 359,000 TPRs.

The logic of the TPR trading documented for Gillette can be conveyed by the numerical example we developed in connection with our discussion of Dutch auction repurchases (DARs). Recall that we postulated a reservation supply price schedule for shareholders:

$$V(r) = 80 + 0.04r \qquad \textbf{(18.6)}$$

In our example for the DAR, if a firm had announced that it would repurchase 20% of its 1,000 shares at a schedule of prices from $80 to $88, the market would have cleared at a price of $88. Using the Kale, Noe, and Gray notation of LR for a low reservation price shareholder and HR for a high reservation price shareholder, we can see that the LR shareholders would have tendered and the HR shareholders would not have tendered. At the end of the DAR the new marginal shareholder would have a reservation price of $88.

But in practice the firm knows that the supply schedule is positively sloped but does not know the price and quantity that would just clear the market with neither prorationing nor an undersubscription to the tender offer. We can illustrate how the use of TPRs solves this problem. Assume that a firm facing the shareholder valuation schedule depicted by Figure 18.1 offered to buy 20% of its shares at a price of $96. Based on the valuation schedule, the number of shares and shareholders who would be interested in selling at $96 would be determined by the equation

$$\$96 = \$80 + 0.04r$$

Solving for r, 400 shares would be offered. But only 200 TPRs were issued. Hence, trading in the TPRs would take place. Shareholders with a reservation price below $88 (the LRs) would place the greatest value on the TPRs and would end up buying TPRs from the shareholders with the higher reservation prices (the HRs). By the end of the trading period when the TPRs would be exercised, the LRs would own the 200 TPRs and the HRs would have been net sellers. Two hundred shares, along with the 200 TPRs, would be put to the company. The result would be that the TPR trading discovered the market clearing price for the 20% of the shares that the company is seeking to repurchase.

Another use of the TPRs is in consolidating the control position of a group. We can identify three types of shareholders: the control group, dissidents fighting for con-

Table 18.4   TPRs and Control

	(1) Before %	(2) Sell	(3) After	(4) After %
1. Control group	34	0.0	34.0	51
2. Dissidents	24	8.0	16.0	24
3. Others	42	25.3*	16.7	25
Total	100	33.3	66.7	100

*25.3 = 14.0 + 11.3.

trol, and others. Before the issuance of TPRs, the ownership position of each group is given in column 1 of Table 18.4. If one TPR is issued for each three shares held, and assuming that the number of shares is identical to the percentages indicated in column 1, 33.3 TPRs would be issued. Column 2 suggests that the control group would sell their TPRs but not their stock. Postulating that the put price represents a substantial premium over the prevailing market price of the stock, the dissidents would be happy to accept the substantial premium. The third group would use the 14 TPRs received plus the 11.3 TPRs purchased from the control group to sell 25.3 of their shares. Column 3 shows the number of shares each group owns after the TPRs plus stock are put to the company. The company now has only 66.7 shares outstanding. Column 4 expresses each group's ownership as a percent of the total number of shares outstanding. The control group has moved from 34% to 51%. The share of the dissidents is unchanged at 24%. The percentage ownership of the other shareholders has dropped from 42% to 25%.

From the illustrative examples, from the real-life cases, and from the theoretical framework, we can understand the advantages of the use of TPRs. The trading in TPRs results in the low reservation price shareholders putting their shares for repurchase. The remaining shareholders will be high reservation price shareholders. Thus, the TPRs are useful as a takeover defense. In addition, the TPRs may rearrange control positions as well.

We conclude this section with a consideration of why the reservation price schedule is upward-sloping. The empirical data presented by Bagwell (1992) is solid evidence of upward-sloping reservation price schedules. We have checked her findings by directly corresponding with a sample of companies that have used Dutch auctions in recent years. Although we do not have permission to publish their data, we can confirm that they are consistent with the data published in Bagwell (1992). So there is no question of the evidence of upward-sloping reservation price schedules. However, in our idealized example, we have used a slope that seems to be higher than that exhibited in the Bagwell data and in the data that we developed. So one question is, How strong is the upward-sloping effect?

A second question is, Why does the upward-sloping schedule exist? Most authors refer to the possibility of a different tax basis for LRs and HRs. Beyond that, shareholder heterogeneity and differing expectations and valuations are possible explanations. This is an area that requires much more investigation.

OPEN-MARKET SHARE REPURCHASES (OMRs)

Studies suggest that open-market share repurchases outnumber the other three methods by a factor of perhaps 10 to 1. Detailed studies of open-market share repurchases are reported by Ikenberry, Lakonishok, and Vermaelen (ILV) (1995) and Ikenberry and Vermaelen (IV) (1996). They begin by observing that the aggregate value of stock repurchases for the period 1980 to 1990 was about one-third the dollar amount of cash dividends. In the late 1980s, repurchases moved up to about one-half the amount paid as cash dividends. The ILV study covered 1,239 open market share repurchases announced between 1980 and 1990 by firms traded on the NYSE, AMEX, or NASDAQ. Over the 11-year period, sample companies announced repurchases for 6.6% of their outstanding shares on average. The percentage was rising over the sample time period. The average market response to the announcement of an OMR was 3.5%. But this average was influenced by a number of factors.

For a window of −2 to +2 days around the announcement date, the market response for the period 1980 to 1986 averaged about 4.2%. For the period 1987 to 1990, the market response was about 2.3%. The mean announcement period abnormal return for repurchase programs for more than 10% of the outstanding shares is 4.51%. For smaller repurchase programs (less than 2.5% of shares), the average market reaction is 2.58%. Ikenberry, Lakonishok, and Vermaelen (1995) interpret the stronger market reaction to larger share repurchase programs as consistent with the traditional signaling hypothesis (TSH). Firms ranked in the two smallest size deciles show the highest abnormal returns of 8.19%. Firms in the largest size deciles show an abnormal return of 2.09%. Viewing firm size as a proxy of information asymmetries, the inverse relationship between size and abnormal returns is consistent with TSH.

A result that ILV emphasize is that, on average, the market underreacts to OMR announcements. Using a buy-and-hold strategy, the four-year abnormal performance following the announcement is more than 12%. Combined with the announcement effect, the total undervaluation is about 15%. They find further that firms ranked in the top book-to-market quintile achieve four-year abnormal performance of 45.3% following the OMR announcement. This measure is net of a benchmark that explicitly controls for size and book-to-market effects in stock returns. Firms in the bottom two quintiles by book-to-market exhibit a long-run performance close to zero. They conclude that the market reaction to new information is not always completed over short time periods. They observe that if the market underreacts to the first announcement of an OMR, managers who judge their shares to be undervalued may make a series of OMRs to gain the benefit of multiple announcement reactions.

So the initial announcement effect of a modest positive 3.5% to an OMR does not fully capture the impact. Subsequent three-year abnormal performance represents an additional 12%. ILV (1995) argue that companies with high ratios of book-to-market that engaged in share repurchases were out of favor, their shares will show higher returns in the future compared with low book-to-market ratio stocks in general. Thus, added to our earlier discussion of the other methods of share repurchase, the in-depth analysis of OMRs over time yields further insights into the significant impact that share repurchases can make on shareholder returns.

Ikenberry, Lakonishok, and Vermaelen (1995, p. 207) draw another conclusion: "This evidence is consistent with other studies which find that managers have market timing ability." Furthermore, announcements of open market share repurchases are somewhat ambiguous. The company announces that it will buy up to X shares over the following Y months. If a major reason for buybacks is that companies believe their shares are underpriced, as share prices rise with the announcement and initiation of a repurchase program the incentives for managers to complete the total OMR are reduced.

A *Wall Street Journal* article on March 7, 1995 ("Heard on the Street," pp. C1, C2) cited a study of how the data on announcements are easier to track than data on actual buyback activity. The article cited a study by Eric T. Miller, chief investment officer at Donaldson, Lufkin & Jenrette, that as of March 7, 1995, only 15% of announced 1993 OMRs had been completed. OMRs of $65 billion had been announced for 1994, but by March 1995 it appeared that only $2 billion to $3 billion of the buyback programs had taken place. The article also quoted Ikenberry as saying, "Once a stock price rises it may not make business sense to keep on buying stock."

Another aspect of management manipulation may be noted in connection with share repurchases. If the companies have a high ratio of market-to-book (a low ratio of book-to-market), the reduction in the book value of shareholders' equity as a result of share repurchases may be very substantial. The original accounting credit was at book; the debit to record the share repurchase can be made at market. For a given level of net income, the reported return on equity (ROE) would be expected to increase substantially. In pure financial theory, increased levels of ROE should not influence stock prices.

A formal model of the empirical findings of Ikenberry, Lakonishok, and Vermaelen discussed above is suggested by Rappaport (1998). If a company's shares are undervalued and if stock is repurchased in OMRs at an undervalued price, nonselling shareholders will earn a rate of return greater than the market-required cost of equity. The relationship can be expressed in a formula, where the symbols are defined as follows:

$$R = \text{rate of return in share repurchase}$$
$$k_s = \text{market-required cost of equity}$$
$$V = \text{intrinsic value}$$
$$P = \text{market price}$$

The initial relationship is shown by the equation

$$\text{Rate of Return in Share Repurchase} = \frac{\text{Cost of Equity}}{1 - \text{Percent Undervaluation}} \qquad \textbf{(18.8)}$$

In symbols:

$$R = \frac{k_s}{1 - (V - P)/V}$$

$$= \frac{k_s}{(V - V + P)/V}$$

$$= \frac{k_s}{P/V}$$

Table 18.5   Basic Relationships

1. Cash flow per year		$300
2. Cost of capital		10%
3. Intrinsic value before share repurchase		$3,000
4. Number of shares		100
5. Intrinsic value per share		$30
6. Market price per share		$20
7. Return on share repurchase	15% × $400 =	$60
8. New cash flow	$60 + $300 =	$360

In words:

$$R = \frac{\text{Cost of Equity}}{\text{Ratio of Actual Market to Intrinsic Value}}$$

For example, let $k_s = 10\%$, $P = \$20$, and $V = \$30$. Then,

$$R = \frac{10\%}{\$20/\$30} = 15\%$$

These relationships can also be used to illustrate the equivalence of the return on a share repurchase and an investment. A share repurchase financed by forgoing value-creating investments makes sense only if the investment would have yielded a rate of return less than the rate of return on a share repurchase, as calculated above. An example illustrates this point. The basic relationships are shown in Table 18.5. An all-equity firm has an annual cash flow of $300, a 10% cost of equity (capital), and therefore an initial intrinsic value of $3,000. With 100 shares outstanding, it has an intrinsic value per share of $30. The market price per share is $20. In open-market purchases it buys 20 shares at $20. In line 7 of Table 18.5 we show that the dollar return on the share repurchase will be the rate of return on the share repurchase as developed in our previous example of 15% times the share repurchase of $400, to achieve an incremental cash flow of $60. So the new cash flow, as shown in line 8, is $360.

In Table 18.6, we can now compare the effect of shareholder intrinsic value of investing in a share repurchase versus a project with an explicit cash flow of $360 per year. The new intrinsic value per share under case 1 of share repurchase directly follows our previous discussion. The annual cash flow remains at $300; capitalized at the 10% cost of capital, it gives an intrinsic value of $3,000. We deduct the investment of $400 made in the share repurchase. The net new equity value is $2,600 (line 4), which, divided by the 80 shares remaining, gives a new intrinsic value of $32.50 per share (line 6).

Case 2 involves an investment that adds $60 to the original cash flows, as shown in line 1. Line 2 capitalizes the cash flow to give $3,600. Net of the investment, the new equity value in line 4 is $3,200; dividing by 100 shares gives the new intrinsic value per share of $32. This result is slightly below the $32.50 under the

Table 18.6   Intrinsic Value Effects of Repurchase vs. Investment

	Case 1 Repurchase $400	Case 2 Invest $400
1. Cash flow	$300	$360
2. Cash flow / cost of capital	$3,000	$3,600
3. Investment	$400	$400
4. New equity value	$2,600	$3,200
5. Number of shares	80	100
6. Shareholder intrinsic value per share	$32.50	$32.00
7. Market value (intrinsic × 0.667)	$1,733	$2,133
8. Market value per share	$21.67	$21.33

case 1 repurchase because the gains in equity value have to be distributed over 100 shares including the 20 shares that otherwise are eliminated by the share repurchase. If the actual market price is one-third below the intrinsic value, the new market price per share under the share repurchase will be $21.67 and $21.33 for the investment. If in the share repurchase a premium of 6.67% had been paid, the number of shares purchased would have been 18.75. The shares remaining would have been 81.25, which divided into the $2,600 new intrinsic equity value, would give $32 per share. This is the same as the investment result. So in order to get equivalent returns, it is necessary to have a share repurchase in which a 6.67% premium is paid over the prevailing market price.

The above numerical examples illustrate the logic behind the results of the empirical studies on the effects of open-market share repurchases. Returns on OMRs can be increased somewhat by the use of puts. For example, a company with a stock selling at $40 sells one year put warrants for 1 million shares at $3 per share, with an exercise price at $40. This $3 million income is net, because the tax code allows corporations to sell options on their stock tax-free. The buyer of the warrants is likely to be a large financial concern, which will hedge the warrant by buying the company's shares in the open market. Using an options-based hedging model, they buy 400,000 shares to cover the 1 million warrants. If the stock price rises, the warrants are worthless, but the stock part of the hedge can be sold in the open market for profit. As the stock rises, the put owner can begin to sell because fewer shares are needed to hedge the position. If the stock falls below the exercise price, the financial concern can exercise the puts at $40 per share, regardless of how low the price of the stock may fall. An example is Microsoft, which has sold 30 million to 40 million puts a year; none has ever been "put" back to the company. According to its 1998 Annual Report, Microsoft had 60 million puts outstanding on June 30, 1998.

SUMMARY

We described four methods of share repurchase:

1. Fixed-price tender offers (FPTs).
2. Dutch auctions (DAs).
3. Transferable put rights (TPRs).
4. Open-market repurchases (OMRs).

We explained the mechanisms and logic behind each of the four types. Each has a different signaling effect and wealth effect. All result in significant positive abnormal returns to shareholders.

A number of hypotheses have been advanced to explain these gains. Tax effects appear to play a small role; gains to shareholders on repurchase are taxed as capital gains rather than as ordinary income in the case of dividends. Share repurchase represents an alternative means of making payouts to shareholders, which becomes even more important during periods of restrictions on dividends. Increased leverage may also be responsible for some of the shareholder wealth increase, especially in debt-financed repurchases, to the extent that there is a tax subsidy on debt interest payments or that the firm has been operating at a suboptimal leverage level. Increased leverage is also related to the information or signaling hypothesis, which is another explanation for the source of gains. By increasing leverage, management signals that it believes cash flows will be sufficiently higher in the future to cover higher interest payments. Also, by repurchasing the shares at a premium over the current market price, management is signaling its belief that the shares are undervalued by the market. And, because corporate insiders typically do not participate in the repurchase, they are increasing their percentage ownership in the firm, another signal that they are optimistic about the firm's prospects. The share repurchase premium also serves as a takeover defense. It may be higher than the premium offered by a raider. Thus, it alerts shareholders that it is not only the raider who sees the potential for increased value in the firm but also the firm's own management. The bondholder expropriation theory suggests that the gains to shareholders come at the expense of the bondholders, but the evidence does not support this hypothesis.

QUESTIONS

18.1 What are four ways to carry out a share repurchase?

18.2 In a tender offer for share repurchase, how is the wealth increase distributed among tendering and non-tendering shareholders?

18.3 What theory most plausibly explains the positive shareholder wealth effect observed in share repurchases?

18.4 A company has 8 million shares outstanding. It offers to repurchase 2 million shares at $30 per share; the current market price of the stock is $25. Management controls 500,000 shares and does not participate in the repurchase. What is the signaling cost of the repurchase if the true value of the stock is $20? If the true value of the stock is $29?

18.5 What is the influence of prorationing or not and OD at risk or not on wealth effects in share repurchases?

18.6 Do open market share repurchases meet the requirements of achieving credible signaling?

Case 18.1 FPL

A Harvard case published on March 15, 1995 (Esty and Schreiber) and an article published in spring 1996 (Soter, Brigham, and Evanson) highlight some aspects of share repurchase. The FPL group is a holding company whose principal operating subsidiary is Florida Power and Light Company (FPL), which serves most of the east coast and lower west coast of Florida, a population of about 6.5 million. Its energy mix consists of purchased power (17%), oil (31%), nuclear (26%), gas (20%), and coal (6%).

Deregulation had been increasing competition in the public utility industry since 1978. The Public Utilities Regulatory Policies Act (PURPA) in 1978 encouraged the creation of power plants using renewable or nontraditional fuels. If specified efficiency and size standards were met, PURPA required local utilities to buy all of their electrical output. In 1992 the National Energy Policy Act (NEPA) was enacted by Congress. It required utilities to permit use of their transmission systems at the same level of quality and at fair cost. In early 1994 some states permitted retail wheeling, under which customers could buy power from utilities other than the local franchise supplier. The local utility would be required to permit competitors' use of its transmission and distribution network. Major utilities in states that proposed to phase in retail wheeling experienced substantial declines in market values. Electric utility companies faced increased competition.

Florida Power and Light embarked on a diversification program into life insurance, cable television, information services, and citrus production between 1985 and 1988. In 1989 the new president emphasized a return to the core utility business. An aggressive capital expenditure program was launched to meet projected demand increases. Quality and efficiency programs increased plant availability above industry averages and lowered operating expenses.

The improved outlook for growth and profitability caused FPL to reassess the relationship between its long-term business strategies and its financial strategies. Increased growth opportunities were associated with increased competitive risks. Increased financial flexibility was required. With increased business risk, financial leverage was reduced.

A major reassessment of dividend policy was also made. With prospects for increased investment requirements and possible acquisition opportunities, a lower dividend payout policy made sense. The traditional utility company policy of consistent annual dividend increases was breached. A share repurchase program was announced. The initial stock price reaction to the dividend cut was negative. The share repurchase program signaled a favorable outlook for FPL and conveyed assurances that management would return cash to shareholders (by share repurchases), if not required by its basic business strategy. In addition, a tax advantage resulted from the maximum personal rate on long-term capital gains at 28% versus a rate on dividend income as high as 39%.

The earnings of FPL continued to improve, and its share price sharply increased above previous high levels. The stock price range in 1994 was $27 to $37; for 1995 it was $34 to $46.50. This case illustrates a number of the elements of share repurchase programs developed in the chapter.

557

QUESTIONS

1. What was the major force that stimulated the diversification program by FPL?
2. How successful were the diversification efforts of FPL?
3. What was the impact of increased competitive risks and increased growth and profitability opportunities on the financial policies of FPL?
4. What caused FPL to reduce its dividend payout?
5. What kinds of signals were conveyed by the announcement of a share repurchase program?

REFERENCES

Bagwell, Laurie Simon, "Dutch Auction Repurchases: An Analysis of Shareholder Heterogeneity," *Journal of Finance,* 47, March 1992, pp. 71–105.

Barber, B. M., and J. D. Lyon, "Detecting Abnormal Operating Performance: The Empirical Power and Specification of Test-Statistics," *Journal of Financial Economics,* 41, 1996, pp. 359–399.

Bradley, Michael, and Lee M. Wakeman, "The Wealth Effects of Targeted Share Repurchases," *Journal of Financial Economics,* 11, 1983, pp. 301–328.

Brickley, James, "Shareholder Wealth, Information Signalling and the Specially Designated Dividend: An Empirical Study," *Journal of Financial Economics,* 12, 1983, pp. 103–114.

Comment, Robert, and Gregg A. Jarrell, "The Relative Signalling Power of Dutch-Auction and Fixed-Price Self-Tender Offers and Open-Market Share Repurchases," *Journal of Finance,* 46, September 1991, pp. 1243–1271.

Dann, Larry, "Common Stock Repurchases: An Analysis of Returns to Bondholders and Stockholders," *Journal of Financial Economics,* 9, 1981, pp. 113–138.

Esty, Benjamin C., and Craig F. Schreiber, "Dividend Policy at FPL Group, Inc.," HBS Case N9-295-059, March 15, 1995.

Gay, Gerald D., Jayant R. Kale, and Thomas H. Noe, "Share Repurchase Mechanisms: A Comparative Analysis of Efficacy, Shareholder Wealth, and Corporate Control Effects," *Financial Management,* 20, Spring 1991, pp. 44–59.

Healy, P., K. Palepu, and R. Ruback, "Does Corporate Performance Improve after Mergers?" *Journal of Financial Economics,* 19, 1992, pp. 135–175.

Howe, K., J. He, and G. Kao, "One Time Cash Flow Announcements and Free Cash Flow Theory: Share Repurchases and Special Dividends," *Journal of Finance,* 47, 1992, pp. 1963–1976.

Ikenberry, David, Josef Lakonishok, and Theo Vermaelen, "Market Underreaction to Open Market Share Repurchases," *Journal of Financial Economics,* 39, October–November 1995, pp. 181–208.

Ikenberry, David L., and Theo Vermaelen, "The Option to Repurchase Stock," *Financial Management,* 25, Winter 1996, pp. 9–24.

Kale, Jayant R., Thomas H. Noe, and Gerald D. Gay, "Share Repurchase Through Transferable Put Rights," *Journal of Financial Economics,* 25, 1989, pp. 141–160.

Kamma, Sreenivas, George Kanatas, and Steven Raymar, "Dutch Auction Versus Fixed-Price Self-Tender Offers for Common Stock," *Journal of Financial Intermediation,* 2, 1992, pp. 277–307.

Lang, L., and R. Litzenberger, "Dividend Announcements: Cash Flow Signaling vs.

Free Cash Flow Hypothesis," *Journal of Financial Economics,* 24, 1989, pp. 181–191.

Liang, J. Nellie, and Steven A. Sharpe, "Share Repurchases and Employee Stock Options and Their Implications for S&P 500 Share Retirements and Expected Returns," working paper, Federal Reserve Board—Division of Research and Statistics, November 1999.

Lie, Erik, and John J. McConnell, "Earnings Signals in Fixed-Price and Dutch Auction Self-Tender Offers," *Journal of Financial Economics,* 49, 1998, pp. 161–186.

Masulis, Ronald W., "Stock Repurchase by Tender Offer: An Analysis of the Causes of Common Stock Price Changes," *Journal of Finance,* 35, 1980, pp. 305–319.

Nohel, Tom, and Vefa Tarhan, "Share Repurchases and Firm Performance: New Evidence on the Agency Costs of Free Cash Flow," *Journal of Financial Economics,* 49, 1998, pp. 187–222.

Perfect, S., D. Petersen, and P. Petersen, "Self Tender Offers: The Effects of Free Cash Flow, Cash Flow Signaling, and the Measurement of Tobin's Q," *Journal of Banking and Finance,* 19, 1995, pp. 409–420.

Rappaport, Alfred, *Creating Shareholder Value,* New York: The Free Press, 1998.

Soter, Dennis, Eugene Brigham, and Paul Evanson, "The Dividend Cut 'Heard 'Round the World': The Case of FPL," *Journal of Applied Corporate Finance,* 9, Spring 1996, pp. 4–15.

Vermaelen, Theo, "Common Stock Repurchases and Market Signalling: An Empirical Study," *Journal of Financial Economics,* 9, 1981, pp. 139–183.

———, "Repurchase Tender Offers, Signaling and Managerial Incentives," *Journal of Financial and Quantitative Analysis,* 19, 1984, pp. 163–181.

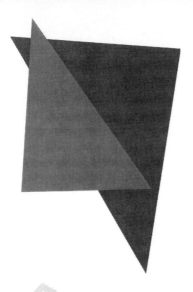

C h a p t e r   1 9

Takeover Defenses

We have documented that the pace of takeovers and mergers greatly increased during 1998 and 1999. Not all merger proposals are welcomed by the target. During the 1980s, arsenals of devices were developed to defend against unwelcome proposals. Examples of resistance to takeover offers abound. We present two illustrative cases. In August 1998 AMP received a cash bid from AlliedSignal. AMP was a leading producer of electronic connectors. AlliedSignal was regarded as an advanced technology company with operations in diversified areas. AMP resisted and ultimately accepted a proposal by Tyco International, another diversified firm.

On November 14, 1999, Vodafone AirTouch (based in Britain) made an unsolicited bid to Mannesmann AG (based in Germany). Despite many defenses put up by Mannesmann, it finally agreed to the Vodafone offer on February 3, 2000.

Multiple issues are raised by the use of takeover defenses. One is whether the target is resisting mainly to get a better price. A second possibility is that management of the target judges that the company will perform better on its own. A third reason might be that management is seeking to entrench itself against loss of authority in the combined firm. So many issues are raised by the subject that we provide a road map in Table 19.1. We discuss each of the topics listed in the sections that follow.

STRATEGIC PERSPECTIVES

In chapter 1, we described how strong change forces like advances in technology and globalization have redefined industries and increased the intensity of competition between firms. It is imperative that management and the board of a company, with the assistance of its legal advisers and its financial advisers, continuously reassess the competitive landscape. Management and the board must evaluate on a continuing basis how all the forms of M&A activities described in the previous chapters may impact the firm both as threats and as opportunities. Wasserstein (1998) describes how large public companies review takeover defense issues on a regular basis (chapter 20). He describes the innovative contributions of Martin Lipton, the founder of Wachtell, Lipton, Rosen, and Katz, who developed the poison pill defense (Wasserstein, 1998, pp. 461–463).

Table 19.1 An Overview of Takeover Defenses

1. Strategic perspectives
2. Financial defensive measures
3. Corporate restructuring and reorganization
   a. Reorganization of assets
   b. Other strategies (leveraged recaps, LBOs, etc.)
4. Duty of directors
5. Greenmail
   a. Wealth effects of greenmail
   b. Antigreenmail developments
6. Methods of resistance
   a. Pac Man defense
   b. White knight
   c. White squire
7. Antitakeover amendments
   a. Supermajority amendments
   b. Fair-price amendments—to avoid two-tier offers
   c. Staggered or classified board of directors
   d. Dual class or create new classes of securities with magnified voting power
   e. Other antitakeover actions
   f. Antitakeover amendments and corporate policy
   g. Antitakeover amendments and shareholder returns
8. State laws
9. Poison pills—right to purchase securities at low prices
   a. Types of plans
   b. Dead-hand provisions
   c. Case studies
   d. Effects on shareholder returns
10. Shareholder activism
11. Poison puts—permit bondholders to put (sell) bonds to the issuer in the event of a takeover
12. Golden parachutes
    a. Rationale
    b. Silver and tin parachutes
    c. Returns to shareholders and golden parachutes

Wide-ranging subjects are covered, including the following:

1. What are the main developments in the industry?
2. Are there opportunities for adding critical capabilities to participate in attractive growth areas?
3. Are there opportunities for rolling up fragmented industries into stronger firms?
4. Is our firm likely to be rolled up?

5. Are sales-to-capacity relationships improving or deteriorating in our industry?
6. Will consolidating mergers to reduce capacity and cost impact our firm?
7. Is one of the top six to eight firms in our industry a likely target for takeover by a competitor whose capabilities would thereby be significantly enhanced?
8. Should our firm make preemptive moves?
9. How should our firm respond to a takeover bid?

In short, every firm needs to reevaluate its strategies on a continuing basis with particular reference to the possibilities of M&A activity that will impact it.

FINANCIAL DEFENSIVE MEASURES

It is often proposed that the best defense against a takeover is for the firm to be highly efficient, its sales growth favorable, and its profitability margins high. However, the firm may become a takeover target of another firm seeking to benefit from an association with such an efficient firm. In addition, if it has long-range investment plans whose payoffs are not reflected in its current stock price, the firm may be viewed as undervalued.

Other characteristics that make a firm vulnerable to a takeover include

➤ A low stock price in relation to the replacement cost of assets or their potential earning power (a low q-ratio).

➤ A highly liquid balance sheet with large amounts of excess cash, a valuable securities portfolio, and significant unused debt capacity.

➤ Good cash flow relative to current stock prices. Low P/EPS ratios.

➤ Subsidiaries or properties that could be sold off without significantly impairing cash flow.

➤ Relatively small stockholdings under the control of incumbent management.

A combination of these factors can simultaneously make a firm an attractive investment opportunity and facilitate its financing. The firm's assets act as collateral for an acquirer's borrowings, and the target's cash flows from operations and divestitures can be used to repay the loans.

A firm fitting the above description would do well to take at least some of the following steps. (1) Increase debt with borrowed funds used to repurchase equity, thus concentrating management's percentage holdings while using up debt capacity. (2) Increase dividends on remaining shares. (3) Structure loan covenants to force acceleration of repayment in the event of takeover. (4) Liquidate securities portfolios and draw down excess cash. (5) Invest continuing cash flows from operations in positive net present value projects or return it to shareholders. (6) Use some of the excess liquidity to acquire other firms. (7) Divest subsidiaries that can be eliminated without impairing cash flow, perhaps through spin-offs to avoid large sums of cash flowing in. (8) Analyze the profitability of all operations in depth to get at the true picture beneath such accounting devices as transfer pricing and overhead allocation, and divest low-profit operations. (9) Realize the true value of undervalued assets by selling them off or restructuring.

Table 19.2   Defensive Corporate Restructuring and Reorganization

1. Reorganization of assets (chapter 11)
   a. Acquisitions
   b. Sell-offs or divestitures
2. Creating new ownership relationships (chapter 12)
   a. Spin-offs
   b. Split-ups
   c. Equity carve-outs
3. Reorganizing financial claims (chapter 13)
   a. Exchange offers
   b. Dual-class recapitalizations
   c. Leveraged recapitalizations
   d. Financial reorganization (bankruptcy)
   e. Liquidation
4. Other strategies
   a. Joint ventures (chapter 14)
   b. ESOPs and MLPs (chapter 15)
   c. Going-private transactions (LBOs) (chapter 16)
   d. Using international markets (chapter 17)
   e. Share repurchase programs (chapter 18)

CORPORATE RESTRUCTURING AND REORGANIZATION

In both academic journals and business magazines, the topics of corporate restructuring and reorganization to increase value have been kept separate from the topics of defensive corporate restructuring and reorganization. After reading both types of literature, the insight came to us that this is really one subject, not two. We will review the topics of value-increasing activities and then show their application and extension in defensive programs. In Table 19.2, we modify Table 11.1 of chapter 11, which outlined the value-increasing topics. From looking at Table 19.2, it is clear that four sections taken together are the headings for chapters 11 to 18. In the initial treatment of those chapters, the emphasis was on the development of value-increasing strategies. Here we use the same framework to demonstrate how the entire panoply of activities can be employed as takeover defenses. We cover each of the four major topics in turn.

Reorganization of Assets

In the earlier discussion, assets were acquired to extend the firm's capabilities. But asset acquisitions can also be used to block takeovers. In 1984 Disney bought the Arvida real estate firm with equity to dilute the ownership position as a defense against Saul Steinberg and his Reliance Group. Acquisitions can also be used to create antitrust problems for the bidder. The Marshall Field department store used this defense several times. For example, when Carter Hawley Hale (CHH) made a tender offer,

Field's directors expanded into the Galleria in Houston and acquired five Liberty House stores in the northwest. Because CHH was active in these areas, on February 22, 1978, it withdrew its tender offer, citing the impact of Field's expansion plan.

In chapter 11 we described how sell-offs and divestitures can be used to move resources to their higher valued uses, creating values for both the seller and buyer. To block a tender offer, however, a firm may dispose of those segments of its business in which the bidder is most interested. This is called "selling off the crown jewels."

In chapter 12 we described how spin-offs, split-ups, and equity carve-outs are used to create more value. These can also involve the "crown jewels" segment of the company, thereby representing takeover defenses.

In chapter 13 we discussed reorganizing financial claims. By using exchange offers, a firm can either increase or decrease leverage. A debt-for-equity expansion can be used to increase leverage to levels that would be unacceptable to the bidder. Dual-class recapitalizations can be used to increase the voting powers of an insider group to levels that would enable it to block a tender offer. Leveraged recapitalizations can be used to unlock potential values for the company. But a firm may also incur huge amounts of debt, using the proceeds to pay a large cash dividend and increase the ownership position of insiders. This tactic has been called a "scorched earth" policy. The crown jewel and scorched earth actions can be combined. The firm sells off attractive segments of the company and adds large amounts of debt, using the cash for a large dividend that may even exceed the tender offer price from the bidder.

Other Strategies

In chapter 14 we described how joint ventures can be used to extend the capabilities of the firm. Joint ventures can also be used to block a takeover. A close involvement with other firms could represent liaisons that the potential bidder might prefer to avoid.

In chapter 15 we explained how ESOPs are often used to block takeovers, and we described the famous example of Polaroid and Shamrock Holdings. Chapter 16 discussed MBOs and LBOs, which are widely used as a defense against an outside tender offer. Sometimes the financing of the MBO or LBO comes from financial institutions. Sometimes the competitive bidder is an LBO specialist firm such as KKR. One of the incentives management may have for turning to the LBO specialist firm is that its stock ownership position may thereby be increased more than in the outside tender offer.

In chapter 17 we discussed how international liaisons and other transactions can be used to defend against unwanted takeovers. A domestic bidder may not offer as great a potential for augmenting the firm's capabilities and growth as an international partner.

In chapter 18 we discussed share repurchase programs. One purpose of share repurchase programs is to signal that the current price of the stock represents undervaluation. But share repurchase programs are widely used to defend against takeovers. They increase the ownership of insiders. With respect to outside shareholders, the low reservation price investors are bought out in a share repurchase program. The tender offer price to succeed, therefore, is higher than it otherwise would be.

Another strategy to avoid a takeover is by a proxy contest as will be discussed in chapter 20. The aim is to change the control group and make performance improvements (Dodd and Warner, 1983; Mulherin and Poulsen, 1998).

We have demonstrated that corporate restructuring and reorganization programs can be used to unlock values and/or to defend against takeovers. Therefore, we can predict what studies of event returns are likely to find. When restructuring improves the firm's efficiency in important dimensions, the probability of favorable stock price movements is improved. When the restructuring represents a scorched earth policy of some type, it predictably will have undesirable effects and result in CARs that are negative.

Bae and Simet (BS) (1998) examined the effects on shareholder wealth of two defensive tactics, leveraged recapitalization (LR) and leveraged buyout (LBO). They used a sample of 72 LBO firms and 37 LR firms for the period 1985 to 1990. They also constructed a sample of 21 matched pairs of LR and LBO firms based on industry and firm size.

Over a two-day period, $[-1,0]$, the mean CARs were highly significant. They were 11.954% and 5.704%, respectively, for the LBO and LR firms, both significant at the 1% level. The difference in the mean was significant at the 1% level. Over a wider period, from day -20 to day 0, the mean CARs were 15.5% for LBOs and 11.7% for LRs, and the difference was significant at the 1% level. The market seemed to respond more favorably to LBO announcements than to LR announcements.

DUTY OF DIRECTORS

It is the duty of directors to approve only a transaction that is fair to the public shareholders and is the best transaction available. Directors have the burden of proof to demonstrate that the best interests of the shareholders have been served (*Moran v. Household International*, 1985).

If the directors reject a takeover offer and choose to remain independent, they must demonstrate to the courts that they have sound business reasons for doing so. For example, when Time was completing its merger, a $200 per share offer from Paramount was rejected. Time argued that a much greater value per share would be produced from the Time–Warner merger over a longer planning horizon. The courts upheld the rejection of Paramount's apparently higher bid, as consistent with the business judgment rule.

When a target company agrees to an acquisition, the directors must demonstrate that the price was fair to shareholders and was the best offer that could be obtained. The courts have elaborated this view in a series of cases. For example, in 1994 the Delaware Supreme Court enjoined the acquisition of Lynch Communication Systems by Alcatel, a French company. One of the Lynch shareholders, Kahn, alleged that Alcatel as a controlling shareholder of Lynch had dictated the terms of the merger and had paid an unfair price. The court held that Lynch had not fully explored independent competitive offers.

A fairness opinion from an investment banking firm on the price received is useful evidence, but it is not sufficient. Examples abound of firms that announce auctions and even encourage multiple rounds of bidding to establish that the best possible price has been obtained.

GREENMAIL

In one sense, greenmail says to the bidder, "Here is some money. Now go away." More formally, greenmail represents a targeted repurchase of a large block of stock from specified shareholders at a premium. The purpose of the premium buyback presumably is to end a hostile takeover threat by the large blockholder or greenmailer. The term **greenmail** connotes blackmail, and both payers and receivers of greenmail have received negative publicity. Proponents of antigreenmail charter amendments or legislation that would prohibit targeted repurchases argue that greenmailers cause damage to shareholders. In this view, the large block investors are corporate "raiders" who expropriate corporate assets to the detriment of other shareholders. Allegedly, raiding takes the form of the raiders using their corporate voting power to accord themselves excessive compensation and perquisites, receiving on their shares a substantial premium over the market price through greenmail or "looting" the corporate treasury in some unspecified manner (Holderness and Sheehan, 1985).

An alternative view is that the large block investors involved in greenmail help bring about management changes, either changes in corporate personnel or changes in corporate policy, or have superior skills at evaluating potential takeover targets (Holderness and Sheehan, 1985). In this view, proposals to prohibit targeted repurchases are antitakeover proposals in disguise (Jensen, 1988). Jensen (1988, p. 41) argued that "management can easily prohibit greenmail without legislation; it need only announce a policy that prohibits the board or management from making such payments." He suggested that managers make greenmail payments to protect themselves from competition in the corporate control market.

Often, in connection with targeted repurchases, a standstill agreement is written. A standstill agreement is a voluntary contract in which the stockholder who is bought out agrees not to make further investments in the target company during a specified period of time (for example, 10 years). When a standstill agreement is made without a repurchase, the large blockholder simply agrees not to increase his or her ownership, which presumably would put him or her in an effective control position.

The St. Regis Paper Company provides an example of greenmail. When an investor group led by Sir James Goldsmith acquired an 8.6% stake in St. Regis and expressed interest in taking over the paper concern, the company agreed to repurchase the shares at a premium. Goldsmith's group acquired the shares for an average price of $35.50 a share, a total of $109 million. It sold its stake at $52 a share, netting a profit of $51 million. Shortly after the payoff in March 1984, St. Regis became the target of publisher Rupert Murdoch. St. Regis turned to Champion International and agreed to a $1.84 billion takeover. Murdoch tendered his 5.6% stake in St. Regis to the Champion offer for a profit.

Wealth Effects of Greenmail

The announcement of a greenmail transaction by a company generally results in a negative abnormal return to shareholders of about 2% to 3%, which is statistically significant (Bradley and Wakeman, 1983; Dann and DeAngelo, 1983; Mikkelson and Ruback, 1991). But further analysis is required. Consider a number of possibilities.

When the large blockholder starts buying the shares that provide him with a threatening position, the price of the company stock is likely to increase. Other empirical studies find that when these initial stock purchases are taken into account, positive abnormal returns are earned both during the initial period when the foothold is being established and in the full "purchase-to-repurchase" period (Holderness and Sheehan, 1985; Klein and Rosenfeld, 1988; Mikkelson and Ruback, 1985, 1991).

But even at the announcement of a greenmail repurchase a decline in stock prices generally does not occur unless the greenmail is associated with a standstill agreement or preceded by a control contest (Mikkelson and Ruback, 1991). The standstill agreements may be viewed as reducing the probability of a subsequent takeover. Nevertheless, even with standstill agreements, about 40% of the firms experience a subsequent control change within three years of the greenmail.

We should not read the empirical results without thinking about some real-world possibilities, such as the hostile bid for Disney in 1984 by Saul Steinberg and his associates. Among other things, Disney paid Steinberg greenmail in the amount of about $50 million, but it was widely recognized that Disney needed some top management changes (Taylor, 1987). After fending off the Steinberg group, a new management team was brought in headed by Michael D. Eisner. Taking into account stock splits, the Disney stock increased from about $6 in 1984 to $34 by 1989, representing a compound rate of increase in the common stock price for shareholders of 41.5%. From 1989 to 1996, Disney stock increased to $60 a share, representing a further compound annual rate of increase of 8.5%. The initial jump in stock prices reflected the ability of Disney directors to make the top management changes needed. The slower rate of growth in stock prices after 1989 may have contributed to the Disney acquisition of Cap Cities/ABC in August 1995.

The moral of this story is that the impact of greenmail can be different depending on the circumstances. If it gives the directors time to work out a better solution, then the market reaction could be positive rather than negative.

Antigreenmail Developments

The negative view of greenmail resulted in efforts to restrict its use. In 1986 Congress included in the tax law changes a provision in Section 5881 of the Internal Revenue Code that imposes a 50% excise tax on the recipient of greenmail payments. In addition, antigreenmail charter amendments began to be enacted by companies.

Antigreenmail charter amendments prohibit or discourage the targeted repurchase by requiring management to obtain the approval of a majority or supermajority of nonparticipating shareholders prior to a repurchase. Proxy statements proposing antigreenmail amendments typically state that greenmailers pressure the company for a premium buyback with "threats of disruption" including proxy contests and tender offers, that greenmail is inherently unfair to the nonparticipating shareholders, and that the decision-making power for any targeted repurchases should be properly transferred to the hands of those most affected by the repurchase decision. According to Bhagat and Jefferis (1991), proxy statements proposing antigreenmail amendments frequently include one or more of (other) antitakeover amendment proposals. Among a sample of 52 NYSE-listed firms proposing antigreenmail amendments in the 1984 to 1985 period, 40 firms also offered one or more antitakeover amendments in the proxy material. In 29 cases, shareholders had to approve or reject the antitakeover provisions and antigreenmail amendment jointly.

For a subsample in which the antigreenmail amendments are not associated with other antitakeover proposals, the antigreenmail amendment itself does not decrease shareholder wealth. Eckbo (1990) demonstrated the complexity of the effects of greenmail prohibitions. He found that the average market reaction to charter amendments prohibiting greenmail payments was weakly negative, indicating some value to retaining managerial flexibility. He found, however, that for a subsample of firms with an abnormal stock price runup over the three months prior to the mailing of a proxy providing for greenmail prohibitions, the market reaction was strongly positive. This was particularly true if the prior runup was associated with evidence or rumors of takeover activity. The logic here is that the prohibition against greenmail would remove a barrier to a takeover with positive gains to shareholders. It would follow that greenmail payments themselves would tend to decrease the firm's value. Eckbo suggested that the possibility of alternative methods for remunerating takeover entrepreneurs.

METHODS OF RESISTANCE

Firms can employ several other types of strategies to resist a particular bidder. These include the Pac Man defense, the use of a white knight, and resort to a white squire.

Pac Man Defense

Making a counterbid for the bidder is similar to the video game from which it gets its name. The Pac Man defense in essence involves the target counteroffering for the bidder. This severe defense is rarely used and in fact is usually designed not to be used. The defense is more likely to be effective if the target is much larger than the bidder, a phenomenon common in the 1980s. The risk of using the defense is that it implies that the target finds combining the two firms desirable but prefers control of the resulting entity. The user of the Pac Man essentially gives up using antitrust issues as a defense.

In most takeovers, target managements that resist maintain that the combination is undesirable. If the Pac Man defense is used, it is extremely costly and could have devastating financial effects for both firms involved. If both firms employ a large amount of debt to buy each other's stock, the resulting entity may be crippled by the combined debt load. Also, there is a risk that under state law, should both firms buy substantial stakes in each other, each would be ruled as subsidiaries of the other and be unable to vote its shares against the corporate parent. Curiously, the severity of the defense may lead the bidder to disbelieve that the target will actually employ the defense.

The famous example of the use of the Pac Man defense involves Bendix and Martin Marietta, among others. On August 25, 1982, Bendix Corporation announced a previously rumored tender offer for Martin Marietta of $43 a share. The case is noteworthy because Martin Marietta became the first firm to remain independent by employing the Pac Man defense. Marietta, with the advice of its investment banker, announced a $75 a share countertender for half of Bendix, with a $55 back-end price.

Although Marietta announced its tender offer after Bendix and would be able to buy Bendix shares only after Bendix could purchase Marietta shares, it believed that it might be able to gain control first due to differences in state laws concerning the calling of a special meeting to approve a merger. United Technologies, a large defense contractor that was interested in the complementary fit of Bendix's automotive business and Bendix's consumer electronics business, later joined Marietta and agreed to tender for half of Bendix for $75 a share and a $50 back-end price.

Efforts to convince Bendix of the seriousness of the counterbid were not effective in getting Bendix to back down. On September 17, Bendix bought 70% of Marietta shares for $48 a share. On September 23, Marietta purchased 42.4% of Bendix shares despite news that Allied Corporation and Bendix would merge. Allied, whose main businesses were oil and gas production and chemicals, had been searching for a profitable company to enable it to use its over $100 million in U.S. federal income tax credits and to reduce its dependence on gas and oil profits.

After Marietta declined Allied's offer to buy both Bendix and Marietta, the two sides agreed to a stock swap at cost. Marietta reacquired some of its shares, but Allied retained possession of a 39% stake in Marietta. Allied signed a 10-year standstill agreement. Due to the purchase of Bendix stock, Marietta had a debt-to-equity ratio of 85%, and the new debt of $930 million raised total debt to $1.3 billion. To raise funds it sold stock, businesses, plants, and other assets. The restructuring included the divestiture of its chemicals, cement, and aggregates businesses. In late 1983 Marietta bought back all its shares held by Allied for $345 million.

White Knight

The white knight defense involves choosing another company with which the target prefers to be combined. An alternative company may be preferred by the target because it sees greater compatibility. Or the new bidder may promise not to break up the target or engage in massive employee dismissals.

Examples of the use of white knights abound. Frequently, T. Boone Pickens would make an offer for a company on behalf of his Mesa Petroleum. For example, in 1982, Mesa made a bid for the Cities Service Oil Company. Cities Service responded with a Pac Man defense. Then Cities Service invited Gulf Oil to make a bid. Gulf made a bid, but when the Federal Trade Commission raised antitrust objections, Gulf dropped out. Ultimately, Cities Service was purchased by Occidental Petroleum. In 1984 Mesa bid for Gulf Oil. Gulf responded by holding an auction. Chevron (then SOCAL) ultimately won the bidding contest.

White Squire

The white squire is a modified form of a white knight, the difference being that the white squire does not acquire control of the target. In a white squire transaction, the target sells a block of its stock to a third party it considers to be friendly. The white squire sometimes is required to vote its shares with target management. These transactions are often accompanied by a standstill agreement that limits the amount of additional target stock the white squire can purchase for a specified period of time and restricts the sale of its target stock, usually giving the right of first refusal to the target. In return, the white squire often receives a seat on the target board, generous dividends, and/or a discount on the target shares. Preferred stock enables the board to tailor the characteristics of that stock to fit the transaction and so is usually used in white squire transactions.

Here is a famous example of a white squire investment. Although Champion International did not face a direct takeover threat, the company became concerned about the possibility of an attempted takeover following the first hostile takeover bid in the paper industry, that of Georgia Pacific for Great Northern Nekoosa in 1989. Champion's management approached Warren Buffett about investing in the company. In December 1989 Buffett purchased $300 million of new Champion convertible preferred stock that carried a 9.25% annual dividend rate. This was about $6 million a year over the market rate of 7% for investment grade convertible preferred stock. Buffett held an 8% voting equity stake, one that he was allowed to raise to 18%.

ANTITAKEOVER AMENDMENTS

Other defense mechanisms are referred to as antitakeover amendments to a firm's corporate charter. These are often called "shark repellents." As with all charter amendments, antitakeover amendments must be voted on and approved by shareholders. Although 95% of antitakeover amendments proposed by management are ratified by shareholders, this may be because a planned amendment may not be introduced if management is unsure of its success (Brickley, Lease, and Smith, 1988). Failure to pass might be taken as a vote of no confidence in incumbent management and may provide a platform for a proxy fight or takeover attempt where none had existed before. The evidence provided by Brickley, Lease, and Smith (1988) indicated that institutional shareholders such as banks and insurance companies were more likely to vote with management on antitakeover amendments than others such as mutual funds and college endowments. Note that the former institutions generally have ongoing business relationships with management and thus are more likely to be influenced by management. Brickley, Lease, and Smith also found that blockholders more actively participate in voting than non-blockholders and may oppose proposals that appear to harm shareholders. This result is consistent with Jarrell and Poulsen (1987), who found that those amendments having the most negative effect on stock price (amendments other than fair-price amendments) are adopted by firms with the lowest percentage of institutional holdings and the highest percentage of insider holdings. Jarrell and Poulsen suggested that these results helped explain how harmful amendments receive approval of shareholders. The evidence also suggested that blockholders do play a monitoring role. Institutional holders are sophisticated and well informed, so they vote in accordance with their economic interest more consistently than less informed small investors.

Antitakeover amendments generally impose new conditions on the transfer of managerial control of the firm through a merger or tender offer or by replacement of the board of directors. There are four major types of antitakeover amendments: supermajority, fair-price, classified boards, and authorization of preferred stock.

Supermajority Amendments

Supermajority amendments require shareholder approval by at least two-thirds vote and sometimes as much as 90% of the voting power of outstanding capital stock for all transactions involving change of control. In most existing cases, however, the supermajority provisions have a board-out clause that provides the board with the power to determine when and if the supermajority provisions will be in effect. Pure supermajority provisions would seriously limit management's flexibility in takeover negotiations.

Fair-Price Amendments

Fair-price amendments are supermajority provisions with a board-out clause and an additional clause waiving the supermajority requirement if a fair price is paid for all purchased shares. The fair price is commonly defined as the highest price paid by the bidder during a specified period and is sometimes required to exceed an amount determined relative to accounting earnings or book value of the target. Thus, fair-price amendments defend against two-tier tender offers that are not approved by the target's board. A uniform offer for all shares to be purchased in a tender offer and in a subsequent cleanup merger or tender offer will avoid the supermajority requirement. Because the two-tier tender offer is not essential in successful hostile takeovers, the fair-price amendment is the least restrictive in the class of supermajority amendments.

Classified Boards

Another major type of antitakeover amendment provides for **staggered,** or **classified,** boards of directors to delay effective transfer of control in a takeover. Management's purported rationale in proposing a staggered board is to ensure continuity of policy and experience. For example, a nine-member board might be divided into three classes, with only three members standing for election to a three-year term each year. Thus, a new majority shareholder would have to wait at least two annual meetings to gain control of the board of directors. Effectiveness of cumulative voting is reduced under the classified-board scheme because a greater shareholder vote is required to elect a single director. Variations on antitakeover amendments relating to the board of directors include provisions prohibiting the removal of directors except for cause and provisions fixing the number of directors allowed to prevent "packing" the board.

Authorization of Preferred Stock

The board of directors is authorized to create a new class of securities with special voting rights. This security, typically preferred stock, may be issued to friendly parties in a control contest. Thus, this device is a defense against hostile takeover bids, although historically it was used to provide the board of directors with flexibility in financing under changing economic conditions. Creation of a poison pill security could be included in this category but is generally considered to be a different defensive device. (We examine the poison pill defense in the following section.)

Other Antitakeover Actions

Other amendments that management may propose as a takeover defense include

1. Abolition of cumulative voting where it is not required by state law.
2. Reincorporation in a state with more accommodating antitakeover laws.
3. Provisions with respect to the scheduling of shareholders meetings and introduction of agenda items, including nomination of candidates to the board of directors.

Another refinement is the passage of lock-in amendments making it difficult to void previously passed antitakeover amendments by requiring, for example, supermajority approval. Shareholders may propose antigreenmail amendments that restrict a company's freedom to buy back a raider's shares at a premium.

Iqbal, Shetty, Haley, and Jayakumar (1999) analyzed whether the termination of overfunded pension plans to deter takeover attempts was viewed negatively by shareholders. Termination could be viewed as a takeover defense because by liquidating the excess assets the firm removes a significant source of cash flow to the bidder firm. The sample analyzed consisted of 123 firms with defined benefit pension plan terminations with excess asset reversions exceeding $1 million during the period May 1980 to October 1990. The event date was defined as the earlier of the *Wall Street Journal* announcement date or the filing date. No other financial news occurred around a six-day window surrounding the event date. The sample was subdivided by managerial ownership level. Of the sample firms, 63 were classified as low ownership (5% or less direct insider ownership) and 60 were considered high ownership (higher than 5% ownership). The sample was also classified by whether they received a takeover bid in a period two years before through two years after the termination date. Twenty-eight firms were classified as takeover-susceptible, whereas the remaining 95 firms were classified as nontakeover firms.

For the event window [−1,0], the full sample had CARs of 0.5% and 0.6% based on filing date and event date, respectively, both significant at the 10% level. The high ownership group exhibited a positive CAR of 1.0%, significant at the 10% level, consistent with the notion that terminations were favorable when managers had a high ownership interest in the firm. The CAR for the takeover-susceptible firms was a positive 1.6%, significant at the 5% level. One explanation given by Iqbal, Shetty, Haley, and Jayakumar was that shareholders viewed takeover attempts as a direct threat to their claim on the excess pension assets.

Additional analysis examined the effects of managerial ownership on the stock price reactions for both the takeover-susceptible and nontakeover sample. For takeover-susceptible firms, high level of ownership had a highly significant CAR of 4.6%, significant at the 1% level. Low level of ownership did not show significant results. For the nontakeover sample, there was no significant reaction for either level of managerial ownership. Thus, stockholders favored terminations only when terminating firms faced takeover and managerial ownership was high in the firm.

Similarly, Boyle, Carter, and Stover (1998) studied antitakeover provisions adopted by mutual savings and loan associations converting to stock ownership (SLAs). For a sample of 51 SLAs receiving conversion approval during 1985 and 1986 (years of highest conversion activity), relatively low insider ownership after conversion was associated with strong antitakeover protection. Firms with relatively high resulting insider ownership adopted less "extraordinary" antitakeover protection; the strength of ownership position appeared to substitute for strong antitakeover provisions.

Antitakeover Amendments and Corporate Policy

The effects of antitakeover statutes on firm leverage were studied by Garvey and Hanka (GH) (1999), based on a sample of 1,203 firms and covering data for the period 1983 to 1993. This is a further test of the previous literature with models in which managers increased debt as a method of reducing the threat of hostile takeovers. By 1982, 37 states had first-generation antitakeover laws that in *Edgar v. MITE* were ruled to be preempted by the federal 1968 Williams Act. In 1987, the Supreme Court reversed in *Dynamics v. CTS,* ruling that state antitakeover laws are enforceable as long as they do not prevent compliance with the Williams Act. After this ruling, a majority of the states passed new antitakeover statutes between 1987 and 1990. Garvey and Hanka compared a sample of firms protected by the second generation of laws with a control sample of firms in states without such laws. Protected firms substantially reduced their debt ratios compared to the control group over a period of four years. The results are not influenced by variations in size, industry, or profitability. GH found weak evidence that protected managers undertake fewer major restructuring programs. They also found that firms eventually covered by antitakeover legislation used greater leverage in the years preceding the adoption of the statutes. This is further evidence of the substitution between increased leverage and protection by the state antitakeover laws.

Johnson and Rao (1997) studied the impact of antitakeover amendments on the financial performance of the firm. Their study was based on the original sample of 649 firms that adopted antitakeover amendments between 1979 and 1985 used in the Jarrell and Poulsen (1987) study. The usable sample was reduced to 421 firms. The firms were classified by whether they adopted fair-price amendments or not. Of the total firms used, 311 firms were fair-price and 110 were not.

The study compared financial attributes before and after the amendment adoption. Specifically, preantitakeover variables based on three-year averages of financial attributes prior to the antitakeover amendment were compared to the postannouncement variables in each of the five years after the adoption. Four categories of financial performance were used in the analysis: income (ratio of operating and net income to total assets), expenses (ratio of operating and overhead expenses to sales), investment (ratio of R&D and capital expenditures to sales), and debt (ratio of debt to total assets). Raw and industry-adjusted data changes were analyzed.

For the overall sample, firms exhibited no significant differences from industry means except for a decline in net income but not in operating income, most likely due to an increase in leverage. For the non-fair-price subsample, there were no significant differences from the industry mean for any of the financial attributes. For the fair-price group, the results were similar to those of the full sample.

Antitakeover Amendments and Shareholder Returns

A substantial literature has studied the effects of antitakeover amendments on shareholder returns (Dodd and Leftwich, 1980; McWilliams, 1990; Pound, 1987; Romano, 1985, 1987, 1993; Ryngaert and Netter, 1988). The first edition of this book presented a review of the effects of several individual antitakeover measures in painstaking detail. Fortunately, a definitive, up-to-date analysis of the subject by Comment and Schwert (1995) enables us to compress our present discussion.

The literature predicts possible positive and negative effects of takeover amendments. Positive effects could result from the announcement of an antitakeover measure as a signal of the increased likelihood of a takeover with gains in value to shareholders of the order of magnitude of 30% to 50%. DeAngelo and Rice (1983) noted that shark repellents may have positive benefits in helping shareholders respond in unison (through management) to takeover bids. Negative effects of antitakeover amendments could result from discouraging or deterring takeovers because managers seek to prevent control changes. This is the management entrenchment hypothesis. Let us look at a review of the evidence.

Malekzadeh, McWilliams, and Sen (1998) analyzed the market reaction to antitakeover charter amendments, taking into account the governance and ownership structure of the firms. They used a sample of 213 firms that proposed antitakeover amendments during the period 1980 through 1987. Regressions showed significantly higher negative abnormal returns to firms where the CEO had a lower share ownership or to firms where the board had a lower share ownership. The relationship was more significantly negative when the CEO was also the board chair.

Loh and Rathinasamy (1997) studied the impact of the adoption of antitakeover devices on the announcement effect of voluntary spin-offs. The sample included in the study consisted of 268 U.S. firms that underwent voluntary sell-offs during the period 1981 to 1991. A firm was classified as a device firm if over a period of six months prior to the sell-off announcement it announced the adoption of an antitakeover device; otherwise, it was classified as a non-device firm. Of the total sample, 104 were classified as device firms. The top three antitakeover devices were poison pills (25 firms), leveraged recapitalizations (15 firms), and fair-price amendments (13 firms).

For the whole sample, the sell-off event generated a CAR of 4.18% from day -1 to day $+1$, significant at the 5% level. The subsample of device firms had an insignificant CAR of 0.65% for the same window. In contrast, the non-device firms had a significant and positive corresponding CAR of 5.37%, significant at the 1% level. The market seemed to interpret the no-device sell-offs as a way for firms to reallocate assets to their higher valued uses. On the other hand, the adoption of antitakeover devices seemed to indicate that the sell-off was part of a managerial entrenchment strategy.

The stock price reactions to antitakeover amendments were studied by McWilliams and Sen (1997) for a sample of 265 firms proposing antitakeover amendments from 1980 through 1990. They focused on board composition. The stock price reaction to antitakeover amendments was significantly lower when the board was dominated by inside and affiliated outside board members. The most negative reaction was when the CEO was also chair of the board and the inside and affiliated outside board members increased their ownership in the firm and their representation on the board.

Sundaramurthy, Mahoney, and Mahoney (SMM) (1997) analyzed a sample of 261 firms that adopted 486 antitakeover provisions (supermajority, classified boards, fair-price, reduction in cumulative voting, antigreenmail, and poison pills) in the period 1984 to 1988. They found that the adoption of antitakeover provisions caused negative CARs, significant at the 1% level, for a range of event windows. The market reacted less negatively when the board of directors had a chairperson who was not the CEO. But the market reacted more negatively to antitakeover provisions adopted by boards with higher proportions of outside members. The implications are that the use of outside directors does not ensure their independence. They might be chosen because they are aligned with top management.

The prior studies reviewed by Comment and Schwert (1995) showed a "typical decline" of less than 1% for most types of antitakeover measures and often under 0.5% (Jarrell and Poulsen, 1987; Karpoff and Malatesta, 1989; Malatesta and Walkling, 1988; Romano, 1993; Ryngaert, 1988). Two other studies found no statistically significant negative effects from the adoption of antitakeover charter amendments (DeAngelo and Rice, 1983; Linn and McConnell, 1983). Furthermore, a later study showed that corporate governance efforts through shareholder-initiated proposals to repeal antitakeover amendments had no statistically significant effects (Karpoff, Malatesta, and Walkling, 1996). The finding that the repeal of antitakeover amendments is a nonevent further buttresses the likelihood of little effect when they were announced in the first place.

Counterevidence is provided by Mahoney and Mahoney (1993). They found that although antitakeover amendments had no significant effects for the period 1974 to 1979, effects were significant for the period 1980 to 1988. However, they studied only classified board amendments and the supermajority provision. For 1980 to 1988 the effects of supermajority provisions were not statistically significant, but the effects of the adoption of a classified board of directors were. These results were the reverse of what logic would suggest. Supermajority provisions could be used to block takeovers by managers with some equity ownership. The effects of time-staggering fractions of director elections would be expected to be somewhat attenuated.

It is difficult to disentangle a number of influences. For example, if antitakeover amendments are adopted after a takeover is already under way, the purpose may be to help management obtain a better deal for the shareholders. Similarly if a takeover is rumored. Also, if one takeover has occurred in an industry, there may be contagion effects. When one takeover is completed, often the financial press observes that other takeovers in that industry are likely to occur. If the positive runup in abnormal returns prior to the announcement of antitakeover amendments is considered, then a possible 1% decline in shareholder wealth should be netted against the prior positive returns. The 1% decline could be viewed as a reflection of the reduced probability of the takeover being completed. If 30% is taken as the average positive wealth effect of mergers and takeovers of all types, a wealth decline of 1% following the adoption of antitakeover amendments would mean a decrease of 3.3% $(0.01/0.30)$ in the probability of the takeover. If the event effect is a -0.5%, the decline in the probability of the takeover would be 1.67%. We concur with the Comment and Schwert judgment that these relationships suggest that even small negative event returns from the announcement of antitakeover measures would have little power to deter takeovers.

STATE LAWS

We discussed the history of state antitakeover laws in the previous section. Here we look at decisions to opt out of the protection of state antitakeover laws. Janjigian and Trahan (JT) (1996) studied the factors that influenced firms to opt out of the Pennsylvania Senate Bill 1310 and the long-term performance of those firms after the bill announcement. The bill severely restricted hostile takeovers and was introduced on October 20, 1989. The sample analyzed was 39 firms incorporated in Pennsylvania. Of these, 21 firms opted out of at least one provision of the bill and the remaining 18 did not opt out of any provision.

Using monthly returns, the mean CARs for the preevent period defined as January 1988 to August 1989 were an insignificant 2.15% for the whole sample, a significant −12.79% (10% level) for firms opting out, and a significant 19.72% (10% level) for firms not opting out. The difference in the mean CARs for the two groups was significant at the 1% level. Six firms were targeted for takeover or rumored to be targets during this preevent period. Excluding these firms resulted in mean CARs that were an insignificant −2.15% for the full sample of 33 firms, a significant −9.50% (10% level) for 20 firms that opted out, and an insignificant 9.15% for 13 firms that did not. The difference in the mean CARs for the two groups dropped to a 10% level of significance. Of the original 21 firms that opted out, seven opted out of all provisions. The mean CAR for these seven firms was −26.4%, significant at the 10% level. The mean CAR for firms that opted out of one or two provisions was an insignificant −4.26%.

Preevent accounting performance in 1989 showed no significant difference between the firms that opted out and those that did not. However, the performance of both groups deteriorated substantially from 1989 to 1992. Nevertheless, firms that opted out had significantly better net profit margins, net return on assets, and operating return on assets in 1992 than firms that did not opt out.

Swartz (1996) examined a larger sample of 120 Pennsylvania firms. The event date was defined as April 27, 1990, the date of the passage of the Pennsylvania Antitakeover Law (Act 36 based on Senate Bill 1310). The mean CAR for the full sample for a 190-day [−130,+60] window was a negative 9.23%, significant at the 5% level. For a narrower window of 80 days, [−60,+20], the mean CAR was an insignificant −0.98%. Approximately 70% of the firms opted out of the legislation. The mean CAR was −5.24% from day −130 to day +60 for the firms that opted out and 0.70% from day −60 to day +20, neither one significant. The firms that did not opt out had a mean CAR of −23.35% for [−130, +60] and of −4.71% for [−60,+20], significant at the 1% and 5% level, respectively. The firms that opted out outperformed the firms that did not in both periods; from day −130 to day +60, the difference in the means was 18.11%, and from day −60 to day +30, the difference was 5.41%. Both differences were significant at the 5% level.

State laws appear to differ in provisions for facilitating takeover defenses. Heron and Lewellen (HL) (1998) studied 364 reincorporations during the period 1980 to 1992. Reincorporations made to establish stronger takeover defenses had significant negative returns. Reincorporations to limit director liability to attract better qualified outside directors had significant positive returns. HL also found that the firms giving limits on director liability as their prime motive actually did expand outside representation on their boards; firms citing other motives did not.

POISON PILLS

Poison pills represent the creation of securities carrying special rights exercisable by a triggering event. The triggering event could be the accumulation of a specified percentage of target shares (like 20%) or the announcement of a tender offer. The special rights take many forms, but they all make it more costly to acquire control of the target firm. Poison pills can be adopted by the board of directors without shareholder approval. Although not required, directors will often submit poison pill adoptions to shareholders for ratification.

Types of Plans

There is considerable jargon involved. The basic distinction is between flip-over and flip-in plans. As an oversimplification, flip-over plans provide for a bargain purchase of the *bidder's* shares at some trigger point. The flip-in plans provide for a bargain purchase of the *target's* shares at some trigger point. Flip-in plans became more widely used after the weakness of the flip-over plans was demonstrated in the Crown Zellerbach case in 1984 to 1985. Crown Zellerbach was a paper and forest products company. Because its market price did not fully reflect the value of its forest lands, it was vulnerable to a takeover. Crown Zellerbach adopted a flip-over poison pill plan that enabled its shareholders to buy $200 worth of stock in the merged firm for $100. The pill was in the form of rights that would be triggered when either (1) an acquirer bought 20% of its stock or (2) a bidder made a tender offer for 30% of its stock. The rights or calls became exercisable when the bidder obtained 100% of the company stock.

Sir James Goldsmith (a famous raider) purchased just over 50% of Crown Zellerbach stock in order to achieve control. The rights were issued when Goldsmith's purchasing program brought him to over 20% of the stock. But the rights never became exercisable because he did not plan to complete the purchase of the company until after the flip-over rights had expired. Crown Zellerbach continued to resist but ultimately agreed to the takeover by Goldsmith.

The ownership flip-in provision allows the rights holder to purchase shares of the target at a discount if an acquirer exceeds a shareholding limit. The rights of the bidder who has triggered the pill become void. Some plans waive the flip-in provision if the acquisition is a cash tender offer for all outstanding shares (to defend against two-tier offers).

Case Studies

The nature of ownership flip-in shareholder rights plans can be illustrated by a case study of the Bank of New York (BONY) pursuit of the Irving Bank Corporation (IB). On September 25, 1987, BONY launched an unsolicited cash bid of $80 a share for 47.4% of IB's shares. The remaining shares would receive 1.9 shares of BONY per IB share. On October 9, 1987, IB rejected the BONY offer as inadequate and adopted a flip-in poison pill. The poison pill rights to the IB shareholders when triggered would permit them to purchase $400 of IB stock for $200. The IB shares held by

BONY would be excluded from the rights distribution. The Bank of New York challenged the pill's legality. On October 4, 1988, the appellate division of the New York State Supreme Court upheld a lower court ruling. This ruling held that the flip-in provision violated New York law that shares of the same class should be treated equally. The court held that BONY should be allowed to buy shares at half price as well. On October 5, 1988, IB accepted BONY's offer. Irving Bank shareholders would receive $15 cash, 1.675 BONY shares, and a warrant to purchase BONY stock. The offer was valued at $77.15 a share. States subsequently modified their antitakeover statutes to exclude the discriminatory effect of flip-in poison pills.

On May 17, 1985, the Delaware court upheld a discriminatory self-tender offer that was essentially a triggered back-end pill employed by UNOCAL against a bid by Mesa Petroleum. The court noted that Mesa had proposed a grossly inadequate coercive two-tier offer. The standard employed by the court was the "business judgment rule." The court stated that unless it could be shown that the directors' decisions were primarily based on perpetuating themselves in office or some other breach of judiciary duty, the court would not substitute its judgment for that of the board. The court's decision drew criticism, and in 1986 the Securities and Exchange Commission changed its rules to prevent discriminatory tender offers of the kind that UNOCAL had employed.

Later in the year, on November 19, 1985, the Delaware Supreme Court in *Moran v. Household International,* again upheld the adoption of the poison pill. It noted that any such defense by the directors must be justified on the basis of protection to the corporation and its stockholders. In 1986 the courts blocked a poison pill adopted by the CTS Corporation. The court held that the board had inadequately considered the bidders' offer and acted without adequate outside consultation. CTS formed a special committee of outside directors and solicited advice from investment bankers and legal counsel. It then adopted another poison pill that was upheld by the courts.

This brief review of court decisions demonstrates that the use of poison pills requires justification. Directors must establish that they were adopted not for their own entrenchment but in the best interests of the shareholders of the corporation. Thus, there remains some ambiguity as to whether the adoption of a poison pill will be effective and also whether it will be upheld by the courts.

Dead-Hand Provisions

A common feature of a poison pill is the board's ability to redeem it. This gives the board flexibility in negotiating with bidders. A hostile bidder can put considerable pressure on the board by making a premium cash bid that is conditional on the redemption of the pill. The board may find it difficult to refuse redemption. A dead-hand provision strengthens the board's position by granting the ability to redeem or amend the pill only by continuing directors—directors on the board prior to a bidder's takeover attempt. The dead-hand provision prevents a bidder from achieving control of the target's board, which then removes the pill.

In the *Bank of New York v. Irving Bank* 1988 case, a New York court invalidated a dead-hand pill. But other state courts have upheld the dead-hand provision. For example, in *Invacare v. Healthdyne Technologies,* a Georgia court in 1997 approved a dead-hand pill. A *Wall Street Journal* article (Plitch, 2000) quotes an estimate that of some 3,000 poison pills nationwide, 200 contained dead-hand features.

Some shareholder groups are critical of poison pills because they can be used to block a takeover carrying a substantial premium. Pension fund TIAA-CREF has described dead-hand poison pills as "a nefarious corporate-governance practice." TIAA-CREF sent letters and made phone calls to 35 companies with dead-hand pills urging them to remove the dead-hand provisions from their pills. Many companies complied; the others are under continuing pressure to do so.

Sometimes stockholder pressure is sufficient to cause a company to eliminate the entire poison pill takeover defense plan. Such was the case with Phillip Morris (Hwang, 1995). In 1989, Philip Morris distributed rights to shareholders to buy additional Philip Morris stock at reduced prices if a third party purchased 10% or more of the company's common stock. Pressure against the poison pill came from the Counsel for Institutional Investors, which represents more than 100 pension funds. Also the International Brotherhood of Teamsters, whose pension funds held 3.38 million Philip Morris shares, described the poison pill as "inappropriate, antiquated and unnecessary." In removing the pill, the president of Philip Morris stated that this was "a prudent course of action given the concern of some of our shareholders." Philip Morris paid its shareholders 1¢ per share to redeem the poison pill rights, adding the penny to its quarterly dividends of 82.5 cents per share. The redemption cost totaled $8.5 million.

Effects of Poison Pills on Shareholder Returns

The early event studies of the wealth effect of poison pills found about a 2% negative impact (Malatesta and Walkling, 1988; Ryngaert, 1988). Comment and Schwert (1995) observed that these studies covered only the earlier one-fourth of adopted pills. The Comment and Schwert paper updated the earlier studies by using the entire population of 1,577 poison pills adopted from 1983 through December 1991. They observed that the wealth effect of a poison pill adoption reflected a number of elements. The possibility that managers may wait to adopt pills until they know that an offer is likely to be made may cause the pill to be viewed as a signal that the probability of a takeover attempt had increased. This would cause the event return to be positive. Also, the poison pill may enable managers to obtain a better price in negotiations with bidders. This also would have a positive influence. But if poison pills deterred takeovers, there would be a negative influence representing the expected present value of future takeover premiums lost.

Datta and Iskander-Datta (1996) examined the valuation effects of poison pill adoption announcements on bondholder and stockholder wealth. The sample analyzed contained 91 poison pill announcements between January 1985 and December 1989. Excess bond returns were calculated by matching the corporate bonds with treasury bonds according to maturity and coupon rate. The two-day $[0,+1]$ bond CAR was -0.67%, significant at the 1% level. In contrast, the $[0,+1]$ stock CAR was an insignificant -0.25%. The stock excess returns were not sensitive to the time period. However, for firms that were the subject of takeover speculations in the year preceding the poison pill adoption, the three-day period $[-1,0,+1]$ stock CAR was a significant -2.253%. The stock CAR for firms that were not targets was an insignificant 0.094%.

Additional long-run analyses of changes in leverage and firm performance during three years centered around the poison pill announcement were performed. The results indicated that the sample firms were not underleveraged compared to the industry median before the poison pill adoption. There was a significant increase in the median debt ratios during the year prior to the announcement, and the median debt ratio remained higher than the industry in the year following the poison pill adoption. Performance measures based on return on assets and profit margins revealed that the sample firms performed consistently worse than the industry during and around the year of the poison pill adoption.

Johnson and Meade (1996) examined the market reactions to the announcement of poison pills used as the first antitakeover measure compared with poison pills enacted after existing antitakeover amendments. Their sample consisted of 191 firms with poison pill announcements from November 1983 through December 1987. Of these 191 firms, 160 had adopted some prior form of antitakeover amendments. Thirty-one firms were implementing poison pills as their first antitakeover device.

Using a two-day $[-1,0]$ event window, the mean CAR for the full sample was 0.21%, not significant. For the subsample with no prior existing antitakeover amendments, the CAR was -0.94%, not significant. For the subsample with one or more preexisting antitakeover amendments, the CAR was 0.43%, not significant. The difference between the mean CARs of the two groups was significant at the 10% level.

The Comment and Schwert (1995) analysis considered several influences using the familiar cumulative abnormal return (CAR) measure and a regression analysis. One variable takes into account whether rumors of a bid or an actual takeover bid made it likely that a control premium was built into the issuer's stock price at the time of the announcement of a poison pill. The wealth effect was about -2%. Another variable accounts for whether merger and acquisition news was announced at the same time as the pill. This test found a positive wealth effect of about 3% to 4%. Dummy variables for the year of adoption distinguished the early pills from the later ones. In the year-by-year results for 1983 to 1991 only 1984 had a negative wealth effect of between 2.3% and 2.9%. For 1985 through 1991 the wealth effect was usually positive by about 1% or less, but it was significant only for the year 1988.

Comment and Schwert (1995) performed various sensitivity analyses, but the main thrusts of their findings remained unchanged. They observed that there were individual cases where potential takeovers were likely to have been deterred by poison pills. But their systematic evidence indicates small deterrence effects. They observe that only the earliest pills (before 1985) were associated with large declines in shareholder wealth. Their new evidence indicated that takeover premiums were higher when target firms were protected by state antitakeover laws or by poison pills. Thus, the gains to targets were increased, raising the cost to bidders. This suggested some deterrence, but they also found that target shareholders gained even after taking into account deals that were not completed because of poison pills.

A major emphasis of the Comment and Schwert study was to evaluate whether the decline in the level of takeover activity that took place in 1991 and 1992 was primarily due to the effectiveness of antitakeover legislation and defensive measures by targets. Their empirical analysis led them to the conclusion that it was more general economic factors that caused the decline in takeover activity, not the widespread use of antitakeover measures adopted by governments and firms. Their conclusion is supported by the evidence we presented in chapter 6. Our data established that by 1995, M&A activity measured in constant dollars had risen even above the previous peak level reached in 1988. Thus, the carefully reasoned analysis of Comment and Schwert successfully predicted the resurgence in M&A activity as the economic environment changed after 1993.

SHAREHOLDER ACTIVISM

Shareholder resolutions to rescind poison pills were studied by Bizjak and Marquette (BM) (1998). They covered 190 shareholder-initiated proposals over the period 1987 to 1993. They start with a sample of firms that received shareholder proposals for poison pill rescissions. They make comparisons with a control sample of firms that had adopted poison pills but did not receive shareholder proposals to rescind them. Using a three-day $[-1,+1]$ event window they find a CAR for the proposal sample of -0.43% relative to a positive 1.35% for the matched sample. The difference is statistically significant. They find that the average flip-in percentage for the rights plan is 14.20% for the proposal sample versus 17.87% for the matched sample. These relationships hold up for various forms of multivariate analysis.

Using different announcement dates and event return windows, they find a negative market reaction to the initial shareholder proposal but a positive market reaction to pill restructurings defined as rescissions or changes in the percentage trigger or similar characteristics. The positive management response to shareholder concerns yields positive information about management quality and indicates that shareholder proposals can influence managers' actions. The authors conclude that shareholders become active when they become concerned about managerial actions to create impediments to the market for corporate control. This activism can influence management to be responsive to shareholder recommendations.

POISON PUTS

Poison puts, or event risk covenants, give bondholders the right to put (sell) target bonds in the event of a change in control at an exercise price usually set at 100% to 101% of the bond's face amount. This poison put feature seeks to protect against risk of takeover-related deterioration of target bonds, at the same time placing a potentially large cash demand on the new owner, thus raising the cost of an acquisition. Merger and acquisition activity in general has had negative impacts on bondholder wealth. This was particularly true when leverage increases were substantial. As a consequence, poison put provisions began to be included in bond covenants beginning in 1986.

Cook and Easterwood (CE) (1994) analyzed the economic role of poison put bonds. They observed that poison puts could be included in corporate debt for three possible reasons. First, the entrenchment hypothesis was that the puts made firms less attractive as takeover targets. Second, the bondholder protection hypothesis was that the poison puts protect bondholders from wealth transfers associated with debt-financed takeovers and leveraged recapitalizations. If the poison puts had this purpose, their use would not reduce the probability of all takeovers, only those involving wealth transfers from bondholders to shareholders. If puts and related covenants did not increase the protection to existing debt, the bondholder protection hypothesis predicted no effect on the price of the firm's outstanding debt.

The impact on stock returns would be the net of two opposite influences. Takeovers motivated primarily by wealth transfers were deterred, which represented a negative influence on shareholder returns. Debt with event risk covenants could be issued at an interest cost lower than unprotected debt. If interest cost savings outweighed the forgone wealth transfers, there would be a nonnegative stock price reaction to the sale of protected debt.

The bondholder protection hypothesis had been tested in two ways. One looked at the difference in yield spreads at the offering date for samples of protected and unprotected bonds. Two empirical studies suggested that the inclusion of event risk protection reduced the required yields on protected bonds by 25 to 50 basis points; a third study found no effect. A second type of test analyzed wealth transfers from bondholders in leveraged buyouts. One study (Marais, Schipper, and Smith, 1989) found no evidence of bondholder losses. Another, by Warga and Welch (1993), found small losses. Other studies showed that whether bondholders lose depends on the covenant protection. Protected bonds did not experience losses, but unprotected debt experienced significant losses. These findings were evidence that alternative contracting technologies could substitute for the use of poison puts.

The third hypothesis was the mutual interest hypothesis. This postulated that both managers and bondholders sought to prevent hostile debt-financed takeovers. The managers sought to protect their control positions, while the bondholders sought to avoid losses from deterioration in credit ratings. Under this hypothesis, stock price reactions would be negative, whereas the effects on the price of existing debt would be positive. The wealth effects for debt and equity would be negatively correlated because more protective puts would make the price response more positive for existing debt and more negative for stock prices. These three alternatives are summarized in Table 19.3.

In their empirical analysis, CE found that the issuance of bonds with poison puts caused negative returns to shareholders and positive returns to outstanding bondholders. A control sample of straight bond issues without poison puts had no effect on stock prices. Note that the finding of no stock price effect of straight bond issues is different from the findings of earlier studies and may be related to the economic environment that prevailed in 1988 and 1989, the years covered by their sample. A cross-sectional regression for the put sample showed a strong negative relation between the returns for stocks and the returns for outstanding bonds. This

Table 19.3   Effects of Poison Puts on Shareholder and Debt Holder Returns

	Managerial Entrenchment Hypothesis	Bondholder Protection Hypothesis	Mutual Interest Hypothesis
Effect on shareholder returns	−	0	−
Effect on outstanding debt	0	0	+

relation was not found for the nonput sample. The study concluded that the empirical results were consistent with the mutual interest hypothesis, which holds that the use of poison put bonds protects managers from hostile takeovers and bondholders from event risk while lowering returns to shareholders.

GOLDEN PARACHUTES

Golden parachutes (GPs) are separation provisions of an employment contract that compensate managers for the loss of their jobs under a change-of-control clause. The provision usually calls for a lump-sum payment or payment over a specified period at full or partial rates of normal compensation. This type of severance contract was increasingly used even by the largest Fortune 500 firms as M&A activity intensified in the 1980s and these firms became susceptible to hostile takeover.

A brief case study will convey the role of golden parachutes. On May 23, 1983, Diamond Shamrock Corporation launched a hostile tender offer for Natomas Company. The offer at $23 a share represented a 25% premium over the closing price of Natomas on May 20, 1983. Natomas began arranging bank financing to defend itself. It also adopted golden parachutes that would give its top four executives a $10.2 million severance payment if they decided to quit within six months after the merger. These four top executives had received $1.3 million in compensation and benefits in 1982. Diamond Shamrock had been in the process of transforming itself from a chemical company into an energy company under W. H. Bricker, its chairman. It was seeking additional oil reserves to feed its refineries. The oil reserves of Natomas in the Pacific Basin were especially attractive to Diamond. On May 29, 1983, a merger agreement was reached between Diamond and Natomas. The new terms were 1.05 shares of Diamond per share of Natomas. Diamond would retain the Natomas management, with Dorman Commons remaining as chairman of Natomas and becoming vice chairman of Diamond. Kenneth Reed would remain president of Natomas. The combination was completed in August 1983. In October 1983 Commons and Reed resigned, departing the company with the severance payments provided by the golden parachutes.

Extreme cases of golden parachutes created a stir among the public and were often viewed as "rewards for failure."[1] An example is the payment of $23.5 million to six officers of Beatrice Companies in connection with its leveraged buyout in 1985. One of the officers received a $2.7 million package even though he had been with the company only 13 months. Another received a $7 million package after being recalled from retirement only seven months before. Also in 1985, the chairman of Revlon received a $35 million package consisting of severance pay and stock options. Even in these extreme cases, the golden parachutes were small compared to the total acquisition prices of $6.2 billion in the Beatrice LBO and $1.74 billion in the Revlon acquisition. Indeed, the cost of golden parachutes is estimated to be less than 1% of the total cost of a takeover in most cases.[2] For this reason, golden parachutes are not considered to be an effective takeover defense.

---

[1]See, for example, *The New York Times,* "Golden Chutes Under Attack," November 4, 1985, p. D1.
[2]*Fortune,* "Those Executive Bailout Deals," December 13, 1982, p. 86.

Excessive use of GPs appears to be infrequent, and a new tax law now imposes specific limits. The Deficit Reduction Act of 1984 denies corporate tax deductions for parachute payments in excess of three times the base amount on a present value basis, where the base amount is the executive's average annual compensation over the five years prior to takeover. An executive has to pay an additional 20% income tax on "excess parachute payments." To be legally binding, the golden parachutes have to be entered into at least one year prior to the date of control change for the entire corporation or a significant portion of the corporation. In many employment contracts, the severance payment is triggered either when the manager is terminated by the acquiring firm or when the manager resigns voluntarily after a change of control. Coffee (1988, p. 131) reported several cases in which the court invalidated or granted preliminary injunctions against the exercise of golden parachutes especially when the payment could be triggered at the recipient's own election.

Rationale

The use of golden parachutes has been defended by some (Coffee, 1988; Jensen, 1988; Knoeber, 1986). One argument is based on the concept of *implicit contracts* for managerial compensation. In general, managers' real contribution to the firm cannot be evaluated exactly in the current period but can be estimated better as time passes and more information becomes available on the firm's long-term profitability and value. In this situation, an optimal contract between managers and shareholders will include deferred compensation (Knoeber, 1986). Seniority-based compensation and internal promotion partly reflect this deferred compensation process. Because detailing all the future possibilities and contingent payments in a written contract is costly and very likely futile, a long-term deferred contract will be largely implicit. Another argument presumes existence of firm-specific investments by managers. When the likelihood of an unexpected transfer of control and the loss of their job is high, managers will not be willing to invest in firm-specific skills and knowledge. A related argument is that the increased risk of losing one's job through a takeover may result in managers focusing unduly on the short-term or even taking unduly high risks (Eisenberg, 1988).

Another rationale for golden parachutes is that they encourage managers to accept changes of control that would bring shareholder gains and thus reduce the conflict of interest between managers and shareholders and the transactions costs resulting from managerial resistance. Berkovitch and Khanna (1991) further analyzed the role of golden parachutes in takeover markets in which the bidder had a choice between a merger and a tender offer. In their model, a tender offer was more desirable for target shareholders as more information was released in tender offers and this frequently led to an auction in which potential acquirers competed for the target. Excessive payment will tend to motivate managers to sell the firm at too low a gain. By tying the payment to synergy gains in the case of mergers, the firm can avoid the misuse of golden parachutes. Stock options that are exercisable in the event of a change of control are an appropriate solution, and in general increased stock ownership by management will tend to reduce the conflict of interest (Jensen, 1988).

Silver and Tin Parachutes

The terms *silver parachutes* and *tin parachutes* have also been employed. Silver parachutes provide less generous severance payments to executives. Tin parachutes extend relatively modest severance payments to a wider coverage of managers, including middle management, and in some cases cover all salaried employees. Tin parachutes were employed by General American Oil of Texas when it faced a takeover threat from T. Boone Pickens in 1982. It adopted tin parachutes that would give all employees at least three months' pay whether they were terminated or chose to leave after any adverse changes in their pay or duties. Workers would be entitled to at least four weeks' pay for each year of service.

There is disagreement on the number of employees to be covered. Focusing on the conflict of interest problem in control-related situations, Jensen (1988) argued that the contract should cover only those members of the top-level management team who would be involved in negotiating and implementing any transfer of control. On the other hand, Coffee (1988) emphasized the implicit contract for deferred payments and the incentive for managers to make investments in firm-specific human capital. This led Coffee to propose that the control-related severance contracts should be extended to members of middle management as well as top management.

Golden Parachutes and Returns to Shareholders

Mogavero and Toyne (1995) formulated three central hypotheses to be tested by the empirical evidence: (1) The **alignment hypothesis** is that prearranged severance agreements reduce conflict of interest between managers and shareholders. Golden parachutes will make executives more willing to support takeover offers beneficial to the firm's shareholders. (2) The **wealth transfer hypothesis** predicts that GPs reduce stock values by shifting gains from shareholders to managers. By increasing costs to bidders, GPs reduce the probability of takeover bids. By providing some insulation from the market for corporate control, GPs reduce the incentives for executives to manage firms efficiently. In addition, GPs may also indicate a level of influence over boards exercised by management that may increase the potential for other forms of executive benefit consumption. (3) Adoption of GPs may *signal* the likelihood of a future takeover, which would be associated with positive gains to shareholders. Alternatively, GPs may signal an increase in management influence over boards, which would have negative implications.

The empirical study by Lambert and Larcker (LL) (1985) covered the period 1975 to 1982. They found that the adoption of GPs resulted in abnormal positive returns to shareholders of about 3%. This finding was consistent with the alignment hypothesis, suggesting that the cost of reducing conflicts of interest between management and shareholders was low relative to potential gains from takeover premiums. Alternatively, the signaling hypothesis might be supported in that from 1975 to 1982 relatively few firms had adopted GPs, so that GPs could be taken as signals of a likely takeover bid. The study by Born, Trahan, and Faria (1993) looked at two samples. One sample for the period 1979 to 1989 contained firms that announced GPs while in the process of being acquired. Hence, there should be no takeover signal effect. If alignment of interests, the returns should be positive; if wealth transfer, the returns should be negative. But no significant abnormal stock returns were found. The second sample from 1979 through 1984 contained firms not in the process of a takeover when the GPs were adopted. They found positive stock returns. The authors argued that the combined evidence is consistent with a takeover signaling hypothesis but not with an alignment hypothesis.

Hall and Anderson (1997) studied the impact of the adoption of golden parachute compensation plans on shareholder wealth. They used a sample of 52 firms that announced the adoption of golden parachutes between 1982 and 1990. The adoptions were for new contracts and not amendments to preexisting contracts. These firms did not experience preexisting takeover bids for the three years prior to the golden parachute adoption. The mean CAR for the whole event window $[-20,+20]$ was a statistically insignificant -1.21%. The mean abnormal return on the announcement day was an insignificant 0.46%. CARs for other event windows were also not significant except for the window $[-5,-2]$, which was -1.19%, significant at the 10% level. When three firms were excluded because of possible outliers, the event window $[-5,0]$ was a significant -1.29% at the 10% level.

The study by Mogavero and Toyne (1995) used a sample of 41 large firms with adoption dates from 1982 through 1990. For their full sample, the CAR was -0.5% but not statistically significant. They divided their sample into two subsamples. The first contained 18 observations from 1982 to 1985 for which the CAR was $+2.3\%$ but not statistically significant. The second subsample was of 23 observations and covered the years 1986 through 1990. Its CAR was -2.7% and statistically significant at the 1% level. This finding was consistent with the wealth transfer hypothesis. The authors noted that the stock returns associated with GPs changed from positive for the 1975 to 1982 period of the LL study to negative for the 1986 to 1990 period of their own study. This change was associated with the initiation of legislative restraints on GPs that may have encouraged boards to adopt them to avoid further restrictions. Thus, shareholders in the later years may have perceived GP adoptions as unfavorable signals of management's ability to control directors in management's interest at the expense of shareholder interest.

SUMMARY

Takeover defenses and antitakeover measures have become part of management's long-range strategic planning for the firm. One view justifies these actions on the basis of the desirability of creating an auction for the target, preventing coercive tender offers, and increasing management's ability to obtain better transaction terms in the bargaining process. Opposing views emphasize the increased cost of takeovers and the resulting inefficiency in the market for corporate control.

Just saying no to a takeover is not that simple. Target directors must present shareholders with a sound business reason to expect that the shareholders will gain more by not accepting the takeover offer. Even if the target company agrees to an acquisition, directors must demonstrate that the price is fair to shareholders and is the best offer that could be obtained.

A firm may be vulnerable to takeovers because of its financial characteristics. The firm's stock price may be low in relation to the replacement cost of assets or its potential earning power. It may possess a large amount of excess cash or unused debt capacity. Such characteristics make it an attractive investment opportunity and facilitate the financing of the takeover. The firm can take defensive adjustments to make itself less attractive. For example, it could sell assets, increase debt, and use its excess cash to increase cash dividends or share repurchases.

A target may counteroffer for the bidder in a Pac Man defense. This is a costly defense and is rarely used. Another defense strategy is for the target to seek a white knight as an appropriate company for the combination. Alternatively, in a white squire transaction, the target could sell a block of its stock to a third party it considers friendly.

Corporate restructuring and reorganizations that increase a firm's value are also extensions to a defensive program. Acquisitions of assets are used to extend a firm's capabilities, to block a takeover by diluting the ownership position of the pursuer, or to create antitrust issues. Sell-offs and divestitures move resources to their higher valued uses but can also involve selling off the "crown jewels." Spin-offs, split-ups, and equity carve-outs can be used to clarify organizational structures and to increase managerial incentives, motivations, and performance.

The target firm can also reorganize its financial claims to make itself less attractive. Exchange offers such as debt-for-equity offers can increase leverage to unattractive levels. Dual-class recapitalizations can increase the voting power of target insiders to levels that make tender offers less likely to succeed. "Scorched earth" tactics such as leveraged recapitalizations may incur a huge amount of debt and increase the ownership position of insiders. Joint ventures could represent liaisons that potential bidders might prefer to avoid. Employee stock ownership plans can pre-vent a successful tender offer by making it difficult to meet supermajority requirements. Management buyouts and LBOs are other leverage-increasing defenses favorable to the managers' stock ownership position. Share repurchase can be used to pay premium prices to shareholders to compete with takeover bids. Low reservation price shareholders will tender, leaving high reservation price shareholders who, with the increased ownership position of insiders, will require higher tender offer prices.

In greenmail transactions, the target firm repurchases a large block of its shares at a premium price from large blockholders to end a hostile takeover threat. A standstill agreement may be included to prevent the greenmailer from making other takeover efforts for a specified period of time. The view that greenmail damages shareholders has prompted tax law penalties and anti-greenmail charter amendments to discourage or prohibit its use. Antigreenmail amendments do not seem to decrease shareholder wealth but appear to remove a barrier to takeovers with positive gains to shareholders.

Antitakeover amendments or "shark repellents" impose new conditions on the transfer of managerial control. Supermajority amendments require shareholders' approval of takeover negotiations by a two-thirds vote or higher. Fair-price amendments hinder two-tier tenders by requiring the bidder to pay the "fair" price to all purchased shares. A staggered, or classified, board of directors can delay effective transfer of control. New securities with special voting rights may be issued to friendly parties in a takeover contest. Previously enacted antitakeover measures can be reinforced with lock-in amendments, making them difficult to void.

The empirical literature on antitakeover amendments is extensive but difficult to interpret because multiple influences are operating. In general, positive returns will result if the announcement of the antitakeover amendment is interpreted as a signal of an increased likelihood of a takeover or is associated with management's intention to obtain a better price in negotiations or a better solution. Negative effects could result if the amendment is interpreted as a management entrenchment tactic. Studies find small declines of about 1% but no statistical significance.

Poison pills are securities carrying special rights exercisable by a triggering event such as the announcement of a tender offer or a specified ownership position in the firm's stock. Poison pills make it more costly to acquire control of the firm and can be adopted without shareholders' approval. But the adoption of poison pills requires justification that they are in the best interests of the shareholders if they are to be upheld by the courts. Studies by Comment and Schwert find small deterrence effects of poison pills. Takeover premiums are higher when target firms are protected by state antitakeover laws or by poison pills. Even the decline in the level of takeover activity in 1991 and 1992 is attributable to general economic factors and not to antitakeover measures.

Poison puts or event risk covenants give bondholders the right to sell target bonds in the event of takeover at a price set at the bond's face value or higher. This feature seeks to protect bondholders' wealth and at the same time place potentially large requirements on the new owner. The negative returns found by Cook and Easterwood are consistent with the mutual interest hypothesis in which bondholders and managers gain at the expense of shareholders.

Golden parachutes (GPs) are severance contracts that compensate managers for losing their jobs after a takeover. Extreme cases of golden parachutes have often been viewed as a reward for failure, but GPs are estimated to be less than 1% of the total cost of a takeover. For this reason, they are not considered to be a strong takeover defense. The rationale for their use is the reduction in the agency problem between managers and shareholders. This reduced conflict or alignment hypothesis is supported by the positive returns found by Lambert and Larcker. But the golden parachute adoption could also be interpreted as a signal of future takeovers. The study by Mogavero and Toyne finds negative returns for the 1986 to 1990 period, indicating some influence over boards exercised by managements, increasing the potentials for wealth transfers from shareholders to managers.

QUESTIONS

19.1 What are three types of antitakeover amendments, and how do they work to defend a target from an unwelcome takeover?

19.2 What is the effect of the passage of antitakeover amendments on stock price?

19.3 What is the role of litigation against a bidder in takeover contests?

19.4 Under what circumstances are share repurchase and exchange offers useful as antitakeover measures?

19.5 How can legislation and regulation serve as merger defenses?

19.6 Explain the difference between flip-in and flip-over poison pills.

Case 19.1 Carter Hawley Hale Versus Marshall Field & Co.

In 1977 the president of Marshall Field & Co. died unexpectedly and was replaced by Angelo R. Arena, the former head of Carter Hawley Hale's (CHH) Neiman-Marcus division. Carter Hawley Hale, which had long been interested in Field, then approached Marshall Field with the idea of a merger and continued to pursue the idea despite Field's lack of interest. On December 10, 1977, Philip Hawley, the CEO of CHH, gave Marshall Field an ultimatum: Either Field's directors would agree to merger negotiations by December 12 or he would make a public exchange proposal. Arena was unwilling to enter into negotiations, and Field directors rejected the $36 a share CHH offer, saying that the merger would not be in the best interests of Field stockholders, employees, and customers and that the price was inadequate. Field filed an antitrust suit.

Carter Hawley Hale was the nation's eighth largest department store group, and Field was the largest of the department store independents. Carter Hawley Hale, which had grown through acquisitions, sought to further expand by taking over Field. Field owned valuable real estate, was established in the Chicago market, possessed large cash reserves, and had a conservative debt-to-equity ratio of 28% even with lease capitalization. Carter Hawley Hale had been looking to break into the Chicago market and believed it could bring operating improvements to Field. The takeover battle drew attention to CHH's highly leveraged position. Carter Hawley Hale had a debt-to-equity ratio of 42%, or 113% with lease capitalization, and was planning to finance the merger on the strength of Field's balance sheet.

Field had previously been targeted for takeover by Associated Dry Goods in 1969,

Federated Department Stores in 1975, and Dayton-Hudson in 1976. In each battle, Field used the antitrust defense and/or made a major acquisition. Under the advice of lawyer Joseph Flom, Field believed expansion would help the firm remain independent. In 1976 CHH had sales of $1.4 billion compared with Field's sales of $610 million. At the time of the offer, Field shares, which had a book value of $27, were trading at $23. In the prior five years, Field earnings per share had fallen by 20% as it struggled with declining profit margins and shrinking market share.

In early February 1978 CHH announced a tender offer of $42 in cash and CHH stock for each share of Field stock tendered. Field's board continued to oppose the merger and agreed to expand into the Galleria in Houston and to acquire five Liberty House stores in the northwest. The two transactions would total $34 million. Carter Hawley Hale already had a store in the Galleria, Neiman Marcus. Field had considered acquiring the Liberty House stores in the context of another takeover battle, but at the time Field's vice president of corporate development judged the earnings potential to be minimal. It was rumored that CHH had also planned to expand to the northwest. Field had the ambitious vision of becoming a national retailer. On February 22 CHH withdrew its proposed tender offer, citing doubts of the impact of Field's expansion plan. Through the expansion program, Field increased its debt, making it less attractive to CHH. Upon announcement of the withdrawal of CHH's offer, Field shares plummeted to $19.

Field's directors were sued by some of its shareholders for resisting the CHH offer regardless of shareholders' interests and breach-

CHAPTER 19

ing their fiduciary duty as directors. The court found that the plaintiffs failed to show that there was a breach of fiduciary duty, and the directors were protected by the business judgment rule.

Under Arena, the number of Field stores tripled and the firm took on $120 million in debt. Problems continued to plague Field, and by 1981 its share price had fallen to under $20 a share. In February 1982 Field came under attack by Carl Icahn. Icahn continued to purchase Field stock despite lawsuits filed against him. Field turned to a white knight, Batus Inc., the American subsidiary of B.A.T. Industries of London. Batus owned the nation's third largest tobacco company as well as Gimbel's and Saks Fifth Avenue. Other bidders included CHH and May Department Stores. Although Batus's initial offer was $25.50 a share, it eventually paid $30 a share for the front and back ends of the offer. Icahn walked away with a profit of $30 million.

QUESTIONS

1. What defensive actions did Marshall Field take in response to Carter Hawley Hale's interest?
2. Why did Carter Hawley Hale want to acquire Marshall Field?
3. Over the years, which defense did Marshall Field employ several times?
4. Which characteristics attracted Marshall Field's suitors to bid for the company?
5. Who was Marshall Field's white knight?

Case 19.2 Mattel–Hasbro*

After some preliminary discussions on January 24, 1996, Mattel made an unsolicited proposal to buy the second largest toy company, Hasbro Inc. Their proposal indicated a fundamental reorganization in the toy industry. The *Financial Times* (January 27, 1996) stated, "Barbie fluttered her eyelashes at GI Joe and all the hearts in Toy Town skipped a beat!" Mattel was strong in dolls with its market leaders Barbie and Ken and was developing joint products with Disney and others. Hasbro was strong in toys for boys such as GI Joe and Tonka trucks as well as in board games. Hasbro's reaction was to cry, "Monopoly" (one of its board games). Both firms had gaps in creating electronic toys in which foreign competitors such as Nintendo and Sony were leaders.

The preannouncement price of Mattel was $32 per share and that of Hasbro was $30.625. The Mattel offer of 1.67 shares for one share of Hasbro placed a value of $53.44 per share on Hasbro, representing a premium of 74%. Because Hasbro objected immediately, the Hasbro price never went above $40. The price of Mattel moved up by about $1. With 225 million shares, the wealth of Mattel shareholders increased about $225 million. For Hasbro, with 97 million shares outstanding, shareholder wealth increased by almost $1 billion.

Negotiations continued, but Hasbro continued to raise antitrust objections. Finally, on February 3, 1996, it was announced that Mattel would withdraw its offer for Hasbro. John Amerman, the Mattel chairman, stated that in a friendly deal the antitrust barriers could have been resolved in about five months (*Wall Street Journal*, February 8, 1996, p. B8).

*This case was written by J. F. Weston, Aaron Cheatham, and Girish Kulai.

But with the obstacles thrown up by Hasbro, the legal complications would have continued for as long as two years. Mr. Amerman stated that at the end of three years the earnings per share for Mattel would have been unchanged from current projections. He concluded by stating, "why raise our risks?"

The Hasbro stock dropped back to $34.625. The Mattel stock stayed at about $33, about $1 above its prebid price. Mattel said that the costs related to the failed bid would lower their earnings per share for 1996 by about 1¢.

QUESTIONS

1. What would have been the business advantages of the combination?
2. Would the combination have created market power in the production and distribution of toys?
3. From the standpoint of U.S. public policy, evaluate the desirability of the combination.

REFERENCES

Bae, S. C., and D. P. Simet, "A Comparative Analysis of Leveraged Recapitalization Versus Leveraged Buyout as a Takeover Defense," *Review of Financial Economics,* 7, 1998, pp. 157–172.

Bagli, Charles V., "A New Breed of Wolf at the Corporate Door: It's the Era of the Civilized Hostile Takeover," *New York Times,* March 19, 1997, pp. C1, C4.

Berkovitch, E., and N. Khanna, "A Theory of Acquisition Markets: Mergers Versus Tender Offers, and Golden Parachutes," *Review of Financial Studies,* 4, 1991, pp. 149–174.

Bhagat, S., and R. Jefferis, "Voting Power in the Proxy Process: The Case of Antitakeover Charter Amendments," *Journal of Financial Economics,* 30, 1991, pp. 193–225.

Bizjak, J. M., and C. J. Marquette, "Are Shareholder Proposals All Bark and No Bite? Evidence from Shareholder Resolutions to Rescind Poison Pills," *Journal of Financial and Quantitative Analysis,* 33, 1998, pp. 499–521.

Born, Jeffery A., Emery A. Trahan, and Hugo J. Faria, "Golden Parachutes: Incentive Aligners, Management Entrenchers, or Takeover Bid Signals?," *Journal of Financial Research,* 16, Winter 1993, pp. 299–308.

Boyle, G. W., R. B. Carter, and R. D. Stover, "Extraordinary Antitakeover Provisions and Insider Ownership Structure: The Case of Converting Savings and Loans," *Journal of Financial and Quantitative Analysis,* 33, 1998, pp. 291–304.

Bradley, M., and L. Wakeman, "The Wealth Effects of Targeted Share Repurchases," *Journal of Financial Economics,* 11, 1983, pp. 301–328.

Brickley, J. A., R. C. Lease, and C. W. Smith, Jr., "Ownership Structure and Voting on Antitakeover Amendments," *Journal of Financial Economics,* 20, 1988, pp. 267–292.

Coffee, J. C., "Shareholders Versus Managers: The Strain in the Corporate Web," chapter 6 in J. C. Coffee, L. Lowenstein, and S. Rose-Ackerman, eds., *Knights, Raiders, and Targets,* New York: Oxford University Press, 1988, pp. 77–134.

Comment, Robert, and G. William Schwert, "Poison or Placebo? Evidence on the Deterrence and Wealth Effects of Modern Antitakeover Measures," *Journal of Financial Economics,* 39, 1995, pp. 3–43.

Cook, Douglas O., and John C. Easterwood, "Poison Put Bonds: An Analysis of Their Economic Role," *Journal of Finance,* 49, December 1994, pp. 1905–1920.

Dann, Larry Y., and Harry DeAngelo, "Standstill Agreements, Privately Negotiated Stock Repurchases, and the Market for Corporate Control," *Journal of Financial Economics,* 11, 1983, pp. 275–300.

Datta, S., and M. Iskandar-Datta, "Takeover Defenses and Wealth Effects on Securityholders: The Case of Poison Pill Adoptions," *Journal of Banking & Finance,* 20, 1996, pp. 1231–1250.

DeAngelo, Harry, and Edward M. Rice, "Antitakeover Charter Amendments and Stockholder Wealth," *Journal of Financial Economics*, 11, April 1983, pp. 329–359.

Dodd, P. R., and R. Leftwich, "The Market for Corporate Control: 'Unhealthy Competition' Versus Federal Regulation," *Journal of Business*, 53, 1980, pp. 259–283.

Dodd, P. R., and J. B. Warner, "On Corporate Governance: A Study of Proxy Contests," *Journal of Financial Economics*, 11, 1983, pp. 401–438.

Eckbo, B. Espen, "Valuation Effects of Greenmail Prohibitions," *Journal of Financial and Quantitative Analysis*, 25, December 1990, pp. 491–505.

Eisenberg, M. A., "Comment: Golden Parachutes and the Myth of the Web," chapter 9 in J. C. Coffee, L. Lowenstein, and S. Rose-Ackerman, eds., *Knights, Raiders, and Targets,* New York: Oxford University Press, 1988, pp. 155–158.

Garvey, G. T., and G. Hanka, "Capital Structure and Corporate Control: The Effect of Antitakeover Statutes on Firm Leverage," *Journal of Finance*, 54, 1999, pp. 519–546.

Hall, P. L., and D. C. Anderson, "The Effect of Golden Parachutes on Shareholder Wealth and Takeover Probabilities," *Journal of Business Finance and Accounting*, 23, April 1997, pp. 445–463.

Heron, Randall A., and Wilbur G. Lewellen, "An Empirical Analysis of the Reincorporation Decision," *Journal of Financial and Quantitative Analysis*, 33, 1998, pp. 549–568.

Holderness, C. G., and D. P. Sheehan, "Raiders or Saviors? The Evidence on Six Controversial Investors," *Journal of Financial Economics*, 14, 1985, pp. 555–579.

Hwang, Suein L., "Philip Morris Throws Away Its Poison Pill," *Wall Street Journal*, March 2, 1995, B8.

Iqbal, Z., S. Shetty, J. Haley, and M. Jayakumar, "Takeovers, Managerial Ownership, and Pension Plan Terminations," *American Business Review*, 17, January 1999, pp. 1–6.

Janjigian, V., and E. A. Trahan, "An Analysis of the Decision to Opt Out of Pennsylvania Senate Bill 1310," *Journal of Financial Research*, 19, Spring 1996, pp. 1–19.

Jarrell, G. A., and A. Poulsen, "Shark Repellents and Stock Prices: The Effects of Antitakeover Amendments Since 1980," *Journal of Financial Economics*, 19, 1987, pp. 127–168.

Jensen, Michael C., "Takeovers: Their Causes and Consequences," *Journal of Economic Perspectives*, 2, Winter 1988, pp. 21–48.

Johnson, D. J., and N. L. Meade, "Shareholder Wealth Effects of Poison Pills in the Presence of Anti-Takeover Amendments," *Journal of Applied Business Research*, 12, Fall 1996, pp. 10–19.

Johnson, M. S., and R. P. Rao, "The Impact of Antitakeover Amendments on Corporate Financial Performance," *Financial Review*, 32, November 1997, pp. 659–690.

Karpoff, Jonathan M., and Paul H. Malatesta, "The Wealth Effects of Second Generation State Takeover Legislation," *Journal of Financial Economics*, 25, 1989, pp. 291–322.

———, and Ralph A. Walkling, "Corporate Governance and Shareholder Initiatives: Empirical Evidence," *Journal of Financial Economics*, 42, 1996, pp. 365–395.

Klein, A., and J. Rosenfeld, "The Impact of Targeted Share Repurchases on the Wealth of Non-Participating Shareholders," *Journal of Financial Research*, 11, Summer 1988, pp. 89–97.

Knoeber, C. R., "Golden Parachutes, Shark Repellents, and Hostile Tender Offers," *American Economic Review*, 76, March 1986, pp. 155–167.

Lambert, R., and D. Larcker, "Golden Parachutes, Executive Decision-Making, and Shareholder Wealth," *Journal of Accounting and Economics*, 7, April 1985, pp. 179–204.

Linn, S. C., and J. J. McConnell, "An Empirical Investigation of the Impact of Antitakeover Amendments on Common Stock Prices," *Journal of Financial Economics*, 11, April 1983, pp. 361–399.

Loh, C., and R. S. Rathinasamy, "The Impact of Antitakeover Devices on the Valuation Consequences of Voluntary Corporate Selloffs," *The Financial Review*, 32, November 1997, pp. 691–708.

Mahoney, James M., and Joseph T. Mahoney, "An Empirical Investigation of the Effect of Corporate Charter Antitakeover Amendments on Stockholder Wealth," *Strategic Management Journal*, 14, 1993, pp. 17–31.

Malatesta, Paul H., and Ralph A. Walkling, "Poison Pill Securities: Stockholder Wealth, Profitability, and Ownership Structure," *Journal of Financial Economics*, 20, 1988, pp. 347–376.

Malekzadeh, A. R., V. B. McWilliams, and N. Sen, "Implications of CEO Structural and Ownership Powers, Board Ownership and Composition on the Market's Reaction to Antitakeover Charter Amendments," *Journal of Applied Business Research*, 14, Summer 1998, pp. 53–62.

Marais, L., K. Schipper, and A. Smith, "Wealth Effects of Going Private for Senior Securities," *Journal of Financial Economics*, 23, 1989, pp. 151–191.

McWilliams, V. B., "Managerial Share Ownership and the Stock Price Effects of Antitakeover Amendment Proposals," *Journal of Finance*, 45, 1990, pp. 1627–1640.

———, and N. Sen, "Board Monitoring and Antitakeover Amendments," *Journal of Financial and Quantitative Analysis*, 32, 1997, pp. 491–505.

Mikkelson, W. H., and R. S. Ruback, "An Empirical Analysis of the Interfirm Equity Investment Process," *Journal of Financial Economics*, 14, 1985, pp. 523–553.

———, "Targeted Repurchases and Common Stock Returns," *The RAND Journal of Economics*, 22, Winter 1991, pp. 544–561.

Mogavero, Damian J., and Michael F. Toyne, "The Impact of Golden Parachutes on Fortune 500 Stock Returns: A Reexamination of the Evidence," *Quarterly Journal of Business and Economics*, 34, 1995, pp. 30–38.

Moran v. Household International, Inc., Del. Ch. 490A. 2d 1059, 1985.

Mulherin, J. H., and A. B. Poulsen, "Proxy Contests and Corporate Change: Implications for Shareholder Wealth," *Journal of Financial Economics*, 47, 1998, pp. 279–313.

Plitch, Phyllis, "Pension Fund TIAA-CREF Targets 'Dead-Hand' Antitakeover Provisions," *Wall Street Journal*, January 31, 2000, p. B12.

Pound, J., "The Effects of Antitakeover Amendments on Takeover Activity: Some Direct Evidence," *Journal of Law and Economics*, 30, October 1987, pp. 353–367.

Romano, Roberta, "Law as a Product: Some Pieces of the Incorporation Puzzle," *Journal of Law, Economics and Organization*, 1, 1985, pp. 225–269.

———, "The Political Economy of Takeover Statutes," *Virginia Law Review*, 73, 1987, pp. 111–199.

———, "Competition for Corporate Charters and the Lesson of Takeover Statutes," *Fordham Law Review*, 61, 1993, pp. 843–864.

Ryngaert, Michael, "The Effect of Poison Pill Securities on Shareholder Wealth," *Journal of Financial Economics*, 20, 1988, pp. 377–417.

———, and J. M. Netter, "Shareholder Wealth Effects of the Ohio Antitakeover Law," *Journal of Law, Economics and Organization*, 4, Fall 1988, pp. 373–384.

Sundaramurthy, C., J. M. Mahoney, and J. T. Mahoney, "Board Structure, Antitakeover Provisions, and Stockholder Wealth," *Strategic Management Journal*, 18, 1997, pp. 231–245.

Swartz, L. M., "The 1990 Pennsylvania Antitakeover Law: Should Firms Opt Out of Antitakeover Legislation?" *Journal of Accounting, Auditing and Finance*, 11, Spring 1996, pp. 223–245.

Taylor, John, *Storming the Magic Kingdom*, New York: Ballantine Books, 1987.

Warga, A., and I. Welch, "Bondholder Losses in Leveraged Buyouts," *Review of Financial Studies*, 6, 1993, pp. 959–982.

Wasserstein, Bruce, *Big Deal*, New York: Warner Books, 1998.

Corporate Governance and Performance

A rich and growing literature on corporate governance has been developing. Fama's paper on the theory of the firm (1980) was followed by the two papers on governance by Fama and Jensen (1983a, 1983b). Further work on these topics was developed in two symposia issues of the *Journal of Financial Economics*. The first, in January–March 1988, was "The Distribution of Power Among Corporate Managers, Shareholders, and Directors" (Jensen and Warner, 1988). The second, in two parts in the fall of 1990, was "The Structure and Governance of Enterprise" (Jensen and Ruback, 1990). A rich abundance of follow-up articles appeared. Book-length studies of corporate governance were published (Chew, 1997; Monks and Minow, 1995). A survey of corporate governance and board effectiveness was developed by John and Senbet (1998). An even broader survey of corporate governance issues was achieved by Shleifer and Vishny (1997).

Enterprise governance is of great significance because it impacts everyone—including you, the reader. The materials are as full of action as a basketball or football game, so they should command great interest as well. Some examples: The virtual collapse of the Russian economy in 1998 resulted in large measure from the weakness of governance mechanisms. The abysmal inefficiency of business operations under state control led to the earlier collapse of the Soviet system. But privatization of industries resulted in a "substantial diversion of assets by managers" (Shleifer and Vishny, 1997, p. 738). Putting the matter less euphemistically, the managers robbed other shareholders, creditors, consumers, the government, the workers—all possible stakeholders. It has been estimated that funds on the order of magnitude of $100 billion were moved out of the country by the predators. The consequent distrust predictably resulted in "the virtual nonexistence of external capital supply to firms." So enterprise governance can shake the very foundations of a society, affecting every member.

In the United States, many complaints are made about corporate governance systems: "The books are cooked to meet or exceed analysts' forecasts; workers are underpaid and executives are overpaid; board members are hand picked by management to help plunder the firm at the expense of shareholders and creditors; etc., etc."

AN OVERVIEW OF CORPORATE GOVERNANCE

The subject matter is clearly important and exciting. It has many dimensions, so we begin with an overview to provide the big picture that will guide the organization of the chapter. To run a business requires funds. Once funds are supplied, what is to prevent the managers from taking advantage of all the other stakeholders? This is the problem of a separation of ownership and control; it has also been termed the agency problem or the relationship between the principal and agents. In theory, the shareholders elect a board of directors to represent their interests. But the managers may subvert this process. If boards are ineffectual, can other mechanisms outside the firm help? Does the stock market serve as a regulator by penalizing poor performance with reduced security prices? Do proxy contests help? Or are M&As—the market for corporate control—the ultimate mechanism for the regulation of corporate governance? Or do completely different governance systems, such as banking control in Germany and Japan, work better? These are the issues covered in the following sections.

CORPORATE GOVERNANCE SYSTEMS IN THE UNITED STATES

In the United States, the system of corporate enterprise that developed was the limited liability public corporation whose ownership in theory was widely dispersed among individual shareholders. After legislation in 1933, commercial banks were not permitted to make equity investments and insurance companies had long been circumscribed in the percentage of their funds they could invest in equities. In contrast, the system that grew up in Germany and Japan was characterized by large equity and loan investments by banks and insurance companies. In addition, substantial cross-holdings of ownership shares among corporations developed. We begin with an analysis of the U.S. model of corporate governance.

Diffuse Stock Ownership

In the United States, for many years the dominant form of corporate ownership was diffuse limited liability ownership of the voting equity shares by a large number of individual investors. The growth of this form of ownership reflected some distinct advantages. Under limited liability, the investor could lose no more than was paid for the equity stock of the corporation. Relatively small investments could be made in a number of corporations, so the individual investor could achieve the benefits of diversification. Asset pricing models hold that diversification enables the investor to ignore the idiosyncratic risks of individual companies to earn the risk-free rate plus a market risk premium weighted by systematic risk, which implies that relatively little direct monitoring of the operations of individual business firms is required by investors.

In addition, the equity ownership shares of the corporation are readily bought and sold in active and relatively liquid markets. In the United States, by tradition and by legislation enacted in the 1930s, commercial banks and insurance companies are limited in their ability to hold large equity positions in individual corporations. Under this idealized scenario, issues of corporate governance and control are muted. However, over time, the effectiveness of this governance system has been questioned. To understand the issues we begin with a brief summary of the theory of the firm.

Contractual Theory of the Firm

The contractual theory of the nature of the firm has become widely held (Alchian, 1982; Alchian and Woodward, 1988; Fama and Jensen, 1983a, 1983b). It views the firm as a network of contracts, actual and implicit, that specify the roles of the various participants or stakeholders (workers, managers, owners, lenders) and defines their rights, obligations, and payoffs under various conditions. The contractual nature of the firm implies multiple stakeholders. Their interests must be harmonized to achieve efficiency and value maximization. A basic issue is the role of market transactions (and their relative costs) versus organization processes as alternative modes of governance (Williamson, 1999).

Although contracts define the rights and responsibilities of each class of stakeholders in a firm, potential conflicts may occur. Contracts are unable to envisage the many changes in conditions that develop over the passage of time. Also, participants may have personal goals as well.

Most participants contract for fixed payoffs. Workers receive wages. Creditors receive interest payments and are promised the repayment of principal at the maturity of debt contracts. The shareholders hold residual claims on cash flows. In recent years, wage earners have been paid in part in the common stock of the firm in ESOPs or in return for wage concessions. Warrants and convertibles add equity options to debt contracts.

In this framework, the literature has expressed concern about the separation of ownership and control (Berle and Means, 1932). In general, the operations of the firm are conducted and controlled by its managers without major stock ownership positions. In theory, the managers are agents of the owners, but in practice they may control the firm in their own interests. Thus, conflicts of interest arise between the owners and managers.

Jensen and Meckling (1976) developed a number of aspects of the divergence of interest between owners (the principal) and management (their agent). They described how the agency problem results whenever a manager owns less than the total common stock of the firm. This fractional ownership can lead managers to work less strenuously and to acquire more perquisites (luxurious offices, furniture, and rugs; company cars) than if they had to bear all of the costs.

To deal with agency problems, additional monitoring expenditures (agency costs) are required. Agency costs include (1) auditing systems to limit this kind of management behavior, (2) various kinds of bonding assurances by the managers that such abuses will not be practiced, and (3) changes in organization systems to limit the ability of managers to engage in the undesirable practices.

Divergent Interests of Stakeholders

Traditionally, corporate governance has focused on the problem of the separation of ownership by shareholders and control by management. But increasingly we have come to recognize a broader framework. Firms must respond to the expectations of more categories of stakeholders. These include employees, consumers, large investors such as pension funds, government, and society as a whole. These diverse interests need to be harmonized. Firms must respond to the expectations of diverse stakeholders to achieve long-run value maximization (Cornell and Shapiro, 1987).

In recent years, externalities such as product safety, job safety, and environmental impacts have increased in importance. A business firm must be responsive to new and powerful constituencies for long-run viability. This point of view argues that business firms must recognize a wide range of stakeholders and external influences.

INTERNAL CONTROL MECHANISMS

We first consider the internal control mechanisms available to balance the interests of the multiple stakeholders. In theory, under widely dispersed ownership, shareholders elect the board of directors to represent their interests. This poses issues of how other stakeholders obtain representation of their views and interests. These problems have not been fully resolved. Increasingly, public expectations look to the board of directors to balance the interests of all stakeholders. Some criticize such a view as soft-headed, unrealistic "do-goodism." An alternative view is that if the needs and goals of the multiple stakeholders—shareholders, creditors, consumers, workers, government, the general public—are not addressed, the political-economic system will not function effectively in the long run. These are matters of great importance with respect to which the board of directors has considerable responsibilities.

Campbell, Gillan, and Niden (CGN) (1999) analyzed how shareholders used the proxy mechanism on issues concerning corporate governance and social policy in the 1997 proxy season. The shareholder proposal rule (Rule 14a-8) allowed shareholders to include a proposal and a 500-word supporting statement in the company's proxy materials subject to certain constraints. CGN's sample consisted of 287 social policy proposals and 582 corporate governance proposals at 394 companies. The data source was the Investor Responsibility Center's compilation of shareholder proposals, the nature of which is described in the following paragraph.

Only 43.3% of all proposals were considered for vote. For the corporate governance proposals, 49.2% were voted on and 35.2% were either omitted or withdrawn. For social policy proposals, 31.4% were voted on and 61.6% were either omitted or withdrawn. For proposals that were submitted to a vote, corporate governance received a higher level of support, with a mean of 23.6% of the votes cast in favor, particularly those related to antitakeover measures, board pensions, and shareholder voting. Low support was associated with executive compensation, board stock ownership, and board tenure. Social policy issues received only weak support, with a mean of 6.6% of the votes cast in favor. CGN conclude that Rule 14a-8 remains an important avenue for shareholders seeking change in corporate behavior on issues of corporate governance and social policy.

ROLE OF THE BOARD OF DIRECTORS

Monitoring by boards of directors can, in theory, deal with at least some problems of corporate governance. But there is the alternative view that boards have been ineffective in recognizing the problems of the firm and standing up to top officers, especially when tough decisions are necessary to solve the problems (Jensen, 1986). External control devices such as hostile takeovers have multiplied because of the failure of the board, according to this view.

The work by Morck, Shleifer, and Vishny (1989) was motivated by these opposing views and provided evidence on when the board could effectively deal with the problems of the firm and when the external control market comes into play. It is the view of Morck, Shleifer, and Vishny that when the company underperforms its relatively healthy industry, it is easier for the board to evaluate top management. But the board's task is much harder when the whole industry is suffering. When the industry is having problems, it is difficult to judge whether the management is making mistakes. The boards of directors of firms in problem industries may be reluctant to force the CEO to take the painful measures (for example, divest divisions, lay off workers, or cut wages) often required in slow growth, mature, or declining industries. Under these circumstances, an external challenge (M&A) to shake up the management and the board may be necessary to enforce shareholder wealth maximization.

Composition of the Board

It is widely believed that outside directors play a larger role in monitoring management than inside directors. Fama (1980), for instance, argues that the inclusion of outside directors as professional referees enhances the viability of the board in achieving low-cost internal transfer of control. This also lowers the probability of top management colluding and expropriating shareholders. Outside directors are usually respected leaders from the business and academic communities and have incentives to protect and develop their reputation as experts in decision control (Fama and Jensen, 1983a).

A study by Weisbach (1988) formally tested the hypothesis that inside and outside directors behave differently in monitoring top management and found that firms with outsider-dominated boards were significantly more likely than firms with insider-dominated boards to remove the chief executive officer (CEO). In Weisbach's study, firms were grouped according to the percentage of outsiders (directors who neither work for the corporation nor have extensive dealings with the company) on the board. In his sample of 367 New York Stock Exchange (NYSE) firms, the proportion of outside directors on the board centered around 50%, with few firms in the tails of the distribution. In the study, outsider-dominated firms (128 firms) were those in which at least 60% of the board were outsiders. Insider-dominated firms (93 firms) had outsiders making up no more than 40% of the directors. Firms with between 41% and 59% outsiders were considered mixed (146 firms). For all the firms in the sample, there were 286 CEO resignations in the period 1974 to 1983. In the actual analysis, CEO resignations for reasons that are clearly unrelated to performance were eliminated from the sample.

When stock returns are used as predictors of CEO removal, the results show a statistically significant inverse relation between a firm's market-adjusted share performance in a year and the likelihood of a subsequent change in its CEO. The responsiveness of the removal decision to stock performance is three times as large for the outsider-dominated boards as for the other board types. Resignations are not sensitive to returns from periods preceding the event by more than a year, which suggests that the board's decision to replace the CEO takes place relatively quickly following poor share return performance. Using accounting earnings changes (net of industry effects) as the performance measure gives similar results. Also, there is an indication that the board of directors looks at accounting numbers (earnings before interest and taxes) to evaluate a CEO's performance, possibly more than at stock returns.

Weisbach (1988) provided evidence that the larger the shareholdings of both the top two officers of the firm and the rest of the board, the smaller the number of outsiders on the board. As expected, increased shareholdings of the CEO reduced the probability that he or she resigned. However, share ownership by noncontrolling directors (that is, directors excluding the top two officers) does not appear to have any explanatory power other than board composition. Thus, Weisbach suggested that the composition of the board rather than its equity ownership was what drove the level of monitoring. He also measured price responses to the announcement of CEO resignations. His results show that the excess returns from a market model are significantly positive and thus imply that new information is revealed by these resignations.

Corporate governance reformers believe that outside directors are better monitors and therefore recommend that nominating committees should be composed of only independent outside directors. Outside directors are not officers of the firm and do not have a direct business relationship with the firm. It was GM's outside board members who played the pivotal role in ousting the chairman, Robert C. Stempel, in November 1992.

Using the *Wall Street Journal's* "Who's News" section, Rosenstein and Wyatt (1990) examined the impact of the announcement that a company is appointing an outside director. The cumulative average prediction error (CAPE) for the total sample was significantly positive, which provided support for the argument that the appointment of outside directors adds to shareholder wealth.

Borokhovich, Parrino, and Trapani (1996) discuss the role of outside directors and CEO selection. They found a positive monotonic relation between the proportion of outside directors and the likelihood that an outsider is appointed CEO. This relation holds after controlling for firm size, firm performance, CEO stock ownership, and regulatory effects. Evidence from the stock returns around the succession announcements suggests that the market views the appointment of an outsider to the CEO position more favorably than the appointment of an insider, especially when the incumbent CEO is forced to resign. A new CEO from outside the firm appears to be perceived as more likely to alter firm policies in a way that benefits shareholders. On average, a significant positive abnormal return is observed when a CEO is replaced by an outsider following either voluntary or forced turnover. In contrast, whereas inside appointments following voluntary successions are associated with small positive abnormal returns, large negative abnormal returns are observed when insiders replace fired CEOs.

Compensation of Board Members

Part of the solution might be a well-structured compensation system. Although director compensation is a relatively recent phenomenon, it goes hand in hand with the increased director responsibility. In the past, directors did little monitoring and their own performance was not evaluated. They received a token fee for their services. Board members today take a greater leadership role by overseeing the appointment and assessment of officers, helping implement strategy, representing shareholders, and seeing that the company fulfills its public responsibilities. Critics of the compensation as a motivating factor model point out that in some fields, particularly nonprofit, many directors volunteer their services without financial compensation.

If compensation is a significant motivating factor for directors, director stock ownership aligns director interests more closely with those of shareholders. Some companies have adopted stock ownership requirements for directors and/or pay part or all of the directors' annual retainer in stock and stock options. Some finance their directors' retirements with stock. Studies find that directors of top-performing companies hold more stock than do their counterparts at poor performers, suggesting a positive link between director stock ownership and company performance.

Evaluating a Board of Directors

Business Week (Byrne, 1996) carried a cover story entitled "The Best & Worst Boards." Boards were rated by how close they came to meeting recommendations, which we summarize into nine items: (1) Evaluate CEO performance annually. (2) Link CEO pay to clear performance criteria. (3) Review and evaluate strategic and operating plans. (4) Require significant stock ownership and compensate directors in stock. (5) Consist of no more than three insiders. (6) Require election each year and mandatory retirement at 70. (7) Have key committees composed of outside directors. (8) Impose limits on number of boards and ban interlocking directorships. (9) Disqualify anyone receiving fees from the company.

The article listed the "best" and "worst" 25 companies based on the above criteria. Such listings throw the glare of publicity on the performance of boards of directors. The article also noted that some pension funds and mutual funds judge boards by the stock market performance of their companies. This is called a "blinkered view." It is argued that sound governance will improve the odds of good performance.

The final sentence in the preceding paragraph is tested by Millstein and MacAvoy (1998). They develop two metrics for board independence and performance, using them to predict whether a company is adding wealth to its shareholders. The first metric for board performance is based on a survey by CalPERS of 300 large corporations in which they requested a response to a questionnaire on board procedures. The responses were graded by CalPERS with ranks from A+ to F based on criteria such as the nine items listed above. In addition, Millstein and MacAvoy assigned an associate to review the responses to the CalPERS questionnaire to develop a binary criterion of board independence. At least one of the following had to be present: a non-executive chairman of the board, meetings of outside directors without management present, and/or substantial adherence to recommended guidelines. These metrics were the independent variables in a regression on the company spread between ROIC (the return on invested capital) and WACC (the cost of capital), using data for 1991 to 1995. Calculations were made using the CalPERS grade of A+ to F and another using the binary measure of board independence. By either metric, the better the board rating, the higher was the geometric mean of the 1991 to 1995 spread of ROIC over WACC. Their study demonstrates that the relationship between board procedures and performance can be quantified.

Similar results were found by Seward and Walsh (1996) in their study of 78 voluntary corporate spin-offs between 1972 and 1987. The new companies were typically headed by an inside CEO from the parent company. The CEO received a market-based performance-contingent compensation contract. The boards of directors in the new entities included a majority of outsiders. Incentive contracts for top managers were designed by a compensation committee composed of a majority of outside directors. Seward and Walsh conclude that the spin-off form of equity reorganizations has been associated with the implementation of efficient internal governance and control practices. As in earlier studies of spin-offs, the event returns were positive, with abnormal returns averaging 2.6%. However, their variables measuring the efficiency of the governance and control of the spin-offs did not explain the positive announcement returns.

OWNERSHIP CONCENTRATION

Equity ownership by managers must balance convergence or alignment of interests versus entrenchment considerations. When management share ownership increases, managers' interests are better aligned with shareholder interests, and thus deviation from value maximization will decline (convergence). But managerial ownership and control of voting rights may give a manager enough power to guarantee his or her employment with the firm and pursue self-interest at the expense of shareholder wealth (entrenchment).

Ownership and Performance

Stulz (1988) formulated a model in which at low levels of management ownership, increased equity holdings improve convergence of interests with shareholders, enhancing firm value. At higher levels of insider ownership, managerial entrenchment blocks takeovers or makes them more costly. This decreases the probability of a takeover, which is likely to decrease the value of the firm.

In Morck, Shleifer, and Vishny (MSV) (1988), performance (measured by the q-ratio) was related to management or insider ownership percentages. As ownership concentration increased from 0 to 5%, performance improved. In the ownership range from over 5% to 25%, performance deteriorated. As ownership concentration rose above 25%, performance improved, but slowly. A simple explanation of this pattern is that in the 0 to 5% range the alignment-of-interest effect improved performance. In the above 5% to 25% range, management entrenchment influence may have a dampening effect on performance. In the over 25% range, incremental entrenchment effects were attenuated. But MSV questioned this simple interpretation. In the 0 to 5% range, they observed that the direction of causality may be reversed. (See also Jensen and Warner, 1988.) High performance firms were more likely to give managers stock bonuses or make it profitable for them to exercise their stock options, resulting in large ownership percentages for management. They also referred to the point made by Demsetz and Lehn (1985) that firms with high performance may have substantial intangible assets that require greater ownership concentration to induce proper management of these assets. Morck, Shleifer, and Vishny agreed that it appeared plausible that above the 25% ownership concentration additional entrenchment effects would be small.

McConnell and Servaes (MS) (1990) replicated the MSV study, which used 1980 data, for the years 1976 and 1986. For 1976, MS found that the relationship between ownership concentration and performance, measured by the q-ratio, was relatively flat with a moderate convergence of interest effect up to 50%, after which the curve appears to flatten and then decline moderately. For their 1986 data, they found that the curve rose relatively sharply to 40%, after which it was relatively flat to 50% followed by a sharp decline. MS also tested for the influence of leverage, institutional ownership, R&D expenditures, and advertising expenditures, concluding that including these control variables did not change their initial findings.

Another follow-up study was made by Cho (1998). Cho, using 1991 data, was able to replicate the MSV patterns using ordinary least squares (OLS) regression. He notes that the previous studies treat ownership structure as given by outside factors (exogenous). He tested for the hypothesis of Demsetz and Lehn (1985) that ownership structure is endogenous—reflecting decisions made by owners based on considerations such as choices between salaries and the receipt of stock options. When Cho estimated a simultaneous equation regression instead of OLS, he found that corporate value affects ownership structure, but not the reverse. This reverses the interpretation of the relationship between ownership structure and corporate value.

Bristow (1998) examined the issues using a new database of consistently derived insider holdings on 4,000 firms covering the years 1986 through 1995. He calculated the relationship between management ownership and performance for each of the ten years. For some years, he obtained the MSV results; for others, he obtained the MS roof-shaped patterns and for still other years, a bowl pattern (inverted roof). Bristow's findings suggest that other economic variables, such as the relative growth rates of industries, differences in demand–supply relationships among industries, the relative value change patterns among industries and firms within them, and stock price movements, may influence the ownership–performance relationship. Bristow's results may also reflect the econometric identification problems discussed by Cho. The true relationship may be that of the Demsetz–Lehn theory of no relationship between ownership and performance. Another possibility is suggested by the considerable literature concluding that corporate governance in the United States had suffered from widely diffused ownership. Holderness, Kroszner, and Sheehan (1999) found that the mean and median percentages of managerial equity ownership increased from 12.9% and 6.5%, respectively, in 1935 to 21.1% and 14.4% in 1995. This is roughly a doubling of managerial ownership, possibly implying a general improvement in corporate governance in the United States.

Other Studies of Ownership Effects

Holderness and Sheehan (1988) analyzed 114 listed firms with ownership concentration of more than 50% but less than 100%. Among the 114 firms, 27 became majority shareholder firms during the period 1978 to 1984, but only 13 ceased to be such firms during the same period. Thus, there was little net outflow from majority ownership. This result is also confirmed for a much larger base of publicly traded firms. It appears that majority ownership was surviving as a viable organizational form. In the sample, the majority shareholders were approximately equally divided between individuals and corporations. Firms with individual majority shareholders were typically smaller than, and firms with corporate majority shareholders slightly larger than, the typical NYSE or AMEX firms.

The average majority holding was 64% (median 60%) for all firms in the sample, which is substantially more than the minimum 50% that ensures voting control. This evidence appears inconsistent with the proposition that majority blocks are held to expropriate minority shareholders. Expropriation-oriented majority shareholders might want to hold above 66% because of supermajority voting provisions in the firm's bylaws or articles of incorporation. However, only 36% of the sample firms involved blocks above 66%, the typical supermajority requirement, and for these firms the authors found no cases in which the requirement was mentioned in proxy statements.

Holderness and Sheehan (1988) also analyzed stock price reaction to 31 announcements of majority block trades to study the effect on firm value of changing shareholders. On average, stock prices increased over the two-day window of the day before announcement and the announcement day by an abnormal 7.3%, and over the 30-day period around the announcement by an abnormal 12.8%. The results also indicated that on average firm value increases more when both the buyer and the seller are individuals rather than corporations. The abnormal return was higher for announcements that involved simultaneous tender offers to minority shareholders (10 out of 31 cases) than announcements with no such tender offers (21 cases). In most of the consummated cases, new directors and officers were appointed after the trades.

When majority shareholder firms were compared to firms with relatively diffuse stock ownership, Holderness and Sheehan (1988) found no statistical difference in investment expenditures, frequency of control changes, accounting rates of return, or Tobin's q. However, there was evidence that *individual* majority shareholder firms underperformed their comparison firms in terms of q-ratios and accounting rates of return, whereas *corporate* majority shareholder firms did not (see also Barclay and Holderness, 1991).

Slovin and Sushka (1993) analyzed the influence of ownership concentration on firm value by studying the effects of the deaths of inside blockholders. They found that the abnormal returns for the two-day event interval from day -1 to the report of the executive's death was a positive 3.01%, statistically significant. They found also that ownership concentration fell and increased corporate control activity followed. A majority of the firms in which an inside blockholder died subsequently became the target of a takeover bid. Two-thirds of the bids were friendly, and three-fourths of them succeeded.

The preceding empirical studies yielded several implications. First, the positive stock price reactions were inconsistent with the proposition that the majority shareholders' primary objective was to expropriate or consume corporate wealth. If the expropriation hypotheses were valid, majority shareholders would not offer to buy out minority shareholders at substantial premiums. Yet such offers were made in one-third of the majority-block trading announcements. Second, majority shareholders or their representatives did not merely monitor management teams but actively participated in management. That the majority shareholder played a central role in management was consistent with the management and board turnover following majority-block trading. Third, the apparent premise for the antagonism toward large block shareholders (reflected in state regulations limiting their voting rights, antitakeover laws, poison pill charter amendments, and other "shareholder rights" initiatives) was not consistent with the empirical evidence.

Managerial Ownership and Bond Returns

The relationships between concentration of managerial ownership and bond returns were tested by Bagnani, Milonas, Saunders, and Travlos (BMST) (1994). They employed the three-stage analysis of Morck, Shleifer, and Vishny (1988) discussed above. Their empirical analysis found no relationship between bond returns and managerial ownership of 0 to 5%, a positive relationship between above 5% to 25%, and a weak negative relationship for ownership above 25%.

Some reasons for these findings were suggested by BMST. The above 5% to 25% range represented a concentration of stock ownership that resulted in increased incentives for managers to act in shareholders' interests, taking risks that were potentially harmful to bondholders. In this range, rational bondholders required higher returns on their bonds.

At ownership above 25%, managers became more risk-averse. As their stake increased, their wealth was less diversified with firm-specific, nondiversifiable human capital and/or they had greater incentives to protect their private benefits and objectives. Thus, their interests were more aligned with those of bondholders, implying lower bond return premiums.

Financial Policy and Ownership Concentration

In share repurchases financed by debt, the amount of equity is reduced. Because the insider group does not tender its shares in the repurchase, its percentage of equity shares is increased. This may increase the convergence-of-interest effect. We have seen in chapter 16 that LBOs and MBOs increase management ownership shares. Incentive effects of high management ownership percentages have played a positive role in LBOs and MBOs.

Safieddine and Titman (1999) studied a sample of 573 firms that successfully resisted takeover attempts during 1982 to 1991. Target stock prices declined an average of 5.14% around the date of the termination announcement. For 328 companies, data were available to calculate effects on leverage. In 207 firms, the median level of the total debt to total book value of assets increased from about 60% one year before the unsuccessful takeover attempt to 71.5% one year later. The increased leverage is one form of defensive strategy. Only 38% of the targets that increased their leverage ratio by more than the median during a three-year window around the initial failed takeover attempt were taken over in the subsequent five years. For the target firms that increased their leverage ratios by less than the median, 57% were taken over during the five-year period.

The higher leverage ratio increases are associated with corporate restructuring activity. The turnover of top management during the three-year window was 30% for the group with low leverage increases and about 37% for the firms with higher leverage increases. In hostile takeover attempts, 44% of the top managers are replaced; in friendly takeover attempts, only 29% are replaced. In addition to management turnover, labor force reductions and asset sales to increase corporate focus take place. Operating performance improves. As a result, the long-run post-termination performance of leverage-increasing targets is superior to that of benchmark control groups. The returns realized by the shareholders of the targets with leverage increases grow by about 55% within five years or within a shorter time if the firm is delisted, possibly because of the takeover. This is approximately the same level of returns that would have been realized by accepting the takeover offer. Shareholders of targets with less than median leverage increases are worse off. The strong long-term abnormal stock price performance indicates that for the leverage-increasing firms, despite the initial drop at the termination announcement, the associated productivity improvements are consistent with target manager behavior aligned with the longer run interests of their shareholders.

Other effects have been noted. The Amihud, Lev, and Travlos (ALT) (1990) study measured whether the likelihood of an acquisition being financed by cash was an increasing function of the managerial ownership in the acquiring firm. Increasing debt, while increasing the probability of bankruptcy, can be used to increase management's equity stake if the debt is used to retire equity held by the public. The ALT sample consisted of firms that appeared on the 1980 list of Fortune 500 companies and made cash acquisitions of over $10 million of other firms during the period 1981 to 1983. The results showed that cash acquisitions are associated with significantly larger insider ownership levels than stock-financed acquisitions.

EXECUTIVE COMPENSATION

We have presented materials on the relationship between managerial concentration of ownership and the convergence of interests of managers with those of owners. Executive compensation plans have also been proposed to achieve alignment of interests.

One view is that the conflict of interest between owners and managers would be substantially reduced if executive compensation plans more tightly related pay to performance. The view is widely held that executive compensation is not closely linked to performance measured by changes in the value of the firm. Jensen and Murphy (1990) found that executive pay changes by only $3 for a $1,000 change in the wealth of a firm, an elasticity of 0.003, or 0.3%. This is argued to demonstrate that executive pay is not linked to performance. But this relationship may be at least partially explained by the large value of the firm in relation to executive compensation.

For example, the Disney Company at the end of 1995 had 524 million shares outstanding. At a price of $60 per share, this represented $31.44 billion. If its top executive received compensation of $10 million, this was 0.0318% of total firm value.

In 1996 its president, Michael Eisner, realized $200 million mainly from the exercise of stock options. From a low of $7 in 1986, the price of Disney stock, adjusted for splits, increased to a high of $64.25 in 1995. Based on the 524 million shares outstanding at the end of 1995, this represented an increase in value to Disney shareholders of approximately $30 billion. Thus, Eisner's salary change in the one unusual year represented about $6.7 for each $1,000 change in the wealth of Disney shareholders, an elasticity of 0.0067 or 0.67%. The result was not greatly different from the Jensen and Murphy relationship. This example suggested that although the elasticity of executive pay in relation to changes in firm value was small, the impact on the wealth position of executives could be very large.

A large impact on executive wealth position could have strong motivational influences. Haubrich (1994), using some reasonable parameter assumptions, derived the Jensen and Murphy results from some leading models of principal-agent theory. Haubrich's analysis led Shleifer and Vishny (1997) to observe that the Jensen and Murphy relationship would generate large swings in executive wealth and require considerable risk tolerance for executives.

Core, Holthausen, and Larcker (CHL) (1999) examined the association between the firm's corporate governance structure and level of CEO compensation and the future performance of the firm. The sample consisted of 495 observations for 205 publicly traded U.S. firms over the period 1982 to 1984. The compensation data were collected by a major consulting firm using mail surveys.

The cross-sectional regression, controlling for the economic factors, showed that board of director characteristics and ownership structure were significantly related to the level of CEO compensation. With regard to board of director variables, CEO compensation was higher when the CEO was also the board chair, the board was larger, there was a greater percentage of outside directors appointed by the CEO, there were more outside directors considered "gray" (he or his employer received payments from the company in excess of his board pay), and outside directors were older and served on more than three other boards. CEO compensation was lower the greater the percentage of inside directors in the board. With respect to ownership variables, CEO compensation was lower when the CEO's ownership stake was higher and when the large blockholders were present (either non-CEO internal board members or external blockholders who owned at least 5% of the equity).

Core, Holthausen, and Larcker used a second set of regressions between the compensation predicted by the board and ownership variables and the subsequent operating and market performance of the firm. They found a significant negative relationship. This result suggested that the board and ownership variables were proxies for the effectiveness of the firm's governance structure in controlling agency problems and not for the determinants of the CEO's equilibrium wage. The board and ownership structures affected the extent to which CEOs obtained compensation in excess of the level implied by the economic determinants. Thus, firms with weaker governance structures had greater agency problems. CEOs of firms with greater agency problems were able to obtain higher compensation. Firms with greater agency problems did not perform as well.

Another criticism of past patterns in executive compensation was that bonuses and stock options had been based on accounting measures rather than on stock market-based performance measures. Rappaport (1986) provided some perspective on the choice of performance measure. He observed that early executive compensation performance plans *were* market-based. However, during the 1970s, stock price movements were essentially flat. The average of daily closing prices for the Dow Jones Industrial Average was 911 for 1965 and was still only 884 for 1982. The broader S&P 500 index also remained essentially flat over the same time period. As a consequence, performance measures for granting options shifted from market-based to accounting-based measures over this period (Rappaport, 1986, p. 177).

However, in recent years, performance is again moving to market-based measures. The data in chapter 16 on leveraged buyouts demonstrate that in going-private transactions top management increased its percentage ownership of equity shares in the company by substantial percentages. This was an important element in the strong motivational influences that led to the well-documented performance improvement in the LBOs during the first part of the 1980s.

Other proposals for improved pay vs. performance policies have been made in recent years:

1. Limit the base salaries of top executives.
2. Base bonus and stock option plans on stock appreciation.
3. Stock appreciation benchmarks should consider
   a. close competitors.
   b. a wider peer group.
   c. broader stock market indexes such as the Dow or the S&P 500.
4. Base stock options on a premium of 10% to 20% over the current market and do not reprice them if the shares of the firm fall below the original exercise prices.
5. Institute company loan programs that enable top executives to buy substantial amounts of the firm's stock so that subsequent stock price fluctuations substantially impact the wealth position of the top executives.
6. Pay directors mainly in stock of the corporation with minimum specified holding periods to heighten their sensitivity to firm performance.

These changes in corporate practice are consistent with the recognition of the need to align the interests of managers with the interests of owners. Recent developments in executive compensation seek to achieve a closer link between executive pay and company performance. To the degree that these efforts are successful, the interests of managers will, to a greater degree, be aligned with those of owners. Other aspects of designing optional executive compensation plans are discussed in Copeland and Weston (1988, pp. 665–672).

OUTSIDE CONTROL MECHANISMS

To this point we have discussed internal control mechanisms for effective corporate governance. We have discussed the role of the board of directors, ownership concentration, and executive compensation. We now turn to outside control mechanisms, which include stock price performance, institutional investors, and proxy contests.

Stock Prices and Top Management Changes

Warner, Watts, and Wruck (WWW) (1988) investigated the relationship between a firm's stock price performance and subsequent changes in its top management including the CEO, president, and chairman of the board. They also provided new evidence on mechanisms for replacing inefficient managers and encouraging managers to maximize shareholder wealth. The data set used by WWW included top management changes for 269 NYSE and AMEX firms in the period 1963 to 1978.

Consistent with studies of CEO changes (Coughlan and Schmidt, 1985; Weisbach, 1988), WWW found that poor stock price performance was likely to result in an increased rate of management turnover. They also documented evidence of several internal control mechanisms such as monitoring by large blockholders, competition from other managers, and discipline by the board.

A number of earlier studies found significant positive price effects of changes in top management. Some found insignificant price reactions. In a later study, Denis and Denis (1995) also found insignificant announcement period abnormal returns for all management changes. However, forced resignations are associated with a positive 1.5% significant period abnormal returns. Normal retirements have insignificant effects. Interestingly, for the preannouncement period of −251 to −2 days, the forced resignations were associated with a −24% CAR. Normal retirements were associated with a −4% CAR but not statistically significant.

Denis and Denis also found that forced top management changes were preceded by significantly large operating performance declines and followed by significant improvements. Forced management changes were associated with significant downsizing measured by declines in employment, capital expenditures, and total assets. Denis and Denis observed that improvements did not result from effective board monitoring. Only 13% of their large sample (853) were forced changes. Over two-thirds of the forced resignations were associated with blockholder pressure, financial distress, shareholder lawsuits, and takeover attempts. They found that 56% of the firms with a forced top executive change became the target of some corporate control activity, generally in the form of a block investment or some form of takeover. They concluded that internal control mechanisms were inadequate to do the job alone and required the pressure of external corporate control markets.

The Shleifer and Vishny (1997) survey does not develop the potential role of the stock market and security price movements in disciplining managers in the United States. Security price movements provide a scorecard for measuring management performance. The evidence is clear that bad scores on the stock market increase managerial turnover. The potential of higher scores may also stimulate superior performance, bringing rewards to all of the stakeholders. The companies with performance like General Electric, Cisco Systems, and Intel do not raise issues of corporate governance.

Public Pension Funds

Public pension funds have the ability and size to become significant factors in corporate governance, yet only a small fraction have involved themselves in these issues. One of the more active pension funds is the California Public Employees' Retirement System (CalPERS), which invests $68 billion in pension funds for nearly 1 million public employees in California. In March 1992 CalPERS publicly announced the names of 12 companies with which it had failed to negotiate the adoption of corporate reforms. CalPERS accused these poorly performing companies of excessive executive pay or failing to maintain independent boards of directors.

In October 1993 the world's largest pension plan with $125 billion in assets, TIAA-CREF (formerly known as the Teachers Insurance and Annuity Association–College Retirement Equities Fund), announced a "corporate governance" policy. Although Chairman John Biggs said he was unwilling to sacrifice more than 0.1 percentage point in the annual return to fight for better corporate governance practices, TIAA encouraged companies to have independent, diverse boards with a majority of independent directors, and to have directors held more accountable to shareholders (Scism, 1994, p. C1).

Carleton, Nelson, and Weisbach (1998) find similar results for TIAA-CREF. They describe the negotiation process between financial institutions and target firms on governance issues. TIAA-CREF contacted 45 firms during the period 1992 to 1996. All the firms agreed to institute confidential voting. Most of the firms contacted added women or minorities to the board. Most of the firms that were asked to limit the use of blank check preferred stock as an antitakeover defense complied.

Wahal (1996) studied the activities of nine activist pension funds, from 1987 to 1993, with assets totaling $424 billion at the end of 1994. He noted that these funds averaged about 1% of the market value of equity of 146 targeted firms. In dollar terms, the ownership ranged from $8 million to $86 million. Inactive institutions as a group own approximately 51% ($3 billion) of the firms targeted by activist pension funds. The average inactive institution owns 0.3% ($14 million) of targeted firms. Takeover-related proxy proposals covered poison pills, greenmail, and antitakeover provisions. Governance-related targeting involved golden parachutes, board composition, and compensation. The activist proposals shifted from takeover-related proxy proposals in the late 1980s to governance-related proposals in the 1990s.

Wahal's results showed approximately a zero average abnormal return for shareholder proposals and small positive abnormal returns for attempts to influence target firms by using shareholder proposals (nonproxy targeting). But no evidence of significant long-term improvement was found in either stock price movements or accounting measures of performance in the post-targeting period.

Strickland, Wiles, and Zenner (SWZ) (1996) studied the United Shareholders Association (USA) from 1986 to 1993. The USA was founded in August 1986 by T. Boone Pickens as a not-for-profit organization for shareholder rights. It was disbanded on October 25, 1993, by a vote of the USA board of directors. USA developed a Target 50 list of firms on the basis of poor financial performance, executive compensation plans not tied to firm performance, and policies that limited shareholder input on governance issues. If the targeted firms did not respond, the USA, through its 65,000 or so members, sought to sponsor proxy proposals to change the governance structure.

Strickland, Wiles, and Zenner recognized that proxy proposals do not bind the firm's board of directors. To judge whether USA was effective, SWZ documented that USA successfully negotiated corporate governance changes covering 53 proposals before inclusion in proxy statements. At the announcement of such negotiated agreements, target firms' shareholders receive a 0.9% abnormal return, representing a wealth increase of $1.3 billion ($30 million per firm). The association was most effective when the target firm was a poor performer with high institutional ownership.

MULTIPLE CONTROL MECHANISMS

Most of the studies reviewed up to now considered the influence of individual control mechanisms. The study by Agrawal and Knoeber (1996) considered seven mechanisms: insider shareholdings, outside representation on the board, debt policy, activity in the corporate control market, institutional shareholdings, shareholdings of large blockholders, and the managerial labor market. Their sample was composed of the 400 largest firms for which they could obtain the data required to measure the seven mechanisms. Firm performance is measured by Tobin's q. Measuring the influence of each separately, the first four control mechanisms are statistically related to firm performance. Considering all of the mechanisms together but not within a simultaneous equation system, the influence of insider shareholdings drops out. Finally, when the interdependence among the mechanisms is accounted for in a simultaneous system estimation, only the negative effect on firm performance of outsiders on the board remains. Agrawal and Knoeber concluded that the control mechanisms are chosen optimally except for the use of outsiders on boards. Most other studies find a positive benefit from the use of outside directors.

PROXY CONTESTS

Proxy contests represent another corporate control mechanism. Proxy contests are attempts by dissident groups of shareholders to obtain board representation. Even though technically most contests are unsuccessful to the extent that the dissident group fails to win a majority on the board of directors, proxy contests can and do have significant effects on target firm shareholder wealth regardless of outcome. Some have argued that a better measure of success is whether the dissident group gains at least two members on the board of directors. "We want one person to propose a motion and a second person to second it. Then discussion of the motion will be in the minutes of the board meeting. In this way, we can monitor the majority group and record our views on important policy issues." This quote summarizes the view we have encountered in our experience with proxy contests.

A major change occurred in October 1992, when the SEC adopted proxy reform rules. Under the old rules, any shareholder who wanted to communicate with more than 10 other shareholders was required to submit the comments for SEC approval prior to circulation. The new rules ease requirements for communications among shareholders not seeking control of the company.

Studies of proxy contests explain the shareholder wealth effects that take place in terms of the disciplinary value of proxy contests in the managerial labor market, the relationship between proxy contests and other forms of takeover activity, and the value of the vote, which takes on greater importance during a proxy contest. The study by Pound (1988) empirically identified the sources of inefficiency of the present system of proxy contests.

Wealth Effects—Early Studies

Dodd and Warner (DW) (1983) examined 96 proxy contests for board seats on NYSE- or AMEX-listed firms over the period 1962 to 1978. They considered several hypotheses to explain why target shareholder returns were positive and significant on average (6.2% over the period from 39 days before the contest announcement through the contest outcome) in spite of the fact that dissidents won a majority on the board in only one-fifth of the cases studied.

First, even minority board representation allows the dissident group to have a positive impact on corporate policy leading to a permanent share price revaluation.

In cases where no board seats change hands, the fact of the challenge itself may cause incumbent management to implement changes in policy that benefit shareholders (Bradley, Desai, and Kim, 1983; the "kick-in-the-pants" hypothesis). Scenarios that hypothesize stock price declines when proxy contests fail were not supported. These hypotheses emphasize the direct costs (in terms of corporate resources) of defending against the dissident group and ignore the possibilities for increased efficiency that may be exposed during the course of the contest. Abnormal returns at the contest outcome announcement were in fact negative for contests in which the dissidents failed to win any seats at all; however, the negative return was only -1.4%, not large enough to offset earlier gains and not significant.

The mechanics of waging a proxy contest almost guarantee that there will be leakage of information about dissident activity well before the proxy contest announcement in the *Wall Street Journal*. This is confirmed by significant abnormal returns of 11.9% over the period starting 60 days before the announcement through the announcement itself. These returns are not attributable to merger activity, because the results are similar whether the dissident group included another firm or not; the sample did not exhibit unexpectedly higher earnings in the preannouncement period. Thus, the positive returns seem attributable to the changes that may be stimulated by the proxy contest itself.

A later study by DeAngelo and DeAngelo (1989) of 60 proxy contests from 1978 to 1985 corroborated many of Dodd and Warner's (1983) results. They found significant positive abnormal returns of 6.02% from 40 days before the contest through the outcome announcement and significant returns of 18.76% in the 40 days preceding any public indication of dissident activity. As in the earlier study, the gains (particularly those in the precontest period) were not dependent on contest outcome. Like DW they found negative returns at the contest outcome when the dissidents failed to win any seats on the board. These negative returns were larger than in the DW study: -5.45% over the two-day outcome announcement period. However, most of these negative returns were shown to result from the means by which the dissidents were defeated. Where the incumbents prevailed in a shareholder vote, the negative return was only -1.73% and not significant; but where the dissidents were defeated by other means, the return was a -7.19% (significant). The other means included the expenditure of corporate assets to buy off the dissidents, a white knight acquisition of the target, or court approval of the validity of the incumbent's defense in the face of which the dissidents withdrew. This result appeared to imply that when the incumbent management was securely entrenched or the probability of future control contests was reduced, the value of vote and/or the expected takeover premium capitalized in the share price declined.

As in the prior study, the dissidents were successful in only about one-third of the proxy contests. However, DeAngelo and DeAngelo (1989) go on to examine events in the target firm for three years after the contest. It was found that by the end of three years fewer than 20% of the target firms remained as independent publicly held corporations under the same management as before the contest. For example, in 20 of the 39 firms in which dissidents failed to win a majority, there were 38 resignations of the CEO, president, or chairman of the board over the next three years. These resignations were clearly linked to the proxy contest either explicitly in the financial press or by the fact that the vacancy was filled by a member of the dissident group. The 60-firm sample included 15 cases where sale or liquidation of the firm in the three-year period following the contest was directly linked to the dissident activity.

In fact, DeAngelo and DeAngelo (1989) concluded that most of the gains to proxy contest activity are closely related to merger and acquisitions activity. The initial gains in the precontest period (approximately 20%) are attributed to the increased likelihood that the firm will eventually be sold at a premium at some time following the proxy contest. To support this conclusion, they divided their sample into two groups: those that were eventually sold or liquidated and those that were not. For the "sold" subsample, abnormal returns over the full period of dissident activity were a significant 15.16%; for the "unsold" group, the gain was a less significant 2.90%. The fact that the initial runup was similar for the two groups simply indicates that the market revises its opinion of the likelihood of a sale as more information becomes available. To the extent that proxy contests are indeed linked to takeover activity, the goal seems to be to get some representation on the board to persuade the rest of the board to sell or liquidate.

Sridharan and Reinganum (1995) sought to explain why tender offers occur in some cases and proxy contests take place in others. Their sample was composed of 79 hostile tender offers and 38 proxy contests. A proxy fight is more likely to take place when target firm performance is relatively poor, measured by return on assets and stock market returns. Managerial inefficiency leads to a proxy contest; failure to pursue new and profitable investment opportunities leads to a tender offer.

When shareholdings of management are high, they are more likely to be able to block a tender offer so dissidents will engage in a proxy contest. Sridharan and Reinganum found that tender offer targets tend to be less leveraged than firms experiencing proxy fights. The reason they give is that the lower the leverage the greater is the supply of shares available for purchase in a tender offer.

Wealth Effects—Later Studies

Borstadt and Zwirlein (1992) sampled 142 NYSE and AMEX firms that were involved in proxy contests waged between July 1, 1962 and January 31, 1986. The sample was further divided into full-control and partial-control subsamples. The dissident success rate was 42% for the full-control subsample and 60% for the partial-control subsample. The turnover rate of top management after the proxy contest was higher than average. On average, shareholders realized a positive abnormal return of 11.4% (significant) during the proxy contest period, defined as 60 days prior to the announcement of the contest through the contest resolution announcement.

Ikenberry and Lakonishok (IL) (1993) tested the hypothesis that the proxy contest, in challenging the management's slate for the board of directors, represents a referendum on management's ability to operate the firm and can act as a disciplinary mechanism. Their sample of 97 election contests during the period 1968 to 1987 came from the *Weekly Bulletin* for NYSE and AMEX firms. Firms not followed by Compustat or cases where there was an earlier election contest within the 60 months prior were eliminated. For the period from month -60 to month -5 relative to the announcement of the contest, the CAR of proxy contest targets was -34.4% (significant). Compared with growth in operating income before depreciation, contest targets underperformed control firms by 39.3% (significant) over the five-year period prior to the announcement of election contests. Thus, proxy contests appear to be stimulated by poor performance.

When the incumbent board members retained all their seats, the CAR was not significantly different from zero for the five-year period following the contest. In cases where dissidents gained at least one board seat, the CAR from month +3 to +24 was −32.4% (significant). The negative returns over the same time period were more severe in cases where the dissidents gained control of the board, −48% (significant). When dissidents gained control of the board, IL speculate that the negative stock price behavior might be explained by either overoptimistic expectations of improved performance or the dissidents' discovery that the company faced more serious problems than anticipated.

The IL findings of abnormal negative returns are different from those of the earlier studies, which found predominantly positive returns associated with proxy contests. Mulherin and Poulsen (MP) (1998) reexamined the shareholder wealth implications in proxy contests. They used a sample of 270 proxy contests for board seats during the period 1979 to 1994. For the event study analysis, day 0 was the date of the contest initiation and day R was the contest resolution date. The event windows analyzed were the initiation period [−20, +5], the postinitiation period [+6, R], the full-contest period [−20, R], and the postcontest period of one year following the contest resolution. For the full sample, using continuous compounding, the CAR in the initiation period was a significant 8.04%; in the postinitiation period it was an insignificant −2.82%; in the full-contest period it was a significant 5.35%; in the postcontest period it was a borderline significant −3.43%. Using simple compounding, the results followed the same patterns except that the postcontest CAR was not significant.

The results contradicted the substantial decline in the postcontest period reported by Ikenberry and Lakonishok (IL) (1993). Further analysis showed that performance measurements were sensitive to the survivorship bias arising from minimum data requirements. IL's requirement that a firm be listed on Compustat in the period around the contest led to a downward bias in estimated wealth changes. This occurred because the Compustat requirement excluded a sizeable number of firms that were acquired in the period surrounding the proxy contest.

The full sample results suggested that shareholders benefited from proxy contests during the full-contest period. MP next looked for the sources of the value created. Subsamples were analyzed according to whether the firm was a takeover target, whether dissidents attained seats, and whether the senior officers of the target firm were replaced.

There were 116 proxy contests accompanied by a takeover bid. The acquisition attempts were successful in 63 of these cases. Both at the contest initiation and in the postinitiation period, the CARs were positive and significant, resulting in an abnormal return of 20.1% for the full-contest period. In the year following the resolution of the contest, the CAR was 12.4%, borderline significant. For the remaining 53 firms for which the acquisition attempt was unsuccessful, the CAR for the full-contest period was a negative and not significant return of −4.88%, followed by a further significant decline of −23.7% in the year following the contest resolution.

For the 154 contests not accompanied by a takeover bid, the full-contest period had a positive and significant CAR of 3.27%. In the year following the contest, the CAR was effectively zero. The subsample of 154 contests not accompanied by takeovers was further analyzed for possible interactions between whether dissidents attained seats and whether the senior officer was replaced within three years of the contest. Of the 85 contests in which dissidents won seats, management was replaced in 68 cases. The contests in which management were replaced experienced an increase in shareholder wealth, a significant 9.56% for the full-contest period but an insignificant 2.55% return in the postcontest period. The remaining 17 firms that retained the incumbent management suffered a significant decline, -13.8% in the full-contest period and -18.5% in the postcontest period. In both cases, the CAR during the initiation period was positive and significant. Investors anticipated that contests in which dissidents won would be followed by management changes. However, if the expectation was not fulfilled, investors revised the firm value downward.

In the 69 cases in which dissidents did not win seats, 25 firms replaced their senior management and experienced an average CAR increase of 5.07% in the full-contest period, not significant, and a significant positive 31.3% in the postcontest period. This postcontest wealth gain was significantly greater than the decline in wealth of -12.7% for the 44 firms that did not replace their senior management. These results demonstrated that management turnover should be an integral part of the interpretation of the changes in shareholders' wealth in the postcontest period. Ikenberry and Lakonishok reported a wealth decline whether dissidents attained seats or not, but they failed to observe that wealth changes following proxy contests were positive when there was management turnover.

THE M&A MARKET FOR CONTROL

In one sense, proxy contests, discussed in the preceding section, represent a form of external control if the dissidents are from outside the company, which is usually the case. The most widely recognized form of external pressure is the market for corporate control. Several empirical measures demonstrate that M&As do indeed impact business firms. One good metric is provided by Mitchell and Mulherin (1996). They analyzed the 1,064 firms listed in the *Value Line Investment Survey* at year-end 1981. By 1989, 57% of these firms either had been a takeover target or had engaged in substantial defensive asset restructuring. That more than half of the universe of firms with a relatively wide investment following were subjected to the pressures of the M&A market is a measure only of the direct impacts. Surely a high percentage of the remaining 43% had to be aware that poor performance would subject them to a possible takeover. Also, superior performance might enable such firms to augment their resources by taking over firms whose performance could be improved.

Furthermore, the proprietary database of Robert Comment with information about all M&As for NYSE- and AMEX-listed target firms from 1975 to 1991 covered 1,814 companies, a substantial number (Schwert, 1996). The total number of M&A announcements tracked by the annual *Mergerstat Review* was 3,510 in 1995, jumping to 9,278 in 1999. Another metric is MBO activity, which represented 11.4% of the main sample of 1,523 firms in the Schwert study.

Thus, the M&A market is clearly a major source of external control mechanisms on business firms. However, the need to resort to the M&A market is an indication of at least some degree of failure in internal control mechanisms.

ALTERNATIVE GOVERNANCE SYSTEMS

A number of studies provide background for assessment of alternative governance systems (Kaplan, 1994; *The Economist,* 1994; Shleifer and Vishny, 1997; Franks and Mayer, 1998; Bruner, 1999; La Porta, Lopez-de-Silanes, and Shleifer, 1999; Logue and Seward, 1999). In the United States, managerial stock ownership has increased over time (Holderness, Kroszner, and Sheehan, 1999). Both large shareholders and small are protected by a well-developed system of laws, court decisions, and financial markets that facilitate efficient transactions in securities, protect minority rights, and enable shareholders to sue directors for violations of their fiduciary responsibilities. Companies are quickly penalized for poor performance and rewarded for excellence in stock market price changes. Although a vigilant stock market facilitates control, it may also have the disadvantage of causing managers to emphasize short-term results rather than longer term strategies. The bankruptcy laws in the United States are highly protective of managers. After entering into bankruptcy, management (the debtor) remains in possession of the company (debtor in possession; DIP). Provision is made for an automatic stay, which provides that no payment of interest or payment on principal need be made until the reorganization is complete. Interest continues to accrue only on fully secured debt. Financing after filing is facilitated, because it has priority status (DIP financing).

Shleifer and Vishny (SV) (1997) observe that in Germany creditors have stronger rights than in the United States, but shareholder rights are weaker. Large shareholders, often the major banks, exercise control over the large firms as permanent investors. SV observe that small investors had virtually no participation in the stock market (p. 770).

Japan is described as falling between the United States and Germany in the degree of protection to shareholder and creditor rights. SV observe that the powerful banks and long-term shareholders in Japan are not as powerful as those in Germany. Anecdotal evidence questions this conclusion. Japanese companies financed in the United States during the earlier periods of time when Japan was supposed to have lower financing costs than in the rest of the world. The reasons given were that the Japanese firms were seeking to avoid the strong controls that came with financing from Japanese banks. In Japan, industrial firms own shares in one another and groups of firms become tied together by cross-shareholdings (Kaplan, 1994). The Japanese governance system has facilitated participation by small investors in the stock market.

The three countries described above have in common a well-articulated set of rules of the game that provide effective legal protection for "at least some types of investors" (SV, p. 770). Studies of Italy indicate that firms are predominantly family-controlled, have difficulty raising outside funds, and finance their investment internally. Most bank financing is state bank financing of state controlled firms.

Limited evidence suggests that most of the rest of the world is similar to Italy. At least in part this would reflect the absence of a system of laws, regulations, and courts to protect minority investors and creditors. The rules of the game are deficient. Large firms are mostly family-controlled, rely on internal financing, or obtain help from government-controlled banks.

Clearly, the United States, Germany, and Japan benefit from having well-formulated rules of the game that are enforced by the courts and regulatory agencies. But Germany and Japan differ in giving banks and financial groups a stronger role. In theory, the large ownership position of owners-lenders with business expertise and high financial stakes will lead to effective monitoring of business performance. In a survey of corporate governance, *The Economist* (January 29, 1994) presented material that raised doubts about the effectiveness of the German and Japanese corporate governance models. The article cited studies that indicate that the banks have not monitored closely the firms to which they have provided both equity and debt capital. These studies suggest that the banks became active only when their client firms experience substantial difficulties.

The Economist also argued that German and Japanese governance appeared to be good only because the earlier economic environment was so favorable. With growing economies, favorable productivity improvements, high employment, and rising exports, stock prices were moving continuously upward. In favorable economies, commitments could be made to provide employees with lifetime employment. Cross-holdings of common stocks lead to an increase in trust among partners. The system works well if all parties have the same long-term interests and goals.

The Economist, in completing its survey of corporate governance, concluded that the increased activism of pension funds in the United States helped make that system work better. An active market for corporate control in the form of mergers and takeovers provides a marketplace test of performance. The strength of the American and British systems of shareholder control is that they are ultimately market-based. In the long run, this is held to be superior to the direct supervision and judgments of the large banking corporations, which have their own governance problems.

SUMMARY

Because there is a substantial body of literature on corporate governance, this summary provides a logical framework for the subject. Traditionally, corporate governance focused on conflicts of interest between managers and owners. It is increasingly recognized that conflicts of interest occur across a wide range of stakeholders: owners with a small number of shares, owners with large ownership positions, creditors, managers, employees, consumers, government, and society as a whole. Most of the literature discusses problems of the separation of ownership and control. Historically, in the United States, the main form of corporate ownership was small ownership stakes diffused among a large number of individual investors. The advantages were limited liability, broad diversification of investments, small monitoring requirements, and easy

purchase or sale of ownership rights. But increasingly, several forms of agency problems became recognized. Managements may act in their own self-interest.

Compensation arrangements and competition among managers provide internal control mechanisms. In addition, poor stock price performance is likely to cause changes in management. In theory, the board of directors monitors management. In practice, boards tend to be dominated by management insiders. The use of outside directors provides for greater independence but does not solve the problem of effective monitoring of managers. The increased activism of large institutional holders of equity such as pension funds has demonstrated increased effectiveness in monitoring corporate managers and their performance.

Increased stock ownership by management has been proposed as a method of reducing conflicts of interest between owners and managers. Some studies suggest that performance improves with rising management ownership share in the 0 to 5% range, deteriorates in the 5% to 25% range, and improves above 25%. Large block purchases have had positive event returns. When the shareholdings of a group are large, monitoring is increased. In addition, large blockholders are more likely to monitor management.

The holding of voting stock that achieves control of the firm commands a price premium. Because control is valued by the capital markets, dual-class recapitalizations are employed by majority owners to further consolidate their control position. Larger managerial holdings can have incentive effects. The voting rights premium may also result from the possibility that in a takeover superior voting rights will receive a higher price.

Proxy contests represent another method of improving managerial performance. In most studies, the initiation of proxy contests is associated with substantial positive event returns. The challenge of a proxy contest may be sufficient to cause incumbent management to improve policies. Minority board representation enables dissidents to have a continuing impact. A strong link has been found between proxy contests and subsequent takeover activity. The positive event returns associated with proxy contests reflect the increased likelihood of improved performance or the eventual sale of the firm at a premium. Mergers and acquisitions represent an important external control mechanism.

Executive compensation plans have been suggested as another mechanism for influencing managerial performance. The elasticity of management compensation in relation to changes in the value of the firm is apparently small. But the elasticity of wealth changes of managers to changes in the value of the firm may be substantial. The increased ownership share of managers and LBOs in the early 1980s demonstrated strong motivational influences. Proposals have been made to improve the influence of executive pay on corporate performance. One is to base bonus, stock, and option plans on benchmark stock price changes. The benchmarks can be based on the stock price performance of close competitors, wider peer groups, broader stock market indexes, or other criteria. Another proposal is to adopt policies that result in substantial stock holdings by executives so that they think more like owners. Also, the bonus and stock ownership arrangements with executives should cause their wealth positions to increase with good performance and to deteriorate with poor performance. These arrangements should be appropriately benchmarked and related to the long-range planning processes of the firm.

Finally, it has been proposed that the alternative governance systems of Germany and Japan provide a better model for improving corporate governance. In these alternative governance systems, commercial banks hold large ownership shares in industrial firms and are major lenders as well. Also, groups of firms become tied together by cross-shareholdings. But some observers state that the alternative governance systems worked well when the general macroeconomic framework was favorable. With reduced economic growth, tensions and conflicts of interest have also arisen in the German and Japanese governance systems. Furthermore, even under favorable macroeconomic conditions, there were strains in the system. Monitoring by the large banking corporations with their own governance problems often was not effective. The strength of the American and British systems of shareholder control is that they are ultimately market-based.

QUESTIONS

20.1 What was the role of enterprise governance in the history of the Russian economy?

20.2 What complaints have been made about corporate governance systems in the United States?

20.3 What are the effects of the size of the fraction of equity share ownership by top management on:
   a. q-ratio?
   b. Agency problems?
   c. Probability of a hostile bid?
   d. Level of premium required for a takeover bid to succeed?

20.4 List five of the *Business Week* criteria for evaluating effective governance by boards of directors.

20.5 What were the findings by Millstein and MacAvoy?

20.6 Discuss the issue of the elasticity of executive pay in relation to changes in firm value versus the impact of incentive executive compensation on the wealth position of executives.

20.7 What is the potential role of the stock market and security price movements in corporate governance?

20.8 Evaluate the potential of activist pension funds for improving corporate governance.

20.9 What effect do proxy contests have on shareholder returns?

20.10 Compare the U.S., Germany, and Japan with respect to protection of shareholder rights and creditor rights.

20.11 What criticisms have been made of corporate governance in Germany?

Case 20.1 Chrysler Corporation Versus Tracinda Corporation— A Struggle for Control

The control struggle between Kirk Kerkorian and the Chrysler Corporation continued over the period from early April 1995 until early February 1996, when a compromise agreement was reached. The battles and skirmishes reflected a number of twists and turns in strategies that involved many episodes. Here is a time line of events:

4/11/95   Robert Eaton, chairman of Chrysler, received a phone call from Kirk Kerkorian that he and former Chrysler chairman Lee

Iacocca were planning a takeover bid of $55 a share totaling $22.8 billion. The stock reaction was a 24% increase, closing at $48.75 on the announcement date, 4/12/95. Kerkorian charged that Chrysler was too conservative in holding cash reserves of $7.5 billion.

4/24/95   Chrysler formally rejected the Kerkorian bid, saying it did not want to gamble with Chrysler's future.

5/31/95   Kerkorian withdrew his bid due to lack of financing but stated that he would continue his efforts to help Chrysler management improve the value of its common stock. Kerkorian hired the investment banking firm Wasserstein Perella & Co. to develop a full range of possible options.

6/26/95 Kerkorian announced his intention to buy 14 million Chrysler shares at $50 each to raise his stake to 13.6%.

7/1/95 Chrysler's board adopted golden parachutes for its 30 highest ranking officers.

7/15/95 Chrysler moved to prevent Iacocca from exercising his Chrysler stock options because he had violated the prohibition from taking actions "which adversely affect the Chrysler Corporation."

8/25/95 Kerkorian achieved his goal of increasing his ownership of Chrysler to 13.6%.

9/5/95 Kerkorian announced that he had hired Jerome York, the CFO of IBM and before that the treasurer of Chrysler, to be his main strategist.

9/7/95 Chrysler's board announced that it would double its share repurchase program to $2 billion.

9/10/95 York stated that Tracinda Corporation was considering a proxy fight. He criticized Chrysler's management for holding too much cash, stating that $4.5 billion would be an ample reserve rather than $7.5 billion. He also stated that $2.5 billion of Chrysler assets were "non-core."

9/20/95 Tracinda hired Ralph Whitworth, widely regarded as an expert on corporate governance and an influential shareholder activist.

10/1/95 Chrysler began a publicity campaign against York's criticisms and called attention to Chrysler's earnings and product successes.

10/25/95 York met with Chrysler's CFO and general counsel, requesting a seat on the board for himself and the addition of two independent members.

11/6/95 Iacocca filed a suit over his Chrysler stock options. Tracinda agreed to cover up to $2 million of his legal fees and make up the difference between $42 million and his award.

11/20/95 Tracinda announced that it would file preliminary proxy-soliciting materials with the SEC including a proposal to replace board member Joseph Antonini with Jerome York.

11/23/95 Antonini announced that he would resign from the Chrysler board.

12/7/95 Chrysler announced a 20% dividend increase, its fifth dividend increase in two years.

1/19/96 Chrysler announced strong fourth quarter earnings.

2/7/96 Chrysler announced that it would recommend for membership on its board John R. Neff, a respected asset manager who had retired in the previous year as manager of the $4.5 billion Windsor Fund.

2/8/96 The two sides agreed to a five-year truce in the form of a five-year standstill agreement. Kerkorian would reserve a board seat to be occupied by James Aljian, a Tracinda executive in return for agreeing not to launch a proxy fight or to increase his shareholdings during the five-year period. Within 30 days, Kerkorian would also terminate his arrangements with Wasserstein Perella, with Ralph Whitworth, and with D. F. King & Co., a proxy-soliciting firm. Chrysler would add another $1 billion to its share repurchase program and would continue its efforts to sell its nonautomotive units. Chrysler would increase the accountability of its board by switching from cash to stock compensation. In exchange for Iacocca's agreement to terminate

his position as consultant to Tracinda and to refrain from publicly criticizing Chrysler for the five-year period, Iacocca's stock option lawsuits would be settled; Chrysler would pay Iacocca $21 million, and Tracinda would contribute $32 million.

5/17/96 Chrysler announced a dividend increase of 17% and a 2-for-1 stock split. The stock closed up $2.25 to $67.125 compared with its price in the low 40s in May 1995, about one year earlier.

QUESTION

1. What are the lessons from the Kerkorian–Chrysler case?

REFERENCES

Agrawal, Anup, and Charles R. Knoeber, "Firm Performance and Mechanisms to Control Agency Problems between Managers and Shareholders," *Journal of Financial and Quantitative Analysis*, 31, September 1996, pp. 377–397.

Alchian, A. A., "Property Rights, Specialization and the Firm," chapter 1 in J. Fred Weston and Michael E. Granfield, eds., *Corporate Enterprise in a New Environment*, New York: KCG Productions, Inc., 1982, pp. 11–36.

———, and S. Woodward, "The Firm Is Dead: Long Live the Firm: A Review of Oliver E. Williamson's *The Economic Institutions of Capitalism*," *Journal of Economic Literature*, 26, March 1988, pp. 65–79.

Amihud, Yakov, B. Lev, and N. G. Travlos, "Corporate Control & the Choice of Investment Financing," *Journal of Finance*, 45, June 1990, pp. 603–616.

Bagnani, Elizabeth Strock, Nikolaos T. Milonas, Anthony Saunders, and Nickolaos G. Travlos, "Managers, Owners, and the Pricing of Risky Debt: An Empirical Analysis," *Journal of Finance*, 49, June 1994, pp. 453–477.

Barclay, Michael J., and C. G. Holderness, "Negotiated Block Trades and Corporate Control," *Journal of Finance*, 46, July 1991, pp. 861–878.

Berle, A. A., Jr., and G. C. Means, *The Modern Corporation and Private Property*, New York: Macmillan, 1932.

Borokhovich, Kenneth A., Robert Parrino, and Teresa Trapani, "Outside Directors and CEO Selection," *Journal of Financial and Quantitative Analysis*, 31, September 1996, pp. 337–355.

Borstadt, Lisa F., and T. J. Zwirlein, "The Efficient Monitoring of Proxy Contests: An Empirical Analysis of Post-Contest Control Changes and Firm Performance," *Journal of*

Financial Management, 21, Autumn 1992, pp. 22–34.

Bradley, Michael, Anand Desai, and E. Han Kim, "The Rationale Behind Interfirm Tender Offers: Information or Synergy," *Journal of Financial Economics*, 11, April 1983, pp. 183–206.

Bristow, Duke K., "Time Series and Cross Sectional Properties of Management Ownership and Valuation," manuscript, May 16, 1998.

Bruner, Robert F., "An Analysis of Value Destruction and Recovery in the Alliance and Proposed Merger of Volvo and Renault," *Journal of Financial Economics*, 51, 1999, pp. 125–166.

Byrne, John, "The Best & Worst Boards," *Business Week*, November 25, 1996, pp. 82–106.

Campbell, C. J., S. L. Gillan, and C. M. Niden, "Current Perspectives on Shareholder Proposals: Lessons from the 1997 Proxy Season," *Financial Management*, 28, Spring 1999, pp. 89–98.

Carleton, Willard T., James M. Nelson, and Michael S. Weisbach, "The Influence of Institutions on Corporate Governance through Private Negotiations: Evidence from TIAA-CREF," *Journal of Finance*, 53, August 1998, pp. 1335–1362.

Chew, Donald H., ed., *Studies in International Corporate Finance and Governance Systems*, New York: Oxford University Press, 1997.

Cho, Myeong-Hyeon, "Ownership Structure, Investment, and the Corporate Value: An Empirical Analysis," *Journal of Financial Economics*, 47, 1998, pp. 103–121.

Copeland, Thomas E., and J. Fred Weston, *Financial Theory and Corporate Policy*, Reading MA: Addison-Wesley Publishing Company, 1988.

Core, J. E., R. W. Holthausen, and D. F. Larcker, "Corporate Governance, Chief Executive Officer Compensation, and Firm Performance," *Journal of Financial Economics*, 51, 1999, pp. 371–406.

Cornell, Bradford, and Alan Shapiro, "Corporate Stakeholders and Corporate Finance," *Financial Management*, 16, Spring 1987, pp. 5–14.

Coughlan, A. T., and R. M. Schmidt, "Executive Compensation, Managerial Turnover, and Firm Performance: An Empirical Investigation," *Journal of Accounting and Economics*, 7, 1985, pp. 43–66.

DeAngelo, Harry, and Linda DeAngelo, "Proxy Contests and the Governance of Publicly Held Corporations," *Journal of Financial Economics*, 23, 1989, pp. 29–60.

Demsetz, H., and K. Lehn, "The Structure of Corporate Ownership," *Journal of Political Economy*, 93, 1985, pp. 1155–1177.

Denis, David J., and Diane K. Denis, "Performance Changes Following Top Management Dismissals," *Journal of Finance*, 50, September 1995, pp. 1029–1057.

Dodd, Peter, and Jerold B. Warner, "On Corporate Governance: A Study of Proxy Contests," *Journal of Financial Economics*, 11, 1983, pp. 401–438.

The Economist, "A Survey of Corporate Governance," January 29, 1994, special supplement, pp. 1–18.

Fama, E. F., "Agency Problems and the Theory of the Firm," *Journal of Political Economy*, 88, 1980, pp. 288–307.

———, and Michael C. Jensen, "Separation of Ownership and Control," *The Journal of Law and Economics*, 26, June 1983a, pp. 301–325.

———, "Agency Problems and Residual Claims," *The Journal of Law and Economics*, 26, June 1983b, pp. 327–349.

Franks, J., and C. Mayer, "Bank Control, Takeovers and Corporate Governance in Germany," *Journal of Banking & Finance*, 22, 1998, pp. 1385–1403.

Haubrich, Joseph G., "Risk Aversion, Performance Pay, and the Principal-Agent Problem," *Journal of Political Economy*, 102, April 1994, pp. 258–276.

Holderness, C. G., and D. P. Sheehan, "The Role of Majority Shareholders in Publicly Held Corporations: An Exploratory Analysis," *Journal of Financial Economics*, 20, 1988, pp. 317–346.

Holderness, Clifford G., Randall S. Kroszner, and Dennis P. Sheehan, "Were the Good Old Days That Good? Changes in Managerial Stock Ownership Since the Great Depression," *Journal of Finance*, 54, April 1999, pp. 435–469.

Ikenberry, David, and Josef Lakonishok, "Corporate Governance Through the Proxy Contest: Evidence and Implications," *Journal of Business*, 66, July 1993, pp. 405–435.

Jensen, Michael C., "Agency Costs of Free Cash Flow, Corporate Finance, and Takeovers," *American Economic Review*, Papers and Proceedings, 76, May 1986, pp. 323–329.

———, and W. H. Meckling, "Theory of the Firm: Managerial Behavior, Agency Costs and Ownership Structure," *Journal of Financial Economics*, 3, 1976, pp. 305–360.

Jensen, Michael C., and Kevin J. Murphy, "Performance Pay and Top-Management Incentives," *Journal of Political Economy*, 98, April 1990, pp. 225–264.

Jensen, Michael C., and Richard S. Ruback, eds., "Symposium on the Structure and Governance of Enterprise," *Journal of Financial Economics*, 27, Part I, September 1990; Part II, October 1990.

Jensen, Michael C., and Jerold B. Warner, eds., "Symposium on the Distribution of Power Among Corporate Managers, Shareholders, and Directors," *Journal of Financial Economics*, 20, January/March 1988.

John, Kose, and Lemma W. Senbet, "Corporate Governance and Board Effectiveness," *Journal of Banking & Finance*, 22, 1998, pp. 371–403.

Kaplan, Steven N., "Top Executive Rewards and Firm Performance: A Comparison of Japan and the United States," *Journal of Political Economy*, 102, June 1994, pp. 510–546.

La Porta, Rafael, Florencio Lopez-de-Silanes, and Andrei Shleifer, "Corporate Ownership Around the World," *Journal of Finance*, 54, April 1999, pp. 471–517.

Logue, Dennis E., and James K. Seward, "Anatomy of a Governance Transformation: The Case of Daimler-Benz," *Journal of Law & Contemporary Problems*, 87 (Summer 1999) pp. 87–111.

McConnell, John J., and Henri Servaes, "Additional Evidence on Equity Ownership and Corporate Value," *Journal of Financial Economics*, 27, 1990, pp. 595–612.

Millstein, Ira M., and Paul W. MacAvoy, "The Active Board of Directors and Performance of the Large Publicly Traded Corporation," *Columbia Law Review*, 98(5), June 1998, pp. 1283–1321.

Mitchell, Mark L., and J. Harold Mulherin, "The Impact of Industry Shocks on Takeover and Restructuring Activity," *Journal of Financial Economics*, 41, 1996, pp. 193–229.

Monks, Robert A. G., and Nell Minow, *Corporate Governance*, Cambridge, MA: Blackwell Publishers, 1995.

Morck, R., A. Shleifer, and R. W. Vishny, "Management Ownership and Market Valuation: An Empirical Analysis," *Journal of Financial Economics*, 20, 1988, pp. 293–315.

———, "Alternative Mechanisms for Corporate Control," *American Economic Review*, 79, 1989, pp. 842–852.

Mulherin, J. H., and A. B. Poulsen, "Proxy Contests and Corporate Change: Implications for Shareholder Wealth," *Journal of Financial Economics*, 47, 1998, pp. 279–313.

Pound, John, "Proxy Contests and the Efficiency of Shareholder Oversight," *Journal of Financial Economics*, 20, 1988, pp. 237–265.

Rappaport, Alfred, *Creating Shareholder Value*, New York: The Free Press, 1986.

Rosenstein, Stuart, and J. G. Wyatt, "Outside Directors, Board Independence, and Shareholder Wealth," *Journal of Financial Economics*, 26, 1990, pp. 175–191.

Safieddine, Assem, and Sheridan Titman, "Leverage and Corporate Performance: Evidence from Unsuccessful Takeovers," *Journal of Finance*, 54, April 1999, pp. 547–580.

Schwert, G. William, "Markup Pricing in Mergers and Acquisitions," *Journal of Financial Economics,* 41, 1996, pp. 153–192.

Scism, Leslie, "Labor Unions Increasingly Initiate Proxy Proposals," *The Wall Street Journal,* March 1, 1994, pp. C1, C16.

Seward, James K., and James P. Walsh, "The Governance and Control of Voluntary Corporate Spin-Offs," *Strategic Management Journal,* 17, 1996, pp. 25–39.

Shleifer, Andrei, and Robert W. Vishny, "A Survey of Corporate Governance," *Journal of Finance,* 52, June 1997, pp. 737–783.

Slovin, Myron B., and Marie E. Sushka, "Ownership Concentration, Corporate Control Activity, and Firm Value: Evidence from the Death of Inside Blockholders," *Journal of Finance,* 48, September 1993, pp. 1293–1321.

Sridharan, Uma V., and M. R. Reinganum, "Determinants of the Choice of the Hostile Takeover Mechanism: An Empirical Analysis of Tender Offers and Proxy Contests," *Financial Management,* 24, Spring 1995, pp. 57–67.

Strickland, Deon, Kenneth W. Wiles, and Marc Zenner, "A Requiem for the USA—Is Small Shareholder Monitoring Effective?" *Journal of Financial Economics,* 40, February 1996, pp. 319–338.

Stulz, R. M., "Managerial Control of Voting Rights: Financing Policies and the Market for Corporate Control," *Journal of Financial Economics,* 20, 1988, pp. 25–54.

Wahal, Sunil, "Pension Fund Activism and Firm Performance," *Journal of Financial and Quantitative Analysis,* 31, March 1996, pp. 1–23.

Warner, J. B., R. L. Watts, and K. H. Wruck, "Stock Prices and Top Management Changes," *Journal of Financial Economics,* 20, 1988, pp. 461–492.

Weisbach, M., "Outside Directors and CEO Turnover," *Journal of Financial Economics,* 20, 1988, pp. 431–460.

Williamson, Oliver E., "Strategy Research: Governance and Competence Perspectives," *Strategic Management Journal,* 20, 1999, pp. 1087–1108.

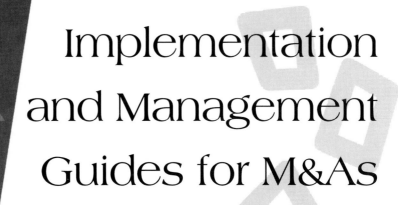

C h a p t e r   2 1

Implementation and Management Guides for M&As

Any organization or individual is subject to continual changes. The economic, political, cultural, and international environments are turbulent. The communications, computer, and Internet developments have changed the way business is conducted. Technologies and processes advance. Interactions with competitors, suppliers, customers, complementary firms, and a wide range of stakeholders must be adjusted. Sometimes the adjustments required are massive, sometimes they represent only fine-tuning. But continual adjustments are necessary for both organizations and individuals.

M&As IN A STRATEGIC LONG-RANGE PLANNING FRAMEWORK

Sometimes M&A activities can help a firm improve its capabilities and performance; but sometimes M&A activities would represent a diversion from the fundamental adjustments that must be made. M&A planning must fit into the framework of the firm's overall strategic planning processes (Chung and Weston, 1982; Weston, 1970).

Goals and Objectives

General goals may be formulated with respect to size, growth, stability, flexibility, and technological breadth. Size objectives are established in order to use effectively the fixed factors the firm owns or buys. Size objectives have also been expressed in terms of critical mass. Critical mass refers to the size a firm must achieve in order to attain cost levels that will enable it to operate profitably at market prices.

Growth objectives may be expressed in terms of sales, total assets, earnings per share, or the market price of the firm's stock. These are related to two valuation objectives. One is to attain a favorable price/earnings multiple for the firm's shares. A second is to increase the ratio of the market value of the firm's common stock to its book value.

Three major forms of instability can be distinguished. The first is exemplified by the defense market, which is subject to large, erratic fluctuations in its total size and abrupt shifts in individual programs. Another form of instability is the cyclical instability that characterizes producers of both industrial and consumer durable

625

goods. Other instabilities are major discontinuities of the type that have taken place in the computer and media industries.

The goal of flexibility refers to the firm's ability to adjust to a wide variety of changes. Such flexibility may require a breadth of research, manufacturing, or marketing capabilities. Of increased interest in recent years is technological breadth. With the faster pace of technological change in the U.S. economy, a firm may consider it important to possess capabilities in the rapidly advancing technologies.

Goals may be stated in general or specific terms, but both are subject to quantification. For example, growth objectives may be expressed in relationship to the growth of the economy or the firm's industry. Specific objectives may be expressed in terms of percentage of sales in specified types of markets. The quantification of goals facilitates comparisons of goals with forecasts of the prospects for the firm. If it is necessary for the firm to alter its product–market mix or range of capabilities to reduce or close the planning gap, a diversification strategy may be formulated.

Efforts to achieve multiple goals suggest a broader range of variables in the decision processes of the firm. Decisions involve trade-offs and judgments of the nature of future environments, the policies of other firms with respect to the dimensions described, and new missions, technologies, and capabilities. In short, to the requirements of operating efficiency and optimal output adjustments has been added the increased importance of the planning processes (Weston, 1972; Weston and Copeland, 1992).

The Role of Strategy

The literature views long-range planning and strategic planning as essentially synonymous (Steiner, 1979). The emphasis of strategic planning is on areas related to the firm's environments and constituencies, not just operating decisions (Summer, 1980). In our view, the modern literature on long-range planning indicates that long-range strategic planning involves at least the following elements:

1. Environmental reassessment for new technologies, new industries, and new forms of competitors.
2. A consideration of capabilities, missions, and environmental interactions from the standpoint of the firm and its divisions.
3. An emphasis on process rather than particular goals or objectives.
4. An emphasis on iteration and on an iterative feedback process as a methodology for dealing with ill-structured problems.
5. Recognition of the need for coordination and consistency in the resulting long-range planning processes with respect to individual divisions, product–market activities, and optimization from the standpoint of the firms as a whole.
6. Recognition of the need to relate effectively to the firm's changing environment and constituencies.
7. Integration of the planning process into a reward and penalty (incentive) system, taking a long-range perspective.

Earlier, the emphasis of long-range strategic planning was on doing something about the so-called gap. When it is necessary to take action to close a prospective gap between the firm's objectives and its potential based on its present capabilities, difficult choices must be made. For example, should the firm attempt to change its environment or capabilities? What would be the costs of such changes? What are the risks and unknowns? What are the rewards of success? What are the penalties of failure? Because the stakes are large, the iterative process is employed. A tentative decision is made. The process is repeated, perhaps from a different management function orientation, and at some point the total enterprise point of view is brought to bear on the problem. At some point, decisions are made and must involve entrepreneurial judgments.

Alternatively, the emphasis may be on broader orientations to the effective alignment of the firm with its environments and constituencies. Different approaches may be emphasized. One approach seeks to choose products related to the needs or missions of the customer that will provide large markets. A second approach focuses on technological bottlenecks or barriers, the solution of which may create new markets. A third strategy chooses to be at the frontiers of technological capabilities on the theory that attractive product fallout will result from such competence. A fourth approach emphasizes economic criteria including attractive growth prospects and manageable instability.

Other things being equal, a preferred strategy is to move into a diversification program from the base of existing capabilities or organizational strengths. Guidance may be obtained by answers to the following questions: Is there strength in the general management functions? Can the company provide staff expertise in the new areas? Does the firm's financial planning and control effectiveness have a broad carryover? Are there specific capabilities such as research, marketing, and manufacturing that the firm is seeking to spread over a wider area?

The firm should be clear on its strengths, its limitations, and the changing environments in which it operates. To remedy weaknesses, the firm should clearly define the specific new capabilities it is seeking to obtain. If the firm does not possess sufficient breadth of capability to use as a basis for moving into other areas, an alternative strategy may be employed, one that would establish a beachhead of capabilities in one or more selected areas. The firm is then in a position to develop concentrically from each of these nuclei.

Changing product requirements and changing market opportunities require new technologies and new combinations of technologies. To illustrate, the aircraft industry moved through stages in which the critical competence shifted from structures, to engine and other propulsion methods, to guidance, and finally to the interaction of structures, propulsion, and guidance as reflected in the concept of aerospace systems. Similarly, in office equipment, products have moved from manual operation to electromechanical, to electric, to electronic, and to the interactions of specialized units in systems. Electronics technology has moved from electron tubes to semiconductors to integrated circuitry, involving a fusion with chemistry and metallurgy. Competitive factors caused Intel to drop its production of memory chips and focus its resources on microprocessors. Telecommunications is shifting from hard wire to microwave, fiber optics, broadband, etc. Internet systems have created many new types of businesses and have impacted many "Old Economy" businesses.

In the consumer nondurable goods industries (such as food, cleaning products, and paper goods), product changes have characteristically been labeled product differentiation, with the unfavorable connotation that fundamental characteristics of products have not been altered. Yet even in these industries, fluctuations in consumer income patterns and tastes have created needs and opportunities for basic changes. For example, the need to understand the nature of the impact of foods on people has increased the requirements for competence in the chemical and biological sciences in the food industry.

The Role of Planning

A number of misconceptions are held with respect to the significance of planning in the firm. The misconceptions range between two extremes. One view holds that we have always planned, that planning is nothing new, as the practice antedates biblical times. This view misses the real significance of modern planning, however. Certainly business firms have been planning for decades, with accounting and financial budgeting activities representing one kind of planning. But the important developments that set the new managerial technology of planning apart from its predecessor activities are (1) coordinating research, sales, production, marketing, facilities, personnel, and financial plans, making them consistent with one another and resolving them into comprehensive planning for the enterprise as a whole; (2) a feedback system; and (3) integration with reward and penalty (incentive) systems. Some U.S. firms developed and practiced such integrated and coordinated planning by the 1920s, but the broad extension of the practice did not occur until after World War II, with substantial gaps still persisting in the understanding and implementation of effective planning among a large number of firms.

The other erroneous view about business planning holds that the heavy investments of capital by large corporations have led them to devise methods for controlling demand and that planning has replaced the market mechanism. Such a view led one author to sweeping generalizations, unsupported by systematic evidence, such as the following: "It is a feature of all planning that, unlike the market, it incorporates within itself no mechanism by which demand is accommodated to supply and the reverse" (Galbraith, 1967, p. 35). This statement represents a basic misconception. Those with experience with purposive organization planning processes recognize that the development of integrated planning is an effort to adapt more responsively to increasingly dynamic environments. Planning and management controls do not remove the uncertainty of market influences; rather, they seek to help the firm adjust more sensitively to change, to new threats, and to opportunities.

Managerial Capabilities Perspective

The capabilities concept encompasses important management technologies including planning, information sciences, computerization of information flows, Internet technologies, formal decision models, problem-solving methodologies, and behavioral sciences. Thus, managerial capabilities include competence in the general management functions of planning, organizing, directing, and controlling, as well as in the specific management functions of research, production, personnel, marketing, and finance. In addition, they include a range of technological capabilities. Another important dimension is coordinating and achieving an effective organization system, aided by real-time information systems.

The development of such a range of capabilities requires substantial investments in the training and experience of people. This includes investments required to hold organizations together during periods of depressed sales. Market demand and supply forces place a high value on executive talent and staff expertise. Their importance in the competitive performance of firms leads to new forms of fixed investment in managerial organizations. The effective utilization of augmented fixed factors leads to firms of larger size and increased diversification. Fixed factors include investments in plant and equipment or the development and holding of a group of scientists, engineers, and other highly trained and experienced executives. The pharmaceutical and Internet industries are clear examples.

The theory of the firm set forth by Coase (1937) predicts these developments. In explaining the role of firms in relation to markets, Coase identified two functions as determinants of the scope and size of firms. One was the relative efficiency of making transactions within the firm compared to conducting transactions in the external marketplace. The other was the effectiveness with which the elements of the firm were coordinated or managed. Coase described possible developments that would affect the size of firms compared to the relative scope of market transactions. Coase's model predicts that the broadening of capabilities encompassed by a firm and developments in managerial technology will result in an increase both in the absolute size of business firms and in the degree of their diversification with respect to capabilities, missions, and markets.

Potential competition has thus been enlarged. Industry boundaries defined by products or production methods become less meaningful than those defined by the ability to perform the critical functions for meeting customers' needs or missions. The ease of entry into industries may be affected because the critical factor for success in changing environments may be a range of technologies, experience developed in international markets, or even more general organizational performance capabilities.

Because of the critical role of managerial capabilities, some firms have emphasized hiring key executives rather than buying companies. This policy may have some validity on theoretical grounds, but it can also stir up ill will in the companies that have been raided. Companies that have succeeded in hiring new top executives with recognized capabilities have experienced an immediate increase in the market value of their common stock.

THE FOUNDATION FOR SOUND M&A DECISIONS

Sound M&A planning must take into account the many factors involved in M&A activities. Of central importance is the understanding that M&As should fit into the broad framework of the firm's overall strategic planning processes. The basic elements of strategic planning include an assessment of the firm's environment and an analysis of the firm's resources and capabilities as they relate to the environment. Goals are formulated, and adjustments, which may include mergers and acquisitions, are made to move the firm closer to these goals. The process is never complete but rather is performed iteratively as the firm's capabilities and environments change over time.

Increasingly, firms are defined less in terms of products and markets and more by their range of capabilities. This creates both opportunities and increasing competitive threats in a dynamic economy. M&As provide a means of preserving the organization capital of those firms that have been less able to adapt to change. They allow more successful firms to acquire needed capabilities faster and with less risk than developing them internally. Even pure conglomerate M&As that start with transferability of only generic management capabilities provide an avenue for the eventual development of increased skills in specific management functions such as production and marketing.

Systematic studies of M&As enable us to draw a number of conclusions:

1. Value is created by mergers, takeovers, and restructuring; acquired firm shareholders gain 25% to 35% of equity value, on average, and acquiring firm shareholders do not lose, on average.
2. M&A profitability and activity is positively correlated with GNP growth and favorable investment opportunities.
3. The use of M&As to achieve firm goals is affected by the availability of alternative investment opportunities.
4. Financial variables (including relative costs of capital, monetary stringency, and risk premiums) are more important for pure conglomerate mergers than for product or market extension mergers.
5. Leverage generally increases following M&As.

M&A decisions involve the use of principles from finance, business economics, and strategy in a dynamic framework. They recognize multiple dimensions of successful business operations. Operating activities must be efficient, but efficient operations must be a part of sound planning processes. The firm must continuously adjust to its changing economic, financial, political, and social environments. It must adjust to, and be proactive toward, potential competitors, suppliers, customers, and complementary firms. A successful firm must be a part of processes that involve many change forces, such as changes in technology, changes in production processes, changes in product quality, new products, and changes in the organization of industry. It is within this broad framework that M&A decisions are made and contribute to increases in the value of organizations.

A FRAMEWORK FOR EVALUATING M&AS

From the principles set forth in previous chapters, and from an analysis of many studies, we have developed a basis for a framework for evaluating mergers or acquisitions. As each merger or takeover is announced, we can evaluate it by reference to the following points:

1. Is total value increased by this merger or acquisition, or is total value decreased? This question uses the data on the initial market reaction to the transaction. Systematic research establishes that, on average, the initial market reaction is a good predictor of the subsequent performance of a merger or acquisition. By initial market reaction, we mean the change in market price per common share of the target company multiplied by the number of shares outstanding plus the change in market price of the acquiring company multiplied by the number of shares outstanding. This sum can be positive or negative. If the market prices of the common shares of acquiring and acquired companies all increase, total value will increase. The market value of the acquired company almost always increases because of the premium paid. So whether total value increases depends on by how much the market value per share of the acquiring firm increases or decreases.

2. If the total market value is increased by the transaction, determine the potential sources of the value increases. Revenues may be increased, asset management may be improved, and other efficiencies may achieve cost savings. Or revenues may be increased by improved marketing or by product improvements. In mergers among financial institutions, savings may be achieved by better utilization of large investments in computer systems. Or economies may be achieved by eliminating overlapping activities.

3. What are the obstacles that are likely to be encountered, and can they be managed effectively? Are the cultures of the two companies different? How will cultural differences be managed over time? Are the cultural differences respected? What plans have been made to adjust to or assimilate cultural differences?

4. Will the companies allocate the requisite management and resources for successful implementation of combining the companies to achieve the potentials for cost savings and/or revenue enhancement?

These are the central issues involved in evaluating an individual merger or acquisition.

Many other factors need to be taken into account also. Formulated as questions, some factors are

1. Is there an opportunity for a turnaround, and are the requisite managerial capabilities and incentive systems available to accomplish it?

2. Are operating synergies likely? What forms of economies of scale or scope are likely? Are there complementarities with respect to both general management functions such as innovation, planning, and control as well as the specific management functions such as production and marketing?

3. Will there be financial synergies? Will the future cash flows of the combined firms exhibit greater stability and growth than the historical patterns of the component firms? Will debt capacity for target or optimal capital structures provide savings in financing costs and taxes?

4. Are the planning, control, and operating systems to be employed applicable to each component or segment of the combined firm? Do product characteristics, production requirements, and marketing strategies require different system designs for different segments?

5. Can the incentive systems of the component firms be harmonized? Do the incentive systems need to be different for different segments of the combined firms? Can the incentive systems employed effectively relate to the history of each segment and relate to critical requirements for motivation in the individual segments?

6. Each segment of the combined firm has a history as a sociological organization. Each segment has created its own individual cultural personality. Will these cultural differences be respected as the component firms are joined? Can the organizational structure of the combined firm accommodate the different cultural histories and patterns? Will management assign the requisite executive capabilities and talent to work toward harmonizing the cultural differences over time, preserving and developing strengths and first accommodating, then muting disharmonies?

7. Will the new organization structures preserve the diverse strengths and organization systems required for product and process innovation in changing environments? Will executive capabilities be assigned to monitor the changing economic, financial, and competitive environments? Will the information, feedback, and adjustment processes in the firm produce an environment that creates and exploits new opportunities for superiorities and new growth opportunities?

8. Will the new organization assign the requisite executive capabilities for effective implementation of decisions on restructuring, combining, divesting, and reorganizing? A merger or takeover is not completed when all the legal steps have been completed. This represents only the first step of many that must be taken to complete the implementation of the decisions made. This applies equally to new programs and reorganizations that take place internally. A well-conceived organizational change including a takeover or merger can fail if not effectively implemented.

9. Have other approaches to value improvements been explored? Could the firm achieve corporate renewal from internal transformations? Have the critical needs of the firm been identified? Effective management is the key to organization success if the existing management team is not achieving results. Downsizing should start with the top management team. Does it contain deadwood? Does it have the right combination of diverse skills and personalities? Have the requisite steps for improvement been identified? Which of the existing executives should be replaced? Has the best qualified executive for each management design been identified? Have efforts been made to hire the best executive talent whether from our competitors or firms in related industries or simply the best in the business world? Have all potential cost-cutting efforts been pursued? Has the emphasis on efficiency and competence been extended through all levels of the organization? Can purchasing costs be reduced by changing the number and types of suppliers? Can inventory costs be reduced by innovations such as "just-in-time" inventory methods? Have effective quality control standards been worked out with suppliers? Can some inventories be obtained on a consignment basis? Can the number of items carried in stock be reduced by improved design and manufacturing processes? Could costs be significantly decreased by reducing the number and type of products without substantial loss of revenues? Have all sources of product definition and design been effectively explored? Has the firm optimized on its product family with respect to cost efficiency and market penetration? Have all types of outlays been evaluated with respect to their contributions to performance? Has this type of review included corporate jets, executive cars, club memberships, and subscriptions? Have consultant services contributed to a coherent long-term corporate strategy, and have they made contributions to improved performance? Would the strengthening of the management team make consultant services unnecessary?

10. Having considered all of the foregoing, will the premium paid for another firm or the costs involved in a restructuring or reorganization yield sufficient savings or future cash flow improvements to make these positive net present value investments? Will the net improvement in future cash flows be sufficient to yield positive returns from the investment outlays required at the applicable cost of capital?

These and other questions should be analyzed in evaluating a prospective investment program whether internal or external. They are applicable to restructuring, reorganizing, new product or investment programs, and to external mergers and takeovers. This checklist of questions reflects the core of the key topics discussed in the preceding 20 chapters of the book.

THE ACQUISITION PROCESS

Within the framework of strategy as process and the relationships between structure and strategy, this section outlines practical aspects of formulating and implementing M&A programs. It is an overview of the central topics. These materials are developed more fully in the other chapters. Many books and articles have been written on the M&A subject. Each appears to recommend a particular approach. Our view is that different approaches are likely to be required by different circumstances.

One logical basis for organizing the acquisition process is to divide it into three categories: strategy, transactions, and implementation. Other groupings might add accounting and tax issues, due diligence, and human resources considerations. Our own emphasis is on a set of dynamic interrelated processes with consideration of the firm's characteristics and needs or goals. We organize the acquisition process into 14 interacting activities:

1. Strategic processes for growth in value
2. The economics of the industry
3. The firm's organization system
4. Multiple strategies for value growth
5. Search processes
6. Economic basis—synergy potentials
7. Restructuring potentials
8. Due diligence—both legal and business
9. Cultural factors
10. Valuation
11. Negotiation
12. Deal structuring
13. Implementation
14. Reviews and renewal processes

Our emphasis is on the dynamic interrelated activities. Feasible strategies are related to the quality of the firm's capabilities and resources. Cisco Systems Inc. successfully implemented an expanding strategy because of the high quality of its management and execution, including a financial information and control system that provides real-time feedback. We discuss each item of the above list in sequence.

Strategy Formulation

The firm must formulate the strategies that define its character and scope. Illustrative approaches are listed in Table 21.1. From this analysis, the firm can articulate its goals. It can then assess its strengths and weaknesses in relationship to its goals. We emphasized in chapter 5 that we begin with a powerful strategic vision. As a refresher to the examples given, we add another illustration here.

Table 21.1 Illustrative Approaches to Merger Programs

Internet companies: Formulate a concept, expand it rapidly by acquisitions—Yahoo!, Amazon.com

High tech: Central technical capability augmented by acquisitions—Cisco Systems, Oracle

A reinvented strategy: Adjust to new technologies by acquisitions—AT&T

Industry consolidation: Combine and reduce capacity—Exxon Mobil

Augment capabilities: Acquire new research competencies—pharmaceutical industry mergers

Globalization: Add products and markets—Daimler Benz-Chrysler

Industry roll-ups: Transform fragmented industries into fewer firms—Waste Management, US Filter

Southwest Airlines changed the landscape of domestic air travel by creating the first successful "no-frills" airline. They cut out the travel agents by doing the ticketing themselves and changed the ticketing process by offering boarding passes without any assigned seating. They lowered overhead by purchasing smaller, cheaper planes and lowered operating expenses by serving minimal, standardized food (little bags of peanuts and pretzels). A favorable culture of good relationships with employees has developed high morale. They have perfected the quick turnaround of airplanes. Similar to our previous examples of Cisco and Dell, a compelling vision has been backed up by efficiency in all aspects of its operations. The result has been the achievement of an innovation in air travel—low-cost, no-frills service.

As we described, strategy deals with problems that cannot be put in neat mathematical equations with solutions readily obtained by the computer. The complex, ill-structured, dynamic environmental changes in competitive thrusts are the challenges that strategy seeks to meet. The central methodological procedure is a rapid review process to identify weaknesses to be eliminated and resources and capabilities to be added to enforce strengths.

The Economics of the Industry

The firm is defined by the business economic characteristics of its industry. Industries are classified in different ways for different purposes. From an economic standpoint some useful distinctions are consumer vs. producer products, durable vs. nondurable, products vs. services vs. information, stage in life cycle, tangible vs. intangible, and the pace of technological and other changes.

All business activities in recent years have been greatly influenced by the increased dynamism of their economic, political, and cultural environments. Rapid change defines the environment of most business activities. Industries have characteristics that influence responses to change. Change is reflected in economic activity measured by rates of growth in gross domestic product (GDP). Some industries are affected more than others. For example, a 5% change in the rate of growth of GDP will be magnified in the growth or decline in durable goods industries but have a smaller impact on nondurable goods industries. The strong upward thrust of growth in high tech industries may dominate cyclical changes in business activity.

The nature of the industry may influence the relative advantages of large and smaller firms. Industry characteristics will influence opportunities for industry roll-ups or the need for consolidation to reduce industry excess capacity. This discussion suggests the many dimensions of industry characteristics; it is not meant to be exhaustive.

An example of an industry assessment is our summary outline of the characteristics of the pharmaceutical industry.

1. Research-intensive—R&D about 11% to 13% of sales.
2. Small investment in plant and equipment; major investment in research Ph.D. staffs; patent protection, but only 11 years after FDA approval.
3. Scale advantages—it costs about $300 million to bring a new drug to FDA approval and takes 7 to 11 years; then "me too" drugs surround them.
4. Many dry holes; even if drugs are approved by the FDA, most are not blockbusters; only about 10% earn their cost of capital.
5. Risk of liability suits—can ruin an otherwise good company.
6. Number of New Chemical Entities (NCEs) per time period—key to market share and profitability.
7. A leader in a therapeutic product class does not hold its position beyond three to five years; needs continual stream of new NCEs to succeed.
8. Generally price-skimming policy; start with high prices and then reduce them as they get "me too'd" and new, better NCEs take their market share.
9. Needs backup of strong marketing and sales effort; key role of detail salespeople.
10. Needs to be worldwide to spread fixed costs; approximately 50% of sales in foreign countries by majors.
11. Purchase decision made by doctor, not by patient; doctor not sensitive to costs; doctor wants it (drug) to be effective and safe; continue with what works.
12. For many decades drug prices increased at a rate less than CPI; in past decade the reverse; index number problem? Also if drugs avoid surgery, long hospital stay, and death, they would be cheap at much higher nominal prices.
13. Accounting profits in recent years have been more than double the average for all manufacturing industries; does not take into account value of capitalized marketing and R&D outlays.
14. Increasingly vulnerable to political scapegoat and pressure. This is aggravated by the demographics—higher percentage of over 65, many of whom spend their income on drugs to keep alive and much of their time on voting to protect their interests. Paradox: Successful drugs extend the life expectancy of people who criticize the drug companies because the aged spend so much on drugs to keep alive longer. If this reduced funds for R&D, could be chopping off the "hands" that are ministering to them.
15. Data on drug industry have "survivor" biases; companies that survive were successful; the companies that died are not in the data. If data on unsuccessful are included, it's a different picture.
16. Exotic new areas like biotechnology.

17. No company strong across full 64 TPCs (therapeutic product class).
18. History of diversifying out of industry, then divesting. Much other merger activity for some companies; less for others.
19. Problems with public attention on prices and profits.
20. Subject to considerable political surveillance and pressure.
21. New research efforts and areas require large investment and outlays. Pressures for larger size. Cause of major mergers.

Because of demographic and political factors, the pressure to keep prices down is strong. Yet the costs of developing new chemical entities continues to rise. Investments required for newer types of research methods such as gene description are large. Individual companies run into periods when research efforts result in "dry holes" and product pipelines begin to empty. So alliances and mergers between pharmaceutical companies have taken place to attain larger size to afford the larger investments for new forms of research. Mergers to reduce costs and to balance product lines are also stimulated. These are some of the factors behind the major drug combinations: Glaxo Wellcome, SmithKline Beecham, Ciba Geigy and Sandoz into Novartis, and Pfizer and Warner-Lambert.

The Organization System

The firm must have an organizational structure consistent with its strategies and operations. It must have resources and capabilities consistent with its product–market activities. It must have an effective information flow system related to meaningful performance measurement. Compensation systems must be based on contributions to value creation.

We have described how the unitary (U) form of organization based on functions such as production, marketing, or geographic areas must change as the scope of a firm's activities expands. The multidivisional (M) form provides a more flexible framework for expanding products and widening geographic areas of operations. We also noted that in the Internet age firms are developing virtual organizations. Through Internet processes, suppliers, for example, become virtual segments of end firm activity. Early examples are Dell and the new arrangements Ford and GM have made with their suppliers.

Thus, a clearly articulated strategic vision and strong organizational framework are required to embrace expanded and new activities. In addition, operational efficiency must be achieved. The firm must have a solid basis for adding capabilities and resources to align more effectively to changes and opportunities through acquisitions. But if the firm is underperforming, it is more likely to be a target for a takeover.

Multiple Strategies for Value Growth

The firm has a wide variety of strategies for growth. Potentials for internal growth through product expansion and new product programs deserve full consideration. Alliances and joint ventures extend possibilities with smaller investment requirements. Licensing from other firms provides knowledge, and licensing to other firms provides revenues with small incremental direct costs. Firms may use divestitures to harvest successes or correct mistakes. Spin-offs may be a source of funds as well as increased corporate focus. Financial policies such as the use of debt and share repurchases may also enhance value.

Search Processes

In a firm that is seeking to grow by acquisitions, how are prospective candidates selected? Our recommendation is that this must be an ongoing activity of the firm. Organizationally, the firm should have a dedicated business development group. It is essential to have a core group that builds up experience and expertise in the acquisition process. Much basic information about the universe of candidate firms can be obtained from Web sites on the Internet. The business development group should train all employees to regard themselves as a source of research information on potential acquisition candidates.

In the ordinary course of business the firm has customers, suppliers, and competitors. Customers can provide information on product and marketing effectiveness in relation to competitors. Continued surveillance of competitors provides information on whether the firm is in the forefront of best practices. Interactions with suppliers can be a source of information on potential product improvements and may uncover opportunities for vertical integration of operations. Trade shows and technical forums provide information. Financial analysts and market analysts develop considerable knowledge about the best practices and superior performance.

Economic Basis—Synergy Potentials

A wide range of valid economic reasons for mergers may be considered. The explosive growth in the Internet sector has been driven by new technologies, new information systems, and new distribution systems. Internet companies such as Yahoo! and Amazon.com have formulated a concept and expanded it rapidly by acquisitions. The high technology area has stimulated acquisition programs based on a critical set of technological capabilities expanded and improved by acquisitions, as illustrated by Cisco Systems and Oracle.

Deregulation has also stimulated acquisition programs. Deregulation usually reflects new technologies and intensified competition, which puts pressure on incumbent firms. AT&T has had to adjust to new technologies, new forms of competition, and changed opportunities by acquisitions to reinvent itself. Excess capacity in the automobile industry and intense product competition have stimulated alliances, joint ventures, and mergers such as the Daimler–Chrysler transaction.

Globalization has created strong pressures for cross-border mergers. Economic reversals in developing countries have resulted in "invasions of the bargain snatchers." Industry roll-ups represent the consolidation of a highly fragmented industry through aggressive programs of acquiring similar businesses. Industry characteristics favorable for a roll-up include initial fragmentation, substantial industry annual revenues, companies with robust cash flows, and economies of scale.

Thus, a wide range of valid economic reasons exist for acquisitions, alliances, and joint ventures. Others can be formulated in terms of management strategies. A classic example is Beatrice Foods. Baker (1992) describes how Beatrice engaged in a dairy industry geographic roll-up under its president, Clinton Haskell. His successor, William Karnes, expanded the roll-up efforts. But Federal Trade Commission intervention against horizontal acquisitions led to diversifying acquisitions. Instead of integrating the more weakly related activities, Karnes moved to a decentralized organizational structure, avoiding intervention in the management of the new divisions.

Karnes extended the logic of the earlier acquisition program. Small firms were acquired to avoid competitive bidders. Many were privately held, family-run firms with relatively informal management procedures. Beatrice provided professional management expertise in functional areas and developed a program of management education for the company managers. This program produced increased efficiency, profitability, and growth for which Beatrice provided the requisite financing. Beatrice also used the knowledge and opinions of managers of previously acquired companies as well as their contacts with other companies to expand horizontally within the new diversified areas. The Beatrice example illustrates how management and organization policies can reinforce the economic basis for making synergistic acquisitions.

Restructuring Potentials

A strong economic rationale for an acquisition can be reinforced by restructuring gains. The collection period for receivables can be moved closer to contractual terms of credit. Inventory costs can be reduced by utilization of Internet arrangements. Investments in fixed assets can be controlled by improved models of production management and material flows. Firms have also demonstrated savings in the management of financing forms and sources. The increased use of share repurchases illustrates innovations in dividend policy. In general, leveraging best practices between both the buying and selling firms can contribute to achieving the kinds of efficiency increases described. Products can be improved, new products developed, and more effective utilization of investments can be achieved through incorporating the knowledge and best practices of the combined firms.

Due Diligence

Due diligence may begin with legal aspects but must be extended to business and management considerations. It involves all of the following. An examination of all aspects of prospective partners should be performed. Firms should be sure there are no legal problems, such as pension funding, environmental problems, or product liabilities. Inspection should determine important factors like the relevance of accounting records, the maintenance and quality of equipment, and the possibility of maintaining cost controls. It should also be determined whether the firm has potentials for product improvement or superiority.

Broader business aspects also need to be taken into account. In particular, management relationships must be analyzed. A business combination should fill gaps in managerial capabilities and also extend capabilities. The firm's resources should be extended in multiple dimensions. Consideration must be given to how the two management systems will fit together and whether managers will have to be hired or fired. Firms should be aware of new developments that will benefit the firm or require adjustments. Ultimately, the acquired unit should be worth more as a part of the acquiring firm than alone or with any other firm.

Cultural Factors

Corporate culture is defined by an organization's values, traditions, norms, beliefs, and behavior patterns. Corporate culture may be articulated in formal statements of organization values and aspirations. Corporate culture is also expressed in informal relationships and networks. Corporate cultures may be reflected in a company's operating style, including both formal and informal influences. More concretely, corporate culture may be conveyed by the kinds of behavior that are rewarded in an organization.

Differences in organization cultures may be illustrated by the following examples:

➤ Strong top leadership versus team approach.

➤ Management by formal paperwork versus management by wandering around.

➤ Individual decision versus group consensus decisions.

➤ Rapid evaluation based on performance versus long-term relationship based on loyalty.

➤ Rapid feedback for change versus formal bureaucratic rules and procedures.

➤ Narrow career paths versus movement through many areas.

➤ Risk-taking encouraged versus "one mistake and you're out."

➤ Big-stakes (bet-your-company) decisions versus low-risk activities.

➤ Learn from the customer versus "we know what is best for the customer."

➤ Narrow responsibility assignments versus "everyone in this company is a source of new or improved product ideas or sources of sales effort or sources of cost efficiencies, and so on."

We argue that a firm must manage its own corporate culture effectively before engaging in merger activity. If its organizational culture house is not in order, combining companies and their cultures will aggravate problems. The firm must be consistent in its formal statements of values and the kinds of actions that are rewarded. The firm must already have a program of proactive employee training and communications systems that convey the importance of the value of individual development and recognition of contributions to organizational effectiveness.

The foregoing emphasizes that in planning for external growth through mergers, alliances, and other relationships, the firm must recognize cultural factors in addition to products, plant and equipment, and financial factors. The firm must be sensitized to recognizing the requirement for pulling together all the systems, informal processes, and cultures required for organizational effectiveness. Due diligence must include coverage of cultural factors in all their dimensions. A wise acquirer puts culture on the table at the earliest planning sessions.

Cultural differences have caused mergers to fail or prevented them from achieving their potentials. Cultural differences are almost certain to be involved when companies are combined. Cultural differences are increasingly important in the rising number of cross-border transactions.

Pitfalls begin with simply ignoring the problem. Another is to promise equal treatment and respect but impose culture from one firm onto another. Problems inherent in inconsistent cultures can escalate to conflict.

Information on how the acquiring firm has handled cultural factors in the past or how the firm has handled organizational change can be developed. Formal tools are available for assessing cultural problems and potentials. Potential partners may be asked to complete a questionnaire describing the cultural dimensions of the prospective merger partners. Focus groups may be employed to conduct sessions with senior officers and directors of the combining firms.

End solutions may take various forms. One is to recognize cultural differences and to respect them. This may occur in firms with vertical relationships in which required management styles may vary at different levels of activity such as research, production, marketing, and finance. Another practice is to exchange executives across the organizations that have been brought together.

Ultimately, the cultures may move toward similarity. Or differences may even be valued as sources of increased efficiency. Diversity of patterns may be the result in different types of industrial activities or between firms with different histories. A general recommendation is to involve the human resources managers in the process so that modern concepts and tools can be used.

Valuation

The purpose of a careful valuation analysis is to provide a disciplined procedure for arriving at a price. If the buyer offers too little, the target may resist and, since it is in play, seek to interest other bidders. If the price is too high, the premium may never be recovered from postmerger synergies. These general principles are illustrated by the following simple model.

The Model

Mergers increase value when the value of the combined firm is greater than the sum of the premerger values of the independent entities.

$$NVI = V_{BT} - (V_B + V_T)$$

where

NVI = Net value increase
V_B = Value of bidder alone
V_T = Value of target alone
V_{BT} = Value of firms combined

A simple example will illustrate. Company B (the bidder) has a current market value of $40 (it is understood that all the numbers are in millions). Company T (the target) has a current market value of $40. The sum of the values as independent firms is therefore $80. Assume that as a Combined Company (CC) synergies will increase the value to $100. The amount of value created is $20.

How will the increase in value be divided? Targets always (usually) receive a premium. What about the bidders? If the bidder pays a premium of less than $20, it will share in the value increase. If B pays a premium larger than $20, the value of the bidder will decline. If the bidder pays $50 for the target, a premium of 25% has been paid to T. The value increases are shared equally.

If B pays $60 for T, all gains go to the target. B achieves no value increase. If B pays $70 for T, the value of B will decline to $30.

The Use of Stock in Acquisitions

A high percentage of the large transactions beginning in 1992 have been stock-for-stock transactions. Some hold the view that this does not represent real money. But that view is not valid.

Suppose B exchanges 1.25 of its shares for 1 share of T. Since B is valued at $40, T will receive 1.25 × $40, which equals $50. The premium paid is 25%. Based on their previous $40 values, B and T each owned 50% of the premerger combined values. Postmerger, the percentages of ownership will remain 50–50.

If B exchanges 1.5 of its own shares per share of T, this is equivalent to paying $60 in value for the target. T shareholders will own 60% of the combined company. None of the synergy gains will be received by the bidder shareholders. Also note that the target shareholders will have 1.5 shares in the new company for every 1.0 share held by the bidder shareholders.

The situation is even worse if B pays more than $60 for the target. Assume B pays $70 for the target. Since the combined company has a value of $100, the value of the bidder shares must decline to $30. The consequences are terrible. The shares of the bidder will decline in value by $10, or 25%. Furthermore, the B shareholders will own only 30% of the combined company; for every 1.0 share that they own, the target shareholders will own 2.3 shares.

Negotiation

We believe that the area of M&As (mergers and acquisitions, alliances, and joint ventures) offers attractive opportunities for principled negotiation. By this we mean using standards of fairness in seeking to meet the interests of both parties. Since firms are being combined, it is important to produce agreements that build good future relationships.

With that foundation in principle, the literature offers guides for negotiation strategy and techniques. A basic requirement is to start with good preparation. Recall the previous topics in this summary statement on the M&A (defined broadly as above) process. We need a strategic vision. The firm needs to assess its strengths and weaknesses. The firm identifies the resources and capabilities required and what it brings to the deal.

A key factor in M&As is realistic identification of gains, synergies, and their sources, whether in revenue enhancement and/or cost reductions and/or possibilities for new and strengthened strategies. This is the basis for developing a solid quantification of the firm's BATNA—best alternative to a negotiated agreement. In merger valuation, quantification of BATNA is facilitated. Value relationships can be analyzed with references to comparable companies and comparable transactions. Other more formal methods of valuation, as described in chapters 9 and 10, can be used. The active markets for buying and selling business entities and segments provide quantitative information. Plus, all the parties can benefit. For the buyer, it is imperative that the premium paid have a sound foundation in estimates of synergy and savings.

Deal Structuring

Deal structuring begins with understanding the tax consequences of combining firms. A second important area is to understand whether the accounting treatment employed has any true economic consequences. A third issue is the method of payment: cash, stock, debt, or a combination thereof. A fourth variable is whether an explicit contingency payout should be used and how the standard for the bonus or penalty should be formulated. The use of cash reduces uncertainty for the seller but has tax consequences. The use of stock makes the actual return to the seller dependent upon the future success of the combination.

Implementation

A key challenge in doing M&As is implementation. Some discussions propose that implementation starts when the merger agreement has been signed. Our view is that implementation starts as a condition for thinking about M&As. The firm must have implemented all aspects of effective operations before it can effectively combine organizations. This means that the firm must have a shareholder value orientation. It must have strategies and organizational structures compatible with its multiple business units.

Companies should pursue only mergers that further their corporate strategy: strengthening weaknesses, filling gaps, developing new growth opportunities, and extending capabilities. Integration leadership is required. The demands of regular business operations and integration are too much for one person to handle. The integration leader should have management experience, experience with external constituencies, and credibility with the various integration participants.

Poor communication distresses employees; good integrators use communication plans that provide early, frequent, and clear integration messages. The company should maintain ongoing communication that clearly addresses the concerns of employees.

M&As may fail because of slow integration. Firms should create cross-functional teams to devote attention to the issues of integration. But the firm should also be sensitive to the need for balance between speed and disruption. Day-to-day operations should not be sacrificed for rapidity of integration. The key is to formulate in advance integration plans that can effectively accomplish the goals of the M&A processes.

Reviews and Renewal Process

Strong change forces in the environments in which a firm operates and the continued impacts of competitors represent continued challenges. No plan or set of policies can remain in force without change for very long. The firm must continuously adjust to new opportunities and challenges.

It is to be hoped that the firm has a broad strategy that guides success in its business markets. For example, Dell Computer began with the central strategy of selling directly to customers. But Dell has continuously integrated new concepts into its operations. The initial vision of Cisco Systems was to provide business customers with Internet routers. From this base, Cisco moved to become a provider of complete data networking solutions. When the new technologies for long distance telephone communications gave cost advantages to the use of microwave and fiber-optic systems, AT&T had to reinvent itself.

In more mature industries such as food and automobiles, similar continuing challenges had to be managed. Food sales are tied to population growth, which in the United States is only 1% to 2% per annum. Growth rates that low would not make it possible for firms to compete for executives seeking promotions and stock options. Nor do low-growth firms receive respect or support from the financial markets. Food companies over a period of years were able to achieve earnings growth at two-digit levels by introducing new products and promoting strong brands and by expanding abroad in faster growing markets. In recent years, this has been increasingly difficult to accomplish. Similarly, the automobile industry has persistently faced a world production capacity of some 80 million units per year, but with quantity demanded at around 60 million units per year. Strong continuing competitive pressures have resulted. Automobile companies have sought to develop innovative new products, such as sport utility vehicles (SUVs). They have also engaged in a wide range of M&A and restructuring activities. The cross-border Daimler–Chrysler merger in 1998 is a notable example. Many consolidating automobile mergers and alliances have taken place in Europe. General Motors has made investments in a number of manufacturers in Asian countries, including mainland China.

So the adjustment processes for firms are a continuous activity. Learn from the past, manage well in the present, and plan imaginatively for the future! These are the precepts that make M&A and restructuring continuing activities. The fundamental characteristic of strategic planning processes are illustrated: assessment of needs; evaluation of alternative strategies; selection of strategies and plans; fast feedback on results; reassessment of strategies, plans, policies, and decisions; modifications and adjustments; and continued repetitions of the process. Alliances, joint ventures, mergers, restructuring, and financial engineering all perform significant roles in these dynamic processes. That is why our subject is highly important for the well-being of firms as well as economies.

THE RULES FOR SUCCESSFUL MERGERS

In his editorial page article in the *Wall Street Journal* of October 15, 1981, Peter F. Drucker set forth "The Five Rules for Successful Acquisition." He noted that the then-current merger movement in the United States paralleled the tremendous wave of acquisitions in Germany in 1920 to 1922, a period of chronic inflation that preceded the chaotic hyperinflation of 1923. He then went on to observe that during periods of severe inflation, fixed assets can be purchased by buying companies at market prices that are well below book value and even further below replacement costs. The low stock market valuations of companies over the previous decade, he argued, were due in large part to sustained underdepreciation of assets because of tax regulations. The basic impetus driving increased merger activity under inflation was said to be the general flight by businesspersons and investors out of money and into hard assets.

Drucker's Merger Rules

But although Drucker (1981) saw the stimulus for mergers as primarily a financial one, he also argued that economically sensible mergers must follow the Drucker five commandments for successful acquisitions:

1. Acquirer must contribute something to the acquired company.
2. A common core of unity is required.

3. Acquirer must respect the business of the acquired company.
4. Within a year or so, the acquiring company must be able to provide top management to the acquired company.
5. Within the first year of merger, managements in both companies should receive promotions across the entities.

Drucker supports his prescriptions by selected examples of successes and failures. The limitation of such a method of proof, of course, is that propositions derived from individual case studies often do not have general validity. There are, however, a large number of systematic empirical studies of mergers that have been performed during the last two decades. We found their results to be consistent with Drucker's analysis and prescriptions for acquisitions.

The dollar value of merger and acquisition activity in the United States in recent years has averaged about 30% of new plant and equipment expenditures. This relationship, furthermore, is statistically significant. Thus, merger activity appears to be subject to the same influences as investment activity generally, and this suggests that there has been some economic rationale to merger activity in recent years in the United States. In short, mergers appear to be influenced by the availability of alternative investment opportunities and, more specifically, by the relative costs of merger compared with direct internal expansion. These investment incentives, however, operate differently in different economic environments.

Extending the Rules

Examination of the evidence suggests that the Drucker rules may be unduly restrictive if interpreted too literally. In essence, the Drucker rules can be boiled down to two statements: (1) Merging companies must have activities that are related in some way, and (2) well-structured incentives and rewards must be held out to the management of both firms to help make the merger work, although the acquiring firm should be prepared to cover the departure of the key management of acquired companies.

A less restrictive interpretation of these rules would include the following commentary on the Drucker pentalogue.

1. Relatedness is a necessary requirement, but complementarities are an even greater virtue. For example, combining a company strong in research but weak in marketing with a company strong in marketing but weak in research may bring blessings to both.
2. Relatedness or complementarities may apply to general management functions such as research, planning and control, and financial management as well as to the more firm-specific operating functions such as production and marketing. This perspective widely increases the basis for relatedness. Thus, companies with cash flows or managerial capabilities in excess of their investment opportunities or available capacity could effectively combine with companies lacking the financial or managerial resources to make the most of the prospects for growth and profits in their industries.
3. Even if the preceding rules are followed, an acquiring firm will experience negative returns if it pays too much. It is difficult to fully and accurately evaluate another organization. There may be great surprises on both sides after the mar-

riage, and the problems of implementing complementarities may be substantial. The uncertainty associated with acquisitions is likely to be greater than the uncertainty attending internal investments made in product market areas more directly related to the firm's current activities. The external investments may appear to offer higher rates of return. But financial theory tells us that higher returns on average are associated with higher risks. The prospective high returns from a merger must be based on real economies, whether operating or financial, expected from the combination. Further, one who expects that a firm can improve the average risk–return relationship in an unfamiliar market or industry is likely to be disappointed.

Anslinger and Copeland (1996) suggest an alternative framework for making seemingly unrelated acquisitions. They studied in depth 21 successful acquirers of two types: diversified corporate acquirers and financial buyers such as leveraged buyout firms. These companies made a total of 829 acquisitions from the early 1980s to the mid-1990s. Although many of the acquisitions seem to be unrelated in some respects, successful acquirers focused on a common theme. Clayton, Dubilier & Rice stockpiled management capabilities used to make turnarounds. Another financial buyer, Desai Capital Management, focused on retail-related industries. Emerson Electric Company looked for companies with a core competence in component manufacturing to exploit cost control capabilities. Sara Lee used branding in retailing as its common thread.

Anslinger and Copeland identified the successful acquirers as those that substantially outperformed benchmarks such as the Standard & Poor's 500 and the Morgan Stanley capital international index by almost 50% during a recent 10-year period. They appeared to employ seven key principles:

1. Acquire companies with a track record of innovative operating strategies.
2. Capable managerial talent is most important for creating values. If current executives are not capable of increasing value, look for managers within the organization who are not yet in leadership positions and/or hire outstanding talent from other firms.
3. Use strong incentive compensation systems such as stock purchase programs so that top managers have holdings in the company that represent a large part of their net worth.
4. Link compensation incentives to future changes in cash flow.
5. Push the pace of change to make turnarounds happen within the first two years of the takeover.
6. Develop information and feedback systems that promote continuing dynamic relationships among owners, managers, and the board.
7. Acquiring firms must use executives with expertise and demonstrated successful experience as deal makers. Their judgments are often critical to the success or failure of the transaction.

The above guidelines are consistent with themes that we have developed throughout this book. They provide useful inputs to the summary guidelines we now set forth.

SUMMARY

Both the case studies and systematic empirical studies suggest the following guidelines for successful merger and acquisition activity:

1. The M&A program must be part of long-range strategic planning.
2. Recognize that in seeking new areas with higher growth potentials and improved opportunities for value enhancement, internal investments and restructuring can be used in conjunction with external investments and M&A activity.
3. Know the industry and its competitive environment as a basis for making projections for the future.
4. Be sure there is an element of relatedness, but don't be too restrictive in defining the scope of potential relatedness.
5. Combine firms that have relatively unique relationships that other firms cannot match, thus avoiding multiple bids that drive up the price of the target to excessively high levels. The acquired unit should be worth more as part of our firm than alone or with some other firm.
6. There is a time to buy. There is a time to sell. Sometimes a firm may seek to augment its position in an industry by acquiring related firms. If the prices received by sellers reflect overoptimistic expectations, it may make sense to reverse the strategy and become a seller rather than a buyer.
7. Top executives must be involved in M&A activity as well as other major investment programs.
8. Combining two companies is an activity that involves substantial trauma and readjustment. Therefore, a strong emphasis on maintaining and enhancing managerial rewards and incentives is required in the postmerger period. The managements of all the companies combined in a merger must receive incentives to stay and to make contributions to the combined company.
9. Communicate as soon as possible when major investment and restructuring decisions are made.
10. Postmerger coordination must be another top management responsibility. This does not happen automatically. Top executives must be involved as well as all members of the organization.
11. For future promotions, distinctions based on employment in different segments of the company should disappear. If employees have to be separated, it should be done in as enlightened a way as possible including assistance with insurance coverages and placement activities. This is ethically sound behavior and has an important impact on the future morale and culture of the firm.

12. Managing the integration of cultures and coordinating all the systems and informal processes of the combining firms are absolute musts. Cultural integration usually works best when the combining firms have similar cultures. When cultures are greatly different, each should be respected for its values. Initially, each component company may be encouraged to operate within its own culture. As each component learns to appreciate the strengths and weaknesses of cultural differences, a blended culture may develop over time.

13. The risk of mistakes stemming from wishful thinking is especially great in mergers. The planning may be sound from the standpoint of business or financial complementarities or relatedness. But if the acquiring firm pays too much, the result will be a negative net present value investment.

14. The restructuring and renewal requirements for an organization represent a continuing challenge to be addressed in the firm's strategic planning processes.

QUESTIONS

21.1 What are the basic principles to keep in mind in mergers and acquisitions planning?

21.2 In evaluating an individual merger or takeover, why is it useful to start with an analysis of the business economics of the industry?

21.3 Why is industry important in influencing the pace of M&A activity?

21.4 According to Coase, what are the determinants of the scope and size of firms?

21.5 What are Drucker's rules for successful mergers?

21.6 Summarize the key principles Anslinger and Copeland gave as the reasons for both corporate and financial buyers in seemingly unrelated acquisitions.

21.7 If you were to formulate ten commandments to guide sound decisions with respect to merger and acquisition activity, what would they be?

Case 21.1 Analysis and Evaluation of Dean Witter Discover's Merger with Morgan Stanley*

OVERVIEW OF DEAL TERMS

In a friendly bid on February 5, 1997, Dean Witter Discover & Co. ("DWD" or "the bidder") announced that it would be merging with Morgan Stanley Group Inc. ("MS" or "the target"), creating a leading global financial services firm with a market capitalization above $23 billion and leading positions in three businesses: securities, asset management, and credit services. The new company will be named Morgan Stanley, Dean Witter, Discover & Company. This transaction will knock Merrill Lynch from the number one spot in market capitalization and assets under management. The new entity will have a total of $270 billion in assets under management including mutual funds and individual accounts, the most of any securities firm.

Expected Completion Date

The combination was expected to be completed in mid-1997. However, joint research efforts on 2,000 stocks had begun even before the merger became final.

Price and Tax Treatment

DWD will make a tax-free exchange of 1.65 of its shares for each MS share. Many believe that DWD got a good deal, paying 11 times MS's 1996 profits and about two times book value. Regional banks have fetched as much as 15 times profits or three times book value, while Banc One paid about 18 times profits for First USA, a credit card company.

Accounting

The merger will be accounted for as a pooling of interests.

Management

Richard B. Fisher, Morgan Stanley's chairman, will become chairman of the executive committee of the new firm's board of 14 directors, half drawn from DWD and half from MS. Phillip J. Purcell, DWD's top executive, will become chairman and chief executive of the combined company. His number two will be John J. Mack, now MS's president.

The merger is expected to be accretive to earnings per share (EPS) for the merged company. Each company has also granted the other an option to acquire shares representing 19.9% of its outstanding shares if a higher bidder comes along, in addition to a $250 million breakup fee. The deal, which was two years in the making, is the biggest ever between two Wall Street firms.

COMPARISON OF MS's AND DWD's BUSINESSES

MS

Morgan Stanley is a major international securities brokerage firm. Its principal businesses include securities underwriting, distribution, and trading; merchant banking; mergers and acquisitions; stock brokerage and research services; asset management; real estate; and trading of futures, options,

---

*This case was written with Angela Zvinakis in early March, 1997. The merger was completed on May 28, 1997, but we retain the write-up we developed shortly after the merger plan was announced.

foreign exchange, and commodities. Its foreign operations account for about 50% of its net revenues. It concentrates on serving very wealthy investors and underwriting securities for big corporations.

DWD

Dean Witter Discover is a diversified financial services organization operating in three main businesses: full-service brokerage, credit services, and asset management. Its Discover card is used by roughly 36.1 million accounts and 2.5 million merchants. Additionally, it is a full-service brokerage firm with about $80 billion under administration, servicing primarily retail clients.

The table below contrasts the companies' businesses:

	Capital	Retail Brokers	Institutional Brokers	Domestic Offices	International Offices	Customer Accounts
MS	$15.7 B	402	268	10	25	70,000
DWD	$ 1.6 B	8,406	169	353	1	3.1 million

Source: *USA Today*, February 6, 1997.

HISTORY OF THE DEAL

Morgan Stanley had been interested in a merger for a while. Three years earlier, it discussed and then dropped a possible merger with S.G. Warburg & Company, the London merchant bank. The history between MS and DWD is also an extended one. Morgan Stanley helped take DWD public in June 1993 and also advised Sears when it reorganized and spun off the brokerage firm. Moreover, MS and DWD had discussed working together intermittently during the last three years. They had also discussed how to structure contractual relationships in which securities underwritten by MS bankers could be sold by DWD brokers. This was the true precursor to the merger.

THE FINANCIAL SERVICES INDUSTRY "SHAKE OUT"

The securities brokerage industry performed remarkably well in 1996. Table 21.2 gives some key statistics on brokerages and investment banks in 1996. Continued pressure for superior performance in the financial services industry has led to an increase in merger activity, especially in the banking sector. No wonder DWD eyed MS in the wake of its impressive 1996 performance. Several factors explain the 1996 and 1997 surge in merger activity in the industry:

- The growing power of the retail market, particularly led by the postwar baby-boom generation, has caught the attention of Wall Street. This sector is where much of the growth will come from in the future. The common belief is that greater profits can be achieved by putting under one roof the underwriting of stocks and bonds for corporate clients and the sale of stocks, bonds, and mutual funds to individual investors.
- Competition will intensify when commercial banks gain a bigger foothold in the securities industry as the rules on underwriting are loosened this year. (Elements of the

Table 21.2 1996 Performance of Selected Brokerages and Investment Banks, for the Twelve Months Ended December 31, 1996

Company	ROE	Sales Growth	EPS Growth	Sales ($mm)	Net Income ($mm)	Profit Margin
Schwab	33.20%	33.60%	31.50%	2,167	217	10.00%
Raymond James	24.30%	30.30%	40.80%	722	66	9.10%
Alex. Brown	29.30%	45.40%	71.40%	1,042	150	14.40%
A.G. Edwards	18.20%	26.30%	39.20%	1,603	201	12.50%
Merrill Lynch	23.00%	14.50%	56.80%	23,703	1,478	6.20%
Bear Stearns	19.20%	27.60%	79.70%	5,126	505	9.90%
MS*	20.90%	17.40%	178.70%	12,720	980	7.70%
Paine Webber	21.20%	12.60%	N/A	5,611	332	5.90%
Salomon Brothers	20.20%	13.30%	500.0+%	9,165	847	9.20%
Lehman Bros.	8.60%	11.10%	74.20%	14,061	357	2.50%

Before any consideration of merger with DWD.
Source: *Forbes,* January 13, 1997.

Depression-era Glass-Steagall Act will be further relaxed later in 1997.) The Federal Reserve has decided to raise the proportion of revenues that banks can derive from a securities subsidiary from 10 to 25%.

- As the market becomes more globalized, Wall Street now believes that the key is to join a well-run distribution network with an investment bank in order to distribute successfully globally.
- Several analysts also believe that the industry is currently suffering from overcrowding. For the level of returns available, there is too much capital in the business.

Possible Future Targets

Many believe that Paine Webber Group, Lehman Brothers, and Salomon Brothers must find partners if they want to compete against the full-service giants that are coming to dominate the financial services industry. Another potential target is the Equitable Companies' Donaldson, Lufkin & Jenrette unit. Additionally, investment banks or commercial banks might also consider A.G. Edwards with its fifth largest retail network in the country.

Goldman, Sachs & Company is rumored to be partnering with Citicorp in the near future. Other commercial banks, like Chase Manhattan, may buy brokerage houses as the regulatory barriers come down. Prudential Securities may even be put up for sale to take advantage of the high prices currently being offered in the industry.

Table 21.3   Announcement Returns

	(per share)				(millions)		
	MW **Close**	**DWD** **Close**	**MS** **Shares**	**DWD** **Shares**	**MS** **Equity** **Value**	**DWD** **Equity** **Value**	**Total**
Feb. 4, 1997	$57.375	$38.625	152.425	321.514	$8,745	$12,418	$21,163
Feb. 5, 1997	$65.250	$40.625	152.425	321.514	$9,946	$13,062	$23,008
Value Created					$1,201	$ 644	$ 1,845

Recent Industry Developments

- Salomon Brothers announced an alliance in January 1997 with Fidelity Investments. Fidelity will gain access to Salomon's stock offerings, whereas Salomon can now reach a retail network with 6.1 million customers.
- Citicorp and American Express discussed a merger late in 1996 and then disregarded the idea.
- PIMCO recently opened 12 of its mutual funds to individual investors.
- Brown Bros. Harriman announced that it would sell its stock funds through the mutual fund supermarkets.

FINANCIAL ANALYSIS OF THE MERGER

Stock Market's Reaction to the Merger

Table 21.3 details the stock market's reaction to the announcement on February 5, 1997, and the combined equity values of the new entity.

The new company will have a stock market value of $23 billion, as seen in Table 21.3. On February 5, 1997, DWD's shareholders, in aggregate, gained approximately $600 million. MS's shareholders gained approximately $1.2 billion! Combined, $1.8 billion was created in market value on February 5, 1997, from this announcement. Table 21.3 also shows how the market prices of the individual stocks adjusted in order to reflect the exchange ratio proposed by DWD: 1.65 shares of DWD for each share of MS. On February 5, 1.65 shares of DWD were valued at $67.03, and 1 share of MS shot up to $65.25. Thus, the values were almost equated. MS's stock did not adjust fully (to $67.03) because there still remained the possibility that the deal would not go through.

Shareholder Returns

In Table 21.4 and Figure 21.1 are calculated the returns for MS shareholders and DWD shareholders for the 30 days preceding the merger announcement and the 12 days after the merger announcement. The findings are summarized in Table 21.5.

Table 21.4 Returns to MS and DWD Shareholders and to the S&P 500 Index

Day	MS Price	MS Actual	MS Predicted*	MS Residual	DWD Price	DWD Actual	DWD Predicted*	DWD Residual	S&P 500 Level	S&P 500 Return
−30	57.2500				33.7500				746.92	
−29	58.3750	1.97%	0.55%	1.41%	33.8750	0.37%	0.55%	−0.18%	751.03	0.55%
−28	59.0000	1.07%	0.64%	0.43%	33.6875	−0.55%	0.64%	−1.19%	755.82	0.64%
−27	58.8750	−0.21%	0.13%	−0.34%	33.6250	−0.19%	0.13%	−0.31%	756.79	0.13%
−26	58.8750	0.00%	−0.39%	0.39%	33.8125	0.56%	−0.39%	0.95%	753.85	−0.39%
−25	57.1250	−2.97%	−1.74%	−1.23%	33.1250	−2.03%	−1.74%	−0.29%	740.74	−1.74%
−24	56.1250	−1.75%	−0.50%	−1.25%	33.1250	0.00%	−0.50%	0.50%	737.01	−0.50%
−23	56.3750	0.45%	1.50%	−1.05%	33.8125	2.08%	1.50%	0.58%	748.03	1.50%
−22	56.5000	0.22%	−0.05%	0.27%	33.8125	0.00%	−0.05%	0.05%	747.65	−0.05%
−21	56.0000	−0.88%	0.75%	−1.63%	34.0000	0.55%	0.75%	−0.19%	753.23	0.75%
−20	56.0000	0.00%	−0.64%	0.64%	33.6250	−1.10%	−0.64%	−0.46%	748.41	−0.64%
−19	55.8750	−0.22%	0.86%	−1.08%	34.0625	1.30%	0.86%	0.44%	754.85	0.86%
−18	55.3750	−0.89%	0.62%	−1.51%	33.8750	−0.55%	0.62%	−1.17%	759.50	0.62%
−17	54.3750	−1.81%	0.00%	−1.81%	34.2500	1.11%	0.00%	1.11%	759.51	0.00%
−16	55.5000	2.07%	1.23%	0.84%	35.1250	2.55%	1.23%	1.32%	768.86	1.23%
−15	55.1250	−0.68%	−0.22%	−0.46%	34.2500	−2.49%	−0.22%	−2.28%	767.20	−0.22%
−14	54.6250	−0.91%	0.25%	−1.16%	34.6250	1.09%	0.25%	0.84%	769.15	0.25%
−13	56.5000	3.43%	0.91%	2.52%	35.5000	2.53%	0.91%	1.61%	776.17	0.91%
−12	57.3750	1.55%	0.07%	1.48%	36.5000	2.82%	0.07%	2.75%	776.70	0.07%
−11	57.2500	−0.22%	0.78%	−0.99%	37.1250	1.71%	0.78%	0.94%	782.72	0.78%
−10	57.2500	0.00%	0.45%	−0.45%	38.0000	2.36%	0.45%	1.91%	786.23	0.45%
−9	57.2500	0.00%	−1.10%	1.10%	37.5000	−1.32%	−1.10%	−0.21%	777.56	−1.10%
−8	57.3750	0.22%	−0.91%	1.12%	37.2500	−0.67%	−0.91%	0.24%	770.52	−0.91%

−7	56.6250	−1.31%	−0.71%	−0.59%	37.0000	−0.67%	−0.71%	0.04%	765.02	−0.71%
−6	56.2500	−0.66%	0.00%	−0.66%	36.6250	−1.01%	0.00%	−1.01%	765.02	0.00%
−5	56.5000	0.44%	0.98%	−0.53%	36.8750	0.68%	0.98%	−0.30%	772.50	0.98%
−4	56.6250	0.22%	1.51%	−1.29%	37.7500	2.37%	1.51%	0.86%	784.17	1.51%
−3	57.1250	0.88%	0.25%	0.63%	38.1250	0.99%	0.25%	0.74%	786.16	0.25%
−2	57.1250	0.00%	0.07%	−0.07%	38.3750	0.66%	0.07%	0.58%	786.73	0.07%
−1	57.3750	0.44%	0.32%	0.12%	38.6250	0.65%	0.32%	0.33%	789.26	0.32%
5-Feb-97 0	65.2500	13.73%	−1.39%	15.12%	40.6250	5.18%	−1.39%	6.57%	778.28	−1.39%
1	66.5000	1.92%	0.24%	1.68%	41.1250	1.23%	0.24%	0.99%	780.15	0.24%
2	67.3750	1.32%	1.21%	0.11%	42.0000	2.13%	1.21%	0.92%	789.56	1.21%
3	67.8750	0.74%	−0.52%	1.27%	41.8750	−0.30%	−0.52%	0.23%	785.43	−0.52%
4	67.5000	−0.55%	0.53%	−1.08%	41.6250	−0.60%	0.53%	−1.13%	789.59	0.53%
5	66.8750	−0.93%	1.67%	−2.60%	40.8750	−1.80%	1.67%	−3.47%	802.77	1.67%
6	68.8750	2.99%	1.13%	1.86%	42.0000	2.75%	1.13%	1.62%	811.82	1.13%
7	68.7500	−0.18%	−0.41%	0.23%	42.3750	0.89%	−0.41%	1.30%	808.48	−0.41%
8	70.8750	3.09%	0.97%	2.12%	43.5000	2.65%	0.97%	1.69%	816.29	0.97%
9	71.8750	1.41%	−0.47%	1.88%	43.7500	0.57%	−0.47%	1.04%	812.49	−0.47%
10	69.8750	−2.78%	−1.19%	−1.59%	42.5000	−2.86%	−1.19%	−1.66%	802.80	−1.19%
11	67.6250	−3.22%	−0.13%	−3.09%	41.2500	−2.94%	−0.13%	−2.81%	801.77	−0.13%
24-Feb-97 12	66.7813	−1.25%	1.06%	−2.31%	40.6250	−1.52%	1.06%	−2.58%	810.28	1.06%
44 trading day total return	16.65%				20.37%			8.48%		
Average daily return	0.38%				0.46%			0.19%		
Return from −30 to −1	0.22%				14.44%			5.67%		
Return from −1 to 0	13.73%				5.18%			−1.39%		
Return from 0 to 12	2.35%				0.00%			4.11%		
Cumulative abnormal return				8.44%				10.91%		

*Used the market adjusted return model in which the predicted return for a firm for a day is just the return on the market index for that day.

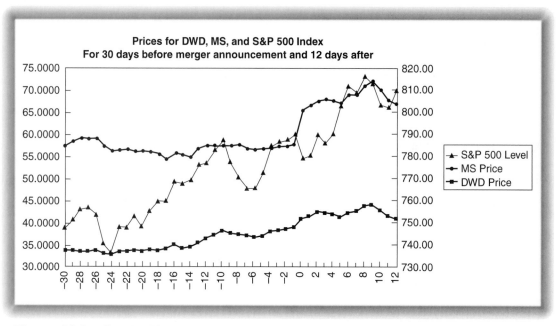

Figure 21.1 Graph of Daily Stock Prices

Table 21.5 Returns to MS and DWD Shareholders

	MS: Target	**DWD: Bidder**	**S&P 500**
44-day total return: from −30 to 12	16.65%	20.37%	8.48%
Runup: Return from −30 to −1	0.22%	14.44%	5.57%
Announcement day return: Return from −1 to 0	13.73%	5.18%	−1.39%
Markup: Return from 0 to 12	2.35%	0.00%	4.11%
Cumulative abnormal return	8.44%	10.91%	N/A

Amazingly, over this 44-day period, *MS's stock rose by less than DWD stock.* This is strange because historically the target's stock experiences a positive return, while the return to the bidder is small or even negative. In support of empirical evidence, however, we do see that *the target stock gained more on the announcement date than the bidder's stock.* Another interesting fact is that *the runup,* the return from day −30 to day −1, *is seen in the bidder's*

stock. So far, *there has also been little cumulative markup in this deal.* As a proxy for the market return, the S&P 500 index is used. Additionally, to calculate the **cumulative abnormal returns (CAR)** over the period, the "market adjusted return method" is used. Once again, DWD's shareholders were better off than MS's shareholders during this 44-day period. *DWD's CAR was 10.91%, whereas MS's CAR was 8.44%.*

Valuation of MS

The following two valuations of MS were done "premerger," ignoring any possible synergies that would occur from the merger with DWD, such as reduced operating expenses.

1. *Spreadsheet/formula approach.* The value of the firm is $146,466 million ($7,887 million in equity and $138,579 million in debt). All of the historical drivers are used for the value going forward and temporary supernormal growth for five years, then no growth. Five years was more applicable than 10, given the cyclicality and riskiness in the investment banking industry. Also, the company's growth in EBIT over the last five years has only been 8.8% annually. The valuation can be viewed in Table 21.6.

2. *Comparable companies approach.* Morgan Stanley premerger is valued by comparing it to other investment banks, using price/book, price/sales, and price/net income ratios. The total value of MS's equity was $7,226 million using this method. The valuation can be viewed in Table 21.7.

Results

Table 21.8 details the results of the two approaches and compares them to the market value of MS's equity on February 4, one day before the merger announcement.

The results are mixed. We cannot say whether MS was being undervalued or overvalued by the markets. The comparable companies approach gave the lowest results because some of the companies in the pool, such as Bear Stearns and Salomon Bros., are not highly valued by the market. The formula approach gives a higher value because it assumes growth higher than MS's growth for the last five years. Based on the 1.65 exchange ratio on February 4, 1997 (DWD share price = $38.625), DWD was offering MS shareholders $9,714 million. This price would go higher as the stock market reacted. This does not necessarily mean that DWD overpaid. This price included a control premium for MS shareholders, and it also took into account possible synergies and cost savings that would result from the merger.

DEAL SYNERGIES

Although many feel that DWD and MS operate at two opposite spectrums of the securities business, the market believed that the merger contained many synergies and was a positive move for both parties. According to DWD's CEO, the deal is "based on powerful franchises, high profitability and opportunities for accelerated growth."

- In securities, it combines MS's strengths in investment banking and institutional sales and trading with DWD's in retail distribution and asset gathering. In asset management, the new entity will manage more than $270 billion, the largest of any securities firm. In credit services, MS's global presence will create opportunities for expansion. Cross-selling of Discover cards to MS clientele may occur.
- The deal creates an entity with unmatched origination and distribution skills and a global presence among both providers and users of capital.
- The deal will enable both firms "to do far more together than either could have done separately," in the words of MS's chairman.
- It enhances the value drivers in this business: preeminent brands, quality professionals, proprietary distribution, multiple channels, broad customer relationships, global platform, size, and scale.
- The deal includes complementary origination and distribution. (1) Morgan Stanley can supply its product through DWD's distribution channels, including its top-ranked research, underwritten equity and

Table 21.6 Valuation of Morgan Stanley (Premerger) Using the Formula Approach, 1988–1995

	(1) Current Assets Total	*(2)* Marketable Securities	*(3)* Current Liabilities Total	*(4)* Debt in Current Liabilities	*(5)* Pretax Income	*(6)* Income Taxes Total
1988	$ 39,312	$24,504	$ 36,951	$ 32,561	$ 637	$ 242
1989	$ 52,366	$24,877	$ 49,565	$ 44,252	$ 738	$ 295
1990	$ 53,009	$15,836	$ 49,201	$ 41,580	$ 470	$ 200
1991	$ 62,951	$17,892	$ 57,314	$ 47,966	$ 772	$ 297
1992	$ 79,610	$23,170	$ 72,896	$ 61,357	$ 793	$ 283
1993	$ 96,127	$29,370	$ 86,305	$ 70,627	$1,200	$ 414
1994	$115,168	$38,029	$103,926	$ 86,762	$ 594	$ 199
1995	$141,841	$47,225	$128,813	$101,470	$ 883	$ 283
Totals					$6,088	$2,213

	Historicals	Projected
$X_0 =$	$6,384	$6,384
$T =$	36.36%	36.36%
$b =$	228.79%	228.79%
$r =$	4.22%	4.90%
$g =$	9.66%	11.21%
$n =$		5
$k =$	3.34%	3.28%
$(1 + h) = (1 + g)/(1 + k) =$	1.061	1.077
Risk free rate	5.40%	5.40%
Market return	12.70%	12.00%
Beta	1.49	1.49
Cost of equity	16.28%	15.20%
Cost of debt[1]	3.97%	3.97%
After tax cost of debt	2.53%	2.53%
$S/(B + S)^2$	5.94%	5.94%
$B/(B + S)^2$	94.06%	94.06%

Note: Data for 1985–1987 was eliminated because Compustat did not separate out marketable securities. Calculations may not compute due to rounding.

[1]*Interest expense/total liabilities (for 1995).*

[2]*Based on 2/4/97 MS market value of equity of $8.745 billion and total debt of $138.579 billion.*
Source: Compustat.
*Calculation of k

$k_s = R_f + (R_m - R_f)\beta$
$\quad = 0.054 + (0.12 - 0.054)1.49$
$\quad = 0.054 + (0.066)1.49$
$\quad = 15.2\%$
$k = k_s(1 - L) + k_b(1 - T)(L)$
$\quad = 0.152(0.0594) + 0.0397(0.6364)(0.9406)$
$\quad = 0.009 + 0.0238$
$k = 0.0328$

(7)	(8)	(9)	(10)	(11)	(12)
Interest Expense	Property, Plant, and Equipment Total (Net)	Net Working Capital $(1-2)-(3-4)$	Total Capital $(8+9)$	Investment (Delta 10)	EBIT $(5+7)$
$1,905	$ 238	$10,419	$10,657		$ 2,541
$3,378	$ 268	$22,175	$22,442	$11,785	$ 4,117
$3,711	$ 385	$29,553	$29,938	$ 7,495	$ 4,181
$3,925	$ 544	$35,711	$36,255	$ 6,317	$ 4,697
$4,362	$ 552	$44,902	$45,454	$ 9,199	$ 5,156
$5,020	$ 778	$51,079	$51,857	$ 6,403	$ 6,220
$5,875	$1,061	$59,975	$61,036	$ 9,179	$ 6,469
$5,501	$1,286	$67,273	$68,559	$ 7,523	$ 6,384
				$57,902	$39,765

Valuation:

$$\text{1st term} = X_0(1-T)(1-b)\sum_{t=1}^{n}\left(\frac{1+g}{1+k}\right)^t = \qquad -\$32,843\ (-22.4\%)$$

$$\text{2nd term} = \frac{X_0(1-T)}{k}\left(\frac{1+g}{1+k}\right)^n = \qquad \$179,309\ (122.4\%)$$

Total value of FIRM =	$146,466 (100.0%)
Debt in current liabilities	$101,470
Long-term debt	$ 9,171
Other liabilities	$ 27,938
Implied Equity Value	$ 7,887

Table 21.7   Comparables Valuation for MS: Premerger

Comparable Companies	Market/Sales*	Market/Book**	P/E = Market/Net Income†
Bear Stearns	0.91	1.43	7.75
A.G. Edwards	1.65	1.97	11.60
Lehman Bros.	0.28	1.03	10.69
Merrill Lynch	0.87	2.64	11.66
Salomon Brothers	0.68	1.43	7.22
Paine Webber	0.64	2.06	9.48
Average	0.84	1.76	9.73
	Sales	**Book Value**	**Net Income**
Morgan Stanley	9,124	4,653	600
	Market/Sales	**Market/Book**	**PE = Market/Net Income**
Equity valuation based on averages (in millions)	$7,648.95	$8,189.28	$5,840.00
Average Equity Valuation	$7,226.08 (in millions)		

Note: Market values are current values as of February 24, 1997.

*Sales are the latest available fiscal year-end sales.

**Book value is from the latest quarter available.

†Net income is from the latest 12 months available.
Source: Bloomberg Investor Services.

Table 21.8   Alternative Equity Valuations of MS

	Value of MS's Equity
Formula approach	$7,887 million
Comparable companies approach	$7,226 million
Equity value of MS on February 4, 1997	$8,745 million

fixed income securities, and its global products. (2) The entity's retail distribution will be strengthened, as account executives' productivity and growth is enhanced. (3) The entity's origination capability is enhanced, leading to increased lead management in underwritings and enhanced corporate relationships.

- The deal builds a powerful asset management platform. Multiple channels and brands are created, the product mix is more balanced, strengths can be leveraged across brands (DWD's mutual funds have not been stellar performers), and the business can expand globally with MS's global presence in Europe and emerging markets. Cost savings are also involved, as much of the trading, research, and back-office operations can be merged.

- In general, cost savings of $250 million are expected, and a loss of 600 jobs has occurred. (On February 24, 1997, DWD fired 600 employees in its New York headquarters.) The savings would come in the merging of data processing systems and reduced employment—in traders, institutional salespeople, research analysts, and back-office support personnel.

REASONS FOR THE DEAL AND DEAL CHALLENGES

Reasons from Both Parties' Perspective

Inevitably, this merger has the potential to create various synergies, including cutting capacity and costs, as duplicate functions at the two firms are erased. This could be one reason why the market reacted so positively. However, DWD's chairman stated: "[Cost savings is] not what we want you to walk away thinking about. The message we're giving you is a message of growth and revenues, not cost savings" (*USA Today,* February 6, 1997).

Reasons from MS's Perspective

MS favored the merger because

- It saw DWD as the perfect pipeline from Wall Street to Main Street.
- It wanted to increase its access to millions of Americans who have been lured to the stock market in recent years; the importance of the retail customer was a key factor in this merger.
- It eyed mutual funds, credit cards, and other retail business as a way to soften the rough cycles of the institutional brokerage business.
- It saw a higher growth potential among small retail investors.
- It saw wider profit margins in the retail business than in the investment banking business.

Reasons from DWD's Perspective

DWD favored the merger because

- Its customers would have access to many new investment choices from MS's stock and bond factory.
- It would be able to use the prestige of the MS name to attract money from ordinary investors.
- It could build its credit business globally with MS's global presence.

Challenges

First, integrating Morgan Stanley's aristocratic culture (although analysts say that "it is one of substance over appearance") with the "meat and potatoes" environment at DWD will prove to be challenging. The firms will mainly steer clear of conflict by their autonomy. Next, mergers of equals are usually very difficult to carry out, and often one party emerges as the dominant force. Dean Witter Discover will have to manage the egos of MS's executives. Finally, retail brokerages might be less inclined to push MS's mutual funds since the funds are now "associated" with competing broker DWD.

CONCLUSION

Overall, the market reacted very positively to this merger. The price paid by DWD was judged to be quite fair. There are many potential synergies and cost savings to be realized. The question remains: Can retail and institutional houses be successful under one roof? So far, only Merrill Lynch has been successful. Additionally, the health of the combined entity still depends greatly on the health of the financial markets.

QUESTIONS

1. What were the key financial industry developments that provided a background for the Dean Witter–Morgan Stanley merger?

2. Was the total market value of the two companies increased or decreased at the announcement of the proposed merger?

3. What are the business and financial factors involved that explain the market reaction to the proposed merger?

4. What are the main implementation challenges that will have to be managed well if the merger is to achieve its objectives?

5. From the data provided in the case, present your judgment of whether Dean Witter paid too much for Morgan Stanley.

6. Evaluate the merger on the basis of performance compared with Merrill Lynch and Salomon Smith Barney/Citigroup from 1997 to the present time.

REFERENCES

Anslinger, Patricia L., and Thomas E. Copeland, "Growth Through Acquisitions: A Fresh Look," *Harvard Business Review,* 74, January–February 1996, pp. 126–135.

Baker, George P., "Beatrice: A Study in the Creation and Destruction of Value," *Journal of Finance,* 47, 1992, pp. 1081–1120.

Chung, Kwang S., and J. Fred Weston, "Diversification and Mergers in a Strategic Long-Range-Planning Framework," chapter 13 in M. Keenan and L. J. White, eds., *Mergers and Acquisitions,* Lexington, MA: D. C. Heath & Co., 1982, pp. 315–347.

Coase, Ronald H., "The Nature of the Firm," *Economica,* 4, November 1937, pp. 386–405.

Drucker, Peter F., "Five Rules for Successful Acquisition," *The Wall Street Journal,* October 15, 1981, p. 28.

Galbraith, John K., *The New Industrial State,* Boston: Houghton Mifflin, 1967.

Steiner, George A., *Strategic Planning,* New York: Free Press, 1979.

Summer, Charles E., *Strategic Behavior in Business and Government,* Boston: Little, Brown and Company, 1980.

Weston, J. Fred, "Mergers and Acquisitions in Business Planning," *Rivista Internazionale di Scienze Economiche e Commerciali,* 17, April 1970, pp. 309–320.

———, "ROI Planning and Control," *Business Horizons,* 15, August 1972, pp. 35–42.

———, "The Rules for Successful Mergers," *Midland Corporate Finance Journal,* 1, Winter 1983, pp. 47–50.

———, and Thomas E. Copeland, *Managerial Finance,* 9th ed., Fort Worth, TX: The Dryden Press, 1992.

Glossary*

Abnormal return In event studies, the part of the return that is not predicted; the change in value caused by the event. Also excess return, benchmark adjusted.

Acquisition The purchase of a controlling interest in a firm, generally via a tender offer for the target shares.

Acquisition MLP Also called start-up master limited partnership; the assets of an existing entity are transferred to an MLP, and the business is henceforth conducted as an MLP. The Boston Celtics' conversion into an MLP is an example.

ACR See *Macroconcentration.*

Adverse selection Without a basis for buyers to identify good products, bad products will always be offered at the same price as good products; said to be a characteristic of the used-car market in which the buyer has to consider the probability that he is being offered a lemon.

Agency problem The conflict of interest between principal (e.g., shareholders) and agent (e.g., managers) in which the agent has an incentive to act in his own self-interest because he bears less than the total costs of his actions.

Anergy Negative synergy. Instead of a "2 + 2 = 5" effect, anergy implies "2 + 2 = 3." Business units actively interfere with each other and may have more value if separated.

Announcement date In event studies, typically, the day information becomes public.

Antigreenmail amendment Corporate charter amendment that prohibits targeted share repurchases at a premium from an unwanted acquirer without the approval of nonparticipating shareholders.

Antitakeover amendment A corporate charter amendment that is intended to make it more difficult for an unwanted acquirer to take over the firm.

Any-or-all offer A tender offer that does not specify a maximum number of shares to be purchased, but none will be purchased if the conditions of the offer are not met.

Appraisal right The right of minority shareholders to obtain an independent valuation of their shares to determine the appropriate back-end value in a two-tier tender offer.

APT See *Arbitrage pricing theory.*

Arbitrage The purchase of an asset for near-term resale at a higher price. In the context of M&As, risk arbitrage refers to investing in the stock of takeover targets for short-term resale to capture a portion of the gains that typically accrue to target shareholders.

Arbitrage pricing theory A general approach to asset pricing that allows for the possibility that multiple factors may be used to explain asset returns, as opposed to the capital asset pricing model. (See *Capital asset pricing.*)

Atomistic competition Numerous small sellers and buyers, none of which have the power to influence market prices or output.

Atomistic shareholders Each shareholder has only a small amount of stock. Small shareholders have less incentive to monitor management than large block shareholders.

Auction Two or more bidders competing for a single target. An auction increases the price target shareholders receive.

Back-end value The amount paid to remaining shareholders in the second stage of a two-tier or partial tender offer.

Bear hug A takeover strategy in which the acquirer, without previous warning, mails the directors of the target a letter announcing the acquisition proposal and demanding a quick decision.

---

*Technical terms used in explanations are defined in their alphabetical position.

Benchmark   A company, group of companies, or portfolio used as a standard of performance.

Beta   In the capital asset pricing model, the systematic risk of the asset; the variability of the asset's return in relation to the return on the market.

Bidder   The acquiring firm in a tender offer.

Blended price   The weighted average price in a two-tier tender offer. The front-end price is weighted by the percent of shares purchased in the first step of the transaction, and the lower, back-end price is weighted by the percent of shares purchased to complete the transaction.

Blockholder   The holder of a significant percentage of the ownership shares.

Board-out clause   A provision in most supermajority antitakeover amendments which gives the board of directors the power to decide when and if the supermajority provision will be in effect.

Bootstrap transaction   A highly leveraged transaction (HLT).

Bottom-up   An approach to firm strategy formulation based on the aggregation of segment forecasts.

Bounded rationality   Refers to the limited capacity of the human mind to deal with complexity.

Brand-name capital   Firm reputation; the result of nonsalvageable investment which provides customers with an implicit guarantee of product quality for which they are willing to pay a premium.

Breach of trust   Unilaterally changing the terms of a contract.

Business judgment rule   A legal doctrine which holds that the board of directors is acting in the best interests of shareholders unless it can be proven by a preponderance of the evidence that the board is acting in its own interest or is in breach of its fiduciary duty.

Bust-up takeover   An acquisition followed by the divestiture of some or all of the operating units of the acquired firm which can be sold at prices greater than their current value.

Buyback   See *Share repurchase.*

Calls   Options to buy an asset at a specified price for a specified period of time.

Capital asset pricing model   Calculates the required return on an asset as a function of the risk-free rate plus the market risk premium times the asset's beta.

Capital budgeting   The process of planning expenditures whose returns extend over a period of time.

Capital intensity   In economics, the ratio of investment required per dollar of sales. In finance, the sales to investment ratio. The steel industry and manufacturing generally are more capital intensive than the wholesale or retail industries.

CAPM   See *Capital asset pricing model.*

CAR   See *Cumulative abnormal return.*

Cash cows   A Boston Consulting Group term for business segments which have a high market share in low-growth product markets and thus throw off more cash flow than needed for reinvestment.

Chinese wall   The imaginary barrier separating investment banking and other activities within a financial intermediary.

Classified board   Also called a staggered board. An antitakeover measure which divides a firm's board of directors into several classes, only one of which is up for election in any given year, thus delaying effective transfer of control to a new owner in a takeover.

Clayton Act   Federal antitrust law originally passed in 1914 and strengthened in 1950 by the Celler-Kefauver amendment. Section 7 gives the Federal Trade Commission (FTC) power to prohibit the acquisition of one company by another if adverse effects on competition would result, or if the FTC perceived a trend which might ultimately lead to decreased competition.

Clean-up merger   Also called a take-out merger. The consolidation of the acquired firm into the acquiring firm after the acquirer has obtained control.

Clientele effect   A dividend theory which states that high-tax bracket shareholders will prefer to hold stock in firms with low dividend payout rates and low-tax bracket shareholders will prefer the stock of firms with high payouts.

Coercive tender offer   Any tender offer which puts pressure on target shareholders to tender by offering a higher price to those who tender early.

Coinsurance effect The combination of two firms whose cash flows are not perfectly correlated will result in cash flows of less variability for the merged firm, thus decreasing the risk to lenders to the firm and thereby increasing its debt capacity.

Collateral restraints Agreements between the parties to a joint venture to limit competition between themselves in certain areas.

Collusion Illegal coordination or cooperation among competitors with respect to price or output.

Complementarity The strengths of one firm offset the weaknesses of another firm with which it combines. For example, one firm strong in marketing combines with one strong in research.

Concentration Measures of the percentage of total industry sales accounted for by a specified number of firms, such as 4, 8, or 20.

Concentric merger A merger in which there is carry-over in *specific* management functions (e.g., marketing) or complementarity in relative strengths among *specific* management functions rather than carry-over/ complementarities in only generic management functions (e.g., planning).

Conglomerate A combination of unrelated firms; any combination that is not vertical or horizontal.

Conjectural variation The reaction of rival firms as one firm, Firm A, restricts output or raises prices. Ranges from -1 to $+1$; a negative conjectural variation indicates competitive behavior, i.e., Firm A's action is offset by the reactions of competing rival firms.

Contingent voting rights Rights to vote in corporate elections which become exercisable upon the occurrence of a particular event. Examples: Preferred stockholders may win the right to vote if preferred dividends are missed; convertible debt may be viewed as having voting rights contingent upon conversion.

Convergence of interests hypothesis Predicts a positive relationship between the proportion of management stock ownership and the market's valuation of the firm's assets.

Cost leadership A business strategy based on achieving lower costs than rivals.

Covenant See *Indenture.*

Crown jewels The most valuable segments of a company; the parts most wanted by an acquirer.

Cumulative abnormal return (CAR) In event studies, the sum of daily abnormal returns over a period relative to the event.

Cumulative voting Instead of one vote per candidate selected, shareholders can vote (the number of share they hold times the number of directors to be elected) for one candidate or divide the total votes among a desired number of candidates. Example: A shareholder has 100 shares; six directors are to be elected. With cumulative voting the shareholder has 600 votes to distribute among six candidates however he or she chooses.

DCF See *Discounted cash flow valuation.*

Decision control Fundamental ownership rights of shareholders to select management, monitor management, and to determine reward/incentive arrangements.

Decision management Decision functions related to day-to-day operations which may be delegated to managers. Includes initiation and implementation of policies and procedures.

Defensive diversification Entering new product markets to offset the limitations of the firm's existing product-market areas.

Defined benefit plan A pension plan which specifies in advance the amount beneficiaries will receive based on compensation, years of service, and so on.

Defined contribution plan A pension plan in which the annual contributions are specified in advance. Benefits upon retirement depend on the performance of the assets in which the contributions are invested.

Delphi technique An information-gathering technique in which questionnaires are sent to informed individuals. The responses are summarized into a feedback report and used to generate subsequent questionnaires to probe more deeply into the issue under study.

De novo entry Entry into an industry by forming a new company as opposed to combining with an existing firm in the industry.

Differential managerial efficiency hypothesis A theory that hypothesizes that more efficient managements take over firms with less efficient managements and achieve gains by improving the efficiency of the target.

Discounted cash flow valuation (DCF) The application of an appropriate cost of capital to a future stream of cash flows.

Discriminatory poison pill Antitakeover plans that penalize acquirers who exceed a given shareholding percentage (the kick-in or trigger point).

Dissident A shareholder or group of shareholders who disagrees with incumbent management and seeks to make changes via a proxy contest to gain representation on the board of directors.

Diversification The holding of assets whose returns are not perfectly correlated.

Divestiture Sale of a segment of a company (assets, a product line, a subsidiary) to a third party for cash and/or securities.

Dividend growth valuation model The application of an appropriate discount factor to a future stream of dividends.

Dividend method dual-class recapitalization Most widely used method of converting to dual-class stock ownership. A stock split or dividend is used to distribute new inferior voting stock. The previously existing common stock is redesignated as superior-vote class B stock.

Dogs A Boston Consulting Group term for business segments characterized by low market shares in product markets with low growth rates.

Dual-class recapitalization Corporate restructuring used to create two classes of common stock with the superior-vote stock concentrated in the hands of management.

Dual-class stock Two (or more) classes of common stock with equal rights to cash flows but with unequal voting rights.

DuPont system A financial planning and control system focusing on return on investment by relating asset turnover (effective asset management) to profit margin on sales (effective cost control).

Dutch auction repurchases (DARs) Shareholders are permitted to put their shares to the company within a range of prices; at a price at which the company's target level of shares is reached, all shares offered receive that price.

Dynamic competition theory A model of industrial organization theory that extends the traditional models of price and output decisions of firms in a static environment to decisions on product quality, innovation, promotion, marketing, and so on in changing environments.

Dynamic oligopoly Although an industry may be dominated by a few large firms (oligopoly), recognized interdependence does not occur because decisions must be made on so many factors that actions and reactions of rivals cannot be predicted or coordinated.

Empirical test Systematic examination of data to check the consistency of evidence with alternative theories.

Employee Retirement Income Security Act (ERISA) 1974 federal legislation regulating pension plans including some ESOPs. Sets vesting requirements, fiduciary standards, minimum funding standards. Established the Pension Benefit Guarantee Corporation (PBGC) to guarantee pensions.

Employee stock ownership plan (ESOP) Defined contribution pension plan (stock bonus and/or money purchase) designed to invest primarily in the stock of the employer firm.

End of regulation A theory hypothesizing that takeovers occur following deregulation of an industry as a result of increased competition, which exposes management inefficiency that may have been masked by regulation.

Entrenchment See *Managerial entrenchment hypothesis*.

Equity carve-out A transaction in which a parent firm offers *some* of a subsidiary's common stock to the general public to bring in a cash infusion to the parent without loss of control.

ERISA See *Employee Retirement Income Security Act*.

ERISA-type ESOP Employee stock ownership plans other than tax credit ESOPs; i.e., includes leveraged, leveragable, and nonleveraged ESOPs recognized under ERISA rather than under the Tax Reduction Act of 1975.

ESOP See *Employee stock ownership plan*.

Event returns   A measure of the stock price reaction to the announcement of significant new information such as a takeover or some type of restructuring.

Event study   An empirical test of the effect of an event (e.g., a merger, divestiture) on stock returns. The event is the reference date from which analysis of returns is made regardless of the calendar timing of the occurrences in the sample of firms.

Excess return   See *Abnormal return.*

Exchange method dual-class recapitalization   Means of converting to a dual-class stock corporate structure. High-vote stock is issued to insiders in exchange for their currently outstanding (low-vote) stock. The remaining low-vote stock, in the hands of outside shareholders, generally receives a higher dividend.

Exchange offer   A transaction that provides one class (or more) of securities with the right or option to exchange part or all of their holdings for a different class of the firm's securities, e.g., an exchange of debt for common stock. Enables a change in capital structure with no change in investment.

Exit-type firm   In Jensen's free cash flow hypothesis, a firm with positive free cash flows. The theory predicts that for such a firm, stock prices will increase with unexpected increases in payout.

Extra merger premium hypothesis   The possibility that a higher price will be paid for superior vote shares if a dual-class stock firm becomes a takeover target causes the price of superior vote stock to be higher even in the absence of a takeover bid.

Failing firm defense   A defense against a merger challenge alleging that in the absence of the merger, the firm(s) would fail. The 1982 Merger Guidelines spell out the conditions under which this defense will be acceptable.

Fair-price amendment   An antitakeover charter amendment that waives the supermajority approval requirement for a change of control if a fair price is paid for all purchased shares. Defends against two-tier offers that do not have board approval.

Fallen angel   A bond issued at investment grade whose rating is subsequently dropped to below investment grade, below BBB.

Financial conglomerates   Conglomerate firms in which corporate management provides a flow of funds to operating segments, exercises control and strategic planning functions, and is the ultimate financial risk taker but does *not* participate in operating decisions.

Financial Institutions Reform, Recovery, and Enforcement Act (FIRREA)   A 1989 law changing the regulatory rules for savings and loan companies as well as other financial institutions.

Financial synergy   A theory that suggests a financial motive for mergers, especially between firms with high internal cash flows (but poor investment opportunities) and firms with low internal cash flows (and high investment opportunities which, absent merger, would require costly external financing). Also includes increased debt capacity or coinsurance effect and economies of scale in flotation and transactions costs of securities.

Fixed-price tender offers (FPTs)   A method of share repurchase in which a put price is specified for a specified number of company shares.

Flip-in poison pill plan   Shareholders of the target firm are issued rights to acquire stock in the target at a substantial discount when a bidder has reached a designated percentage ownership trigger point.

Flip-over poison pill plan   Shareholders of the target firm are issued rights to purchase the common stock of the surviving company at a substantial discount when a bidder has reached a designated percentage ownership trigger point.

Formula approach   A discounted cash flow valuation in which key variables or value drivers are used to calculate the net present value of a project or firm.

Four-firm concentration ratio   The sum of the shares of sales, value added, assets, or employees held by the largest four firms in an industry. A measure of competitiveness according to the structural theory.

Free cash flow   Cash flows in excess of positive net present value investment opportunities available.

Free cash flow hypothesis   Jensen's theory of how the payout of free cash flows helps resolve the agency problem between managers and shareholders. Holds that bonding payout of current (and future) free cash flows reduces the power of management as well as subjecting it more frequently to capital market scrutiny.

Free-rider problem   Atomistic shareholder reasons that its decision has no impact on the outcome of the tender offer and refrains from tendering to free-ride on the value increase resulting from the merger, thus causing the bid to fail.

Front-end loading   A tender offer in which the offer price is greater than the value of any unpurchased shares. Resolves the free-rider problems by providing an incentive to tender early.

Full ex post settling up   A manager's compensation is frequently adjusted over the course of his or her career to fully reflect his or her performance, thus eliminating an incentive to shirk.

Gambler's ruin   An adverse string of losses that could lead to bankruptcy, although the long-run cash flows could be positive.

Game theory   An analysis of the behavior (actions and reactions) of participants under specified rules, information, and strategies.

General Utilities doctrine   An IRS rule that allowed firms to not recognize gains on the distribution of appreciated property in redemption of its shares (e.g., in a "legal" liquidation). Repealed by the Tax Reform Act of 1986.

Generic management functions   Those functions that are not industry-specific and are thus transferrable even in conglomerate mergers. Include planning, organizing, directing, and controlling.

Going-concern value   The value of the firm as a whole over and above the sum of the values of each of its parts; the value of organization learning and reputation.

Going private   The transformation of a public corporation into a privately held firm (often via a leveraged buyout or a management buyout).

Golden parachute   Provision in the employment contracts of top managers providing for compensation for loss of jobs following a change of control.

Goodwill   The excess of the purchase price paid for a firm over the book value received. Recorded on the acquirer's balance sheet, to be amortized over not more than 40 years (amortization not tax-deductible).

Greenmail   The premium over the current market price of stock paid to buy back the holdings accumulated by an unwanted acquirer to avoid a takeover.

Gross present value   An appropriately discounted stream of future cash flows before the deduction of investment costs.

Growth–share matrix   A guide to strategy formulation that emphasizes attainment of high market share in industries with favorable growth rates.

Harassment hypothesis   Ellert's theory that Federal Trade Commission antitrust complaints are brought against firms with abnormally good stock price performance at the instigation of the firms' competitors who are threatened by their superior performance.

Hart-Scott-Rodino Antitrust Improvements Act of 1976   Expands power of Department of Justice in antitrust investigations; provides for waiting period (15 days for tender offers, 30 days for mergers) following submission of information to Department of Justice and Federal Trade Commission before transaction can be completed; expands power of state attorneys general to institute triple damage antitrust lawsuits on behalf of their citizens.

Herfindahl-Hirschman Index (HHI)   The measure of concentration under the 1982 Merger Guidelines, defined as the sum of the *squares* of the market shares of *all* the firms in the industry.

HHI   See *Herfindahl-Hirschman Index.*

Hidden equity   Undervalued assets whose market value exceeds their depreciated book value but is not reflected in stock price.

Highly leveraged transaction (HLT) Use of debt in relation to equity in excess of average industry ratios.

High yield bond See *Junk bond.*

Holding company An organization whose primary function is to hold the stock of other corporations but that has no operating units of its own. Similar to the multidivisional organization, which has profit centers and a single central headquarters. However, the segments owned by the holding company are separate legal entities that in practice are controlled by the holding company.

Holdup Whenever a resource is dependent on (specialized to) the rest of the firm, there may be a temptation for others to try to expropriate the quasi-rent of the dependent resource by withholding their complementary resources; this is holdup. However, each resource in the team (firm) may be dependent on all the others, and thus all are vulnerable to expropriation.

Horizontal merger A combination of firms operating in the same business activity.

Hostile takeover A tender offer that proceeds even after it has been opposed by the management of the target.

Hubris hypothesis (Winner's curse) Roll's theory that acquiring firm managers commit errors of overoptimism in evaluating merger opportunities (due to excessive pride, animal spirits) and end up paying too high a price for acquisitions.

IAA See *Investment Advisers Act of 1940.*

ICA See *Investment Company Act of 1940.*

Implicit claim A tacit rather than contractual promise of continuing service and delivery of expected quality to customers and job security to employees.

Incentive stock option (ISO) An executive compensation plan to align the interests of managers with stockholders. Executives are issued options whose exercise price is equal to or greater than the stock price at the time of issue and thus have value only if the stock price rises, giving managers incentives to take actions to maximize stock price.

Increased debt capacity hypothesis A theory that postmerger financial leverage increases are the result of increased debt capacity (as opposed to the firms involved having been underleveraged before the merger) due to reduced expected bankruptcy costs.

Indenture The contract between a firm and its bondholders that sets out the terms and conditions of the borrowing and the rights and obligations of each party (covenants).

Industry life cycle A conceptual model of the different stages of an industry's development. (1) Development stage—new product, high investment needs, losses. (2) Growth stage—consumer acceptance, expanding sales, high profitability, ease of entry. (3) Maturity stage—sales growth slows, excess capacity, prices and profits decline—key period for merger strategy. (4) Decline stage—substitute products emerge, sales growth declines, pressure for mergers to survive.

Inferior-vote stock In dual-class stock firms, the class of common stock that has less voting power, e.g., may be able to elect only a minority on the board of directors; may be compensated with higher dividends.

Information asymmetry A game or decisions in which one party has more information than other players.

Initial public offering (IPO) The first offering to the public of common stock (e.g., of a former privately held firm) or a portion of the common stock of a hitherto wholly owned subsidiary.

In play Because of a bid or rumors of a bid, the financial community regards the company as receptive or vulnerable to takeover bids.

Insider trading Some parties take action based on information not available to outside investors.

Internal rate of return (IRR) A capital budgeting method that finds the discount rate (the IRR) that equates the present value of cash inflows and investment outlays. The IRR must equal or exceed the relevant risk-adjusted cost of capital for the project to be acceptable.

Investment Advisers Act of 1940 (IAA) Federal securities legislation providing for registration and regulation of investment advisers.

Investment Company Act of 1940 (ICA) Federal securities legislation regulating publicly owned companies in the business of investing and trading in securities; subjects them to SEC rules. Amended in 1970 to place more controls on management compensation and sales charges.

Investment requirements ratio A firm's investment expenditures (or opportunities) in relation to after-tax cash flows.

IPO See *Initial public offering.*

IRR See *Internal rate of return.*

ISO See *Incentive stock option.*

Joint production Production using complementary inputs in which the output cannot be unambiguously attributed to any single input and in which the output is greater than the sum of the inputs (i.e., synergy). Problems in assigning returns may arise if the inputs are not owned by the same entity.

Joint venture A combination of subsets of assets contributed by two (or more) business entities for a specific business purpose and a limited duration. Each of the venture partners continues to exist as a separate firm, and the joint venture represents a new business enterprise.

Junk bond High yield bonds that are below investment grade when issued, that is, rated below BBB (Standard & Poor's) or below Baa3 (Moody's).

Kick-in or trigger point The level of share ownership by an acquiring firm that activates a poison pill antitakeover defense plan.

Kick-in-the-pants hypothesis Attributes the increase in a takeover target's stock price to the impetus given by the bid to target management to implement a higher valued strategy.

Latent debt capacity hypothesis A theory that postmerger increases in financial leverage are due to underleverage in the premerger period.

LBO See *Leveraged buyout.*

LCO Leveraged cash-out. See *Leveraged recapitalization.*

Learning-by-doing A means of transferring knowledge that is complex or embedded in a complex set of technological and/or organizational circumstances and thus difficult or impossible to transfer in a class-room setting. May motivate knowledge acquisition joint ventures.

Learning curve An approach to strategy formulation that hypothesizes that costs decline with cumulative volume experience, resulting in competitive advantage for the first entrants into an industry.

Leveraged buyout (LBO) The purchase of a company by a small group of investors, financed largely by debt. Usually entails going private.

Leveraged cash-out (LCO) See *Leveraged recapitalization.*

Leveraged ESOP An employee stock ownership plan recognized under ERISA in which the ESOP borrows funds to purchase employer securities. The employer then makes tax-deductible contributions to the ESOP sufficient to cover both principal repayment and interest on the loan.

Leveraged recapitalization A defensive reorganization of the firm's capital structure in which outside shareholders receive a large one-time cash dividend and inside shareholders receive new shares of stock instead. The cash dividend is largely financed with newly borrowed funds, leaving the firm highly leveraged and with a greater proportional ownership share in the hands of management. Also called leveraged cash-out.

Life cycle model of firm ownership A theory that suggests that firms will attract different shareholder clienteles (high or low tax bracket investors) over different periods of firm development depending on changing investment needs and profitability.

Line and staff An organizational form characterized by the separation of support activities (staff) from operations (line).

Liquidation Divestiture of all the assets of a firm so that the firm ceases to exist.

Liquidation MLP The complete liquidation of a corporation into a master limited partnership.

Lock-in amendment A corporate charter amendment that makes it more difficult to void previously passed (antitakeover) amendments, e.g., by requiring supermajority approval for a change.

Lock-up option   An option to buy a large block of newly issued shares that target management may grant to a favored bidder, thus virtually guaranteeing that the favored bidder will succeed. Target management's ability to grant a lock-up option induces bidders to negotiate.

Logical incrementalism   A process of effecting major changes in strategy via a series of relatively small (incremental) changes.

M-form   See *Multidivisional corporation*.

Macroconcentration   An overall measure of the share of sales or value added by a specified number of firms; their share is the aggregate concentration ratio (ACR).

Management buyout (MBO)   A going-private transaction led by the incumbent managers of the formerly public firm.

Managerial conglomerates   Conglomerate firms that provide managerial expertise, counsel, and interaction on decisions to operating units. Based on the transferability of generic management skills even across nonrelated businesses.

Managerial entrenchment hypothesis   A theory that antitakeover efforts are motivated by managers' self-interests in keeping their jobs rather than in the best interests of shareholders.

Managerialism   A theory that managers pursue mergers and acquisitions to increase the size of the organizations they control and thus increase their compensation.

Marginal cost of capital (MCC)   The relevant discount factor for a current decision.

Market-adjusted return   The return for a firm for a period is its actual return less the return on the market index for that period.

Market extension merger   A combination of firms whose operations had previously been conducted in nonoverlapping geographic areas.

Market model   In event studies, the most widely used method of calculating the return predicted if no event took place. In this method, a clean period (with no events) is chosen, and a regression is run of firm returns against the market index return over the clean period. The regression coefficient and intercept are then used with the market index return for the day of interest in the event period to predict what the return for the firm would have been on that day had no event taken place.

Market value rule   The principle that all decisions of a corporation should be judged solely by their contribution to the market value of the firm's stock.

Mark-to-market accounting   At statement dates, assets and liabilities are restated to measures of their current market values.

Markup return   The event return measured from the announcement date to various designated dates thereafter.

Master limited partnership (MLP)   An organizational form in which limited partnership interests are publicly traded (like shares of corporate stock) while retaining the tax attributes of a partnership.

Matrix organization   Company that has functional departments assigned to subunits organized around products or geography. Employees report to a functional manager as well as a product manager.

Maximum limit offer   A stock repurchase tender offer in which all tendered shares will be purchased if the offer is undersubscribed, but if the offer is oversubscribed, shares may be purchased only on a pro rata basis.

MBO   See *Management buyout*.

Mean adjusted return   The actual return for a period less the average (mean) return calculated for a time segment before, after, or both in relation to the event.

Merger   Any transaction that forms one economic unit from two or more previous units.

Mezzanine financing   Subordinated debt issued in connection with leveraged buyouts. Sometimes carries payment-in-kind (PIK) provisions, in which debt holders receive more of the same kind of debt securities in lieu of cash payments under specified conditions.

Microconcentration   A measure of the market share of individual firms or groups such as the four-firm concentration ratio or a measure of inequality of market shares such as the HHI.

Minority squeeze-out The elimination by controlling shareholders of noncontrolling (minority) shareholders.

Misappropriation doctrine A rationale for insider trading prosecution of outsiders who trade on the basis of information that they have "misappropriated," e.g., stolen from their employers or obtained by fraud.

MLP See *Master limited partnership.*

MNE See *Multinational enterprise.*

Money purchase plan A defined contribution pension plan in which the firm contributes a specified annual amount of cash as opposed to stock bonus plans in which the firm contributes stock, and profit-sharing plans in which the amount of the annual cash contribution depends on profitability.

Monopoly A single seller.

Moral hazard One party (principal) relies on the behavior of another (agent), and it is costly to observe information or action. Opportunistic behavior in which success benefits one party and failure injures another, e.g., high leverage benefits equity holders under success and injures creditors under failure.

Muddling through An approach to strategy formulation in which policy makers focus only on those alternatives that differ incrementally (i.e., only a little) from existing policies rather than considering a wider range of alternatives.

Multidivisional corporation (M-form) An organizational form to achieve greater efficiency via profit centers to reduce the need for information flow across divisions and to guide resource allocation to the highest valued uses. Benefits from large fixed investment in general management expertise (especially strategic planning, monitoring, and control) spread over a number of individual decentralized operations (at which level decision making on specific management functions takes place).

Multinational enterprise (MNE) A business organization with operations in more than one country, beyond import–export operations.

NAAG See *National Association of Attorneys General.*

NASDAQ Stock quotation system of the National Association of Securities Dealers for stocks that trades over the counter as opposed to on an organized exchange.

National Association of Attorneys General (NAAG) An organization of state attorneys general.

Negotiated share repurchase Refers to buying back the stock of a large blockholder (an unwanted acquirer) at a premium over market price (greenmail).

Net operating loss carryover Tax provision allowing firms to use net operating losses to offset taxable income over a period of years before and after the loss. Available to firms that acquire a loss firm only under strictly specified conditions.

Net present value (NPV) Capital budgeting criterion that compares the present value of cash inflows of a project discounted at the risk-adjusted cost of capital to the present value of investment outlays (discounted at the risk-adjusted cost of capital).

Niche opportunities A business strategy that aims at meeting the needs or interests of specific consumer groups.

NOL carryover See *Net operating loss carryover.*

Nolo contendere A legal plea in which a defendant, without admitting guilt, declines to contest allegations of wrongdoing.

Nondiscriminatory poison pill Antitakeover defense plans that do not penalize acquirers exceeding a given shareholding limit. Include flip-over plans, preferred stock plans, and ownership flip-in plans that permit cash offers for all shares.

Nonleveraged ESOP An employee stock ownership plan recognized under ERISA that does not provide for borrowing by the ESOP. Essentially the same as a stock bonus plan.

Normal return In event studies, the predicted return if no event took place, the reference point for the calculation of abnormal, or excess, return attributable to the event.

No-shop agreement The target agrees not to consider other offers while negotiating with a particular bidder.

NPV See *Net present value.*

Oligopoly A small number (few) of sellers.

Omnibus Budget Reconciliation Act of 1993 (OBRA) A tax law that included the conditions under which the excess purchase price over the accounting value of a target could be amortized as a tax-deductible expense.

Open corporations Fama and Jensen's term for large corporations whose residual claims (common stock) are least restricted. They identify the following characteristics: (1) They have property rights in net cash flows for an indefinite horizon; (2) stockholders are not required to hold any other role in the organization; (3) common stock is alienable (transferrable, saleable) without restriction.

Open-market share repurchase Refers to a corporation's buying its own shares on the open market at the going price just as any other investor might buy the corporation's shares, as opposed to a tender offer for share repurchase or a negotiated repurchase.

Operating synergy Combining two or more entities results in gains in revenues or cost reductions because of complementarities or economies of scale or scope.

Opportunism Self-interest seeking with guile, including shirking, cheating.

Organization capital Firm-specific informational assets that accumulate over time to enhance productivity. Includes information used in assigning employees to appropriate tasks and forming teams of employees, and the information each employee acquires about other employees and the organization. Alternatively, defined by Cornell and Shapiro as the current market value of all future implicit claims the firm expects to sell.

Organization culture An organization's "style" or approach to problem solving, relations with employees, customers, and other stakeholders.

Organization learning The improvement in skills and abilities of individuals or groups (teams) of employees through learning by experience within the firm. Includes managerial learning (generic, as well as industry-specific) and nonmanagerial labor learning.

Original plan poison pill Also called preferred stock plan. An early poison pill antitakeover defense in which the firm issues a dividend of convertible preferred stock to its common stockholders. If an acquiring firm passes a trigger point of share ownership, preferred stockholders (other than the large blockholder) can put the preferred stock to the target firm (force the firm to redeem it) at the highest price paid by the acquiring firm for the target's common or preferred stock during the past year. If the acquirer merges with the target, the preferred can be converted into acquirer voting stock with a market value no less than the redemption value at the trigger point.

Ownership flip-in plan A poison pill antitakeover defense often included as part of a flip-over plan. Target stockholders are issued rights to purchase target shares at a discount if an acquirer passes a specified level of share ownership. The acquirer's rights are void, and his or her ownership interest becomes diluted.

Pac Man defense The target makes a counterbid for the acquirer.

Parking A securities law violation in which traders attempt to hide the extent of their share ownership (to avoid the 5% trigger requiring disclosure of takeover intentions and keep down the price of target stock) by depositing, or parking, shares with an accomplice broker until a later date, e.g., when the takeover attempt is out in the open.

Partial tender offer A tender offer for less than all target shares; specifies a maximum number of shares to be accepted but does not announce bidder's plans with respect to the remaining shares.

Payment-in-kind (PIK) provision A clause that provides for issuance of more of the same type of securities to bondholders in lieu of cash interest payments.

Payroll-based ESOP (PAYSOP) A type of employee stock ownership plan in which employers could take a tax credit of 0.5% of ESOP-covered payroll. Repealed by the Tax Reform Act of 1986.

Pension plan A fund established by an organization to provide for benefits to plan participants (e.g., employees) after their retirement.

Perfect competition Set of assumptions for an idealized economic model: (1) Large numbers of buyers and sellers so none can influence market prices or output; (2) economies of scale exhausted at relatively small size and cost efficiencies are the same for all companies; (3) no significant barriers to entry; (4) constant innovation, new product development; (5) complete knowledge of all aspects of input/output markets is costlessly available.

PIK provision See *Payment-in-kind provision*.

Plasticity (Alchian and Woodward) Resources are considered plastic when a wide range of discretionary uses can be employed by the user. If monitoring costs are high, moral hazard problems are likely to develop.

Poison pill Any antitakeover defense that creates securities that provide their holders with special rights (e.g., to buy target or acquiring firm shares) exercisable only after a triggering event (e.g., a tender offer for or the accumulation of a specified percentage of target shares). Exercise of the rights would make it more difficult and/or costly for an acquirer to take over the target against the will of its board of directors.

Poison put A provision in some new bond issues designed to protect bondholders against takeover-related credit deterioration of the issuer. Following a triggering event, bondholders may put their bonds to the corporation at an exercise price of 100% to 101% of the bond's face amount.

Pooling of interests accounting Assets and liabilities of each firm are combined based solely on their previous accounting values.

Portfolio balance strategy A balance in business segments based on market growth–market share criteria. Combine high growth–high market share (stars), low growth–high market share (cash cows), low growth–low market share (dogs) segments to achieve favorable overall growth, profitability, and sufficient internal cash flows to finance positive NPV investment opportunities.

Potential competition Firms not in an industry at the present time but that could enter.

Predatory behavior A theory that holds that a dominant firm may price below cost or build excess capacity to inflict economic harm on existing firms and to deter potential entrants.

Premium buyback Refers to repurchasing the stock of a large blockholder (an unwanted acquirer) at a premium over market price (greenmail).

Price-cost margin (PCM) Defined as (Price minus Marginal Cost) divided by Price. That is, operating profit as a percentage of price. A zero PCM reflects perfect competition, i.e., Price = Marginal Cost.

Price pressure A theory that the demand curve for the securities of an individual company is downward sloping and that this causes negative stock price effects of large supply increases such as large block offerings.

Price trader Outside investors who trade in response to price changes in securities regardless of whether or not they understand the cause of the price change.

Product breadth Carryover of organizational capabilities to new products.

Product differentiation The development of a variety of product configurations to appeal to a variety of consumer tastes.

Product-extension merger A type of conglomerate merger; a combination between firms in related business activities that broadens the product lines of the firms; also called concentric mergers.

Product life cycle A conceptual model of the stages through which products or lines of business pass. Includes development, growth, maturity, and decline. Each stage presents its own threats and opportunities.

Production knowledge A form of organization learning; entrepreneurial or managerial ability to organize and maintain complex production processes economically.

Profit-sharing plan A defined contribution pension plan in which the firm's annual contributions to the plan are based on the firm's profitability.

Proxy contest An attempt by a dissident group of shareholders to gain representation on a firm's board of directors.

Public Utilities Holding Company Act of 1935 Federal securities legislation to correct abuses in financing and operation of gas and electric utility holding company systems.

Purchase accounting The total assets of the combined firm reflects the purchase price of the target.

Pure conglomerate merger A combination of firms in nonrelated business activities that is neither a product-extension nor a geographic extension merger.

Puts An option to sell an asset at a specified price for a designated period of time.

q-ratio (Tobin's q-ratio) The ratio of the market value of a firm's securities to the replacement costs of its physical assets.

Quasi-rent The excess return to an asset above the return necessary to maintain its current service flow.

Racketeer Influenced and Corrupt Organizations Act of 1970 (RICO) Federal legislation that provides for seizure of assets upon accusation and triple damages upon conviction for companies that conspire to defraud consumers, investors, and so on.

Recap See *Leveraged recapitalization.*

Recapture of depreciation The amount of prior depreciation that becomes taxable as ordinary income when an asset is sold for more than its tax basis.

Redistribution hypothesis A theory that value increases in mergers represent wealth shifts among stakeholders (e.g., a wealth transfer from bondholders to shareholders) rather than real increases in value.

Residual analysis The examination of asset returns to determine if a particular event has caused the return to deviate from a normal or predicted return that would have resulted if the event had not taken place. The difference between the actual return and the predicted return is the residual.

Residual claims The right of owners of an organization to cash flows not otherwise committed.

Restricted vote stock In dual-class stock firms, the stock with inferior voting rights.

Restructuring Significant changes in the strategies and policies relating to asset composition and liability and equity patterns as well as operations.

Retention ratio The percentage of free cash flows retained in the firm.

Returns to scale As scale of operations becomes larger, marginal and average costs decline.

Reverse LBOs Firms, or divisions of firms, that go public again after having been taken private in a leveraged buyout transaction.

Reverse mergers The uncombining of firms via spin-offs, divestitures, and so on.

RICO See *Racketeer Influenced and Corrupt Organizations Act of 1970.*

Risk-free rate The return on an asset with no risk of default. In theory, the return on short-term government securities.

Risk premium The differential of the required return on an asset in excess of the risk-free rate.

Roll-out MLP Also called spin-off MLP. A corporation transfers some of its assets to an MLP to avoid double taxation, for example, MLP units are initially distributed to corporate shareholders, and corporate management serves as the general partner.

Roll-up MLP The combination of several ordinary limited partnerships into a master limited partnership.

Royalty trust An organizational form used by firms that would otherwise be taxed heavily (due to declining depreciation and increasing pre-tax cash flows) to transfer ownership to investors in low tax brackets.

Runup return The event return measured for some period ending with the announcement date.

Sample selection bias Criteria for sample may exclude some relevant categories. Examples: Completed spin-offs will not include spin-offs announced but not completed. Measures of industry profitability will not include firms that have failed. Studies of leveraged buyouts that have a subsequent public offering will represent the most successful and exclude the failures or less successful.

Saturday night special A hostile tender offer with a short time for response.

Scale economies The reduction in per-unit costs achievable by spreading fixed costs over a higher level of production.

Schedule 13D A form that must be filed with the SEC within 10 days of acquiring 5% or more of a firm's stock; discloses the acquirer's identity and business intentions toward the target. Applies to all large stock acquisitions.

Schedule 14D A form that must be filed with the SEC by *any* group or individual making solicitations or recommendations that would result in its owning more than 5% of the target's stock. Applies to public tender offers only.

Scorched earth defenses Actions taken to make the target less attractive to the acquiring firm and that may also leave the target in weakened condition. Examples are sale of best segments (crown jewels) and incurring high levels of debt to pay a large dividend or to engage in substantial share repurchase.

Secondary initial public offering (SIPO) The reoffering to the public of common stock in a company that had initially been public but had then been taken private (e.g., in an LBO).

Second-step transaction Typically the merger of an acquired firm into the acquirer after control has been obtained.

Securities Act of 1933 (SA) First of the federal securities laws of the 1930s. Provides for federal regulation of the sale of securities to the public and registration of public offerings of securities.

Securities Exchange Act of 1934 (SEA) Federal legislation that established the Securities and Exchange Commission (SEC) to administer securities laws and to regulate practices in the purchase and sale of securities.

Securities Investor Protection Act of 1970 (SIPA) Federal legislation that established the Securities Investor Protection Corporation empowered to supervise the liquidation of bankrupt securities firms and to arrange for payments to their customers.

Securities parking An arrangement in which a second party holds ownership of assets to avoid identification of the actual owner in order to avoid rules and regulations related to securities trading.

Sell-off General term for divestiture of part or all of a firm by any one of a number of means—sale, liquidation, spin-off, and so on.

Shareholder interest hypothesis The theory that shareholder benefits of antitakeover defenses outweigh management entrenchment motives and effects.

Share repurchase A public corporation buys its own shares, by tender offer, on the open market or in a negotiated buyback from a large blockholder.

Shark repellent Any of a number of takeover defenses designed to make a firm less attractive and less vulnerable to unwanted acquirers.

Shark watcher A firm (usually a proxy solicitation firm) that monitors trading activity in its clients' stock to detect early accumulations by an unwanted acquirer before the 5% disclosure threshold.

Shelf registration The federal securities law provision in Rule 415 that allows firms to register at one time the total amount of debt or equity they plan to sell over a two-year period. Securities can then be sold with no further delays whenever market conditions are most favorable.

Sherman Act of 1890 Early antitrust legislation. Section 1 prohibits contracts, combinations, conspiracies in restraint of trade. Section 2 is directed against actual or attempted monopolization.

Short-swing trading rule Federal regulation under Section 16 of the Securities Exchange Act that prohibits designated corporate insiders from retaining the profits on any purchase and sale of their own firms' securities within a six-month period.

SIC See *Standard Industrial Classification*.

Signaling An action that conveys information to other players; for example, seasoned new equity issues signal that the stock is overvalued.

Silver parachutes Reduced golden parachute provisions extended to a wider range of managers.

SIPO See *Secondary initial public offering*.

Sitting-on-a-goldmine hypothesis Attributes the increase in a takeover target's stock price to information disclosed during the takeover process that the target's assets are undervalued by the market.

Small numbers problem When the number of bidders is large, rivalry among bidders renders opportunistic behavior ineffectual. When the number of bidders is small, each party seeks terms most favorable to it through opportunistic representations and haggling.

Specialized asset An asset whose use is complementary to other assets. For example, a pipeline from oil-producing fields to a cluster of refineries near large consumption markets.

Specificity The degree to which an asset or resource is specialized to and thus dependent on the rest of the firm or organization.

Spin-off A transaction in which a company distributes on a pro rata basis all of the shares it owns in a subsidiary to its own shareholders. Creates a new public company with (initially) the same proportional equity ownership as the parent company.

Split-off A transaction in which some, but not all, parent company shareholders receive shares in a subsidiary in return for relinquishing their parent company shares.

Split-up A transaction in which a company spins off all of its subsidiaries to its shareholders and ceases to exist.

Spreadsheet approach Analysis of data over a number of past and projected time periods.

Squeeze-out The elimination of minority shareholders by a controlling shareholder.

Staggered board Also called a classified board. An antitakeover measure that divides a firm's board of directors into several classes only one of which is up for election in any given year, thus delaying effective transfer of control to a new owner in a takeover.

Stakeholder Any individual or group who has an interest in a firm; in addition to shareholders and bondholders, includes labor, consumers, suppliers, the local community, and so on.

Stake-out investment Preliminary investment for a foothold in anticipation of the future possibility of a larger investment.

Standard Industrial Classification (SIC) The Census Bureau's system of categorizing industry groups, mainly product- or process-oriented.

Standstill agreement A voluntary contract by a large block shareholder (or former large blockholder bought out in a negotiated repurchase) not to make further investments in the target company for a specified period of time.

Start-up MLP Also called acquisition MLP. The assets of an existing entity are transferred to a master limited partnership, and the business is henceforth conducted as an MLP. The Boston Celtics' conversion into an MLP is an example.

Stepped-up asset basis The provision allowing asset purchasers to use the price paid for an asset as the starting point for future depreciation rather than the asset's depreciated book value in the hands of the seller.

Stock appreciation right (SAR) Part of an executive compensation program to align managers' interests with those of shareholders. SARs are issued to managers giving them the right to purchase stock on favorable terms; the exercise price can be as low as 50% of the stock price at issuance; maximum life is 10 years.

Stock bonus plan A defined contribution pension plan in which the firm contributes a specified number of shares to the plan annually. The benefits to plan beneficiaries depend on the stock performance.

Stock lockup An option to buy some fraction of the target stock at the first bidder's initial offer when a rival bidder wins.

Strategy The long-range planning process for an organization. A succession of plans (with provisions for implementation) for the future of a firm.

Strip financing A type of financing, often used in leveraged buyouts, in which all claimants hold approximately the same proportion of each security (except for management incentive shares and the most senior bank debt).

Structural theory An approach to industrial organization that argues that higher concentration in an industry causes less competition due to tacit coordination or overt collusion among the largest companies.

Stub New shares issued in exchange for old shares in a leveraged recapitalization.

Subchapter S corporation A form of business organization that provides the limited liability feature of the corporate form while allowing business income to be taxed at the personal tax rates of the business owners.

Superior-vote stock In dual-class stock firms, the class of stock that has more power to elect directors; usually concentrated in the hands of management.

Supermajority A requirement in many anti-takeover charter amendments that a change of control (for example) must be approved by more than a simple majority of shareholders; at least 67% to 90% approval may be required.

Supernormal growth Growth due to a profitability rate above the cost of capital.

Swaps Exchanges of one class of securities for another.

SWOT Acronym for Strengths, Weaknesses, Opportunities, and Threats; an approach to formulating firm strategy via assessments of firm capabilities in relation to the environment.

Synergy The "2 + 2 = 5" effect. The condition of the output of a combination of two entities being greater than the sum of their individual outputs.

Take-out merger The second-step transaction that merges the acquired firm into the acquirer and thus "takes out" the remaining target shares that were not purchased in the initial (partial) tender offer.

Takeover A general term that includes both mergers and tender offers (acquisitions).

Takeover defenses Methods employed by targets to prevent the success of bidders' efforts.

Target The object of takeover efforts.

Targeted share repurchase Refers to repurchasing the stock of a large blockholder (an unwanted acquirer) at a premium over market price (greenmail).

Tax credit ESOP (TRASOP, PAYSOP) An employee stock ownership plan that allowed employers to take a credit against their tax liability for contributions up to a specified amount, based on qualified investment in plant and equipment (TRASOP) and/or covered payroll (PAYSOP). Repealed by the Economic Recovery Tax Act of 1981 and the Tax Reform Act of 1986.

Tax-free reorganization A takeover transaction in which the primary consideration paid to obtain the voting stock or assets of the target must be the voting stock of the acquiring firm. (In fact, tax is deferred only until target shareholders sell the stock received.)

Team effects A form of organization capital; information that helps assign employees for an efficient match of capabilities to tasks and that helps to match managers and other employees to form efficient teams.

Team production Alchian and Demsetz's distinguishing characteristic of a firm. Team output is greater than the sum of the outputs of individual team members working independently (synergy): increased output cannot be unambiguously attributed to any individual team member.

Tender offer A method of effecting a takeover via a public offer to target firm shareholders to buy their shares.

Termination fee The payment or consolation prize to unsuccessful bidders.

Third market Trading conducted off the organized securities exchanges by institutional investors.

Time trader Investors who buy or sell because of events unrelated to stock price fluctuations, e.g., for portfolio adjustment needs.

Tin parachutes Payments to a wide range of the target's employees for terminations resulting from a takeover.

Tobin's q The ratio of the current market value of the firm's securities to the current replacement costs of its assets; used as a measure of management performance.

Toehold The initial fraction of a target firm's shares acquired by a bidder.

Top-down planning An approach to overall firm strategy based on companywide forecasts from top management, versus aggregation of segment forecasts.

Total capitalization The sum of total debt, preferred stock, and equity.

Total capital requirements A firm's financing requirements. Two alternative measures: (1) Total capital = Current Assets minus Noninterest-Bearing Debt plus Net Fixed Assets; (2) Total Capital = Interest-Bearing Debt plus Shareholders' Equity.

TPRs See *Transferable put rights.*

Transaction cost The cost of transferring a good or service across economic units or agents.

Transferable put rights (TPRs) A share repurchase plan in which puts for a limited time period issued to current shareholders can be resold to others.

TRASOP See *Tax credit ESOP.*

Trigger point The level of share ownership by a bidder at which provisions of a poison pill antitakeover defense plan are activated.

Trust Indenture Act of 1939 (TIA) Federal securities regulation of public issues of debt securities of $5 million or more. Specifies requirements to be included in the indenture (the agreement between the borrower and lenders) and sets out the responsibilities of the indenture trustee.

Two-tier tender offer Tender offers in which the bidder offers a superior first-tier price (e.g., higher or all cash) for a specified maximum number of shares it will accept and simultaneously announces its intentions to acquire remaining shares at a second-tier price (lower and/or securities rather than cash).

Type A, B, C reorganization Forms of tax-free reorganizations. Type A: Statutory mergers (target merged into acquirer) and consolidations (new entity created). Type B: Stock-for-stock transaction in which target is liquidated into the acquirer or maintained as separate operating entity. Type C: Stock-for-asset transaction in which at least 80% of fair market value of target's property is acquired; target then dissolves.

Undervaluation A firm's securities are selling for less than their intrinsic, or potential, or long-run value for one or more reasons.

Underwritten offerings Public securities issues that are sold by a firm to an investment banker at a negotiated price; the investment banker then bears the risk of price fluctuations before the securities are sold to the general public.

Unitary company (U-form) An organization form that is highly centralized under the president. Departments are organized by functions such as research, manufacturing, and marketing. It facilitates rapid decision making. Difficulties arise with multiple products.

Value additivity principle (VAP) A quality of the NPV method of capital budgeting that enables managers to consider each project independently. The sum of project NPVs represents the value added to the corporation by taking them on.

Value chain An approach to strategy that analyzes the steps or chain of activities in the firm to find opportunities for reducing cost outlays while adding product characteristics valued by customers.

Value drivers Operating measures that have a major influence on the value of a firm.

Vertical merger A combination of firms that operate in different levels or stages of the same industry; e.g., a toy manufacturer merges with a chain of toy stores (forward integration); an auto manufacturer merges with a tire company (backward integration).

Virtual organization The links of the value chain are brought together by contracts the company makes with its suppliers and customers. This is a form of virtual integration facilitated by a networked computer system or through the Internet.

Voting plan A poison pill antitakeover defense plan that issues voting preferred stock to target firm shareholders. At a trigger point, preferred stockholders (other than the bidder for the target) become entitled to supervoting privileges, making it difficult for the bidder to obtain voting control.

Voting trust A device by means of which shareholders retain cash flow rights to their shares while giving the right to vote those shares to another entity.

WACC See *Weighted-average marginal cost of capital.*

Wealth transfer The gain of one type of stakeholder in relation to the associated losses of other stakeholders.

Weighted-average marginal cost of capital (WACC) The relevant discount rate or investment hurdle rate based on targeted capital structure proportions.

White knight A more acceptable merger partner sought out by the target of a hostile bidder.

White squire A third party friendly to management who helps a company avoid an unwanted takeover without taking over the company on its own.

Williams Act of 1968 Federal legislation designed to protect target shareholders from swift and secret takeovers in three ways: (1) Generating more information during the takeover process; (2) requiring minimum period for tender offer to remain open; (3) authorizing targets to sue bidders.

Winner's curse The tendency that in a bidding contest or in some types of auctions, the winner is the bidder with the highest (overoptimistic) estimate of value. This explains the high frequency of negative returns to acquiring firms in takeovers with multiple bidders.

WOTS UP Acronym for Weaknesses, Opportunities, Threats, and Strengths; a technique to identify these key elements as part of the iterative process used to develop strategy.

Author Index

Subject Index